EIGHTH EDITION

Characteristics of Emotional and Behavioral Disorders of Children and Youth

James M. Kauffman
University of Virginia

PEARSON

Merrill
Prentice Hall

Upper Saddle River, New Jersey
Columbus, Ohio

Library of Congress Cataloging-in-Publication Data

Kauffman, James M.
   Characteristics of emotional and behavioral disorders of childern and youth / James M. Kauffman—8th ed.
      p. cm.
   Includes bibliographical references and index.
   ISBN 0-13-111817-X
   1. Behavior disorders in children.   2. Emotional problems of childern.   I. Title.

   RJ506.B44K38 2005
   618.92'89'002437—dc22

                                                                    2004000061

Vice President and Executive Publisher: Jeffery W. Johnston
Acquisitions Editor: Allyson P. Sharp
Editorial Assistant: Kathleen S. Burk
Development Editor: Heather Doyle Fraser
Production Editor: Sheryl Glicker Langner
Production Coordination: Wendy Druck/*The GTS Companies*
Design Coordinator: Diane C. Lorenzo
Photo Coordinator: Valerie Schultz
Cover Designer: Thomas Borah
Cover image: Corbis
Production Manager: Laura Messerly
Director of Marketing: Ann Castel Davis
Marketing Manager: Autumn Purdy
Marketing Coordinator: Tyra Poole

This book was set in Garamond ITC by *The GTS Companies*/York, PA Campus. It was printed and bound by R. R. Donnelley & Sons Company. The cover was printed by The Lehigh Press, Inc.

Photo Credits: Anthony Magnacca/Merrill, pp. 4, 26, 71, 92, 205, 263, 317, 369; Bettmann/Corbis, p. 43; Scott Cunningham/Merrill, pp. 125, 185, 235, 435; Kathy Kirtland/Merrill, p. 164; Barbara Schwartz/Merrill, p. 284; Anne Vega/Merrill, pp. 333, 392, 411.

Pearson Education Ltd.   Pearson Education Australia Pty. Limited
Pearson Education Singapore Pte. Ltd.   Pearson Education North Asia Ltd.
Pearson Education Canada, Ltd.   Pearson Educación de Mexico, S.A. de C.V.
Pearson Education—Japan   Pearson Education Malaysia Pte. Ltd.

10 9 8 7 6 5 4 3
ISBN: 0-13-111817-X

For my children, Tim and Missy, and their children,
Emma, Rachel, and Loren

▶▶ EDUCATOR LEARNING CENTER: AN INVALUABLE ONLINE RESOURCE

Merrill Education and the Association for Supervision and Curriculum Development (ASCD) invite you to take advantage of a new online resource, one that provides access to the top research and proven strategies associated with ASCD and Merrill—the Educator Learning Center. At **www.EducatorLearningCenter.com** you will find resources that will enhance your students' understanding of course topics and of current educational issues, in addition to being invaluable for further research.

How the Educator Learning Center will help your students become better teachers

With the combined resources of Merrill Education and ASCD, you and your students will find a wealth of tools and materials to better prepare them for the classroom.

Research

- More than 600 articles from the ASCD journal *Educational Leadership* discuss everyday issues faced by practicing teachers.
- A direct link on the site to Research Navigator™ gives students access to many of the leading education journals, as well as extensive content detailing the research process.
- Excerpts from Merrill Education texts give your students insights on important topics of instructional methods, diverse populations, assessment, classroom management, technology, and refining classroom practice.

Classroom Practice

- Hundreds of lesson plans and teaching strategies are categorized by content area and age range.
- Case studies and classroom video footage provide virtual field experience for student reflection.
- Computer simulations and other electronic tools keep your students abreast of today's classrooms and current technologies.

Look into the value of Educator Learning Center yourself

A four-month subscription to Educator Learning Center is $25 but is **FREE** when used in conjunction with this text. To obtain free passcodes for your students, simply contact your local Merrill/Prentice Hall sales representative, and your representative will give you a special ISBN to give your bookstore when ordering your textbooks. To preview the value of this website to you and your students, please go to **www.EducatorLearningCenter.com** and click on "Demo."

>> PREFACE

This book, like its earlier editions, is an introductory text in special education for children and youth with emotional and behavioral disorders (those called *emotionally disturbed* in federal regulations). Because emotional and behavioral disorders are commonly observed in children and youth in all special education categories, the book will also be of value in courses dealing with the characteristics of mental retardation, learning disabilities, or students in cross-categorical special education. Students in school psychology, educational psychology, or abnormal child psychology may also find the book useful.

Several comments are necessary to clarify my intent in writing this book. First, developmental processes have been an important concern of mine in understanding the problem of emotional and behavioral disorders. I have tried to integrate the most relevant parts of the vast and scattered literature on child development and show their relevance to understanding the children and youth who have these disorders. In struggling with this task, I have attempted not only to summarize what is known about why disorders occur but also to suggest how emotional and behavioral development can be influenced for the better, particularly by educators. Second, in concentrating primarily on research and theory grounded in reliable empirical data, I have revealed my bias toward social learning principles. I believe that when we examine the literature with a willingness to be swayed by empirical evidence rather than ideology, then a social learning bias is understandable. Third, this book is not, by any stretch of the imagination, a comprehensive treatment of the subject. An introductory book must leave much unsaid and many loose ends that need tying. Unquestionably, the easiest thing about writing this book was to let it fall short of saying everything, with the hope that readers will pursue the information in the works cited in the references.

I have tried to address the interests and concerns of teachers and of students preparing to become teachers. Consequently, I have described many interventions, particularly in the chapters in part 4. However, I emphasize that the descriptions are cursory. This text does not provide the details of educational methods and behavioral interventions that are necessary for competent implementation by teachers. This is not a methods nor a how-to-do-it book.

NEW TO THIS EDITION

- Over 300 new reference citations, updating research findings and further supporting ideas and recommendations
- Questions for additional reflection at the end of the Personal Reflections features, providing additional thought-stimulating items for discussion

- Accompanying case book with introductions and questions, providing further exercises in applying knowledge to actual children and youth
- For each chapter, a consistent number of questions to keep in mind while reading (five advance organizers), giving students greater focus on key issues
- More concise coverage of topics and condensation of the history of the field with more attention to current issues and trends

Users of previous editions will notice significant updates and revisions in the eighth edition. I have updated citations and information on many topics, although I have retained many citations of earlier research because newer findings have not refuted them.

Some of the Personal Reflections features are new. In addition, I have added questions for further reflection at the end of each Personal Reflections feature.

A new case book is now available to accompany the text. I have moved some of the case material previously included in the text into this case book and added new cases as well. The case book will provide students opportunities for further discussion of the emotional and behavioral disorders of actual children and youth.

This text urges readers to engage in self-questioning while reading. In this edition, I have made the number of questions opening each chapter consistent in number (5). I hope this will make the reading more manageable and help students focus on important information without limiting the scope of the questions they might ask themselves or others.

This edition is somewhat shorter than the previous one, and I have accomplished this reduction in overall length by striving to be comprehensive yet concise in my coverage of topics. The attention devoted to the history of the field in chapter 3 has been substantially reduced, with more emphasis on current issues and trends.

Readers may also note that chapters 5 and 6 on assessment were revised by Frederick J. Brigham. Chapters 8 and 14 were revised by Devery Mock. Rick Brigham is a colleague of mine at the University of Virginia who teaches courses in assessment. Devery Mock is a former advisee of mine who completed her Ph.D. program at the University of Virginia and is now a faculty member at the University of Iowa.

ORGANIZATION OF THE TEXT

The organization of this book differs noticeably from that of most other texts. My emphasis is on clear description of emotional and behavioral disorders and interpretation of research on the factors implicated in their development. I did not organize this book around theoretical models or psychiatric classifications but around basic concepts: (1) the nature, extent, and history of the problem and conceptual approaches to it; (2) assessment of the problem; (3) major causal factors; (4) the many facets of disordered emotions and behavior; and (5) a personal statement about teaching pupils with these disorders. I hope this organization encourages students to become critical thinkers and problem solvers.

Part 1 introduces major concepts and historical antecedents of contemporary special education for children and youth with emotional and behavioral disorders. Chapter 1 begins with vignettes to orient the reader to disorders and the ways in which they disturb others. The vignettes are followed by discussion of the problems in defining these disorders, especially for educational purposes. In chapter 2, prevalence is discussed from a conceptual, problem-solving perspective rather than as an exercise in remembering facts and figures. Chapter 3 traces the development of the field—how it grew out of the disciplines of psychology, psychiatry, and public education—and summarizes major current trends. Chapter 4 abstracts the major conceptual models that guide thinking about educating students with emotional and behavioral disorders and provides a sketch of the conceptual model underlying the orientation of the book.

Part 2 deals with procedures and problems in assessing emotional and behavioral disorders. Chapter 5 reviews not only the problems in screening student populations but also the difficulties encountered in classifying disorders. Chapter 6 takes up evaluation for eligibility and intervention, with attention to social validation and the individualized education program.

Part 3 examines the origins of disordered behavior, with attention to the implications of causal factors for special educators. Chapter 7 discusses biological factors, chapter 8 the role of the family, chapter 9 the influence of the school, and chapter 10 cultural factors. Each chapter integrates current research findings that may help us understand why children and youth acquire emotional or behavioral disorders and what preventive actions might be taken.

Types of disorders are discussed in Part 4. The chapters are organized around major behavioral dimensions derived from factor analyses of behavioral ratings by teachers and parents. Although no categorical scheme produces unambiguous groupings of all disorders, the chapters are devoted to the behavioral dimensions emerging most consistently from empirical research. Each chapter emphasizes issues germane to special education, including definition, assessment, and intervention.

Part 5 contains only one chapter—my interpretation and application of all of the preceding material to teaching practices. This is a personal statement intended only to suggest some basic assumptions about teaching pupils who exhibit seriously troublesome behavior.

SUPPLEMENTS

Case book to accompany *Characteristics of Emotional and Behavioral Disorders of Childern and Youth*, 8th edition.   A new case book now accompanies the text and includes cases that enhance and extend the content in each of the 18 chapters of the text. In addition, each case ends with thought-provoking reflective questions to spur discussion and further the reader's understanding of content.

Instructor's Manual with Test Items.   Each of the 17 chapters in the instructor's manual contains the following: chapter focus questions, a list of key terms, over 45 test questions, learning activities, and case-based activities.

PowerPoint Slides.   These visual aids display, summarize, and help explain core information presented in each chapter. Instructors can download these slides from the Companion Website and use them as a PowerPoint slide presentation or print/copy them onto acetates and use them as transparencies for overhead projectors.

Companion Website.   The Companion Website, located at *http://www.pren-hall.com/kauffman,* is a valuable resource for both the instructor and the student.

- *For the Instructor:* The Instructor Resources section is a pass-code–protected area of the Companion Website for instructors only. Each chapter contains PowerPoint slides relevant to chapter content that instructors can download and customize. In addition, the on-line version of the instructor's manual is available here. The Companion Website also features a Syllabus Builder, which enables instructors to create and customize syllabi on-line. To obtain a pass-code to enter the Instructor Resources section of the site, professors should contact the local Prentice Hall sales representative or call faculty services at 1-800-526-0485.
- *For the Student:* The Companion Website helps you—the student—gauge your understanding of chapter content through the use of focus questions, Web links, case-based activities, interactive self-assessments, and discussion starters.

ACKNOWLEDGMENTS

Any shortcomings of this book are my responsibility alone, but its worth has been enhanced substantially by others who have assisted me in a variety of ways. I am especially grateful to Education Editor Allyson Sharp and others at Merrill/Prentice Hall who provided guidance and technical services for this revision. I thank the reviewers of the seventh edition, who offered advance suggestions for the eighth edition. The perceptive suggestions of Gwendolyn W. Garrison, Clark Atlanta University; Sharon Lynch, Sam Houston State University; Christopher Murray, DePaul University; and Annette C. Robinson, Seattle Pacific University, resulted in substantial improvements in my work. Many other users of the book, both students and instructors, have given me helpful feedback over the years. I encourage those who are willing to share their comments on the book to write or call me with their suggestions. I am also grateful to the contributors of the Personal Reflections features for their willingness to share their knowledge and views on important questions. Finally, I offer special thanks to Rick Brigham for revising chapters 5 and 6 and to Devery Mock for revising chapters 8 and 14, helping me locate recent literature, and preparing the Instructor's Manual and Companion Website.

J. M. K.
Charlottesville, Virginia

⟫ BRIEF CONTENTS

>> CONTENTS

CHAPTER 4
Conceptual Models: Approaches to the Problem   71

PART 2   89

CHAPTER 5
Screening and Classification   92

PART 4   261

CHAPTER *11*
Attention and Activity Disorders   263

CHAPTER *12*
Conduct Disorder: Overt Aggression   284

Note: Every effort has been made to provide accurate and current Internet information in this book. However, the Internet and information posted on it are constantly changing, and it is inevitable that some of the Internet addresses listed in this textbook will change.

Part 1

The Problem and Its History

Introduction

In one of his best-known short stories, the humorist James Thurber described the private fantasies of Walter Mitty. While Walter Mitty's wife was getting her hair done and he ran errands, while he drove and she prattled about things to which he paid no attention, he fantasized that he was a daring naval pilot, an eminent surgeon, a debonair marksman on the witness stand in a sensational murder trial, and a captured soldier facing execution with nonchalance. Walter Mitty's imaginings are both humorous and adaptive. His internal dialogue is a way of coping with his life circumstances and enhancing his self-image. An actual person who thinks and behaves like Walter Mitty is not likely to be described as having serious emotional or behavioral problems. Fantasy has a legitimate and helpful place in normal mental life, as long as someone knows the difference between the imaginary and the real.

Thinking about emotional or behavioral disorders requires asking many questions about the way in which people think and behave. Such thinking requires imagination, in which you ask yourself questions and try out various answers—a kind of fantasy. One of the most effective strategies for learning about any topic is making yourself try to answer the questions you ask. Once you begin asking questions, you are likely to find that the answers aren't as simple as they seemed at first, at least not if you're the one trying to answer. Much of my thinking about my professional work is an internal dialogue in which I imagine myself being asked questions about things I am presumed to know or expected to learn about.

Many of the questions I fantasize asking myself are unanswerable. I struggle to refine my answers, never feeling entirely satisfied with my responses. In some cases I can think of no better statement than "I don't know."

I hope that reading this book will launch you on an adventure of self-questioning. If reading my text helps you formulate answers to questions, it should also help you raise more questions, some that neither you nor anyone else is likely to answer in a lifetime of study. In the introductions to the five parts of this book, I present some of the questions I've asked myself—and tried to answer, with only partial success—in the chapters that follow. This book is about difficult questions regarding people's emotions and behavior. There are no simple, easy answers to these questions, and few of the answers are unequivocal. That is the nature of the topic of emotional or behavioral disorders. It is not an appealing area of study for students who feel a need for more answers than questions or who want straightforward answers to complex problems. We don't know much compared to what we need to know, partly because the field of study is relatively young and the necessary research hasn't been done. In addition, some of the important questions we might ask call for value judgments and can't be answered directly by research or require considering both values and research. For answers to many questions, we have to be satisfied with educated guesses or personal opinions.

As you begin your study of emotional or behavioral disorders, you should be asking yourself some of the most obvious yet profound questions about this field of inquiry. For example: What is an emotional or behavioral disorder? As you will see in chapter 1, we have a very difficult problem right off the bat. As simple as this first question might seem, we're immediately faced with an ambiguous answer and continuing controversy.

In chapter 2, we turn to questions such as: What is the scope of the problem? What is the percentage of students with emotional or behavioral disorders in most schools? How do we estimate the number of such students in a district, a state, or the country? Why should we? As you may already have asked yourself, How can we measure accurately the extent of a problem we can't define precisely? Reading chapter 2 should help you formulate questions about what might be required to meet the needs of students with emotional or behavioral disorders if there are as many such students as we estimate there are.

How and where did special education for children and youth with emotional or behavioral disorders begin? What influences shaped the field into what it is today? What are the implications of current trends in the field? Historical analysis should enable us to answer the first of these questions rather precisely, it would seem. As I indicate in chapter 3, however, the beginning of the field is difficult to describe precisely, partly because it is submerged in the beginnings of related professions. If finding the roots of the field is difficult, predicting where it is going is more so. I hope reading chapter 3 will prompt you to ask many questions when you read about "new" developments: Have we heard this before? Who had this idea, and how did it work out? If this is a "recycled" idea, what is different about it as it is being presented today?

Before you finish reading chapter 3—probably before you finish reading chapter 1—you will be asking yourself questions about a framework for thinking about emotional or behavioral disorders. It is frustrating to try to discuss something with someone who is on a different wavelength. The experience is much like listening to a badly tuned radio that picks up two stations at once. So you might be asking: What are the major frequency bands that I can tune in to? Other ways of asking this are: What foundation concepts and principles guide people's thinking about emotional or behavioral disorders? How do we make sense of behavior that people call "crazy," "sick," or "deviant"? In chapter 4, I summarize some of the major theories (conceptual models) that scholars have used to explain both strange and commonplace behavior. These theories have value for our purposes primarily because they help us when we ask: How do we conceptualize efforts to help students who exhibit unacceptable behavior? The way in which we think about things—how we go about analyzing problems and testing solutions—will have a profound effect on what we do with students.

Perhaps the questions I've posed for part 1 seem basic. They are. But basic questions are often among the most difficult to answer. Their seeming simplicity is deceptive; complete and satisfactory answers to them have eluded the best minds for generations. As you begin reading this book, I hope you will bring curiosity about how researchers and teachers have tried to address these questions and excitement about the questions you might ask yourself or others.

CHAPTER ONE

DEFINITION

THE NATURE OF THE PROBLEM

As you read this chapter, keep these guiding questions in mind:

- Why should an emotional or behavioral disorder be considered a disability?

- What is the difference, if any, between emotional or behavioral disorder and serious emotional disturbance?

- What criteria should one use in deciding that behavior is disordered or abnormal?

- Why is defining emotional or behavioral disorder so difficult?

- Why is the judgment of teachers or a multidisciplinary team a necessary part of any school-based definition of emotional or behavioral disorder?

This book is about children and youth who arouse negative feelings and induce negative behavior in others, including teachers. The reaction of most other children and adults is to withdraw from them to avoid battles. As a result, these children and youth do not learn to behave acceptably. "In the case of [the] rejected child, parents, teachers, and peers simply withdraw from the child, and thus 'teaching opportunities' are greatly reduced, along with the opportunity for the rejected child to redeem himself in the eyes of parents, teachers, and mainstream peers" (Ialongo, Vaden-Kiernan, & Kellam, 1998, p. 210). These are not children and youth who can be depicted accurately in the sanitized language described by Diane Ravitch in *The Language Police* (2003).

The children and youth we are considering may be socially withdrawn, but most are aggressive toward others. Typically, they experience academic failure in addition to social rejection or alienation. They usually are not popular or leaders among their peers. If they have status among their peers, it is usually because of their antisocial behavior. Their friends, if they have any, are usually antisocial or social misfits. They may make friends initially but do not know how to keep them. Emotional and behavioral problems of all types are interrelated, and we seldom find that a child or youth has difficulties of only one type.

Most of the children and youth we are describing are boys. However, research is showing more clearly that aggression, disruptive behavior, and peer rejection, as well as social withdrawal, are also problems of girls. Many of the youngsters we are considering can be identified before they enter school or in the primary grades. However, most are not identified for special education until they have exhibited very serious behavioral and academic problems in school for several years.

Most adults choose to avoid these children and youth as much as possible because their behavior is so persistently irritating to authority figures that they seem to be asking for punishment or rebuke. Even in their own eyes, these children and youth are usually failures; they obtain little gratification from life and repeatedly fall short of their aspirations. They have disabilities: Compared to nondisabled individuals, their options in important aspects of daily living are highly restricted. Their disabilities are the result of their behavior, which is discordant with their social–interpersonal environments. Their behavior costs them many opportunities for gratifying social interaction and self-fulfillment. They present serious social problems that our society wants to have solved (Walker et al., 1998; Walker, Ramsey, & Gresham, 2004).

TERMINOLOGY

Nearly everyone agrees that emotional and behavioral disorders should be prevented whenever possible. However, many special educators and professionals in related fields, as well as many laypersons in our society, are unwilling to take preventive action. We discuss the many reasons for this reluctance in chapter 3, but chief among them is the issue of labeling (Kauffman, 1999c, 2003a). None of the labels used to describe these disorders has a positive connotation.

Table 1.1
Combinations of Terms

Column A	Column B
Emotionally	Disturbed
Behaviorally	Disordered
Socially	Maladjusted
Personally	Handicapped
	Conflicted
	Impaired

Emotionally disturbed is the label currently used in federal legislation and regulations regarding special education. However, *behaviorally disordered* is preferred by some professionals in the field of special education because it is a more accurate descriptor of the socialization difficulties of children and youths. *Behaviorally disordered* also seems to many people to be a less stigmatizing label than does *emotionally disturbed*. Yet in the professional literature and in the laws and regulations of various states, many additional terms refer to the same population. For the most part, these terms combine one of the terms in Table 1.1's column A with another from column B. Thus, in one state, the label may be *emotionally handicapped* or *emotionally impaired,* whereas in another it may be *behaviorally impaired*. Occasionally, combinations of two words from column A appear with one from column B: *socially and emotionally maladjusted, socially and emotionally disturbed, personally and socially maladjusted,* and so on. The point is that the terminology of the field is confused—sometimes as confused as the children and youth to whom we apply the labels.

Confusing combinations of terms may eventually give way to a commonly accepted label for this category. The term *emotional or behavioral disorders* was adopted in the late 1980s by the National Mental Health and Special Education Coalition, a group formed in 1987 to foster collaboration among various professional and advocacy organizations (Forness, 1988a; Forness & Knitzer, 1992). By 1991, more than 30 professional and advocacy organizations were members of the coalition. The terminology *children and youth with emotional or behavioral disorders* may eventually be widely accepted, and I use it in this book with the understanding that it is the language now preferred by many parent and professional organizations. The mental health and special education coalition chose *emotional or behavioral disorders* over other possible labels simply to indicate that the children and youth to whom it refers may exhibit disorders of emotions or behavior, or both. It is a more clearly inclusive term than are many others. Unfortunately, it is not yet the term used in federal laws and regulations.

DEVELOPMENTAL NORMS VERSUS SOCIOCULTURAL EXPECTATIONS

Some of the behaviors that disabled children and youth exhibit are recognized as abnormal in nearly every cultural group and all social strata. Muteness, serious self-injury, eating feces, and murder are examples of disorders that are seldom considered culture specific. These disordered behaviors represent discrepancies from nearly universal developmental norms. However, children and youth are sometimes considered deviant simply because their behavior violates standards peculiar to their culture or the social institutions in their environment, such as their school. Academic achievement, various types of aggression, sexual behavior, language patterns, and so on will be judged deviant or normal depending on the prevailing attitudes in the individual's ethnic and religious group, family, and school. Failing to read, hitting others, taking others' belongings, and swearing, for example, are evaluated according to the standards of the child's community. A given act or pattern of behavior may be considered disordered or deviant in one situation or context but not in another simply because of differences in the expectations of the people with whom the child or youth lives. The majority of emotional or behavioral disorders are defined by such sociocultural expectations, not by truly universal developmental norms. Research now indicates, however, that behaviors violating some sociocultural expectations may also be developmental disorders. Hyperaggression, covert antisocial behavior, and socialization to the norms of deviant peers, for example, are disorders of conduct that not only violate social expectations but also create developmental risk (Farmer, Farmer, & Gut, 1999; Kazdin, 1995, 1998, 2001; Walker et al., 2004).

BEHAVIOR SHAPED BY ITS SOCIAL CONTEXT (ECOLOGY)

Many emotional or behavioral disorders, though not all, originate in or are made worse by the child's or youth's social interactions. The disorders are learned through modeling, reinforcement, extinction, and punishment—learning processes that shape and maintain much of everyone's behavior, both normal and deviant (Bandura, 1986, 1995b). Adults and youngsters in the child's or youth's environment may accidentally arrange conditions that cause and support undesirable, inappropriate behavior. Ironically, the same adults who unwittingly shape inappropriate behavior may then initiate action to have the child or youth labeled *disturbed, disordered,* or *maladjusted.* The child or youth might behave quite differently if these adults changed their own behavior in relation to the youngster's or if he or she were placed in a different social environment. The problem in these cases is partly, and sometimes mostly, in the caretakers' or peers' behavior.

One might be tempted to conclude that the child or youth with an emotional or behavioral disorder is not "to blame" for the way others react. But youngsters' behavior influences the actions of their parents, their teachers, their peers, and others who interact with them. Researchers have realized for many years that children "teach" their parents, teachers, and peers how to behave toward them as surely as they are taught by these others (Bell & Harper, 1977; Emery, Binkoff, Houts, & Carr, 1983). Therefore, it is not appropriate to ascribe fault exclusively to either the youngster with an emotional or behavioral disorder or to others in the environment. Teaching and learning are interactive processes in which teacher and learner frequently, and often subtly, exchange roles (Kauffman, Mostert, Trent, & Hallahan, 2002). When a youngster has difficulty with teachers, peers, or parents, it is as important to consider their responses to the behavior as it is to evaluate the youngster's reactions to others.

An ecological perspective takes into account the interrelationships between the child or youth and various aspects of the environment. The problem of emotional or behavioral disorders is not viewed simply as a youngster's inappropriate actions but as undesirable interactions and transactions between the youngster and other people. For example, a child's temper tantrums in school could indeed be a problem. An ecological perspective demands that the behavior of the child's teachers, peers, and parents—their expectations, demands, and reactions to the child's tantrums and other behavior, as well as the child's social goals and strategies—be taken into consideration to explain and deal with the problem (Farmer et al., 1999; Kazdin, 2001; Walker, 1995; Walker et al., 2004).

TYPES OF DISORDERS AND CAUSES

The environmental conditions under which children and youth display disordered emotions and behavior vary widely. Some youngsters endure extremely adverse circumstances, including abuse, neglect, and pervasive disadvantage, without developing emotional or behavioral disorders. Others succumb to adverse circumstances, whereas some develop disorders in environments that are clearly conducive to normal development (Katz, 1997).

Although environmental conditions affect how children and youth behave, biological factors also exert a strong influence. We do not know precisely why some children are relatively vulnerable and others invulnerable to environmental conditions. A wide variety of causal factors may give rise to a wide variety of emotional or behavioral disorders. The relationships among causes and disorders are exceedingly complex, as will become apparent in subsequent chapters. We can seldom determine for certain the cause of the disorder in individual cases.

Examples of Disordered Emotions and Behavior

Children and youth can cause negative feelings and reactions in others in many different ways. As we will see in the following chapters, disordered emotions or behaviors may be described according to two primary dimensions: *externalizing* (aggressive, acting-out behavior) and *internalizing* (social withdrawal). The cases presented here and in the accompanying case book illustrate the range in types of emotional or behavioral disorders and the variety of factors that can cause children and youth to become disabled. We have chosen these examples to show that disordered emotions and behaviors have been reported in the literature for centuries and that the nature of these problems has not changed over the decades, although our labels for some of them have changed. Compare these cases to anything you might encounter in the media today, and you will understand that we are talking about persistent human problems. Moreover, these problems appear in young children as well as adolescents; they are exhibited by individuals who have grown up in privileged homes with caring parents as well as by those who have been reared in poverty or under abusive conditions.

They are often accompanied by lower than average intelligence but sometimes by intellectual brilliance. They may be characterized by externalizing (acting out) or internalizing (withdrawn) behavior or alternation between the two, and they may be described from the perspective of an observer or of the self.

The case of Alan is particularly interesting because, like so many students with emotional or behavioral disorders, he has not been labeled as having a disability, nor, apparently, has he been evaluated for placement in special education. He is described as a "discipline problem," and he has been placed in an alternative school described as a "repository for the worst disciplinary cases" (O'Hanlon, 1998, p. 10). His behavior is thought to be connected somehow to the breakup of his parents' marriage, but this is speculation. Even in the alternative school, he is seen as a difficult student with many emotional and behavioral problems.

≫ *Alan*

At age 13, Alan has a long history of involvement in incidents in the neighborhood school and on the bus that adults describe as misbehavior but he interprets differently. For example, a teacher reports that he was making inappropriate gestures (mimicking masturbation), but he says that he was just shaking his hand the way you do to dry it in the air. He scratched the face of another student who, Alan says, he wanted to beat up because he's dumb. He tore up the toast he was served for breakfast and threw the little pieces on the floor. He was caught passing notes in class in which, as he explains, "I called this girl a bitch,

because she was making me mad" (O'Hanlon, 1998, p. 10). He seems to have a ready explanation justifying every misbehavior of which he is accused. And on May 14, the last straw. Or rather, the last two straws: "Inappropriate behavior. Refused to move away from another student when requested by a teacher." Followed by: "Disrespect. Alan told Mr. Combs to shut up and that he was stupid. Due process hearing scheduled for 5/21 at 10:00."

Actually, Alan explains, he didn't call Mr. Combs stupid. "He said that I had pushed somebody when I hadn't. I just said, 'This is stupid.'" (p. 10)

Very occasionally, a young child may have *schizophrenia,* a disorder that is usually diagnosed in young adulthood and affects about 1 in 100 adults. Schizophrenia is a mental illness with physiological causes that are poorly understood. It involves major disorders of thought processes and perceptions, such as delusions or hallucinations, and it is often episodic—people with it may go through alternating periods of acute illness and remission. Treatment with psychotropic drugs is the primary form of intervention in schizophrenia, although certain forms of psychotherapy can be helpful in some cases, and support from the child's family is critical. For children and youth, appropriate education is also an extremely important part of treatment. In the following case, an anonymous youth provides a first-person account of what it is like to experience schizophrenia as a child. (We will return to Elizabeth's experience in the accompanying case book.)

>> *Elizabeth*

I have schizophrenia. Actually I have childhood-onset schizophrenia. This is a very rare form of schizophrenia, especially in girls.

I have had problems ever since I started school. I remember trying to hide under the tables in kindergarten so I wouldn't have to do any work. In first grade I was in the top reading group, even though my mom and grandma had to come to school every day to make sure I got my work done. By the third grade I was in the bottom reading group. I started the fourth grade, and I was doing better because I was taking Ritalin. But something happened in October. All of a sudden I couldn't read or write or do math anymore. Everything was so confusing because I couldn't understand anything that was going on around me. By November I was so sick I couldn't go to school anymore. On November 13 I went to the hospital and I stayed there for 2 months.

I got on a medicine called Mellaril and that helped me on my way to recovery. A doctor told my family that one third of schizophrenia patients get well all by themselves, one third can be helped with medicine, and one third cannot be helped by medicine. But getting better took me a long, long time. In the middle of the seventh grade, I was proclaimed to be in remission. . . .

I have been in remission for over 2 years. Whenever we ask either my psychiatrist or my psychologist what my future will be, they say they just don't know. Childhood schizophrenia is just too rare (especially in girls), and my recovery and improvement have been like miracles. My psychologist says I am high functioning. I don't know exactly what he means. But every night I pray that I will stay in remission. So far that has worked, along with my therapy, my medicine, and all the help I get from my family and some of my teachers. (Anonymous, 1994, pp. 587, 589–590)

A severe mental illness such as schizophrenia does not necessarily exclude a child or youth from participation in typical activities or preclude a successful career, given that the illness can be treated successfully and necessary family and school supports are provided. The following information about Elizabeth puts her account into perspective and strikes a very hopeful note.

>> *Elizabeth* (continued)

Elizabeth was in 10th grade when this was written [with the help of her mother]. She is now a senior in high school and has been able to mainstream all academic classes while maintaining a B average. Every weekday afternoon she tutors two fourth-grade students at her former elementary school who are having difficulty with reading. She is looking forward to attending a junior college next year. It is her dream to be an elementary school teacher. (Anonymous, 1994, p. 590)

Other descriptions of disordered emotions and behavior and their treatment are scattered throughout this book and are included in the accompanying case book. We must not only consider the unpleasant or disturbing features of the youngster's behavior but in each case also the circumstances that may have contributed to the problem and the reactions of both peers and adults. Children and youth with emotional or behavioral disorders should not be viewed merely as youngsters who cause others to experience anger, grief, anxiety, or other unpleasantness. They are troubled as well as troubling, and they often must live in situations that are not conducive to satisfactory interpersonal relations. Teachers must be sensitive to the students' pain, even while they themselves are being pained by the youngsters' misbehavior, puzzling responses, or academic failures in their classrooms.

PROBLEMS OF DEFINITION

The cases you have read about so far may clearly illustrate what children and youth with emotional or behavioral disorders can be like; nevertheless, descriptions are not a definition. These youngsters' problems may seem obvious, but the way they should be categorically defined is not obvious.

The children and youth who are this book's topic etch pictures in one's memory that are not easy to erase. The foregoing discussion and descriptions (and those in the case book) provide the basis for an intuitive grasp of what an emotional or behavioral disorder is, but the definition of such a disorder—the construction of guidelines that will foster valid and reliable judgments about who does and does not have it—is anything but simple. One reason it is so difficult to arrive at a reliable definition is that an emotional or behavioral disorder is not a thing that exists outside a social context but is a label assigned according to cultural rules. A science of behavior exists, and science is our best tool for figuring things out. However, the objective methods of natural science sometimes play a secondary role in designating someone as deviant (Kauffman, 1999d, 2002; Landrum, Tankersley, & Kauffman, 2003). An emotional or behavioral disorder is whatever behavior a culture's chosen authority figures designate as intolerable. Typically, it is behavior that is perceived to threaten the stability, security, or values of that society. This does not mean that the identification of emotional and behavioral disorders is indefensible, just that it must be seen as a human social process.

Defining an emotional or behavioral disorder is unavoidably subjective, at least in part. We can be objective and precise in measuring specific responses of individuals, and we can be painstakingly explicit in stating social norms, cultural rules, or community expectations for behavior. But we must ultimately realize that norms, rules, and expectations, and the appraisal of the extent to which particular individuals deviate from them, require subjective judgment. The problem of definition is made all the more difficult by differences in conceptual models, differing purposes of definition, the complexities of measuring emotions and behaviors, the range and variability of normal and deviant behavior, the relationships among emotional or behavioral disorders and other exceptionalities, the transience of many problems during human development, and the disadvantages inherent in labeling deviance.

One objection to the recognition of emotional and behavioral disorders, as well as some of the other categories of special education, is that it is a social construct.

However, the fact that something is a social construct—something defined by societal rules and, therefore, open to redefinition or new understanding—does not make it insubstantial, unimportant, or indefensible. It is wise to remember that all of the following are social constructs: justice, poverty, ethics, childhood, adolescence, love, and family. We could give many other examples. The point is simply this: Emotional and behavioral disorders are social constructs, but so are many of the things we hold dear in a benevolent society. To say that emotional and behavioral disorders are social constructs should not be assumed to mean that they are merely figments of imagination, are dispensable, or are unwise or uncivil (see Kavale & Mostert, 2003).

Differences in Conceptual Models

Distinctly different conceptual models have been developed to guide intervention. Psychodynamic, biological, sociological, behavioral, ecological, psychoeducational, educational, and phenomenological models have been described. (See McDowell, Adamson, & Wood, 1982; Smith, Wood, & Grimes, 1988; Van Hasselt & Hersen, 1991a, 1991b, for descriptions of models; see Kauffman, 1999d, 1999f; Sasso, 2001; Vaughn & Damman, 2001; Walker, Forness, et al., 1998, for discussions of the role of science in conceptual models.) Each conceptual model includes a set of assumptions about why children behave as they do and what must be done to correct disorders. Not surprisingly, a definition derived from the tenets of one conceptual model does little but baffle or disappoint those who hold the assumptions of a different model. Writing a definition to which all can subscribe, regardless of conceptual persuasion, may be impossible. An additional problem is that many concepts about the emotional or behavioral disorders of children and youth are merely adaptations of conceptual models of adult psychopathology and do not consider the developmental differences of youngsters at various ages. We discuss conceptual models more fully in chapter 4; suffice it to say here that people who disagree about what emotional or behavioral disorders are at a theoretical or philosophical level are unlikely to agree on a practical definition. It is important to note that these people are unlikely to agree on what should be prevented and how to best implement prevention (Kauffman, 1999c, 2003b).

Differing Purposes of Definitions

Definitions serve the purposes of the social agents who use them. Courts, schools, clinics, and families rely on different criteria for definition. Courts give greatest attention to law-violating behavior, schools focus primarily on academic failure, clinics use reasons for referral, and families concentrate on behavior that violates their rules or strains their tolerance. Formulating a single definition that is useful to all the various social agents who are responsible for youngsters' conduct is impossible. In this book, our concern is with definitions that serve the purposes of public education. Our focus is on school-related issues, and often we refer to the children and youth in question as students.

Surveys reveal that the definitions of state education agencies often include statements regarding the supposed causes of emotional or behavioral disorders (e.g., Cullinan & Epstein, 1979; see also Epstein & Cullinan, 1998). States' regulations

often cite biological or family factors as probable causes. They may include requirements for certification that a youngster has a disorder or specify who may legitimately classify the child or youth. State regulations may include exclusions, such as
a statement that the disorders cannot be caused by mental retardation or serious
health impairments. School administrative definitions vary so much that a student
might be classified in one state but not in another. Clearly, definitions are problematic if a student changes from "normal" to "disturbed" merely by moving across a
state line. The problem is not a matter of two people disagreeing about whether a
particular behavior is in evidence but is in states' differing policies about what a particular behavior means.

States may be moving slowly toward aligning their definitions with the definition
used in federal regulations; nevertheless, great variability remains in terminology and
definition from state to state. Moreover, the current federal definition itself presents
serious problems, as we will see.

Difficulties in Measuring Emotions and Behavior

No tests measure personality, adjustment, anxiety, or other relevant psychological constructs precisely enough to provide a sound basis for defining emotional or behavioral
disorders. Psychometric tests may contribute to understanding a youngster's behavior,
but the tests' reliability and validity are inadequate for purposes of identification.
Although the problems of reliability and validity are especially great for projective tests,
which purportedly measure unconscious mental processes, these problems also occur
in personality inventories, behavior rating scales, and screening tests designed to sift
out students who may have a disorder (Epstein & Cullinan, 1998; Merrell, 1994).

Some of the difficulty in measurement is a result of attempts to assess supposed
internal states or personality constructs that cannot be observed directly. Direct
observation and measurement of behavior reduce reliance on indirect measurement,
but these newer assessment techniques have not resolved the problem of definition.
It may be more useful for a teacher to know how frequently a student hits classmates
or sasses an adult than it is to know the student's responses to psychometric tests,
but there is no consensus among teachers or psychologists as to what frequency of a
given behavior indicates a disorder. Local norms for given behavior problems may be
useful in screening, but they do not provide a general definition.

To compare students for purposes of classification, behavior must be measured
under specified environmental conditions. This standard is required because behavior
is typically sensitive to social context: Students behave differently under different circumstances. But even if environmental conditions are specified and students' behaviors
are measured directly and reliably under those conditions, we are still not likely to
derive a satisfactory definition. The reason is, that given a single set of environmental
circumstances, disordered and adaptive behaviors are defined by more than behavioral
frequencies. Adaptive and disordered behaviors are defined by the student's ability or
inability to modulate his or her behavior in everyday environments to avoid the censure
of others and to obtain their approval. The problem of measurement here is analogous
to that in the fields of vision and hearing. Central visual acuity and pure-tone auditory

thresholds can be measured precisely under carefully controlled conditions, but these measures do not indicate (except within very broad limits) how efficiently one sees or hears in one's everyday environment. For example, two people with the same auditory acuity may function quite differently—one as hearing (using oral language almost exclusively) and the other as deaf (relying mostly on manual communication). Visual and auditory efficiency must be assessed by observing how the individual adapts to the changing demands of the environment for seeing and hearing. Behavioral adaptation must also be judged by observation and according to how well one meets environmental demands that often change subtly. This judgment calls for experienced "clinical" appraisal, which includes precise measurement of behavior going beyond quantitative assessment, and also demands knowledge of cultural influences on behavior.

Range and Variability of Normal and Deviant Behavior

A wide range of behavior may be considered normal; the difference between normal and disordered behavior is usually one of degree rather than kind, and there is no sharp line between the two. Most children and youth do nearly everything done by those who have emotional or behavioral disorders, but they perform these acts under different conditions, at a different age, or at a different rate. Crying, throwing temper tantrums, fighting, whining, spitting, urinating, screaming, and so on are behaviors that can be expected of all youngsters. Only the situations in which children and youth with emotional or behavioral disorders perform these acts or the intensity and rate at which they do them sets them apart. Longitudinal studies and surveys of youngsters' and parents' perceptions of problem behavior show clearly that a large number of children and youth who are considered "normal" show disturbing behaviors such as tantrums, destructiveness, fearfulness, and hyperactivity to some degree and at some time during their development. Most students are considered to have a behavior problem at some time by one of their teachers. The problem of definition involves comparison against a nebulous and constantly changing standard. There are inadequate quantitative norms for most behaviors to which we can compare a student's behavior.

There is also great variability in deviant behavior. Deviant acts can range from physical assault on others to extreme withdrawal. An individual may exhibit behavior that alternates between these extremes, and the degree of deviance may change markedly over time or with changes in the environment. It is inappropriate to consider most classifications of human behavior as mutually exclusive such that one must be considered either aggressive or nonaggressive, withdrawn or gregarious, and so on. It is extremely difficult to write a definition that deals adequately with the many types and degrees of disorder.

Relationships Among Emotional or Behavioral Disorders and Other Exceptionalities

Decades ago, Hallahan and Kauffman (1977) pointed out that there are many similarities among students with mild mental retardation, learning disabilities, and emotional or behavioral disorders. Students with severe disabilities in these three categories have many common characteristics. There is considerable literature regarding emotional or behavioral disorders in individuals with mental retardation (Barrett, 1986; Epstein, Cullinan, & Polloway, 1986; Lee, Moss, Friedlander, Donnelly, & Honer, 2003; Menolascino, 1990) and communication disorders (Rogers-Adkinson & Griffith, 1999). It is often difficult not only to distinguish among students with pervasive developmental disorders such as autism or mental retardation, but in some cases it may also be difficult to distinguish very young children with severe emotional or behavioral disorders from those who are deaf, blind or who have suffered brain damage from cerebral palsy or traumatic brain injury.

A student may have more than one type of disability. Disordered behavior may occur in combination with any other type of exceptionality; indeed, emotional or behavioral disorders probably occur more frequently in combination with other disabilities than alone. Defining emotional or behavioral disorders in a way that excludes other handicapping conditions is unrealistic. A disorder should be defined specifically enough for its definition to be of value in working with children and youth whose single or primary disability is maladaptive emotions or behavior but broadly enough to admit its coexistence with other disabilities. This is not easy.

Transience of Many Emotional and Behavioral Problems

Emotional and behavioral problems are often transitory. Behavioral problems exhibited by young children seem likely to disappear within a few years unless the problems are severe or include high levels of hostile aggression and destructiveness. Definitions must take into account age-specific and developmentally normal problems that do not persist over a long period of time.

Disadvantages in Labeling Deviance

A problem associated with the issue of definition is the unavoidable practice of labeling—attaching a diagnostic or classifying label to the student or behavior (Burbach, 1981; Hallahan & Kauffman, 2003; Kauffman, 1999c, 2002, 2003a, 2003b; Kauffman & Pullen, 1996). Assigning any label is dangerous because the label is likely to stigmatize and can significantly alter the youngster's opportunities for education, employment, and socialization. This seems to be true regardless of the conceptual foundation of the definition with which the label is associated or the semantics of the label. Furthermore, once a student has been labeled, changing the label may be difficult or impossible. However, we cannot talk about things, including disabilities, without using labels (language) to describe them. Our definitions should be couched in language that will minimize damage to students when they are identified as members of a particular deviant group, but reducing stigma depends on changing social attitudes toward what we label, not on changing the label referring to undesirable characteristics (see Kauffman, 2003a).

Importance of Definition

The issue of definitions may not appear serious at first. If a student has an emotional or behavioral disorder when adult authorities say so, then why not concern ourselves with the more important issue of effective intervention and leave the question of definition to those who enjoy arguing about words? Serious reflection leads us ultimately to conclude that definition is too important to leave to chance or whim (Cullinan, 2004; Forness & Kavale, 1997).

The definition we accept reflects how we conceptualize the problem and therefore what intervention strategies we consider appropriate. A definition succinctly communicates a conceptual framework that has direct implications for practitioners. Medical definitions imply the need for medical interventions, educational definitions imply the need for educational solutions, and so on. Furthermore, a definition specifies the population to be served and thereby has a profound effect on who receives intervention, as well as how they will be served. It follows that if a definition specifies a population, then it will provide the basis for estimates of prevalence. Finally, decisions of legislative bodies, of government executives, and of school administrators concerning allocation of funds and training and employment of personnel are guided by the implications of working definitions. Vague and inappropriate definitions contribute to confused and inadequate legislation, foggy administrative policies, non-functional teacher training, and ineffective intervention. Definition is a crucial as well as a difficult problem, and it behooves special educators to construct the soundest possible definition.

A case in point—definitional problems affecting services to students—is the current federal definition that has been widely criticized for a variety of reasons as inadequate or inappropriate. The federal definition seems to indicate that a student must be failing academically to be classified as "emotionally disturbed" for special education purposes. This feature of the definition may result in denial of services to a large number of students with serious disorders but with academic skills judged adequate for their grade placement (Forness & Kavale, 1997; Kauffman, 1986a, 1999c; Morse, 1985; Smith, Wood, & Grimes, 1988; Wodrich, Stobo, & Trca, 1998).

The Current Federal Definition: Its Derivation and Status

During the past 40 years, numerous definitions of emotional or behavioral disorders have been constructed. Each definition has served the particular purposes of the writer, but none has resolved the problems of terminology, specificity, clarity, and usefulness that we have discussed. Only one definition, Bower's (1981), has had a significant influence on public policy at the national level. The current federal definition derives from Bower's research in the 1950s involving thousands of students in California. Although Bower's definition is a logical interpretation of his findings, the version that was adopted by the U.S. Department of Education has been widely criticized as illogical (see Bower, 1982; Council for Children with Behavioral Disorders Executive Committee, 1987; Forness & Knitzer, 1992; Kauffman, 1986a). To understand the issues, one must first understand Bower's definition and then compare it to the federal version, point by point.

In a classic treatise on definition and identification, Bower (1981) defined "emotionally handicapped" students as those exhibiting to a marked extent and over a period of time one or more of five characteristics (pp. 115–116):

1. An inability to learn that cannot be explained by intellectual, sensory, or health factors
2. An inability to build or maintain satisfactory interpersonal relationships with peers and teachers
3. Inappropriate types of behavior or feelings under normal conditions
4. A general, pervasive mood of unhappiness or depression
5. A tendency to develop physical symptoms, pains, or fears associated with personal or school problems.

According to Bower, the first of these characteristics, problems in learning, is possibly the most significant school-related aspect of emotionally handicapped youngsters' behavior. He goes on to explain that another important feature of his definition is the inclusion of degree or level of severity. Bower's definition has many good points, particularly its specification of five characteristic types of behavior. Still, it does not easily enable one to determine that a particular child or youth is or is not emotionally handicapped (see Epstein & Cullinan, 1998). There is much latitude in terms such as *to a marked extent* and *over a period of time*. There is also a need for subjective judgment about each of the five characteristics. Consider the problems in answering these questions:

Just what is an inability to learn? Is it evidenced by a one-year lag in achievement? Six months? Two years? Does it include the inability to learn appropriate social behavior, or only academic skills?
How do you establish that an apparent inability to learn is not explainable by intellectual or health factors? Do health factors include mental health factors?
Exactly what are satisfactory interpersonal relationships with peers?
What is inappropriate behavior and what are normal conditions?
When is unhappiness pervasive?

Bower's definition is widely criticized because it obviously lacks the precision necessary to take subjectivity out of decision making. This may not be a fault of his definition. It may be the nature of the problem of definition. Bower's definition has had a tremendous impact on public policy not because of its accuracy but primarily because it is included, with a few changes, in the rules and regulations governing implementation of Public Law 94–142 (now the Individuals With Disabilities Education Act—IDEA). The federal definition of "emotionally disturbed," with the most significant differences between it and Bower's definition, indicated by italics, reads:

(4)   Emotional disturbance is defined as follows:

(i)   The term means a condition exhibiting one or more of the following characteristics over a long period of time and to a marked degree *that adversely affects a child's educational performance:*

(A)   An inability to learn that cannot be explained by intellectual, sensory, or health factors.

(B) An inability to build or maintain satisfactory interpersonal relationships with peers and teachers.
(C) Inappropriate types of behavior or feelings under normal circumstances.
(D) A general pervasive mood of unhappiness or depression.
(E) A tendency to develop physical symptoms or fears associated with personal or school problems.

(ii)   *The term includes schizophrenia. The term does not apply to children who are socially maladjusted, unless it is determined that they have an emotional disturbance.*

Bower's term *emotionally handicapped* was changed to *emotionally disturbed*. As the italics show, the federal rules and regulations contain three statements not found in Bower's original definition. These added statements do not make the definition clearer; in fact, they come close to making nonsense of it. The additional clause "which adversely affects educational performance" is particularly puzzling. One might speculate that it is a pro forma statement (i.e., set up in advance) that the regulation is concerned only with educational matters. The clause is redundant, however, with Characteristic A, "An inability to learn," if educational performance is considered to mean academic achievement. Moreover, a student is extremely unlikely to exhibit one or more of the characteristics listed to a marked degree and for a long time without adverse effects on academic progress. But what should one conclude about a student who exhibits, for example, Characteristic D, "A general, pervasive mood of unhappiness or depression" and is academically advanced for his or her age and grade? If educational performance is interpreted to mean academic achievement, then the student would seem to be excluded from the category of emotionally disturbed. However, if educational performance is interpreted to include personal and social satisfaction in the school setting, then the clause is superfluous.

Even greater confusion is created by part ii regarding schizophrenia and social maladjustment. Any youngster with schizophrenia would clearly be included under the original definition. That is, any such child or youth will exhibit one or more of the five characteristics listed (especially B or C, or both) to a marked degree and over a long period of time. Therefore, the addendum is unnecessary. The final addendum regarding social maladjustment is incomprehensible. A youngster cannot be socially maladjusted by any credible interpretation of the term without exhibiting one or more of the five characteristics (especially B, C, or both) to a marked degree and over a long period of time. Neither logic nor research supports the discrimination between social maladjustment and emotional disturbance (Bower, 1982; Cline, 1990; Costenbader & Buntaine, 1999; Walker et al., 2004). Many professionals are very unhappy with the current definition because of the limitations we have discussed and hope that it will soon be replaced.

PERSPECTIVES ON DEFINITION

In the early part of the 20th century, psychiatric perspectives on definition tended to be accepted with little question by school personnel. Bower's work in California public schools in the 1950s and 1960s and the growth of special education programs for students with emotional or behavioral disorders led to definitions that were more closely related to students' behavior in the classroom. Most professionals recognize that a given definition is never adequate for all purposes. As Knitzer (1982) commented, "it is hard to talk about children and adolescents who need mental health services. Terms like 'mentally ill,' 'behaviorally disordered,' or 'psychotic' take away their uniqueness and pain" (p. 3). The most useful definition for educators is one that clearly focuses on the behavior problems of school students.

Ironically, the current federal definition may be contributing to the underservice of students with emotional or behavioral disorders. The addenda to Bower's definition allow so many interpretations that students who need services can be easily excluded. Some can be excluded because they are not academically retarded, others because they are judged to be socially maladjusted but not emotionally disturbed. Legal arguments continue over issues such as whether a student must be academically retarded under the definition and whether adjudication as delinquent qualifies a juvenile as emotionally disturbed.

The definition of emotional or behavioral disorders remains partly subjective, even though several relevant characteristics of a student's behavior can be described clearly. The definition of disturbance or disorder eludes complete objectivity for the same reasons that happiness and depression defy completely objective definition. This does not mean that the effort to devise more objective means of identifying students must be abandoned (as we discuss further in part 2). Nor does it mean that it is impossible to improve the definition. For the definition to be most useful to educators, however, the subjective judgments that go into identifying students must include those of the teachers who work with them. In decisions made by groups of professionals, the teacher, not the psychologist, social worker, or psychiatrist, should be viewed as the most important "imperfect test" in determining that a student needs help in school (Gerber & Semmel, 1984). Reliance on teachers' judgments puts great responsibility on teachers for moral and ethical conduct in decision making, but it is a responsibility they cannot avoid (Howe & Miramontes, 1992; Kauffman, 1992, 2002, 2003b).

An Emerging Definition

The problems presented by the current federal definition have been recognized for many years. Although professionals have been able to reach agreement on a substitute definition, they have not been able to persuade the U.S. Congress to adopt a new one. The National Mental Health and Special Education Coalition created a working group assigned to propose a new definition. The working group represented more than a dozen different professional associations and advocacy groups, assuring that the proposed definition would initially have a strong base of support. The definition proposed in the 1980s reads as follows:

I. The term emotional or behavioral disorder means a disability characterized by behavioral or emotional responses in school programs so different from appropriate age, cultural, or ethnic norms that they adversely affect educational performance, including academic, social, vocational or personal skills, and which:

(a) is more than a temporary, expected response to stressful events in the environment;

(b) is consistently exhibited in two different settings, at least one of which is school related; and

(c) persists despite individualized interventions within the education program, unless, in the judgment of the team, the child's or youth's history indicates that such interventions would not be effective.

Emotional or behavioral disorders can co-exist with other disabilities.

II. This category may include children or youth with schizophrenic disorders, affective disorders, anxiety disorders, or other sustained disturbances of conduct or adjustment when they adversely affect educational performance in accordance with section I. (Forness & Knitzer, 1992, p. 13)

This definition obviously does not solve all the problems in identifying and serving children and youth with emotional or behavioral disorders. Nevertheless, the coalition and many of its member organizations believe it is a significant improvement over the federal definition. Forness and Knitzer (1992) noted the following:

1. It uses terminology that reflects current professional preferences and concern for minimizing stigma.
2. It includes both disorders of emotions and disorders of behavior.
3. It is school centered but acknowledges that disorders exhibited outside the school setting are also important.
4. It is sensitive to ethnic and cultural differences.
5. It does not include minor or transient problems or ordinary responses to stress.
6. It acknowledges the importance of prereferral interventions but does not require slavish implementation of them in extreme cases.
7. It acknowledges that children and youth can have multiple disabilities.
8. It includes the full range of emotional or behavioral disorders of concern to mental health and special education professionals without arbitrary exclusions.

A major problem of the current federal definition is its exclusion of many antisocial children and youth who need special education and related mental health services.

The coalition and many of the more than 30 professional and advocacy groups have formally endorsed the proposed definition and are working toward its incorporation into federal laws and regulations. Those who support the definition hope that it will eventually become the standard adopted by the states as well.

SUMMARY

Children and youth with emotional or behavioral disorders are disabled by behaviors that are discordant with their social–interpersonal environments. The definition of these disorders is a difficult matter complicated by differences in conceptual models, differences in the purposes of various social agencies, problems in measuring social–interpersonal behavior, variability in normal behavior, confusing relationships among emotional or behavioral disorders and other exceptionalities, the transience of many childhood disorders, and the effects of pejorative labels. No definition can be made completely objective. No definition has been universally accepted. The most common definition used in educational contexts is the one proposed originally by Bower and incorporated into the federal rules and regulations for IDEA. This definition specifies marked and persistent characteristics having to do with the following:

1. School learning problems
2. Unsatisfactory interpersonal relationships
3. Inappropriate behavior and feelings
4. Pervasive unhappiness or depression
5. Physical symptoms or fears associated with school or personal problems

Inclusion and exclusion clauses of questionable meaning have been appended to these characteristics in the federal definition. Although improvements in definition are possible, and more objective criteria for identification are being developed, teachers' responsibility for judging students' behavior cannot be avoided.

A new definition has been proposed by the National Mental Health and Special Education Coalition using the term *emotional or behavioral disorder*. The proposed definition has been endorsed by many organizational members of the coalition, who hope to incorporate the new definition into federal laws and regulations. Major points of the proposed definition are

1. Emotional or behavioral responses in school
2. Difference from age, cultural, or ethnic norms
3. Adverse effect on educational performance (academic, social, vocational, or personal)
4. Responses to stress that are more than temporary or expected
5. Consistent problem in two different settings, including school
6. Persistent disorder despite individualized interventions
7. Possibility of coexistence with other disabilities
8. Full range of disorders of emotions or behavior

CASE FOR DISCUSSION (SEE CASEBOOK FOR ADDITIONAL CASES)

Where Does He Fit?
Allan Zook

I did not realize they were shopping for the ideal class for their son when Allan's parents came to observe my classroom. Just before their observation, Allan had qualified for special education services as a student with multiple disabilities. But neither the school system nor the parents could decide where he could best be served. A week after their visit, my supervisor brought me Allan's folder and directed me to meet with the parents that week and develop an individualized education program for him. "You win!" she said as she patted my shoulder. My question was "Why?"

My "prize" was 7 years old. He had received speech and language services since he was 2, took massive doses of anticonvulsant medication, and thought compliance with adults' requests or commands was disabling. He also had a repertoire of behaviors guaranteed to distress his teachers and peers. For example, he liked to pick his nose and wipe the results on teachers or students. He routinely exposed himself during the time he spent in mainstream classes. He was big for his age, aggressive, and had justifiably earned the description of "bully." I was not surprised to observe that he played by himself

and did not approach other students. They did not approach him either.

Testing Allan was, according to the school psychologists who had tried, an extraordinary challenge. The full-scale IQ of 73 was to be taken with a grain of salt, because his responses were "unusual." Allan's academic skills were as delayed as his social skills. Most of the normative and curriculum-based measurement data placed him 2 to 3 years behind his age mates in reading and math. His fine motor skills were almost nonexistent, and any required handwriting, cutting, or painting was for him a fate worse than death. "It's too hard," he always whined before he threw a tantrum.

Individual and small-group instruction was almost impossible for Allan. Even when he tried to pay attention (which wasn't very often), he was distracted by anything and everything—people walking by the room, other students shifting in their seats, a newly decorated bulletin board, someone's clothing, or a strange noise.

Some days he came to school late because he had experienced a seizure earlier in the day. On those days, he was subdued and not so eager to misbehave, but neither did he remember many of the skills he had mastered before the seizure. If he had a seizure in school, which happened occasionally, the rest of the day was a waste as far as academic work was concerned.

"So, why me, Lord?" I asked myself repeatedly. Allan's parents and the special education administrators had considered classes designed for kids with learning disabilities, physical disabilities, and emotional disturbance, but they decided my class of kids with mild mental retardation was the best place for him. They liked my highly structured, directive program. They liked the fact that my kids were happy and learning lots of social and academic skills. They believed he'd fit in better in my class than in any of the others. Besides, I had room to take another student in my class without asking for a state waiver. So I won the lottery.

Questions About the Case

1. Does Allan fit the definition of "emotional disturbance" in IDEA? Does he fit the definition of "emotional or behavioral disorder" of the National Mental Health and Special Education Coalition?

2. How would you determine which of Allan's disabilities was foremost for purposes of education?

3. Was Allan's placement in this class appropriate? Was it legal under IDEA? (You may want to revisit this question after you have read chapter 6.)

>> PERSONAL REFLECTIONS

Definition

Steven R. Forness, EdD, was principal of the inpatient school and an educational psychologist in the outpatient clinic at UCLA Neuropsychiatric Hospital. He was also a professor in the Department of Psychiatry and Biobehavioral Sciences at UCLA. He is now professor emeritus at UCLA.

Why should an emotional or behavioral disorder be considered a disability?

Children who have emotional or behavioral disorders are disabled in an especially critical way. They are cut off in one way or another from the fullness of life itself. A boy with schizophrenia may at times be so bombarded by "voices in his head" that he can pay only intermittent attention to what the real people around him are saying. A girl with clinical depression may feel so withdrawn or sad that she can scarcely get out of bed in the morning, let alone enjoy the company of others. An adolescent with an anxiety disorder may be so fearful or preoccupied with what others may think that he or she avoids a whole variety of wonderful situations that are part of growing up. A young boy with an attention deficit may be so hyperactive or impulsive that the simplest of school tasks becomes arduous and cannot be finished without tremendous and exhaustive effort at concentration. Even a youngster with a conduct disorder may be so impelled to follow his or her own instincts as to be constantly drawn into conflicts, arguments, or physical aggression, even with close family members. Children like these have real and tragic disabilities.

These children may also have associated problems that add to their disability, especially in school. As many as half of them have serious academic problems. I have had almost daily contact with youngsters whose schooling has been interrupted by their emotional or behavioral disorders for a wide variety of reasons. Some are so depressed or anxious that they never even make it to school for days or weeks at a time. Others are so prone to verbal conflict or physical aggression with classmates or teachers that they are frequently truant or suspended from school. Still others show behavioral or emotional responses to typical situations that are so unusual or bizarre that their schoolmates either begin to shun their company or, worse yet, tease them unmercifully. School becomes a particularly unhappy place for them. When someone asks the degree to which these youngsters are disabled, I answer as a special educator that a great many are perhaps even *more* disabled than children or adolescents with learning disabilities or mental retardation. As a matter of fact, recent annual reports by the U.S. Department of Education have shown that the long-term outcomes for youngsters with emotional or behavioral disorders are among the worst in special education and that we are serving only the most seriously impaired in this category.

Why and how are these children disabled?

To answer that question, one has only to ask their parents, their teachers, and even the youngsters themselves. They will tell you not only of the devastating personal distress and stigma that go with having these disorders but also of the abysmal failure of education, mental health, child welfare, juvenile justice, and health insurance agencies to ease their plight. It is indeed this current combination of personal anguish and public neglect that leads me to see emotional or behavioral disorders as one of the most disabling conditions of the children with whom I work.

Why do professionals find it so difficult to agree on a definition?

I have observed the process of definition and diagnosis of emotional or behavioral disorders from several vantage points. I worked as a special educator in a psychiatric setting for over 30 years. For several years, I also have been a member of the National Mental Health and Special Education Coalition, a group of about 30 professional associations representing school and mental health professionals, as well as families of youngsters with emotional or behavioral

23

disorders. I have also worked with others on the revision of the American Psychiatric Association's diagnostic manual. All these experiences lead me to wonder how we ever arrive at *any* definition of emotional or behavioral disorders.

Part of the problem stems from the limited perspective of each professional discipline. Parents tend to focus on the problems of living with their children, teachers often see only classroom management or academic issues, social workers tend to view family interactions as a primary focus, psychologists sometimes are preoccupied with the child's inner world or behavioral interactions that can be shaped and modified, and psychiatrists may concentrate on a search for effective medication. Seldom, if ever, does everyone sit in the same room and pool these fragments of knowledge. It is also exceedingly rare that professionals are trained in a truly interdisciplinary fashion. More often than not, they are taught in a multidisciplinary fashion, where they work side by side yet seldom interact with each other in any significant way.

Part of the problem also involves how we determine when an emotional or behavioral response actually crosses the line and becomes "deviant." Psychiatric diagnoses are not very reliable and often consist of selecting a critical but limited number of symptoms from a larger list of common characteristics of a particular disorder. Emotional or behavioral rating scales often depend on a rather arbitrary clinical cutoff point determined from a limited sample of patients. Projective tests depend greatly on the skill of individual clinicians who determine whether responses are outside normal limits. Case histories of a child with a potential emotional or behavioral disorder are frequently filtered through both the selective memories of parents or guardians and the biases of the interviewing clinician.

Finally, society itself shifts its tolerance for deviant behavior from generation to generation (witness the difference between the button-down era of the 1950s and the wild rebelliousness of the 1960s), from community to community (behavior that seems quite common to residents in an inner-city neighborhood may seem intolerable to those living in a wealthy suburb), and from age to age (behavior tolerated from a preschooler becomes unacceptable just a few years later). Given all of these barriers to consensus, the definition of emotional or behavioral disorders will continue to be the most elusive category in special education.

Is it useful to draw distinctions between emotional disorders and behavioral disorders?

In actual fact, it is sometimes difficult if not impossible to separate emotional from behavioral disorders. When I read case histories of children admitted to our psychiatric hospital for so-called emotional disorders, such as depression, the first thing that parents or teachers noticed in many cases was not necessarily the emotion of sadness but a behavior, such as the child's acting agitated or aggressive or withdrawing from social situations. We often have to infer emotional states from a child's overt behaviors. I have also studied a rather large group of children with depression in our outpatient clinic and found that more than half of them had a separate diagnosis of conduct or attention deficit disorder in addition to their underlying depression. This comorbidity or co-occurrence of two disorders in the same child may be much more common in children referred for services (i.e., the ones referred for special education or mental health services). Dick Mattison, a psychiatrist whom I helped to train at UCLA, has done extensive research on children referred to special education for emotional or behavioral disorders. He found that nearly half of these students had two different diagnoses, usually an emotional and a behavioral disorder. Having one disorder does not confer any immunity from developing a second disorder; it may in fact even predispose a child to having another disorder. Seldom do disorders come in nice tidy packages.

Differentiating between these two types of disorders may be useful or even possible only at the extremes. Historically, the primary public school term for these disorders in federal special education law was "serious emotional disturbance." Most mental health clinicians and special educators nonetheless realize that it is not useful, and most of the time not even possible, to make these distinctions.

Are there other points you would like to make about this topic?

Three things about these children continue to amaze me. One is the incredible diversity of this population. We had from 20 to 40 children in our psychiatric hospital at any given time, ranging in age from 2 to early 20s. Most presented challenging problems, even for an experienced special education teacher. Our inpatient school, therefore, had a variety of small preschool, elementary, and secondary classrooms to address the functional levels of these youngsters' learning and behavioral problems, with a variety of special or remedial curriculum materials and individualized token economy systems. But we also had an elementary classroom and a secondary classroom in which we had regular textbooks, put relatively little or no emphasis on token or checkmark systems, and focused more on academic progress than on classroom behavior or social skills. Kids who attended these latter two classrooms did so because they had been admitted to a psychiatric hospital for a range of serious psychiatric disorders. The expression of their particular emotional or behavioral disorders just didn't seem to affect their ability to comply with most school expectations or do academic work. The educators in their community schools were completely (and probably appropriately) unaware that these children had serious psychiatric disorders such as schizophrenia, anxiety disorder, or depression.

Second, the children we served often needed many different types of services. I spoke earlier of comorbidity (i.e., two or more psychiatric disorders occurring in the same child). It turns out, however, that many of the children I worked with had what I call trimorbidity (i.e., two or more psychiatric disorders along with a learning disability or even mental retardation). Several also came with histories of child abuse and even chronic medical disorders in addition to their emotional or behavioral disorders. Almost daily I came across kids who needed the services of at least four or five professionals when they left the hospital, for example, a psychiatrist to regulate their medication, a psychologist to assist their parents in developing and monitoring a home behavioral management system, a social worker for family therapy sessions,

perhaps one of these three or even a fourth person to also be the child's therapist, a consulting special education teacher for learning disability materials in school, and even a pediatrician for medical problems that may be related to physical or sexual abuse or for a chronic medical problem that may be unrelated. It was not all that unusual for a single case to require the coordination of agencies for mental health, special education, child welfare, health services, and juvenile justice.

Third, time and time again, even after reading what looked like a catastrophic case history and steeling myself for the worst, the kid I met was essentially just a kid. Relatively seldom was his or her behavior especially bizarre. More often than not the behavioral or emotional responses we saw were crying, tantrums, mouthing off, fighting, and other things that most kids occasionally do in the course of growing up. Kids with emotional or behavioral disorders do these things but do them much more frequently and with less provocation. Emotional or behavioral disorders are, in all but a few cases, mostly a matter of degree. What separates them is the frequency (not the kind) of emotional or behavioral response. In most cases, there is just a kid underneath all that behavioral or emotional excess, a kid who is hurt or scared or misunderstood, either because of what has happened in the past or because of the insidiousness of the disorder itself. Some few disorders are, of course, extreme and require very specific treatments. In every case, however, we do well to remember that we treat a child, not a disorder.

>> QUESTIONS FOR FURTHER REFLECTION

1. How would you respond to someone who suggested that youngsters who act out are bad kids, not kids with disabilities?
2. How would you explain to someone who is unfamiliar with special education and child psychology what is wrong with the youngsters we say have emotional or behavioral disorders?
3. How would you make the case that some youngsters who exhibit problem behavior should be excluded from the definition of emotional or behavioral disorders?

CHAPTER TWO

PREVALENCE

THE EXTENT OF THE PROBLEM

As you read this chapter, keep these guiding questions in mind:

- In what sense does identification of students with emotional or behavioral disorders require arbitrary decisions?

- What is the difference between prevalence and incidence?

- Why have special educators been more concerned with prevalence than with incidence?

- What arguments can one use to defend the position that 2% of the student population is a conservative estimate of prevalence?

- Approximately what percentage of the public school population is now served by special education under the "emotionally disturbed" category?

Nearly all children and youth at some time, in some social context, could be said to exhibit an emotional or behavioral disorder. But classifying nearly all children and youths as disabled by these isolated, transitory, or minor problems would be silly. Indeed, suggestions that 20% or more of children and youth have serious psychological problems create public disbelief and professional skepticism. A typical reaction is that bleeding hearts are making much ado about the normal pains of growing up, bemoaning the usual slings and arrows that people must suffer as part of their daily lives.

The general public and administrators tend to dismiss teachers' reports of problems as unreliable. Teachers do sometimes mistake their own ineptitude in teaching and managing behavior for the emotional or behavioral disorders of students, and skeptics use this fact to discount all teachers' opinions. If we want to argue convincingly for special services, we must present the strongest possible case that the emotional and behavioral problems we are concerned about are unusual, debilitating, and are not the result of teachers' inadequacies.

How frequently do students' emotional or behavioral problems clearly stand out from the usual difficulties of childhood and youth and seriously limit their options for social and personal development despite adequate teachers? The answer cannot be entirely objective. Addressing the question requires that we establish arbitrary criteria. These criteria may be quite objective, but choosing them requires subjective judgment. Consider similar questions: How heavy (or thin or tall or short) must a person of a given age be to qualify as exceptional for medical purposes? How little income must a person have to be considered poor for purposes of public assistance? How different from the average in intelligence and social adaptation must a student be to qualify as having mental retardation (or giftedness) for special education purposes? In each case, we can "make" more people deviant—obese, poor, retarded, or disturbed, for example—simply by changing an arbitrary definition. Physicians, economists, social workers, psychologists, or educators may make their case for a given criterion, and their arguments may be convincing to legislators or others who make public policy or establish standards for judgment. The standards and policy are merely a matter of consensus, and they can be changed at will.

The number or percentage of children and youth who are judged to have emotional or behavioral disorders, then, is a matter of choice. Disordered emotion or behavior is not a "thing," an objective entity that can be detached from the observer. Emotional or behavioral disorder—like poverty or love or justice—is a social reality that we construct on the basis of our judgment as to what is tolerable and what is desirable (Kauffman, 1999g, 2003b; Kauffman, Gerber, & Semmel, 1988). Our task as professionals is to struggle with issues of prevalence, to make the most intelligent and caring choices we can about the lives of children and youths. We must seek to identify those students—and only those—for whom the risks associated with identification (such as social stigma) are outweighed by the advantages (effective intervention). This is not easy. Although we can and must make difficult judgments about the risks and advantages entailed in identification, we can seldom be absolutely certain that our judgment of the individual case is correct.

Try to decide which of the students described in the accompanying casebook has an emotional or behavioral disorder. The descriptions are very brief, and you probably believe you should have more information before making judgments. You should, in fact, have more information; anyone should, and anyone would probably be unprofessional in making a judgment based solely on this information.

WHO HAS A DISORDER?

The descriptions of cases in the accompanying case book are based on actual case histories. Some of the children and youth were labeled as having an emotional or behavioral disorder; others were not. Some were placed in regular classrooms, others in special classes or institutions. These brief case descriptions illustrate the difficulties even experts face in deciding who does and does not have an emotional or behavioral disorder. Here, we present only the case of T. J.

>> *T. J.*

T. J. is an 11-year-old fifth grader. His IQ is 115. He has no significant physical anomalies and no history of developmental delay in motor development or language. He had no particular difficulties academically until fourth grade. His academic performance was about average until last year, when his grades suddenly began to deteriorate. This year he is earning mostly Ds and Fs.

T. J. was not known as a problem child in school until last year. But every teacher who has dealt with him in the past 18 months has commented on his frequent misbehavior. He is difficult to manage because of his high rates of out-of-seat behavior, talking out, teasing, and temper outbursts. He is usually defiant of teachers and argumentative with his peers. These problems are, in the opinion of his current teachers, increasing. His belligerence recently resulted in several fights in and around school, including one in which another child was injured and required medical attention. Two weeks ago he was caught shoplifting a bag of candy from the local drugstore. Ratings by his teachers on a problem checklist indicate that his behavior is a problem more often than that of 90% of his schoolmates.

T. J. has no close friends, although he is sometimes tolerated briefly in school situations by other boys who exhibit similar behavior patterns. He and his two older brothers live with his mother and stepfather, who provide little supervision or control. His parents have never shown any interest in his school progress or lack of it, and they have refused to recognize that any of his behavior, including the fights and shoplifting, is a problem.

T. J.'s current teachers are quite concerned about him for several reasons. He does not complete most of his academic work and is failing in most subjects. He disrupts the class frequently by hitting or taunting other students or mumbling complaints about the teacher and assignments. He spends a lot of his time in class drawing tattoos on his arms with felt-tip pens. None of his three experienced teachers, who manage 63 fifth graders as a team, has been able to establish a close relationship with T. J. or produce significant improvement in his behavior. (Kauffman, 1984, p. 62)

For special education purposes, should one consider T. J. to have a disorder? On the basis of the information presented, experts may disagree. Of course, one may argue that additional information is necessary to justify a decision. But regardless of how much additional information one might amass, the decision would probably remain questionable. Some would argue that T. J. presents a problem but does not have an emotional or behavioral disorder. Perhaps he needs help but not in the form of special education. Some might suggest that his home life and his teachers' lack of expertise are responsible for his behavior. T. J. and everyone else involved would have more to lose than to gain by his being identified as a student with an emotional or behavioral disorder. His problems can best be addressed through consultation with his regular class teachers on how to manage his behavior in the classroom and by providing social workers to help his parents do a better job at home.

Others would argue that T. J. shows all the classic signs of a student in trouble, one who is unlikely to improve without direct intervention. He is certainly headed for more social and academic trouble unless something is done, probably through provision of special education and related services. Special educators are the most appropriate professionals to deal with the situation, and the benefits of identifying him for special education would clearly outweigh the risks. He can be taught academic and social skills most effectively through placement in a special program for part of the school day with a smaller group of students and a teacher specially trained to manage such problems. After weighing all the outcomes—for T. J., his classmates, his teachers, and his parents—the greatest benefits and least damage will be done by providing special education.

Understandably, heated arguments about prevalence will continue into the foreseeable future. After all, the issues are both complex and emotional; they include economics, statistics, law, public policy, and concern for the welfare of children.

THE MEANING OF PREVALENCE AND INCIDENCE

Prevalence refers to the total number of individuals with X disorder in a given population. The prevalence of a disorder is calculated for a given period or for a point in time. Federal reports typically include the number of students with emotional or behavioral disorders counted at a particular time during the school year. Prevalence is often expressed as a percentage of the population; the total number of cases is divided by the total number of individuals in the population. Thus, if 40 students out of a total student population of 2,000 in a school or school district are identified as having emotional or behavioral disorders, then the prevalence rate is 2%.

Incidence refers to the rate of *inception*—the number of new cases of X disorder in a given population. *Cases* can refer to individuals or to episodes of the disorder (which means that an individual might be counted more than once during the incidence period if he or she exhibits the disorder, subsequently does not exhibit the disorder or goes into remission, and then again exhibits the disorder). Incidence, like prevalence, may be expressed as a percentage of the population, but this can be misleading when episodes rather than individuals are counted. Incidence addresses the question: How often does this disorder occur? whereas prevalence addresses the question: How many individuals are affected?

For special education purposes, prevalence has usually had more meaning than incidence. Prevalence has been the statistic of interest because most exceptionalities with which special educators deal have been assumed to be developmental, lifelong characteristics. Consequently, teachers and school administrators have most often been concerned about knowing or estimating the number of students who have emotional or behavioral disorders or mental retardation or some other disability in any given school year.

Incidence of certain disorders or problems is often also important, however, particularly when making judgments regarding trends in the school population. The incidence of pregnancy, suicidal behavior, or drug and alcohol use among public school students, for example, may be critical for planning and evaluating intervention programs. Moreover, special educators are becoming increasingly aware that exceptionalities can be episodic. A student may function quite differently in one grade compared with another or even change rather drastically over a period of weeks or months. Emotional or behavioral disorders, as well as giftedness, mental retardation, and learning disabilities, are not necessarily immutable characteristics. To the extent that disorders are transient or episodic, incidence becomes equally as important as prevalence.

Prevalence and Incidence Estimates: Why Should We Care?

Prevalence and incidence estimates have little meaning for the classroom teacher. When your responsibility is to teach a certain number of difficult children and you know that many teachers or parents are anxiously awaiting the day when their child can receive your services, what difference does it make whether 2, 5, or 10% of the school's students have emotional or behavioral disorders?

For those who plan and administer special education programs at a districtwide, statewide, or nationwide level, however, prevalence and incidence are extremely important. Prevalence estimates and incidence rates are the basis for requesting budgets, hiring staff, planning inservice programs, and so on. Frequently, school boards or school administrators decide to cut budgets or allocate additional funds because the percentage of children served by a program is more or less than that of neighboring school districts or state or national averages. Thus, although prevalence issues may seem irrelevant or purely academic to classroom teachers, these issues can ultimately affect their working conditions.

Problems of Estimation

Estimates of the prevalence of emotional or behavioral disorders vary from about 0.5% of the school population to 20% or more. It is easy to see why estimates are varied and confused. First, because the definition is unsettled, the number of students cannot be determined accurately or reliably. It is difficult, if not impossible, to count the instances of a phenomenon that has no precise definition. Second, there are numerous ways to estimate the number of students with emotional or behavioral disorders, and differences in methodology can produce drastically different results. Third, the number of students counted by any definition and methodology can be influenced more by powerful social policy and economic factors than by professional training or clinical judgment. Judgments about who is and is not disabled for special education purposes are surely influenced by social consequences and their economic implications (Kauffman, 1999c, 2003b). We will discuss each of these problems—definition, methodology, and policy and economic factors.

Lack of a Standard Definition

Research clearly shows that identification rates are in part a consequence of the diagnostic criteria that are used (Cluett et al., 1998). Even using a standard written definition, people seem to carry their own private definitions in their heads; they differ greatly in how they match the written definition to students' behavior.

Estimation, False Positives, and False Negatives

Prevalence and incidence are usually estimated from a sample of the population in question. It is not feasible to count every case in an entire state or nation or even in an extremely large school district. The estimate must be generated from standard screening procedures applied to a carefully selected sample. The methodological problems are similar to those of conducting a poll or making a projection during an election. Different numbers will tend to be obtained depending on how the sample is selected and what questions are asked.

In either estimating or identifying students as having emotional or behavioral disorders (or anything else), it is a given that there will be *false negatives* (students who should be but have not been identified) and *false positives* (students who have been identified but should not have been). Put another way, we can say:

False negative—overlooked or missed
False positive—wrongly identified

As Kauffman (1999c, 2003b, 2003c, 2004) points out, the preference for false negatives and the fear of false positives are often sufficient to stop prevention, although it is the false negative that should give us most concern. Which is most common, the false positive or the false negative? If we believe the U.S. surgeon general's report on children's mental health (U.S. Department of Health and Human Services, 2001) and many prevalence studies, then we must conclude that false negatives (children overlooked who should have been identified) far outnumber the false positives (children falsely identified).

Social Policy and Economic Factors

At any given time, 2% is a very modest estimate of the school population whose emotional or behavioral disorders deserve special education. We have very good reason to believe that the percentage of the child population needing mental health services is much higher, and this is likely also an indication of the percentage needing special education for emotional or behavioral disorders (see U.S. Department of Health and Human Services, 2001, Walker, Ramsey, & Gresham, 2004). However, reports from the U.S. Department of Education indicate that only about 1% of the school population receive special education in the "emotionally disturbed" category (U.S. Department of Education, 2002). Because the Individuals with Disabilities Education Act (IDEA) requires that all children with disabilities be identified and provided with special education, we might expect that several times more than 1% should be identified. The percentage served is much lower than the percentage estimated to need services.

The definition of emotional disturbance is sufficiently vague and subjective so that just about any student can be included or excluded as long as inclusion or exclusion serves a useful purpose. School systems and states find it useful to stay within their budgets. Official nonidentification is a convenient way for many school officials to avoid the hassles, risks, and costs of expanded services. In addition, many professionals find it easy to rationalize nonidentification of students (Kauffman, 1984, 1988, 1999c, 2003a, 2004; Walker et al., 2004).

Reasonable Estimates of Prevalence

The most relevant question is: What is a reasonable estimate of the percentage of students whose behavior is so persistently troublesome that special education is desirable? Reasonable estimates based on decades of population surveys are in the range of 3 to 6% of the student population (see Achenbach & Edelbrock, 1981; Anderson & Werry, 1994; Brandenburg, Friedman, & Silver, 1990; Costello, Messer, Bird, Cohen, & Reinherz, 1998; Cullinan, Epstein, & Kauffman, 1984; Graham, 1979; Juul, 1986; U.S. Department of Health and Human Services, 2001).

At the beginning of the 21st century, the U.S. surgeon general released a report indicating that at least 5% of children and youth have serious mental health needs and that only about 1 in 5 receives any mental health services (U.S. Department of Health and Human Services, 2001). We may safely assume that at least half of the children and youths with serious mental health needs (i.e., 2.5%) should be identified for special education—more than double the percentage receiving special education in the category "emotionally disturbed."

Several findings are consistent across a variety of studies spanning nearly half a century. First, most children and youth exhibit seriously troublesome behavior at some time during their development. Second, more than 2% of school-aged youngsters are considered by teachers and other adults—consistently and over a period of years—to exhibit disordered behavior and to fit the federal definition of *emotionally disturbed*. For example, the 7.4% of the child population that Rubin and Balow (1978) found to be consistently identified as having behavior problems over a period of three years appears to fit a reasonable definition: When compared to other children, they scored significantly lower on achievement tests in language, reading, spelling, and arithmetic, in addition to their persistently and pervasively troublesome behavior in school. These children also scored significantly lower on tests of intelligence, were classified in significantly lower socioeconomic levels, totaled significantly higher numbers of grade retentions, and required more special services (remedial reading, speech therapy, psychological evaluation, and so on), all of which are characteristics associated with emotional or behavioral disorders. Students now in programs for students with emotional or behavioral disorders, as well as those not identified but showing similar characteristics, have serious academic and social difficulties that are not likely to be overcome without intervention.

Trends in Prevalence Estimates and Percentage of Students Served by Special Education

During the decade of the mid-1970s to the mid-1980s, the percentage of the public school population receiving special education services under the "seriously emotionally disturbed" category grew from about 0.5 to about 1.0%, however, since 1986, growth in the percentage served has been negligible or even declined, according to federal reports. The percentage of students served varies drastically from state to state and among school districts (Hallahan, Keller, & Ball, 1986; National Research Council, 2002).

Social policy and economic realities have effectively precluded the public schools' identification of 2% or more of the school-aged population as having emotional or behavioral disorders. Consider the economic realities. In the 1970s, nearly a billion more dollars per year would have been needed from the federal government, plus nearly 1.4 billion more dollars from state and local sources, to serve 2% of the students in public schools (Grosenick & Huntze, 1979). These figures did not include funds for training personnel or allowances for inflation. Today, services for 2% of the public school population would require several billion more dollars per year from federal sources alone than is currently budgeted. It is highly unlikely that federal or state legislatures or local schools will make the required amounts of money available for training personnel and operating programs for the 2% of the public school population classified as emotionally disturbed.

Faced with a shortage of adequately trained personnel and insurmountable budget problems, what can we expect of school officials? They cannot risk litigation and loss of federal funds by identifying students they cannot serve. It is reasonable to expect that they will identify as many students as they can find resources to serve. The tragedy is that social policy (IDEA) mandates the impossible and that the public—and a growing number of professionals—are likely to change their perceptions to match economic realities. The social policy mandate changes the question, at least for those who manage budgets, from, How many students with emotional or behavioral disorders are there in our schools? to How many can we afford to serve? And to save face and try to abide by the law, it is tempting to conclude that there are, indeed, precisely as many students with emotional or behavioral disorders as one is able to serve.

Pressures not to identify students as having emotional or behavioral disorders are powerful (Kauffman, 1986b, 1988, 1999c, 2004; Peacock Hill Working Group, 1991). Distaste for identifying students as exceptional and for providing special programs outside the regular class, even on a part-time basis, has led to efforts to merge or restructure special and general education, known since the 1990s as the *full inclusion movement* (Fuchs & Fuchs, 1994, 1995; Kauffman & Hallahan, 2005a, 2005b; Mock &

Kauffman, 2002, 2003). Proponents of full inclusion argue that most students now considered disabled are either not disabled at all or have such mild disabilities that we can expect regular classroom teachers, with little additional training or assistance, to deal with them effectively. This viewpoint, however well intentioned, has a strong negative effect on the recognition of emotional or behavioral disorders as disabilities for which special education and related services are appropriate (Kauffman, Bantz, & McCullough, 2002; Kauffman, Lloyd, Baker, & Reidel, 1995). The trend appears to be toward identification of only those students whose behavior offends or disturbs others most egregiously—those with the most severe disorders (Kauffman, 1999c, 2004; Landrum & Kauffman, 2003). We do not seem to be nearing the day when special education and related services will be provided even for most of the 3% of the child population that Morse (1985) many years ago called "very seriously impaired" (p. ix).

In 1986, a meeting of education and mental health experts resulted in the following conclusions regarding underservice of students with emotional or behavioral disorders by special education (National Mental Health Association, 1986):

- A majority of SED [seriously emotionally disturbed] children are never identified as such and consequently do not receive the services they need. The reasons for this underidentification are many:
- There is concern about the stigma of labeling a child as "severely emotionally disturbed."
- No clear definition of SED eligibility exists in the law; therefore, states have had to operationalize a definition, resulting in a tremendous disparity among states.
- A lack of uniformity in identification procedures exists in states and localities.
- Because of funding constraints, states may set limits on the number of SED children they will identify.
- Children may not be identified, not only because of limited funding, but also because few or no appropriate services may be available in their community or because communities lack confidence in their ability to develop appropriate services due to lack of funding or because this is a difficult population to serve.
- A lack of clarity among clinicians in the mental health field on definitions and diagnoses compounds the difficulty educators have in making an assessment that a child is severely emotionally disturbed.
- The law explicitly excludes children who are "socially maladjusted," yet the distinctions between socially maladjusted and severely emotionally disturbed are confusing and meaningless. This confusion in labeling can result in some children not being identified or served.
- There is a tendency to identify children who present significant behavioral problems, and to overlook those who do not act out. In some communities, this, in part, results in an over-representation of black males identified as SED and an under-identification of females of all races, who may not be labeled as troublesome.
- There are limited outreach efforts by schools and education systems to parents and professionals in the community to identify SED youths.
- There are also differences for SED children, compared to other populations with handicaps, in the degree of their handicap. SED children tend to be more disturbed before they are identified; those with mild or moderate disturbances may never be identified. (p. 5)

Nothing has changed in the intervening time that makes these statements inaccurate. In fact, as the need for services for more children and youth with emotional or behavioral disorders has grown, American society's response has been to trim funding for social programs, including special education, that provide services to those in need (see U.S. Department of Health and Human Services, 2001).

FACTORS AFFECTING PREVALENCE AND PLACEMENT FOR SERVICES

Assuming that we can agree about the definition of children and youth who should be identified as having emotional or behavioral disorders, what are the factors that might increase or decrease the prevalence of these disorders? This is the primary question we address in the four chapters in part 3.

At this point it is sufficient to note that a variety of biological, family, school, and cultural conditions might make emotional or behavioral disorders occur more frequently. Thus, we might expect that these disorders will be somewhat more prevalent in some communities and schools than in others. Nevertheless, these factors that might be expected to affect prevalence do not explain the extreme range of rates of service (from 0.05% of the school population in one state to more than 2% in another).

Emotional or behavioral disorders are not identified at the same rate across age groups, partly because of the nature of these disorders and the way our society responds to them. As shown in Figure 2.1, the distribution of students identified as having emotional or behavioral disorders at different ages is a mirror image of the distribution for students with learning disabilities, and it is quite unlike the relatively flat distribution for those with mental retardation. Although the data depicted in Figure 2.1 are from the 1989–1990 school year, there is no reason to believe that the distributions across age groups have changed significantly.

We might speculate that the age trends for students with emotional or behavioral disorders are related to the increasing social difficulties they face as they enter adolescence, which is a stressful period for all youngsters. Students with learning disabilities and mental retardation may tend to have more obvious academic difficulties early in their school careers. Those with mental retardation show steady and persistent school difficulties through adolescence, and some of those with learning disabilities begin to find a resolution of their difficulties by early adolescence.

The patterns shown in Figure 2.1 are consistent with other indications that the problems of children with emotional or behavioral disorders tend to be overlooked or neglected for as long as possible—until they become painfully obvious and intolerable to adults. By the time these children obtain services, they are older and their problems are more severe than those identified in other categories. Adults tend to respond to them by being more demanding and punitive. This may account, in part, for the fact that students with emotional or behavioral disorders leave school at higher rates and are placed more frequently in more restrictive settings than are students in other categories (see Cullinan, 2002; Kauffman, 2004; Kauffman, Lloyd, Hallahan, & Astuto, 1995a).

Emotional or behavioral disorders are not identified in the same proportion across all ethnic groups. African American students are about 1.5 times as likely to be identified as are Caucasian students (Coutinho & Oswald, 1998; National Research Council, 2002;

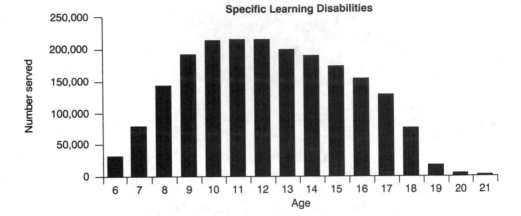

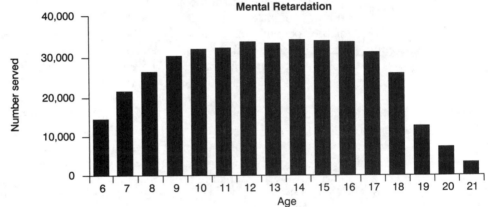

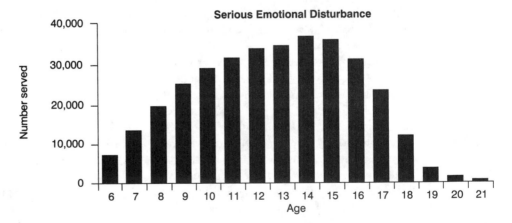

Figure 2.1
Number of students in three special education categories receiving special education
services in 1989–1990.
Source: From U.S. Department of Education (1991). Thirteenth annual report to Congress on the implementation of the Individuals with Disabilities Education Act *(p. 11). Washington, DC: Author.*

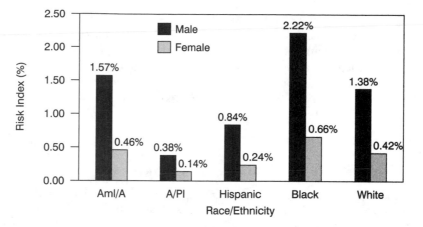

Figure 2.2
Ethnicity and gender breakdown for emotional disturbance: 1998 OCR data
Source: National Research Council (2002). *Minority students in special and gifted education.* (M. S. Donovan & C. T. Cross, Eds.) Washington, DC: National Academy Press, p. 73.

Oswald, Coutinho, Best, & Singh, 1999; Osher, Cartledge, Oswald, Sutherland, Artiles, & Coutinho, 2004). However, students of Hispanic or Asian–Pacific Island ethnic groups are considerably less likely than are Caucasian students to be identified as emotionally disturbed. Males are much more likely to be identified as emotionally disturbed than are females (Oswald, Best, Coutinho, & Nagle, 2003). Figure 2.2 shows the comparative risk of identification of males and females in various ethnic groups.

Disproportionality in identification is a serious matter and could be the result of a variety of factors, including bias in assessment. Moreover, there is pronounced variation from state to state in the disproportion of various ethnic groups' disproportionality. However, research has not yet provided answers to why such disproportionality exists (National Research Council, 2002; Osher et al., 2004).

One might note that the percentage of no ethnic or gender group identified as emotionally disturbed exceeds the estimated prevalence of emotional disturbance among children and youth. However, the combined issues of prevalence and ethnic disproportionality do clearly suggest that although all ethnic groups are underserved, some ethnic groups are more underserved than are others. More specifically, false negatives seem clearly to be more of a problem than false positives among all ethnic groups, and false negatives appear to be a greater problem among ethnic groups that are not African Americans (Kauffman, 2003c).

Prevalence and Incidence of Specific Disorders

So far we have considered emotional and behavioral disorders in the general case. But because there are many types of disorders, it is possible to estimate the prevalence of some specific problems. Unfortunately, many of the same difficulties of estimation we have discussed for the general case also arise when considering more specific disorders. The classification of emotional or behavioral disorders is almost as problematic as the general definition. In addition, the methodology of estimation is at least as varied for many specific disorders as for the general case. Consequently, estimates of prevalence and incidence of specific disorders vary and are confusing. Whenever possible, we will provide prevalence estimates in chapters dealing with specific disorders.

SUMMARY

Nearly all children and youth sometimes exhibit behavior that is problematic. Emotional and behavioral problems are a part of normal development. Labeling 20% or more of the child population as having an emotional or behavioral disorder, however, results in disbelief by the general public and alternative explanations by educators. Prevalence figures must be accompanied by convincing arguments that members of the identified population are in need of special services because their problems are highly unusual and debilitating, and not the result of teacher inadequacy. Establishing criteria for identification, however, requires arbitrary judgment regarding what degree of difference is tolerable, as well as a judgment about the relative risks of identification and nonidentification.

Prevalence refers to the number or percentage of individuals exhibiting a disorder at or during a given time. *Incidence* refers to the number of new cases of a disorder occurring during a given interval. Prevalence has been of greatest interest to special educators because most disabilities have been assumed to be developmental and to entail lifelong characteristics. However, special educators are increasingly aware that types of disability, particularly some disorders of learning and behavior, are episodic. Consequently, incidence is becoming of greater interest. Prevalence and incidence may seem irrelevant to the everyday work of the teacher, but they are important issues for those who plan and administer programs, with consequent implications for the teacher's working conditions.

Estimates of prevalence and incidence are made difficult by the lack of a standard definition, methodological problems, and social policy and economic factors. If no standard definition is accepted, then it is difficult to count cases.

Reasonable estimates based on the best available research are that 3 to 6% of the school-aged population is in need of special education and related services because of emotional or behavioral disorders. Although the percentage of students served increased from about 0.5 to about 1% from the mid-1970s to the mid-1980s, it does not seem probable that dramatic increases in the percentage will occur in the foreseeable future. Economic factors and other constraints, such as the full inclusion movement and other pressures toward nonidentification, appear likely to limit future estimates of prevalence. Most students with emotional or behavioral disorders who are receiving special education are in the 12- to 17-year age range. Ethnic disproportionality in identification is a serious and as yet unexplained problem.

CASE FOR DISCUSSION

Is This a Sick County?
Carrie Dobbs

Marion County school board member Frank Lott scowled at the county special education director, Carrie Dobbs. "Ms. Dobbs, I simply don't understand. Here we are in Marion County with 2 percent of our kids identified as seriously emotionally disturbed, and right next to us in the Circle City schools only 1 percent of the kids are identified. And if I'm to believe the consultants you brought in, only about 1 percent of the public school population nationwide is identified. Now, why should we have *double* the rate of identification of other places, including the school system next to us? Are you telling me that something about this county makes kids emotionally disturbed?"

"No, Mr. Lott, I think we use better identification procedures than do Circle City and most other school systems in the country, and we're doing our best to serve all of our students who need special education because of their emotional or behavioral problems."

School board member Sandi Mosher leaned back in her chair, staring intently at Carrie Dobbs. "Like Mr. Lott, I don't understand what's happening. But I know we're spending a lot more money on these kids than Circle City is. I wonder if that isn't because you use the term 'behavior improvement' instead of 'seriously emotionally disturbed.'"

"That might be part of the reason, I admit," Carrie said cautiously. "But we think BI is a better choice than SED. It carries less stigma, and we'd rather label a program than kids."

"But that's just the point, isn't it?" asked Mr. Lott. "You make it easier to identify students, so parents are more likely to go along with it—until they find out that the kids are actually labeled "emotionally disturbed" in our reports to state and federal authorities, and then they're really upset."

"Besides," Ms. Mosher joined in, "it seems to me you're including a lot of kids who are just behavior problems, but they're not really seriously emotionally disturbed. I don't like this BI label, and I don't think it's reasonable for us to be identifying kids in this county who wouldn't be identified in most other systems and using labels in this county that aren't consistent with state and federal language."

"I respectfully disagree, Ms. Mosher. The students we've identified have serious and persistent behavior problems that put them at a severe disadvantage in school. They're very likely to fail or drop out of school without a special program. We feel the BI program is the most effective and least stigmatizing way of providing the needed services. Our identification procedures and our prevalence are consistent with the best available research."

Questions About the Case

1. If you were a school board member, what line of questioning would you pursue in challenging Ms. Dobbs?

2. If you were Ms. Dobbs, how would you defend serving 2% of the school population in a behavior improvement (BI) program?

3. If you were asked to investigate the BI program in the Marion County schools, what would you want to know to help you understand whether serving 2% of the students is justified?

Prevalence

Teresa Zutter, MEd, is director of the Office of Alternative School Programs in the Fairfax County Public Schools, Fairfax, Virginia.

Why is it important for you as an administrator to be able to estimate the number of students who will be identified as having emotional or behavioral disorders?

Obviously, school administrators need to plan many months in advance of the beginning of a new school year. An accurate estimate of how many students will need services at various grade levels and the degree of support each will need is invaluable in deciding how many teachers to hire. We have to budget for textbooks, materials, supplies, and equipment for each student. We have to provide physical accommodations in compliance with federal and state requirements as well. At cofacilities like ours, use of communal areas such as the lunchroom, the gymnasium, the playing fields, and the auditorium must be discussed with the general education administrators for smooth coexistence and integration of our programs and students. Transportation must be budgeted for as well, and this is especially complex when one facility is serving a wide area in a particular district.

Teaching every student is our most important task, but the preliminary steps of initial referral, screening, evaluation, eligibility, placement, and follow-up triennial reviews are also crucial. Furthermore, in-service training for both special educators and general education teachers is required for comprehensive educational services. We can manage our time efficiently only if all involved personnel know in advance approximately how many students must be accommodated in planning these other crucial components of special education. Finally, prevalence figures can be enormously helpful when planning for community-based programming. Negative community attitudes about a program, especially if they are based on exaggeration or rumor, can intensify the fears and uncertainties of students and parents. We administrators are responsible for communicating to the public how many students will be served at a particular site in the course of explaining the educational program.

Why is a higher percentage of students identified in some school districts and states than others?

Some states and localities still see public education as a critical element of a strong community. The local high school football games are still attended every fall Friday by families, friends, and neighbors. There is community spirit and concern for the young. These people still feel free to care for and watch over each other's children. These communities may be urban or rural, and the citizens of them may be highly educated or relatively uneducated. But one characteristic differentiating these communities from others is their willingness to provide for the well-being of others. This public attitude affects the establishment and support of community- and school-based services, the quality of public employees, and the degree to which educators are professionally and financially rewarded for their work. Prevalence may be higher in these caring communities because the process of identification is sound.

In the best of circumstances, a school district has the financial and political backing of its citizens to honestly and objectively assess the needs of its young people. Although the risk of false positives may be greater in these communities, the risk of false negatives is lower because eligibility criteria may be less stringent. When a public service is well established and well run, it stands a higher chance of being used regularly and more comfortably. High-quality services promote accuracy in assessing needs. Citizens with disabled children often choose to move into a particular district or state because of its fine reputation for readily accessible and high-quality public school special education services.

High prevalence may also be due to the difficulty of school personnel in discriminating true emotional or behavioral disorders from serious general student difficulties. Many general education teachers have never taken even an introductory special education course. Most general education teacher training does not include a course in behavior management. In school districts where teachers are poorly trained and unsupported, "problem children" are at higher risk for being incorrectly labeled as disabled. Lack of professional training and competence in basic classroom behavior management skills can contribute directly to high prevalence rates.

Many teachers report seeing disturbing behaviors in more of their students today than they saw in the past. Many highly competent teachers worry that more of today's children are exhibiting behaviors that warrant identification as a disorder or disability. Some suggest that this is because of the overall dysfunction, chaos, and moral decay in contemporary American society. It is important to recognize that some states and localities have higher rates of poverty and other environmental conditions that we know contribute to emotional and behavioral disorders.

What factors do you think account for the increasing prevalence of and behavioral disorders?

There appear to be a multitude of reasons that might explain it. Unfortunately, the explosion of student referrals is because of many factors that fall beyond the control of the public schools. There appears to have been a fundamental change in children's basic sense of security. Many children are afraid of the future. They worry that they will not live out a natural life span, and they express pessimism regarding the future of Earth itself. Many have adopted the attitude, What's the use? We're all going to die anyway!

Learned helplessness seems to be sweeping the nation as children recognize at younger and younger ages that the chances of a successful lifelong marriage and prosperous life may be extremely difficult or impossible to attain and sustain. The fairy tale endings of previous generations have evaporated in the light of harsh realities being portrayed through music, media, and the daily exposure to "role models" who lead increasingly frenetic lives. Even in the midst of increasingly crowded areas, children experience loneliness, isolation, and depression. Large numbers of children seem to be mourning the loss of certain fundamental human social elements without being able to express exactly what is missing. Technological developments and family priorities and structure rob many children of opportunities to learn about interpersonal intimacy, acquire social skills, and achieve psychological and

physiological well-being. Many developmentally significant social traditions are being diminished in frequency and importance. It appears that the lack of stability, permanence, and unwavering commitment in so many areas of young people's lives has contributed to mistrust on their part that anyone is really in control.

Children affected by their mothers' use of drugs during pregnancy and by drug use in their homes are reaching school age in significant numbers. Drug abuse in the home or neighborhood is often accompanied by child neglect, violence, poverty, and the inevitable deterioration of the fabric of family and community. Ineffective teaching methods and rising teacher burnout exacerbate the situation. Most teachers have neither the training nor the desire to be surrogate parent, psychologist, and social worker in addition to teacher. One response is to place students in special education where, theoretically, there is more time to pay attention to the serious symptoms of a societal problem that is larger than any school system can successfully overcome.

On a more positive note, reports of higher prevalence of emotional and behavioral problems also may be because of a more open attitude nationwide that no longer allows children's problems to be swept under society's rug. Instead of being hidden away, these children are being acknowledged and assisted by effective school programs. These children have always been a part of the public school scene, but there may be more public support to help troubled children before their destructive behaviors become a way of life. In part, this may be because of adult citizens feeling the same unease or even outright fear, commonly expressed by youth that our society is raging out of control. Although it may be a sobering experience for a nation to contend openly with its suffering children, the rational and reasonable approach of attacking today's concerns head-on is to be applauded.

What are the major reasons that fewer students have been identified than we would expect based on prevalence studies?

Demographic fluctuations may be a contributing factor. Budgets for education initiatives may shrink as the population of taxpayers changes. For instance, if households with no school-aged children outnumber those with children, then a school bond vote might be defeated in favor of other public spending, such as new roads. A school system faced with a budget crisis, inadequately trained personnel, poorly defined procedures, rigid criteria for eligibility, or a weakness in available programs may underidentify students. Limited services may be provided to only the most obviously in need.

Second, when money is tight, special education may have to compete with other worthy education programs for limited resources. For example, a region may become popular for immigrants from a war-torn country. Costly programs for incorporating these new students may force another look at current funding. With no hard-and-fast rules for eligibility for many programs, including special education and English as a Second Language, school districts may manipulate identification procedures to raise or lower prevalence to more closely fit the available local funding.

A lower identification rate does not necessarily stem from such negative situations. Another notable possibility includes implementation of extremely effective in-service training of general education teachers. Teachers who are supported and rewarded for success with children who might otherwise be referred for special education may lower the prevalence of disabilities. The actual number of at-risk children in a particular area may remain the same, but more children escape the disability label because of

efficient prereferral assistance in the regular classroom setting. Likewise, identified children who are properly educated by special educators and then mainstreamed back into general education may be found ineligible for services at the next triennial review. In these circumstances, the school system may have chosen to invest in proactive educational strategies, with less emphasis on sustaining large numbers of children in long-term separate programs.

Finally, the phenomenon of "resilient children" has only recently been examined closely on a national level. Researchers have always wondered why some children successfully overcome extremely distressful and traumatic circumstances, whereas others succumb to emotional despair and ineffective coping mechanisms. However, more attention is now being given to learning how we can help more children achieve personal success despite incredible adversity. States or districts that promote innovative research and program development to foster resiliency in children may exhibit lower prevalence because of a true decrease in the number of students who, without this assistance, might otherwise be identified.

>> QUESTIONS FOR FURTHER REFLECTION

1. If you were responsible for planning special education services for students with emotional or behavioral disorders in a school district, what information would you try to obtain, and from what sources?
2. If you were an administrator, what types of in-service would you want to provide to make sure

that your teachers were ready and able to recognize the early signs of emotional or behavioral disorders and intervene effectively to keep them from getting worse?
3. Over what factors affecting the prevalence of emotional or behavioral disorders do teachers have the greatest control?

CHAPTER THREE

HISTORY OF THE PROBLEM
DEVELOPMENT OF THE FIELD
AND CURRENT ISSUES

As you read this chapter, keep these guiding questions in mind:

- What events in the late 1700s set the stage for more humane and effective treatment of children and youth with emotional or behavioral disorders?

- What were major issues involving children with emotional and behavioral disorders in the nineteenth century?

- In the first half of the 1900s, what were the predominant emphases in programs for children and youth with emotional or behavioral disorders?

- What are the major recent trends in the field?

- How are current issues related to historical developments?

We are tempted to believe that in an earlier era, when life was supposedly simpler, the issues involving emotional and behavioral disorders were less difficult. Perhaps life was simpler long ago, but much of the historical literature suggests that identifying social deviance and responding to it have always been perplexing (see cases in the accompanying case book).

Current issues must be seen in the light of past and, perhaps, perpetual problems. We cannot understand today's difficulties very well if we assume that they emerge from present circumstances alone. Although knowledge of history is no guarantee that we will not repeat mistakes, our ignorance of history virtually ensures that we will make no real progress (Kauffman, 1993, 1999e, 2002; Kauffman & Smucker, 1995).

Teachers have always been challenged by the problem of disorderly and disturbing student behavior. Throughout history, some youngsters' behavior has angered and disappointed their parents or other adults and violated established codes of conduct. However, special education for this population is a relatively recent phenomenon. A purely educational history of the field is not possible because the conceptual foundations of special education lie for the most part in the disciplines of psychology and psychiatry. Its historical origins cannot be separated entirely from the histories of other fields (Lewis, 1974).

A BRIEF HISTORY OF THE FIELD

The 19th Century

Following the American and French revolutions in the closing years of the 18th century, kind and effective treatment of the "insane" and "idiots" (terms then used to designate people with mental illness and mental retardation) appeared. In that era of political and social revolution, near the beginning of the 19th century, emphasis on individual freedom, human dignity, philanthropy, and public education set the stage for humane treatment and education of people with disabilities.

The literature of the 19th century is meager by current standards. However, most histories of childhood emotional or behavioral disorders consistently contain certain inaccuracies and distortions that lead to underestimating the value of the 19th-century literature in approaching present-day problems (Kauffman, 1976). Some psychiatrists of the early 19th century identified etiological factors in youngsters' emotional or behavioral disorders that are today given serious consideration, such as the interaction of temperament and child rearing, overprotection, overindulgence, and inconsistency of discipline. Although biological causes of emotional or behavioral disorders were recognized during the first half of the 19th century, the emphasis was on environmental factors, especially early discipline and training. It is not surprising that interventions in that period centered on environmental control—providing the proper sensory stimulation, discipline, and instruction.

Many children and youth, including those with emotional or behavioral disorders, were neglected and abused in the 19th century. Bremner (1970, 1971), Hoffman (1974, 1975), and Rothman (1971) amply document the cruel discipline, forced labor, and other inhumanities suffered by children and youth in the 1800s (see also Forehand & McKinney, 1993). Although many 19th-century attempts at education and treatment were primitive compared to today's best, some youngsters with emotional or behavioral disorders in the 19th century received considerably better care than many such children receive today. If we concentrate on neglect and abuse in institutions, schools, detention centers, and homes in the early 21st century, we might conclude that the plight of children and youth has not improved much in the past century. Contrasting the best contemporary thinking and treatment to the worst of the 19th century creates a dark and distorted vision of that century. Many 19th-century leaders in the treatment of children with emotional or behavioral disorders were more enlightened than their critics have assumed. Unfortunately, some of their brightest successes have been ignored (Kauffman, 1976).

The 19th century cannot be viewed as a unitary or homogeneous historical period. Between 1850 and 1900, important changes took place in attitudes toward severe and profound emotional or behavioral disorders and mental retardation. Optimism, pragmatism, inventiveness, and humane care, associated with moral treatment and model social programs in the first half of the century, gave way to pessimism, theorizing, rigidity, and dehumanizing institutionalization after the Civil War. The failure of private philanthropy and public programs to solve the problems of "idiocy," "insanity," and delinquency and to rectify the situations of the poor led to cynicism and disillusionment. More and larger asylums and houses of refuge were not the answers. Things do not always get better for a society's poor and sick citizens; sometimes they get worse. The many, complex reasons for the regression in social policy in the last part of the 19th century included economic, political, social, and professional factors (Bockoven, 1956, 1972; Caplan, 1969; Deutsch, 1948; Grob, 1973; Kanner, 1964; Menninger, 1963; Rothman, 1971; Ullmann & Krasner, 1969). The same factors operate today—economic, social, political, and professional forces (see Heward, 2003; Heward & Silvestri, 2004; Jakubecy, Mock, & Kauffman, 2003; Kauffman, 1999f, 2002, 2003b, 2003c, 2004).

By the end of the 19th century, several textbooks had been published about the psychiatric disorders of children and youth. These books dealt primarily with etiology and classification and tended toward fatalism—the idea that there is not much we can do to help (Kanner, 1960). Psychiatric disorders were assumed to be the irreversible results of widely varied causes such as masturbation, overwork, hard study, religious preoccupation, heredity, degeneracy, or disease. The problems of obstreperous children and juvenile delinquents had not been solved, but new efforts were being made.

Early Twentieth Century: The Establishment of Intervention Programs

Concern for the mental and physical health of children expanded greatly in the early 20th century (Ollendick & Hersen, 1983). The first teacher training program in special education began in Michigan in 1914. By 1918, all states had compulsory education laws, and in 1919, Ohio passed a law for statewide care of handicapped children. By 1930, 16 states had enacted laws allowing local school districts to recover the excess costs of educating exceptional children and youths (Henry, 1950). Educational and psychological testing were becoming widely used, and school psychology, guidance, and counseling were emerging. Mental hygiene and child guidance clinics became relatively common by 1930. By that time, child psychiatry was a new discipline (Kanner, 1973). According to Kanner, child guidance clinics of this era made three major innovations: (1) interdisciplinary collaboration; (2) treatment of any child whose behavior was annoying to parents and teachers, not just the severe cases; and (3) attention to the effects of interpersonal relationships and adult attitudes on child behavior (Kanner, 1973, pp. 194–195). These are similar to today's innovations.

Two professional organizations that are particularly important to the education of children with emotional or behavioral disorders were founded in the 1920s. The Council of Exceptional Children, organized in 1922, was then made up primarily of educators but included other professionals and parents. The American Orthopsychiatric Association, dominated by the professions of child psychiatry, clinical psychology, and social work but including education and other disciplines as well, was founded in 1924.

The Depression and World War II necessarily diverted attention and funds from the education of students with disabilities. Nevertheless, more students with disabilities were receiving special education in 1940 than in 1930; and by 1948, 41 (of the then 48) states had enacted laws authorizing or requiring local school districts to make special educational provisions for at least one category of exceptional children (Henry, 1950). The vast majority of special classes were for children with mild mental retardation. Programs for students with emotional or behavioral disorders were relatively few and were designed primarily for acting-out and delinquent children, and youth in large cities.

The first psychiatric hospital for children in the United States, the Bradley Home (now the Emma Pendleton Bradley Hospital), was established in Rhode Island in 1931 (Davids, 1975). In the 1940s, Leo Kanner of Johns Hopkins University Medical School identified the syndrome now known as autism, or *autistic spectrum disorder* (he called it early infantile autism).

Lauretta Bender pioneered the education of children with schizophrenia in the 1930s. By the end of the 1930s, the literature on children's emotional or behavioral disorders had grown to sizable proportions (Baker & Stullken, 1938). Attempts had been made to define emotional disturbance and to delineate several subclassifications. Surveys of children's behavior problems and teachers' attitudes toward misbehavior had been completed, and there had been efforts to estimate the prevalence of emotional or behavioral disorders (Martens & Russ, 1932; Wickman, 1929). Various plans of special education, such as special rooms, schools, classes, and consultative help, had been tried.

Mid to Late 20th Century: Elaboration of Intervention Programs

A wave of interest in educating children with emotional or behavioral disorders arose in the middle of the 20th century. Education of students with emotional or behavioral disorders became a field of specialization in its own right. Before the end of the 1950s, the first book describing classroom teaching of children with emotional or behavioral disorders appeared (Kornberg, 1955) and researchers recognized that systematic procedures were needed to identify students with emotional or behavioral disorders in the public schools (Bower, 1960). A nationwide survey of special classes was conducted in the early 1960s (Morse, Cutler, & Fink, 1964), and professionals banded together in 1964 to form a new division of the Council for Exceptional Children: the Council for Children with Behavioral Disorders (see Wood, 1999, for details). Preparation of personnel to work with children with emotional or behavioral disorders received federal support in 1963. The Autism Society of America (initially called the National Society for Autistic Children) was founded in 1965.

In the last half of the 20th century, various conceptual models were developed. Landmark volumes edited by Rhodes and Tracy (1972a, 1972b) and Rhodes and Head (1974) detailed the various conceptual approaches to working with youngsters who have emotional or behavioral disorders. These models varied in the extent to which they recommended that special educators address the supposed underlying psychological disturbances or unconscious motivations of behavior and the extent to which they considered behavior itself to be the problem (Van Hasselt & Hersen, 1991a, 1991b).

During the 1960s and 1970s, there was a dramatic increase in interest and effort to educate children and youth with severe disabilities, including those with severe emotional or behavioral disorders. The intervention gaining widest acceptance in this era and proving to be most effective with students having severe disabilities was behavior modification, now better known as applied behavior analysis.

Many special projects with long-range implications for children and youth with emotional or behavioral disorders were conducted in the 1970s, 1980s, and 1990s, and important new organizations were founded. These included a project on classifying children for special education (Hobbs, 1975a, 1975b), a national needs analysis in emotional disturbance (Grosenick & Huntze, 1979, 1983), and the formation of the National Mental Health and Special Education Coalition (Forness, 1988a). The coalition proposed a new definition and terminology (Forness & Knitzer, 1992), and its continuing efforts are geared toward improving mental health and special education legislation and increasing collaboration among disciplines. Another important milestone in the field was the organization in 1989 of the Federation of Families for Children's Mental Health. The federation now offers support and advocacy for parents and families of children and youth with emotional or behavioral disorders.

During the late 1980s, calls were made for greater integration of special and regular education for all students with disabilities. In fact, some proposed a merger of regular and special education or called for the abandonment of pull-out programs in which students are taught in any setting other than the regular class. These ideas grew into the full inclusion movement in the 1990s. Although inclusion in general education is desirable in many cases, the full inclusion movement also generated criticism for its lack of consideration of individual needs and the interventions feasible only in other environments (see Kauffman, Bantz, & McCullough, 2002; Kauffman, Lloyd, Baker, & Riedel, 1995; Kavale & Forness, 2000; Mock & Kauffman, 2003). The issue of special education's service to very young children with emotional or behavioral disorders also emerged in the 1980s. In 1986, Congress passed P.L. 99–457, which includes incentives for states to develop early intervention programs for disabled infants and infants at risk, from birth to age 36 months.

In the 1990s, the federal government attempted to establish a national agenda for the education of children with emotional or behavioral disorders. Such students typically have low grades and other indications of unsatisfactory academic outcomes, have higher dropout and lower graduation rates than other student groups, are often placed in highly restrictive settings, are disproportionately from poor and minority families, and frequently encounter the juvenile justice system (Chesapeake Institute, 1994; U.S. Department of Education, 1994). By 1992, the national agenda consisted of seven interdependent, strategic targets (notice that the terminology in federal legislation at the time was "serious emotional disturbance," or SED):

> Target 1 *Expand Positive Learning Opportunities and Results:* To foster the provision of engaging, useful, and positive learning opportunities. These opportunities should be result-driven and should acknowledge as well as respond to the experiences and needs of children and youths with a serious emotional disturbance.
>
> Target 2 *Strengthen School and Community Capacity:* To foster initiatives that strengthen the capacity of schools and communities to serve students with serious emotional disturbance in the least restrictive environments appropriate.
>
> Target 3 *Value and Address Diversity:* To encourage culturally competent and linguistically appropriate exchanges and collaborations among families, professionals, students, and communities. These collaborations should foster equitable *outcomes* for all students and result in the identification and provision of services that are responsive to issues of race, culture, gender, and social and economic status.
>
> Target 4 *Collaborate with Families:* To foster collaborations that fully include family members on the team of service providers that implements family-focused services to improve educational *outcomes*. Services should be open, helpful, culturally competent, accessible to families, and school-based as well as community-based.
>
> Target 5 *Promote Appropriate Assessment:* To promote practices ensuring that assessment is integral to identification, design, and delivery of services for children and youths with SED. These practices should be culturally appropriate, ethical, and functional.
>
> Target 6 *Provide Ongoing Skill Development and Support:* To foster the enhancement of knowledge, understanding, and sensitivity among all who work with children and youths who have or who are at risk of developing SED. Support and development should be ongoing and should aim at strengthening the capacity of families, teachers, service providers, and other stakeholders to collaborate, persevere, and improve outcomes for children and youths with SED.
>
> Target 7 *Create Comprehensive and Collaborative Systems:* To promote systems change resulting in the development of coherent services built around the individual needs of children and youths who have or who are at risk of developing SED. These services should be family-centered, community-based, and appropriately funded. (U.S. Department of Education, 1994, pp. 119–120)

Whether sufficient resources were or will be allocated to make achievement of these targets possible, and whether the agenda was sufficiently specific to guide needed changes, are questionable (Kauffman, 1997). In spite of the stated intentions of those writing the agenda, it appears that there is considerable resistance to early identification and early intervention (Kauffman, 2003b, 2003c, 2004).

CURRENT ISSUES

Current issues and trends in the field seem to suggest a heightened level of attention to the empirical and conceptual foundations for special education. Given this circumstance, it is tempting to believe that we are finally emerging into an era of enlightenment in which progress will be coherent, dramatic, and sustained. Perhaps we are entering such an era, but careful analyses of current trends and issues in the light of history will remind us that today's issues are not new, nor are current suggestions for addressing them likely to be completely successful.

Special education has perpetual issues, including who should be served and how and where they should be served (Bateman, 1994). Many or most of the issues of today have been issues for well over half a century, as reflected in the following: early identification (e.g., Brown, 1943), placement options (e.g., Berry, 1936; Postel, 1937), similarities between general and special education (e.g., Baker, 1934), early identification and prevention (Martens & Russ, 1932), and training in social skills (e.g., Farson, 1940). Our approaches to these issues may be somewhat more sophisticated today, but we clearly do not have the wisdom or the technical knowledge to put these problems entirely behind us. Although the issues and trends we review here may be prominent in the early years of the 21st century, they all have historical roots many decades deep and will likely remain vexing problems for many decades to come. These issues and trends are not entirely separate and distinct. Inevitably, we find that addressing one demands that we consider others simultaneously.

Early Identification and Prevention

A persistent and self-defeating response of educators and parents is to let emotional or behavioral problems fester until they become disorders of serious if not dangerous proportions. The problems inherent in early identification and prevention have been well understood for more than 50 years (Bower, 1960; Martens & Russ, 1932), yet few measures to address the problems have been taken. We know that the early signs of emotional and behavioral disorders can be detected through careful observation or use of reliable screening instruments (Bierman et al., 2002; Conroy, Hendrickson, & Hester, 2004; Denham, Blair, Schmidt, & DeMulder, 2002; Ialongo et al., 1998; Loeber et al., 1992, 1998a, 1998b; Strain & Timm, 2001; Tobin & Sugai, 1999; Walker, Kavanagh, et al., 1998; Walker & Severson, 1990; Walker, Severson, & Feil, 1994). In discussing the implications of their massive longitudinal study of antisocial boys, Loeber et al. (1998a) concluded: "Interventions should deal with early problem behaviors in an attempt to prevent their escalation to serious levels. Particular candidates are physical fighting, covert behaviors, and chronic disobedience, which we assume . . . are keystone behaviors in the development of more serious acts" (p. 267).

Walker and Sprague (1999b; see also Kingery & Walker, 2002) charted the path leading from risk factors to negative, destructive long-term outcomes, as shown in Figure 3.1. The first maladaptive behaviors leading to negative outcomes are clear, and I discuss these

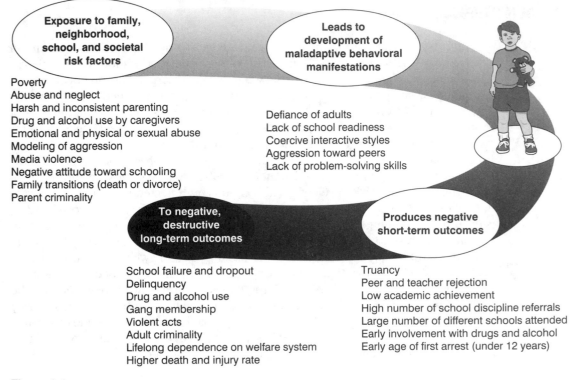

Figure 3.1
The path to long-term negative outcomes for at-risk children and youth
Source: Walker, H. M. & Sprague, J. R. (1999). The path to school failure, delinquency, and violence: Causal factors and some potential solutions. *Intervention in School and Clinic, 35,* 68. © 1999 by PRO-ED, Inc. Reprinted with permission.

in detail in later chapters. However, the fact that we know the path to long-term negative outcomes does not mean that we will intervene early to change the child's course.

There is now, as there has been for decades, recognition that we need intervention that is early in two ways: we need to catch problems when the child is young, and we need to catch the early stages of misbehavior regardless of the person's age (Hester & Kaiser, 1998; Kamps & Tankersley, 1996; Kauffman, 1999a, 1999c, 2003b, 2004; Strain & Timm, 2001; Walker, Ramsey, & Gresham, 2004; Walker & Sprague, 1999b). Early intervention—both types—is the essence of prevention; yet early identification, intervention, and prevention remain unresolved problems.

Will schools use the knowledge and tools we have to identify students early, before problems become very serious? Having identified the students, will schools take preventative action? These are the same questions raised by Bower in 1960 and by many others in the intervening years. The answers are in doubt for reasons that are both readily apparent and exasperating, as discussed in detail by Kauffman (1999c, 2003a, 2003b, 2003c, 2004):

- Many people are tempted to maintain a "developmental optimism" in the face of signs that a young child is at high risk. "He'll grow out of it," "Don't worry; it's just a passing phase she's going through," and similar explanations provide a convenient excuse not to intervene.

- Others worry about the stigma associated with any identification of deviance or risk status. Their concern about avoiding the stigma of identification prevents intervention, not the development of the disorder. Identification requires labeling—words used to describe the particular group of children under consideration. People who oppose all labeling also oppose all identification and therefore all procedures not used with all children. Universal interventions play an important role in primary prevention, but they are insufficient to address the problems of students for whom secondary prevention is necessary.

- Still others point to the less-than-perfect prediction that any early identification procedure or preventative effort entails. Early screening and prevention inevitably mean that some children are misidentified because no such system is perfect, and the chance of making an error can be used as an excuse not to identify a child and intervene.

- Some people worry that to predict or anticipate something is to make it happen. However, it is impossible to prevent what we are unwilling to anticipate.

- Some people are loathe to see disability as undesirable (they may suggest that disability is merely a difference, and all differences should be celebrated). We will not prevent what we do not see as a disaster, or at least something that we do not see as undesirable.

- Another complicating factor is concern about bias. If a disproportionate number of children belonging to any particular group of concern is identified—those who are poor or male or who belong to an ethnic, religious, or color group, for example—then early identification and prevention may be undermined by charges of discrimination.

- Finally, early screening, identification, and intervention are interrelated and costly. Screening makes no sense if children are not identified; identification makes no sense in the absence of intervention; intervention, other than the procedures used indiscriminately with all children, cannot be provided without identification. All cost money. There is always competition for public funds, and many taxpayers and their governmental representatives seem to prefer paying the costs of problems that cannot be skirted to paying the costs of preventing problems that are still avoidable. Many agree to pay for prisons but not for early intervention.

The denial of deviance is common today among people of all colors, both sexes, adults and children, and people of vastly different political persuasion. It has become politically unacceptable to define any behavior that someone views as merely "cultural" or typical of a given group as deviant (Hendershott, 2002). Moreover, "what is judged to be 'mild' deviance is often ignored, while those acts viewed as 'very deviant' elicit demands for severe sanctions" (Hendershott, 2002, p. 82). Thus, early intervention is stopped in its tracks.

Consider the case of adolescents charged with murder. Rocky, age 19, is described as having had minor run-ins with the law and as being somewhat depressed after he quit taking his antidepressants. "Prior to his recent arrest, Rocky . . . had been convicted of trespassing in a January 2001 break-in at . . . [a] church. Authorities said several items were stolen and that a dead bird had been placed in a communion plate on an altar" (Williams, 2003, p. A8). His sister Jessica, age 16, had spent time in a juvenile facility for truancy. The father of Rocky and Jessica downplayed police discovery of gruesome images on the computer of one of the suspects in the case, a companion of Rocky and Jessica. The police found "dozens of computer pictures of torture and executions" that "bore striking similarities" to the killing, but the father did not think they were significant: "'That's what kids are into these days,' he said" (Williams, 2003, p. A8). And of Jessica, the mother said, "'Jesse was studying Wicca, what they call white magic. But a lot of kids do that'" (Williams, 2003, p. A8). However, not everyone agrees. A letter to the editor about these youngsters' behavior said: "It is my belief that, together, these teenagers' interests and activities raise blatant warning signs that were apparently missed" (Woodson, 2003, p. A8).

But warning signs are often ignored, and minor deviance is allowed to escalate to hurtful if not lethal levels before action is taken. "Better safe than sorry" is not a bromide often applied to the questionable behavior of children and youth—unless safety is defined as not having questioned something said to be cultural or normative (therefore, safety means not risking a charge of bigotry or prudishness). Of course, the world does have its bigots and prudes, and it is better not to be one. But the fear of a false accusation or the false identification of problem behavior loads identification in favor of letting things go until they turn tragic.

Early identification and prevention are compelling ideas embraced by many special educators and psychologists in the new millennium (see Bierman et al., 2002; Eddy, Reid, & Curry, 2002; Walker & Shinn, 2002). Turning the ideas into coherent, consistent, sustained action will require scientific and political finesse that previous generations could not muster. Children are unlikely to be identified for special services until their problems have grown severe and have existed for a period of years. This is the opposite of prevention, but it remains the norm.

Education of Antisocial and Violent Students

Antisocial, delinquent, and violent behavior in schools and communities has been a perplexing issue for a very long time. In late-20th-century American culture, youth violence became a major problem demanding intervention on multiple fronts (American Psychological Association, 1993; Flannery, 1999; Flannery & Huff, 1999; Kauffman, 1994b; Kauffman & Burbach, 1997; Walker et al., 2004). In fact, the education of antisocial and violent students became a central issue in both general and special education in the 1990s.

Youth violence remains a great concern, although violent crime has been on a downward trajectory in the early 21st century (Furlong, Morrison, & Jimerson, 2004). Youths seldom engage in violent behavior without warning signs, so research and recommendations sometimes focus on the precursors of violent acts. Precursors are usually defined to include such things as aggressive talk, talk of aggression, threats, intimidation, and various forms of bullying. Best practices suggest that we should intervene to stop such precursors of more serious problems (e.g., Lerman & Vorndran, 2002; Sheras, 2002; Smith & Churchill, 2002). Violent behavior and its precursors are complex and demand that we struggle with difficult questions, including the following:

- When is antisocial, violent behavior legitimately declared a disability, and when should it be considered criminal or delinquent behavior for which special education is inappropriate? There is great controversy about the kind of behavior that demonstrates a disability and that which merely demonstrates delinquency, criminality, or moral failure.
- What level of antisocial and violent behavior can be tolerated in a general education classroom? No doubt, behavior that is tolerated in many classrooms today would not have been in decades past. Moreover, conduct varies widely from school to school and from class to class. There is much disagreement about the kind of behavior that should be tolerated or accommodated in general education classrooms. Because behavior cannot be separated from the student who exhibits it, there is much controversy about which students, if any, should be removed from general education classrooms.
- If students cross the line of what is tolerable in a classroom or school, then where and how should their education be continued? Alternative schools, special classes, homebound instruction: These placement options and the kinds of instruction offered in them are matters of much conflict.
- What are legitimate means of controlling antisocial and violent behavior? Punishment of various types and the legitimate uses of it provide the basis of heated arguments about the treatment of children and youth.
- How can schools best function as a part of a larger community effort to lessen antisocial and violent behavior? Most people today seem to recognize that the problem of antisocial and violent behavior is not one the schools can handle alone. However, there is much disagreement about just what schools can and should do and how they can best work with other social agencies to address the problem.

Decades of research suggest how some of these issues might be addressed (American Psychological Association, 1993; Kazdin, 1998, 2001; McMahon & Wells, 1998; Walker et al., 2004). However, the educational treatment of students who bring weapons to school, threaten and intimidate their peers or teachers, disrupt the education of their classmates, or are incarcerated will likely be controversial for decades to come. Discipline of students with disabilities, especially those with learning disabilities or emotional and behavioral disorders, is a controversial and critical issue involving the Individuals with Disabilities Education Act (IDEA) and other education laws (Dupre, 1996, 1997, 2000; Huefner, 2000; Yell, 1998; Yell, Rogers & Rogers, 1998; Yell & Shriner, 1997).

Comprehensive, Collaborative, Community-Based Services

A strong trend beginning in the 1990s is the integration of a variety of services for children and families, "wrapping services around" children in their homes and communities rather than sending them to a succession of intervention programs in other environments. These attempts to coordinate and improve the effectiveness of multiple social service programs such as special education, child protective services, child welfare, foster care, and so on are built on the observation that individual programs are seldom sufficient to meet children's needs and that a closer working relationship of all service providers is required (e.g., Armstrong & Evans, 1992; Clark & Clarke, 1996; Clarke, Schaefer, Burchard, & Welkowitz, 1992; Eber & Keenan, 2004; Epstein, Kutash, & Duchnowski, 1998; Nelson & Pearson, 1991; Quinn, Epstein, & Cumblad, 1995; Rosenblatt & Attkisson, 1992; Zanglis, Furlong, & Casas, 2000). Making the school a center for social welfare programs of all kinds, an idea now at least four decades old (cf. Rothman & Berkowitz, 1967), is part of the current trend.

The idea of comprehensive, coordinated social services, including general and special education, delivered through the neighborhood school, is compelling. It is particularly appealing in the case of children whose lives are in great disarray, as are the lives of many children who have emotional or behavioral disorders and are also in foster care (Smucker, Kauffman, & Ball, 1996). However, implementing the ideas and demonstrating that the service delivery system is effective are far from simple. At this point, we understand relatively little about how to design and evaluate research on such complex service delivery systems (see Bickman, Heflinger, Lambert, & Summerfelt, 1996; Henggeler, Schoenwald, & Munger, 1996; Kauffman, 1997; Knapp, 1995). The issue is likely to be kept alive for decades to come for several reasons:

- Simply combining inadequate services will solve few problems, and in many communities the services to be integrated are insufficient in quantity and quality. If individual agencies have too few resources to be "wrapped around" children, then the combined or integrated service delivery system, too, will leave many children ill served.

- Creating the needed expertise and availability of services, integrated and collaborative or not, is an expensive proposition that voters in many states and communities appear unwilling to fund. If wraparound services are going to be found adequate in the long run—after the initial hyperbole about reform, restructuring, and systems change have given way to reality—then they must have highly trained personnel who can coordinate a sufficient number of adequately trained direct-service personnel. Serving the needs of difficult children and youth is a highly personnel-intensive proposition, and there is no real shortcut or cheap path to addressing these needs.

- The proposition to provide varied services through local schools inevitably becomes enmeshed in controversies about what schools are for—the scope of their mission in their communities. In many communities, schools are poorly funded even to accomplish their academic goals for students, and those who control the schools seem reluctant to expand their mission to include collaborative work with other social agencies.

The ideal of comprehensive, collaborative, community-based services is highly appealing but not new. Whether such services become a reality in many American communities will depend on how Americans come to view their schools and value their children. Barring a dramatic change in the political will of the nation, the promise of the ideal will remain unfulfilled for decades to come (cf. Epstein et al.,

1998; Knitzer & Aber, 1995). There is a huge gap between rhetoric and practice. "In reality, services are often provided in a series of uncoordinated, unmeasured interventions. . . . schools tend to rely on interventions that are short-term and narrowly focused when responding to students who create disruptions or experience serious problems and disabilities" (Dwyer & Bernstein, 1998, p. 278).

Focus on Academic and Social Skills

Since the report of Knitzer et al. (1990), there has been increased concern about the quality of instruction in special education programs for students with emotional or behavioral disorders. Knitzer and her colleagues suggested that in far too many classrooms serving these students the emphasis is almost exclusively on controlling acting-out behavior, meaning that students are being given neither the academic proficiency nor the social skills they need to be reintegrated into general education or become employable adolescents and adults.

It is widely recognized that effective instruction is at the heart of both effective special education (e.g., Kauffman, 1994a) and behavior management (e.g., Kauffman, Mostert et al., 2002; Kerr & Nelson, 2002; Lane, 2004; Walker et al., 2004; Witt, Van Der Heyden, & Gilbertson, 2004). In fact, researchers long ago devised procedures in which teachers approached predictable misbehavior as an instructional problem and devised teaching procedures for desirable behavior similar to those used for academic instruction (Colvin, Sugai, & Patching, 1993; Kavale, Mathur, & Mostert, 2004; Polsgrove & Smith, 2004). Emphasis on teaching will likely continue as a trend in special education programs for at least two reasons:

1. Good instruction is now known by researchers to be the first line of defense in behavior management. That is, a good instructional program prevents many behavior problems from arising, and an emphasis on instruction is compatible with the clearest mission of public schools. For several decades, beginning in the early 1960s, special educators working from a behavioral model emphasized the use of consequences to alter problem behavior (e.g., Haring & Phillips, 1962). More recently, it has become apparent that the antecedents of behavior—the events preceding an act and the context or setting in which it occurs—are powerful teaching tools that have been neglected in working with students with problem behavior (Alberto & Troutman, 2003; Kerr & Nelson, 2002; Trout, Nordness, Pierce, & Epstein, 2003). Researchers are helping teachers understand how the classroom conditions they create and the instructional procedures they use may contribute to behavioral problems and their resolution (e.g., Kerr & Nelson, 2002; Walker et al., 2004; Wehby & Lane, 2003).

2. Empirical evidence to support an instructional approach to behavioral problems is accumulating, and a clear consensus may be reached that teaching appropriate behavior explicitly is a central mission of special education programs (Kauffman & Landrum, 2005). Given that teaching both academics and appropriate social behavior are seen as the central role of schools, there may be less tolerance for programs in which the objectives are merely behavioral containment. This trend in special education may be one of the most promising,

but it is not without controversy and danger. If students who are antisocial, disruptive, and violent are disqualified for special education and seen as simply "bad," then they may be expelled or placed in alternative programs designed to be more punitive than instructive. The controversy is whether such students should be considered to need special education; the danger is that they will be found to deserve only exclusion from general education and that their school experience, if they continue to have one, will not emphasize instruction in academic and social skills.

Functional Behavioral Assessment

In a *functional behavioral assessment* (FBA), the teacher or researcher determines what specific purposes or goals the student's behavior may have. The objective then becomes teaching the student to achieve essentially the same goal but with different and more acceptable behavior (Alberto & Troutman, 2003; Cullinan, 2002; Kerr & Nelson, 2002; O'Neill, Horner, Albin, Sprague, Storey, & Newton, 1997). Although FBA, in concept at least, is as old as behavioral psychology, the current trend toward widespread implementation in schools began in the 1990s.

The emphasis on FBA is a result of considering the communicative intent of behavior—the function the behavior has in telling others what one likes, dislikes, wants, cannot tolerate, and so on. It grows out of work with individuals who have severe mental retardation or other disorders that prevent them from using oral language, but it applies also to verbal individuals who are inept at communicating their goals appropriately through language. It is also a way of responding nonpunitively to behavior. Whereas a less thorough behavioral analysis may suggest using punishing consequences for misbehavior, an FBA is an attempt to respond with support for appropriate alternatives to misbehavior.

An emphasis on FBA is completely consistent with increased attention on the academic and social skills curricula. It is also a more explicit and narrow focus on the environmental events that trigger undesirable social behavior and what the student obtains as a consequence of behaving in a given way. Functional assessment may reveal, for example, that a student misbehaves out of frustration, boredom, or overstimulation. It may uncover the fact that misbehavior is maintained because of the attention it garners or because it allows the student to avoid difficult tasks or unpleasant demands. Although it is a highly useful tool in teaching, conducting an FBA and basing teaching procedure on it requires careful training, especially in the case of students whose behavioral problems are severe or long-standing (see Alberto & Troutman, 2003; Armstrong & Kauffman, 1999; Cullinan, 2002; Fox & Gable, 2004; Kerr & Nelson, 2002; Walker et al., 2004). Consider these potential limitations:

- FBA is not necessarily simple. Identifying the function of the behavior—what it "says" or the role it plays in the student's life—may require extensive assessment by trained observers. Without support staff trained in functional analysis, teachers may be unable to carry out the required observations and other evaluation procedures (Scott & Nelson, 1999).

- Intervention procedures suggested by an FBA are sometimes difficult for class-room teachers to carry out without extra help (Gable, 1999; Scott & Nelson, 1999; Sugai, Horner, & Sprague, 1999).
- Functional assessment and functional analysis procedures were developed primar-ily in nonschool settings using very frequent observations of behaviors that occurred often. These procedures may not generalize to the school problems of many students with emotional or behavioral disorders, which include many serious behaviors that occur only infrequently (see Gresham, Quinn, & Restori, 1999; Nelson, Roberts, Mathur, & Rutherford, 1999).

Nevertheless, research on FBA will likely provide increasingly effective teaching procedures and become an important part of special education teachers' repertoire. It will be up to special educators to figure out just what the term *functional behav-ioral assessment* means and how to implement it in school settings in which students exhibit problem behavior of all types (Armstrong & Kauffman, 1999; Bateman & Linden, 1998; Huefner, 2000; Sasso, Conroy, Stichter, & Fox, 2001; Yell, 1998; Yell & Shriner, 1997). It will no doubt also continue to be a controversial topic for many years to come.

Continuum of Alternative Placements

The inclusion of students with disabilities in general education classrooms is perhaps one of the most controversial and divisive issues in education in the 1990s (Crockett & Kauffman, 1999; Hallahan & Kauffman, 2003; Kauffman & Hallahan, 1997, 2005a, 2005b; Kavale & Forness, 2000; Mock & Kauffman, 2002, 2003). Inclusion of students with emotional or behavioral disorders is particularly controversial (Kauffman & Lloyd, 1995; Kauffman, Lloyd, Baker, & Riedel, 1995; Kauffman, Lloyd, Hallahan, & Astuto, 1995b). The controversy is not generated by suggestions that *some* students with emotional or behavioral disorders should be included in regular classes, but by the suggestion that *all* students should be accommodated in general education (e.g., Lipsky & Gartner, 1991; Stainback & Stainback, 1991; Van Dyke, Stallings, & Colley, 1995).

Many different definitions of *inclusion* have been offered, and much confu-sion about the term and its meaning persists. Virtually no one opposes the partial or total inclusion of most students with disabilities in as normal an educational experience as possible. In fact, placement in the least restrictive environment (LRE) has been a basic concept in special education for at least several decades. What has become a central issue of the new century is whether, as some reform-ers propose, the regular classroom should be considered the LRE for literally all students (cf. Kauffman, 1995; Kauffman & Hallahan, 2005a; Mock & Kauffman, 2003; Palmer et al., 2001). Proponents of full inclusion often discuss special edu-cation with little or no reference to the different types and levels of disabilities represented and assume that no students will fail to benefit from placement in a regular classroom (e.g., comments by Sapon-Shevin in O'Neil, 1995). Federal law (the Individuals with Disabilities Education Act) and regulations mandate a continuum of alternative placements, which has included the following options since the early 1960s:

- Regular classroom with supports, including aides, counselling, or mental health services
- Crisis or resource teachers in regular schools, including consultation with regular classroom teachers and students spending minimum time in the resource room
- Self-contained special classes in regular schools, including mainstreaming for part of the school day
- Special day schools, including those organized on a cooperative or regional basis
- Day treatment or partial hospitalization programs attached to hospitals or residential centers, including those placing some students in regular classrooms in the community
- Residential treatment centers and inpatient hospitals, including those sending some students home on weekends and to regular classrooms in the community
- Homebound instruction, in which teachers visit students' homes to provide instruction
- Schools in juvenile detention centers and prisons. (Kauffman & Smucker, 1995, pp. 36–37)

Reformers' suggestion that this continuum be abandoned in favor of one (i.e., regular classroom in the neighborhood school) or very few placement options is seen by many special educators as ill advised, unworkable, and detrimental to many students with disabilities, especially to many with emotional or behavioral disorders (e.g., Diamond, 1993; Kauffman, et al., 1995; Mock & Kauffman, 2003; Morse, 1994). In addition, under IDEA, it is illegal not to maintain the continuum of alternative placements and to make placement decisions on the basis of each individual student's needs (Bateman & Chard, 1995; Crockett & Kauffman, 1999; Huefner, 1994; Jakubecy, Mock, & Kauffman, 2003; Kauffman & Hallahan, 2005a; Yell, 1998). Nevertheless, as ideological and political pressures for full inclusion build, maintenance of placement options becomes a serious concern.

Throughout history, the purposes of placement have been to create and control social ecologies that are conducive to appropriate behavior and mental health, both of the children and their families (Jakubecy, Mock & Kauffman, 2003). Kauffman and Smucker (1995) list the following purposes:

- Protecting others (family, community, schoolmates) from children's uncontrolled or intolerable behavior
- Protecting children from themselves or others
- Educating or training children in academics and other life skills and appropriate emotional responses, attitudes, and conduct
- Educating or training children's families or teachers and peers in order to provide a more supportive environment
- Keeping children available and amenable to therapies—psychotherapy, pharmacotherapy, or behavioral therapy
- Providing opportunity for observation and assessment of children's behavior and its contexts. (p. 37)

It is extremely unlikely that these purposes can be achieved without a continuum of alternative placements (cf. Crockett & Kauffman, 1999; Farmer, 2000; Kauffman, Bantz, & McCullough, 2002). Furthermore, meta-analyses (i.e., systematic statistical comparison of evidence from many studies) indicate that students placed in self-contained classrooms have been more likely than those placed in general education to show improved achievement and decreases in disruptive behavior (e.g., Carlberg & Kavale, 1980; Stage & Quiroz, 1997). However, advocates for students with emotional or behavioral disorders will undoubtedly fight a continuing battle to maintain placement options in the face of reform proposals that would eliminate or severely limit them (Kauffman, 2004; Kauffman, Bantz, & McCullough, 2002).

Transition to Work or Further Education

Since 1990, IDEA has required that individual plans be written for the transition of older students with disabilities from high school to higher education or work (Hallahan & Kauffman, 2003). IDEA, in combination with societal concern for education of the workforce and efforts to reform public schooling, has thus made transition an issue sure to continue.

The primary controversial issues in transition have to do with the curricular and placement options that should be available to students with disabilities at the secondary level (Bullis & Cheney, 1999; Cheney & Bullis, 2004; Edgar & Siegel, 1995). Plans for the transition of students with emotional or behavioral disorders, as well as other disabilities, may founder on the following points, as Edgar (1987) has noted:

- The college-bound secondary curriculum may be inappropriate for the interests, life goals, and abilities of some students with disabilities, even with special supports in regular classes. Forcing students into these classes not only fails to prepare them for technical education or work but creates an environment in which students are likely to misbehave, fail, and drop out.
- Any alternative curriculum or placement option makes the student vulnerable to stigma, neglect, and second-class status. Any alternative to inclusion in the regular, college-bound curriculum is open to charges of discrimination, tracking, and abuse. The early 1990s saw reports of the National Longitudinal Transition Study (NLTS), a major effort to assess the outcomes of secondary education for students with disabilities. As noted by the U.S. Department of Education (1995), the NLTS shows that secondary school programs can produce post-school benefits for students with disabilities—but only for students who can succeed in them. Perhaps the greatest positive contribution schools can make to the post-school success of students with disabilities is to contribute to the in-school success of those students, regardless of their placement. As the inclusion movement gains momentum, great care must be paid to issues of quality and support. (p. 88)

Differentiated education is always controversial. If all students are not treated equally, we assume that some are treated unfairly. We have great difficulty reconciling difference and equality in spite of our commitment to individualization. The dilemmas inherent in helping secondary students plan for life after school are not easily resolved; perhaps they are unresolvable. They are likely to be issues with which every generation will continue to struggle throughout their professional lives.

Multicultural Special Education

The rapidly changing age, social class, and ethnic demographics of the United States brought multicultural concerns to the forefront of educators' thinking in the 1990s. Teaching students with any type of exceptionality demands understanding of multicultural issues (Gay, 1998; Gibbs & Huang, 2003; Hallahan & Kauffman, 2003). Teaching students with emotional or behavioral disorders requires particularly keen attention to the distinctive cultural aspects of behavior and behavioral change, as well as to the principles that are common to all cultures (Anderson & Webb-Johnson, 1995; Osher, Cartledge, Oswald, Sutherland, Artiles, & Coutinho, 2004; Peterson & Ishii-Jordan, 1994; Trent & Artiles, 1995; Vasquez, 1998).

It is difficult to know exactly how to define culture for purposes of multicultural education. Banks (1997) has suggested the concepts of microculture and macroculture. The *macroculture* is a national or shared culture to which smaller microcultures belong. For example, American culture is made up of many *microcultures* based on gender, social class, race, ethnicity, disability, religion, region, and so on. Gay and lesbian youths may be considered to have their own microculture (McIntyre, 1992). Microcultures may differ in a variety of ways relevant to special education, including the discipline procedures they recommend, condone, or reject (McIntyre & Silva, 1992). Moreover, a basic concept of multiculturalism is that there is enormous individual variation among the members of any microculture. Although a culture, however defined, may have identifiable group characteristics, any individual member may or may not share those characteristics.

Regardless of the microculture under consideration, the multicultural aspects of special education for students with emotional or behavioral disorders raise difficult questions that point to continuing controversies:

- How can behavior be assessed without cultural bias? Behavior cannot be assessed without a cultural perspective, so it is critically important to understand one's own cultural frame of reference and how it might affect perceptions and judgments.
- What behavior is normative and what behavior is deviant in the student's culture? Clearly, cultures differ in their standards and expectations for the behavior of children and youth, what they consider acceptable and what they consider inappropriate or intolerable. It is essential to understand the cultural demands of the child's family and community.
- What interventions are acceptable in the culture of the student? Cultures vary considerably in what is considered appropriate behavior of adults toward children. Educators must understand how proposed interventions will be viewed by students' parents and communities.
- How might racism, sexism, and other forms of discrimination have contributed to and how might they still contribute to the creation, labeling, and inappropriate treatment of "deviance"?
- Whose culture should be the standard for making judgments about behavior and interventions?

The challenge of multicultural education is not new. Americans have always faced the daunting task of dealing with cultural diversity (Banks, 1995, 1997; Banks & Banks, 1997; Johnson-Powell, Yamamoto, Wyatto, & Arroyo, 1997; National Research Council, 2002). Historically, we Americans have failed, as have most if not all other nations of the world, to provide a macroculture that is inviting and supportive of all of our desirable microcultures. The next few decades may determine whether a humane, democratic American macroculture exists and can be sustained (see Glazer, 1997). If a macroculture welcoming of differences is to thrive, it must focus on the common humanity of all people regardless of their cultural differences (see Britt, 1999; Kauffman, 1999b, 2002, 2004; Raspberry, 1999; Singh, 1996).

PAST AND FUTURE

It is easy to be discouraged by the history of the treatment of children and youth with emotional or behavioral disorders. Not a single critical issue seems to have been truly resolved; current issues and trends seem only to be a recycling of those that have been with us for well over a century (cf. Kauffman, 1976, 1981, 1999c, 1999f, 2002, 2004; Kauffman, Brigham, & Mock, 2004; Kauffman & Smucker, 1995; Simpson, 1999; Walker, Forness, et al., 1998; Whelan, 1999). In spite of the best intentions of those who have struggled with the problems of educating students with emotional or behavioral disorders, the most promising innovations nearly always seem to have gone awry, to have produced results that are disappointing in the eyes of some, or to have been abandoned at least temporarily. Our disappointment may be partly a result of unrealistic expectations and partly a result of our failure to see that good intentions are not enough to ensure success.

It is difficult to define success in special education, especially in the education of students with emotional or behavioral disorders. If special education really works, then what would we expect the outcomes to be? For many or most students who have severe disorders of conduct, it is unrealistic to expect a "cure" if intervention is not begun early (Kauffman, 1999c, 2002; Walker et al., 2004). How much improvement under what conditions would we define as success? These are important questions that are seldom directly, explicitly addressed among special educators. Too often, perhaps, our expectations are simply not reasonable, and we define ourselves or our programs as failures by criteria that are quixotic—extravagantly, unreasonably idealistic.

Many of the efforts special educators have made have been at least moderately successful by a reasonable standard; but few have been spectacularly successful, and none has been totally successful. Charges of failure and calls for radical reform have been based in some cases on distorted perceptions of the effects special education might be expected to produce, given the resources allocated to the effort (Kauffman, 1994a, 2002; Kauffman & Hallahan, 2005b; Kauffman, et. al., 1995b; Walker, Forness, et al., 1998). We must constantly strive to balance the recognition that special education needs improvement and should produce better outcomes than it does for children, with the acknowledgment that special education has a history of improving the lives of many students. In a sense, our situation is like that of the students with whom we work: we need to recognize our failures, limitations, and need for improvement without becoming unrealistic in our expectations for change, success, or approximations of perfection.

The road special education has traveled from eugenics to euphemisms in the past century has been paved with good intentions. The people who, in retrospect, we may see as monsters who set out to stigmatize, dehumanize, and disenfranchise children and youth with disabilities are bogeymen, not the real people who chose labels, built institutions, established special classes, emptied institutions, tinkered with new labels, mainstreamed students, and called for full inclusion, or wrote the laws and regulations we see as cumbersome, inadequate, or counterproductive. Their intentions were good, but good intentions are not and never have been enough to make hope a reality.

If it had succeeded as planned, special education's history would be a tale of success—of cures and caring, fully realized potential, freedom from stigma and discrimination, efficient management, and social harmony. Well-laid, best-intentioned plans can miss their mark for many reasons, including the failure of planners to see their designs in a social-historical context and to adhere strictly to what is actually known at the time about intervention in human behavior. Our failure to see how our own designs are enmeshed in the context of current sociopolitical trends and our false claims of knowledge about our interventions could make us the bugbears of future generations. If we are going to avoid many mistakes of the past, then we need to proceed with greater awareness of our history, more caution in assuming that any change will bring real progress, and heightened attention to staying within the scientific foundations of our work (Crockett, 2001; Kauffman, 1993, 1999d, 1999f, 2002, 2004; Simpson, 1999; Walker, Forness, et al., 1998; Walker, Zeller, Close, Webber, & Gresham, 1999).

SUMMARY

Children and youth with emotional or behavioral disorders have been recognized throughout history. Efforts to educate these students began in the 19th century. The second half of the 20th century was a period of rapid growth in educational interventions. Diverse theories and divergent educational practices were proposed. Many current issues are a recycling of concerns that have never been and may never be completely resolved.

The history of the field cannot be captured merely by reviewing a chronology of events, but a chronology can help one grasp the development of ideas and trends. Some of the important events in the history of the field are listed in Table 3.1.

Definition, prevalence, and terminology remain current issues of great importance to special educators. Issues of increasing importance revolve around the settings in which students with emotional or behavioral disorders should be taught. Proposals to merge or radically integrate regular and special education have, however, met with considerable skepticism, particularly as such integration might be applied at the secondary level. Extension of special education to incarcerated youths and provision of special services to very young children with emotional or behavioral disorders are emerging trends. Conceptual models are evolving into more sophisticated and integrated approaches that address students' behavior and cognitions in social systems. New coalitions of parents, professionals, and advocates and a new organization for parents and families have brought renewed hope to the field.

In the early 21st century, issues and trends include early identification and prevention; education of antisocial and violent students; comprehensive, collaborative, community-based services; a focus on instruction in academic and social skills; functional assessment of behavior; maintaining a continuum of alternative placements; transition of students to work or further education; and multicultural education.

Table 3.1

Chronology of important events relating to children with emotional or behavioral disorders, 1799–2004

Year	Event
1799	Itard publishes his report of the wild boy of Aveyron
1825	House of Refuge, first institution for juvenile delinquents in the United States, founded in New York; similar institutions founded in Boston (1826) and Philadelphia (1828)
1841	Dorothea Dix begins crusade for better care of the insane
1847	State Reform School for Boys, the first state institution for juvenile delinquents, established in Westborough, Massachusetts
1850	Massachusetts incorporates school for idiotic and feebleminded youths at urging of Samuel Gridley Howe; Edward Seguin moves to the United States
1866	Edward Seguin publishes *Idiocy and Its Treatment by the Physiological Method*
1871	Ungraded class for truant, disobedient, and insubordinate children opens in New Haven, Connecticut
1898	New York City Board of Education assumes responsibility for two schools for truant children
1899	First U.S. juvenile court established in Chicago
1908	Clifford Beers publishes *A Mind That Found Itself*
1909	National Committee for Mental Hygiene founded; Ellen Key publishes *The Century of the Child;* William Healy founds the Juvenile Psychopathic Institute in Chicago
1911	Arnold Gesell founds the Clinic for Child Development at Yale University
1912	Congress creates the U.S. Children's Bureau
1919	Ohio passes law for statewide education of the handicapped
1922	Council for Exceptional Children founded
1924	American Orthopsychiatric Association founded
1931	First psychiatric hospital for children in the United States founded in Rhode Island
1935	Leo Kanner publishes *Child Psychiatry;* Loretta Bender and others begin school for psychotic children at Bellevue Psychiatric Hospital in New York City
1943	Leo Kanner describes early infantile autism
1944	Bruno Bettelheim opens the Orthogenic School at the University of Chicago
1946	New York City Board of Education designates 600 schools for disturbed and maladjusted pupils; Fritz Redl and David Wineman open Pioneer House in Detroit
1947	Alfred Strauss and Laura Lehtinen publish *Psychopathology and Education of the Brain-Injured Child,* based on work at Wayne County Training School in Northville, Michigan
1950	Bruno Bettelheim publishes *Love is Not Enough*
1953	Carl Fenichel founds the League School, first private day school for severely emotionally disturbed children, in Brooklyn
1955	Leonard Kornberg publishes *A Class for Disturbed Children,* first book describing classroom teaching of disturbed children
1960	Pearl Berkowitz and Esther Rothman publish *The Disturbed Child,* describing permissive, psychoanalytic educational approach
1961	William Cruickshank et al. publish *A Teaching Method for Brain-Injured and Hyperactive Children,* reporting results of a structured educational program in

Table 3.1 *continued*

	Montgomery County, Maryland; Nicholas Hobbs and associates begin Project Re-ED in Tennessee and North Carolina
1962	Norris Haring and Lakin Phillips publish *Educating Emotionally Disturbed Children,* reporting results of a structured program in Arlington, Virginia; Eli Bower and Nadine Lambert publish *An In-School Process for Screening Emotionally Handicapped Children* based on research in California
1963	PL 88–164 provides federal money for support of personnel preparation in the area of the emotionally disturbed
1964	William Morse, Richard Cutler, and Albert Fink publish *Public School Classes for the Emotionally Handicapped: A Research Analysis;* Council for Children with Behavioral Disorders established as a division of the Council for Exceptional Children
1965	Nicholas Long, William Morse, and Ruth Newman publish *Conflict in the Classroom;* Autism Society of America founded; first annual Conference on the Education of Emotionally Disturbed Children held at Syracuse University
1968	Frank Hewett publishes *The Emotionally Disturbed Child in the Classroom,* reporting use of an engineered classroom in Santa Monica, California
1970	William Rhodes begins Conceptual Project in Emotional Disturbance, summarizing theory, research, and intervention
1974	Association for Persons with Severe Handicaps founded
1975	Nicholas Hobbs publishes *Issues in the Classification of Children and the Futures of Children,* reporting the work of the Project on the Classification of Exceptional Children
1978	PL 94–142 (enacted in 1975) requires free, appropriate education for all handicapped children, including the seriously emotionally disturbed; federal funding for National Needs Analysis studies at University of Missouri
1986	PL 99–457 enacted, extending provisions of PL 94–142 to all handicapped children 3 to 5 years of age by school year 1990–1991; statistics show that about 1% of students enrolled in public schools are receiving special education services as seriously emotionally disturbed, only about one half a conservative estimate of prevalence
1987	National Mental Health and Special Education Coalition formed; C. Michael Nelson, Robert B. Rutherford, and Bruce I. Wolford publish *Special Education in the Criminal Justice System*
1989	Federation of Families for Children's Mental Health founded; National Juvenile Justice Coalition formed
1990	Individuals With Disabilities Education Act (IDEA) amends PL 94–142; National Mental Health and Special Education Coalition proposes new definition and terminology
1997	National Agenda for Students With Serious Emotional Disturbance proposed; IDEA amended; "seriously" dropped from the designation of "emotionally disturbed" in federal language
2004	IDEA reauthorized

CASE FOR DISCUSSION

She's All Yours
Cindy Lou

I began my teaching career in a special self-contained class in a small town in the South. I was not certified to teach, but the school district was desperate for someone to take positions in special education. Two days before my first students arrived, the principal handed me a cumulative folder and said, "Mrs. Jones and I have decided that this young man would do better in your room." He offered no verbal or written explanation about why the young man in question would do better in a class for students with mild mental retardation. As the year progressed, I began to understand how students qualified for my class. If the principal and the regular classroom teacher agreed, they pulled that child's folder from behind the regular classroom teacher's name in the file drawer and placed the folder behind my name. He or she was then "retarded." It was that simple—a process uncluttered by procedures the teacher and principal deemed unnecessary.

The most interesting student in my class that year was Cindy Lou, one of the few who had actually had a score on an IQ test. Her full-scale score, obtained 4 years before she came to my class, was 92.

Cindy Lou always sat in the back of the room in spite of my best efforts to place her anywhere else. I soon learned to appreciate her self-imposed exile. Whenever she completed seat work, she talked and muttered to herself constantly. Sometimes she supplemented this soliloquy with yells and threats directed at anyone unfortunate enough to catch her eye. Early on, some of my other students laughed at her or teased her about talking and muttering to herself. But they soon learned to keep a healthy distance from Cindy Lou. She was a big girl and not above punching someone who offended her. And it soon became apparent that she didn't require an excuse to knock someone into the middle of next week. Any insult, real or imagined, would suffice.

In spite of Cindy Lou's angry outbursts, she was the best student in my room—when she was there. She was always first to grasp a concept, completed her work first, and answered oral and written questions correctly. But even with my efforts combined with those of her mother, the principal, and the school social worker, Cindy Lou was absent at least 1 day each week.

Cindy Lou was a seventh grader who had been retained twice. She was large, full-bosomed, and sexually active. It wasn't long before the town madam called me to say, "Listen here, you restrain that Cindy Lou!" According to her, Cindy Lou waited outside her establishment, offering herself for less money than the whores inside. "She's undercutting my girls. And furthermore, I'll have you know I run a clean establishment. None of my girls is under age!" she bellowed.

Just before Christmas, Cindy Lou brought me a pretty glass candle holder shaped like a star. Since we spent part of every day in angry confrontation with each other, I was touched that she would give me a present. An hour later, the principal asked me to come to his office. The manager of a store was there. He had seen Cindy Lou take the candleholder. When he confronted her, she had become violent, and he had retreated. There were other witnesses, and he intended to press charges unless someone paid for the candleholder. I was new, unskilled, and a bit stupid. I paid for the candleholder.

Questions About the Case

1. In what historical period do you think this case could have taken place? Why?

2. In what historical period do you think this case did take place? What developments in the field lead you to this conclusion?

3. Historically, what attempts have been made to guard against misidentification and misplacement of students with special needs? Can you propose better safeguards than have been devised so far?

>> PERSONAL REFLECTIONS

History

Richard J. Whelan, EdD, is professor emeritus at the University of Kansas. He was the Ralph L. Smith Distinguished Professor of Child Development and a professor of special education and pediatrics at the University of Kansas Medical Center, where he also directed the education of children.

What do you think are the most important current forces influencing the direction of the field of special education for children with emotional and behavioral disorders?

There are four forces that are major influences in the field today. The first is the long overdue coalition among mental health service providers and special education professionals. I also include in this group parent organizations that are now making every effort to have their needs identified and responded to at the federal and state levels.

The second force is legislation that is largely the product of lobbying efforts by the coalition and parent groups. Legislation (and changes in regulations supporting federal initiatives) will continue to provide money for preparing professional personnel in education and for supporting research and demonstration projects that show how an integrated approach to mental health services and education can be developed at the local level. This effort will take the form of transdisciplinary or interdisciplinary efforts between community-level mental health personnel and special educators in local school systems. If such interdisciplinary, integrated service functions successfully at the local level, it should be implemented at the state and national levels. Local initiatives that are successful and efficient have a higher probability of growth and spread to state and national levels. If we have learned anything about the integration of educational and mental health services over the past 40 years, it is that top-down laws without local acceptance are rarely successful in bringing about deep change as contrasted to surface compliance.

A third force is an initiative to decertify certain students as eligible for special education. This initiative has its foundations in efforts among administrators—of general and special education programs, plus some professionals in the field—to separate students with conduct problems from students who are identified

as seriously emotionally disturbed. The rationale behind this movement is that youngsters with conduct problems are capable of deciding or differentiating among behavior patterns that are acceptable to society and those that are not: If students with conduct problems do not make the right behavioral choices, they should be held accountable to the rules and regulations of the school system and society at large with the same consequences for them as are imposed on other students. Although on the surface this approach seems to make sense, the question is whether the so-called general education personnel are capable of serving the very complex needs of youngsters who act out their affectively based problems. In all likelihood, the general education organization is not capable at this time of offering these students what they need in the way of counseling or specialized instruction. Unfortunately, one of the propelling forces that is driving this decertification movement is economic. Perhaps both general education and special education administrators believe that by limiting the number of children served under the category of "emotionally disturbed" they can reduce the special education budget. This force is also paradoxical, because the numbers of emotionally disturbed children currently being served in special education programs are far fewer than the federal government's estimated 2%. However, if this decertification movement is successful, the young people who are denied services at a time when special education might make a difference will surely be frequent and comprehensive users of the mental health system as adults.

Finally, the fourth force is one of educational restructuring to produce payoffs of large achievement gains for the majority of students. On the surface, who wants to challenge reforms that may increase learning? But beware, special educators, because

66

reformers are looking at disability-targeted dollars to reduce teacher–pupil ratios in general education classrooms (see Odden, Monk, Nakib, & Picus, 1995). After all, if 12% of the students are using 25% of the education dollars, some may say, "Let's just redistribute the funds to reduce teacher–pupil ratios from 1:25 to 1:13." And who will provide instruction to students with disabilities in these smaller classrooms? General education teachers, of course. This is "back to the past" thinking, yet it is one more way to support an agenda called "reform" on the backs of students who are few in number and have little political clout to protect their interests. It is a reversal of the hard-won rights embodied in IDEA.

Furthermore, research findings on smaller class size do not support the assumption of benefits to be gained by the dollar redistribution, nor does research support the assumption that general educators are competent in teaching extremely diverse student groups. Instead, the Kappan article lists a reference on service coordination to support a statement that there is conclusive research that special education dollars produce few achievement effects. The source listed doesn't address program efficacy, but it does argue for coordinated services, a worthwhile goal. The implication for special educators is that we must look behind the assertions of reformers for a foundation of evidence. If the evidence to support an assertion is not there or is distorted, then we must be prepared to respond strongly and quickly. Students with special needs deserve no less than our strongest possible response to protect their rights to an appropriate education that is equitable, but not necessarily identical, when compared to the education that general education students receive.

What are the relationships among these four forces? The answer is self-evident. Two of the forces, the coalition and federal legislation, combine to produce integrated mental health and special education services initiatives at national, state, and local levels. Thus, these two forces are positive, if not downright progressive, in their goals and effects. When joined, the other two forces—excluding students with conduct problems from the schools and high-stakes educational reform schemes—may counter the gains of the first two. In that sense, these two forces are negative if not downright regressive. If my assertions that the last two forces are destructive stimulates incredulity, think through the discipline provisions of IDEA–97. They have given school administrators great flexibility in dispensing long-term suspensions to students who do not fit the prescribed conduct mold. And these same adminis-

trators are even now asking the U.S. Congress for additional flexibility to make unilateral decisions about students who can stay in school and students who are not acceptable in that setting. Will these two sets of forces coexist for a number of years, or will one set prevail? I believe that the progressive forces will win in the long term, and I also believe that the regressive forces will be blunted by the development—a return, if you will—of small, well-run residential treatment centers. These centers will serve students the schools cannot accommodate until they can return as functional learners. Isn't this a far better scenario than increasing the numbers of school pushouts and dropouts, who perpetually use scarce tax dollars in prisons and become lifetime drains on welfare programs? I think so, but time will determine whether my views on this become policy and practice.

How do you think the field will be different in the the 21st century?

This question reminds me of a statement that Albert Einstein made: "I never think of the future. It comes soon enough." Nevertheless, if our society wants to reduce the number of children with serious emotional and behavioral disorders, it will have to function differently from the way it functions today. I believe the current trends are moving in the right direction. For example, if the federal government and states will carry through current initiatives to expand Head Start services, perhaps we can finally move into prevention rather than wait to initiate treatment at the point of crisis or after several crises have occurred in a child's life. Prevention must include a strategy of care that begins during pregnancy and follows throughout the child's educational experience. This means that our local, state, and national governmental agencies must provide instruction for parents and potential parents in healthy living, child development, and other topics that will ensure that their children have the capacity and skills to respond to the vagaries of everyday living.

When children come to school unprepared to deal with teaching and learning environments, the cost of that neglect is an increased frequency of serious affective problems that forever influence children's ability to respond appropriately in situations that require cognitive, social, and related competence. Neither the children nor we as a society in general are served well by such neglect, and as citizens of a demographically diverse nation that requires capable citizens for its very existence, we must insist that this neglect stop now. The 21st century should see not only responsive intervention programs in the public schools and at the preschool level but also a necessary emphasis on the prevention of childhood emotional problems. This prevention must take a proactive approach in terms of children acquiring knowledge and skills to allow them to be resilient and adaptive to the problems they confront in everyday life.

In your professional lifetime, what do you think have been the most important developments affecting the education of children with emotional or behavioral disorders?

In addition to my responses to your earlier questions, I think one of the most important changes in the field since I began, 50 years ago, is the willingness of professionals to look at various ways of understanding children's behavior and the interventions designed to deal with them. When I started there were two, perhaps three, very divergent approaches to understanding and treating the problems children presented to mental health personnel and to professionals in the schools. Unfortunately, there was very little understanding of positions or the language used by the major supporters of each philosophy or theory. Over the past 50 years, there has been a steady progression toward integration of theories—understanding of causes and methods of intervention—to the point at which professionals who adhere to different theoretical approaches can now converse with a more common language and compare research findings associated with their particular positions. The common language that I have seen adopted across theoretical models is that of measurement, particularly that brought to the profession by the strategies and tactics of applied behavior analysis (ABA). It is now relatively common, for example, to use ABA measurement procedures to test the efficacy of a life-space interview approach with students. I view this as a healthy change, because an increased understanding of other views often leads to effective communication, which in turn results in useful approaches to prevention and intervention. Also, children in pain could not care less about the theory espoused by their teacher or counselor; they want relief and help toward a better life.

Another development of critical importance is the role of the federal government in providing programs to serve children with emotional and behavioral disorders. Without the federal catalytic initiatives to provide dollars to serve children and support teacher education, I believe that our field would not have progressed very much since the late 1950s. In the late 1950s, there were fewer than 15 programs in the

United States preparing teachers to serve this group of children. The federal initiative to prepare large numbers of professional personnel has increased service options manyfold. No longer are children and their advocates faced with the choices of no intervention or total hospitalization; there is a continuum of choices between the two extremes. And the federal government has backed up access to these increased services by a strong system of due-process protections and guarantees for a free, appropriate public education. But our field must be forever vigilant, because during economic hard times the hard-won rights of children with special needs can be lost easily. Children can't vote, and professional voices are rarely loud enough or numerically sufficient to counter voices that call for the dismantling of effective programs upon the altars of "wasteful spending" and "bootstrap" slogans.

Perhaps the most important development is the recognition that special education has something to offer in the way of therapeutic experiences for children with emotional and behavioral disorders. No longer do we hear statements like this from our colleagues in mental health: "We will fix the youngsters and send them back to you teachers, and you need not worry about the therapy process." Now we teachers are viewed as important, essential people on the transdisciplinary or interdisciplinary team and function as equals with mental health personnel. After all, the business of children is school; next to home, they spend more hours per day in the school environment than anyplace else. Even if a home situation is dysfunctional, there is still hope that the hours in school can be used to instill within a child the skills, strength, and resilience to cope successfully with life outside of school.

What are the most important lessons to be learned from the history of our field?

Clarence Darrow once remarked, "History repeats itself, and that is one of the things that is wrong with history." I hope that Mr. Darrow was wrong in his analysis of history. Certainly there are important lessons to be learned from our past, and we should avoid the obvious errors we've made. At the same time, we must be selective in pulling from our history those achievements that are still functional today and will be long into the future. In using the past to learn lessons, we must avoid the pitfall of wanting to predict the future so precisely that we alter the past to make our prediction true. After all, we don't know whether our present projections of the future are correct until they become the present. If we are going to learn from our past, then let's be sure that we don't change it to fit our present needs and plans for the future. There must be a careful balance between the positions of "seeing is believing" and "believing is seeing"; either position alone may produce policy errors of considerable magnitude. For example, must the best of 24-hour intervention models be closed because a current paradigm declares that community-based services are best for all children with disabilities? Of course not; but if conventional wisdom based on one-sided policy visions prevails, intensive intervention programming could be unavailable for children with 24-hour needs. Add to this the reality that community service models—no matter how functional the grand plan—have rarely had access to the human and dollar resources required to deliver the services they were designed to provide. Commitment to provide services for children with special needs is the essential vision. Now let's bring historical fact plus balancing of policies to the process of realizing this vision.

Perhaps the most important lesson that we can learn from our history relates back to the concept of preventing the high prevalence of children with emotional and behavioral disorders. We somehow have not arrived at the position of knowing that early commitment of resources functions to preclude even larger commitments of them in the future. The citizens and leaders of our country seem not to be able to operate over the long term; instead, they are making crisis decisions that at best serve as Band-Aids for fundamental problems in our society. Clearly, the goals of the president and the Governors' America 2000 Initiatives are important. Very few people can argue with the position that every child should come to school ready to learn. But unless our society is willing to back up that goal with funding for validated programs, we will not have learned critical lessons from our history.

Another lesson is that we must prepare all educators to be mental health providers in the sense that we offer children nurturing environments with opportunities to learn and time in which to do it. We must abandon our lockstep notion that the curriculum and the time available to teach it must be the same for all children. Having a set curriculum and a set time in which to complete it is simply not responsive to the needs of all children. Just as children's needs vary, so must curriculum and teaching time vary to get that all-important fit between them. If this can be accomplished, many of the affective and cog-

nitive problems that children present today can be prevented from becoming realities tomorrow.

In your recent work in schools, what problems do you see?

In January 2000, I retired from the University of Kansas and its Medical Center. I spent 37 years at the university and, prior to that, 10 years at the Children's Division of the Menninger Clinic in Topeka, Kansas. Since retiring, I have worked part-time as an ombudsman and program consultant at a large school district. My other part-time job is a complaint investigator for Student Support Services (i.e., special education) for the Kansas State Department of Education. I will mention only three of the problems I see.

First, the schools have become the service provider of both first and last resort without additional infusions of dollars and trained personnel to take on that role. Our state residential hospitals have closed or are about to be closed without a concurrent buildup of community-based 24-hour care. I am not referring to the less than 1% of students with "serious emotional disturbance" being served under the Individuals With Disabilities Education Act. Instead, I am referring to the 20% of children and adolescents who have diagnosable mental disorders, and the probable 12% of school-aged children who qualify under the definition of "serious emotional disturbance." These children have limited functional abilities to participate meaningfully in family, school, and community settings.

Where do these children go for help? According to the President's New Freedom Commission on Mental Health, about 70% of the children identified are not receiving the therapeutic interventions they need. School counselors, school psychologists, and teachers (general and special) work hard to meet the affective, social, and cognitive needs of these children. These dedicated professionals could do even more if a functional system of collaboration and coordination between school and other mental health providers was supported by national and state policies.

Second, I rarely hear colleagues discuss so called evidence-based interventions developed by university-based researchers and disseminated by them in teacher education programs. There appears to be a disconnect between university and school professionals that must be connected if "research to practice" means anything more than words in print. In other words, "what works" doesn't seem to thrive, or even survive for that matter, as well as it should from discovery to daily application. For example, I hear my consultant peers, who are highly qualified and experienced, lament new staff members' lack of knowledge about observing, recording, and displaying student performance data as part of an ongoing instructional program for students with cognitive, social, and affective disorders. This knowledge base is simple to teach and master, but it is an absolute requirement for using complex interventions to produce positive outcomes.

Third, except for my colleagues who work closely with students who, by label or behaviors, display "serious emotional disturbance," school personnel are so burdened with multiple demands upon their time and energies (e.g., adequate yearly progress, Section 504, IDEA, IEPs, safe schools, No Child Left Behind, national and state assessments, zero tolerance, teacher accountability) that they have little of either (time or energy) left over to consider the affective lives of their students. They are so pressed to produce student achievement in a never-ending stream of yearly progress that aperiodic (unpredictable) signals from students that all is not well emotionally are simply not received, or if they are, are put in the electronic schedule machine as something to consider later. Unless educators and colleagues from the mental health professions can somehow come together to balance these demands in the mission of providing services for children and adolescents, I believe that in a few short years we may come to believe that the status quo is progress, a sad state of affairs indeed.

I end this part of my personal reflections by mentioning a second and even a third part of my professional life. For over 25 years, I was an IDEA due process hearing officer and trainer. I am also a Kansas Supreme Court mediator and trainer. So, I have learned a few "legalisms" over the years that just might apply to the word picture I attempted to draw in these comments. Right now, general and special educators are the de facto providers of mental health services. If we are to be effective as mental health service providers, and if that is what is expected of us, then make us so de jure as a matter of public policy and provide the resources to allow us to get on with the mission with confidence and commitment to succeed.

Finally, I am optimistic by nature and will remain that way. We optimists may be wrong as often as are pessimists, but we have more fun. More important, my colleagues in general and special education are optimists also. How else could they survive? So, even though the concerns described are serious, they in no way reflect on the dedication and caring I observe each and every day among professionals in the schools. If any group of professionals can solve the problems associated with these concerns, our education colleagues can. Give them time, support, and resources, and they will do it. If I didn't believe this to be true, I probably would become a pessimist.

>> QUESTIONS FOR FURTHER REFLECTION

1. Why are many "old" issues never resolved but are "recycled," appearing again and again, usually in slightly different form?

2. What do you think will be the "new" or contemporary and controversial issues 10 years from now, and how will they be related to today's current issues?

3. How would you judge whether a new movement or idea is likely to lead to improvement of the lives of children and youth with emotional or behavioral disorders? On what basis would you resist the adoption of a new idea?

CHAPTER FOUR

CONCEPTUAL MODELS

APPROACHES TO THE PROBLEM

As you read this chapter, keep these guiding questions in mind:

- How are beliefs about human nature linked to one's choice of intervention strategies?

- How are the assumptions underlying a biological model the same as or different from those underlying a psychodynamic model?

- From the perspective of a behavioral model, what is the most important strategy in changing maladaptive behavior?

- What is the most important concept underlying social-cognitive theory, and what implication does it have for understanding the disordered emotions and behavior of children and youth?

- What are the most obvious strengths and weaknesses of each conceptual model (biological, psychodynamic, psychoeducational, behavioral, social-cognitive, postmodern)?

People in every culture have ideas about the causes of disturbing human behavior. They try to link presumed causes to procedures that they assume will eliminate, control, or prevent deviant acts. From the innumerable causes and remedies that have been suggested over the centuries, we can identify several conceptual themes. These themes have remained remarkably consistent for thousands of years, and contemporary versions are merely elaborations and extensions of their ancient counterparts (Kauffman, 1974). For purposes of explanation and control of behavior, humans have been variously conceptualized as spiritual beings, biological organisms, rational and feeling persons, and products of their environments.

Educators have always struggled with how human behavior—both troublesome and desirable—should be conceptualized. What we believe people *are* determines what explanations of behavior we seek and accept. If people are thought to be spiritual beings, then mystical or religious approaches to changing their behavior will be adopted. If people are conceptualized as biological organisms, then medical, surgical, or dietary treatments will be prescribed. If people are said to be rational and feeling persons, then cognitive and affective interventions will be attempted. And if people are analyzed as products of environmental events, then antecedent and consequent events will be controlled in efforts to modify behavior. How we respond to disordered behavior is linked to what we believe about the nature and causes of human conduct.

Today we recognize so many possible causes of troublesome behavior that sorting through them has become a troubling task. It does not take professional training to see how nearly all aspects of young people's lives are fraught with potential for psychological problems. Adults now recognize that children and youth feel stress in everyday life and that school experiences can be particularly stressful. Recognizing that children and youth face stress, however, does not bring understanding of the causes of disordered emotions or behavior or a remedy. It is one thing to recognize stress; it is quite another to articulate a coherent view of how stress affects human development and to determine what kinds are most significant. It is one thing to note that self-concept is an important aspect of emotional and behavioral development; it is quite another to understand how self-esteem fits into the web of other influences on behavior.

To have more than a superficial understanding of emotional and behavioral disorders, we need a complex set of organizing principles—a *conceptual model,* or framework, for organizing and making sense of the vast array of ideas and information about causes and cures. Any simple explanation of human behavior will have its day in the popular imagination, but all such oversimplifications have a common fate: They become today's cliché and tomorrow's jest.

One popular notion is that emotional and behavioral problems, if not disorders, are caused by stress and that finding coping mechanisms is critical to mental health. Few children, it seems, will escape the curse of our stress-ridden society. The only apparent solution is a radical change in societal values to relieve the stress our children and youth are experiencing. Too often, such observations are turned into a popular, simplistic formula: Stress causes emotional or behavioral problems; if we want to reduce these problems, we must alleviate stress. We must go beyond a simple formula to learn how youngsters cope with stress—why some succumb to a given stressor but others don't—and to discover why some sources of stress are particularly debilitating but others are not.

Another popular idea is that emotional and behavioral problems are reflections of low self-esteem. The suggested cure, as you might expect, is lifting self-esteem. Among the most popular views of our era is the assumption that low self-esteem is the origin of every human foible and that raising self-esteem will solve every problem from the poor academic performance of schoolchildren to the mismanagement of corporations. Low self-esteem, some suggest, is behind delinquents' behavior (which is interpreted as an attempt to enhance their self-esteem by showing off), the motivation for "sin" (and also the basis for self-righteousness), the basis for underachievement (and overachievement) and aggression (and passivity)—any behavior that is seen as undesirable. Psychologists, ministers, business executives, and educators may be naively optimistic about the curative effects of higher self-esteem. The simplistic view of self-esteem as a universal cause and cure may give feeling good about oneself a bad name.

Among the hottest issues in the early 21st century is youth violence, especially its causes and cures. It remains a hot topic in spite of the fact that indices of violent crime show that it is decreasing, not increasing. In many popular and professional journals and books, we are told that violence has no single cause and no single cure, that we must integrate what we know about biological, psychological, sociological, and all other verifiable influences on behavior if we are to understand the causes of violence and address the problem effectively (e.g., Flannery, 1999; Flannery & Huff, 1999; Manno, Bantz, & Kauffman, 2000). This is not a simplistic view. However, some articles in the popular press focus on particular explanations of violent behavior that many are tempted to oversimplify. Evolutionary psychologists study the interplay of behavior, neurochemicals, and the individual's environment—how each affects the other and how behavior has been shaped through genetic processes during human evolution. However, glib statements about evolutionary psychology can be seriously misleading and be broadened to explain nearly all human emotional or behavioral problems.

Nearly every reader of this book will know that there are alternative theories of behavior (or schools of psychology). Each conceptual model offers an explanation of human behavior and suggests how to change it. The challenge we face is choosing or constructing a defensible theory and using it consistently to evaluate alternative conceptual models. More simply, the challenge is to decide what is believable and what is helpful to understand about human behavior.

I offer three different levels of analysis or grouping of ideas. First, I provide a traditional exposition of models. Teacher educators and researchers have provided a traditional grouping of concepts: biogenic, psychodynamic, psychoeducational, humanistic, ecological, and behavioral (see Van Hasselt & Hersen, 1991a, 1991b). Second, I discuss a conceptual model derived primarily from social learning principles. Third, I describe a model that integrates classification, causal factors, assessment, and intervention.

TRADITIONAL EXPOSITION OF CONCEPTUAL MODELS

Following is a brief description of the basic assumptions of several conceptual models. Keep two cautions in mind as you read these expositions and the accompanying cases:

- The descriptions of these models are cursory, and much additional reading is required to obtain a full understanding of each model.
- The descriptions and cases are purposely unidimensional and do not reflect the multiple perspectives that competent practitioners typically bring to bear.

The descriptions and cases (in the accompanying case book) are purposeful oversimplifications intended to highlight particular conceptual models. Very seldom would a competent teacher, psychologist, or psychiatrist view a child or youth in only one way. Finally, we should note that each of these models has gone through periods of popularity and disrepute. Some are being gradually abandoned as evidence to support them fails to materialize; others are being gradually strengthened through the accumulation of scientific evidence. Some are more readily applicable to certain disorders than to others (e.g., a biogenic approach may be more relevant to schizophrenia and autism than to conduct disorder). We do not give case examples involving the psychodynamic and humanistic approaches simply because so little evidence indicates their effectiveness in working with troubled youngsters.

Psychodynamic Approach

Dynamic psychiatry is concerned with hypothetical mental mechanisms and their interplay in the developmental process. *Psychodynamic models,* sometimes called *psychoanalytic models* because psychoanalytic theory provides so many of their tenets, rest on the assumption that the essence of emotional and behavioral disorders is not the behavior itself but a pathological imbalance among the dynamic parts of one's personality (the id, the ego, and the superego). Disturbed behavior is merely symptomatic of an underlying mental illness; the cause of mental illness is usually attributed to excessive restriction or excessive gratification of the individual's instincts at a critical stage of development or to early traumatic experiences. Interventions based on a psychodynamic model stress the importance of individual psychotherapy for the child (and often for the parents as well) and the necessity of a permissive, accepting classroom teacher. Problems in relating to youngsters, whether as teacher or therapist, are often interpreted in terms of the adult's own unconscious conflicts. Extreme importance is placed on understanding the unconscious motivation for behavior on the assumption that, once it is understood (and not until), the problem will be resolved. Another assumption is that if the underlying unconscious conflict is not understood and resolved, then any improvement in the symptomatic behavior is trivial or even harmful, and the symptom will be replaced by another (see Remschmidt & Quaschner, 2001).

Humanistic Approach

Humanistic education draws heavily from humanistic psychology; the social–political movement of the late 1960s and early 1970s known as the counterculture or countertheory movement; and the free school, open education, alternative school, and deschooling ideas of the same era. A humanistic approach emphasizes self-direction, self-fulfillment, self-evaluation, and free choice of educational activities and goals; but the theoretical underpinnings of humanistic models are hard to identify. A teacher who devises education based on a humanistic model will be more a resource and a catalyst for learning than a director of activities. The teacher is unauthoritarian and promotes a classroom atmosphere best described as open, free, nontraditional, affectively charged, and personal. An assumption underlying most humanistic approaches is that youngsters will find their own solutions to their problems if they are merely freed to do so in a loving and supportive environment.

The humanistic model of the 1960s and 1970s is an apparent precursor of what is now called *postmodernism* or *deconstruction* (e.g., Danforth, 1997, 2001; Danforth & Rhodes, 1997; Gallagher, 2004; see Burke, 1972; Dennison, 1969; Knoblock, 1970, 1973, 1979, 1983; Neill, 1960; Rogers, 1983, for description of a humanistic approach before postmodernism became popular). Some of the elements of affective education and some characteristics of alternative schools (sometimes called schools of choice) fit the model of humanistic education (see Fizzell, 1987; Knoblock, 1983). The *holistic education* of the 1990s, which rejects the traditional mechanistic view of the natural sciences and emphasizes one's personal construction of reality, appears in many ways to be an extension of the humanistic approach of the 1960s and 1970s or a blending of psychoeducational and humanistic elements. These approaches emphasize qualitative (as opposed to quantitative) research, although little qualitative research on behavioral disorders has actually been done (Sabornie, 2004). The shortcomings of postmodern and holistic ideas in education are discussed by Heward (2003); Heward and Silvestri (2004); Kauffman (2002); Kauffman, Brigham, and Mock (2004); Mostert, Kauffman, and Kavale (2003); Polsgrove and Ochoa (2004); and Sasso (2001).

The *life-impact curriculum* described by Rhodes and Doone (1992) and Blair (1992) has as its objectives changing students' higher-order thinking abilities by (a) awakening children to the pattern of meaningful experiences that they project and build into an object, space, time, and causal reality; (b) teaching mental patterning and projection skills that give children a greater sense of control over the development of themselves; and (c) extending the range of variability and flexibility in the acceptance and projection of reality in their actual world, both in and out of school (Rhodes & Doone, 1992, p. 13).

Biogenic Approach

Human behavior involves neurophysiological mechanisms; that is, a person cannot perceive, think, or act without the involvement of his or her anatomy and physiology. One set of conceptual models begins with one or both of two hypotheses:

1. Emotional or behavioral disorders represent a physiological flaw.
2. These disorders can be brought under control through physiological processes.

Some writers suggest that disorders such as autism, hyperactivity, depression, or hyperaggression are manifestations of genetic factors, brain dysfunction, food additives, or biochemical imbalance. Some suggest that emotional or behavioral disorders of most types are responsive to or most easily ameliorated by drugs or, in rare cases, neurosurgery. According to these models, recognition of the underlying biological problem is critical; however, successful treatment may or may not be aimed at resolving the physiological flaw. In many cases, we know of no way to repair or ameliorate the brain damage, genetic process, or metabolic disorder. Consequently, we must be satisfied with understanding the physiological cause of the disorder and making appropriate adaptations to it. Some management strategies are based on hypotheses about physiological processes but do not address known physiological disorders. For example, students may be given drugs to help control hyperactivity or schizophrenia, or they may be taught biofeedback techniques to help them gain self-control, even though the physiological cause(s) have not been isolated. Interventions associated with a biogenic approach include drug therapy, dietary control, exercise, surgery, biofeedback, and alteration of environmental factors that exacerbate the physiological problem (see Forness & Kavale, 2001a; Forness, Kavale, Sweeney, & Crenshaw, 1999; Forness, Walker, & Kavale, 2003; Konopasek & Forness, 2004; Kutcher, 2002; and the case, *Elizabeth,* continued, in the accompanying case book).

Psychoeducational Approach

The *psychoeducational model* shows concern for unconscious motivations and underlying conflicts (hallmarks of psychodynamic models) yet also stresses the realistic demands of everyday functioning in school, home, and community. A basic assumption of the psychoeducational model is that teachers must understand unconscious motivations if they are to deal most effectively with academic failure and misbehavior. This does not mean that they must focus on resolving unconscious conflicts as a psychotherapist might. It means focusing on how to help the student acquire self-control through reflection and planning. Intervention based on a psychoeducational model may include therapeutic discussions, or *life-space interviews,* later renamed *life-space crisis intervention* to help youngsters understand that what they are doing is a problem, recognize their motivations, observe the consequences of their actions, and plan alternative responses to use in similar future circumstances. Emphasis is on the youngster's gaining insight that will result in behavioral change, not on changing behavior directly (see Dembinski, Schultz, & Walton, 1982; Fagen, 1979; Fenichel, 1974; Heuchert & Long, 1980; Long, 1974; Long et al., 1998; Long & Newman, 1965; Long, Wood, & Fecser, 2001; Morse, 1974; Redl, 1966; Rezmierski, Knoblock, & Bloom, 1982; Rich, Bock, & Coleman, 1982; Wood, 1990; Wood & Long, 1991, and the case, *Aaron,* in the accompanying case book).

Ecological Approach

An *ecological model* is based on concepts in ecological psychology and community psychology. In its early years, the approach drew also on the model of European educateurs, who work with youngsters in their homes and communities as well as their schools. The student is considered an individual enmeshed in a complex social system, both a giver and a receiver (excitor and responder) in social transactions with other students and adults in a variety of roles and settings. Emphasis is on study of the child's entire social system, and intervention is directed, ideally, toward all facets of the student's milieu. Interventions used in ecological programs have tended to emphasize behavioral and social learning concepts and the ways in which they can be used to alter an entire social system (see Daly, 1985; Hobbs, 1966, 1974; Lewis, 1982; Muskal, 1991; Rhodes, 1965, 1967, 1970; Schroeder, 1990; Swap, 1974, 1978; Swap, Prieto & Harth, 1982; Votel, 1985; and the case, *Emelda,* in the accompanying case book).

In the 1980s and 1990s, the melding of ecological concepts and social learning or behavioral theory has been described as *ecobehavioral analysis* (see Kamps, Leonard, Dugan, Boland, & Greenwood, 1991; Schroeder, 1990; Teare, Smith, Osgood, Peterson, Authier, & Daly, 1995). An ecobehavioral analysis is an attempt to identify and use naturally occurring, functional events more skillfully and consistently to improve instruction and behavior management. If naturally occurring strategies, such as peer tutoring, can be validated as effective and applied consistently, then supportive, habilitative social systems might be built or strengthened with less reliance on artificial interventions that tend to be more costly, intrusive, temporary, and unreliable.

Behavioral Approach

Two major assumptions underlie a *behavioral model:*

1. The essence of the problem is the behavior itself.
2. Behavior is a function of environmental events.

Maladaptive behavior is viewed as inappropriate learned responses; therefore, intervention should consist of rearranging antecedent events and consequences to teach more adaptive behavior. A behavioral model derives from the work of behavioral psychologists. With its emphasis on precise definition and reliable measurement, careful control of the variables thought to maintain or change behavior, and establishment of replicable cause–effect relationships, it represents a natural science approach. Interventions based on a behavioral model consist of choosing target responses, measuring their current level, analyzing probable controlling environmental events, and changing antecedent or consequent events until reliable changes are produced in the target behaviors (see Hewett, 1968, 1974; Kazdin, 2001; Kerr & Nelson, 2002; Lewis, Lewis-Palmer, Stichter, & Newcomer, 2004; Malone, 2003; Rhode, Jenson, & Reavis, 1992, Walker, 1995; Walker, Ramsey, & Gresham, 2004; and the case, *Sven,* in the accompanying case book).

COMPARING AND ELIMINATING MODELS

Cullinan, Epstein, and Lloyd (1991) have compared important features of three of these conceptual models: psychoeducational, behavioral, and ecological. Figure 4.1 shows their evaluation of the three models on causation (the extent to which each

Feature	Psychoeducational	Behavioral	Ecological
Causation			
Formal principles	●	●	○
Past events	●	○	○
Internal determinants	●	○	○
Holistic view	○	○	●
Intervention			
Replicability	◐	●	○
Efficiency	○	●	◐
Breadth	●	●	○
Scientific			
Empirical emphasis	◐	◐	○
Restricted effectiveness	○	●	○
Extended effectiveness	○	○	○

● High   ◐ Medium   ○ Low

Figure 4.1
Comparison of models of behavior disorder
Source: Cullinan, D., Epstein, M. H., & Lloyd, J. W. (1991). Evaluation of conceptual models of behavior disorders. *Behavioral Disorders, 16,* 150.

relies on formal principles, past events, internal determinants, and a holistic view to explain behavior), intervention (the extent to which each suggests methods that are replicable, efficient, and have broad applicability), and scientific rigor (the extent to which each relies on empirical data, shows evidence of behavior change restricted to the treatment setting, and shows evidence that treatment effects extend to environments other than the treatment setting). This kind of comparison among conceptual models helps us see the particular strengths and weaknesses of various frameworks for special educators.

Cullinan et al. (1991) did not include the psychodynamic model because it has been largely abandoned. They did not include the biological model because the new medical model to which Forness and Kavale (2001a) referred is a relatively recent development that has grown out of advances in drug therapies and brain imaging (see also Konopasek & Forness, 2004). However, both of these models could be evaluated using the framework provided by Cullinan et al. (1991).

The new medical model is worth considering in more detail. *Medical model* was a derogatory term for special education in which medical diagnoses and psychiatric interventions took precedence over education. The term is sometimes still used to condemn special education for imitating medicine in any way. However, medicine is based on science, and *medical model* can be interpreted to mean a model of scientific inquiry and practice (Kauffman & Hallahan, 1974).

Special education is really patterned much more on law than on medicine (see Kauffman, 1999c, 2004). The new medical model refers to both adopting a scientific approach to education and considering contemporary medical practice (Forness & Kavale, 2001a). The new medical model is not meant to replace but to supplement behavior management (see Konopasek & Forness, 2004). The intention is to integrate behavior management and medicine, which are both based on scientific principles.

Concepts that are relatively new to special education are postmodernism or deconstructivism. The terms *postmodern* and *deconstruction* are poorly defined, even by the people who use them (see Kauffman, 1999f, 2002, 2003a, 2004). Nevertheless, some have proposed a postmodern or deconstructivist approach to special education, including the education of students with emotional or behavioral disorders (e.g., Danforth, 2001; Danforth & Rhodes, 1997; Elkind, 1998; Gallagher, 2004). Postmodernism has been proposed in fields related to special education, including psychology (e.g., Gergen, 2001). We do not consider postmodernism further here because it seems to be a rejection of scientific thinking about problems. As one psychologist critic put it, "All it can offer, by its own admission, is word games—word games that lead nowhere and achieve nothing. Like anthrax of the intellect, if allowed into mainstream psychology, postmodernism will poison the field" (Locke, 2002, p. 458). Likewise, it will poison special education if it is allowed to become the dominant way of thinking about disability. Forness (2002) has noted that postmodernism "stands almost as the antithesis of evidence-based practice" (p. 6; see also Heward, 2003; Kauffman, 2002; Kavale & Forness, 2000; Krueger, 2002; Kruger, 2002; Mostert et al., 2003; Sasso, 2001; Walker et al., 1998). Polsgrove and Ochoa expressed the issue well: "No social reconstruction of reality can alter the fact that problems presented by children with EBD are real and that we need the best and most advanced practices available to address their needs" (2004, p. 176).

DEVELOPING AN INTEGRATED MODEL

The education of children and youth with emotional or behavioral disorders is not now governed by a consistent philosophy or conceptual model that is linked to instructional methodology. Although slavish devotion to a single conceptual model is not desirable, and diverse theories can be the basis for productive debate, our field would be advanced by a more integrated, less haphazard conceptual approach.

In practice, few professionals adhere rigidly to a single conceptual model. Most realize that multiple perspectives are needed for competent practice. Yet there is a limit to the degree to which one can be eclectic (picking and choosing concepts and strategies from various models) without being simple-minded and self-contradictory (see Kauffman, 2002). Some conceptual models are not complementary; they suggest radically different and incompatible approaches to a problem. Acceptance of one set of assumptions about human behavior sometimes implies rejection of another.

Selection and Use of Conceptual Models

We have several distinct options in treating the issue of *conceptual models*. First, we can adopt a single model as an unvarying theme, a template by which to judge all hypotheses and research findings. Although this option has the advantages of consistency and clarity, it is disconcerting to many careful thinkers because it rests on the questionable assumption that reality is sufficiently encompassed by one set of hypotheses about human behavior.

Second, we can take a nonevaluative stance, a posture that treats all concepts equally, as deserving the same attention and respect. This option has immediate appeal in its acknowledgment that every model has limitations, and it allows the reader to choose from an unbiased treatment of all contestants. There are, however, many drawbacks. Under the guise of eclecticism, this option rests on the implicit assumption that we have no sound reasons for discriminating among ideas. It fosters the attitude that behavior management and education, like religion and political ideology, are better left to personal belief than to scientific scrutiny; and it leads inevitably to witless self-contradiction. Finally, it supports fads based on little more than a bold assertion that something is true or works, and such fads are a serious impediment to progress in education (cf. Heward & Silvestri, 2004; Kauffman, 1999d, 2002; Sasso, 2001).

A third option, and the one I chose for this book, is to focus on hypotheses that can be supported or refuted by replicable and public empirical data—ideas that lend themselves to investigation by the methods of natural science (see Cook, Landrum, Tankersley, & Kauffman, 2003; Crockett, 2001; Kauffman, 1999d, 2002; Landrum & Tankersley, 1999; Tankersley, Landrum, & Cook, 2004, for elaboration). The result of this choice is that most of the discussion is consistent with a social-cognitive model, and useful concepts from other models are discussed as they are related to social learning. Psychodynamic, humanistic, and postmodern approaches are ignored, for the most part, because so little reliable evidence (from a natural science point of view) is available to support them (see Rutherford, Magee, & Mathur, 2004). Biogenic models are discussed because they are open to empirical investigation, but these models are not treated extensively because of their relatively limited implications for the work of educators.

My choice for this book does not mean I believe there is only one way of knowing; I do believe, however, that some ways of knowing are better than others for certain purposes. For educators who work with troubled children and youth, I believe the natural science tradition provides the firmest foundation for competent professional practice. The most useful knowledge is derived from experiments that can be repeated and that consistently produce similar results—in short, information obtained from investigations conducted according to well-established rules of scientific inquiry.

Not every problem can be approached through scientific experiment, and in such cases one must rely on other sources of wisdom: clinical experience, intuition, expert opinion, logical analysis, and so forth. But to the extent that reliable, quantitative, experimental evidence is available or can be obtained, I believe educators should make it the basis for their practice (see Crockett, 2001; Heward, 2003; Heward & Silvestri, 2004; Kauffman, 1987, 1993, 1994a, 1999d, 2002; Sasso, 2001, for further discussion). Furthermore, the most useful scientific information for teachers is that which is derived from controlled experiments that reveal how the social environment can be arranged to modify behavior and how individuals can be taught self-control.

Biological experiments have relatively few implications for the work of teachers. Teachers do not choose students' genes, perform surgery, prescribe drugs, control diet, or do physical therapy. Teachers do, however, have enormous power over the social environment of the classroom as well as a significant measure of control over how they think about behavioral and emotional problems and how they act. Therefore, my emphasis is on social learning.

A Social-Cognitive Approach

Social-cognitive theory is an attempt to explain human behavior from a natural science perspective by integrating what is known about the effects of the environment (the behaviorist position) and what is known about the role of cognition (cognitive psychology). Scientific research indicates indisputably that the consequences of our behavior—environmental responses created by our actions—affect the way we are likely to behave in the future. But behavioral research alone cannot explain the subtleties and complexities of human conduct. Social-cognitive theory emphasizes *personal agency:* the ability of humans to use symbols for communication, to anticipate future events, to learn from observation or vicarious experience, to evaluate and regulate themselves, and to be reflectively self-conscious. Personal agency or social context adds a needed dimension to a behavioral analysis and provides a more complete explanation of human behavior (see Bandura, 1995a, 1995b; Bandura & Locke, 2003; Capara, Barbarnelli, Pastorelli, Bandura, & Zimbardo, 2000; Harrington, 2001; Mahoney, 1995; Malone, 2003; Meyers & Cohen, 1990).

Social-cognitive theory is not, however, merely a combination of behavioral and cognitive psychology. It is also a reconceptualization of the direction, interaction, and reciprocality of effects. It suggests that people are not merely products of their environments, nor are they simply driven to behave as they do by internal forces. It suggests that behavior results from reciprocal influences among the environment (both social and physical), personal factors (thoughts, feelings, perceptions), and the individual's behavior itself. This "triadic reciprocality," described by Bandura (1977, 1978, 1986), is depicted in the center of Figure 4.2, showing that behavior (B), person variables (P), and environment (E) constantly influence one another.

Under some conditions, one of the three factors shown in Figure 4.2 may play a more influential role than another, but usually all three elements are involved. As Bandura (1986) noted, "reciprocality does not mean symmetry in the strength of bidirectional influences. Nor is the patterning and strength of mutual influences fixed in

Figure 4.2
Triadic reciprocality in social-cognitive theory. Environment (E), behavior (B), and person variables (P) influence each other reciprocally. Solid lines connecting B, P, and E represent strong reciprocal effects; dashed lines represent weaker influence. Circles represent environment, behavior, and person variables and their shared (intersecting) reciprocal effects.

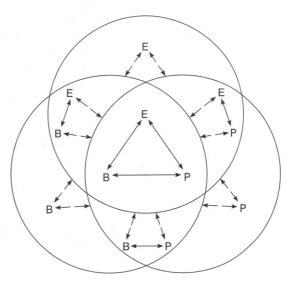

reciprocal causation. The relative influence exerted by the three sets of interacting factors will vary for different activities, different individuals, and different circumstances" (p. 24).

Thus, the three sets of interacting factors might be depicted as in the outer portions of Figure 4.2. Under many circumstances, all three factors exert reciprocal influence, as shown by the central part of the figure in which the three circles (representing sets of factors) intersect. Under other circumstances, the intersections of and interactions between two of the sets of factors, or the effects of only one set, are of primary concern.

An example of strong reciprocal causal connections between two factors, with only weak connection to the third, is the extremely fearful child who will not make any approach to dogs. In this case, environment and person variables intersect and are closely tied, as shown in the upper right section of Figure 4.2. Environment (E) and person variables (P) interact reciprocally, as shown by the solid line connecting them, but the connection to behavior is weaker, as indicated by the broken lines connecting them to behavior (B). Dogs may arouse great fear in the child, and the fear may lead the child to avoid environments that include dogs and seek dog-free environments, which effectively reduce anxiety. But the child's behavior involving dogs may be extremely limited, consisting almost entirely of stereotyped avoidance rather than varied and adaptive responses (see Kauffman, 1979; Kauffman & Kneedler, 1981).

An example of person variables affecting each other reciprocally but having only weak connections to behavior and environment is an individual who becomes more and more anxious on the basis of thoughts and affective states. "In the personal realm of affect and thought, there exist reciprocal escalating processes, as when frightening thoughts arouse internal turmoil that, in turn, breeds even more frightening thoughts" (Bandura, 1986, p. 25). Such processes are represented in the lower right section of Figure 4.2, in which an isolated subset of person variables (*P*) is connected to behavior and environment by dashed lines, indicating weaker causal connections.

As I use the term in this book, *social-cognitive theory* also takes into consideration the developmental features of behavior. That is, we recognize that behavior must be evaluated in the context of normal development. There is continuity across developmental stages in the type of behavior that is adaptive or maladaptive, yet the same behavior may have different meanings at different ages. For example, a pronounced lack of social skills may be maladaptive at all developmental stages, but the particular behaviors that indicate social retardation may differ considerably, depending on the child's age and social circumstances (see Strand, Barnes-Holmes, & Barnes-Holmes, 2003; Sugai & Lewis, 2004).

A detailed exposition of social-cognitive theory is far beyond the scope of this book. Full understanding of the theory demands study of the work of its foremost proponent, Albert Bandura (see, for example, Bandura, 1977, 1978, 1986, 1995a, 1995b; Bandura & Locke, 2003). We have sketched the theory here merely to provide a framework for later discussion. The primary concept to keep in mind is Bandura's notion of *triadic reciprocality.* An important implication of this concept is that emotional or behavioral disorders are comprehensible only in the contexts, both personal and social, in which they occur. For example, studies of how teachers control their students' behavior must be extended to include students' effects on teachers—that is, *transactions,* or mutual influences. The emphasis of social-cognitive theory on reciprocality of effects in human transactions is entirely consistent with an ecological approach.

STRUCTURE FOR DISCUSSION

Given a social-cognitive model for conceptualizing human behavior, what is the best way to structure a coherent discussion of the characteristics of the emotional or behavioral disorders of children and youth? As Bandura (1986) noted, it is impossible to study all possible reciprocal actions at once; trying to examine all causal factors simultaneously paralyzes scientific study because the task is overwhelmingly complex. We must study behavior, its assessment, its causes, and its effects in simpler, more manageable segments. This is true whether one is conducting research or summarizing and interpreting it.

Figure 4.3 indicates that assessment and intervention are overlapping activities. It also indicates that types of disorders and causal factors are interconnected. We might choose to analyze a particular slice of the model, such as the assessment of genetic factors in depression, but we can never completely separate the particular problem we are analyzing from all other problems. If we are studying the assessment of genetic factors in depression, then we cannot totally ignore the assessment of temperament as a causal factor and the design of interventions involving peers and parents. Although we focus on one particular topic, we must be aware of its connection to others. Our focus in the following chapters will first be on assessment (part 2), then on

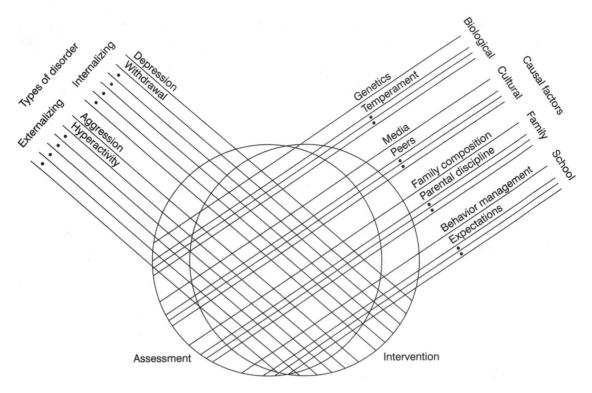

Figure 4.3
Structure for analysis of emotional or behavioral disorders

causal factors (part 3), then on types of disorders (part 4), and finally on a personal statement about teaching (part 5).

SUMMARY

Beliefs about the nature of human beings determine what explanations one seeks for behavior and the strategies one uses in approaching emotional or behavioral disorders. Throughout history, people have been conceptualized as spiritual beings, biological organisms, rational and feeling individuals, and products of their environments. Each conceptualization has led to intervention approaches. Conceptual models, which help organize and interpret information, are necessary for making sense of the vast array of ideas and information about the causes and cures of disordered emotions or behavior. Traditional expositions of conceptual models include descriptions of biogenic, psychodynamic, psychoeducational, humanistic (now perhaps known as postmodern), ecological, and behavioral models. Although practitioners and scholars seldom employ one model exclusively, they must have a rational basis for choosing among models; some are logically incompatible and suggest opposite courses of action. A model derived from scientific experiments in social learning and self-control provides the most defensible basis for professional practice. A social-cognitive approach, which emphasizes triadic reciprocity among behavior, person variables, and environment, provides a consistent theme for this book.

CASE FOR DISCUSSION

Where Do You Start with One Like This?
Derrick Yates

Derrick is a 12-year-old placed in a class of high-average and gifted fifth graders, although his academic skills are at about third-grade level. He has been known as a terror, as unmanageable, by every teacher he has had in his school career. He is large for his age and is described as a "scary kid" with crooked, bucked teeth, a chilling laugh, and an odd look in his eyes. Because of his disruptive behavior, he has been allowed to attend school for only half days for protracted periods. The school's teacher assistance team has recommended that he be evaluated for possible special education services.

At home, Derrick's behavior is also highly problematic, threatening, and intimidating. His mother and father are divorced, and Derrick lives with his mother and younger sister and brother. He is enraged about the divorce and blames his mother for the family's breakup. The school social worker reports that Derrick killed the family dog with a butcher knife—beheaded and dismembered the dog and scattered the parts in the yard. His mother has had locks installed on the kitchen drawers for fear that Derrick would use knives and other kitchen utensils to harm her or his siblings. She has also had double locks installed on her bedroom door and lets the two younger children sleep with her for fear of Derrick. She reports that in a fit of rage stemming from her not asking him to talk with his father (who had called regarding child support) on the phone, Derrick one night assaulted her bedroom door with a butcher knife. Derrick's mother is at her wit's end, terrified of him and not able to get help from social services or mental health services.

Derrick's teacher this year is an experienced special educator who asked for reassignment to a general education classroom. Although she is well aware of Derrick's history, she has agreed to take Derrick in her class until the evaluation for special education is completed. Derrick knows that teachers and other students are afraid of him. He says that he likes to do mean things and glories in his bad reputation. However, for the first few days of this school year his teacher has kept her cool, seemed unafraid of him, and observed no serious misbehavior. One day he approached her with this question: "You don't know about me, do you?"

Source: This case was adapted from Kauffman, Mostert, Trent, and Hallahan (2002).

Questions About the Case

1. What conceptual model offers the best understanding of the cause(s) of Derrick's behavior?
2. How would you describe the most important behavior, environment, and person variables (using a social-cognitive model) in the case of Derrick, and how are these variables interrelated?
3. Were you to design an intervention strategy for working with Derrick, where would you begin, and why?
4. What concepts would you draw on in deciding how best to respond to Derrick's question to his teacher?

>> PERSONAL REFLECTIONS

Conceptual Models

Frank H. Wood, Ph.D., is professor emeritus of educational psychology and special education at the University of Minnesota.

How would you describe the importance of theoretical concepts for teachers' everyday work?

Theories are interrelationships among complex ideas expressed in a condensed form. Being so condensed, with complex ideas often signified by single key words, theories often seem "unfriendly" at first meeting. Getting to know them takes work, requires learning a new vocabulary, or, more often, learning a new meaning for old vocabulary. For example, in behavioral psychology, *reinforcement* means reward, and thus *negative reinforcement* must have something to do with reward rather than punishment.

Our impatience with the time it takes to learn how to read a theoretical statement is frequently compounded by the perception that, once learned, the statement does not tell us anything we didn't already know. It's not surprising that many educators feel that theories are hard-to-understand descriptions of the obvious. But the value of theories should not be so quickly dismissed. Theories help us recognize common patterns in differing situations. They help us pull out and remember the most significant details in situations. They help us predict what will happen if key factors in a situation are manipulated. When theories help us to do these things, they're useful to us.

No theory that has been seriously put forward by people who have carefully studied human behavior is entirely lacking in value, but some theories are certainly more useful than others to teachers. "Usefulness" is an appropriate criterion against which an educational theory can be measured. The usefulness of a theory depends on *who* wants to use it and for *what*. Given those constraints, "by whom" and "for what," any theory can be evaluated for its usefulness to us as educators. The theory we are studying at the moment may appear to have no application in our particular classroom, but to dismiss all theories as irrelevant and impractical would deprive us of very useful tools. As a matter of fact, there is almost no teacher—certainly no good teacher—who does not use theories or some of their component parts, principles, or models, in generating ideas useful for instruction. Often, we may simply be unaware that we are doing so.

For you personally, what are the most important guiding concepts for teachers of children with emotional or behavioral disorders?

Consider a well-known principle of human learning, sometimes called the law of effect: A response that is followed (timing factor) by a reward (reward factor) will increase in strength and frequency of occurrence. Many of the behavior management procedures good teachers use in their classrooms are well-timed applications of an effective reward. Teachers praise students who are working on assigned tasks, predicting that this verbal reward will strengthen their application to their work. Teachers give higher grades to students whose work is of higher quality, predicting that all students will be motivated to produce higher-quality work. In each case, teachers are demonstrating a belief in the relevance and usefulness of the law of effect.

Most of the time teachers can apply the law of effect and other important theoretical principles of learning without knowing they are doing so. However, for especially challenging situations—such as when we plan an intervention program for a student who is not responding well to praise or grades— it is often helpful to bring to mind this theoretical principle of the effect of reward. Considering alternative applications of the principle may help us develop a strategy for solving the problem. Perhaps the reward is not being applied at the right time or in the right manner. The student may be embarrassed by praise given in front of others but respond to praise given quietly or privately at a later time. More fundamentally, perhaps praise and grades are not effective

86

rewards for this student. Opportunities to earn free time or time at the computer may stimulate greater efforts to achieve. The law of effect tells us that the nature of the reward and its timing are important. Exploring alternative patterns of timing and reward can help us come up with a combination that will make the principle work for this student.

Often the interrelationship of several different concepts or principles can be illustrated in a diagram that is easier to remember than the ideas in their written form. An example shown elsewhere in this book (see Figure 4.2) is the diagram illustrating the concept of triadic reciprocality. Such a diagram is a graphic representation of the principle that persons and environments affect and are reciprocally affected by each other. Try writing out in words what this diagram illustrates and you will see how usefully the diagram summarizes several complex ideas.

I ask teachers to learn the diagram of triadic reciprocality before using it to understand, in a systems context, the behavior of individual students. I think several other diagrams efficiently capture theoretical concepts that are useful to teachers. One is the familiar "Antecedents → Behavior ← Consequences" diagram summarizing the theoretical concept that behavior (B) is influenced by events that precede (A for antecedents) and follow it (C for consequences). The A and C of this diagram are both aspects of the E (for environmental factors) of the triadic reciprocality diagram. We can add a personal dimension (P from the triadic reciprocality diagram) to our diagram by differentiating between (1) As and Cs that are characteristic of the setting in which the behavior occurs and the behavior of the people in that setting and (2) As and Cs that are characteristic of the individual whose behavior is the focus of attention. In the second sense, As may include what the individual brings to the setting, such as physical characteristics and previously learned behavior, whereas Cs are the meaning the individual gives to his or her behavior in the context of the responses (consequences) for that behavior. Again, most of us will find it easier to understand and remember these ideas by studying the figure than by reading the words. Translating pieces of theories into figures makes them easier to remember and apply; it makes them more useful to us.

There are many other theoretical models with which teachers should be familiar because they are useful in the same sense as those I've already discussed: In a school setting, they help teachers understand present student behavior more adequately and suggest ways in which they may promote student growth. Theoretical models provide mental frameworks on which teachers can organize the enormously complex information they acquire about an individual student or group in ways that help it make sense. Used this way, theories are useful and relevant to the work of the teacher—well worth knowing about.

What basic values do you think should guide teachers of children with emotional or behavioral disorders?

Ethical principles incorporating values provide another example of the application of theoretical ideas to real-world situations. I'll mention just two such principles. First, there is the *professional's commitment to serve.* The basic ethical commitment made by all people who take on the special role of providing professional service to others is to give a higher priority to the needs of those they serve than is expected in human relationships in general. Thus, parents are expected to give a higher priority to the general care of their children than are other members of the lay public. Medical professionals give a higher priority to healing sick persons than is expected by others in the society. Teachers are expected to give a higher priority than others to helping their students develop and use their abilities to acquire useful knowledge and skills.

I carefully say "a higher priority than is expected in human relationships in general" because this ethical commitment is sometimes misunderstood as meaning that teachers should give to the growth of their students a priority that is absolute. Such an idealized commitment has been described in fiction, but in practice it cannot be maintained for long. Teachers who neglect too seriously the meeting of their own needs often become exhausted and disillusioned. They may eventually find it difficult to meet their minimal professional obligations to their students. This is particularly the case when the students behave in ways that cause discomfort or injury to others and arouse a strong sense of disapproval or anger in the teacher. Teachers must learn to balance their high professional commitment with their care for their own physical and mental well-being.

Professional teachers must ask themselves two important questions. The first is what may be called the professional question: "Am I doing more to help my students develop and use their abilities to acquire useful knowledge and skills than those in their lives who make no claim to be professional teachers?" The professional answer must be yes. The second question is the personal question: "Am I successfully balancing the effort required to teach with my own mental, emotional, and physical resources so that I can continue to be an effective teacher for as long as I wish?" The answer to this question should also be yes, but it makes no sense to ask it if we have not already answered the professional ethics question affirmatively.

Second, there are the *limits of the service provided*. Educating means arranging experiences for students that encourage them to learn. Among the most difficult of the decisions educators must make are those about the limits to be placed on the experiences provided. Some experiences from which students might learn cannot be ethically used because they are too stimulating, too frightening, or too physically dangerous to students. The use of punishment to discourage the expression of problem behavior provides a good test case. How much discomfort or stress can teachers ethically apply in managing problem behavior? This decision is especially difficult for educators who teach students with emotional and behavioral disorders because these students are characteristically vulnerable to fear- or anger-producing situations.

Is there an ethical principle that can help us make wise decisions when punishing procedures may be necessary to control the behavior of a student? Can the same principle help us decide whether or not to continue remaining immediately available to a student who refuses to respond positively to any request or task unless our constant attention is given (knowing that withdrawing our attention will lead to severe and prolonged tantrums)?

Ann and Rud Turnbull provide a thoughtful discussion of this important issue in *Families, Professionals, and Exceptionality* (1990). Although they discuss several alternatives, the rule they recommend as helpful in the widest variety of situations is the principle of "empathetic reciprocity," a secular version of the principle of the Golden Rule, common to all the great religious traditions. Paraphrased, this rule asks that we take the perspective of the student and then respond to the question: "In this setting, given the alternatives available and the probable outcomes of each, what experience would be the best one for me?" The ultimate responsibility for the effects of the action we take always rests with us, but thoughtfully applying the principle of empathetic reciprocity helps us make decisions consistent with the high priority we professional educators must give to meeting the needs of our students.

>> QUESTIONS FOR FURTHER REFLECTION

1. On what basis would you choose to embrace a particular conceptual model and make it the primary basis for your work with students?
2. What would be sufficient to convince you that a particular conceptual model offers little or nothing to practitioners and should be abandoned?
3. How would you explain the fact that some individuals (of any given age) have emotional or behavioral disorders and others do not, even though their life experiences have been very similar?

Part 2

Assessment

Introduction

As you read the next two chapters, I hope your self-questioning will turn to important practical matters having to do with intervention. If we are going to do something about emotional or behavioral disorders, we must be able to determine who has a disorder. We must also decide what kind of information we are going to rely on in screening, classifying, and teaching the students we believe have a disorder. The major problems we address in part 2 might be expressed as two questions:

- How do we turn a definition into practical procedures for identifying students who have disorders and classifying their disorders in a useful way?
- How do we get and use information about students that will help us teach them most effectively?

We begin chapter 5 by discussing the reliability and validity of assessment procedures. These are foundational concepts by which all assessment procedures must be evaluated. We do not go into the details of calculation of reliability and validity. Our presentation is designed to give readers the ideas of reliability and validity and suggest how to interpret test results or other assessment data with these criteria in mind. We try to address these questions: Why do people do assessments? How would we know a good assessment from one that is not good?

We then turn to issues in screening and classification. At first blush, screening seems an easy problem to tackle. After all, children and youth with severe emotional or behavioral disorders are usually easy for anyone to identify. They typically stand out immediately and clearly as different—obviously peculiar or deeply troubled in most people's perceptions. Rational people do not typically have much difficulty reaching a consensus that certain ways of behaving are deviant, and most people will admit that clearly deviant behavior requires some sort of intervention. If we were interested only in children and youth with severe disorders, screening would be a snap. But the majority of emotional or behavioral disorders are not so severe, nor are youngsters with them so readily identified.

Most emotional or behavioral disorders of children and youth are not so severe that they are immediately obvious to the casual observer. They are serious enough that at least one adult is upset or concerned. But they are mild enough that someone might argue that most of the youngster's behavior is within the normal range and that the problem will work itself out with little or no help. Indeed, mild disorders fade into normal behavior in a haze of conjecture about where to draw the line or what to make of a particular behavior. Differences of opinion about whether an individual should be identified as having an emotional or behavioral disorder are common, even among experts. Consequently, it is often helpful to use screening procedures to help focus attention on the marginal cases. Screening procedures are designed to answer questions like these:

- Which students should we be most concerned about?
- How should we select those we are going to study more carefully?
- How do we decide that one student has problems but doesn't need special education, but that another student with problems does need special education?

The variety of youngsters' perplexing behavior is dazzling, even to people who have had many years of experience working with those who have emotional or behavioral disorders. Saying that a student has an emotional or behavioral disorder and needs special education is thus not very informative. "What kind of disorder does this student have?" is a reasonable question to ask, and the answer must be a category or classification. The classifications we use should tell us more about what kind of behavior the student exhibits—the problems we might expect. We cannot treat every individual in *every* respect as a unique case. We must identify the similar or critical features of cases so that we have some basis for communicating about types of problems and deciding what interventions to try. Classification is not just basic to all science; it is essential for effective communication and intervention. The issue, then, is this: What is the most helpful way to categorize or classify the types of problems we encounter? In chapter 6, we get to important questions about how assessment is related to what we do in the classroom:

- What kinds of information are most helpful in planning an educational program?
- How should I use the information I have about a student in writing an educational plan, choosing a curriculum, and evaluating progress?

Significant changes in the assessment of exceptional children and youth have occurred in recent years. One change is a shift in terminology. Psychologists and educators still occasionally use the term *diagnosis,* and psychiatrists typically use that term with reference to emotional or behavioral disorders. However, *diagnosis* has largely been replaced in the language of educators by *evaluation* or *assessment,* because *diagnosis* connotes the classification of disease. In the vast majority of cases, there is no evidence that disordered emotions or behavior is a disease in any physiological sense. *Evaluation* and *assessment* are more appropriate for educational purposes because they connote measurement of nonphysiological and nonmedical factors related to social learning and adaptation.

During the past several years, there has been a large increase in the availability of assessment devices and technical information about the assessment process. If you are preparing to teach students with emotional or behavioral disorders, you will need to study assessment procedures in greater detail than this book provides.

Besides the increase in available instruments and technical information, legal issues have recently taken a prominent place in assessment. A student who is referred for special education must be evaluated to determine whether he or she is eligible for services under the Individuals with Disabilities Education Act and related state legislation. Federal regulations require that this assessment be completed by an interdisciplinary team of qualified specialists because the results will be useful not only for determining eligibility for special education but also for planning instruction regardless of the student's placement in special or general education classes. If the student receives special education, then the evaluation data must be used in writing an individualized education program (IEP). The law now also requires a functional behavioral assessment, meaning that special educators must try to figure out why the student is behaving inappropriately and devise a positive, proactive behavior intervention plan to address the student's needs as part of the IEP.

The assessment of a student's abilities and problems is no easy task. It can easily be botched in either of two ways. On the one hand, it is easy to be too imprecise—so subjective and so reliant on general impressions that we miss important details or end up with a decision that simply does not fit the objective facts of the case. On the other hand, it is easy to get so absorbed in precise measurement and quantitative details that we miss the big picture or ignore the affective, human aspects of the case. Perhaps assessment is the task that presents the greatest challenge to maintaining balance between objective data and subjective interpretation. I think the challenge of becoming skilled at assessment is much like the challenge of becoming a sensitive scientist, and I hope you will complete your reading of the next two chapters with an appreciation of the difficulty of giving balanced attention to what can be recorded objectively and what can only be sensed.

CHAPTER FIVE

SCREENING AND CLASSIFICATION

Revised by Frederick J. Brigham

As you read this chapter, keep these guiding questions in mind:

- Why are reliability and validity so important for educational assessments?

- What is *treatment utility* and how might increased attention to this aspect of assessment affect the kinds of assessments used to identify students with emotional or behavioral disorders (EBDs)?

- Why are so many measures that lack treatment utility used in assessment of students with EBDs?

- Why does detecting emotional or behavioral disorders usually involve secondary rather than primary prevention?

- How should teachers engage in prereferral procedures for students suspected of having emotional or behavioral disorders? Why are they important?

In general, students suspected of having disabilities or students who have been identified as having disabilities are assessed for one of two purposes (Yell & Drasgow,
2000). The first is to determine whether a student is eligible for special education. The
second is to plan the student's educational program. Although these are compatible
goals, the instruments and procedures used for each purpose are sometimes different.
Typically, assessment directly linked to intervention is the most useful for teachers who
must plan and implement instruction (Brigham, Tochterman, & Brigham, 2001).
However, the legal mandates of identifying a specific group of children who are to receive special treatment appears to be most efficiently conducted through norm-
referenced assessments (Landrum, 2000). Currently, there is some movement away
from exclusive reliance on norm-referenced instruments toward more informal and ostensibly more useful procedures (McMaster, Fuchs, Fuchs, & Copton, 2002). However,
we can learn much about a student from norm-referenced instruments, despite the criticisms leveled at them (e.g., Sacks, 1999). Eliminating them from the repertoire of
educational and psychological evaluators would be premature (Kauffman, 2002). This
chapter focuses on the procedures most often used to determine eligibility for special
education. The next chapter emphasizes assessment procedures most suitable for planning and monitoring classroom instruction. Although there is some overlap between
the chapters, this chapter focuses more on norm-referenced procedures than the informal procedures that are the focus of the next chapter.

The procedures for assessment, identification, and classification of students with
disabilities are very important. In fact, according to Huefner (2000), it is difficult to
overstate the importance of a full assessment prior to the development of the individualized education program (IEP). Huefner's emphasis on the importance of good
assessment is based on the understanding that an accurate evaluation of the child's
strengths, weaknesses, and current levels of performance is the basis for all that will
follow. Assessment involves procedures to identify the distinguishing features of an
individual case. Classification involves placing the cases in groups on the basis of
those features (Kamphaus & Frick, 1996). Accurate classification is based on good assessment, and assessment of children and youth with emotional and behavioral disorders must include psychiatric and psychological as well as educational evaluations
(Mattison, 2004).

GENERAL CRITERIA FOR ACCEPTABLE ASSESSMENTS

All usable assessments must meet a basic set of requirements. Among these are: (a) They
must assess what they say they are assessing; (b) the assessment domain must reflect
agreed on definitions of the target behavior(s) or constructs; (c) the assessment must be
as free from error as possible; and (d) the assessment should yield similar results when
administered by different evaluators or at reasonably close time periods. The foregoing
list of desirable test characteristics is far from complete. The Council for Exceptional
Children (Council for Exceptional Children, 1997–1999), the American Educational
Research Association, the American Psychological Association, and the National Council
for Measurement in Education have all developed statements regarding assessment

requirements and competencies for assessment professionals (see American Educational Research Association, American Psychological Association, & National Council on Measurement in Education, 1985). A complete discussion of those standards is beyond the scope of this chapter. However, professionals who are engaged in formal assessment procedures would be wise to become familiar with the principles illustrated in the professional standards of those organizations.

The characteristics of assessment can be lumped roughly into two areas: reliability and validity. Issues of random measurement error and the stability of measures over time or evaluators are related to the reliability of the measure. The extent to which a test measures what it says it does in a manner that is consistent with agreed on definitions of the phenomenon and without bias are related to the validity of the procedure.

Reliability and validity are interrelated, but you cannot have validity without reliability. One can have a reliable test that is not valid, for example, measuring something that is the incorrect target, like checking the gas in your car by using an air pressure gauge on your tires. Everytime someone measures in this manner, he or she would get the same result (reliability). However, the measurement would not be related to the intended measurement, in this case the amount of fuel remaining (validity). One cannot, however, have a valid measure that is unreliable. Imagine a thermometer used to take the temperature of a patient in a physician's office. Suppose that in measures separated by short intervals of time, the thermometer registered changes in body temperature of plus or minus 10 degrees. Most people would doubt that the thermometer was really measuring the individual's temperature because there is little reason to believe that body temperature actually varies that much in a short time. Therefore, the wise conclusion is that one can never really be sure what an unreliable measure is measuring. Thus, all valid measures possess a certain amount of reliability, but not all reliable measures are valid for the purposes for which they are used. We turn first to a brief discussion of reliability, then to validity.

Reliability in Assessment

The short definition of reliability is "the degree of consistency with which a test measures what it measures" (Baumgartner & Jackson, 1991, p. 479). However, a basic assumption of measurement is that measurement contains error (Brigham et al., 2001). Nevertheless, assessment and classification must be as free from bias and random error as possible. When assessments are characterized by lots of error or bias, they waste time, money, have the potential to harm students, and undermine the credibility of those attempting to help individuals with EBDs. Random results and bias are both forms of error, but bias is discussed in the validity section because it tends to be consistent, and thus is related more to validity than to reliability.

Classification should be based on relatively stable characteristics. That is, it should be based on characteristics that have persisted for a relatively long time and are likely to continue. Not only should classification be consistent over time, but across different evaluators as well. The stability of classification across time and evaluators is referred to as reliability. The importance of reliability is underscored by the Individuals with Disabilities Education Act (IDEA), which states, "The term [emotional disturbance] means a condition exhibiting one or more of the following characteristics *over a long period of time and to a marked degree* that adversely affects a child's educational performance" (emphasis added; see discussion of the definition in chapter 1). Several different types of reliability can be considered, including test–retest reliability, alternate forms reliability, and interrater reliability.

Types of Reliability

Test–retest reliability means that the assessment of the same person yields similar results at different times. This is an important point for characteristics that are unlikely to change quickly. Intelligence tests and measures of general functioning should have good test–retest reliability.

For some assessments, reliability is indicated by *alternate forms reliability*. This means that two forms of the same instrument (e.g., a behavior rating scale) yield the same results, usually at a closer period of time than is considered for test–retest reliability. Some achievement tests use alternate forms to show that they have adequate reliability. However, not all tests have alternate forms of the same instrument. In that case, test–retest reliability is often the measure of choice.

The level of sensitivity to change that characterizes an instrument is related to reliability. Instruments that measure constructs in a more general fashion often have greater reliability than highly sensitive measures, at least for measures obtained at a given point in time. Norm-referenced tests are usually produced to tap stable characteristics across a wide section of the population. Therefore, they are relatively insensitive to small changes. Also, they may be undesirable measures for characteristics that are highly changeable or exhibited only under certain conditions. For such circumstances, we usually consider reliability as the extent that different individuals rate the same event or behavior the same way. This is called *interrater reliability*. This kind of reliability is very important in behavioral observation and other assessments that may have a great deal of subjectivity (e.g., judging writing assignments).

Reliability measures are usually expressed as correlation coefficients. The coefficients range from -1.0 through zero to $+1.0$. A negative coefficient indicates that there is some level of systematic disagreement between the measures (i.e., high scores on one measure are associated with low scores on the other measure, and vice versa). A positive coefficient indicates that there is some level of systematic agreement between the measures (i.e., high scores on one measure are associated with high scores on the other measure, and low scores on one measure are associated with low scores on the other measure). Correlation coefficients at zero indicate that there is no systematic relation between the measures. Depending on the particular instruments being compared, a positive or a negative correlation can indicate high reliability. The point to remember is that a bigger difference from zero indicates a stronger relationship and, thus, greater reliability.

Interpreting Reliability Data

Several authors have suggested guidelines for acceptability of reliability measures. For example, Webb (1983) suggested that instruments with reliabilities of $\pm.80$ or less are weak, and instruments with reliabilities of ±.91 or higher are strong. However, there are no absolute rules for evaluating instruments' reliability, other than stronger indications of reliability (i.e., greater difference from zero) are better (Gay & Airasian, 2003).

Interrater reliability data is usually expressed as a percent of agreement between raters and across observation or evaluation opportunities. Agreement of 100% indicates perfect agreement on all opportunities; less than 100% indicates the extent to which there is disagreement among the raters. As with test reliabilities, the rule is that higher agreement coefficients are more desirable than lower coefficients. For our purposes, it is sufficient to state that evaluators should be aware of the reliability estimates of the instruments that they use and select the most reliable tools they can.

Standard Error of Measure

There are simply no perfect measures of human behavior. Variations in test scores can be attributed to factors such as motivation, the situation in which the measure is taken, the person taking the measure, or random errors in administration and scoring, to name but a few. The variation of the observed measure from what the true measure should have been is called error. We can estimate the typical variability of any measure of development. Such an estimate is called a *standard error of measurement* (SEM). An SEM is usually expressed as a range of scores (plus or minus a certain number from the obtained score) within which the individual is likely to score on a readministration of the measure. We can estimate the likelihood that the attained score will fall within this range. The estimate is called a confidence interval (CI) and is usually expressed as a percent (e.g., 68%). The CI tells us that on repeated administrations of the same measure to the same individual, a certain percent of scores can be expected to fall within a given range. For example, if a student attains a score of 85 on a given measure and the SEM for the 68% CI is 5, we estimate that 68% of measures of this individual with this instrument would yield scores between 80 and 90 (85 ± 5).

The SEM is a fairly complex topic, and our discussion of it here can only alert new teachers to its existence and remind experienced practitioners of its importance. The SEM is a very important consideration when one is considering cutoff scores for eligibility. Consider a measure with an SEM of ±3 at the 68% CI. Failing to take the SEM into account will result in some false positives receiving special education placements and services simply because their scores fall one or two points below a cutoff when it is quite likely that another measure would yield a score that could be two or three points higher. The number of false positives is probably small, because students tend to be referred for good reasons (Gerber & Semmel, 1984). Conversely, a student with a score only one point above a cutoff score (and who really needs services) will be denied the services even though a measure on another occasion could yield a score two or three points lower. This student will be a false negative. The error estimate in an SEM is usually considered to be random, so scores are equally likely to be higher or lower within the CI. This means that professional judgment should be a factor in eligibility decisions, particularly when an individual's scores are near the point that separates those who are eligible for a classification, service, or even a high school diploma from those who are not. Unfortunately, we are unable to specify the exact actions that should be taken in the face of uncertainty (Beyth-Marom, Lichtenstein, & Marom, 1985); however, failure to consider the error of a given measure falls far short of standards for professional practice in educational and psychological evaluation.

Validity

The short definition of validity is "The degree to which a test measures what it is intended to measure, a test is valid for a particular purpose or group" (Gay & Airasian, 2003, p. 593). Concerned individuals must share a high level of agreement about definitions and characteristics of the disorders in question. Otherwise, we abandon the idea that they exist. For example, in the early to mid-20th century, some individuals were diagnosed with "hysterical paralysis." Few practitioners today believe there is such a thing. Assessments of "hysterical paralysis" would today be regarded with suspicion or disbelief by most professionals. Conversely, conditions such as depression, although often dismissed in the past, are now well supported by research. Assessments for depression now appear in the repertoires of many mental health workers and educators.

Another issue is the ability to isolate particular behaviors or behavioral clusters from other aspects of the person (e.g., socioeconomic status, ethnicity, gender, educational opportunity, and language abilities and differences). Most professionals consider measures that fail to isolate the target skill or behavior to be contaminated by other influences—error or biases.

A clear example of measurement contaminated by additional factors is a test requiring children to read and solve mathematical word problems. For students with adequate reading ability, the measure primarily taps their ability to conceive of the mathematical situation described and use operations leading to a solution. However, the picture is much more complicated for students with limited reading ability. Failure to perform under such circumstances could be related to a student's reading deficiencies, the student's mathematical ability, or an interaction of these factors. Validity requires freedom from bias, measuring the target variable instead of some extraneous factor, measuring variables that are sensible, and measuring with accuracy.

Types of Validity

Four traditional types of validity are: (a) construct validity (what the test is really measuring); (b) concurrent-criterion-related validity (the degree to which scores on one test are similar to scores on another test administered at the same time); (c) predictive-criterion-related validity (the extent to which a test can predict how well a person will perform in a future situation; and (d) content validity (the extent to which a test measures its intended content area; Good & Jefferson, 1998).

Different indications of validity are used for different purposes. For example, if one is attempting to identify children whose behaviors are not yet highly problematic but are likely to become so without intervention, then a high degree of predictive validity is required. If one desires a standardized measure of achievement that indicates how well the child is progressing through school learning tasks, then high content validity is essential. Concurrent validity indicators are often used by producers of new tests attempting to demonstrate the adequacy of their instrument. If a new procedure yields scores that are highly similar to another, well-accepted procedure, then the publisher is able claim that the new test is at least as useful as the older procedure. Finally, construct validity is normally invoked to demonstrate the importance of the phenomenon under consideration.

Some authors have suggested that these characteristics of validity do not go far enough. In addition to these traditional forms of validity, many researchers and assessment professionals have called for additional validity indicators. Two of these additional validity indicators are *outcomes criteria* (Reschley, 1988) and *treatment utility* (Hayes, Nelson, & Jarrett, 1987, 1989). Outcomes-criteria validity is related to the extent that meaningful student outcomes are enhanced as a result of given assessment procedures. Treatment-utility validity describes the extent to which a given assessment leads to selection of effective interventions (Good & Jefferson, 1998). Although there is some disagreement in the field regarding the extent to which these goals are possible (Braden & Kratochwill, 1997), it is clear that many of our current assessments are not linked directly to important instructional or behavioral treatments (F. J. Brigham et al., 2001; Hess & Brigham, 2000).

Interpreting Validity Data   As with reliability calculations, hard and fast rules about validity in measurement are difficult to specify. Assessments that have strong indications of validity for the purpose for which they are used can be quite useful in identifying children who are in need of special education and suggesting appropriate treatments for them. Tests that lack reliability and validity for their purposes and the people for whom they are used will be of no constructive value to educators or the students that they serve. Worse, some of these measures actually can be detrimental to children by promoting misclassification, providing misleading results, or focusing attention on fruitless educational or behavioral treatments.

The Importance of Reliable and Valid Measures for Students with EBDs

Students with disabilities are entitled to certain rights that do not apply to their peers who do not have disabilities (Yell, 1998; Yell & Drasgow, 2000). Among these are procedural safeguards including: (a) informed parental consent for initial assessment and any reevaluations that are to be conducted; (b) use of a variety of assessment tools that are validated for their purpose and administered in the child's native language or mode of communication, unless it is not feasible; (c) tests administered by trained personnel in accordance with the instructions provided by the test producer; and (d) assessment in all areas of suspected disability. In addition, federal law requires assessment yielding information directly relevant to the team that determines the educational needs of the student. Many of the procedures and instruments used to determine eligibility of students with EBDs can provide insight into the general educational needs of a given student. However, the fine-tuning of education is often better accomplished by the procedures described in chapter 6.

SCREENING

Ideally, the identification and evaluation procedure should move from brief, general measures applied to large groups—screening—through a series of more elaborate and focused steps converging on a classification and determination that a given student is eligible for special education services. These increasingly focused procedures have been called multiple gating procedures (Walker et al., 1988). Many times, however, schools do a poor job of screening for EBDs in the general population, preferring to wait until a student's behavior can no longer be ignored or tolerated to begin evaluation procedures (Kauffman, 1999c, 2003b, 2004; Landrum, 2000). When individuals exhibit highly unusual or intolerable behaviors, school personnel may omit screening. In this section, we describe the rationale for screening as well as some of the procedures for screening preschool and school-aged students.

Screening is a brief procedure that samples a few behaviors across skills or a domain (Overton, 2003). Information from a screening can be used to determine the need for additional assessment. However, because screening samples no areas in depth, the information generated is inappropriate for anything but selecting students for more study. Screening is economical and efficient. Therefore, a large number of students can be screened with minimal expense and time, allowing schools to identify students who may be in need of assistance long before their behaviors become so intolerable that they arouse the concerns of even the most hardened observer (Kauffman, 1999c, 2004).

Early Identification and Prevention

Screening is often justified by the argument that early identification will lead to prevention. Although this argument is both rational and supported by research, translating concern for prevention into effective screening is difficult. Chief among the difficulties are defining the disorders to be prevented and separating serious from trivial problems. Effective screening must eliminate concern for common problems that do not carry serious consequences or that are virtually certain to resolve themselves without intervention. Efforts to prevent problems demand a developmental perspective that takes into account developmental milestones associated with chronological age, life events, different environments, and intervention strategies (Forness & Kavale, 1997).

The purpose of screening for emotional or behavioral disorders is usually *secondary prevention* as opposed to *primary prevention*. Primary prevention keeps disorders from occurring at all. It involves the universal application of safety and health maintenance interventions that reduce risk. If primary prevention is successful, then secondary prevention is not needed. Once a disorder has emerged (is detectable), primary prevention is no longer possible for that individual. Then the issue is secondary prevention. Secondary prevention is designed to stop the disorder from getting worse and, if possible, to reverse or correct it. *Tertiary prevention* is designed for disorders that have reached advanced stages of development and seem likely to have significant side effects or complications. Tertiary prevention is intervention designed to keep the disorder from overwhelming the individual and others in his or her environment (Kauffman, 1999c, 2003b, 2004; Walker & Sprague, 1999).

Screening for EBDs among infants and preschool children is particularly problematic. Children with pervasive developmental disorders such as autism have often been perceived by their parents as "different" from birth or from a very early age. Pediatricians often identify these and other cases in which extremely troublesome behavior is part of a pervasive developmental disorder. But trying to select infants and preschoolers who need special education and related services because of relatively mild disorders is quite another matter. Several factors make selection difficult. First, large and rapid changes occur during development from infancy to middle childhood. Infants and preschoolers have not yet acquired the language skills that are the basis for much of the older child's social interaction. Second, a child's behavioral style or temperament in infancy interacts with parenting behavior to determine later behavior patterns. For example, "difficult" behavior x at the age of 10 months is not predictive of inappropriate behavior y at 6 years. Behavior management techniques that parents and teachers use from 10 months to 6 years need to be taken into account. (Thomas & Chess, 1984; Thomas, Chess, & Birch, 1968). Third, parents vary markedly in their tolerance of emotional and behavioral differences in children. Because a problem *is* a problem primarily by parental definition in the preschool years, it is difficult to decide on a standard set of behaviors that are deviant (Achenbach & Edelbrock, 1981; Campbell, 1983, 1995). (Exceptions, as we have said, are obvious developmental lags.) Finally, the school itself is a potential source of problems. Its structure, demands for performance of new skills, and emphasis on uniformity may set the stage for disorders that simply do not appear until the child enters school. Nevertheless, it is now possible to identify children in the primary grades or even in preschool who are at high risk for developing antisocial behavior and other serious behavioral problems (see Feil, 1999; Hester & Kaiser, 1998; Ialongo, Vaden-Kiernan, & Kellam, 1998; Loeber, Green, Keenan, & Lahey, 1995; McConaughy, Kay, & Fitzgerald, 1998; Walker, Ramsey, & Gresham, 2004; Walker, Kavanagh, Stiller, Golly, Severson, & Feil, 1998).

Despite our increased ability to identify children at risk for EBDs at earlier ages, the data do not support the idea that schools are actually doing so (Walker, Nishioka, Zeller, Severson, & Feil, 2000). School-referrral data collected by the federal government from the 1993–1994 school year to the 1998–1999 school year show a stable pattern of referral. Further, the referral rates are quite low for young children, with rates rising as the students age and a peak in the referral rate at the ages of 14 and 15. Walker et al. (2000) suggested that "(a) the majority of behaviorally at risk students are not identified until well after the point where early intervention could have a substantive, positive impact on their problems; and (b) by deferring the point of referral, school personnel allow destructive patterns of student behavior to develop and expand to the point where they exceed the tolerance levels and accommodation capacities of teachers within mainstream classroom settings" (p. 30).

There is also evidence that many of the students who would benefit from EBD services are actually identified as eligible for special education but placed in programs for students with learning disabilities (Forness & Kavale, 2001b). This is a truly unfortunate situation because credible evidence suggests that with primary prevention efforts, even interventions that are of short duration can not only improve mental health in Headstart preschool classrooms but prevent or at least delay the onset of emotional or behavioral disorders in many children who are at risk for developing these problems (Serna, Lambros, Nielsen, & Forness, 2002; Serna, Nielsen, Lambros, & Forness, 2000).

Criteria for Selecting and Devising Screening Procedures

Some screening procedures are more effective and efficient than others. Care is required to select procedures that meet reasonable psychometric and practical criteria for use in schools. Walker et al. (1995) suggested four criteria for screening and identifying antisocial behavior, and the same criteria could be applied to all types of emotional or behavioral disorders:

1. The procedure should be proactive rather than reactive. The school should take the initiative in seeking out students who are at high risk for exhibiting disorders, not simply wait for these students to demonstrate serious maladaptive behavior and then respond.
2. Whenever possible, a variety of people (e.g., teacher, parent, trained observer) should be employed, and students' behavior should be evaluated in a variety of settings (e.g., classroom, playground, lunch room, home). The objective should be to obtain as broad as possible a perspective on the nature and extent of any problems that are detected.
3. Screening should take place as early as possible in students' school careers, ideally at preschool and kindergarten levels. If screening is to serve its intended function well, then target students need to be identified and intervention programs begun before the child develops a history of maladaptive behavior and school failure.
4. Teacher nominations and rankings or ratings are appropriate in the beginning of the screening process but should be supplemented, if possible, by direct observation, examination of school records, peer or parent ratings, and other sources of information that might be available. The process should be increasingly broad and thorough at successive stages to minimize the chances of misidentification.

Alternative Screening Instruments

Hundreds of behavioral rating scales are available, nearly all of which are potentially useful as screening instruments. Many other procedures, including self-reports, sociometrics, direct observation, and interviewing, are used in assessing children's social–emotional behavior (Hersen & Ammerman, 1995; Merrell, 1994; Overton, 2003; Taylor, 1997). We cannot discuss the whole range of instruments that might be used for screening emotional or behavioral disorders but will concentrate on several representative instruments. Use and interpretation of these instruments require careful study of the test materials and manuals.

Strength-Based Assessment

One emerging concept is strength-based assessment (Epstein, 2000). Strength-based assessment can be defined as "the measurement of those emotional and behavioral skills, competencies, and characteristics that create a sense of personal accomplishment; contribute to satisfying relationships with family members, peers, and adults; enhance one's ability to deal with adversity and stress; and promote one's personal, social, and academic development" (Epstein & Sharma, 1998).

Strength-based assessment can be conducted in an informal or formal manner. Examples of informal assessments are strength chats—semistructured interviews between a teacher and parent or teacher and student (Van Den Berg & Grealish, 1996). It is likely that many educators and clinicians have practiced strength-based assessments in an informal manner.

Epstein and Sharma (1998) have formalized strength-based assessment in an instrument known as the Behavioral and Emotional Rating Scale (BERS). The instrument has 52 items organized into five separate subscales:

1. *Interpersonal strengths*, which measures the ability to control emotions or behaviors in social situations
2. *Family involvement*, which measures the individuals' participation and relations within the family
3. *Intrapersonal strength*, which assesses the individual's perception of competence and accomplishment
4. *School functioning*, which measures the individual's competence in school and classroom tasks
5. *Affective strengths*, which measures the individual's ability to accept affect from others and to express her or his own emotions.

Each item on the individual BERS scales is rated from 0 to 3 (0 = not at all, 1 = not much like the child, 2 = like the child, and 3 = very much like the child). Higher scores indicate areas of greater perceived emotional and behavioral strengths. In addition, the respondent is asked to complete a set of eight open-ended questions (e.g., "At a time of need, to whom would the child turn for support?")

The BERS has norms for children 5 to 18 years old. Separate norm tables are provided for children without disabilities as well as for children with EBDs. Correlations among the BERS and the Achenbach *Teacher Report Form* (Achenbach, 1991) and the *Walker–McConnell Scale of Social Competence and School Adjustment* (Walker & McConnell, 1988) were in the moderate to high range, suggesting that the BERS has adequate concurrent validity with these instruments (Epstein, 2000). A reliability study showed test–retest correlations in the moderate to high range, indicating that the measure taps relatively stable characteristics (Epstein, Hertzog, & Reid, 2001).

The BERS was administered to three groups of students: (a) students with no identified learning or behavior problems, (b) students identified with learning disabilities (LDs), and (c) students identified with EBDs. It discriminated the individuals with EBDs from the group without disabilities, but not from the group with LDs. The BERS did not reliably and statistically discriminate the group with LDs from typical students. However, students without disabilities attained higher scores than students with LDs, who attained higher scores than the students with EBDs (Reid, Epstein, Pastor, & Ryser, 2000).

The authors of the BERS suggested that the scale is useful in identifying students with EBDs and for identifying emotional and behavioral strengths in students with LDs. The authors speculated that the inability to discriminate the students with LDs from either students with no disabilities or the group with EBDs may be because of a wide variability in the behavior of students with LDs. Some students with LDs demonstrate no behavioral difficulties, and others demonstrate serious behavioral problems in addition to their learning disabilities (see Hallahan, Lloyd, Kauffman, Weiss, & Martinez, 2005). Many students with EBDs are classified as having LDs. There may have been a substantial number of students in the LD group who have EBDs as well.

Other Instruments

Flowers, Lanclos, and Kelly (2002) developed the Children's Version of Screen for Adolescent Violence Exposure (KID-SAVE). They suggested that the KID-SAVE could be a particularly useful tool for screening children for exposure to violence. They examined the self-report data from both a group of children from Grades 3 through 7 and their parents using the KID-SAVE (Flowers, Hastings, & Kelley, 2000). All of the participants in this study were African Americans living in a high-crime neighborhood where exposure to violence was considered to be likely. The KID-SAVE is a downward extension of the Screen for Adolescent Violence Exposure (SAVE; Hastings & Kelley, 1997). It is a self-report scale containing 34 items arranged into three subscales: Traumatic Violence, Indirect Violence, and Physical/Verbal Abuse. Each item is rated on a pair of 3-point scales. The first rating asks about frequency of exposure (0 = never, 1 = sometimes, and 2 = a lot). The second scale asks about the impact of the exposure to the individual (0 = not at all upsetting, 1 = somewhat upsetting, and 2 = very upsetting).

The parent version of the KID-SAVE is a rewording of the children's version but has yet to receive sufficient research attention to warrant any strong claims about its adequacy. Reliability data for the KID-SAVE places it in the moderate range of acceptability. Furthermore, reports of exposure to violence on the KID-SAVE were positively correlated with problematic ratings on the Child Behavior Checklist (CBL; Achenbach, 1991). In particular, higher frequency reports on the Indirect Violence Scale was associated with parental reports of social problems, and frequency of events on the Traumatic Violence Scale was predictive of indications of problems on the Anxious/Depressed, Delinquent Behavior, and Aggressive Behavior subscales of the CBL. Thus, the KID-SAVE appears to be promising for screening children from similar backgrounds who may need additional assessment and intervention. However, the high-risk nature of the sample in the studies to date limits the direct generalizability of the KID-SAVE to groups with dissimilar demographic characteristics.

The Scale for Assessing Emotional Disturbance (SAED) is a standardized, norm-referenced scale designed to assist in the identification of students who qualify for special education under the federal category of "emotional disturbance" (Epstein & Cullinan, 1998). It can be administered by teachers or other school personnel, and it is constructed specifically to fit the federal definition (see chapter 1). Thus, it is perhaps the instrument most directly tied to the school environment and the adverse effects of the characteristics of emotional disturbance on school performance.

Other instruments that may be useful in screening include the Behavior Rating Profile (Brown & Hammill, 1990), the Behavior Assessment System for Children (BASC; Reynolds & Kamphaus, 1992), and the Child Behavior Checklist (CBCL; Achenbach & Edelbrock, 1991).

The instrument known as Systematic Screening for Behavior Disorders (SSBD; Walker & Severson, 1990) deserves particular attention as a screening device. It is designed for use in elementary schools based on the assumption that teacher judgment is a valid and cost-effective (though greatly underused) method of identifying students with emotional or behavioral disorders (Walker, Severson, Nicholson, Kehle, Jenson, & Clark, 1994). Teachers tend to overrefer students who exhibit externalizing behavior problems—those who act out or exhibit conduct disorder. Teachers tend to underrefer students with internalizing behavior problems—those who are characterized by anxiety and social withdrawal (Gresham & Kern, 2004). To make certain that students are not overlooked in screening and to minimize time and effort, a three-step, or "multiple gating," process is used (Walker et al., 1988).

In the first step, or "gate" of the SSBD, the teacher lists and rank-orders students with externalizing and internalizing problems, listing those who best fit descriptions of externalized problems and internalized problems, and ranking them from most like to least like the descriptions. The second step requires that the teacher complete two checklists for the three highest-ranked students on each list—those who have passed through the first "gate." One checklist asks the teacher to indicate whether the pupil exhibited specific behaviors during the past month ("steals," "has tantrums," "uses obscene language or swears"). These items constitute a Critical Events Index (CEI) of behaviors that, even if they occur at a low frequency, constitute "behavioral earthquakes" that place children at very high risk of being identified as having an emotional or behavioral disorder (Gresham, MacMillan, & Bocain, 1996). The other checklist requires that the teacher judge how often ("never," "sometimes," "frequently") each student shows certain characteristics ("follows established classroom rules," "cooperates with peers in group activities or situations"). The third step requires observation of students whose scores on the checklists exceed established norms—those who have passed through the second "gate." Students are observed in the classroom and on the playground by a school professional other than the usual classroom teacher (a school psychologist, counselor, or resource teacher). Classroom observations indicate the extent to which the student meets academic expectations; playground observations assess the quality and nature of social behavior. These direct observations, in addition to teacher ratings, are then used to decide whether the student has problems that warrant full evaluation for special education.

Table 5.1
Means and standard deviations by risk status for groups on the CEI

Groups	Year of Observation	
	Grade 3	Grade 4
Controls		
Mean	.67	.25
Standard Deviation	1.32	.77
At-Risk		
Mean	1.91	.78
Standard Deviation	2.11	1.30
EBD		
Mean	4.42	6.33
Standard Deviation	3.35	3.40

Source: Lambros, K. M., Ward, S. L., Bocain, K. M., MacMillan, D. L., & Gresham, F. M. (1998). Behavioral profiles of children at-risk for emotional and behavioral disorders: Implications for assessment and classification. *Focus on Exceptional Children, 30*(5), 5. Reprinted by permission of Love Publishing Company.

The procedures that Walker and his colleagues devised are the most fully developed screening system currently available for use in school settings. The Critical Events Index (CEI) alone has been used to reliably distinguish typical children from those at risk and those who have been identified as having emotional or behavioral disorders. Table 5.1 shows differences between control, at-risk, and EBD students in Grades 3 and 4 in a study by Lambros, Ward, Bocain, MacMillan, and Gresham (1998). Note that the students at risk exhibited about three times the number of critical events, or "behavioral earthquakes," of their normal peers and that the number of such events was much higher yet for those identified as having EBDs.

The Early Screening Project (ESP) is a downward extension of the SSBD (Walker, Severson, & Feil, 1994). It is designed and normed specifically for children ages 3 to 5. As noted by Feil (1999), "the beginning of antisocial behavior patterns can be identified at an early age, and these behaviors can be prevented from escalating into more serious and intractable problems" (p. 53). Nevertheless, as Kauffman (1999c, 2003b, 2004) has noted, there are strong forces working against prevention, including resistance to the idea of identifying young children as exhibiting serious problem behavior.

The School Archival Records Search (SARS) is designed to code and quantify existing school records of elementary students (Walker, Block-Pedego, Todis, & Severson, 1991). It involves collecting and systematically coding certain information from a student's school records. Eleven variables are examined: demographics, attendance, achievement test information, school failure (i.e., retentions in grade), disciplinary contacts, within-school referrals, certification for special education, placement out of the regular classroom, receiving Chapter 1 services, out-of-school referrals, and negative narrative comments. The SARS was originally intended as a fourth level of screening in the SSBD, but it can be used for a variety of other purposes. Because it is a systematic way of searching out important data about a student's school career, however, the SARS can be used to assist in three other decision-making tasks: identifying students who are at risk for dropping out of school, validating school assessments, and determining eligibility for special programs. It has been shown to be useful in identifying students in sixth grade who are highly likely to have further difficulties in school (Tobin & Sugai, 1999).

Screening as Convergence and Confirmation of Concerns

A key provision of professional practice in assessment is that no single procedure or data source should ever be used to make important decisions (Brigham, Brigham, & Lloyd, 2002). The risk of one person reaching an unjustified conclusion about a student is too great to be ignored. It is often difficult for an individual who holds an unsupported opinion to reanalyze the evidence and alter his or her conclusion without external supports (Pinker, 2002). Furthermore, all tests and measures are characterized by a certain amount of error, leading to random fluctuation of scores taken at specific times or with specific instruments (Sternberg & Grigorenko, 2002). Therefore, one person's opinion or a single score on a rating scale or other instrument should never be considered adequate for screening. A student should be selected for evaluation only when several observers share the suspicion that he or she may have a disorder and their shared suspicion is confirmed by data obtained from structured observations or ratings. Otherwise, the risk is too high that the student will be unnecessarily labeled and stigmatized, that his or her privacy rights will be violated, and that resources will be wasted on fruitless evaluations.

The goal of screening should be to obtain information from a variety of sources and to use instruments that facilitate hypotheses regarding the reciprocal influence of the behavior, the environments in which it occurs, and the student's personal perspectives. This goal is consistent with an ecological approach and with a social-cognitive conceptual model.

A special concern in screening and identification is the accommodation of cultural diversity and individual differences. Students who are members of some ethnic or cultural minorities are at particularly high risk for identification as having disabilities requiring special education or other special services, whereas other ethnic groups are at risk of underidentification (see Osher, Cartledge, Oswald, Sutherland, Artiles, & Coutinho, 2004; Oswald, Coutinho, Best, & Singh, 1999; Peterson & Ishii-Jordan, 1994). On the one hand, behavioral differences that are not truly disorders may be misinterpreted if the person doing the assessment is not sensitive to cultural or ethnic patterns of behavior. On the other hand, misperception or misunderstanding of cultural or ethnic patterns of behavior could lead to serious behavioral problems being overlooked or dismissed as of little consequence. Bias about the characteristics of various cultural groups could thus result in overidentification or underidentification of students with these characteristics. Teachers often need guidance in how to evaluate the influence of cultures on students' behavior. The available data suggest that African American students, especially those in urban middle schools, are at risk of overidentification and that children from Hispanic or Asian American families are at risk of underidentification (Coutinho & Oswald, 1998; Crijnen, Achenbach, & Verhulst, 1997; National Research Council, 2002).

Using Functional Behavioral Assessment in Screening

Functional behavioral assessment (FBA) has been suggested as a useful tool for identifying children with EBDs at an early age. FBA is a procedure required in IDEA to address challenging school behaviors that are likely to result in severe disciplinary actions or removal from the schools. However, researchers have begun to consider the application of FBA procedures to younger children (Conroy & Davis, 2000; Conroy, Davis, Fox, & Brown, 2002).

FBA helps practitioners answer two important questions: (1) What is the outcome of the child's behavior? (2) Does the child obtain something of value (e.g., a tangible reinforcer such as food, access to an activity, or attention), or does the child escape something, such as a demanding task? After answering these questions, FBA practitioners design interventions that alter or eliminate factors supporting the undesirable behavior. At present, no single FBA procedure exists, and the law does not identify specific strategies for conducting FBA (Conroy et al., 2002). However, it is possible to identify several steps shared by most FBA procedures. These are (a) defining the target behavior clearly and specifically, (b) determining broad environmental events and factors that may increase the occurrence of the behavior, (c) identifying antecedents and consequences of the behavior, (d) developing hypotheses regarding the function of the behavior, (e) testing the hypothesis through experimental manipulation, and (f) developing and implementing behavioral interventions that address the contributing and maintaining factors (Dunlap & Kern, 1993; Dunlap et al., 1993).

Conroy and her colleagues (2002) adapted the functional behavioral assessment model to create a multigating, multilevel system of assessment that can be used to identify children with EBDs. It contains three levels. At Level 1, a broad environmental assessment is conducted, and interventions that should benefit all children in the classroom are implemented. By ensuring that elements of the environment (both the physical and the instructional environment) that support undesirable behavior are reduced and elements that support positive behavior are increased, minor problems can be eliminated, secondary problems can be prevented, and the number of false positives greatly reduced (Brigham & Kauffman, 1998). Evaluations at level one are conducted through interviews, checklists, and sometimes direct observation of the environment in which the problem behavior occurs across several days. Aspects of the environment that are identified as potential contributors to problem behavior are addressed, and the behavior of the target children is observed.

For many but not all children who exhibit undesirable behavior in the school, Level 1 intervention is sufficient. However, some children continue to exhibit undesirable behavior after Level 1 environmental intervention has been implemented. These students are the focus of assessment at Level 2. Level 2 assessment focuses on high-risk behavior and intervention. To identify children who are at risk for development of EBDs at this level, Conroy et al. (2002) suggested using standardized screening instruments (e.g., Walker, Severson, & Feil, 1994) or informal techniques such as teacher nomination. At his stage, identification focuses on examination of the social and communication skills of the target children. Behavioral problems can be the result of skill deficits (Wehby, Symons, & Canale, 1998). Children who are determined to have deficits in skills can be provided with training in social and communication skills, as well as general compliance training (Brown, Musick, Conroy, & Schaffer, 2001; Ford, Olmi, Edwards, & Tingstrom, 2001).

Children who resist interventions at Levels 1 and 2 and who continue to exhibit undesirable behaviors are candidates for further assessment and intervention at Level 3 of the Conroy et al. (2002) assessment model. During Level 3 screening procedures, FBA procedures are employed to target the specific antecedents and consequences of target behaviors and to develop, implement, and monitor behavioral interventions for the child in question. Assessment procedures at this level are far more intensive, time-consuming, and individually focused than were efforts at Levels 1 and 2. It is likely that only a very few children will need this type of attention, and it is probable that those children will fall into the group of children identified as having EBDs.

PREREFERRAL STRATEGIES

Before students are evaluated for special education services, teachers must try to accommodate their needs in regular classes. These efforts must be documented and must show that the student is not responding well to reasonable adaptations of the curriculum and the behavior management techniques used in the regular classroom. Prereferral strategies aim to reduce the number of false positives (i.e., to avoid the misidentification of those who do not actually have a disorder) and to avoid wasting effort on unnecessary formal evaluations. The functional behavioral approach to screening for EBDs (Conroy et al., 2002) described earlier in this chapter contains many elements of prereferral activities as a part of the screening procedure itself. The case of Amy summarizes what a teacher must do before referring a student for a full evaluation (see accompanying case book).

One element of prereferral intervention success is the support provided for such activities by the school administration (Burns & Symington, 2002; Kovaleski, Gickling, Morrow, & Swank, 1999). Schools in which adequate training and support are provided often report effects of prereferral intervention that are far superior to many other schools. Furthermore, involvement of university-based consultant teams also appears to be associated with positive outcomes for prereferral interventions (Burns & Symington, 2002).

Screening should result in prompt attempts to find solutions to the problems of selected students in general education without evaluating them for special education. Failure to find solutions within a reasonable time should result in prompt referral for evaluation; eternal hope should not spring from failure (see Kauffman, 1999c). Furthermore, specialized prereferral procedures should not be conducted without parental consent, and keeping students in general education classrooms when prereferral procedures have not been successful could be a violation of IDEA (see Katsiyannis, 1994). When has a teacher done enough to circumvent referral? The answer requires careful consideration of the individual, as the cases of Don and Bill illustrate in the accompanying case book. Suggestions are provided in Box 5.1.

Box 5.1

What Do I Do Before Making a Referral?

Before making a referral, you will be expected to document the strategies you have used in your class to meet the student's educational needs. Regardless of whether the student is later found to have a disability, your documentation will be useful in the following ways: (a) You will have evidence that will be helpful to or required by the committee of professionals who will evaluate the student, (b) you will be better able to help the student's parents understand that methods used for other students in the class are not adequate for their child, and (c) you will have records of successful or unsuccessful methods of working with the student that will be useful to you and any other teacher who works with the student in the future.

Your documentation of what you have done may appear to require a lot of paperwork, but careful record keeping will pay off. If a student is causing you serious concern, then you will be wise to demonstrate your concern by keeping written records. Your notes should include items such as the following:

* Exactly what you are concerned about
* Why you are concerned about it
* Dates, places, and times you have observed the problem
* Precisely what you have done to try to resolve the problem
* Who, if anyone, helped you devise the plans or strategies you have used
* Evidence that the strategies have been successful or unsuccessful

Prereferral strategies sometimes result in successful management of the student in a general education classroom without the need for special education. Early detection of problems increases the likelihood of finding effective solutions without removing the student from the problem situation. Even with the best available prereferral strategies and flawless teamwork of general and special educators, however, some students' needs will not be met in regular classes (see Bateman & Chard, 1995; Brigham & Kauffman, 1998; Kauffman, Bantz, & McCullough, 2002; Mock & Kauffman, 2003).

CLASSIFICATION

Classification should be based on reliably observed phenomena, and the classification of a given disorder should have a clear relationship to its nature, origin, course, and treatment. Ideally, a classification system should include *operationally defined categories*—categories defined in such a way that the behaviors forming them can be measured. The system should also be reliable: An individual should be classified consistently by different observers, and the assignment of someone to a category should be consistent over a reasonable period of time. The categories should be valid: Assignment to a category should be determinable in a variety of ways (by a variety of observational systems or rating scales), and it should be highly predictive of particular behaviors (recall our previous discussion of reliability and validity).

We shall briefly discuss two major types of classification: psychiatric and dimensional. Of the alternative systems available, psychiatric classification typically carries the greatest legal authority, but dimensional classification has greatest relevance for educators and most closely approximates the ideal system.

Psychiatric Classification

Psychiatry, mimicking the empirical classification of diseases in physical medicine, has devised systems of classification based on demonstrated or presumed *mental diseases*. Historically, many psychiatric classifications have been unreliable and have had few or no implications for treatment, particularly educational interventions (Achenbach, 1985; Kratochwill & McGivern, 1996; Sinclair, Forness, & Alexson, 1985). However, psychiatric classifications are widely used, and educators will encounter psychiatric labels in working with students with emotional or behavioral disorders. Much progress has been made in psychiatric classification in recent decades. Categories are now more objective and reliable than they were a quarter century ago. Nevertheless, psychiatric categories are not aligned with eligibility criteria for special education. That is, students are not identified for special education through psychiatric diagnosis.

The most widely accepted psychiatric system of classification is the one devised by the American Psychiatric Association. The standard psychiatric diagnoses are those included in the most recent edition of the American Psychiatric Association's *Diagnostic and Statistical Manual of Mental Disorders,* or *DSM*. The fourth edition of the manual has been revised and is known as *DSM–IV–TR* (American Psychiatric Association, 2000). Besides the classifications it lists, the *DSM–IV–TR* system includes multiaxial assessment that is designed to help in planning treatment and predicting outcomes. Multiaxial assessment is a way of organizing information on five axes or strands of information. The five axes are an attempt to include all relevant information and to see the problem in the context of its biological and social ecologies.

Axis I: Clinical disorders are listed, including not only the primary presenting complaint but all other conditions that may be a focus of clinical attention. On this axis, the clinician lists the diagnostic category or categories of the individual's psychopathology (e.g., conduct disorder; attention deficit–hyperactivity disorder, hyperactive-impulsive type).

Axis II: Personality disorders and mental retardation are listed on a separate axis to make sure that these are not overlooked when the primary complaint is a more florid disorder listed on Axis I.

Axis III: General medical conditions includes the current medical conditions that might be relevant to understanding or managing the disorder(s) listed on Axes I and II (e.g., physical illnesses that might be related to anxiety or depression).

Axis IV: Psychosocial and environmental problems are meant to indicate factors that might affect the diagnosis, treatment, or prognosis of disorders listed on Axes I and II.

These would include categories such as problems with a primary support group or educational, occupational, or economic problems. The purpose is to take into account the life circumstances of the individual that may be relevant to the diagnosed disorder.

Axis V: Global assessment of functioning is the clinician's estimate of the client's overall functioning in everyday life.

The actual diagnostic categories are listed under 18 broad headings, the first of which is "Disorders Usually First Diagnosed in Infancy, Childhood, or Adolescence." Although children and youth may receive diagnoses from other categories, they are most likely to be categorized under this general heading. The first four categories under this heading are mental retardation, learning disorders, motor skills disorder, and communication disorders. These disorders may, indeed, accompany emotional or behavioral disorders of other types, but they are typically considered in detail in books or chapters devoted exclusively to them (e.g., Hallahan et al., 2005).

For purposes of this book, we will examine the *DSM–IV–TR* listing of diagnostic categories and subcategories beginning with the fifth major category, pervasive developmental disorders (see Table 5.2). We shall not attempt to define all of these categories here. Definitions of all are found in the glossary, and most are discussed in later chapters. In the *DSM–IV–TR*, each category and subcategory is associated with a number (e.g., autistic disorder is 299.00), which we have not included. Many categories include a subcategory of NOS, for "not otherwise specified," a catchall that, as we discuss later, is necessary in any comprehensive diagnostic system.

Hartman et al. (2001) examined the statistical structure of several classifications of the DSM and concluded that although the scales generally were useful in identifying individuals with various disorders, they nevertheless failed to explain a lot of variation in classification. Furthermore, Hartman et al. (2001) reported that many syndromes were characterized by the presence of many symptoms that are diagnostically ambiguous. Therefore, diagnoses based on these scales may be somewhat variable among practitioners and fail to capture important elements of the diagnosed individual's behavior.

All of the categories and subcategories listed in the *DSM–IV–TR* are accompanied in the manual by extensive diagnostic guidelines that include explicit criteria for inclusion and exclusion. These guidelines and criteria have done much to improve the reliability of psychiatric diagnosis (cf. Waldman & Lillenfeld, 1995). However, just because a child or youth carries a *DSM–IV* diagnosis does not mean that he or she is eligible for special education services. Although many of those who carry psychiatric labels are eligible for special education, it is important to remember that identification for special education is independent of and uses criteria different from those in any *DSM* classification system (Duncan, Forness, & Hartsough, 1995; Forness & Kavale, 1997).

Behavioral Dimensions

Psychiatric classification is focused primarily on differentiating among *kinds* of disorders. Dimensional classification indicates how much individuals differ in the degree to which they exhibit a type of behavior (Waldman & Lillenfeld, 1995). Behavioral

Table 5.2
Selected *DSM–IV* categories of disorders usually first diagnosed in infancy, childhood, or adolescence

Pervasive developmental disorders
    Autistic disorder
    Rett's disorder
    Childhood disintegrative disorder
    Aspergers Syndrome
    Pervasive development disorder NOS

Attention-deficit and disruptive behavior disorders
    Attention deficit–hyperactivity disorder
        Combined type
        Predominantly inattentive type
        Predominantly hyperactive-impulsive type
    Attention deficit–hyperactivity disorder NOS
    Conduct disorder (Specify type: childhood-onset type/adolescent-onset type)
    Oppositional defiant disorder
    Disruptive behavior disorder NOS

Feeding and eating disorders of infancy or early childhood
    Pica
    Rumination disorder
    Feeding disorder of infancy or early childhood

Tic disorder
    Tourette's disorder
    Chronic motor or vocal tic disorder
    Transient tic disorder (specify if: single episode/recurrent)
    Tic disorder NOS

Elimination disorders
    Encopresis
        With constipation and overflow incontinence
        Without constipation and overflow incontinence
    Enuresis (not due to a general medical condition, specify type: nocturnal only/
        diurnal only/nocturnal and diurnal)

Other disorders of infancy, childhood, or adolescence
    Separation anxiety disorder (specify if: early onset)
    Selective mutism
    Reactive attachment disorder of infancy or early childhood (specify type: inhibited type/disinhibited type)
    Stereotyped movement disorder (specify if: with self-injurious behavior)
    Disorder of infancy, childhood, or adolescence NOS

dimensions are descriptions of behavioral clusters (highly intercorrelated behaviors). Statistical procedures, such as factor analysis, are used to find behavioral dimensions based on behavior ratings. The statistical analyses reveal which behavior problems tend to occur together to form a dimension. In early studies (e.g., Ackerson, 1942; Hewitt & Jenkins, 1946), behavior traits were obtained from reports in children's case histories. The behaviors were listed and then clustered by visual inspection of the data. Current statistical analyses are much more precise.

Studies of behavioral dimensions or types have generally found two major classifications, or *broadband* problems. One of these is typically referred to as **externalizing** *problems* (sometimes also called *undercontrolled*). It is characterized by aggression, striking out against others, impulsive and disobedient behavior, and delinquency. The other is typically called **internalizing** *problems* (sometimes called *overcontrolled*). It is characterized by anxiety, social withdrawal, and depression. More specific problems, such as hyperactivity, delinquency, depression, conduct disorder, and so on are often referred to as *narrowband* problems. We discuss some of these more narrowly defined disorders in subsequent sections of this book.

Although the broadband types called externalizing and internalizing appear in many studies, they are not mutually exclusive (see Achenbach, 1985, 1991; Achenback & Edelbrock, 1981, 1989, 1991; Achenbach, Howell, Quay, & Conners, 1991; Waldman & Lillenfeld, 1995). That is, a given individual may have multiple types of problems, sometimes including multiple types of more narrowly defined disorders, some of the externalizing and some of the internalizing type. Individuals may show more than one disorder simultaneously or alternate between types. For example, a student can have conduct disorder (an externalizing type) and also be depressed (an internalizing type). Of course, we can compare groups also, not just individuals, in the types of behavioral problems they exhibit.

One instrument tapping the externalizing, internalizing, and hyperactive dimensions of behavior is the Social Skills Rating System—Teacher (SSRS–T; Gresham & Elliott, 1990). This instrument includes teacher ratings of students' social skills (30 items), problem behavior (18 items), and academic competence (9 items). Lambros et al. (1998) compared the SSRS–T ratings of elementary-aged children who were at low risk or high risk for behavioral disorders and a control group. Table 5.1 shows comparisons of the three groups in the domains of academic competence, problem behavior, and social skills. Figures 5.1 and 5.2 show how the groups were different from each other in externalizing, internalizing, and hyperactive behavior. Consistent with many other studies of such groups, the children at highest risk for behavioral disorders were lower in academic competence and social skills but higher in problem behavior, and they exhibited more problem behavior of several types—externalizing, internalizing, and hyperactive—than did those at lower risk or a control group not considered at risk.

Gresham, Elliott, and Evans-Fernandez (1993) have also developed a self-concept scale on which students rate their self-perceptions. Studies with this instrument indicate that students with emotional or behavioral disorders are a heterogeneous group. Some do have low self-esteem. Others, however, see themselves very unrealistically—as much more socially and academically competent than they are. In effect, their self-esteem is bloated; they see themselves in glowing terms totally at odds with their actual behavior or social standing and academic achievement (Lambros et al., 1998).

An important concept underlying the classification of behavioral dimensions is that all individuals exhibit the characteristics of all the dimensions but to varying degrees (Waldman & Lillenfeld, 1995). As we suggested earlier, an individual may be rated high on more than one dimension. Many students with emotional or behavioral

Figure 5.1
SSRS–T scales by group averaged over three
points in time
Source: Lambros, K. M., Ward, S. L., Bocain, K. M.,
MacMillan, D. L., & Gresham, F. M. (1998). Behavioral
profiles of children at-risk for emotional and behavioral
disorders: Implications for assessment and
classification. *Focus on Exceptional Children, 30*(5), 14.
Reprinted by permission of Love Publishing Company.

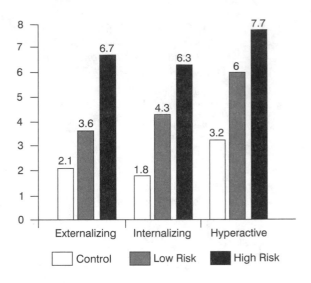

disorders have multiple problems, and they may receive high ratings on several dimensions (Tankersley & Landrum, 1997). Students' behavior is classified according to certain statistical clusters of items on the rating scale; individuals are not classified. Although the same perspective is taken in some psychiatric classifications (that is, disorders are classified, not people), dimensional classification has the advantage of being based on more reliable, empirically derived categories.

These observations bring us back to a foundational concept related to the definition of disorder: Emotional or behavioral disorder is not an all-or-nothing phenomenon. How different an individual's behavior must be from that of others before we

Figure 5.2
SSRS–T problem behavior subscales by group
averaged over three points in time
Source: Lambros, K. M., Ward, S. L., Bocain, K. M.,
MacMillan, D. L., & Gresham, F. M. (1998). Behavioral
profiles of children at-risk for emotional and behavioral
disorders: Implications for assessment and classification.
Focus on Exceptional Children, 30(5), 14. Reprinted by
permission of Love Publishing Company.

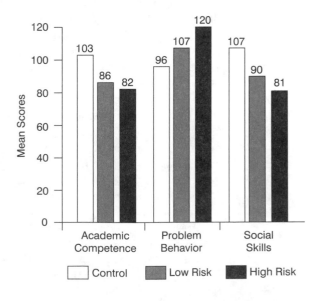

invoke the label "disordered" is a matter of judgment, an arbitrary decision based on an explicit or implicit value system. The same concept applies to the subclassification of disorders within the general category. How high an individual's rating must be on a particular factor or dimension before his or her behavior is said to be problematic is a matter of judgment. That judgment may be guided by statistical analyses, but the statistics themselves are not sufficient. Classification using a dimensional system, like psychiatric classification, is not by itself sufficient to make a child or youth eligible for special education services.

In the abstract, screening and identification or classification are often easier than when we have to apply the ideas to an individual student. Lambros et al. (1998) present several cases for consideration, one of which is the case of José (see Box 5.2).

As you study the case of José, note the discrepancies between the teacher's perceptions of him and his own, much higher self-perceptions. Notice also that he was not referred to the student study team until he was in the third grade. Why were his problems not identified earlier? What are the multicultural aspects of this case, and how might they have been addressed more effectively? Notice the delay in providing the help of a resource specialist, identification of his disabilities, and preparation of an IEP. José is typical in many ways of students eventually identified as having emotional or behavioral disorders. In the Lambros et al. (1998) study, he was identified as HR—a high-risk student. These students' early difficulties are usually ignored or merely noted, or intervention is minimal and insufficient to address the student's problems. José illustrates in many ways how we do not practice prevention but wait until problems become severe before intervening, when we then provide too little intervention (Kauffman, 1999c, 2003b).

Multiple Classifications and the Issue of Comorbidity

Regardless of whether psychiatric or dimensional classification systems are used, researchers and clinicians frequently find that children and youth exhibit more than one type of problem or disorder (see Forness, Kavale, & Lopez, 1993; Richardson, McGauhey, & Day, 1995; Tankersley & Landrum, 1997). Multiple classifications may be more common than single classifications. For example, a youngster who exhibits conduct disorder may also be depressed, one with schizophrenia may exhibit conduct disorder as well, a pervasive developmental disorder may be accompanied by an elimination disorder, or a child may be rated high on both externalizing and internalizing items because his or her behavior vacillates quickly from one extreme to the other.

A word commonly used to describe the co-occurrence of disorders is *comorbidity*. Waldman and Lillenfeld (1995) cautioned that comorbidity is a medical term referring to the co-occurrence of well-understood physical diseases and may be misleading when applied to emotional or behavioral disorders. Nevertheless, the term is used frequently, and children and youth who are referred for special education or other clinical services often carry multiple diagnostic labels.

Some researchers have identified patterns of comorbidity that put children at particularly high risk of school failure and later incarceration. Lynam (1996) and Gresham, MacMillan, Bocain, and Ward (1998) described youngsters who might be called fledgling psychopaths. These children and youth have problems focusing attention on appropriate tasks, are hyperactive, lack impulse control, and have additional conduct problems (exhibit other antisocial behavior). In addition, researchers have identified patterns of comorbidity surrounding children with attention deficit–hyperactivity disorder (ADHD) that have strong implications for treatment (see Hallahan, Lloyd, Kauffman, Weiss, & Martinez, 2005).

In a relatively large study of treatment effects for children with ADHD, strong positive effects were found for most children following a medication management program (usually methylphenidate, known by the trade name Ritalin) with a small additional effect for medical management combined with intensive behavioral treatment. However, children with parent-defined comorbid anxiety disorders, particularly those with overlapping disruptive disorder, were more effectively served by combined behavioral and medical interventions (Jensen et al., 2001). This finding suggests that failing to examine children for comorbid conditions could easily have resulted in the selection of a less effective or even an ineffective treatment. Finally, Forness and Kavale (2001b) have suggested that many students who should be considered to have EBDs are actually identified and served as students with learning

---

Box 5.2

Behavioral Profile for José, High-Risk Student for EBD

José was referred to a SST in the third grade for difficulty in all academic areas. Specifically, teachers noted his lack of reading and writing skills in both Spanish, his primary language, and English. At the time of our initial contact in the third grade, he had trouble spelling his first and last names and reversed letters and numbers. His teachers noted poor peer interactions and attributed this to a lack of self-esteem. José had more difficulty than most working with others in a cooperative group setting.

The SST recommended bilingual classroom services and decided that his externalizing behaviors would reduce with help. José was already working with a bilingual teacher in his classroom, however, and the SST recommendation did not change delivery of instructional services. By the end of third grade, José's acting out behaviors were escalating and were accompanied by teasing from his peers and symptoms of depression, such as a severe lack of interest in activities that previously were of interest.

These behaviors continued through the fourth grade. Academically, his teachers reported little to no growth in reading and writing. Teacher observations indicate that he was easily frustrated, quit without trying, and had developed obsessive-compulsive behaviors.

By the fifth grade, José still was reading at a preprimer level, and formal assessment indicated that José qualified as having a specific learning disability that was not because of cultural or language issues. The IEP team believed that 4 to 6 hours a week with a resource specialist would be an appropriate placement. The RSP teacher's academic interventions included use of direct instruction and a multisensory interactive approach with concrete materials. Behavioral Interventions included isolating José's desk from his peers and utilizing logical consequences.

José is typical of our HR group in that his appraisal of self-concept (SSCS) was at or above the mean, despite low ratings in every dimension of classroom behaviors from teacher and peers alike. José described himself as well liked, able to handle social situations successfully, a good student, and able to turn in work on time. His teachers countered with observations that peers avoided José, he had low social skills, low academic competence, and required frequent reminders to complete assignments. Although this discrepancy points to José's misperception of his behavior, he is not completely oblivious to environmental signals. Unique to José profile, as seen in Figure 5.3 is a decline in perceived self-concept scores that coincided with a placement into special education.

Upon follow-up, José had transitioned into a middle school, where he receives all classes except physical education and his elective in a special day class. His teachers report that he has tantrums, uses obscene language, continues to exhibit sad affect, and remains neglected by peers.

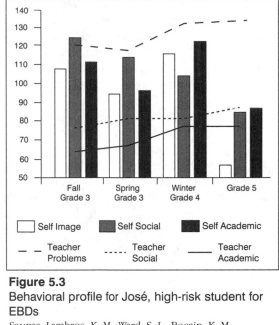

Figure 5.3

Behavioral profile for José, high-risk student for EBDs

Source: Lambros, K. M., Ward, S. L., Bocain, K. M., MacMillan, D. L., & Gresham, F. M. (1998). Behavioral profiles of children at-risk for emotional and behavioral disorders: Implications for assessment and classification. *Focus on Exceptional Children, 30*(5), 12. Reprinted by permission of Love Publishing Company.

disabilities. In such cases, the comorbidity of behavioral and learning problems makes effective treatment of one in the absence of treatment for the other extremely difficult, if not impossible.

Classification of Severe Disorders

Behavior along the different dimensions can vary from minor, even trivial, to extremely serious problems; however, some youngsters' behavior is characterized by differences that appear to be qualitatively as well as quantitatively different. These children are frequently described as inaccessible to others, as unreachable or out of touch with reality, or as having mental retardation. They are often unresponsive to other people, have bizarre language and speech patterns or no functional language at all, exhibit grossly inappropriate behavior, lack everyday living skills, or perform stereotypical, ritualistic behavior. There is not much debate about whether children can exhibit the severe disorders that are often referred to in the general case as *psychosis* (cf. American Psychiatric Association, 1994). Prior and Werry (1986) provided a nontechnical definition of psychotic behavior: "The interpretation of oneself, of the world, and of one's place in it, is so seriously at variance with the actual facts of the matter as to interfere with everyday adaptation and to strike the impartial observer as incomprehensible" (p. 156). Many of the children classified as having a pervasive developmental disorder fit such a description.

There is considerable debate about how to subdivide severe disorders in a reliable and helpful way (Gottesman, 1991). The most common distinction between two major groups is made on the basis of age of onset, a concept decades old but not outmoded. If the onset of the disorder occurs before the child is about 3 years old, the label *autistic disorder* is typically applied; if it occurs after the age of 3, the youngster is usually said to have *schizophrenia*, a psychosis usually seen in adults and very rare in young children. Although we can see much overlap in the behavioral characteristics of children with autism and those with schizophrenia, the reason for the distinction by age of onset is easy to understand. One need only examine the age distribution of first-observed symptoms. Figure 5.4 shows that onset is more frequent before the age of about 3 and after the age of 12 than between those ages.

Parents describe many children with autism as seeming odd or obviously different from birth: aloof, cold, and unresponsive. According to the data in Figure 5.4, the onset of psychotic behavior during middle childhood is quite unusual. Thus, autism (onset before the age of 3) and schizophrenia (onset in later childhood or adolescence)

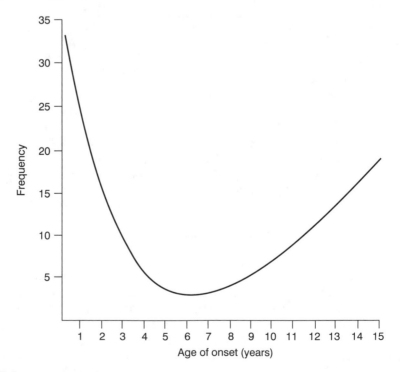

Figure 5.4
Approximate distribution of cases of childhood psychotic behavior by age of onset
Source: Curve sketched from data in Rutter, M., (1974), The development of infantile autism, *Psychological Medicine, 4,* 148.

are typically differentiated primarily on the basis of first appearance of symptoms. However, Rutter and Schopler (1987) note several other important distinctions between autism and schizophrenia. Shizophrenia tends to run in families, autism rarely does; delusions and hallucinations are characteristic of schizophrenia but rare in autism; schizophrenia is often episodic (periods of normal or near normal functioning interspersed with psychotic behavior). Autism is characterized by persistent symptoms, and epileptic seizures are seen in about 25% of children with autism. However, youngsters with schizophrenia rarely have seizures.

Confusion and disagreement regarding diagnostic classification persist. Debate about just what is necessary and sufficient to distinguish psychotic behavior from mental retardation goes back more than a century and continues today. Autism is considered a pervasive developmental disorder because the characteristics are present from birth or from a very early age and affect all or nearly all areas of functioning. But uncertainty about exactly what characteristics distinguish autism from other pervasive developmental disorders and early childhood onset schizophrenia is common (see Gottesman, 1991; National Research Council, 2001; Prior & Werry, 1986; see also Rogers-Adkinson, 1999; Schopler & Mesibov, 1994, 1995).

Aside from an apparent consensus that someone can have both mental retardation and autism or schizophrenia, and that autism is distinguished from schizophrenia primarily by age of onset, there is little agreement. However, when the onset of symptoms of schizophrenia takes place during childhood or adolescence, the child's condition may be indistinguishable from schizophrenia as it occurs in adults (Gottesman, 1991; Asarnow, Tompson, & Goldstein, 1994). Moreover, children with autism are sometimes diagnosed with schizophrenia as adolescents or adults.

Schizophrenia is fundamentally a disorder of thinking and perception. Children or youth with schizophrenia may exhibit bizarre behavior, delusions, and distorted perceptions, sometimes including hallucinations, and their affect is typically inappropriate in many social circumstances. They may believe they are being controlled by alien forces. Delusions and hallucinations are rare in preadolescents, but they are sometimes a part of severe disorders such as schizophrenia. The case of Elizabeth (see the accompanying case book) illustrates the experience of hallucinations by a preadolescent with childhood onset schizophrenia.

NECESSITY OF CLASSIFICATION

The search continues for reliable, valid classifications with relevance for intervention. Although classification of disordered behavior carries the risk that individuals will be needlessly stigmatized by labels for their differences, it would be foolish to abandon the task of classifying people's problems. Giving up all uses of classification is tantamount to abandoning the scientific study of social and behavioral difficulties. Indeed, we need labels for problems to communicate about them and to take preventive action (Forness & Kavale, 2001b; Kauffman, 1999c, 2002, 2003a, 2003b; Waldman & Lillenfeld, 1995). Nevertheless, we must try to reduce the social stigma of the words that describe behavioral differences.

Complexity and Ambiguity of Classification

Classification is a complex undertaking, and scholars frequently disagree about how particular behavioral characteristics should be categorized. Furthermore, any set of categories yet devised leaves the categorical home of some behaviors in doubt. All comprehensive systems of classification produce a residual or miscellaneous category for behavioral odds and ends, or they result in arbitrary assignment of certain behaviors to a category of questionable homogeneity. As we shall see in parts 3 and 4, both the disorders of behavior and their causes are usually multidimensional. Life seldom refines disorders or their causes into pure, unambiguous forms. Youngsters seldom show teachers or researchers a single disorder uncontaminated by elements of other problems, and the cause of a disorder is virtually never found to be a single factor. As a case in point, consider the interrelationships among *hyperactivity, conduct disorder*, and *delinquency*. Hyperactivity is a prominent feature of the behavior of many children who have a conduct disorder. Conduct disorder and delinquency are overlapping categories because conduct disorder is characterized by overt aggression or covert antisocial behavior, such as stealing, lying, and fire setting; delinquency is also often characterized by such behavior but involves breaking the law. The same factors that cause conduct disorder and delinquency may also contribute to hyperactivity. Thus, grouping specific types of disorders is necessarily somewhat subjective, and classifications always contain a certain amount of ambiguity.

SUMMARY

Instruments used for screening and classification must be selected carefully using criteria that apply to any measurement. Reliability refers to the stability of the measured characteristic across time, observers, and forms of an instrument. Validity refers to the extent to which an instrument measures what it supposedly measures. Understanding the concepts of reliability and validity is important for selecting the means by which individuals will be screened and problems will be classified.

Screening means narrowing the field to those students most likely to have emotional or behavioral disorders. It involves becoming a good "suspection," so that incipient cases and those that are not immediately obvious are reliably identified. Although IDEA requires the identification of all children with disabilities, few school systems use systematic screening procedures to identify students with emotional or behavioral disorders. If schools were to use such screening procedures, they would be likely to identify more students than could be served by special education.

One rationale for screening is that early identification will result in effective early intervention. Although this rationale is supportable, translating concern into screening procedures is difficult. Screening for emotional or behavioral disorders involves, for the most part, secondary prevention: preventing complications and exacerbation of existing problems. Effective screening of infants and young children with mild disorders is particularly difficult for educators because young children's behavior is sensitive to parental management, and parents, not teachers, define preschoolers' problem behavior. Criteria for selecting screening instruments include proactive (rather than reactive) procedures, information obtained from a variety of sources, implementation in the early grades, and use of teacher identification followed by additional procedures such as direct observation and ratings by parents and peers.

Many rating scales and other instruments can be used for screening. Screening should never consist of a single individual's judgment or be based on data from a single instrument. Convergence of judgments based on confirmation from a variety of sources should be the basis for screening decisions. Accommodation of cultural diversity and individual differences is necessary to avoid bias in screening children and youth who are members of ethnic or cultural minorities.

Prereferral strategies are a necessary intermediate step between screening and referral for evaluation. Before formal evaluation for special education, school personnel must make documented efforts to resolve the student's problems and provide appropriate education in the regular classroom. When prereferral strategies fail, the teacher should not delay in referring the student for evaluation. Functional behavioral assessment may be thought of as one type of prereferral intervention.

Classification is basic to any science, including the science of human behavior. Classifications should help us understand the nature, origin, and course of whatever is being classified. Psychiatric classification systems have not been especially useful to educators because they are not highly reliable or valid for teaching purposes. Teachers will probably encounter the most widely accepted psychiatric classification system, that of the American Psychiatric Association (various editions and revisions of the *DSM*, the official diagnostic and statistical manual).

Dimensional classifications more closely approximate the ideal system in terms of reliability, validity, and utility in education. An assumption underlying the dimensional approach is that all individuals exhibit behavior that is classifiable but to varying degrees; thus, we classify behavior, not individuals. The broadest categories in a quantitative, dimensional approach to disordered behavior are internalizing (withdrawal) and externalizing (acting out). Within these broad dimensions, more specific categories have been described. Students with emotional or behavioral disorders typically obtain higher ratings on all or most problem dimensions than do students in other special education categories. Boys usually obtain higher problem scores than girls. Differences between categories of students tend to be greatest for the conduct disorder dimension.

The most severe disabilities present particular difficulties for classification. Two common categories are autism and schizophrenia. Autism is distinguished from schizophrenia primarily by age of onset, although other differences may be noted as well. Children whose characteristics are first noticed before the age of about 3 are usually considered to have autism; if the onset is later, then the child or youth is usually said to have schizophrenia. Children with autism often lack functional language and do not usually show the disordered thought patterns of those with schizophrenia, which may include hallucinations or delusions.

Classification cannot be avoided because categories and labels are essential for human communication about disorders. All systems of classification include some miscellaneous categories and ambiguities. Many children and youth with emotional or behavioral disorders exhibit more than one type or dimension of disorder. The co-occurrence of disorders is often referred to as comorbidity.

CASE FOR DISCUSSION

A Problem or a Disorder?
Laura Brown

Laura Brown enjoys her 20 second graders, an interesting mix of general and special education students. Her class has equal numbers of males and females, with both genders including students of Caucasian, African American, Hispanic, and Chinese descent. But she is concerned about Song, an 8-year-old girl who is an only child and the daughter of Chinese immigrants who arrived in the United States about 2 years before she was born. Song is bilingual and seems to be just another American child in this culturally diverse class. However, she exhibits a variety of problem behaviors, both academic and social, that are not typical of her classroom peers.

Much of the time, Song appears to be off in her own little world, oblivious to everything going on around her. She usually does not respond to Laura's instructions. Even more troubling to Laura, Song seldom initiates interactions with her peers during free time or recess and is frequently left out of her peers' games and activities. On numerous occasions, Laura has found Song in the classroom after all of the other children have left, simply because Song has not paid attention to directions to prepare for recess, lunch, music, or some other activity and to line up with the other children. Song seldom begins work on assignments until she has been given numerous prompts and reminders, and she typically fails to complete assignments once she has begun working on them. She spends most of her time reading at her desk or on the floor. Laura sees Song as a bright child, and her scores on IQ and achievement tests suggest that she may be gifted. Nevertheless, Song's academic performance is lagging because of her deficits in following directions and completing assignments.

Song is not well liked by her peers, in part because she pretends to be a chicken (squawking and making chickenlike movements) or impersonates the voices and actions of video game characters with such frequency that her peers find her irritating. At first, these behaviors elicited laughter from her peers, but now the other children are expressing exasperation with her.

Laura has sent notes home to Song's parents expressing her concern about Song's failure to pay attention, follow instructions, and complete assignments, but she has received no replies. She has made one home visit, during which Song's parents were polite and concerned, but they had no suggestions for helping Song be more compliant or complete her work. At this point, Laura attributes much of Song's behavior to what she calls the "Little Princess" syndrome. Song is not only the only child of her parents but is surrounded by a large extended family of grandparents, aunts, and uncles who dote on her and allow her so much freedom to do as she pleases that she is not accustomed to meeting specific expectations. Perhaps, Laura thinks, Song's behavior is merely a reflection of her home life and cultural background. Still, she worries that unless Song learns to pay attention to the teacher, comply with requests, complete assignments, and interact positively with her peers, she is at very high risk of academic and social failure. Source: Information for this case was contributed by Laura Brown.

Questions About the Case

1. How might Laura proceed to determine whether Song should be referred for evaluation for special services?

2. How would you describe Song's behavior within the framework of a dimensional classification system?

3. What are the possible multicultural aspects of this case, and what steps could Laura take to make sure she neither mistakes cultural variation for problem behavior nor mistakes a serious problem for cultural variation?

4. Given that Laura and other school personnel are committed to early identification and prevention, what steps might they take at this point?

Screening and Detection of Behavior Disorders

Hill M. Walker, Ph.D., is director of the Center on Human Development and co-director of the Institute on Violence and Destructive Behavior at the University of Oregon.

How would you describe the signs that a child is likely to develop antisocial behaviors?

Antisocial behavior refers to the persistent violation of social norms relating to appropriate, expected behavior in a range of settings (home, school, or community, for example). This behavior pattern is usually expressed as very aggressive behavior directed either toward persons (i.e., coercion, victimization, aggression, and so on), property (e.g., stealing, property destruction, fire setting), or both. The frequency of antisocial behavior has escalated dramatically in our society over the last several decades, and it is the best predictor of future delinquent behavior. Delinquency, especially chronic delinquency, in turn, is highly predictive of adult criminality.

The behavioral signs of antisocial behavior can be either overt or covert in nature. Overt indicators include adult defiance, problems with rule-governed behavior, aggression that often results in assault, humiliation of peers, bullying, and extreme forms of noncompliance and oppositional behavior. Covert indicators are lying, cheating and stealing, drug and alcohol abuse at very early ages, and very serious offenses such as burglary, shoplifting, and fire setting. Children who are likely to adopt one or both of these behavior patterns typically come from home environs that are characterized by (a) harsh and inconsistent discipline; (b) ineffective and infrequent monitoring of children's activities, whereabouts, and peer affiliations; (c) low levels of parent involvement in the child's life; (d) infrequent use of positive family management techniques; and (e) poor conflict-resolution and crisis-management skills. Families displaying this profile are often under intense pressures from risk factors such as unemployment; physical, sexual, or psychological abuse; and drug and alcohol use.

These conditions provide a nurturing context for the development of antisocial behavior patterns. If antisocial behavior persists into the school setting and is maintained therein, it is very likely that affiliation with deviant peers will occur by about the fourth or fifth grade. Once a member in good standing of such a peer group, a child's first felony arrest occurs within 2 years in about 60 to 70% of cases. So it is extremely important to identify this problem early and to intervene in home, school, and community settings in order to try preventing its full-scale development. Once established, antisocial behavior is extremely difficult to change.

Why did you devise a screening procedure for students' emotional and behavioral disorders?

Actually, part of the reason has to do with my answer to your first question. Our best approach is the early identification and prevention of these disorders. We have the means and resources to screen for antisocial behavior patterns and other disorders that disrupt the development of academic and social-behavioral competence. However, we rarely do so in a systematic or standardized manner.

School provides an ideal setting for the regular screening of children who may be at risk for developing behavioral problems and disorders that can have a dramatically negative impact on their lives and those around them, yet schools do not usually assume responsibility for the early and proactive screening in this domain. They prefer, instead, to rely on the idiosyncratic referrals of regular teachers to identify children in need of assessment, diagnosis, and intervention. Studies show that teachers typically underrefer students with acting-out behavioral problems (disruption, aggression) and rarely refer students with personality problems (depression, social isolation).

My colleagues and I developed a systematic screening procedure for behavioral disorders to facilitate the earliest possible identification of students at risk for the development of social-behavioral adjustment problems. We think teachers can play a very important role in this screening process, and we have incorporated their judgments, along with other information sources, into our screening procedures.

Why do so few schools use systematic screening procedures?

The answer to this question remains partially a mystery to me. My best guesses are as follows: (a) if you don't screen for and identify problems, then you avoid having to address them; (b) social-behavioral problems are often viewed by school authorities as child- and parent-owned problems rather than as school-owned; and (c) schools are so overwhelmed with the current demands on their skills, capacity, and resources that the prospect of adding any number of additional demands through systematic and regular screening for behavioral disorders is viewed as unfeasible or unrealistic. Unfortunately, both children and teachers suffer as a result of these policies and views.

What do you see as the most useful subcategory or classification in emotional and behavioral disorders?

There are many exotic and esoteric classification systems for describing disorders of emotions and be-havior. In my view, many of these systems are only tangentially related to school-based behavioral disorders. I think the bipolar *externalizing–internalizing* classification scheme developed by Alan Ross and Thomas Achenbach is the best system for use in dealing with school-related disorders. *Externalizing* refers to acting-out problems that involve excessive behavior that is problematic. Disorders such as aggression, disruption, oppositional behavior, noncompliance, and negativism are illustrative of externalizing disorders. In contrast, *internalizing* refers to insufficient amounts of behavior that often involve skill deficits. Examples of internalizing disorders are depression, social isolation and neglect, phobias, anxiety, and immaturity.

Unless classification schemes become more fine-grained and reliable than bipolar systems of this type, their usefulness will continue to be limited in school settings by an inability of professionals to agree on which categories best represent an individual child's problems. Externalizing problems suggest a behavioral reduction and a replacement–intervention strategy, whereas internalizing problems suggest a skill-building, proactive strategy. I believe educators would be well served in adopting this type of bipolar classification scheme in dealing with school-related emotional or behavioral disorders.

>> QUESTIONS FOR FURTHER REFLECTION

1. Why should teachers be concerned about students whose problems are primarily internalizing and are not disruptive in class?
2. What are the things that federal, state, and local governments could do to encourage early identification and prevention of emotional and behavioral disorders?

3. Given that affiliation with deviant (antisocial) peers is one of the early signs that a student will have later difficulties, what are the implications for schools? That is, what could schools do to decrease students' affiliation with deviant peers and increase affiliation with nondeviant (appropriately socialized or prosocial) peers?

CHAPTER SIX

EVALUATION FOR INSTRUCTION

Revised by Frederick J. Brigham

As you read this chapter, keep these guiding questions in mind:

- How is evaluation for eligibility different from and similar to evaluation for intervention?

- What is a functional behavioral assessment, and why is it an important aspect of evaluation for instruction?

- What is a behavior intervention plan, and why must it be a positive plan?

- What are the advantages of an instructional approach to assessment?

- How do direct observation, curriculum-based evaluation, and social validation relate to writing individualized education programs (IEPs)?

In the previous chapter, we examined assessments used in screening and classification of emotional and behavioral disorders. In this chapter, we turn to assessment for instruction. Assessments for screening and classification answer questions related to how behavior deviates from normative samples or the extent to which it is similar to the behavior of other individuals with EBDs. Assessments for instruction are intended to answer questions about what a student has learned and needs to learn.

The concepts regarding reliability and validity of measures that we described in the preceding chapter apply to assessment for instruction as well. With measures designed for classification, score stability is a very important characteristic. It is difficult to imagine that classification procedures based on unreliable scores could withstand legal or professional scrutiny. To attain the kind of stability of scores needed for classification decisions, many measures sacrifice sensitivity to small changes in performance. This characteristic makes the measures useful for classification, but it renders them ineffective in guiding classroom instruction. Assessments that are useful for classroom instruction must be sensitive to small changes in behavior so that the teacher can use them to guide decisions about the instruction.

Teachers of students with EBDs routinely collect information on both academic and social or interpersonal behavior. In addition, they often monitor outcomes of medical interventions and related services such as speech and language therapy. There are many formal, commercially produced measures on the market; however, informal, teacher-created measures are often more effective for guiding instruction.

CURRENT TRENDS IN EDUCATIONAL ASSESSMENT

Few educational issues are currently in the spotlight as much as assessment. It is difficult to follow a leading newspaper for longer than a week without seeing at least one feature on American schools, their faults, the current standards-based reforms that are intended to improve them, and the tests that accompany these reforms. The news is rarely flattering for educators. News of the accomplishments of special educators is even less often satisfactory than for general educators.

Several very strong instructional technologies clearly could lead to higher student achievement (Lloyd, Forness, & Kavale, 1998). Selecting the proper instructional tool for the job requires a clear determination of the instructional needs of individual students. Most students with EBDs present several instructional problems. It is sometimes easier to identify the problems facing a given student than to prioritize them to decide which will receive intervention. One reason for the difficulty in prioritizing intervention is that different teachers, schools, and communities put higher values on certain aspects of educational programming than they do on others (Zigmond, 1996). One report on educational outcomes (Chubb et al., 2003) suggested that educators should have clear goals and accurate measures. The authors continued that the measures should be directly linked to incentives and to the school's contribution to student learning. Such language is clear and actually in line with the way many successful businesses operate. However, attaining consensus on the goals of education is very difficult (Cuban, 2000).

Schools vary widely from one community to another, but they nevertheless command the endorsement of their constituents. For example, some schools stress creativity and expression, whereas others stress basic skills or demanding academic curricula. It should not be surprising that test manufacturers have responded to the various niches created by these school models. Consequently, the sheer number of tests available is overwhelming. Worse, the claims regarding many of the tests on the market are, to be kind, overstated. Teachers are often told that a certain test can identify not only specific educational needs, but also the precise methods by which a given student should be taught. Let us be clear: As of 2003, any credible evidence for such a claim simply does not exist.

Rather than looking for a test that will provide guidance about how to teach a given student, the teacher must approach instructional decision-making as a scientific problem-solving task. Typically, the first step in any problem-solving task is to define the problem. Behavioral issues are usually defined as excesses or deficits in particular skills or classes of behavior. Academic achievement problems exist primarily as deficits in skills, the ability to use the skills, the individual's fund of general information, or some related topic. It is also a very good idea to consider the academic strengths of a given student. Part of the process of defining the problem is collecting evidence to validate the decisions that are being made. All of the procedures that are used to generate evidence regarding the nature and extent of the problem, finding its possible causes and exacerbating factors, designing methods for changing it, and monitoring the outcome are considered to be assessments. Tests are one form of assessment, but assessment of individuals with EBDs can include many more tools. For example, observations of the student's behavior in different settings and contexts should be included. Often interviews of the target student, members of the student's peer group, family, and teachers lead to insights unavailable through other means.

A variety of techniques are available to educators of students with EBDs. To ensure that a complete picture of the student's educational needs is developed, teachers should carefully consider the evidence they require and select a variety of tools to collect and cross-check their data. This type of evaluation is an ongoing process that is an integral part of teaching and intervention.

The focus of initial evaluation is clearly a yes-or-no decision for special education and related services, whereas the primary concerns of ongoing evaluation are designing the intervention and measuring progress. Evaluation for eligibility must be multidisciplinary, with emphasis on ruling out as many causes of the problem as possible. Evaluation for intervention, on the other hand, focuses more on classroom and school performance and what can be done to improve the student's behavior. The general rules for evaluation for special education are explained in the next section.

WHAT GENERAL RULES APPLY TO EVALUATION FOR SPECIAL EDUCATION?

The general rules governing evaluation for special education are laid down by federal law in the Individuals With Disabilities Education Act (IDEA) and its accompanying code of regulations. State rules may be no less strict than the federal rules;

however, state rules may mandate requirements that are more stringent than the federal rules.

Parent Participation

Parents must be members of the teams making decisions about eligibility for special education, writing individualized education programs, and choosing placements. The school must include parents in the initial assessment. Parent participation can include identifying areas of particular concern or strength, identifying settings or events that are problematic for the target student as well as those in which the student exhibits acceptable behavior, and a variety of other roles. Parents may also participate in reevaluations of the student. Some parents may decline to participate in the assessment–evaluation process, but all should be invited to do so. If assessment proceeds without parental involvement, then the school must document its good-faith efforts to include the parents (Yell & Drasgow, 2000).

Multiple Disciplines Must Be Involved

An evaluation entails individualized assessment of the student's educational needs. It typically includes four components: medical, psychological, social, and educational. All evaluation procedures must be completed before the student's eligibility for special education can be determined. The assessment must be completed by a group of professionals qualified to evaluate the student's problems, at least one of whom must be a teacher or specialist qualified to teach students with disabilities like the one the child is suspected of having.

All Known or Suspected Disabilities Must Be Assessed Accurately and Fairly

The student must be assessed in each area of known or suspected disability. Evaluation must be done using methods or tests that are not racially or culturally discriminatory, and it must be done in the student's native language or usual mode of communication. The tests must be reliable and valid for the purposes for which they are used. Furthermore, no single test or method of evaluation can be used as the sole criterion for determining the student's eligibility for special education. After parental permission for evaluation is obtained, the school must complete all components within 65 days. (Note: Sixty-five days is a federal requirement; some state laws set a limit of less than 65 days.)

Assessment Results Must Be Confidential

The test results and other records about the student must be kept confidential. No one but teachers and other professionals who work with the student is allowed to review the records without parental permission. It is unprofessional and illegal to share information from the evaluation with professionals who are not directly involved with the student's education. However, parents must, by law, be informed of the results of the evaluation in language they can understand, and the school must allow parents to see their child's records if they so request. In addition, regulations of the Individuals with Disabilities Education Act provide that each regular and special education teacher and service provider responsible for implementing a child's IEP must (a) have access to the child's IEP and (b) be informed of his or her specific responsibilities under the IEP, and of the specific accommodations, modifications, and supports that must be provided for the child in accordance with the IEP.

Parents Have a Right to Mediation or a Due Process Hearing

If parents disagree with the school's evaluation data, they have a right to have their child evaluated somewhere else and present the results to the school. Then, if parents and the school cannot reach an agreement about an accurate evaluation, by law either party may request a hearing. Mediation of disputes about evaluation issues is encouraged, but participation in mediation must be voluntary and cannot be used to delay or avoid a due process hearing.

Periodic Reevaluation Is Required

After a student is placed in special education, his or her progress is assessed at least annually. Usually, the teacher or the specialist providing the services to meet the relevant educational goals or objectives conducts evaluations rather than assembling an entire team of evaluation specialists. However, a reevaluation involving an interdisciplinary team must be completed at least every 3 years. This is called a *triennial* evaluation and is done to decide whether the student's placement is still appropriate. During triennial evaluations, assessment teams review the assessment data collected during the student's recent evaluations to determine the adequacy of the information. The team may decide to either accept the information currently available about the student or to administer assessments to update previously obtained information or to obtain new data regarding a given student.

Transition Planning Must Be Part of the IEP for Students Age 14 or Older

Plans for making the transition to further education or to work must be included in the IEP for students age 14 or older. This requires assessment of the student's probable educational and employment futures. In addition, older students should be active participants in planning transition programs to ensure that the student's interests and preferences are included (Wehmeyer, 2001).

Students with EBD Must Be Included in General Assessments of Educational Progress

All students with disabilities, including those with EBDs, must be included, if appropriate, in any state- or districtwide standardized or general assessment of educational progress. If appropriate, the student with a disability must be included with adaptations or accommodations for his or her disability.

Positive Behavior Intervention Plans Based on a Functional Behavioral Assessment Must Be Included in IEPs

If a student's behavior is interfering with his or her learning (a given in the case of a student with an EBD), then the IEP must include a plan to use positive strategies (i.e., not merely a plan for punishment of misbehavior) to address or prevent the problem behavior. The behavior intervention plan must be based on a functional behavioral assessment (FBA). These legal requirements come into the picture around disciplinary issues involving suspension, expulsion, or change of placement. However, the intent of the law clearly is to have FBAs included in IEPs before such disciplinary actions are contemplated (Cipani, 1999; Yell, Bradley, & Shriner, 1999). Furthermore, the FBAs must be meaningful. Many school districts have adopted procedures that create a document called an FBA, but too often the document is an exercise in checking boxes on preprinted forms to accomplish superficial compliance with state and federal regulations. Many times, such documents are filed without consideration of the results in terms of the child's educational program or disciplinary decisions. It is unlikely that such practices will withstand legal challenges (Yell, Katsiyannis, Bradley, & Rozalski, 2000).

Whether evaluation is for eligibility or intervention, two considerations are important: the source of referral and the initial appearance of a problem. Young children almost never refer themselves for evaluation; even youths seldom do. Children and youth are usually brought to the attention of mental health workers or special educators by their parents, teachers, or other adults. The evaluation is thus almost always prompted by adults' judgments of youngsters' behavior rather than by the children's opinions of themselves. Adult referral of children and youth has two immediate implications:

1. The evaluation must involve appraisal of at least one referring adult as well as the youngster. Appraisal of the adult who refers the child or youth is necessary to validate the concern about the disturbing behavior and to discover how the adult's responses to the student might be contributing to the problem.
2. Attempts must be made to determine the youngster's own view of the situation.

No humane and ethical approach to the disorder can disregard or trivialize the child's opinions of his or her problems and treatment. Some youngsters' opinions are not accessible because of their lack of communication skills, and some young people's opinions must be overruled because they are clearly not in their own best interests. Nevertheless, the rights of children and youth must be protected, and their opinions, when they can be determined, should be weighed seriously in decisions about identification and treatment.

Emotional or behavioral problems are not always what they seem at first. Sometimes an explanation is difficult to find, not because the disorder is buried deep in the individual's psyche but simply because some of the most relevant facts are hard to extract from the situation (see the cases of Ray and Mark in the accompanying case book). Sometimes evaluation focuses too much on the student's behavior and does not tap some critical item of information, which is often difficult to obtain. If the student's behavior is understood in the context of the circumstances of his or her life, then decisions regarding eligibility and intervention can be made with greater confidence.

EVALUATION FOR ELIGIBILITY

Federal regulations require that evaluation for eligibility involve multiple sources of data and assessment by a multidisciplinary team (MDT). One of the most important tools to guide the assessment team is the definition that is used to determine the population with EBDs. The definition that school must use is, of course, found in IDEA. A starting point for identifying the students eligible for service under the category of EBD is the five subpoints of the EBD definition in IDEA. Assessment procedures should generally address the extent to which the student exhibits:

1. An inability to that which cannot be explained by intellectual, sensory, or health factors
2. An inability to build and maintain satisfactory interpersonal relationships with peers and teachers
3. Inappropriate types of behavior or feelings under normal circumstances
4. A general, pervasive mood of unhappiness or depression, or
5. A tendency to develop physical symptoms or fears associates with personal or school problems.

Landrum (2000) pointed out that the field of behavioral disorders has yet to adequately define the population of students with whom we are working. Consequently, the determination that a student is or is not eligible for services under the EBD category is often controversial and difficult to make except for the more extreme instances.

Consider each of the subpoints of the definition. Learning is clearly an important issue for the schools, and one would certainly fall short of any professional standard in ascribing learning problems to emotional disturbance when they were indeed caused by another problem. Therefore, evaluation of academic performance is critical because most students suspected of or identified as having emotional or behavioral disorders have serious academic problems as well as problems of social adjustment (Walker, Ramsey, & Gresham, 2004; see also chapter 9). Evaluations of physical status and cognitive development are also important because problems in one of these areas can contribute substantially to emotional or behavioral disorders. Evaluations of the social environment of the home and the student's emotional responses to parents, teachers, and peers are essential for understanding the social influences that may be contributing to the problem (see Epstein & Cullinan, 1998). We now recognize that language disorders and emotional or behavioral disorders are often closely linked (Hooper, Roberts, Zeisel, & Poe, 2003; Nelson, Benner, & Rogers-Adkinson, 2003). Students with EBDs often have difficulty understanding the meanings of others' language and behavior and have difficulty expressing themselves appropriately and effectively (Rogers-Adkinson & Griffith, 1999). Ideally, the MDT carefully weighs information obtained from evaluations in all these areas before deciding the student's eligibility for special education.

Unfortunately, the MDT seldom functions with ideal care and reliability (Bateman & Linden, 1998). In practice, decisions are often made with information from limited sources, and the decision-making process tends to be unreliable—not predictable on the basis of objective data from tests and observations alone. One reason for the lack of predictability is the absence of guidelines specifying exactly how the MDT must function. Another reason is the lack of clear criteria for defining disorders. Still another reason is the tendency of some evaluation procedures to turn up irrelevant or unhelpful information; for example, physiological or psychological tests may have little value for educational decisions. Decision-making might become more objective along some dimensions by tightening the criteria for definition and by using expert systems, in which computer programs use multiple sources of data to establish complex and entirely objective criteria. Such efforts to objectify the decision-making process do not, unfortunately, take into consideration the fact that the definition of disordered behavior is necessarily subjective, as we discussed in chapter 1. More objective and reliable instruments and computer programs may help people make better decisions, but they cannot become the sole bases for decision making.

A major problem in evaluation is that the decisions of those who declare a student eligible for special education tend to be unreliable (unpredictable or inconsistent) when judged against criteria such as standardized test scores and objective behavioral observations. Different groups and different individuals may evaluate according to different criteria; they may use different criteria for students who differ in sex, race, socioeconomic status, and so forth. Inconsistency is a serious concern because it can indicate bias or inappropriate discrimination in evaluation. However, the solution is not to make the judgments conform to objective psychometric criteria alone (such as test scores or quantitative values in computer programs), nor is it to abandon the goal of more reliable, predictable, or consistent decisions. The most desirable response is to stress professional responsibility in decision making (see Bateman, 1992; Bateman & Linden, 1998; Merrell, 1994; Taylor, 1997; Yell, 1998). These are key actions in discharging that responsibility:

- Obtaining inservice training in appropriate evaluation procedures
- Refusing to use evaluation procedures that you are not qualified to use and refusing to accept evaluation data from unqualified personnel
- Functioning as a member of an MDT to ensure that a single individual does not make the eligibility decision
- Insisting that multiple sources of data be made available to the MDT and that the eligibility decision be made on the basis of all relevant data
- Requiring implementation of documented prereferral strategies before evaluation for eligibility
- Involving the parents and, if appropriate, the student in the eligibility decision to be sure they are informed of the nature of the problem and the implications of identification
- Documenting disordered behavior, its adverse effects on the student's education, and the need for special education and related services
- Considering the interests of all parties affected by the eligibility decision: student, peers, parents, and teachers

- Estimating the probable risks and benefits of identifying and not identifying the student for special education
- Ensuring that any special education program proposed as a result of identification is likely to confer educational benefits on the student
- Remaining sensitive to the possibility of bias in the use of procedures and interpretation of data.

EVALUATION FOR INTERVENTION

Adequate evaluation for the purpose of intervention requires careful attention to a wide range of factors that may be important in the origin and modification of problem behavior. Many educators consider the evaluation process to be synonymous with testing. However, testing is usually considered to be focused on the demonstration of a single behavior or skill under controlled circumstances, whereas assessment and evaluation are broader collections of techniques for collecting evidence to support decision making. All tests are assessments, but because assessment can include activities such as interviews and observations of student behavior, not all assessments are tests. Thus, whenever possible, information must be obtained from parents, teachers, peers, the student, and impartial observers.

Evaluation for special education interventions also requires focusing on the student's problems as they are manifested in school. The data obtained during screening may be helpful in further evaluating the student for intervention. Procedures for evaluating referred students should include at least standardized tests of intelligence and achievement, behavior ratings, assessment of peer relations, interviews, self-reports, and direct observations (Landrum, 2000). An important approach to evaluation, particularly of academic achievement, is curriculum-based assessment (CBA, Crawford & Tindal, 2002; Jones, Southern, & Brigham, 1998; Shinn, Shinn, Hamilton, & Clarke, 2002). CBA may also be applied to social skills.

An important question to answer in evaluation is: What purpose or function does the behavior serve in the student's life? A *functional behavioral assessment* is an approach to assessment designed to answer this question (Fox & Gable, 2004; McConnell, Cox, Thomas, & Hilvitz, 2001; O'Neill, Horner, Albin, Sprague, Story, & Newton, 1997). The function of behavior is a critical issue to be addressed in an evaluation, and a competent functional behavioral assessment may draw on all of the types of assessment information we discuss in this section.

Finally, we might approach the assessment of behavior much the same as we do the assessment of academic skills. Social–emotional behavior can be analyzed as an instructional problem: How can we teach the student a better way of behaving? A clear focus on teaching helps educators tie assessment directly to instruction, prevent misbehavior from occurring, and keep a focus on a positive plan for intervention. Ultimately, the goal of assessment should be *precorrection*—guiding the student away from misbehavior and toward the desired response through skillful, carefully planned instruction linked directly to assessment (Colvin, Sugai, & Patching, 1993; Walker et al., 2004).

Standardized, Norm-Referenced Tests of Intelligence and Achievement

In assessment, standardization means simply that the measure or procedure is carried out the same way with each individual on whom it is used. Standardization is necessary if we are to compare the results of one student's assessment to other students or to compare the results of a given assessment procedure on the same student from one administration to another. Norm referencing refers to the way in which meaning is assigned to the scores yielded by the test. In a norm-referenced test, the student's performance is evaluated by the extent to which it is different from the mean score of the norm group for the test. In most classroom tests, an individual's score is compared to some preset criterion for passing. In a criterion-referenced test, the number of items for which an individual provided the target responses is important. In a norm-referenced test, the number of target responses provided by an individual is important but only relative to the number of target responses provided by the comparison group for the student. Comparison groups, to be useful, must be composed of individuals who are like the test taker in some important and task-relevant way. Age and grade level are often used for academic and intellectual measures. For some measures, the gender of the participant may be important.

Whenever a teacher uses information from a norm-referenced measure, the extent to which the norm group is reasonable for making comparisons in evaluating a given student should be considered. If the reading abilities of young children were compared to older children, they would probably be rated quite poorly. In order to make a meaningful comparison of how well a student reads compared to a peer group, the peer group should be composed of individuals at the same age, grade level, or with similar amounts of reading instruction. In each case, the specification of the norms group would be necessary to interpret the scores. Students who have been retained may have a better standing relative to the norm group when compared to individuals in the same grade or with similar amounts of reading instruction than when compared to their age mates who have not been retained and therefore received more reading instruction. This example is fairly straightforward; however, selecting the proper norm group is often more difficult. For example, it can be argued that cultural norms for different ethnic groups should be considered in evaluating an individual's behavior. In addition, some researchers point to differences in cognitive development of males and females at different points in their education. Selecting norm groups of only members of certain ethnicities or one gender may have advantages under some conditions but may also exacerbate perceptions of differences based on superficial characteristics alone.

Standardized tests can be used to estimate what a student has learned and to compare his or her performance to the norms of age mates. They can provide a description of current abilities and point to general areas in need of instruction. A test of intelligence provides evidence of a student's learning in general skill areas that are predictive of performance in schooling; a test of academic achievement taps more specific skills. Neither type of test, however, provides much information about just what a student should be taught.

There are good reasons for using standardized intelligence and achievement tests. It is helpful, for example, to know how a student's progress in learning skills compares to other students' progress in a national sample. However, one must avoid serious pitfalls, which include possible bias in favor of certain cultural, ethnic, or socioeconomic groups (bias in terms of a disproportionate number of students from one of these groups who score within a certain range on a given test). Other pitfalls include (a) failure to consider the margin of error in the scores students achieve at a given testing, (b) the ability of a measure to detect changes in scores over time or after instruction, (c) failure to consider the match between an achievement test and the instructional expectations of the student's class, and (d) failure of the scores to predict important outcomes.

All measures are composed of at least two parts, the true ability we are attempting to measure and measurement error. Measurement specialists consider all measures to carry a certain amount of error. When error is directional and systematic (either to the benefit or the detriment of the examinee), it is considered to be bias. A great deal of effort has gone into removing obvious sources of bias from assessments in the past few decades, although much more work needs to be done in this area. Even if a test is completely free of systematic bias, nonsystematic, random error is present. Such error is neither consistently to the benefit nor to the detriment of the examinee but can influence a score upward on one occasion or suppress the score on another occasion. It is possible to estimate the amount of random error present on any test for individuals of particular characteristics (e.g., ages or grade levels). The estimate of the error present on the test is called the *standard error of measurement* (SEM). When educators are considering whether scores represent meaningful growth (e.g., tests administered at the beginning and again at the end of the year), they must ensure that the differences exceed the SEM. For example, if a given test is considered to be accurate to an SEM of plus or minus three points, changes of three points or less can easily be the result of measurement error and not actual improvement in performance.

Measures used to evaluate student performance vary in their ability to detect changes in scores over time or after instruction. Norm-referenced tests often can not detect small changes in student behavior because such tests are general enough to be used across the entire nation. Consequently, variations in curriculum, activities, and teacher background tend to be averaged out of the test. In addition, norm-referenced, standardized measures usually cover a very large age span so that there are too few items on any scale to accurately and reliably detect small changes in student behavior. Classroom tests and curriculum-based measurement of student performance can help guide instruction and provide students with feedback about their progress far better than can standardized, norm-referenced tests, which are better suited to detecting larger changes in behavior across long time periods (Brigham, Tochterman, & Brigham, 2000).

Failure to consider the match between an achievement test and the instructional expectations of the student's class can lead to senseless interpretation of test results. Although general curriculum standards have recently been established in most states, considerable variability exists among teachers of the same course, even within the same school. Teachers who want measures that reflect their own instruction should use curriculum-based measurement rather than norm-referenced, standardized tests. To be meaningful, measurement of instruction must be tailored directly to actual instruction (Plasencia-Peinado & Alvarado, 2000).

One of the largest problems in educational measurement is the failure of scores to consistently predict important outcomes. For example, an IQ derived from a standardized test is not a measure of intellectual potential, nor is it static or immutable; it is merely a measure of general learning in certain areas compared to the learning of other students of the same age who formed the normative sample. An IQ is only a moderately accurate predictor of what a student is likely to learn in the future if no special intervention is provided. Remember that a student's performance on a given test on a given day can be influenced by many factors. Even under the best conditions, the score is an estimate of a range in which the student's true score is likely to fall.

Considering the pitfalls in standardized testing is particularly important in evaluating students with emotional or behavioral disorders. These disorders tend to interfere with learning and academic performance during both instruction and testing. Consequently, students with such disorders are likely to perform below their true abilities on standardized tests. As a group, they tend to score lower than average on intelligence and achievement tests. Careful evaluation of their abilities is warranted, therefore, to avoid mistakes in setting expectations for their performance.

Objections to well-known intelligence and achievement tests, as well as to other standardized measures, are often based on criticism of the inappropriate use and interpretation of test scores—unintelligent or unprofessional psychometric procedures that can ruin the value of any evaluation procedure. The value and limitations of standardized and normative testing have been discussed in detail (see Brigham, Tochterman, & Brigham, 2000; Taylor, 1997; Wallace, Larsen, & Elksnin, 1992). Despite their limitations, standardized tests of intelligence and achievement, used with appropriate caution, can be helpful in assessing important areas of strength, weakness, and progress in students with emotional or behavioral disorders (Kauffman, 2002; Kauffman & Hallahan, 2005b; Kaufman & Ishikuma, 1993).

Behavior Ratings

The behavior rating scales described in chapter 5 are commonly used in the evaluation of emotional or behavioral disorders. Sometimes several individuals (parents and teachers, for instance) complete rating scales, and then the ranges are compared to assess the level of agreement about the student's behavior. In fact, one should be very wary of making judgments based on the ratings of a single observer, be it parent or teacher (McConaughy, 1993). Ratings by several individuals should be aggregated to reduce the possibility of bias (Merrell, 1994). The scores obtained on rating scales can be compared to norms that are helpful in judging whether behavior demands intervention and in describing or classifying the types of problems a child or youth exhibits (Gresham, 2000).

In addition to their usefulness for description and classification, rating scales can be administered repeatedly and the scores used to evaluate progress in reaching intervention goals. However, behavior ratings are not adequate for pinpointing specific behaviors as targets for change, something for which direct observation is required (Alberto & Troutman, 2003; Merrell, 1994).

Rating scales are subject to the same dangers of misuse and misinterpretation as any other standardized assessment instrument regarding reliability, validity, inappropriate application, and bias (cf. Piacentini, 1993; Reitman, Hummek, Franz, & Gross, 1998). Another possible misuse is to ask teachers who are not sufficiently acquainted with a student to complete a behavior rating scale.

Direct Observation and Measurement

A large body of behavioral research supports the commonsense practice of observing students in the environments in which problems are reported (Alberto & Troutman, 2003; Barrios, 1993; Beck, 1995; Greenwood, Carta, & Dawson, 2000). Direct observation means that an observer (e.g., teacher, psychologist, parent) sees the behavior as it occurs; direct measurement means that the occurrence of the behavior is recorded immediately. Thus, direct observation and measurement yields information on the frequency, rate, percent of opportunities, and so on with which a behavior occurs rather than a rating. A rating represents cumulative subjective judgment reduced to a number; direct observation and measurement represents objective reporting of the occurrence of behavior. Behavior observations have the additional benefit of sensitivity to small changes in behavior (Alberto & Troutman, 2003; Gresham, 2000; Walker et al., 2004). Thus, improvements or deteriorations in a student's behavioral functioning may be detected earlier by observational methods than by rating scales.

Direct observation and measurement involve not only recording the behavior of the student in question but also selecting the setting(s) or context(s) in which behavior will be measured, a systematic method of observing and recording, procedures designed to ensure reliability of observation, and means of accumulating, displaying, and interpreting the data. In addition to observation of the behavior itself, the immediate antecedents (what happens just before) and consequences (what happens just after) are typically observed and recorded in an initial assessment. The reason for recording antecedents and consequences is that these are often conditions or events that help to explain why the behavior occurs and that, if altered, may change the behavior.

An extensive technology of direct observation and measurement has been developed, much of which is directly applicable to teaching. As Barrios (1993) noted, however, observation and measurement systems can become very complex and costly, resulting in their being used only by specialists. Keeping observation and recording systems simple and inexpensive enough to be used in everyday teaching practice is a major goal in assessment strategies. Such teacher-friendly systems are readily available for use in classroom intervention (see Alberto & Troutman, 2003; Kerr & Nelson, 2002; Kerr, Nelson, & Lambert, 1987). Moreover, computer-assisted observation systems allow highly accurate recording and summarizing of events that are critical to understanding behavior in classroom settings (Greenwood et al., 2000).

Direct observation is a particularly important approach to evaluating disorders that involve externalized problems—those in which the student strikes out at and disturbs others. Regardless of the type of behavior involved, direct observation can address questions like these:

- In what settings (home, school, math class, or playground) is the problem behavior or behavioral deficit exhibited?
- With what frequency, duration, or force does the behavior occur in various settings?
- What happens immediately before the behavior occurs? What seems to set the occasion for it?
- What happens immediately after the behavior occurs that may serve to strengthen or weaken it?
- What other inappropriate responses are observed?
- What appropriate behavior could be taught or strengthened to lessen the problem?
- What does the student's behavior communicate to others?

Direct observation requires careful definition of observable target behaviors and frequent (usually daily) recording of occurrence. Some interventions and evaluation procedures depend on this methodology. A behavioral approach to teaching makes direct observation a central feature of intervention. Curriculum-based assessment depends on direct observation and recording of academic and social behavior, and direct observation is a required part of functional analysis. Direct observation is also an important aspect of many interventions derived from a social-cognitive model. Thus, of all the alternative means of evaluation for intervention, direct observation and measurement of behavior is perhaps the most central in importance.

Interviews

Interviews vary widely in structure and purpose. They can be freewheeling conversations or can follow a prescribed line of questioning for obtaining information about specific behaviors or developmental milestones. They can be conducted with verbal children as well as with adults, including school staff, parents, and others who may have contact with the target student (Scott, Liaupsin, Nelson, & Jolivette, 2003). They may be designed to assess a wide range of problems or to assess particular types of disorders such as depression or anxiety (Hodges & Zeman, 1993; Merrell, 1994; Taylor, 1997) or to help discriminate between skill acquisition, performance, and fluency deficits (Gresham, 2000).

Skillful interviewing is no simple matter. When troublesome behavior is in question, it is not easy to keep the interviewee(s) from becoming defensive. Differences in the cultural backgrounds of the interviewer and interviewee may foster miscommunication, and an interview in which answers represent half truths, misleading information, avoidance, or misunderstandings will not be much help in evaluation. Furthermore, one must maintain a healthy skepticism about the accuracy of interview responses that require memory of long-past events. It is also important to weigh carefully the interviewees' subjective opinions, especially when their responses are emotionally charged or seriously discrepant from other subjective reports or objective evidence. Finally, extracting and accurately recording the most relevant information from an interview requires keen judgment and excellent communication skills (Merrell, 1994).

Interviews should help the evaluator get an impression of how the student and significant others interact and feel about each other. They should also help members of the evaluation team decide what additional types of information they need. But interviews can accomplish these ends only to the extent that the interviewer has great interpersonal skills, the experience and sensitivity to make sound clinical judgments, and the ability to focus on information about the relevant behavior and its social contexts.

Descriptions of behavior, competencies, environmental conditions, and consequences obtained from interviews may be helpful but are often inaccurate and cannot be relied on without verification from other sources. It is important to note discrepancies between reports given to interviewers and information obtained from direct observation because those discrepancies can sometimes be crucial in designing interventions. If, for example, teachers or parents report that they frequently praise appropriate behavior and ignore misconduct but direct observation shows the opposite, then the adults' misperceptions must be taken into account in designing an intervention plan.

ASSESSMENT OF PEER RELATIONS

Interaction with and acceptance by the peer group are necessary for normal social development. Students with emotional or behavioral disorders often do not develop normal peer relations (Sabornie, 1985; Sabornie & Kauffman, 1985; Walker et al., 2004). Some are socially withdrawn and maintain a low profile with their classmates by avoiding peer interaction. Others are aggressive toward peers. A disruptive influence in any group activity, they maintain a high profile with their classmates, although their peers actively reject them. More recently, researchers have noted that students with conduct problems may in fact have friendships, but their friends tend to be other deviant students (Farmer, 2000; Farmer, Farmer, & Gut, 1999; Farmer, Leung, Pearl, Rodkin, Cadwallader, & Van Ackar, 2002; Miller-Johnson, Coie, Maumary-Gremaud, Lochman, & Terry, 1999; Poulin & Boivin, 1999; Shores, 1987; Shores & Wehby, 1999; Xie, Cairns, & Cairns, 1999). In any case, the student ends up alone because he or she does not have the necessary social skills for the positive reciprocal exchanges that characterize friendships, or he or she develops friendships with others who are a negative influence.

Assessment of peer relations is a critical aspect of research and practice, including the identification of subtypes of disorders, determining social status, selecting students for social skills training, judging the outcomes of intervention, and predicting long-term outcomes (Farmer et al., 1999; Gresham & Little, 1993). Peer relations may be evaluated by a variety of methods. Some screening instruments include rating scales that are completed by peers; some include sociometric questions for assessing acceptance or rejection among peers or patterns of peer affiliation. Sometimes interviews regarding social relationships are also employed. Sociometric techniques are not necessarily part of a screening procedure but are often used in research and evaluation in which peer relations are a central concern. Direct observation is sometimes used to measure how often the student makes social initiations or responds appropriately to peers' initiations. Brown, Odom, and Buysse (2002) observed that differing methods of assessment of peer relations often provide different results. Consequently, they suggested that multiple strategies be employed in assessment of peer relations to yield different but related types of information.

Self-Reports

Self-reports typically require students to respond to checklists, rating scales, or interviews in which they describe their behavior or feelings. How students perceive themselves and how they respond emotionally to various circumstances is an important part of the assessment of *person variables,* the cognitive processes and affective states that are part of Bandura's (1986) social-cognitive model (see chapter 4). Self-reports are particularly important when evaluating disorders such as substance abuse, anxiety, fears, and depression—disorders that involve high levels of affect and often are not open to direct observation (Merrell, 1994; Reynolds, 1993). Self-reports are of limited value, however, for youngsters who are nonverbal or unable to organize their responses coherently. In addition, self-reports are vulnerable to intentional over- or underreporting for a number of reasons, including the tendency of the reporting student to provide the examiner with the information they desire or the desire for the reporting student to present himself or herself in a particular way. Therefore, self-report data should be corroborated by other sources of data.

Some behavior rating scales include self-reports, along with ratings by teachers and parents, and may yield scores on multiple dimensions of behavior. Other self-report scales are designed to tap particular self-perception, affective, or behavioral domains such as self-concept, loneliness, alcohol use, depression, and so on. Like all other assessment strategies, self-reports must be interpreted with caution regarding their reliability and validity and in the context of other sources of information.

Curriculum-Based Evaluation

An evaluation methodology involving frequent, direct measurement of students' performance using their typical curriculum materials emerged in the mid-1980s (Deno, 1985, 2003; Howell & Hyatt, 2004). It has been called *curriculum-based measurement* (CBM), *curriculum-based assessment* (CBA), and *curriculum-based evaluation* (Howell, Fox, & Morehead, 1993; Howell & Hyatt, 2004).

There are several differences between curriculum-based assessment (CBA) and the traditional forms of norm-referenced testing described earlier in this chapter (Deno, 2003). Most important is that in CBA the curriculum materials relevant to the assessed student are used as the test stimuli. In traditional testing, items are constructed to create a general representation of the curriculum. However, the purpose of most norm-referenced procedures is to rank individuals relative to a group. Therefore, items in norm-referenced tests are selected for their ability to spread the performance of individuals out rather than to tap actual curricular goals. CBA, in contrast, tracks differences in progress within the individual rather than between individuals (but, of course, the performance of other individuals is ultimately important, too, as we note below; see also Kauffman & Hallahan, 2004).

Curriculum-based assessment is a general term used to refer to any information-gathering procedure that obtains information about student performance in the curriculum. Curriculum-based measurement (CBM) is a specialized set of procedures within CBA that are used to measure student growth in basic skills (Deno, 2003).

Curriculum-based measurements are typically short, frequently administered measures of performance on a single task. Because the measures are repeated, it is important that the tasks selected are appropriate for repeated measure. Tasks that require extended practice are usually the best candidates for repeated measures. Reading fluency and arithmetic computations are two such skills. In secondary content classes, measures of content-related vocabulary have proven to be valid and reliable indicators of progress (Busch & Espin, 2003). Individual students' performances are compared to those of others in the same school using the same curriculum. For example, students might be asked to read aloud for 1 minute from a passage in their usual reader, perhaps three times per week. Their reading rates (words read correctly per minute, errors per minute, or both) are then recorded. To evaluate written language, students might be asked to provide a 3-minute sample of their writing in response to a topic sentence. Math performance might be evaluated by asking students to complete as many computation problems as they can in 2 minutes, with the problems taken from their basal text. The results of these assessments are displayed on a graph and progress is compared to a line of expected progress called an aim line. See Figure 6.1 for an example of a CBM chart. Teachers can intervene by altering the educational program when a student's performance falls below the aim line for a specified number of observations (usually three or four). Note that the aim line (dashed line) in Figure 6.1 is ascending from left to right. In this case, the goal is to increase the target behavior, and problematic performance is indicated by student

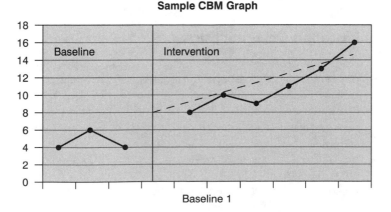

Figure 6.1
Sample curriculum-based measurement graph

data points below the aim line. If the goal was to decrease the target behavior, the aim line would descend across the graph and problematic performance would result in student data points above the aim line.

Many teachers are resistant to using CBM in their classrooms (Deno, 2003). Sometimes, teachers resist CBM because they believe that the focus on discrete units of measure (e.g., accuracy in oral reading) is somehow an illegitimate measure of progress. A great deal of accumulated research suggests that this fear is unfounded. Lloyd, Forness, and Kavale (1998) reported that CBM is among the more effective tools available to educators. Other teachers express reluctance to use CBM because it is quite different from the measurement systems with which they are familiar. This reluctance is truly unfortunate because IEPs developed from CBM data are far more likely to be legally correct and beneficial to the students with disabilities for whom they are designed (Yell & Stecker, 2003).

Curriculum-based evaluation is important because most students who receive special education because of emotional or behavioral disorders have academic deficits (see Kerr & Nelson, 2002; Walker et al., 2004). Furthermore, proponents of curriculum-based methods include social skills among measurable performances (Germann & Tindal, 1985; Howell, 1987; Howell & Hyatt, 2004). A student's and his or her classmates' specific behavioral problems or social skills (such as hitting classmates, making derogatory comments about self, making positive social initiations, and taking turns) can be recorded systematically for comparison. If the student's behavior is significantly different from that of other students, then he or she may be identified as needing a special teaching procedure to change the targeted behavior, and the results can be evaluated by noting changes in the student's behavior compared to the peer group. The significant difference between this kind of curriculum-based evaluation and direct observation is this: A curriculum-based approach assumes that the school is using a coherent social skills curriculum—that is, that social skills are being taught systematically. Unfortunately, social skills curricula are not yet well developed, and many schools have not implemented existing curricula (Hollinger, 1987; Walker et al., 2004).

Manifestation Determination

Manifestation determination assessment procedures are intended to ascertain whether or not a student's misbehavior and disability are related. This is often a very difficult task. Nevertheless, a manifest determination (MD) is required when disciplinary procedures used by school officials result in a change in the student's placement or result in suspension from school for more than 10 consecutive days or expulsion form school.

Yell and Drasgow (2000) suggested that MD assessments should include (a) examinations of school records to examine educational history; (b) interviews of parents, teachers, the target student and other students; and (c) observations of the student's behavior in different contexts (e.g., playground, different classrooms or classroom activities, cafeteria). Parents may also submit assessment data (e.g., evaluations by a private psychologist or a physician) to the MD team. After collecting relevant data, the team must first determine whether or not the student's IEP was appropriate relative to the behavior of concern. That is, the behavior was adequately addressed in the IEP if it was an aspect of the student's disability. If the IEP is appropriate, the team must then determine if services are being provided in accordance with the IEP. If the answer to either of these questions is no, the team must redesign the IEP and institute services to prevent future episodes of the behavior. In such a case, the MD action ends because the behavior and disability are considered to be related by virtue of the inappropriate IEP or the failure to enact its services. If the answer to these questions is yes, the MD team must then consider whether or not the student's disability impaired his or her ability to (a) understand the consequences of the action and (b) control the target behavior. If the behavior is determined to be related to the disability, schools are required to address the behavior through the IEP rather than simply punishing it.

Functional Behavioral Assessment

Since the early 1990s, increasing emphasis has been placed on analyzing the function of students' behavior (Cipani, 1999; O'Neill et al., 1997). A *functional behavioral assessment* (FBA) is a process of obtaining and analyzing assessment data to better understand the nature and causes of problem behavior and develop more effective and positive interventions. The goal of an FBA is to improve the effectiveness and efficiency of behavioral supports for students by linking intervention directly to the function of the behavior (Sugai, Horner, & Gresham, 2002). An FBA is also sometimes referred to as the *functional analysis* of behavior. Walker (1995) noted:

> Functional analysis has three main goals: (1) to describe the undesirable or problem behavior in operational terms, (2) to predict the occasions and situations in which the behavior of interest is and is not likely to occur, and (3) to identify and define the purpose(s) the problem behavior serves. (p. 77)

The purposes of an FBA are straightforward, but the implementation is somewhat controversial (Fox, & Gable, 2004; Sasso, Conroy, Stichter, & Fox, 2001). The way in which a functional assessment is conducted is not mysterious, but, done well, it is time-consuming and requires knowledge of a variety of assessment strategies. It usually begins with a structured teacher interview (or self-interview) in which the objective is to clarify the nature of the problem behavior (including its form, frequency, duration, and intensity) and the contexts (e.g., time, situations) in which it tends to occur. The responses of others to the student's behavior are assessed, including the responses of peers, teachers, and parents. The student's behavior is tracked throughout the day to see how, when, and where it occurs and what consequences it produces—what it gets for the student and what it allows the student to avoid. Then, in the light of all the assessment data, the teacher forms a hypothesis about why the behavior is occurring and what might be altered to resolve the problem.

An FBA may be more difficult for older students, those with greater cognitive abilities and those students with more complex social–emotional problems. Sometimes it is very difficult to find an activity that the student prefers but is consistent with program goals. However, functional analyses provide the basis for arranging classroom conditions and instructional procedures that give students maximum freedom and self-control while resolving their behavior problems. Knowing the function served by a certain behavior can also increase the empathy of teachers toward their students (Rao, Hoyer, Meehan, Young, & Guerrera, 2003), but it is of little other use unless it leads to a behavioral intervention plan based on the function (Scott et al., 2003).

Positive Behavior Intervention Plan

By law (the IDEA), if a disabled student's behavior is interfering with his or her educational progress, then the IEP team must write a positive *behavior intervention plan* (BIP) as part of the IEP, and the BIP must be based on an FBA of the problem (see Bateman & Linden, 1998; Yell, 1998; Yell et al., 1999). A positive BIP is one that is focused clearly on conditions that maximize the likelihood that the student will exhibit the desired, appropriate behavior rather than on eliminating behavioral problems. Behavioral problems may, in the process, be reduced or eliminated; but that desirable outcome is achieved indirectly through encouragement of desirable behavior.

Assessment as an Instructional Problem: Precorrection as a Positive BIP

Teachers often forget that the most effective strategies for teaching academic skills can be applied to teaching appropriate social-emotional behavior. Whether the instructional problem is academic or social–emotional, taking careful note of the situations or contexts in which a particular mistake is most likely to occur is the first step in resolving the problem. Having noted the likely context of a typical error, the teacher may then modify the context to make the error less likely. Other techniques for decreasing the chances that the student will make an error include helping the student rehearse (practice) the correct response, reinforcing (rewarding) correct responses, prompting (reminding or assisting) the student to give the correct response when necessary, and monitoring the student's progress. This approach—combining assessment with proactive teaching strategies—may be used to prevent much misbehavior. Therefore, Colvin, Sugai, and Patching (1993) used the term *precorrection* to describe strategies for avoiding the need to correct behavior.

An example provided by Gina Stetter, a teacher of at-risk second graders, helps clarify the concept and procedures of precorrection (Stetter, 1995). Stetter observed that her students frequently forgot necessary items (e.g., eating utensils, napkins) when going through the cafeteria serving line. Consequently, they often left the lunch table, returning to the serving line to retrieve these items. This may seem an insignificant matter to those uninitiated into teaching students who are at high risk of school failure—students Rhode, Jenson, and Reavis (1992) referred to as "tough kids." However, the experienced teacher knows that more serious problems often grow around such mundane, seemingly trivial behavior. Leaving one's place and food at the lunch table, returning to (and, likely, butting into) the serving line, and coming back to the table are events rife with possibilities for conflict (e.g., pushing, accusations, verbal confrontations, tussles that may escalate to more serious antisocial conduct). Stetter's approach to assessment focused on the question, How can I teach the desired behavior? rather than, How can I put a stop to the problem behavior? Her observations indicated that students tended to forget items in the context of preparing to leave the classroom for lunch and entering the cafeteria line; therefore, she decided to work on teaching students to remember all necessary items while going through the line so that they would not need to return. Her teaching procedures were straightforward:

- *Emphasize the expected behavior.* Remember all needed items while in the serving line.
- *Modify the context.* In the classroom before leaving for lunch, list all items needed (milk, fork, napkin, straw, etc.).
- *Conduct behavioral rehearsal.* Ask students to repeat the list of needed items.
- *Provide strong reinforcement.* Give students rewards such as small candies, points, or extra recess time for remembering everything.
- *Prompt desired behavior just before performance.* Just before entering the cafeteria, provide the reminder, "Now, be sure to remember everything you need."
- *Monitor performance.* Keep count of the number of times students return to the serving line.

Ms. Stetter's assessment of the problem and her teaching procedures related to the assessment—her precorrection plan—resulted in an immediate and dramatic drop in the number of students returning to the serving line. During the 10 school days before she implemented her precorrection plan, she observed six or seven returns daily; during the 10 days following her implementation of the plan, she observed two returns on the first day and one or zero returns thereafter. Furthermore, after she implemented her precorrection plan, she observed her students engaging in prosocial behavior, such as sharing items appropriately or reminding each other not to forget items. She described the advantages as follows:

> I spent time setting up the expectations, prompting, and following through on the reward. I did not, however, spend time "fussing" or correcting children. If they chose to go back, so be it; they would just not get a treat. I did not cajole or discourage their behavior. They made their own choices and very often made the "right" choice. It was a positive experience for both me and the children.

We discuss precorrection further in chapter 12 because it is a particularly useful strategy for managing antisocial behavior.

ADAPTATIONS FOR INCLUSION IN GENERAL EDUCATION ASSESSMENTS

During the 1990s, federal and state authorities became very concerned about the perceived general decline in student achievement, and such concern continues in the 21st century. This resulted in emphasis on "standards-based" reforms or creating standards of academic achievement measured by standardized tests. Reformers feel that teachers' expectations have been too low and that all students should be held to higher standards of performance. Because special education is an integral part of our system of public education and special educators place such heavy emphasis on participation in general education, students with disabilities are included in the quest for higher standards. The expectations are judged to be too low for students in special education; reformers conclude that students with disabilities should not only be expected to learn the general curriculum but be expected to perform at a level comparable to that of students without disabilities on assessments of progress. Moreover, reformers argue, no school or state should be allowed to avoid responsibility for demonstrating that its students with disabilities are making acceptable progress in the general education curriculum. Failure to teach students with disabilities the same things that are taught in general education has been interpreted to mean that the expectations for these students are lower, resulting in their low achievement and failure to make a successful transition to adult life (see Hallahan & Kauffman, 2003).

Actually, we have little information about how students with disabilities have been progressing compared to general norms or how education reforms might affect them (Gronna, Jenkins, & Chin-Chance, 1998; Vanderwood, McGrew, & Ysseldyke, 1998). We have evidence that more students with disabilities are participating in statewide testing and that the states are improving in their ability to document the participation and performance of students with disabilities in such assessments (Thompson & Thurlow, 2001). Many controversies have been generated by the standards-based reform movement:

- What should the standards be?
- How high should they be?
- In what areas of the curriculum should they be set?
- Who should set them?
- How should progress toward them be measured?
- What should be the consequences for students—and for schools or states—if standards are not met?

For students with disabilities, additional questions arise:

- Should all standards apply to all students, regardless of their disability?
- Should state or district standards in age-appropriate academic disciplines take precedence over remedial or vocational education or education in self-care?
- What should be the consequences of failing to meet a given standard if the student has a disability?
- Under what circumstances are alternative standards appropriate?
- Under what circumstances should special accommodations be made in assessing progress toward a standard?

Answering questions like these requires professional judgment in the individual case (see Kauffman & Hallahan, 2005b).

The law recognizes that some students with disabilities have educational needs that are not addressed in the general education curriculum. However, each student's

IEP must include a statement of measurable annual goals, including benchmarks or short-term objectives related to

1. Meeting the child's needs that result from the child's disability to enable the child to be involved in and progress in the general curriculum
2. *Meeting each of the child's other educational needs that result from the child's disability.*

Thus, the IEP team for each child with a disability must make an individualized determination regarding how the child will participate in the general curriculum, and what, if any, educational needs that will not be met through involvement in the general curriculum should be addressed in the IEP. This includes children who are educated in separate classrooms or schools.

Accommodations for evaluation procedures might involve altering the time given for responding, changing the setting in which the assessment is done, or using an alternative format for either the presentation of tasks or the type of response required. Although such accommodations may make a significant difference in how students with some disabilities are able to perform on standardized tests (Tindal, Heath, Hollenbeck, Almond, & Harniss, 1998), accommodations are often difficult to select and sometimes do not actually help students (Fuchs & Fuchs, 2001; Fuchs, Fuchs, Eaton, Hamlett, Binkley, & Crouch, 2000; Kauffman, McGee, & Brigham, in press). Consider a student with problems maintaining on-task behavior for extended periods of time. For such a student, providing extended time to complete the test may actually be detrimental. A better approach might be to break the test up into smaller sections delivered at different times. Selection of appropriate test accommodations must always be based on the characteristics of the individual student and the demands of the test (Bielinski, 2001).

EVALUATION AND SOCIAL VALIDATION

Those who are responsible for assessing students must be concerned with the scientific or technical quality of their work, as well as the social validity of the outcomes. *Social validity* means that the clients (parents, teachers, and students) who are ostensibly being helped, as well as those who intervene, are convinced that (a) a significant problem is being addressed, (b) the intervention procedures are acceptable, and (c) the outcome of intervention is satisfactory (cf. Schwartz & Baer, 1991). Social validation is the process of evaluating the clinical importance and personal, or social, meaningfulness of intervention. Social validation involves social comparison and subjective evaluation (i.e., comparison to peers who do not exhibit the disorder). It requires subjective judgments of specially trained or nonprofessional persons about the client's behavior.

To the extent that a student's behavior is markedly different from that of a valid comparison group before intervention but indistinguishable from the comparison group's behavior after intervention, social validity is established by social comparison. (This is consistent with curriculum-based methodology.) And to the extent that clients and trained observers perceive that the quality of the student's behavior is unacceptable before intervention but markedly improved or desirable after intervention, social validity is indicated by subjective evaluation. Social validation is a particularly important issue for special educators when radical reform or the merging of general and special education is proposed.

USE OF EVALUATION DATA IN WRITING INDIVIDUALIZED EDUCATION PROGRAMS

Evaluation for special education carries legal as well as professional implications. Ultimately, evaluation data must be used to arrive at legitimate decisions about the student's identification, instruction, and placement. At the center of the federal law known as IDEA is the requirement that every student who has a disability and needs special education because of the disability will have a written individualized education program describing the appropriate education the student will receive (Bateman & Linden, 1998).

There has been much misunderstanding of the process of writing and using IEPs, and we cannot provide all of the relevant information here (see Bateman & Linden, 1998; Yell, 1998, for detailed discussion of IEPs). Writing IEPs demands not only knowledge of what an IEP is but of the requirements regarding who writes the IEP and how the IEP team functions. Some of the basic questions about IEPs are answered in the following.

Notes on the IEP

What is an IEP? An IEP is a written agreement between the parents and the school about what the student needs and what will be done to address those needs. It is, in effect, a contract about services to be provided for the student. By law, an IEP must include the following:
- The student's present levels of academic performance
- Annual goals for the student, including short-term instructional objectives or benchmarks
- The special education and related services that will be provided
- The extent to which the student will participate in general state- or districtwide assessment of educational progress
- The extent to which the student will not participate in general classroom and school activities with nondisabled peers
- For students whose behavior is a problem, particularly if disciplinary action is contemplated, a positive behavior intervention plan based on a functional behavioral assessment
- For older students, specific plans for transition to work or further education

- Plans for starting the services and the anticipated duration of the services
- Appropriate plans for evaluating, at least annually, whether the objectives are being achieved

   Who writes the IEP? For the student's first IEP, the following must be involved:

- The student's general education teacher
- One or both of the student's parents or someone acting legally as the parent
- A representative of the public agency or school other than the student's teacher who is qualified to provide or supervise special education
- The student, if appropriate
- Other individuals at the discretion of the student's parent or the school
- At least one person who was a member of the team that evaluated the student or someone who is knowledgeable about the evaluation procedures used with the student
- A representative of each agency involved, if transition services are being considered

   Are teachers legally liable for reaching IEP goals? Teachers are not legally liable for reaching IEP goals. Federal law does not require that the stated goals be met. However, teachers and other school personnel are responsible for seeing that the IEP is written to include the required components, that the parents have an opportunity to review and participate in developing the IEP, that it is approved by the parents before placement, and that the services called for in it are actually provided. Teachers and other school personnel are responsible for making a good-faith effort to achieve the goals and objectives of the IEP.

   All types of evaluation procedures may yield relevant information about a student's education. Several procedures are particularly important, however, for the IEPs of students with emotional or behavioral disorders. Although not every acceptable IEP includes them, direct observation, curriculum-based evaluation, and social validation procedures offer rich sources of information that should be the basis for instructional planning. Direct observational data allow the teacher to choose specific behavioral targets for intervention and to set quantitative goals and objectives for behavioral change. Curriculum-based procedures allow the teacher to be precise about academic goals and objectives in the student's everyday curriculum. A curriculum-based approach also encourages the teacher to select or devise a social skills curriculum, an essential area of learning for students with emotional or behavioral disorders. Both direct behavioral observation and curriculum-based evaluation encourage appropriate social comparisons and provide the basis for social validation. The legal mandates for involving a multidisciplinary team in the eligibility decision and encouraging parents to participate in development of the IEP require at least a minimal level of social validation.

   IEPs differ greatly in format, level of detail, and conceptual orientation. This may be understandable, given the freedom of schools to choose their formats, the backlash against against excessive paperwork requirements leading schools to streamline IEP forms to the minimum requirements of federal regulations (Thompson, Thurlow, Esler, & Whetsone, 2001), the range of conceptual models in the field of emotional or behavioral disorders, and the differences in individual students' needs as well as their parents' wishes and demands. However, a legally correct and useful IEP must contain certain types of information:

- The student's unique characteristics or needs
- The special education, related services, or modifications that must be made to accommodate these characteristics or needs
- The beginning date and duration of the special education and related services that are to be provided
- The present levels, short-term objectives or benchmarks, and annual goals related to the special education and related services

Figure 6.2 is a segment from an actual IEP for Curt, a low-achieving ninth grader who was considered poorly motivated and a disciplinary problem with a "bad attitude." Figure 6.3 is a segment from an IEP for Aaron, a third grader who exhibited troubling behavior. The same categories of information are included in Figures 6.2 and 6.3, although the formats differ.

The full IEPs for Curt and Aaron are considerably longer than the segments shown in Figures 6.2 and 6.3 because the full IEPs include characteristics and instructional strategies for academic as well as behavioral problems. Figures 6.2 and 6.3 are not presented as excerpts from perfect IEPs but as illustrations of how behavioral problems and intervention plans can be presented in legally defensible and educationally useful ways. A variety of publications offer help in writing IEPs. However, our view is that Bateman and Linden (1998) provided the most reliable and helpful guide.

THE IEP AND PLACEMENT

The educational placement of students with disabilities, especially those with emotional or behavioral disorders, is one of the most controversial issues in special education. The issues regarding placement are complex, and we cannot explore all of them here (see Crockett & Kauffman, 1999; Dupre, 1996, 1997; Jakubecy, Mock, & Kauffman, 2003; Kauffman & Hallahan, 2005b; Kauffman & Landrum, 2005; Mock & Kauffman, 2003). However, it is critically important that administrators and teachers understand the following requirements of federal law (IDEA) and regulations:

1. Schools must provide a full continuum of alternative placements, ranging from placement in general education with needed supports to placement in residential treatment centers and hospitals. It is illegal to place all students in a single type of setting regardless of their disabilities or to refuse to provide a particular alternative (e.g., a special self-contained class) that will meet the student's needs.
2. Students must be placed in the least restrictive environment in which their appropriate education can be offered. Potential negative effects of a placement on the student and on regular classroom peers must be considered in making placement decisions.

Unique Educational Needs, Characteristics, and Present Levels of Performance (including how the disability affects the student's ability to progress in the general curriculum)	Special Education, Related Services, Supplemental Aids and Services, Assistive Technology, Program Modifications, and Support for Personnel (including frequency, duration, and location)	Measurable Annual Goals and Short-Term Objectives or Benchmarks (Including how progress toward goals will be measured) • To enable the student to participate in the general curriculum • To meet other needs resulting from the disability
Present level of social skills: Curt lashes out violently when not able to complete work, uses profanity, and refuses to follow further directions from adults. *Social needs:* • To learn anger management skills, especially regarding swearing • To learn to comply with requests	1. Teacher and/or counselor consult with behavior specialist regarding techniques and programs for teaching skills, especially anger management. 2. Provide anger management instructions to Curt. *Services 3 times/week, 30 minutes.* 3. Establish a peer group that involves role playing, etc., so Curt can see positive role models and practice newly learned anger management skills. *Services 2 times/week, 30 minutes.* 4. Develop a behavioral plan for Curt that gives him responsibility for charting his own behavior. 5. Provide a teacher or some other adult mentor to spend time with Curt (talking, game playing, physical activity, etc.). *Services 2 times/week, 30 minutes.* 6. Provide training for the mentor regarding Curt's needs and goals.	Goal: During the last quarter of the academic year, Curt will have 2 or fewer detentions for any reason. Obj. 1: At the end of the 1st quarter, Curt will have had 10 or fewer detentions. Obj. 2: At the end of the 2nd quarter, Curt will have had seven or fewer detentions. Obj. 3: At the end of the 3rd quarter, Curt will have had four or fewer detentions. Goal: Curt will manage his behavior and language in a reasonably acceptable manner as reported by faculty and peers. Obj. 1: At 2 weeks, when asked at the end of class if Curt's behavior and language were acceptable or unacceptable, 3 out of 6 teachers will say "acceptable." Obj. 2: At 6 weeks, when asked the same question, 4 out of 6 teachers will say "acceptable." Obj. 3: At 12 weeks, asked the same question, 6 out of 6 teachers will say "acceptable."

Figure 6.2
IEP for Curt

Source: Bateman, B. D., & Linden, M. A. (1998). *Better IEPs: How to develop legally correct and educationally useful programs* (3rd ed., pp. 127–129). Longmont, CO: Sopris West. Reprinted with permission.

151

Study skills/organizational needs:
How to read text
   Note taking
   How to study notes
   Memory work
   Be prepared for class, with materials
   Lengthen and improve attention span and on-task behavior

Present level:
Curt currently lacks skills in all these areas.

1. Speech/language therapist, resource room teacher, and content area teachers will provide Curt with direct and specific teaching of study skills, i.e.:
   Note taking from lectures
   Note taking while reading text
   How to study notes for a test
   Memorization hints
   Strategies for reading text to retain information
2. Assign a "study buddy" for Curt in each content area class.
3. Prepare a motivation system for Curt to be prepared for class with all necessary materials.
4. Develop a motivational plan to encourage Curt to lengthen his attention span and time on task.
5. Provide aide to monitor on-task behaviors in first month or so of plan and teach Curt self-monitoring techniques.
6. Provide motivational system and self-recording form for completion of academic tasks in each class.

Goal: At the end of academic year, Curt will have better grades and, by his own report, will have learned new study skills.

Obj. 1: Given a 20–30 min. lecture/oral lesson, Curt will take appropriate notes as judged by that teacher.

Obj. 2: Given 10–15 pgs. of text to read, Curt will employ an appropriate strategy for retaining info.–i.e., mapping, webbing, outlining, notes, etc.– as judged by the teacher.

Obj. 3: Given notes to study for a test, Curt will do so successfully, as evidenced by his test score.

Goal: Curt will improve his on-task behavior from 37 to 80%, as measured by a qualified observer at year's end.

Obj. 1: By 1 month, Curt's on-task behavior will increase to 45%.

Obj. 2: By 3 months, Curt's on-task behavior will increase to 60%.

Obj. 3: By 6 months, Curt's on-task behavior will increase to 80% and maintain or improve until end of the year.

Academic needs/written language: Curt needs strong remedial help in spelling, punctuation, capitalization, and usage.

Present level:
Curt is approximately 2 grade levels behind his peers in these skills.

1. Provide direct instruction in written language skills (punctuation, capitalization, usage, spelling) by using a highly structured, well-sequenced program. Services provided in small group of no more than four students in the resource room, 50 minutes/day.

2. Build in continuous and cumulative review to help with short-term rote memory difficulty.

3. Develop a list of commonly used words in student writing (or use one of many published lists) for Curt's spelling program.

Goal: Within one academic year, Curt will improve his written language skills by 1.5 or 2 full grade levels.

Obj. 1: Given 10 sentences of dictation at his current level of instruction, Curt will punctuate and capitalize with 80% accuracy (checked at the end of each unit taught).

Obj. 2: Given 30 sentences with choices of usage, at his current instructional level, Curt will perform with 80% accuracy.

Obj. 3: Given a list of 150 commonly used words in writing, Curt will spell with 80% accuracy.

Adaptations to regular program:
• In all classes, Curt should sit near the front of the class.
• Curt should be called on often to keep him involved and on task.
• All teachers should help Curt with study skills as trained by spelling/language specialist and resource room teacher.
• Teachers should monitor Curt's work closely in the beginning weeks/months of his program.

Figure 6.2 (Continued)

Unique Educational Needs and Characteristics (including how the disability affects the student's ability to progress in the general curriculum)	Special Education, Related Services, Supplemental Aids and Services, Assistive Technology, Program Modifications, and Support for Personnel (including frequency, duration, and location)	Present Levels of Performance (PLOP), Measurable Annual Goals, and Short-Term Objectives or Benchmarks (including how progress toward goals will be measured) • To enable student to participate in the general curriculum • To meet other needs resulting from the disability

1. Aaron talks and draws inappropriately about monsters, torture, blood, etc.	1. Behavioral intervention, including:
	  a. Behavior contract—to be implemented immediately
	  b. Social skills program—1 hour weekly for 3 months, beginning 9/20/99
	  c. In-room display of appropriate work
		PLOP: 10–20 times daily
		Obj. 1: No more than twice daily by 10/1/99
		Obj. 2: No more than once weekly by 10/15/99
		Goal: Appropriate talking and drawing

2. Aaron makes many errors in reading and doesn't seem to recognize that the errors interfere with proper comprehension.	2. Remedial reading with emphasis on accuracy of decoding and monitoring comprehension—30 minutes daily, beginning 9/15/99	PLOP: Reads 3rd-grade material at 80–100 WPM with 5–12 errors and 30% accuracy on factual questions. Obj. 1: Reduce errors to 0–2 at 50–80 WPM by 11/1/99 Obj. 2: Read 3rd-grade material at 80–100 WPM with 0–2 errors by 12/15/99 with 70% accuracy on factual questions
3. Aaron has great difficulty in attempting cursive writing.	3. Timed manuscript probes (only legible letters to be counted) self-selected contingencies—minimum of two 1-minute probes daily. Implemented immediately and continuing throughout the school year.	Goal: Grade level decoding and comprehension PLOP: 8–10 legible manuscript letters per minute Obj. 1: 15–20 per minute by 11/15/99 Obj. 2: 20–25 per minutes by 3/15/00 Goal: 35 per minute by 6/1/00

Figure 6.3
IEP for Aaron

Source: Bateman, B. D., & Linden, M. A. (1998). *Better IEPs: How to develop legally correct and educationally useful programs* (3rd ed., p. 131). Longmont, CO: Sopris West. Reprinted with permission.

3. Placement decisions must be individualized, be based on the student's IEP, and be made after appropriate education is described in the IEP. Placements must be chosen on the basis of the student's individual educational needs, not on the basis of a label or category.

SUMMARY

Significant changes have occurred in the evaluation of exceptional students: Terminology has shifted from diagnosis to assessment and evaluation, available information has increased dramatically, and legal mandates have influenced the evaluation process. Evaluation should produce helpful information for deciding eligibility for special education and planning for intervention. Youngsters seldom refer themselves for evaluation, and problems are often not what they first appear. Thus, evaluation must include the adult(s) who referred the student as well as the student's own perceptions of the problem, and the evaluator must seek all relevant information.

Evaluation for eligibility must be handled by a multidisciplinary team. Ideally, the MDT considers all relevant information and makes unbiased, reliable decisions. In practice, MDTs do not always make predictable, unbiased decisions. Although better evaluation instruments and expert systems may help to improve the reliability of eligibility decisions, improving reliability and reducing bias will also depend on individuals' commitment to higher professional standards of conduct.

Evaluation for intervention should typically include standardized tests of intelligence and achievement, behavior ratings, assessment of peer relations, interviews, self-reports, and direct behavioral observations. An emerging approach is curriculum-based evaluation, in which students' performance is measured frequently using the curriculum materials in which they are working. Curriculum-based methods can be applied to social skills as well as to the traditional academic curriculum. Whenever a student's behavior results in disciplinary actions that are likely to result in a change in placement or removal from school, teams are required to make a manifestation determination about the relation of the behavior to the student's disability and the adequacy of the IEP and the services provided through it. Functional behavioral assessment may indicate how classroom conditions and instructional procedures may be arranged to give students maximum freedom and self-control while resolving their behavioral problems. An instructional approach to assessment, known as precorrection, helps integrate assessment and teaching procedures and allows teachers to prevent many behavioral problems. A positive behavior intervention plan is consistent with the idea of precorrection. Students with disabilities must be included, with appropriate accommodations, in general assessments of educational progress that are administered state- or districtwide. Selections of effective and appropriate accommodations must be made in consideration of the characteristics of individual students and the requirements of specific tests.

Social validation is an evaluation strategy involving comparisons between behavior-disordered students and their peers as well as comparisons between the target student's behavior before and after intervention. It emphasizes obtaining objective evidence and consensus among the principal parties that (a) the problem is important, (b) the intervention is appropriate, and (c) the outcome is satisfactory.

Evaluation data should be useful in writing the IEP for a student who is placed in special education. Direct observation, curriculum-based evaluation, and social validation are procedures with special relevance for the IEPs of students with emotional or behavioral disorders. IEPs vary greatly in format and content, but all must contain certain elements: unique characteristics or needs; special education, related services, or modifications; beginning date and duration of services; and present levels, short-term objectives, and annual goals. Schools must offer a full continuum of placement options. Students must be placed in the least restrictive environment in which an appropriate education can be provided. Placement decisions must be individualized and must be made after, not before, appropriate education is described.

CASE FOR DISCUSSION

Challenging Behavior, Indeed!
Sal

Sal is brooding again. Brooding followed by agitation and a blowup seem to be his typical pattern. Today, as usual, all of us—teachers and support personnel in this special unit in a middle school—are wondering and worrying aloud whether he and we will be able to make it through the day. Everyone is cringing at the prospect of the next struggle, realizing that today will likely be another one of those days when we end up in a physical struggle. Physical struggles with seventh graders like Sal do not make you feel good, competent, or wise. They make you feel defeated and stupid. I think Sal knows that.

The rage Sal carries around seems to have no end. We are struggling to try to find its beginning. Venting his rage on his hapless victims appears to be highly reinforcing to Sal. Our first goal is to keep him from hurting someone. I often think we must seem like a commando team, positioned along the hallway ready for the inevitable punch, push, or flying chair that will mark the beginning of Sal's seething, full-blown tantrum. "Fuck you! Fuck everybody! Nobody better try to stop me! That's not a threat, that's a PROMISE!" Screaming, ripping books, overturning desks . . . we all hope that in the process of restraining Sal nobody, including Sal, gets hurt; that we'll be able to contain him more quickly than last time; and that we'll soon find some way to reduce the frequency and severity of his tantrums.

I've heard people refer euphemistically to behaviors like Sal's as "challenging." Challenging, indeed! We are challenged to find out how to change it. Whatever academic task we give Sal, whatever academic expectation we set, he seems to follow the same pattern: brooding, becoming more and more agitated, eventually engaging the teacher or other staff in a full-tilt struggle. We've tried modifying his assignments, lowering our expectations, requiring only a minimum amount of work. So far, Sal's been "winning" in that he doesn't conform to any expectations we set for doing actual school work. Maybe if we just left him alone, let him sit there in the classroom without being asked to do anything. . . . But he'd be winning then, too, wouldn't he?

Questions About the Case

1. If you were to work with Sal, what assessment strategies would you emphasize?
2. Write an IEP segment based on the information given in this case.
3. Imagine that you are interviewing Sal's parents and teachers. What questions would you ask of them that, if answered, might help you find a way of teaching him more successfully?

Evaluation for Instruction

José Luis Alvarado, Ph.D., is an assistant professor at San Diego State University. He has taught students with emotional and behavioral disorders and has worked as a behavior specialist serving a multidistrict region in southern California.

Should the assessment information that teachers use to design an intervention be different from the information used to determine the student's eligibility for special education?

In an ideal world, assessment for eligibility would be comprehensive enough to contain assessment information helpful for teachers to use in designing interventions. Unfortunately, in reality too much emphasis is placed on formal standardized assessments in meeting the federal requirement of multiple sources of data for eligibility decisions. Not enough informal assessment, such as curriculum-based measurement, is done in determining eligibility; so although the student may be found eligible based on assessment, the data aren't very helpful in designing an intervention. Data used in eligibility decisions are used to determine entitlement to services, whereas informal assessments provide the level of specificity needed to develop effective academic and behavioral interventions.

When I developed interventions for my students, I used a variety of assessments that went beyond eligibility. At times I had teachers and parents complete behavior rating scales. I conducted direct observations of the student's behavior and the ecological variables surrounding it. When appropriate, I interviewed other teachers and parents. I assessed peer relations and conducted curriculum-based assessment. If the behavior was difficult to address with traditional management techniques, then I conducted a functional analysis of the behavior.

What assessment information is most useful in writing an IEP or a positive behavior intervention plan?

I have found that in developing effective IEPs and behavior intervention plans, it is essential to have specific information about the student's current levels of academic and behavioral performance. In developing IEPs, performance information taken from both formal and informal assessments allows me to develop long-term goals as well as short-term objectives specifically addressing the student's areas of academic and behavioral need as well as incorporating the student's strengths. In developing positive BIPs, I have found it most useful to have access to current levels of performance as well as documentation of past performance and information from direct observations, interviews, and review data from others. Ultimately, the positive BIP should include (a) information from the functional assessment; (b) a description of the challenging behaviors and the positive behaviors that are to replace them; (c) goals and objectives related to the BIP; (d) a description of the behavioral interventions; (e) schedules for recording information about the behaviors and interventions, and specific criteria for discontinuing the use of the intervention for lack of effectiveness or replacing it with an identified and specified alternative; (f) criteria by which the interventions will be phased out or less intense, less restrictive interventions or techniques will be used; and (g) specific dates for periodic review by the IEP team of the efficacy of the program.

What is a functional behavioral assessment (required by IDEA), and how is it done?

When the IDEA amendments were drafted and functional behavioral assessment was added to the law, an attempt was made to strike a careful balance between a school's duty to ensure that educational environments are safe and conducive to learning for all children and the school's continuing obligation to ensure that children with disabilities receive a free appropriate public education. Functional behavioral assessment is a data-based approach that holds tremendous potential as a tool for achieving this balance. It is also a tool for addressing the behavioral needs of students with disabilities and preventing the escalation of problems.

Functional behavioral assessment, when applied to a problem such as the school failure of students with emotional or behavioral disorders, describes the ecological variables of classroom practices that may have an adverse effect on student behavior. Functional behavioral assessment includes the full range of procedures that can be used to identify the antecedents and consequences of behavior, including ecological and environmental factors. The components that make up a functional assessment are (a) systematic observation of the occurrence of the targeted behavior, providing accurate description of its frequency, duration, and intensity; (b) systematic observation of the immediate antecedent events associated with each instance of the display of the targeted behavior; (c) systematic observation and analysis of the consequences following the display of the behavior to determine the function the behavior serves for the student (i.e., the communicative intent of the behavior is identified in terms of what the individual is either requesting or protesting through the display of the behavior); (d) ecological analysis of the settings in which the behavior occurs most frequently; (e) review of records for health and medical factors that may influence behaviors; and (f) review of the history of the behavior to include the effectiveness of previously used behavioral interventions. Factors to consider in an ecological analysis should include the physical setting, social setting, nature of instruction, scheduling, quality of communication between the student and staff and other students, degree of the student's independence, participation in a variety of activities, degree of choice, and amount and quality of social interaction. Once all of the data are gathered and a BIP is implemented, the analysis phase is initiated. That is, the teacher keeps observational data documenting the effectiveness or ineffectiveness of the BIP. Through this assessment process, variables are identified and directly manipulated to verify or clarify the hypothesized relationships between ecological variables and the problem behavior.

You entered school speaking only Spanish. As someone who has experienced the process of adapting to a different culture, what do you think are the most important things teachers should be aware of in evaluating students from cultural backgrounds different from their own?

To add context to my response, I find it necessary to briefly share with you my background. It is difficult to remember the details of something that happened so long ago, yet the struggles I had and the emotions I experienced in the process of learning a new language and adapting to a different culture remain fresh in my mind. My family immigrated to the United States when I was 10 years old. It was an economic decision my parents made because they understood that we would have greater opportunities in this country. I started the fourth grade in an English-only classroom where the teacher did very little to make me feel a part of the class. She relegated all of her responsibilities to a Spanish-speaking instructional assistant who worked with me in the back of the room. At times, the instructional assistant seemed to struggle with having to translate the lesson and assignments for me. I recall few interactions with that teacher, and I was never a part of classroom activities, with the exception of art and physical education. I felt invisible in that class. I did receive English as a Second Language (ESL) pull-out services for 1 hour every day. That, to me, was the most exciting time of the day. I had opportunities to be engaged with a teacher and fellow students who spoke my language, who shared similar experiences, but, most important, showed a genuine concern for me as a person. I was not invisible while I was in Mrs. Marquez's ESL class. I felt accepted, understood. I belonged. Even though I received minimal instruction from my fourth-grade teacher, I had the advantage of having attended schools in Mexico until the third grade. Consequently, I was a fluent reader in Spanish and had mastered the math concepts that were being covered in fourth grade.

Teachers must understand that a cultural and linguistic difference does not constitute a deficiency on the student's part. Certainly, there are students who have areas of academic or behavioral needs even when language and culture are considered. Yet it is a dangerous and devastating assumption to believe that students who come from different cultures and speak languages other than English are unintelligent and do not have the innate ability to succeed. When teachers are evaluating students whose language and cultural background are different from their own, they must look beyond those differences and consider the child, first and foremost, as an individual. Teachers must be aware of the student's strengths and must make reasonable efforts to include all students in their instruction. It is not enough to have these students physically integrated in classrooms; they must also be instructionally integrated. From my own experience, I would have felt a part of my fourth-grade class if the teacher had acknowledged, or noticed, that I was able to perform the math that my English-speaking peers were learning. Instead, I sat in the back of the class and worked by myself. This process of exclusion and marginalization could lead students with greater behavioral needs to exhibit more disruptive behaviors, which will hinder their academic progress.

What do you see as the most challenging aspects of assessing students with emotional and behavioral disorders?

The most challenging aspect of assessing students with emotional and behavioral disorders is being able to conduct assessments that have minimal teacher–observer bias or subjective judgment. That is, being able to differentiate between the student's *disturbing* behavior and *disturbed* behaviors. Teachers are human; hence, we have certain "buttons" that can be pushed by particular behaviors or circumstances surrounding a particular set of behaviors. Teasing out what is disturbing to us and what behaviors truly have a debilitating effect on students' performance is key in arriving at effective and accurate assessment and identification of students with emotional and behavioral disorders. I have read student records in which an observer referred to an African American student as walking in a "disruptive manner." But was the student drawing undue attention from peers, or was this an issue concerning the teacher's tolerance for the student's way of walking? In another instance, a teacher wanted a student to be evaluated for special education because she claimed that he talked too much and was disruptive in her class. In my first observation, I discovered that the student was an English-language learner who was limited in his speaking abilities in English. To the teacher, he seemed to understand the language well enough to understand the lesson and directions. The reality was that the student had a basic handle on the conversational aspect of the language but needed to speak to other students in Spanish so that they could explain to him what the assignment or activity was. What the teacher perceived as disruptive and talkative was the student's means of trying to understand what was going on in class.

>> QUESTIONS FOR FURTHER REFLECTION

1. What information contained in IEPs is most essential for a teacher to have?
2. If you are teaching a student and he or she is having very little or no success, what should you do?
3. How would you judge that assessment for instruction for a particular student is free of cultural bias?

Part 3

Causal Factors

Introduction

Disturbing behavior is a puzzle. When we see it, we wonder why people act the way they do. We search for a conceptual model that will help us understand what has gone wrong. In part, perhaps, we want to know what or whom to blame. We believe that we will then know how to correct the problem and perhaps prevent future occurrences. In the chapters in this section, we discuss the four most frequent answers to the "why" question about emotional or behavioral disorders: biology, family, school, culture. As you read these chapters, keep the following questions in mind:

- How are causal factors interrelated?
- How is knowledge of cause related to intervention?
- What are the implications of the way we assess blame?

The fact that we discuss biological, family, school, and cultural causal factors in separate chapters does not mean that they are entirely separate issues. In fact, biological, family, school, and cultural factors are all interrelated. Seldom, if ever, does one factor alone cause an emotional or behavioral disorder. Seldom can we answer the "why" question about emotional or behavioral disorders with much confidence. Only rarely can we pinpoint a single cause. In most cases, we should think about how causal factors work together—what each factor contributes to the individual's risk or vulnerability. As we consider the factors that heighten an individual's risk for emotional or behavioral disorders, we should also be thinking about those factors that offset risk—the conditions that build a person's resilience and help to prevent disorders. We need to ask not only, What supporting role do these factors play in creating conditions under which emotional or behavioral disorders are likely to develop? but also, What events and conditions help to counteract risk factors?

Often we assume that knowing the cause of troublesome behavior will help us find a better way of dealing with it. If we believe an individual's behavior is a sign of "illness" or "disorder," we may hope that finding the cause will lead to a cure, but finding a contributing cause does not always lead us directly to an intervention because we may have no feasible way of changing the causal condition. We may know that watching lots of television programs is associated with increases in the aggressive behavior of already hyperaggressive children, but we may not have effective means of controlling these children's television watching. Furthermore, finding an effective cure or intervention does not necessarily imply that we know the cause.

We might find that medication reduces a child's hyperactivity, but we cannot necessarily conclude from that finding that this child's hyperactivity has a biochemical cause. Some medications work even though physicians do not understand how they are related to the cause of the illness. Reasoning backward from effective treatment to a cause is a common error of logic: *post hoc, ergo propter hoc* (after the fact, therefore because of it). To take an example from medicine, the observation that penicillin cures strep throat does not lead logically to the conclusion that a lack of penicillin causes strep throat. Similarly, in classroom practice, the observation that praise for a student's on-task behavior increases attention to task does not necessarily support the conclusion that lack of reinforcement for on-task behavior caused this student's inattention. In considering what we know about causal factors, you might ask yourself these questions:

- What does knowing or suspecting this cause suggest that I should do?
- Are there effective ways of dealing with this problem even if we don't know the cause?

These are important questions for teachers, and at the end of each chapter in this section, I summarize the implications for educators of what we know about causal factors. How we think about blame or responsibility for behavior is crucial in determining the interventions we choose for children and youth who are troubling to us.

The relationship between presumed cause and blame has important implications not only for our choice of intervention but for the survival of a humane society. An enduring moral precept of our society is that we do not hold people responsible for misfortunes that are beyond their control. Sick people are not usually blamed for their illness. To the extent that we assume children or youth are suffering from mental illness or social circumstances beyond their control, we do not blame them for their misconduct. In the present-day United States and in most Western cultures, we seldom blame children or youth for serious misconduct. In most cases, we shift blame to something other than the individual—to a biological disorder, parental mismanagement or abuse, dissolution of the family, peer pressure, teachers' incompetence, bad school organization, or social decadence. The extent to which we are prone to look for ways to absolve ourselves of blame for our own behavior and give others an excuse for inappropriate behavior is illustrated by the insistence of a character in a popular television situation comedy of the 1990s, *Designing Women*, that she is a helpless victim of "obnoxious personality disorder."

To what extent should we depersonalize blame and attribute misbehavior to external factors? Under what conditions should we view young people who exhibit unacceptable behavior as victims of their environments or biology rather than as responsible persons who should be held accountable for their choices? The depersonalization of blame may carry substantially different implications, depending on the nature, seriousness, and severity of social deviance and the age of the person who exhibits it. Blaming children and youth with autism or schizophrenia—assuming that they choose to behave the way they do and holding them morally responsible for their deviant behavior—hardly seems justifiable on any grounds, partly because evidence so clearly connects these disorders with biological processes. Nevertheless, children and youth who exhibit disorders in which biological factors are less obvious and personal volition is more clearly involved—conduct disorders and juvenile delinquency, for example—might be expected to share some measure of moral responsibility for their behavior. Perhaps a teenage sniper or a youth who shoots up a school cannot usually be held blameless. But what of a youth who has schizophrenia and, as part of his determination to get money for a surgical procedure that he only *imagines* he needs, robs a bank?

Questions about the attribution of cause and personal responsibility are pervasive and critical issues in the field of emotional or behavioral disorders. They are at the heart of the controversy regarding whether students with conduct disorders or "social maladjustment" should be considered to have a handicapping condition or to behave in ways that merit prosecution and punishment. The personalization of blame almost certainly accounts for the punitive approaches to dealing with most students who misbehave in school and the underidentification of students who have emotional or behavioral disorders. Yet the depersonalization of blame may also have undesirable outcomes, including disproportionate increases in social attention and benefits to youngsters who misbehave and a depreciation of individual integrity. In an era of concern for individual responsibility and self-actualization, special educators must weigh carefully the evidence that individual students are able to exercise self-control, as well as the evidence that they are victims of circumstances and have little or no personal, moral responsibility for their behavior. Perhaps blame can be assessed, but if so it must be done with careful judgment.

CHAPTER SEVEN

BIOLOGICAL FACTORS

As you read this chapter, keep these guiding questions in mind:

- Why do biological factors have such great appeal as explanations of deviant behavior?

- Under what conditions is it most likely that a person will develop schizophrenia?

- What can one conclude about the relationship between brain damage or dysfunction and emotional or behavioral disorders?

- What is temperament, and how might it affect pupil–teacher interactions?

- What are the primary implications of biological causes of emotional or behavioral disorders for educators?

APPEAL OF BIOLOGICAL FACTORS AS CAUSAL EXPLANATIONS

A biological view of emotional or behavioral disorders has particular appeal. On the one hand, psychological models of behavior cannot account for all behavioral variations in children (Pinker, 2002). On the other hand, advances in genetics, physiology, and medical technologies such as imaging and medications make the suggestion of a biological basis for all emotional or behavioral disorders seem plausible (see Weiner, 1999; Wilson, 1998).

Completion of the Human Genome Project was announced on April 14, 2003 (Collins, 2003; Collins, Green, Guttmacher, & Guyer, 2003). That is, the "mapping" of all the genes in human DNA was completed. This accomplishment may well allow preventive medicine to make great progress and even have benefits for the prediction and early treatment of certain mental disorders. It was said by its director·to have "great potential to revolutionize medicine throughout the world" (Collins, 2003, p. A19). However, enthusiasm for advances in understanding genetic codes has to be tempered with the understanding that genes alone do not determine the way people behave.

The central nervous system is undeniably involved in all behavior, and all behavior involves neurochemical activity. Furthermore, scientists long ago established that genetic factors alone are potentially sufficient to explain all variation in human behavior (Eiduson, Eiduson, & Geller, 1962; see also Weiner, 1999). It may seem reasonable to believe, therefore, that disordered emotion or behavior always implies a genetic accident, bacterial or viral disease, brain injury, brain dysfunction, allergy, or some other biochemical imbalance (Linnoila, 1997). And we can find cases in which serious antisocial behavior is attributable to such neurological problems as brain tumors (e.g., Burns & Swerdlow, 2003), or biological factors provide a predisposition to develop antisocial behavior (Dodge & Pettit, 2003).

Attractive as biological explanations may appear on the surface, however, the assumption that disorders are simply a result of biological misfortune is misleading, as is the suggestion that disorders are simply a result of social or cultural conditioning. Although biological processes have a pervasive influence on behavior, they affect behavior only in interaction with environmental factors (see Jensen et al., 2001; Leve, Winebarger, Fagot, Reid, & Goldsmith, 1998; Pinker, 2002; Plomin, 1995; Rutter, 1995). In the case of genetics, Plomin (1995) noted, "Twenty years ago, the message from behavioural genetics research was that genetic factors play a major role in behavioural/dimensions and disorders. The message today is that these same data provide strong evidence for the importance of environmental factors as well as genetic factors" (p. 34). Research in cloning in the 21st century underscores Plomin's observation. An identical genetic code does not result in identical behavior, simply because environment also shapes behavior (see Pinker, 2002).

Knowing that a disorder has a biological cause does not always lead to a prescription for treatment. This does not mean that biologically based disorders are untreatable; it means that scientists may not be able to devise a biological treatment designed to reverse the cause but may only be able to treat its effects, the symptoms of the biological process. Furthermore, because biological and environmental processes are interactive, sometimes the best treatment for a biological disorder is an alteration of the environment—arrangement of the social environment to ameliorate the effects of the biologically based disorder. For example, Tourette's disorder, a neurological disorder with symptoms including tics and often accompanied by obsessions, compulsions, hyperactivity, distractibility, and impulsivity, may be treated with a combination of medication and cognitive-behavioral approaches involving changes in the social environment. The social environment may have significant effects on the symptoms of Tourette's disorder, although the basic cause of the disorder is neurological. Medication may be the single most effective treatment alternative for most children with attention deficit–hyperactivity disorder (ADHD), but for many, especially those showing defiant and disruptive behavior in addition to ADHD, the combination of medication and psychosocial intervention (behavior therapy) is better (Jensen et al., 2001).

The biological processes involved in behavioral deviance are extremely complex, and new discoveries are being made rapidly. Moreover, nearly every type of biological factor has been suggested as a possible cause of nearly every type of psychopathology (see Klorman, 1995; Werry, 1986a). We may conclude that the effects of biological factors on behavioral development are considerable but frequently neither demonstrable nor simple. And although biological factors influence behavior, environmental conditions modify biological processes. Knowledge of biological causes may carry significant implications for prevention or medical treatment, but such knowledge usually has few direct implications for the work of educators. Educators work almost exclusively with environmental influences, relying on biological scientists and medical personnel to diagnose and treat the physiological aspects of emotional or behavioral disorders. Thus, educators should have basic information about biological factors but focus primarily on how the environmental conditions they may be able to control might affect students' behavior.

With these points in mind, we discuss several biological factors that may contribute to the development of disordered emotions or behavior: genetics, brain injury or dysfunction, malnutrition and allergies, and temperament. We cannot discuss the role of every possible biological factor in every type of disorder. Clearly, such things as substance abuse of the mother during pregnancy *can* contribute to emotional or behavioral problems in children. However, our discussion is brief and focused on representative examples of known or presumed biological causes and disorders in which such factors may play a role.

GENETICS

Children inherit more than physical characteristics from their parents; they also inherit predispositions to certain behavioral characteristics. Not surprisingly, genes have been suggested as causal factors in every kind of emotional or behavioral difficulty, including criminality, attention deficits, hyperactivity, schizophrenia, depression, Tourette's disorder, autism, and anxiety (see Asarnow & Asarnow, 2003; Levy & Hay,

2001). Research indicates that, indeed, genes have a strong influence on the development of all types of behavior, both desirable and undesirable (see Leve et al., 1998; McGuffin & Thapar, 1997; Pinker, 2002; Weiner, 1999). In fact, the evidence that there are significant genetic influences on behavior is now so overwhelming that "genetic studies are moving away from establishing the *fact* of heritability and toward explaining the *how* of heritability" (Carey & Goldman, 1997, p. 250, emphasis in original).

Genes linked to some specific diseases or vulnerabilities have been identified, but gene therapy, in which genes are manipulated, has been oversold by some scientists and the news media. However, genetically determined differences in children's behavior are observed by scientists not only in their research but also in their everyday lives. Compare the following quotation from the eminent biologist Seymour Benzer, who saw dramatic differences in the behavior of his two daughters, Barbie and Martha, to the personal reflections of Dixie Jordan at the end of chapter 8:

> When you have one child, it behaves like a child," Benzer told a lecture audience not long ago, accepting the Crafoord Prize in Stockholm for his work on genes and behavior. "But as soon as you have a second child you realize from Day One that this one is different from the other." (Weiner, 1999, p. 65)

In the early 21st century, we are learning that cloned animals (and, by extension, humans) do not necessarily have the same behavior as their genetic match. The same is true for identical twins (naturally occurring clones). Scientists have very good reason to understand that behavioral characteristics are not determined solely by genes. Environmental factors, particularly social learning, play an important role in modifying inherited emotional or behavioral predispositions.

Furthermore, at the level of specific behaviors, social learning is nearly always far more important than genetics. Little or no evidence supports the suggestion that specific behaviors are genetically transmitted; however, some type of genetic influence obviously contributes to the major psychiatric disorders of children and adolescents and to many other disorders as well. What is inherited is a predisposition to behave in certain ways, a tendency toward certain types of behavior that may be made stronger or weaker by environmental conditions. The predisposition is created by a very complex process involving multiple genes. Seldom do emotional or behavioral disorders involve a single gene or an identifiable chromosomal anomaly. Moreover, comorbidity—multiple disorders involving complex gene interactions—is common (Hay & Levy, 2001).

Genetic factors are suspected in a wide variety of disorders. However, a disorder in which genetic transmission is particularly well recognized is schizophrenia. The onset of schizophrenia occurs only rarely in young children, but onset in middle and late adolescence is not uncommon (Asarnow & Asarnow, 2003; Remschmidt, Schulz, Martin, Warnke, & Trott, 1994). In most cases, the first symptoms of schizophrenia are observed in people ranging from 15 to 45 years of age. The features of schizophrenia are similar in children and adults, although onset in childhood may be associated with a severe form of the disorder (Alaghband-Rad et al., 1995; Russell, 1994; Spencer & Campbell, 1994). The major characteristics are delusions, hallucinations, disorganized speech, and thought disorders (see chapter 17 and the case of Chad in the accompanying case book for further discussion).

The exact genetic mechanisms responsible for a predisposition to schizophrenia are still unknown, but research decades old clearly shows an increase in risk for schizophrenia and schizophreniclike behavior (often called *schizoid* or *schizophrenic spectrum behavior*) in the relatives of schizophrenics. More recent research has not overturned the basic findings of a genetic link. The closer the genetic relationship between the child and a schizophrenic relative, the higher the risk that the child will develop the condition. Heightened risk cannot be attributed to the social environment or interpersonal factors alone. Figure 7.1 shows the long-known increased level of risk that goes with increasingly close genetic relatedness to a person who has schizophrenia. Having an identical twin who has schizophrenia increases an individual's risk of developing schizophrenia by a factor of 46; having a sibling with schizophrenia carries 10 times the risk of the general population (see also Pinker, 2002).

Many people misunderstand the implications of increased risk for schizophrenia or other disorders. Does a heightened genetic risk for schizophrenia mean a person will necessarily develop the disorder? Do the genetic factors in schizophrenia mean that prevention is impossible? The answer to both questions is no. "Not all people with the genetic potential to become schizophrenic will actually develop the clinical disorder" (Nicol & Erlenmeyer-Kimling, 1986, p. 33). Plomin (1995) pointed out that although genetic relatedness increases risk for schizophrenia dramatically, the chance

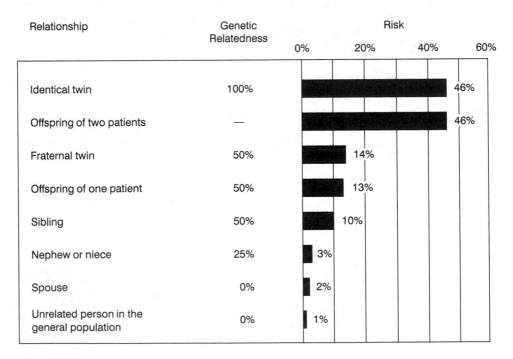

Figure 7.1
Lifetime risk of developing schizophrenia
Source: Nicol, S. E. & Gottesman, I. (1983). Clues to the genetics and neurobiology of schizophrenia. *American Scientist, 71,* 399. Used with permission.

that someone will develop schizophrenia is less than 50% even for those at highest genetic risk—those having an identical twin or both parents with schizophrenia (see also Pinker, 2002). Furthermore, risk factors can be lowered by altering the social environment and avoiding circumstances that might trigger the disorder.

The causes of schizophrenia are likely multiple and complex, with genetic factors being only one predisposing factor. However, schizoid behavior or full-blown schizophrenia can apparently be triggered by a bad drug trip as well as environmental stressors. Those at highest risk for schizophrenia (i.e., those with close blood relatives with the disorder) would be well advised to avoid experimenting with drugs (Gottesman, 1987, 1991).

Implications of Genetic Factors

A common misperception is that disorders arising from genetic accidents are not treatable—that once the genetic code is set, the related deviant behavior is immutable. But this is not necessarily the case (Gottesman, 1991; Hay & Levy, 2001; Plomin, 1995; Wilson, 1998). As with schizophrenia, environmental as well as biological factors are involved in the causation of deviant behavior. When the biochemical mechanisms underlying genetic transmission are discovered, there is hope that effective interventions will be found to prevent or alter the course of behavioral development.

Genetic factors are known to contribute to a variety of emotional and behavioral disorders, perhaps even to most (see Pinker, 2002; Weiner, 1999; Wilson, 1998). In some severe disorders, such as schizophrenia, the level of the genetic contribution is clear, but how the gene system works remains obscure. For most types of emotional or behavioral disorders, the genetic contributions remain unclear and environmental factors appear to be far more important for educators (see Leve et al., 1998).

Evolutionary biology strongly suggests that many behaviors are influenced by genetic makeup and the mixing of genes from unrelated individuals. Genetic mixing ordinarily helps species perpetuate their kind. However, genetic mutations—random changes or errors in genes—also occur (Judson, 2002). Sometimes these are destructive and do not help a species survive. We do not really know which emotional or behavioral disorders are mutations and which, if any, help to perpetuate *Homo sapiens*.

BRAIN DAMAGE OR DYSFUNCTION

The brain can be traumatized in several different ways before, during, or after birth, and such damage may contribute substantially to antisocial behavior (Dell Orto & Power, 2000). Physical insult during an accident or during the birth process may destroy brain tissue. Prolonged high fever, infectious disease, and toxic chemicals (such as drugs or poisons taken by the child or by a woman during pregnancy) may also damage the brain. A frequently suspected or known cause of brain damage in children, however, is *hypoxia* (also known as *anoxia*), a seriously reduced supply of oxygen. Hypoxia often occurs during birth but can also occur during accidents or as a result of disease or respiratory disorders later in life.

The brain may function improperly for a variety of reasons. Tissue damage from traumatic injury may cause dysfunction. In the case of traumatic brain injury (TBI), we know that the brain's function has been impaired by documented damage at a specific location or locations. However, the brain may not function properly because of structural anomalies (i.e., malformation of certain parts of the brain) that are present at birth or are part of a disease process or because of a neurochemical imbalance resulting from a disease or drugs. In some cases, scientists do not know exactly why the brain is not working as it should, although it obviously is not. For example, autism (or autistic spectrum disorder) has been clearly established as a brain disorder, but we do not yet know exactly what is wrong with the brain of a person who has autism (Klinger, Dawson, & Renner, 2003; National Research Council, 2001).

A very wide range of emotional or behavioral disorders has been attributed to known or suspected brain damage or dysfunction (Light, McCleary, Asarnow, Zaucha, & Lewis, 1998). Learning disabilities and the related problems of hyperactivity, impulsivity, and inattention have historically been assumed to be caused by brain injury or dysfunction, although the exact nature of the injury or dysfunction has not been demonstrated (Hallahan, Lloyd, Kauffman, Weiss, & Martinez, 2005). Subtle brain injury before, during, or shortly after birth is an important contributing cause of serious juvenile delinquency and adult criminality, according to some researchers (B. Bower, 1995). Nearly every sort of serious emotional or behavioral problem could be hypothesized to be, at some level, a matter of structural or chemical problems of the brain. For purposes of illustration, however, we focus on two disability categories that were made separate special education categories under federal law in 1990: traumatic brain injury and autism or autistic spectrum disorder.

Traumatic Brain Injury

Synonymous terms for the same general type of neurological damage include *traumatic head injury, cerebral trauma,* or *craniocerebral trauma.* However, *traumatic brain injury* is the term used in federal laws related to special education. TBI is not a new type of disability, but it was made a separate category for special education because it is an increasingly frequent cause of neurological impairment in children and youth (Hallahan & Kauffman, 2003). Furthermore, it presents unique educational problems that have been poorly understood and often mismanaged, and recent medical advances have greatly improved its diagnosis and treatment.

TBI does not include all types of brain damage. The term means the following:

- There is injury to the brain caused by an external force.
- The injury is not caused by a degenerative or congenital condition.
- There is a diminished or altered state of consciousness.
- Neurological or neurobehavioral dysfunction results from the injury (Begali, 1992; Dell Orto & Power, 2000; Snow & Hooper, 1994; Tyler & Mira, 1999).

TBI may involve open head injuries from causes such as a fall, a gunshot, an assault, a vehicular accident, or surgery; there is a penetrating head wound. TBI may also involve closed head injuries, which may be caused by a variety of events, including a fall, an accident, or abuse such as violent shaking; there is no open head wound, but the brain is damaged by internal compression, stretching, or other shearing motion of neural tissues within the head.

The educational definition of TBI focuses on impairments in one or more areas important for learning, such as cognition, language, speech, memory, information processing, attention, reasoning, abstract thinking, judgment, problem solving, perceptual abilities, psychosocial behavior, or physical abilities (Tyler & Colson, 1994; Tyler & Mira, 1999). The various *sequelae* (consequences) of TBI create a need for special education; the injury itself is a medical problem.

The effects of TBI depend on a variety of factors, including the part(s) of the brain damaged; the severity of the damage; the age of the individual when the damage occurs; and the medical, psychological, and educational treatment the student receives. The effects may range from very mild to profound and be temporary or permanent. Sometimes all of the effects are immediately apparent, but some effects may not be seen at all immediately after the injury; some may appear months or even years afterward. About half of the children and youth who experience serious TBI will require special education, and those who return to regular classes will require modifications if they are to be successful (Allison, 1992; Tyler & Mira, 1999).

The effects of TBI may be misattributed to other causes if the brain injury is not diagnosed and understood. In many cases, violence and other disturbing behavior cannot be connected to brain damage, and it is important not to attribute such behavior to brain damage in the absence of medical evidence of damage. However, we also know that TBI can cause violent aggression, hyperactivity, impulsivity, inattention, and a wide range of other emotional or behavioral problems, depending on just what parts of the brain are damaged. The possible effects of TBI include a long list of other psychosocial problems, some of which we list here (see Deaton & Waaland, 1994; Dell Orto & Power, 2000; Light et al., 1998):

- Inappropriate manners or mannerisms
- Failure to understand humor or read social situations
- Becoming easily tired, frustrated, or angered
- Unreasonable fear or anxiety
- Irritability
- Sudden, exaggerated swings of mood
- Depression
- Perseveration (getting stuck on one thought or behavior)

The emotional and behavioral effects of TBI are determined by more than the physical damage. These effects also depend on the student's age at the time of injury and the social environment before and after the injury occurs. Home, community, or school environments that foster misbehavior of any child or youth—disorganization, lack of adult supervision, dangerous circumstances, lack of safety precautions, for example— are known to be associated with higher risk for acquiring TBI. Such environments are extremely likely to make any emotional or behavioral problem resulting from TBI worse.

Creating an environment that is conducive to and supportive of appropriate behavior is one of the great challenges of dealing effectively with the sequelae of brain injury

(Bergland & Hoffbauer, 1996; Suzman, Morris, Morris, & Milan, 1997). Medical treatment usually cannot undo the effects of TBI. Emotional or behavioral problems may be known to have resulted from brain injury, but these problems must be addressed primarily through environmental modifications—changing other people's demands, expectations, and responses to behavior.

TBI often shatters an individual's sense of self. Recovering one's identity may require a long period of rehabilitation and may be a painstaking process requiring multidisciplinary efforts (see Crimmins, 2000). Effective education and treatment often require not only classroom behavior management but family therapy, medication, cognitive training, and communication training.

AUTISTIC SPECTRUM DISORDER

Autism is a rare, severe developmental disorder first described by Kanner (1943). It was initially known as Kanner's syndrome or *early infantile autism*. Kanner described the parents of children with autism as being emotionally cold. His observations were seized on by psychoanalytic theorists, and for decades autism was attributed primarily to the psychopathology of parents (e.g., Bettelheim, 1967). The psychoanalytic view of the cause of autism has been thoroughly discredited, and we now recognize that autism is a disorder caused by brain dysfunction.

The nature of the damage or biochemical irregularity is still a mystery, and environmental conditions can make an enormous difference in the behavior of an individual with autism. Moreover, the term now in vogue, *autistic spectrum disorder,* now covers a wide range of related disabilities. As described by the National Research Council (2001):

> Autism is best characterized as a spectrum of disorders that vary in severity of symptoms, age of onset, and associations with other disorders (e.g., mental retardation, specific language delay, epilepsy). The manifestations of autism vary considerably across children and within an individual child over time. There is no single behavior that is always typical of autism and no behavior that would automatically exclude an individual child from a diagnosis of autism, even though there are strong and consistent commonalities, especially in social deficits. (p. 9)

The spectrum of autistic disorders includes the following:

- *Asperger syndrome* or *Asperger's disorder* (AS)—probably a mild form of autism, but usually without significant delays in cognition and language
- *Rett's disorder*—normal development for 5 months to 4 years, then regression and mental retardation (but may include some behaviors characteristic of autism)
- *Childhood disintegrative disorder*—normal development for at least 2 and up to 10 years, followed by significant loss of skills (also may include behaviors characteristic of autism)
- *Pervasive developmental disorder—not otherwise specified (PDD–NOS)*—pervasive delay in development that does not fit into any of the other diagnostic categories (see American Psychiatric Association, 1994, 2000; National Research Council, 2001).

Autism is rare, as are all the other developmental disabilities listed as part of the spectrum, but both autism and Asperger's disorder are now diagnosed more frequently than in previous decades (National Research Council, 2001; see also Gross, 2003; Sheehan, 2003). Probably the increase in diagnosis is in part because of increased awareness of such disorders. For the sake of simplicity, we consider only autism more specifically, as the biological factors causing it are probably shared to a large degree with other disorders in the autistic spectrum.

The major features of autism are qualitative impairment in social interaction, communication, and symbolic play (see Klinger et al., 2003; we discuss autism and other severe disorders more fully in chapter 17). Children with autism may, for example, avoid eye-to-eye gaze, fail to develop social or emotional reciprocity with their parents or peers, lack spoken language or adopt stereotyped language patterns, be preoccupied with objects or rituals, or adopt stereotyped postures or movement patterns. The onset of the disorder is before the age of 3. In short, from a very early age, children with autism fail to develop normal social behavior and communication. Distinguishing between autism and mental retardation or other severe developmental disorders is often difficult. The behavior of children with autism is usually extremely debilitating, and many of these children are severely disabled throughout their lives.

Speculation about the biological causes of autism has included many hypotheses regarding anomalies of various brain structures and functions and biochemistry. At the turn of the millennium, there was speculation that the increasing prevalence of autism may be related to vaccinations. Some studies using electroencephalography (EEG, a measure of the electrical activity of the brain, or brain waves) have reported differences between normally developing children and those with autism. However, newer techniques of studying the brain, such as magnetic resonance imaging (MRI), may yield more definitive findings. As yet, no definitive findings point to a particular brain problem, although the neurological base of the disorder is no longer in doubt (see Klinger et al., 2003; National Research Council, 2001).

Brain damage or dysfunction can produce a wide variety of emotional and behavioral disorders. Brain damage or dysfunction is not the only cause of such disorders, however, and it is important to remember that environmental factors can make a significant difference in the effects of brain injury on behavior.

MALNUTRITION, ALLERGIES, AND OTHER HEALTH-RELATED ISSUES

We have known for decades that severe malnutrition can have catastrophic effects on children's cognitive and physical development. Malnutrition is especially devastating to the development of very young children (Brennan & Mednick, 1997; Brown & Pollitt, 1996; Tanner & Finn-Stevenson, 2002). It reduces the child's responsiveness to stimulation and produces apathy. The eventual result of serious malnutrition (especially severe protein deficiency) is retardation in brain growth, irreversible brain damage, mental retardation, or some combination of these effects. Apathy, social withdrawal, and school failure are expected long-term outcomes if children are severely malnourished. Furthermore, it is well recognized that hunger and inadequate nutrition interfere with the ability to concentrate on academic and social learning. Thus, the concern for children's adequate nutrition in poor families is well justified (Tanner & Finn-Stevenson, 2002).

The belief that less severe nutritional inadequacies (such as not enough vitamins or minerals) or excesses (such as too much sugar or caffeine) cause children to misbehave has been popular for many years (see Pescara-Kovach & Alexander, 1994; Wolraich, Wilson, & White, 1995). Disorders ranging from hyperactivity to depression to autism to delinquency have been attributed by some to what youngsters eat or do not eat. Hypoglycemia (low blood sugar), vitamin or mineral deficiencies, and allergies can influence behavior; and teachers should be aware of these potential problems (McLoughlin & Nall, 1994). However, the role of specific foods and allergies in causing cognitive, emotional, or behavioral problems has often been exaggerated.

Although we know that some children are allergic to certain foods and a variety of other substances (e.g., medications, pollens, dust, insect stings), there is little evidence that these allergies are often causes of emotional or behavioral problems. However, teachers, like parents, often prefer the belief that diet is a major factor in causing misbehavior (McLoughlin & Nall, 1994, p. 206).

Nutrition and allergies can affect behavior, but there is little evidence that they play a major role in causing emotional or behavioral disorders except in extreme cases. Biases and expectations appear to maintain the superstition that foods and allergies often cause behavioral or emotional problems. Adequate nutrition is crucial; excluding or severely restricting certain food substances seldom is.

A wide variety of other health-related disorders are found in the child population, including obesity, sleep disorders, injuries, and diseases (Peterson, Reach, & Grabe, 2003). In some cases, these involve emotional or behavioral disorders as well as health problems. However, it is important not to assume that all health-related problems are created by emotional or behavioral disorders.

TEMPERAMENT

Beginning in the 1960s, researchers began to explore the centuries-old notion of *temperament*. The definition and measurement of temperament and the stability or continuity of temperament across time are matters of considerable controversy (Bates & Wachs, 1994; Garrison & Earls, 1987; Kagan, Gibbons, Johnson, Reznick, & Snidman, 1990; Keogh, 2003; Teglasi, 1998). Temperament has been variously defined as "behavioral style," or the "how" rather than the "what" and "how well" of behavior; as the "active and reactive qualities" of infant behavior; and as "measurable behavior" during infancy. It has been measured by questionnaires given to parents or teachers and by direct observation of children's behavior. In spite of differences in the ways in which researchers define and measure it, we can describe the concept of temperament in general terms: Individuals tend to have consistent, predictable reactions to certain types of circumstances or events, and their typical way of responding—their temperament—is partly determined by basic biological processes as well as environmental factors (see Carey, 1998; Keogh, 2003).

The point is that infants begin life with an inborn tendency to behave in certain ways. The newborn has a behavioral style that is determined predominantly by biological factors, and how a baby behaves at birth and in the first weeks and months thereafter will influence how others respond. But temperament can be changed by the environment in which the child develops; what the child experiences and how the child is managed may change temperament for better or worse (Bates & Wachs, 1994; Carey, 1998; Chess & Thomas, 2003; Keogh, 2003). A difficult temperament may increase the child's risk for emotional or behavioral disorders. However, temperament is an initial behavioral style that may change in interaction with environmental influences. Based on their now classic longitudinal study, Thomas, Chess, & Birch, (1968) described nine categories of temperamental characteristics (see also Garrison & Earls, 1987; Keogh, 2003):

1. *Activity level:* how much the child moves about during activities such as feeding, bathing, sleeping, and playing
2. *Rhythmicity:* the regularity or predictability with which the child eats, sleeps, eliminates, and so on
3. *Approach or withdrawal:* how the child responds initially to new events such as people, places, toys, and foods
4. *Adaptability:* how quickly the child becomes accustomed to or modifies an initial reaction to new situations or stimuli
5. *Intensity of reaction:* the amount of energy expended in reacting (positively or negatively) to situations or stimuli
6. *Threshold of responsiveness:* the amount or intensity of stimulation required to elicit a response from the child
7. *Quality of mood:* the amount of pleasant, joyful, and friendly behavior compared with unpleasant, crying, and unfriendly behavior exhibited by the child
8. *Distractibility:* the frequency with which extraneous or irrelevant stimuli interfere with the ongoing behavior of the child in a given situation
9. *Attention span and persistence:* the length of time a child will spend on a given activity and the tendency to maintain an activity in the face of obstacles to performance.

Thomas et al. (1968) found that children with any kind of temperament might develop emotional or behavioral disorders, depending on the child-rearing practices of their parents and other adults. Besides the characteristics listed, other more inclusive or general temperaments have been described. As Keogh (2003) pointed out, some children may be described as "easy". An easy temperament is characterized by regularity, adaptability, positive response to new stimuli, mild or moderate intensity of response, positive mood. Children with "difficult" temperaments are more likely to develop troublesome behavior. A difficult temperament is characterized by irregularity in biological functioning, mostly negative (withdrawing) responses to new stimuli, slow adaptation to changes in the environment, frequent displays of negative mood, and mostly intense reactions. Some children can be described as "slow-to-warm-up" in temperament. Other temperament types include "undercontrolled," "inhibited," "confident," "sluggish," and "well adjusted."

Keogh (2003) pointed out that the "difficulty" of a child depends on the social context in which the child is behaving—the particular situation or circumstances and the cultural expectations. The key point is that what is perceived as a "difficult" temperament may elicit negative responses from a child's caretakers: A baby with a difficult temperament is not easy to care for and may increase parents' irritability, negative mood, and tendency to ignore or punish the child. If infant and parents adopt a pattern of mutual irritation, their negative interactions may increase the probability that the youngster will exhibit inappropriate or undesirable behavior in future years. Longitudinal research by other investigators has also shown that difficult temperament at an early age is predictive of behavioral problems in adolescence (Caspi, Henry, McGee, Moffitt, & Silva, 1995). Moreover, an easy or positive temperament has been found to be associated with children's resilience in responding to stress (Keogh, 2003; Smith & Prior, 1995).

The concept of difficult temperament has its critics (see Garrison & Earls, 1987). Some suggest that what researchers believe are inborn biological characteristics of infants are merely the subjective interpretations of mothers' reports. That is, "difficult temperament" reflects social perceptions of an infant's behavior and may not be within-the-individual characteristics. A baby is said to have a difficult temperament on the basis of the mother's report rather than more objective evaluations; therefore, the mother's perceptions (and the researcher's) are being assessed rather than a biological characteristic of the baby. Thomas, Chess, and Korn (1982), Keogh (2003), and others, however, interpret their research as confirming the reality of inborn behavioral characteristics or temperaments that are altered by environmental conditions (see Rutter, 1995). Carey and McDevitt (1995) noted the consensus regarding the interaction of environmental and inborn factors in shaping children's behavior:

1. Environmental effects such as family dysfunction, neighborhood violence, poor schools, and other unfortunate conditions are responsible for a substantial proportion of children's behavioral disorders.
2. Intrinsic factors explain some disorders formerly thought to be caused by the social environment. We now understand, for example, that autism and learning disabilities and perhaps other problems such as obesity are caused primarily by biological processes. These disorders are likely to exist under a wide range of environmental conditions.
3. A poor fit between a child's normal temperament and the values and expectations of the child's caregivers can cause stress leading to emotional or behavioral disorder.

Both environmental and intrinsic, biological factors contribute to emotional or behavioral disorders. Environmental and intrinsic factors combine to shape temperament. Moreover, a mismatch of social environment and the child's behavioral style can exacerbate a difficult temperament. A difficult temperament may increase a child's risk of exhibiting an emotional or behavioral disorder, but the risk may be either heightened further or lowered by the way in which parents and teachers manage the child's behavior (Henderson & Fox, 1998; Keogh, 2003; Kochanska, 1995).

A few researchers have investigated teachers' ratings of children's temperaments in the classroom (see Keogh, 2003, for a review). Their general findings are that children do exhibit a consistent behavioral style or temperament in the classroom and that teachers tend to take children's temperaments into account in planning, instruction, and management. Moreover, teachers have a temperament, which may be a good or bad fit with the child's temperament.

Temperament may play a significant role in the development of emotional or behavioral disorders, but it does so only in interaction with environmental conditions. A consistent behavioral disposition or temperament such as irritability or impulsivity may heighten risk for emotional or behavioral disorders. Research does not indicate that temperament is the direct or exclusive result of biological factors, but it does suggest that students exhibit a consistent behavioral style that teachers recognize and should consider in instruction and accommodation of behavioral diversity among students (Henderson & Fox, 1998; Keogh, 2003; Martin, 1992).

IMPLICATIONS FOR EDUCATORS

The biological factors that may have a significant negative effect on behavior are many and complex. It is important for educators to understand how genetics, parental neglect or abuse, malnutrition, and neurological damage may be linked to school failure and impulsive or antisocial behavior. Biological and social risk factors together offer the best explanations of the causes of antisocial behavior, and the same applies to other forms of emotional and behavioral disorders. Genetic predisposition, neglect, abuse, malnutrition, and brain injury all are more likely to be significant contributors to maladaptive behavior when they are accompanied by inconsistent or ill-suited behavior management at home and school.

However, it is erroneous to assume that all emotional or behavioral disorders have a biological origin and that therefore all such disorders are best handled by medical intervention. Not only is the tie between many of these disorders and specific biological causative factors tenuous, but a biological cause may have no direct implications for change in educational methodology. Educators should work with other professionals to obtain the best possible medical care, nutrition, and physical environment for their students. However, educators cannot provide medical intervention, and they have only very limited influence over their students' physical health. Although teachers should be aware of possible biological factors and refer students for evaluation by other professionals when appropriate, they must not allow speculation regarding biological etiologies to excuse them from teaching appropriate behavior when they can—the academic and social skills that will enable students to be happy and successful in everyday environments.

Pharmacological treatment of many emotional and behavioral disorders is becoming more common, systematic, and effective (Forness, Kavale, Sweeney, & Crenshaw, 1999; Hallfors, Fallon, & Watson, 1998; Konopasek & Forness, 2004; Kutcher, 2002; Pomeroy & Gadow, 1998; Sweeney, Forness, Kavale, & Levitt, 1997). Medications can be extremely helpful in controlling some emotional or behavioral disorders. Unfortunately, there appears to be a strong antimedication bias among many educators. Part of this bias may be because of teachers' lack of awareness of the purposes and possible benefits of medications and to their failure to understand that careful monitoring of classroom behavior is necessary to determine whether the drug is working, should be discontinued, or needs a dosage adjustment to obtain maximum benefits with minimum side effects.

Although the teacher is not able to prescribe medications or adjust dosages, the teacher's observations provide critical information for the physician. Teachers should be aware of the major types of drugs that may be prescribed for their students and the possible effects and side effects those drugs may have on classroom behavior and performance. Table 7.1 provides examples of four major types of medication and some of their possible effects. The generic (chemical) name is shown in parentheses under the brand or trade name for each example listed.

Table 7.1 provides only a limited amount of information. Teachers should seek additional facts relevant to particular cases. There are many other categories and

Table 7.1
Four Types of Psychotropic Medication and Some Possible Classroom Effects

Class of Drugs	Examples	Possible Classroom Effects
Stimulants[a]	Ritalin (methylphenidate) Adderall (mixed amphetamine salts) Dexedrine (dextroamphetamine)	Increased attention and decreased need for teacher control; effects usually evident within the first hour after ingestion; effects may last for up to 10 hours with time-release capsules; possible side effects include headaches, stomach aches, or increased irritability; too high of a dosage can decrease learning.
Antipsychotics (neuroleptics or major tranquilizers)	Haldol (haloperidol) Risperdal (risperidone) Zyprexa (olanzapine) Seroquel (quetiapine)	Effects usually gradual; decreased aggression or agitation and decreased hallucination within days; increased socialization within 3 to 4 weeks; decreased thought disorder within 2 months; side effects may include tremors, drowsiness, decreased attention.
Antidepressants	Prozac (fluoxetine) Zoloft (sertraline) Celexa (citalopram) Wellbutrin (buproprion) Effexor (venlafaxine)	Classroom effects not yet extensively studied; improved sad affect; may increase communication and attention to tasks, decrease disruptiveness; effects may not be seen for 2 to 3 weeks; side effects vary widely with drug.
Mood stabilizers	Lithium Depakote (divalproex) Neurontin (gabapentin) Topamax (topirimate)	Decreased mood lability and extremes of anger; side effects vary with drug; all but lithium are also used as anticonvulsants.

[a]Nonstimulant medications that are also used to treat attention deficit–hyperactivity disorder include Strattera (atomoxetine), Catapress (clonidine), and Tenex (guanfacine).
Source: I am grateful to Richard Mattison, M.D. for the information in this table.

subcategories of psychotropic drugs, new drugs are constantly being introduced, and the effects and side effects of a given drug may vary greatly depending on the dosage level and the individual. The teacher should consult a nurse, a physician, or professional publications for more detailed information about specific drugs and dosages (e.g., Forness et al., 1999; Konopasek, 1996; Konopasek & Forness, 2004; Sweeney et al., 1997). A student's parents or physician should inform the teacher that the student is taking a particular medication and ask the teacher to monitor its effects on the student's classroom behavior and academic performance. If the teacher is not so informed and is not asked to participate in evaluating the drug's classroom effects but becomes aware that the student is taking a psychotropic medication, he or she should approach the parents or the school nurse about monitoring the way in which the student is responding to the drug.

SUMMARY

Biological factors have special appeal because all behavior involves biochemical, neurological activity. Among the many biological factors that may contribute to the origins of emotional or behavioral disorders are genetics, brain damage or dysfunction, malnutrition or allergies, and temperament.

Genetic factors have been suggested as the causes of nearly every type of disorder. Genetics are known to be involved in causing schizophrenia, but little is known about how the gene system that causes the disorder works. Environmental factors appear to trigger schizophrenia in individuals who are genetically vulnerable. The fact that a disorder has a genetic cause does not mean that the disorder is untreatable. Brain damage or dysfunction has been suggested as a cause of nearly every type of emotional or behavioral disorder. Traumatic brain injury involves known damage to the brain and may cause a wide variety of emotional and behavioral problems. Autism is now recognized as a biological disorder, although neither the exact nature nor the reason for the brain dysfunction are known. In both TBI and autism, environmental conditions can be significant in managing the disorder.

Severe malnutrition has devastating effects on young children's development. However, the popular notion that many emotional or behavioral disorders are caused by diet or allergies has not been supported by a consistent body of research. Teachers should be aware of possible dietary problems and allergies of students, but concern for these possible causes should not distract attention from instructional procedures.

Temperament is a consistent behavioral style or predisposition to respond in certain ways to one's environment. Although temperament may have a biological basis, it is shaped also by environmental factors. Skillful management by parents and teachers can lower the risk of emotional or behavioral disorders associated with difficult temperament.

When biological factors contribute to emotional or behavioral disorders, they do not operate in isolation from or independently of environmental (psychological) forces. The most tenable view at this time is that biological and environmental factors interact with one another to cause disorders. It seems reasonable to propose a continuum of biological causes ranging from minor, undetectable, organic faults to profound accidents of nature and a related continuum of emotional or behavioral disorders, ranging from mild to profound, to which these biological accidents contribute. Implications of biological factors for the day-to-day work of teachers may in some cases be nil, but teachers should be aware of possible biological causes and refer students to other professionals when appropriate. Teachers should be aware of the possible effects and side effects of psychotropic medications and be involved in monitoring drug effects.

CASE FOR DISCUSSION

She Goes On and On
Elizabeth (continued)

Sometimes I go on and on when I talk, and people have a hard time understanding what I am talking about. My family is always saying to me, "You're going on and on." This is supposed to be a clue to me to stop talking, or that nobody is understanding what I am talking about. My brother says that nobody wants to hear all the things I have to say, but brothers talk that way to sisters all the time.

Actually that was one of the first clues my doctor had as to what was wrong with me. I had lots of problems, but they didn't have a name. My first psychiatrist thought I had attention deficit disorder because I had so much trouble paying attention and getting my work done. But one time when I was going on and on, my mother said that the listener had to share the experience with me to be able to understand what I was talking about, and even then it was hard. My doctor said that was a serious symptom and then he asked if I was hearing voices. When I said yes, he said I needed to be hospitalized for evaluation, and that was a very serious problem. My parents were scared out of their wits.

I still go on and on. I have trouble writing too. I leave words out of sentences, or I don't finish writing a word. Then, of course, the sentences don't make any sense. Sometimes my sentences get really long. I guess I go on and on in writing too. I cannot write more than one or two paragraphs because I get really confused.

Source: This case is taken from Anonymous (1994), p. 589.

Questions About the Case

1. Imagine that Elizabeth is in your 10th-grade class. Would knowing that she has schizophrenia and is taking medication for it make a difference in how you respond to her going on and on? If not, why not? If so, how?

2. As her teacher, what strategies might you try to help Elizabeth learn to converse more normally (i.e., not to go on and on)?

3. If Elizabeth were a student in a regular 10th-grade class, how would you help her classmates respond kindly and helpfully to her when she goes on and on?

>> PERSONAL REFLECTIONS

Biological Factors

Richard E. Mattison, M.D., is professor of (child) psychiatry and director of school consultation in the Department of Psychiatry and Behavioral Science at the State University of New York at Stony Brook.

What emotional or behavioral disorders have a known biological cause?

Although science is progressively learning the neurobiology of psychiatric disorders, most causes are still to be determined. Advances in methodologies to study the brain have brought us a long way from early observations that stimulated research into brain-disorder connections, such as the observed association of frontal lobe injuries with rages, impulsivity, decreased cognitive function, mood dyscontrol, reduced attention, loss of social skills, or all of these symptoms. The general neurobiology of several psychiatric disorders has now been outlined, especially the important brain regions and neurotransmitters.

The majority of child and adolescent diagnoses that occur most commonly in special education students classified with emotional or behavioral disorders (EBDs) have candidate brain regions or systems, neurotransmitters, or genes. For example, for the most frequent disorder in these students, attention deficit–hyperactivity disorder (ADHD), converging studies point to the frontal lobe and the basal ganglia of the brain as primary candidate regions, which are rich in the neurotransmitter dopamine. In turn, suspect single genes have been identified that affect dopamine neurotransmission, although a polygenic (multiple genes) solution will be the probable outcome, as is likely in most psychiatric disorders. However, these guideposts represent only an early stage in deciphering the complex neurobiology of this disorder.

Advances in the study of the brain from several disciplines have contributed to our progressive understanding of the neurobiology of psychiatric disorders, at times in ways that might surprise EBD teachers. Most impressive have been the contributions from brain imaging. First, magnetic resonance imaging (MRI) allowed scientists to identify structural differences in greater detail between children with and without a specific psychiatric disorder. More recently, functional MRI (fMRI) has shown differences between such groups of children in the real-time metabolism of brain systems (interconnected regions) that operate as children perform carefully designed tasks that represent specific brain functions. Thus, "malfunctioning" brain regions or systems are gradually being identified, which can then be investigated for a variety of causative factors. Potential etiologies for such deficits might include structural or neuronal damage from some trauma during prenatal neurodevelopment, as well as genetic defects that disrupt the production of neurotransmitters. Or, intriguingly, neuroscience has also begun to show that environmental experiences may skew the neurobiology of brain function. For example, abuse has been demonstrated to affect the underlying neurobiology of children's stress response, which can in part explain much of the clinical picture that EBD teachers observe in many of their students who have been physically abused.

This advanced understanding of the neurobiology of psychiatric disorders has also led to treatment discoveries with interesting implications for EBD teachers. For example, obsessive-compulsive disorder (OCD) is especially associated with dysfunction in the right caudate nucleus. When a person with OCD takes a selective serotonin reuptake inhibitor (SSRI) medication such as fluoxetine (i.e., Prozac), brain imaging shows that the abnormal hyper-metabolism of that brain area decreases. Moreover, the same neuroradiological improvement also occurs after a course of specific behavioral therapy. Thus, brain change in this disorder is accomplished directly by medication and indirectly by a psychotherapeutic intervention. Not surprisingly, more lasting improvement often results from a combination of both therapies. Such findings will quite likely hold true for a variety of disorders in students with EBDs: Not only will therapeutic brain

181

changes require medication, but such changes will also be dependent on consistent cognitive-behavioral intervention by their teachers.

Thus, as science has begun to establish the neurobiology of brain function and thereby psychiatric disorders, our understanding of nature–nurture interaction has also matured. EBD teachers may at one time have been leery that the discovery of neurobiological causes for emotional and behavioral disorders would lead to biological treatments that would make their work less relevant. In fact, much the opposite is being found.

What are the most important signs that a child's parents should be encouraged to obtain a neurological examination or consider medication?

Parents should not initially worry whether their child has problems that may require a neurological examination or medication, which may unfortunately deter them from seeking necessary help. Rather, the first step a parent should take if they are concerned that their child may have a behavioral or emotional disorder is to honestly consider how much dysfunction the child is experiencing with family or friends or at school—is he or she suffering or are other people around him suffering during their interaction with the child? If the answer is yes, then an evaluation should be sought.

Parents who have reached this conclusion should begin with an evaluation by a clinician who specializes in such disorders or, at the least, talk to their pediatrician or family doctor. That professional can then determine whether a neurological examination is necessary, which primarily occurs if there is very noteworthy history like an unusual headache pattern for the child or deterioration of already acquired skills, for example, loss of language or motor abilities. Children with most psychiatric disorders rarely require neurological examinations—a review of their medical and neurological history by the clinician will usually suffice. However, a more intensive medical and neurological investigation is appropriate for a few uncommon child psychiatric disorders, such as autism and psychosis.

Similarly, a parent need not initially consider whether their child has a condition that requires medication. Such a discussion should take place after the evaluation. Even if a parent seeks initial evaluation for their child's psychopathology with a nonphysician clinician, at the end of the evaluation the parents should expect the mental health professional's diagnosis or explanation for the child's psychopathology and if or when medication might be indicated. In this day and age, all clinicians should be quite proficient at addressing such questions since medications are indicated for several child psychiatric disorders, either as an initial treatment component or as a subsequent addition if nonmedication therapy is not successful.

If a parent is concerned that their child has ADHD and may require a medication, then the parent should contact a physician in their community who specializes in treating such children. Such a referral can be gained from the family doctor or pediatrician, or often schools or parent groups such as CHADD will know which doctors in the community treat ADHD children well. When medication is indicated for non-ADHD psychiatric disorders, especially where depression, anxiety, or anger outbursts are severe or chronic, then a parent may wish to seek further evaluation or consultation by a child psychiatrist, that is, the specialist with the widest knowledge and experience of medications used for child or adolescent psychiatric disorders. If indicated, the child psychiatrist may begin an initial prescription and establish a beneficial dosage, with the plan that the medicine can subsequently be prescribed and monitored by the child's pediatrician with consultation backup, if the psychiatrist and pediatrician are both comfortable that this is within the pediatrician's ability. Such consultation arrangements are common because the various pediatric specialists are usually few in number; for example, the number of practicing child psychiatrists in our nation is fewer than 8,000.

Finally, parents should realize that in most cases medication is only part of the treatment plan. Medications do not cure child psychiatric disorders, but at this point only stabilize their symptoms. At a minimum, parents will require thorough education about the disorder and practical understanding of how to handle typical accompanying problems. Furthermore, parents of EBD students should expect that combination treatment is especially necessary for their children who usually have complicated, serious, or chronic disorders.

If a student is taking medication, what are the responsibilities of the teacher?

During their training, EBD teachers should be taught an appropriate working knowledge of psychiatric disorders, including medications that are commonly used for specific disorders and both the positive effects that can be expected from specific medications as well as the most common side effects. For example, if a parent or a community physician informs a teacher that a student is being started on an SSRI for a depressive disorder, then the teacher should be able to monitor depressive symptomology in school for change. The teacher should be aware that no positive effect may be observed for 2 or more weeks with SSRIs. Finally, worsening irritability or agitation should be reported to the parent or doctor immediately, as should any abrupt reversal of mood toward silliness.

When an EBD teacher first meets the parent(s) of a new student, the teacher should make clear that he or she wishes to help any community therapist or physician who evaluates or treats the child by supplying observations about the student's functioning in school. If the new child is currently receiving treatment, then the teacher should have the parent sign a consent form (established by the special education agency) for the teacher to provide information to the community professional. If the community clinician does not contact the teacher after the student's next appointment to request information in some form, then the teacher should contact the professional to initiate collaboration.

I realize this view is aggressive. However, students with EBDs will very frequently require medication(s) as part of their overall treatment plan for their common ADHD, depressive, or conduct (aggressive) disorders. Furthermore, they often have comorbid disorders that additionally complicates medication decision-making, and once they are on more than one medication (polypharmacy) the issue of side effects mimicking symptoms increases. Therefore, EBD teachers can increase the chances that their students are on the best possible regimen of medication by proactively ensuring that prescribing physicians (both psychiatrists and nonpsychiatrist physicians) have sufficient school data to make well-informed medication decisions. Otherwise, in my experience as well as the literature, community physicians will too often make medicine decisions with no input from teachers, or with only feedback about school from parents who may not be sufficiently aware of their child's true status at school.

The most common method that prescribing physicians use to gain information from teachers is behavior checklists (both general and specific). Such instruments can objectively supplement differential diagnosis and outcome assessment, and can provide effective communication (to replace phone tag). The more working knowledge that teachers have about a student's diagnosis and prescribed medication, the more helpful they can be with their ratings and also through their written comments, which are typically encouraged at the end of such instruments. If a teacher is not contacted about a student, I would encourage her or him to mail to the treating clinician a preselected general behavior checklist (chosen with the help of the school psychologist or psychiatric consultant).

Finally, EBD teachers should be able to work appropriately with parents about medication. Parents are more likely to ask the EBD teacher about medication ("Is it necessary?" and "Is it working?") than the doctor treating their child because they often have a more established relationship with the teacher. As part of their professional role, EBD teachers should also be able to raise with parents the issue of diagnoses that may need medication. Their handling of such situations can be crucial to a student's progress. If a teacher does not feel adequately trained to deal with such parental interaction, he or she should refer such questions to the family's doctor or psychiatrist, or seek coaching from a consultant psychiatrist on how to answer such questions most constructively.

Are there other points you would like to make about the topic?

My career has offered me a unique viewpoint. I am a child psychiatrist with a "minor" in special education. Both my clinical and research careers have focused on students with EBD. As a school consultant to EBD staffs, I have continually dealt with making psychiatric knowledge relevant and practical for special educators. They have taught me much about this issue, which has greatly influenced my answers to the preceding questions.

As a researcher, I have investigated characteristics of students with EBDs from a modern psychiatric perspective, their function and outcome over time in EBD classes, and predictors of their educational outcome. I have been adapting methodology from my research training in child psychiatry, and simultaneously I have become conversant in techniques used by EBD researchers. Most striking to me is how both fields avoid the other, like the proverbial two ships passing in the night, despite the growing relevancy of one for the other.

Consequently, I would also point out that, much as advances in the neurobiology of brain function and psychiatric disorders have increased meaning and implications for EBD teachers (as I have already described), the same holds true for EBD researchers. Thus, they must more actively determine what advances need to become more common research variables in their work. For example, they could ask such questions as: What psychiatric diagnosis, medication use, or environmental stresses affect children's neurobiological function? Also, EBD researchers should increasingly both design and participate in collaborative research with allied disciplines, to which they must more aggressively contribute their invaluable expertise about student function in school, combined with their skills at objective observation and specific intervention plans. Otherwise, the situation is much as I've described between community physicians and EBD teachers. For example, a child psychiatrist researcher who is examining the effect of a new medication or combination therapy may either not measure school function or not do it adequately. The participation of a well-trained EBD researcher could make the difference in whether or not the true effectiveness of the intervention is ascertained. Unfortunately, this situation is an ongoing problem in medication rescarch for non-ADHD disorders.

Furthermore, teachers will increasingly look toward researchers and trainers of EBD teachers for guidance on how to incorporate neurobiological advances. Such progress by other disciplines can no longer be dismissed as irrelevant, nor can special education depend on other disciplines to make the case for such advances. Their value for EBD teachers must be translated by EBD researchers and trainers of teachers, and EBD researchers must more proactively help to set a collaborative research agenda that includes relevance for EBD teachers.

>> QUESTIONS FOR FURTHER REFLECTION

1. How can a teacher best stay abreast of developments in brain imaging and medication?
2. What are the greatest advantages and disadvantages of medication for emotional or behavioral disorders?
3. How should knowledge of a biological cause of a student's behavior affect the way you work with that student as a teacher?

CHAPTER EIGHT

FAMILY FACTORS

Revised by Devery R. Mock

As you read this chapter, keep these guiding questions in mind:

- What are the implications of an interactional–transactional model of family influence for families with abused children?

- How could one characterize the most and least desirable types of parental discipline?

- What is a negative reinforcement trap?

- How are coercive family interactions related to the development of antisocial behavior?

- How can parents foster school success or school failure?

APPEAL OF FAMILY FACTORS AS CAUSAL EXPLANATIONS

When youngsters misbehave, our natural tendency is to blame parental mismanagement or family disintegration. Given the primacy of family relations in children's social development, it is understandable that we have sought the origins of emotional and behavioral disorders in the structure, composition, and interactions of family units. These elements do not, however, provide a straightforward recipe for predicting emotional or behavioral disorders. Like other causal factors, those related to the family are complex and influenced by genetic factors as well as a wide variety of environmental events (Pinker, 2002; Plomin, 1995). We must guard against adopting facile explanations of "familial determinants" of emotional and behavioral disorders and rely instead on those factors that researchers have reliably identified as predictors of child psychopathology (Reitman & Gross, 1995, p. 87).

Family characteristics appear to predict emotional and behavioral development only in complex interactions with other factors, such as socioeconomic status, sources of support outside the family, and the child's age, sex, and temperamental characteristics. The concept of **risk** is important here: The idea that in examining causal factors we are dealing with probabilities and that particular events or conditions may increase the probability that there will be a particular outcome for the child, such as an emotional or behavioral disorder. When several risk factors occur together—for example, poverty, parental antisocial behavior, community violence, and difficult temperament—their effects are not merely additive but multiplicative, more than doubling the probability that a child will develop a disorder. If a third factor is added, the chance of disorder is several times higher yet (Garmezy, 1987; Quinn & McDougal, 1998; Serbin, Rohde, Lewinsohn, & Clarke, 2002).

Rutter's reviews of research on maternal deprivation (1979) and attachment (1995) and Plomin's (1995) and Pinker's (2002) reviews of the role of genetics in children's experiences in the family highlight some of the complexities in family influences. For example, it is not always the case that separation of the child from one or both parents impairs a child's psychological and behavioral development. In an intact family, parental discord may exert a more pernicious influence than parental separation. A good relationship with one parent may sustain a child even in the face of parental discord or separation. The interaction of the child's constitutional or temperamental characteristics with parental behavior may be more important than parental separation or disharmony. In addition, factors outside the home (school, for instance) may lessen or heighten the negative influence of family factors.

For some reason, some children do not succumb to extreme disruption or disintegration of their families. We do not know precisely why some children are vulnerable and others invulnerable to negative family influences. A positive, or easy, child temperament (recall our discussion of temperament in chapter 7) and maternal warmth appear to be factors that may heighten resilience (Smith & Prior, 1995), but these factors may be insufficient to buffer children against psychopathology in violent families (McCloskey, Figueredo, & Koss, 1995). Research also suggests that high cognitive skills, curiosity, enthusiasm, ability to set goals for oneself, and high self-esteem are associated with resilience (Hanson & Carta, 1996). Many intervention programs now focus on reducing risk factors and fostering resilient behaviors in at-risk children (Beardslee, Versage, Van de Velde, Swatling, & Hoke, 2002; Olsson, Bond, Burns, Vella-Brodrick, & Sawyer, 2003; Place, Reynolds, Cousins, & O'Neill, 2002).

Conversely, we know that certain features of family relationships, especially parental deviance and discord, harsh and unpredictable parental discipline, and lack of emotional support, increase children's risk for developing emotional or behavioral disorders (Reid & Eddy, 1997). Yet a family environment that creates high risk does not necessarily cause a child to have a disorder. Causation is more complex than that (see the cases of Sylvain and Jack in the accompanying case book for illustrations of family involvement in emotional and behavioral disorders).

The concept of *heightened risk,* as opposed to a simple cause–effect relationship, is important in disordered behavior. Consider what happens in families in which risk of emotional or behavioral disorder is high. We can answer this question in general terms, but we cannot make confident predictions of outcomes for individual children for two reasons. First, each child is affected individually by the family environment. A younger, more compliant child may experience her family quite differently than her older, more disobedient brother (Plomin, 1989). Second, whether life circumstances or environmental conditions are positive or negative for a child, and whether they heighten or reduce the child's risk of emotional or behavioral disorders, depends on the processes involved. Processes or mechanisms—not merely the presence of risk variables but how children cope with degrees and patterns of exposure to those variables—determine how vulnerable or resilient a child will be. The shared family context does not offer uniform experiences (Jenkins, Rasbash, & O'Connor, 2003; Pinker, 2002).

We understand little about the processes involved in producing vulnerability and resilience, but a key ingredient for each individual appears to be the pattern, sequence, and intensity of exposure to stressful circumstances. We do know that the accumulation of stressful life events is an important factor in determining how a child will be able to cope. Stressful life events may occur within the family, but they are related to the larger social environment in which the family itself must function as a unit. Therefore, it is important to consider both the interpersonal transactions that occur between the child and other family members and the external pressures on the family that may affect those interactions.

Whereas the research of 30 years ago tended to focus on the general processes thought to be the basis for the development of child psychopathology, recent research has examined more specific, focused interactions that may contribute to causing emotional or behavioral disorders or intensify them (Dadds, 2002). The empirical evidence increasingly points to *social learning* as the basis for many emotional and behavioral disorders; research suggests that parental *modeling, reinforcement,* and *punishment* of specific types of behavior hold the keys to how families influence children's behavioral development. For example, researchers have documented that children who demonstrate high levels of anxiety often have families in which caution and avoidance are modeled and reinforced (Dadds, 2002). In such instances parents may reward avoidance of risk and social disengagement and thereby foster the development and expression of fear and anxiety.

Evidence from longitudinal studies increasingly points to families as critical factors, but not the only factors in the development of antisocial and delinquent behavior. In a sample of approximately 1,500 boys, Loeber, Farrington, Stouthamer-Loeber, and Van Kammen (1998a) found a correlation between early onset of behavioral problems and deviant parental behavior. However, these authors also argued that such findings demonstrated a clear need for interventions aimed at introducing protective factors in the lives of these at-risk youth. Thus, familial factors may be critical, but they are not sufficiently powerful to set a child's fate.

Having considered the effects of family structure, we turn to interaction in families. Families may influence school success or school failure, and we note how they may do so. In turn, family interactions may be shaped by external influences; thus, we discuss the powerful influences of factors such as poverty and parental employment. Finally, we discuss the implications for educators of what we know about families, especially families of children with emotional or behavioral disorders. The scope and complexity of family-related research are enormous, and many details of the topic are left untouched in our review.

FAMILY DEFINITION AND STRUCTURE

Although the intact mother–father–children concept of family remains the ideal in mainstream American culture, a variety of diverse family forms fit the realities of contemporary life (Hanson & Carta, 1996; Hetherington & Camara, 1984; Reitman & Gross, 1995). Radke-Yarrow (1990) suggested that function is more important than structure in defining family and that the essential functions of families are to do the following:

- Provide care and protect children
- Regulate and control children's behavior
- Convey knowledge and skills important for understanding and coping with the physical and social worlds
- Give affective meaning to interactions and relationships
- Facilitate children's self-understanding

Hanson and Lynch (1992) proposed that regardless of how families define themselves, the key elements of the definition of family are that "the members of the unit see themselves as a family, are affiliated with one another, and are committed to caring for one another" (p. 285). Given these considerations, it may be important to examine whether or to what extent family structure affects children's behavior.

The effects of family size and birth order on behavioral development have been studied extensively, but such elements of family configuration are far outweighed by factors related to divorce and other circumstances resulting in single-parent homes or other nontraditional family structures (cf. Hetherington & Martin, 1986; Zigler & Finn-Stevenson, 1997). Family composition or configuration may have an effect on children's behavior (Achenbach, Howell, Quay, & Conners, 1991; Najman, Behrens,

Andersen, Bor, O'Callaghan, & Williams, 1997), but other factors involving interactions among family members and the social contexts in which they live appear to be far more important contributors to behavior problems. However, we briefly examine the effects of single-parent families and substitute care (e.g., foster care, adoption, care by relatives other than parents) on children's behavior.

Single-Parent Families

A substantial proportion of children are now reared in single-parent families, usually because of divorce but also often because of out-of-wedlock births. Census data from the year 2000 indicated that nearly one fourth of U.S. families with children under the age of 18 were headed by single parents. Thus, we must ask whether the presence of only one parent in a family puts children at risk for emotional or behavioral disorders. We begin by considering the effects of divorce on children's behavior.

Divorce is traumatic, not only for parents and children but also for extended family and friends. The lasting psychological pain and fear felt by many children whose parents divorce are well-known (Bolgar, Zweig-Frank, & Paris, 1995; Wallerstein, 1987). Yet the overwhelming finding is that most children adjust to divorce and go on with their lives without developing chronic emotional or behavioral problems. "Most children manifest some disturbances—often a combination of anger, anxiety, depression, dependency, and noncompliance—in the immediate aftermath of divorce; however, most children and adults also recover and adjust to their new life situation by about three years after divorce" (Hetherington & Martin, 1986, p. 340).

How children adjust to divorce depends on factors beyond family dissolution. These factors are numerous and include concerns such as: the child's age when the divorce occurs, characteristics of the custodial parent, and the child's cognitive and affective characteristics related to coping with stress (see Johnson, 1986; Zigler & Finn-Stevenson, 1997). There is no general formula for predicting child psychopathology following divorce, but it is clear that many children and adolescents whose parents are divorced have lower scholastic aptitude, perform less well in school, and have less confidence in their academic abilities than do youngsters from intact families (Watt, Moorehead-Slaughter, Japzon, & Keller, 1990).

The absence of fathers in homes and families is a distressing feature of contemporary life, particularly as it affects African Americans (see King, 1999). Boys in families headed by mothers alone may be at risk for developing aggressive behavior (Vaden-Kiernan, Ialongo, Pearson, & Kellam, 1995). Among the family configurations found by Achenbach et al. (1991) to be significantly related to higher behavioral problem ratings of children were "fewer adults in the household; more unrelated adults in the household; parents who were separated, divorced, or never married to each other" (p. 92). These findings are of concern, but far more important are the conditions accompanying a household headed by a single parent, which is typically the mother.

Economic hardship or impoverishment, with its attendant deprivations, parental substance abuse or criminality, interpersonal conflict and violence, and lack of parental supervision and nurturing—these factors appear to shape children's behavior more significantly, regardless of whether the family contains one parent or two (Baumrind, 1995; Ellwood & Stolberg, 1993). Rutter (1995) noted:

> Early writings on the risks associated with parental divorce and family break-up focused on the role of "loss" because that had received such an emphasis in early writings on attachment. Empirical findings have made clear, however, that the main risks do not stem from loss as such but rather from the discordant and disrupted relationships that tend to precede or follow the loss. . . . Loss is a risk indicator but it is not the major player in most risk mechanisms. (pp. 563–564)

Substitute Care

Children in foster care and those living with relatives who are not their parents appear to be at high risk for emotional or behavioral disorders and school-related problems (Pilowsky, 1995; Smucker, Kauffman, & Ball, 1996; Stein, Raegrant, Ackland, & Avison, 1994). Sheehan's (1993a, 1993b) description of foster care in New York City provides graphic details about the stresses many foster children and foster parents face.

Some children are placed in substitute care because of the death or incapacitation of their parents, but the great majority—and an increasing percentage—are placed under the care of the child protection system because of their parents' neglect and abuse. Virtually never are children placed in any form of substitute care unless they have suffered trauma that is highly likely to result in at least short-term emotional or behavioral problems (except in the case of adopted infants). Abused children are known to have more behavioral problems than those who are not maltreated (Feldman, Salzinger, Rosario, Alvardo, Caraballo, & Hammer, 1995). Yet much remains unknown about why and how children are placed in protective care.

A major problem in providing substitute care is finding or training caregivers who are highly motivated and skilled in child rearing (Evans, Armstrong, Dollard, Kuppinger, Huz, & Wood, 1994; Moore & Chamberlain, 1994). Many foster parents have little or no training for the task, and few are well trained in dealing with difficult children. Although long-term foster care has demonstrated positive outcomes (Minty, 1999; Reddy & Pfeiffer, 1997) many foster children are placed for short periods in many different foster homes, and the risk for negative behavioral and emotional outcomes appears to increase with the number of different placements (see Smucker et al., 1996). The lack of stability, continuity, attachment, and nurturing that goes with numerous foster placements and unskilled foster parents is likely to promote emotional or behavioral disorders (Clark, Prange, Lee, Boyd, McDonald, & Stewart, 1994).

Adoptive families, like biological families, have a variety of structures. The influence of adoptive families on children's emotional and behavioral development can be predicted to parallel the influence of biological families. Controversy sometimes arises regarding the adequacy of adoption by single parents or adoptive families that involve differences in sexual orientation (e.g., gay fathers or lesbian mothers) or differences in the color or ethnicity of children and parents (e.g., Caucasian parents adopting children of color). Here, too, we might expect familial determinants to function as they do in any other family structure. For example, Tasker and Golombok

(1995) found that being raised by a lesbian mother did not necessarily cause children to be maladjusted or to become gay or lesbian.

Research clearly suggests that family form by itself has relatively little affect on children's emotional and behavioral development. Although children reared in single-parent families may be at heightened risk, the risk factors appear to be conditions associated with a single-parent family structure, not single parenting itself. Being reared by substitutes for one's biological parents may be associated with heightened risk but only insofar as abuse, neglect, or other traumatic circumstances affect children before they are removed from their biological parents or after they enter foster care. Far more important than family structure is what happens in the family—the interactions among family members, regardless of how the family is constituted.

FAMILY INTERACTION

When we think of family factors, our tendency is to ask: What kinds of families produce children with emotional or behavioral disorders? However, it is also reasonable to ask: What kinds of families do children with emotional or behavioral disorders produce?

Child developmentalists now realize that children's influence on their parents' behavior is significant in determining family interactions. A child from a broken family may well exhibit behavioral characteristics that would break nearly any family (see Pinker, 2002). Researchers found decades ago that undesirable parenting behavior and negative family interactions are in part a reaction of family members to a deviant youngster (e.g., Bell, 1968; Bell & Harper, 1977; Martin, 1981; Patterson, 1982, 1986a, 1986b; Patterson, Reid, & Dishion, 1992; Reid & Eddy, 1997; Sameroff & Chandler, 1975). Reciprocity of influence can be observed from the earliest parent–child interactions, strengthening and manifesting in all subsequent interactions. This dynamic is especially evident in child management and child abuse.

Child Management

Parental management or discipline comes up as a topic for discussion in children's emotional or behavioral disorders of every description. We shall return to family interactions as potential causal factors in each of the chapters in part 4. Here, we review general findings on parental management of children but focus on the role of family interactions in causing the disorder people usually consider first in discussions of family factors: the impulsive, aggressive, acting-out behavior generally known as *conduct disorder*. In fact, we know more about the effects of parental discipline on disruptive, oppositional, aggressive behavior than we do about the effects of parental behavior on children's anxiety, fear, and depression (Ehrensaft, Wasserman, Verdelli, Greenwald, Miller, & Davies, 2003; O'Leary, 1995).

The effects of discipline techniques are complex and not highly predictable without considering both the parents' and the child's general behavioral characteristics and ongoing stress in the family (Campbell, 1995; Rutter, 1995). Nevertheless, we can suggest some general guidelines for discipline that can help parents avoid the types of interactions that research strongly suggests are mistakes, and these principles may hold across all cultural groups. For example, O'Leary (1995) identified three types of mistakes typically made by mothers of 2- to 4-year-old children: laxness, overreactivity, and verbosity. "Laxness includes giving in, not enforcing rules, and providing positive reinforcement for misbehavior. Overreactivity includes anger, meanness, and irritability. Verbosity involves the propensity to engage in lengthy verbal interactions about misbehavior even when the talking is ineffective" (O'Leary, 1995, p. 12). Parents can be very "nice" to their children but ineffective in discipline because they are unable or unwilling to set consistent, firm, unambiguous limits. These parents may use long, delayed, gentle (but imprudent) reprimands that actually make the child's behavior worse. Others may make the mistake of using harsh reprimands but pay little attention to the child when he or she is behaving well.

Baumrind (1995) reviewed what decades of research on parental discipline in nonabusive middle-class families has shown (see also Campbell, 1995). Researchers describe two primary dimensions of discipline: *responsiveness* (which involves warmth, reciprocity, and attachment) and *demandingness* (involving monitoring, firm control, and positive and negative consequences for behavior). Parents who provide optimal management of their children are both highly responsive and highly demanding; they are highly invested in their children (Baumrind, 1996). More specifically, parents who discipline most effectively are sensitive to their children's needs, empathic, and attentive. They establish a pattern of mutually positive, reciprocal interactions with their children, and their warmth and reciprocity form the basis for emotional attachment or adult–child bonding. These parents are also demanding of their children. They monitor their children's behavior, providing appropriately close supervision for the child's age. They confront their children's misbehavior directly and firmly rather than attempt to manipulate or coerce their children. They provide unambiguous instructions and demands in a firm but nonhostile manner and consistently follow through with negative but nonabusive consequences for misbehavior. They provide positive reinforcement in the form of praise, approval, encouragement, and other rewards for their children's desirable behavior.

Parental discipline that is both demanding and responsive is sometimes referred to as *authoritative* (as opposed to *authoritarian* discipline, which is demandingness without responsiveness) and is typically found to have the best effects on children's behavioral development. Researchers have even found a relationship between authoritative parenting and decreased tobacco and alcohol usage among children and youth, decreased violence among adolescents, and decreased levels of anger and alienation among middle school students (Adamczyk-Robinette, Fletcher, & Wright, 2002; Jackson, Henriksen, & Foshee, 1998). Authoritative discipline balances what is asked of the child with what is offered to the child, and this balance may be the key characteristic of effective parental discipline in various cultures (Abrams, 1995). It may be, in fact, the key to effective discipline by all caretakers of children, but it is not the pattern of interaction typically found in families of children who exhibit antisocial behavior.

The work of Patterson and his colleagues gives insight into the characteristics of interactions in the families of antisocial youngsters (Patterson, 1973, 1980, 1982, 1986a, 1986b; Patterson, Reid, Jones, & Conger, 1975; Patterson et al., 1992; Reid &

Eddy, 1997). His research group's methods involve direct observation of parents' and children's behavior in the home, revealing an identifiable family pattern. They show that interaction in families with aggressive children is characterized by exchange of negative, hostile behaviors, whereas the interaction in families with nonaggressive children tends to be mutually positive and gratifying for parents and children. In the families with aggressive children, not only do the children behave in ways that are highly irritating and aversive to their parents, but the parents rely primarily on aversive methods (hitting, shouting, threatening, and so forth) to control their children. Thus, children's aggression in the family seems both to produce counteraggression and to be produced by punitive parenting techniques.

Patterson (1980) studied mutually aversive interactions between mothers and children, particularly in families of aggressive children, and found that many of the behaviors are maintained by negative reinforcement. Time and further research have not proven his analysis false but only strengthened it. *Negative reinforcement* involves escape from or avoidance of an unpleasant condition, which is rewarding (negatively reinforcing) because it brings relief from psychological or physical pain or anxiety. An example of negative reinforcement in mother–child interactions is shown in Table 8.1. Patterson calls these interactions *negative reinforcement traps* because they set the stage for greater conflict and coercion; each person in the trap tends to reciprocate the other's aversive behavior and to escalate attempts to use *coercion*—controlling someone by negative reinforcement. Patterson and his colleagues have found that, unlike

Table 8.1
Some Reinforcement Traps

Negative Reinforcement Arrangement		
Neutral Antecedent: **Time Frame 1**	**Time Frame 2**	**Time Frame 3**
Behavior: Mother ("clean your room")	Child (whine)	Mother (stops asking)
	Short-Term Effect	Long-Term Effect
Mother	The pain (child's Whine) stops	Mother will be more likely to give in when child whines
Child	The pain (mother's Nag) stops	Given a messy room, mother less likely to ask him to clean it up in the future
Overall	The room was not cleaned	Child more likely to use whine to turn off future requests to clean room

Explanation: The child's room is messy, an aversive condition for the mother. When the mother asks the child to clean room, the child whines. The child's whining is painfully aversive to the mother, so the mother stops asking or nagging. The mother's nagging is painfully aversive to the child, who finds that his or her whining will stop the mother's nagging. In the short run, both mother and child escape pain—child stops whining and the mother stops nagging— but the child's room is not cleaned. In the long run, the mother avoids asking the child to clean the room and the child learns to use whining to stop the mother's nagging. Both mother and child are negatively reinforced by the avoidance of or escape from aversive consequences. However, the problem condition (the messy room) still exists as potential source of future negative interactions.

Source: Patterson, G. R. (1980). Mothers: The unacknowledged victims. *Monographs of the Society for Research in Child Development, 45*(5, Serial No. 186), 5. © 1980 by the University of Chicago Press. Reprinted by permission.

normal children, problem children tend to increase their disruptive behavior in response to parental punishment. Predictably, therefore, the families of aggressive children seem to foster undesirable child behavior.

In effect, the members of families with aggressive children "train" each other to be aggressive. Although the major training occurs in transactions between an aggressive child and parent(s), it spills over to include siblings. Patterson (1986b) reported that siblings of an aggressive child are no more aggressive toward their parents than are children in families without an aggressive child. Interactions between siblings in families of antisocial youngsters, however, are more aggressive than those in families without an aggressive child. Coercive exchanges between aggressive children and their parents appear to teach siblings to be coercive with each other. Not surprisingly, these children then tend to be more aggressive in other social contexts, such as school. In fact, school conflict and school failure are frequently associated with antisocial behavior at home (cf. Kazdin, 1998; Kerr & Nelson, 2002; Patterson, 1986b; Stevenson-Hinde, Hinde, & Simpson, 1986; Walker, Ramsey, & Gresham, 2004).

It is difficult to delineate the development of overt behavioral disorders; however, the model emerging from Patterson's research group suggests that they arise from "failure by parents to effectively punish garden-variety, coercive behaviors" (Patterson, 1986b, p. 436). The child begins winning battles with the parents, and parents become increasingly punitive but ineffective in responding to coercion. Coercive exchanges escalate in number and intensity, increasing to hundreds per day and progressing from whining, yelling, and temper tantrums to hitting and other forms of physical assault. The child continues to win a high percentage of the battles with parents; parents continue to use ineffective punishment, setting the stage for another round of conflict. This coercive family process may occur in concert with other conditions associated with high risk for psychopathology: social and economic disadvantage, substance abuse, and a variety of other stressors such as parental discord and separation or divorce. During the process, the child receives little or no parental warmth and is often rejected by peers. School failure is another typical concomitant of the process. Understandably, the child usually develops a poor self-image (Patterson & Capaldi, 1990).

Patterson's suggestion that parents of aggressive children do not punish their children effectively does not mean he believes punishment should be the focus of parental discipline. Instead, his work suggests that parents need to set clear limits for children's behavior, provide a warm and loving home environment, provide positive attention and approval for appropriate behavior, and follow through with nonhostile and nonphysical punishment for coercive conduct.

Patterson and other researchers have shown that the pattern of coercive exchanges characterizing families of antisocial children can be identified early (Loeber, Green, Lahey, Christ, & Frick, 1992; Patterson, 1986b; Patterson et al., 1992; Reid, 1993; Reid & Eddy, 1997; Shaw & Winslow, 1997; Stevenson-Hinde, Hinde, & Simpson, 1986; Waters, Hay, & Richters, 1986). In addition, these and other findings suggest that conduct-disordered children are at risk from an early age, partly because they are infants with difficult temperaments and have parents who may lack coping skills (cf. Campbell, 1995; Kazdin, 1998; Patterson, 1986b). For children demonstrating disordered behaviors, inconsistent discipline and family conflict often become the norm (Campbell, 1995; Farrington, 1995; Hetherington & Martin, 1986; Kazdin, 1998; Rutter, 1995, 1997). Although data do not support the conclusion that punitive parents cause their children to become aggressive—the relationship does not appear that direct—researchers have observed that parent education can, in some circumstances, modify children's aggression (Patterson et al., 1975, 1992; Reid, 1993; Serbin, Stack, Schwartzman, Bentley, Saltaris, & Ledingham, 2002; Willis, Swanson, & Walker, 1983).

Child Abuse

We may now know something about how coercive interactions begin and are sustained in families of aggressive children and how parents can provide ineffective or counterproductive discipline. However, we must not forget that "there are probably many routes to becoming a 'good parent' which vary with the personality of both the parents and children and with pressures in the environment with which one must learn to cope" (W. C. Becker, 1964, p. 202). When is ineffective child management abusive or neglectful? This question is not easily answered (Baumrind, 1997; Haugaard, 1992). Much depends on the developmental level of the child, specific circumstances, professional and legal judgments, and cultural norms. If there is a consensus about how to define *child abuse,* it likely is centered on parental behavior that seriously endangers or delays the normal development of the child (Baumrind, 1995; Cicchetti & Toth, 1995; Janko, 1994; Widom, 1997). Azar and Wolfe (1998) suggested that for treatment purposes, child abuse and neglect be defined "in terms of the *degree to which a parent uses aversive or inappropriate control strategies with his or her child and/or fails to provide minimal standards of caregiving and nurturance*" (p. 502, italics in original).

Given the difficulty in defining *abuse,* it is not surprising that reliable estimates of child abuse and family violence are difficult to find (Cicchetti & Toth, 1995). Nevertheless, without belaboring the issue, we may conclude that family violence and child abuse—physical, psychological, and sexual—are problems of great magnitude; it very likely involves more than a million children per year in the United States (Azar & Wolfe, 1998; Baumrind, 1995; Cicchetti & Toth, 1995; Wolfe, 1998). Although abuse of all types is serious and has important sequelae, we focus our discussion here on physical abuse.

Most people give little thought to children's and parents' interactive effects on each other in cases of abuse. Child abuse is often seen as a problem of parental behavior alone, and intervention has often been directed only at changing parents' responses to their children. The *interactional–transactional model* considers abused children's influence on their parents and suggests that intervention deal directly with the abused child's undesirable behavior as well as with the parents' abusive responses (see Patterson, 1980, 1982; Walker et al., 2004; Zirpoli, 1986). This perspective is valuable even when the child is not initially an instigator of abuse but has been drawn into an abusive relationship and is exhibiting inappropriate behavior. Intervention typically needs to be directed toward the entire family and its social context (Baumrind, 1995; Janko, 1994; see also Reppucci, Britner, & Woodard, 1997).

One hypothesis about parent–child interaction in child abuse is that their children's responses to punishment inadvertently "teach" parents to become increasingly punitive (recall our prior discussion of how family members may train each other to be aggressive). For example, if the child exhibits behavior that is aversive to the parent (perhaps whining), the parent may punish the child (perhaps by slapping). If the punishment is successful and the child stops the aversive behavior, then the parent is negatively reinforced by the consequence; the parent is, in effect, rewarded by the child's stopping the aversive behavior. The next time the child whines, the parent is more likely to try slapping to get relief from the whining. If at first the child does not stop whining, the parent may slap harder or more often to try to make the child be quiet. Thus, the parent's punishment becomes increasingly harsh as a means of dealing with the child's increasingly aversive behavior. Although abusive parents are not usually successful in punishing their child, they continue to escalate punishment. They seem not to understand or be able to use alternative means of control. Although abused children suffer in the bargain, they often hold their own in the battle with their parents; they may stubbornly refuse to knuckle under to parental pressure. Parent and child are trapped in a mutually destructive, coercive cycle in which they cause and are caused physical or psychological pain (see Shaw & Winslow, 1997; Webster-Stratton, 1985).

The negative reinforcement trap can escalate behavior to the level of abuse. Such a coercive struggle is characteristic of conduct disorder, and the developmental consequences for children are severe (Patterson et al., 1992; Walker et al., 2004). Moreover, if abuse is transmitted across generations, it is likely through such processes because children with conduct disorder are likely to become parents with antisocial behavior and poor child management skills. For example, Serbin et al. (2002) conducted a longitudinal study spanning approximately 25 years and documented that "the more aggressive a mother was as a child, the more aggressive her child was observed to be" (p. 57). Of course, such observations could also confirm genetic tendencies (see Pinker, 2002; we discuss the transmission of antisocial behavior across generations further in chapter 12.)

The conclusion that the child's behavior is always a reciprocal causal factor in an abusive relationship with a parent is not warranted, however. Abusive relationships are extremely varied, both in abusive behaviors and in abused–abuser relations. Sexual abuse in families, for example, takes many forms and may involve incestuous relationships between siblings, parent and child, or other family members (for example, stepparent or grandparent) and child. Because it is a social problem surrounded by many taboos, sexual abuse is a difficult, yet not impossible, topic to research (Haugaard, 1992; Parker & Parker, 1986). Existing research studies have failed to demonstrate that children contribute to their sexual victimizaton, particularly when the abused child is very young. A history of sexual abuse or observation of overt sexual behavior may cause some children to be sexually provocative, which may contribute to, but not cause, their further abuse.

Much has been written about the characteristics of abusive parents, and stereotypes abound. One stereotype is that they are socially isolated; another is that they themselves were abused as children; still another is that they are mentally ill.

Although all three impressions hold for some cases, none is supported by research as an abusive parent prototype (cf. Baumrind, 1995; Thompson & Wilcox, 1995). Nevertheless, we can point to several psychological characteristics that frequently accompany abusive parenting. For example, in addition to an external locus of control, abusive parents tend to exhibit deficits in empathy, role taking, impulse control, and self-esteem, and an external locus of control (Baumrind, 1995).

Children who are abused by their parents have been shown by research to be at risk for the full range of emotional and behavioral disorders, including both internalizing problems such as depression and externalizing problems such as conduct disorder (Cicchetti & Toth, 1995; Widom, 1997). Teachers, parents, and peers are all likely to see higher levels of behavioral problems in physically abused than in non-maltreated children (Feldman et al., 1995). Bolger, Patterson, and Kupersmidt (1999) found that type of maltreatment related to the nature of the child's maladjustment. For example, sexual abuse predicted low self-esteem, and emotional abuse predicted difficulties in peer relationships. The negative effects of abuse may be compounded further if the child already has an emotional or behavioral problem (Levendosky, Okun, & Parker, 1995).

In devising intervention programs for abused children and youth, it is important to recognize that their behavior may be directly related to family violence and that attempting merely to modify their behavior in school may be insufficient. Teachers, as well as others with responsibility for children's welfare, must report suspected abuse and work toward comprehensive services that meet all of the student's needs. These individuals can play pivotal roles in cultivating the resilience of children suffering from abuse (Doyle, 2003).

FAMILY INFLUENCES ON SCHOOL SUCCESS AND FAILURE

Because the responsibility for children's learning is regularly delegated to schools, the family's contribution to school performance often plays a secondary role. Parents nevertheless contribute to or detract from their child's success at school in several ways: their expressed attitudes toward education; their own school experience; and their attitudes toward appropriate school-related behaviors, such as attending regularly, completing homework, reading, and studying. Gesten, Scher, and Cowen (1978) found that "homes characterized by lack of educational stimulation appear to produce children who are prone to learning problems" (p. 254). In addition, the social training children receive at home may be an important factor in determining school success. Moreover, poor peer relations in school, especially rejection by peers, is highly predictive of academic problems (Coie, 1990; DeRosier, Kupersmidt, & Patterson, 1995; Patterson et al., 1992; Reid & Eddy, 1997; Walker et al., 2004; Wentzel & Asher, 1995).

Parental discipline, parent–school relations, and parent–child relationships play important roles in school success and school failure (Dornbusch, Ritter, Leiderman, Roberts, & Fraleigh, 1987). The authoritative parental discipline described previously (both responsive and demanding) is likely to support students' achievement (cf.

Baumrind, 1995; Campbell, 1995; Rutter, 1995). Parents who are positively involved with their child's education tend to have youngsters who perform at a higher academic level (Stevenson & Baker, 1987). Conversely, families in which a coercive process is at work are likely to send students to school unprepared to comply with teachers' instructions, to complete homework assignments, or to relate well to their peers. Unprepared for the demands of school, these students are virtually certain to fail to meet reasonable expectations for academic performance and social interaction (Patterson, 1986b; Patterson et al., 1992; Walker et al., 2004).

EXTERNAL PRESSURES AFFECTING FAMILIES

Family interactions are influenced by external conditions that put stress on parents and children. Poverty, unemployment, underemployment, homelessness, community violence—it is not surprising that these conditions influence the ability of families to cope from day to day, of parents to nurture children, of children to behave well at home and perform well in school (Janko, 1994; Pungello, Kupersmidt, Burchinal, & Patterson, 1996; Walker et al., 2004). Homelessness affects not only entire families but, in some cases, adolescents alienated from their families, sometimes because of external influences that destroyed parent–child bonds (see Schweitzer, Hier, & Terry, 1994).

Poverty is perhaps the most critical problem undermining families today (see Fujiura & Yamaki, 2000; Hodgkinson, 1995; Knitzer & Aber, 1995). The 2000 census reported that approximately 17% of children live below the poverty level, with children younger than five representing the largest group. Severe economic hardship is known to be associated with abusive or neglectful parental behavior and children's maladaptive behavior (Achenbach et al., 1991; Bolger, Patterson, & Kupersmidt, 1995; Felner, Brand, DuBois, Adan, Mulhall, & Evans, 1995; Janko, 1994). Poverty often means that families live in inadequate or dangerous housing (if they are not homeless) in neighborhoods rife with substance abuse and violence. These neighborhood conditions often contribute to parents and children being victimized and to their feelings of inadequacy, depression, and hopelessness (DuRant, Getts, Cadenhead, Emans, & Woods, 1995).

Predictably, there is a substantial link between poverty and risk of disability (Fujiura & Yamaki, 2000). Neighborhoods characterized by low family income, high unemployment, transient populations, high concentrations of children living in single-parent families, and high rates of violence and substance abuse are places in which families are at high risk of dysfunction and disintegration, and children are at high risk for psychopathology and school failure (Coulton, Korbin, Su, & Chow, 1995; DuRant et al., 1995; Fitzgerald, Davies, & Zucker, 2002; Kupersmidt, Griesler, DeRosier, Patterson, & Davis, 1995; McCloskey, Figueredo, & Koss, 1995). Violent victimization, whether by family members or others, puts children and youth at risk for emotional and behavioral disorders and school problems of wide variety (Boney-McCoy & Finkelhor, 1995). Furthermore, in communities characterized by danger of victimization, restrictive parenting may be adaptive (Jackson, 1995; Zayas, 1995).

A common misperception of poor families is that the parents typically are unemployed or uninterested in work. Although unemployment and lack of work skills are problems of a substantial percentage of poor parents, the majority of poor parents are workers. Parental unemployment is a stressor of enormous proportions, but parental employment that does not pay a decent wage is not far behind in its effects. Employment of both parents places stress on middle-class families and requires extraordinary parental efforts to provide adequate monitoring and nurturing for children, but when such employment does not allow the family to escape poverty the stress is multiplied. Poverty and the social and personal problems stemming from it are issues our society must address more effectively if we wish to reduce family stress and child psychopathology (Freedman, 1993; Knitzer & Aber, 1995).

IMPLICATIONS FOR EDUCATORS

We must begin with a strong cautionary note. In their national survey of behavioral problems and competencies of children, Achenbach et al. (1991) found higher ratings on behavioral problem scales for children living in homes in which a family member was receiving mental health services. This should not be interpreted to mean that all children with behavioral problems have parents with mental illness, nor that all parents with mental illness have children with behavioral problems. Familial factors in behavioral problems are multiple, complex, and interactive—they are seldom direct and straightforward (Pinker, 2002).

With what we know about the family's role in children's emotional or behavioral disorders, educators would be foolish to ignore the influence of home conditions on school performance and conduct. Still, blaming parents of troubled students is unjustified. Very good parents can have children with very serious emotional or behavioral disorders. The teacher must realize that the parents of a youngster with an emotional or behavioral disorder have undergone a great deal of disappointment and frustration and that they, too, would like to see the child's behavior improve, both at home and at school. We find the strongest indicators for family causal contributions to antisocial behavior. However, even for conduct disorder and delinquency, we should not assume that parents are usually the primary cause.

Educators must be careful not to become entangled in the same coercive process that may characterize the antisocial student's family life. Harsh, hostile, verbal, or physical punishment at school is likely to function as a new challenge for antisocial students who may have been trained, albeit inadvertently, by their parents to step up their own aversive behavior in response to punishment. To win the battle with such students, school personnel must employ the same strategies that are recommended for parents: clearly state expectations for behavior; emphasize positive attention for appropriate conduct; and punish misbehavior in a calm, firm, nonhostile, and reasoned manner (Kauffman, Mostart, et al., 2002; Pullen, 2004; Walker, 1995; Walker et al., 2004). Teachers need to be both responsive and demanding. They must not allow their student's disadvantaged home lives to become an excuse for poor teaching.

For far too long, educators, and many others in our society as well, have not only blamed parents for students' emotional or behavioral difficulties but viewed parents as likely adversaries rather than potential sources of support for their troubled children. More positive views of parents and their role in helping their children is in large measure a result of effective parent advocacy. The organization of the Federation of Families for Children's Mental Health in 1989 brought parents together to advocate more effectively for mental health and special education programs for their children. Parent groups in many states have established resource centers that provide information and guidance for parents who want to become more actively involved in seeing that their children get appropriate education and mental health services (e.g., Friesen & Stephens, 1998; Jordan, 1995; Jordan, Goldberg, & Goldberg, 1991). Hanson and Carta (1996) suggested that teachers enlist the help and support of other professionals to do the following:

- Provide critical positive interactions with students and demonstrate these for parents
- Find and support the strengths of individual families
- Help families find and use informal sources of support from friends, neighbors, coworkers, or others in the community
- Become competent in understanding and valuing cultural differences in families
- Provide a broad spectrum of coordinated services so that families receive comprehensive, flexible, and usable services that address their needs.

SUMMARY

Although many look to the family as a likely source of deviant behavior, the factors that account for children's disordered behavior are multiple and complex. Some family factors, notably conflict and coercion, are known to increase a youngster's risk for developing an emotional or behavioral disorder. We do not fully understand why some children are more vulnerable to risk factors than others.

Families are best defined by their function. They provide protection, regulation, knowledge, affect, and self-understanding to children. Family structure, by itself, appears to have negligible effects. Divorce does not usually produce chronic disorders in children, although we can expect temporary negative effects. Children living in single-parent families may be at risk for behavioral problems, but we do not know precisely why. When children are cared for by substitutes for their biological parents, any negative effects stem primarily from traumas experienced before their separation or from a continuation of dysfunctional parenting.

An interactional–transactional model of family influence suggests that children and parents exert reciprocal effects; children affect their parents' behavior as surely as parents affect their children's. Parental discipline is a significant factor in behavioral development. Discipline that is authoritative—characterized by high levels of responsiveness and demandingness—usually produces the best outcomes. Ineffective discipline often involves lax supervision, harshness, and inconsistency.

We can view both conduct disorder and child abuse in terms of the interactions and transactions of parents and their children. In both cases, parent and child become involved in an aversive cycle of negative reinforcement, escalating aversive behavior and obtaining reinforcement through coercion. A child's difficult temperament and a parent's lack of coping skills may contribute to the initial difficulty; the coercive process then grows from nagging, whining, and yelling to more serious and assaultive behavior such as hitting.

Parental behaviors affect children's school performance and conduct. External factors such as poverty and employment may have substantial effects on family functioning. Many children grow up in poverty, even if their parents work, and their living conditions put them at risk for a variety of emotional and behavioral disorders.

Educators should be concerned about the family's influence on children's conduct at school, but they must not blame parents for children's misbehavior. School personnel must avoid becoming enmeshed in the same coercive process that antisocial students are probably experiencing at home and should use the same intervention strategies that are recommended for parents. Educators must work with other professionals to obtain comprehensive services for families.

CASE FOR DISCUSSION

He's Our Son, You Know
Weird Nick

Earlier in the day I had taken Nick to the principal's office because he had refused to restore the classroom computer password. He was a genius at computers, and it had taken no time at all for him to discover the school password and replace it with one only he knew. He liked the power this action had given him, knowing it had infuriated me. He loved it when people took his bait, as I had, whether it was in the form of a bomb threat, a detailed drawing of a stabbing, or his consistent proclamation that "Satan rules!"

Nick had sat quietly in the principal's office. He looked the part of a satanic cultist in his black jeans, black shirt, and black shoes. His black hair hung in stringy curls over his pale face. His fingers were busily drawing a pentagram. Was this just the image building of a middle school student plagued by self-doubt, or was it really an expression of belief in the occult?

I remembered how Nick seemed to get a special kick out of leaving the school building, forcing support staff to track him visually, walkie-talkies in hand. He knew that leaving the school grounds would necessitate our calling the police, so he would walk the perimeter of the property, running ahead if an adult came too close. All the other kids were afraid of "Weird Nick," as they called him. They kept their distance from this tall, powerful loner. And he distanced himself from his family, his classmates, and his teachers, unable to connect with anyone. All of us on the staff shared the concern that someday we would be hearing about Nick on the evening news.

Now his mother sat with me and the principal in my classroom after school, nervously twisting her gloves as if wringing out a rag, staring out the window at the freezing rain and growing darkness. "I just don't know what to do with him. I take him to church with me every chance I get. You know I go to church every day. Why is he doing this to me? He knows that his fascination with satanism hurts us deeply. Is he going to hurt us? He's our son, you know. What are we supposed to do?"

Questions About the Case

1. If you were Nick's teacher, how would you respond to his mother's obvious distress?
2. Given Nick's pattern of behavior, what focus would you suggest for his school program? That is, what would be your primary concerns and teaching or management strategies?
3. Would you advise Nick's teacher and principal to make special efforts to work with Nick's parents? Why or why not? If so, how?

>> PERSONAL REFLECTIONS

Family Factors

Dixie Jordan is the parent of a son with an emotional and behavioral disorder. She is director of the Families and Advocates Partnership for Education at the PACER Center in Minneapolis (a resource center for parents of children with disabilities) and is a founding member of the Federation of Families for Children's Mental Health. She is also a Systems of Care coach for Four Directions Consulting.

Why do you think there is such a strong tendency to hold parents responsible for their children's emotional or behavioral disorders?

I am the parent of two children, the younger of which has emotional and behavioral problems. When my firstborn and I were out in public, strangers often commented on what a "good" mother I was to have such an obedient, well-behaved, and compliant child. Frankly, I enjoyed the comments and really believed that those parents whose children were throwing tantrums and generally demolishing their environments were simply not very skilled in child rearing. I recall casting my share of reproachful glances in those days and thinking with some arrogance that raising children should be left to those of us who knew how to do it well. Several years later, my second child and I were on the business end of such disdain, and it was a lesson in humility that I shall never forget. Very little that I had learned in the previous 3 years as a parent worked with this child; he was neurologically different, hyperactive, inattentive, and noncompliant even when discipline was consistently applied. His doctors, his neurologist, and finally his teachers referred me to parenting classes as though the experiences I had had with my older child were nonexistent; his elementary principal even said that there was nothing wrong that a good spanking wouldn't cure. I expected understanding that this was a very difficult child to raise, but the unspoken message was that I lacked competence in basic parenting skills, the same message that I sent to similarly situated parents just a few years earlier.

Most of us in the world today are parents. The majority of us have children who do not have emotional or behavioral problems. Everything in our experience suggests that when our children are successful and obedient, it is because of our parenting. We are rein-forced socially for having a well-behaved child from friends, grandparents, even strangers. It makes sense, then, to attribute less desirable behaviors in children to the failure of their parents to provide appropriate guidance or to set firm limits. Many parents have internalized that sense of responsibility or blame for causing their child's emotional problems, even when they are not able to identify what they might have done or be doing wrong. It is a very difficult attitude to shake, especially when experts themselves cannot seem to agree on causation. With most children, the "cause" of an emotional or behavioral disorder is more likely a complex interplay of multiple factors than it is parenting styles, biology, or environmental influences as discrete entities; but it is human nature to latch onto a simple explanation—and inadequate parenting is, indeed, a simple explanation. When systems blame parents for causing their child's emotional or behavioral disorders, the focus is no longer on services to help the child learn better adaptive skills or appropriate behaviors but on rationalizing why such services may not work. When parents feel blamed, their energies shift from focusing on the needs of their child to defending themselves. In either instance, the child is less well served.

Another reason people hold parents responsible for their children's emotional or behavioral disorders is that parents may be under such unrelenting stress from trying to manage their child's behavior that they may resort to inappropriate techniques because of the failure of more conventional methods. A parent whose 8-year-old hyperactive child smashes out his bedroom window while taking time out for another problem may know that tying the child to a chair is not a good way to handle the crisis, but that parent may be out of alternatives. It may not have been the "right" thing for the parent to do, but it is not what was responsible for causing the child's problems in the first place. It would be a mistake to attribute the incidence of abuse or neglect as "causing" most emotional or behavioral disorders without consideration that difficult children are perhaps more likely to be abused because of their noncompliant or otherwise difficult behaviors.

What are the most important things for teachers to understand about being the parent of a child with emotional or behavioral disorders?

Teachers need to try to understand the isolation that many families may feel when raising a child with emotional or behavioral problems. Parents may not have amicable relationships with their extended families or with the neighbors because of their child and may not have a single person with whom they can freely discuss their child's problems or seek solutions to them. They may not have a sitter to watch their child for a few hours in the evening so they can take a break. They may on occasion feel physically threatened by their own child. Raising a child with an emotional or behavioral disorder is hard work—exhausting work—and families in many instances operate as little islands in their communities, cut off by their child's behavior from extended families, friends, or community supports.

Parents of children with emotional or behavioral disorders bring with them a historical perspective not only of their child's problems but perhaps of the failure of other systems to adequately address those problems before the child ever gets into school. By the time their children are enrolled in elementary school, many parents have lost confidence in any system to truly help them. They may be suspicious and distrustful of schools; When personalized, this leads to suspicion and distrust of teachers. Innocuous comments such as "What is going on at home with your child?" may be interpreted as "What are you doing wrong at home with your child?" It can be difficult for teachers to understand that the anger parents sometimes direct toward schools may stem from a frustration with systems in general and not with a specific program or person.

Teachers also need to understand that not all parents will be able to help their child with homework or school activities, especially if homework causes a great deal of stress or anxiety for the child. When the problem gets to be one of providing either academic support or emotional support because providing both is not possible, it may become more important to parents to support the child emotionally and to skip the homework. This should be negotiated with each family and based on the needs and abilities of each child, but the inability to help a child with homework should not be automatically viewed as lack of parental concern or involvement.

What key steps can teachers take in working more effectively with parents who have children with emotional or behavioral disorders?

One of the greatest fears expressed by parents regarding their child's school program is that if they disagree with any part of the program, the teachers will take it out on their child. If I were a special education teacher, my first step each year would be to call each parent and let them know that I am interested in their child and need their help in developing a program. I would explain to them that we might not always agree about what to do, but that they could call me and know that I would listen, and that no matter what they said I would never punish any child for the parents' displeasure with the program. As an advocate, I must say that fear of complaining is the single most important reason—according to the parents I've heard from—that they do not openly disagree with their child's school program, even when they believe it does not meet their child's needs.

A second key to building trust with parents is being honest with them about their child's needs. Parents may opt for a special education program with the expectation that it is for a few weeks or months, although the teacher knows or is at least reasonably sure that the placement may be for a few years and that the goal of total remediation of academic and behavioral deficits may never be achieved. Many parents, especially of younger children, may not see their child's problems as a disability but as a transitory phase of development. Although that certainly may be true for some children, there are many others for whom an educated guess would be that their problems will be chronic and of long duration. If parents have an understanding of the longitudinal nature of their child's disability and of the possibility of the long-term need for special education services, they will be less apt to get discouraged or angry when their child continues to need services.

Many parents report that the only time they hear from their child's teacher is when there is trouble at school. It is very important for teachers to communicate regularly with parents. There is no easier or more effective way to establish a relationship of trust and open communication with families than with frequent (and at least 50% positive) communication.

Another suggestion for teachers is to learn to apologize when a mistake has been made. Most parents expect that teachers and other school professionals will make mistakes from time to time in dealing with their child, but it is the wise teacher who is ready with an apology for wrongly accusing or for misunderstanding a situation in which the child was disciplined unfairly.

Most teachers truly do not understand how stressful IEP (individualized education program) planning meetings can be for parents. Attention at such meetings is generally focused on the problems a child is having, and parents are nearly always outnumbered by professional educators. A common occurrence at such meetings is for the teachers to refer to the parents as "Dad" or "Mom," which many parents report interpreting as denigrating or disrespectful. Careful planning of such meetings with an eye to the comfort and ease of parents can help increase their participation and their sense of power.

Parents are the true experts on their child, and the information they bring, if it can be tapped, can be invaluable in planning an appropriate program. Parents may not be specialists in behavior management, but they know their child across years and across environments, and if they do not know what techniques will work with a particular child, they at least know what has *not* worked. It can be helpful for teachers to consider the honorable intentions when they are dealing with angry or uncooperative parents. Why are the parents upset? What are they trying to convey (regardless of how inappropriately) about the needs of their child? It is human nature to become defensive, but many such stalemates are resolved by teachers who recognize first that an angry parent is one who is concerned about his or her child's school program; the teacher can then respond to the concern and not the anger. Recognizing honorable intentions, especially in forced relationships such as those at IEP planning meetings, can greatly facilitate open communication between parents and teachers.

>> QUESTIONS FOR FURTHER REFLECTION

1. How would you talk with parents whom you suspect are abusive toward their child?
2. How could you best express empathy for parents whose child is exhibiting behavior that is troublesome to you?
3. How would you approach parents who do not see their child as exhibiting troublesome behavior, although you see their child's behavior as very worrisome?

CHAPTER NINE

SCHOOL FACTORS

As you read this chapter, keep these guiding questions in mind:

- Why should educators consider how the school might contribute to the development of disordered behavior?

- With what academic skill levels should teachers of students with emotional or behavioral disorders be prepared to deal?

- What characteristics of student behavior are most likely to be associated with success in school? What are those associated with school failure?

- How might inconsistent management in the classroom produce results similar to those produced by a coercive family process?

- How does ineffective instruction in critical academic and social skills contribute to emotional and behavioral problems?

THE APPEAL OF SCHOOL FACTORS AS CAUSAL EXPLANATIONS

Besides the family, the school is probably the most important socializing influence on children and youth. In our culture, success or failure at school is tantamount to success or failure as a person; school is the occupation of all children and youth in our society—and sometimes it is their preoccupation. Academic success is fundamentally important for social development and opportunities outside of school. As nearly any student, teacher, or parent can tell you, certain types of behavior are unacceptable in school. Yet many people, including many educators, seem to be unaware of how the school environment can inadvertently foster the very behavior that teachers, parents, and students find objectionable.

The school environment is the causal factor over which teachers and principals have direct control. Some youngsters develop behavior problems before they begin school; some develop problems because of events outside of school. Even so, educators should consider how the school might ameliorate the problem or make it worse. And because many youngsters do not exhibit emotional or behavioral disorders until after they enter school, educators must recognize the possibility that the school experience could be a significant causal factor.

An ecological approach to understanding behavior includes the assumption that all aspects of a youngster's environment are interconnected; changes in one element of the ecology have implications for the other elements. Success or failure at school affects behavior at home and in the community; effects of school performance ripple outward. Consequently, success at school assumes even greater importance if a youngster's home and community environments are disastrous. Furthermore, prereferral strategies, required before a student is evaluated for special education, imply that the current classroom environment might be involved as a cause. Special educators recognize the importance of eliminating possible school contributions to misconduct before labeling the student as having a disability.

Before discussing social–interpersonal behavior and its school and classroom contexts, we must consider the characteristics of students with emotional or behavioral disorders that are relevant to a central mission of the school: academic learning. Intelligence and academic achievement are the two characteristics most closely linked to the way in which students respond to the expectations and demands of the school.

INTELLIGENCE

Intelligence tests are most reasonably viewed as tests of general learning in areas that are important to academic success. IQ refers only to performance on an intelligence test. IQs are moderately good predictors of how students will perform academically and how they will adapt to the demands of everyday life. Standardized tests are the best single means we have to measure general intelligence, even though performance on a test is not the only indicator of intelligence and may not tap abilities in specific areas that are important in everyday life (see Gould, 1996).

The definition and measurement of intelligence are controversial issues, with implications for the definition of giftedness, mental retardation, and other exceptionalities for which special education may be needed (see Hallahan & Kauffman, 2003; Reschly, 1997). Psychologists agree that intelligence is comprised of a variety of abilities, both verbal and nonverbal. The ability to direct and sustain attention, process information, think logically, perceive social circumstances accurately, and understand abstractions, for example, are distinguishable parts of what makes a person "smart." But psychologists continue to debate the merits of the concept of *general intelligence* versus the idea of *multiple intelligences* (e.g., Gardner & Hatch, 1989; Grinder, 1985; Sternberg, 1991; White & Breen, 1998), and debating these issues is beyond the scope of this book. Goleman (1995) popularized the notion of *emotional intelligence,* which may have particular relevance to children and youth with emotional or behavioral disorders.

Intelligence of Students with Mild or Moderate Disorders

Authorities on emotional and behavioral disorders have traditionally assumed that students with such disorders fall within the normal range of intelligence. If the IQ falls below 70, the student is considered to have mental retardation, even when behavioral problems are a major concern. Occasionally, however, students with IQs in the retardation range are said to have emotional or behavioral disorders or learning disabilities rather than mental retardation, on the presumption that emotional or perceptual disorders prevent them from performing to their true capacity (cf. Hallahan, Lloyd, Kauffman, Weiss, & Martinez, 2005).

The average IQ for most students with emotional or behavioral disorders is in the low normal range, with a dispersion of scores from the severe mental retardation range to the highly gifted level. Over the past 40 years, numerous studies have yielded the same general finding: Average tested IQ for these students is in the low 90s (Bortner & Birch, 1969; Bower, 1981; Duncan, Forness, & Hartsough, 1995; Graubard, 1964; Kauffman, Cullinan, & Epstein, 1987; Lyons & Powers, 1963; Motto & Wilkins, 1968; Rubin & Balow, 1978). We have accumulated enough research on these students' intelligence to draw this conclusion: Although the majority fall only slightly below average in IQ, a disproportionate number, compared to the normal distribution, score in the dull normal and mild mental retardation range, and relatively few fall in the upper ranges. Research findings suggest a distribution like that in Figure 9.1. The hypothetical curve for most students with emotional or behavioral disorders shows a mean of about 90 to 95 IQ, with more students falling at the lower IQ levels and fewer at the higher levels than in the normal distribution. If this hypothetical distribution of intelligence is correct, then we can expect a greater than normal frequency of academic failure and socialization difficulties for these students.

Intelligence of Students with Autism and Schizophrenia

Severe emotional or behavioral disorders occur across the entire spectrum of intelligence, but they are most frequently accompanied by a lower than average IQ. Mental

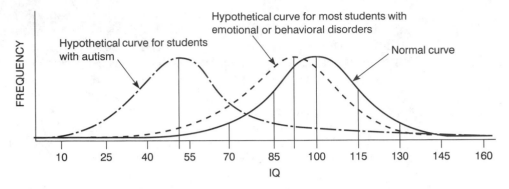

Figure 9.1
Hypothetical frequency distributions of IQ for most students with emotional or behavioral disorders and students with autism as compared to a normal frequency distribution

health professionals long suspected that children with autism are not really characterized by mental retardation, even though they function at a retarded level in most areas of development. Kanner's (1943) description of autism strengthened the belief that such children are potentially normal in intelligence. DeMyer (1975) summarized Kanner's reasons for believing that children with autism have normal intelligence:

> The reasons for his belief were the presence of splinter skills, "intelligent" faces, few reports of motor dysfunction, and "refusal" to perform when age-appropriate items from intelligence tests were presented to them. One widely held theory advanced to explain these "facts" was that most if not all autistic . . . children had anatomically normal brains and that relatively high splinter skills were a "true" reflection of their potential intelligence. If the right treatment key could be found, then the seriously delayed verbal intelligence would advance in an accelerated fashion to catch up with the splinter skills and with the norms of the child's chronological age. (pp. 109–110)

Within the past 30 years, data have been accumulated to indicate that the IQs of most children with autism can be reliably determined and that the majority score in the moderate to severe range of mental retardation (Charlop-Christy, Schreibman, Pierce, & Kurtz, 1998; DeMyer, 1975; DeMyer, Barton, Alpern, Kimberlin, Allen, & Steele, 1974; Green, Fein, Joy, & Waterhouse, 1995; Lovaas, Koegel, Simmons, & Long, 1973; Prior & Werry, 1986; Rutter & Schopler, 1987). On the basis of available data, the distribution of intelligence for these students is hypothesized as shown in Figure 9.1. The average IQ is probably near 50, with the vast majority of students falling between about 35 and about 70. Nevertheless, we know much more about the nature of the cognitive abilities and disabilities associated with autism today than we did a quarter century ago.

Autism may vary from mild to severe, and the cognitive problems associated with the condition are varied. As Grandin (1995), a highly intelligent and creative adult with autism explained, "autism is a heterogeneous disorder with subtypes along a continuum ranging from highly verbal classical Kanner's syndrome, to nonverbal regressive/epileptic types with poor receptive speech" (p. 153). Individuals with autism may be particularly adept at some skills, particularly those requiring visual–spatial and sensory–motor abilities (Green, Feir, Joy, & Waterhouse, 1995; see also Sacks, 1995, Sheehan, 2003, for extensive case descriptions). The cognitive impairments associated with autism are often severe, but they tend to be problems in specific types of cognitive processes. Green et al. (1995) concluded that "autistic children have specific impairments in the selectivity and shifting of attention, executive functioning, abstraction of information and reasoning, language (particularly the social aspects), and social cognition" (p. 25).

Although the intelligence of students with schizophrenia is generally higher than that of students with autism, the distribution for students with schizophrenia is probably below that for the general population. If we were to plot a hypothetical distribution for students with schizophrenia, it would approximate the distribution for most students with emotional or behavioral disorders. The cognitive difficulties of these students are primarily problems of attention and information processing—not paying attention to the right things, not making sense of information, not thinking logically, and not understanding social relationships.

Implications of Low IQ

Research clearly suggests that students with emotional or behavioral disorders tend to be lower than normal in IQ and that the most severely disabled students also tend to be the lowest in IQ. The correlation between intelligence and level of disorder does not imply a causal relationship. Even so, the IQs of students with emotional or behavioral disorders appear to be the best single predictor of educational achievement and later adjustment (see Prior & Werry, 1986). DeMyer (1975) and Rutter and Bartak (1973), for example, reported that their participants' IQs at initial evaluation were good predictors of academic and social skill achievement of children with autism. The predictive power of IQ for less severely disabled students' academic achievement and future social adjustment probably approximates the predictive power of IQ for students in the normal distribution: significant but far from perfect.

ACADEMIC ACHIEVEMENT

Although academic achievement is usually assessed by standardized achievement tests, it is dangerous to place too much confidence in them because they are not highly accurate measures of academic aptitude nor highly precise measures of the academic attainment of the individual student (Reschly, 1997). Scores on achievement tests do, however, allow comparisons between the performances of normative and non-normative groups, which are valuable in assessing and predicting students' school success.

Achievement of Most Students with Emotional or Behavioral Disorders

The academic achievement of disturbed and delinquent students has been studied for many years (Bower, 1981; Graubard, 1964; Motto & Wilkins, 1968; Rubin &

Balow, 1978; Silberberg & Silberberg, 1971; Stone & Rowley, 1964; Tamkin, 1960; Trout, Nordness, Pierce, & Epstein, 2003; see also Walker, Ramsey, & Gresham, 2004). Collectively, research leads to the conclusion that most such students are academically deficient, even taking into account their mental ages, which are typically slightly below those of their chronological age-mates. Although some students with emotional or behavioral disorders work at grade level and a very few are academically advanced, most function a year or more below grade level in most academic areas.

Achievement of Students with Pervasive Developmental Disorders

Compared to their age-mates, few students with autism and other pervasive developmental disorders are academically proficient. Many require training in self-help skills (toileting, dressing, feeding, bathing, grooming), language, and play skills. The highly intelligent, academically achieving student with autism is a relative rarity; most are severely behind their age-mates in academic attainment and require prolonged, directive instruction in a carefully controlled teaching environment to attain functional academic skills (Charlop-Christy et al., 1997; S. L. Harris, 1995a, 1995b; Lovaas, 1987; Schopler, Mesibov, & Hearsey, 1995).

The behavioral characteristics of children diagnosed with schizophrenia tend to persist into adulthood (Howells & Guirguis, 1984; Werry et al., 1994). Although there are few data specific to academic learning, students with schizophrenia might be expected to have problems in academic achievement on the basis of their lower than average IQs; problems with language, attention, perception, and logic; and their deficits in social skills (Prior & Werry, 1986).

Implications of Academic Underachievement

Low achievement and behavior problems go hand in hand; they are highly related risk factors (Kupersmidt & Patterson, 1987). In most cases, it is not clear whether disordered behavior causes underachievement or vice versa. Sometimes the weight of evidence may be more on one side of the issue than the other, but in the majority of instances the precise nature of the relationship is elusive. As we will see, there is reason to believe that underachievement and disordered behavior affect each other reciprocally. Disordered behavior apparently makes academic achievement less likely, and underachievement produces social consequences that are likely to foster inappropriate behavior (B. Bower, 1995; Walker et al., 2004). In any case, we have known for decades that the effects of educational failure on future opportunity should cause alarm for the plight of students with emotional or behavioral disorders:

> Educational attainment and opportunity are linked in many ways. Abundant evidence supports the view that education affects income, occupational choice, social and economic mobility, political participation, social deviance, etc. Indeed, educational attainment is related to opportunity in so many ways that the two terms seem inextricably intertwined in the mind of the layman and in the findings of the social scientist. (Levin, Guthrie, Kleindorfer, & Stout, 1971, p. 14)

Some students with autism and others with pervasive developmental disorders may require an instructional focus on self-care and daily living skills. If they do not achieve these nonacademic skills, they may be consigned to lives of stunted development and continuing dependence.

SOCIAL SKILLS

Interest in the social skills that make people attractive to others and enable them to cope effectively with difficult interpersonal circumstances is many decades, if not centuries, old. Obviously, people who are considered to have emotional or behavioral disorders lack certain critical social skills. However, it is often not so obvious just what those skills are, and how to teach people the skills they lack is even less apparent (see Blake, Wang, Cartlege, & Gardner, 2000; Hallahan et al., 2005).

Social skills related to schooling may be those that allow a student to establish and maintain positive interpersonal relationships, be accepted by peers, and get along well in the larger social environment (Walker et al., 2004). Students with emotional or behavioral disorders often do not know how to make and keep friends. They frequently behave in ways that anger and disappoint their teachers and classmates. They find it difficult or impossible to adjust to changing expectations when they move from one social environment to another (cf. Farmer & Hollowell, 1994; Guevremont & Dumas, 1994; Hundert, 1995; Kavale, Mathur, & Mostert, 2004; Walker, Schwarz, Nippold, Irvin, & Noell, 1994).

A list of the most important social skills encompasses many that are necessary for academic and social success in school. They include listening to others, taking turns in conversations, greeting others, joining in ongoing activities, giving compliments, expressing anger in socially acceptable ways, offering help to others, following rules, being adequately organized and focused, and doing high-quality work. Knowing what these skills are is important; assessing the extent to which individual students have mastered them is critical in dealing effectively with antisocial behavior (Kavale et al., 2004; Walker et al., 2004).

At the heart of social skills is the ability to communicate verbally and nonverbally—to use language competently. In fact, a large percentage of students with emotional or behavioral disorders is known to have language disorders (Rogers-Adkinson & Griffith, 1999). Although these students may have problems in any area of language competence (e.g., they may have difficulty with word sounds, word forms, grammar, and so on), they tend to be particularly deficient in *pragmatics*—the practical, social uses of language. Acting-out youngsters may know how to use language very effectively to irritate, intimidate, and coerce others, but they do not have skills in using language effectively for positive, constructive social purposes. A functional analysis of their language skills is likely to indicate that they need to learn to use language to obtain desired consequences in ways that are socially acceptable. Withdrawn students lack the sophisticated language repertoires their normal peers have for engaging others in discourse. We may conclude that a lack of social skills, especially pragmatic language skills, may underlie many of the behavior problems that are predictive of school failure. Students with emotional or behavioral disorders may need instruction in specific language-based social skills such as these:

- Identifying, labeling, and expressing needs, wants, and feelings
- Describing and interpreting emotions of oneself and others
- Recognizing incipient emotions, providing control over them, and integrating them into appropriate social behavior.

Behavior Predictive of School Success and Failure

Educational researchers have become interested in identifying the overt classroom behavioral characteristics associated with academic accomplishment in the hope that teachers can teach those behaviors. For instance, if attentiveness is found to correlate positively with achievement, then teaching students to pay better attention might improve academic performance. Similarly, if achievement correlates negatively with certain dependence behaviors, then reducing dependency behaviors might be successful. Implicit here is the assumption that the identified behavioral characteristics will have more than a correlational relationship to achievement; there will be a causal link between certain overt behaviors and achievement.

The causal relationship between overt classroom behavior and academic success or failure is not entirely clear. Although a frequent strategy of teachers and educational researchers has been to modify behavior (such as task attention) in the hope of improving performance on academic tasks, direct modification of academic skills has proved most effective in preventing failure or remediating deficits (Lloyd, Hallahan, Kauffman, & Keller, 1998). For decades, we have known that in some cases direct reinforcement of academic performance eliminates classroom behavior problems (Kauffman, Mostert, Trent, & Hallahan, 2002). Increasing a student's correct academic responses is often effective in reducing classroom behavior problems (Gunter, Hummel, & Conroy, 1998; Trout, Epstein, Mickelson, Nelson, & Lewis, in press). Nevertheless, classroom success or failure is determined by more than academic competence; doing the academic work is critical, but it is not the whole story (see Walker & McConnell, 1988).

Success and failure in school correlate with a variety of academic and social characteristics. Students who are low achieving and socially unsuccessful tend to exhibit

- Behavior requiring teacher intervention or control, such as teasing, annoying, or interfering with others
- Dependence on the teacher for direction
- Difficulty paying attention and concentrating
- Becoming upset under pressure
- Sloppy, impulsive work
- Low self-confidence

High-achieving and popular students, on the other hand, tend to exhibit

- Rapport with the teacher, including friendly conversation before and after class and responsiveness in class

- Appropriate verbal interaction, asking relevant questions, volunteering, and participating in class discussions
- Doing more than the minimum work required, taking care to understand directions and to master all details
- Originality and reasoning ability, quickness to grasping new concepts and apply them
- Sensitivity to the feelings of others.

However, we must also consider the teacher's expectations and responses to students' behavior. Sometimes, as we shall discuss further, the mismatch between a student's and teacher's temperaments seems to be the primary reason for academic failure (Keogh, 2003).

School Failure and Later Adjustment

Low IQ and academic failure often foretell difficulty for students. A higher proportion of those with low IQ and achievement than of students with high IQ and achievement will experience adjustment difficulties as adults; those with low IQ are disproportionately represented among people who commit criminal acts (Bower, 1995). A high proportion of schizophrenic and antisocial adults are known to have exhibited low academic achievement as children (Bower, Shellhammer, & Daily, 1960; Kazdin, 1998; Robins, 1966, 1986; Watt, Stolorow, Lubensky, & McClelland, 1970).

However, low IQ and achievement alone do not spell disaster for later adjustment. Most youngsters with mild mental retardation, whose achievement may lag behind even their mental ages, do not turn into social misfits, criminals, or institutional residents in adult life; they are considered problems only during their school years (Edgerton, 1984). The same can be said of most youngsters with learning disabilities, whose academic retardation usually marks them as school failures (see Hallahan et al., 2005). Even among children and youth with emotional or behavioral disorders, the prognosis is not necessarily poor just because the student has a low IQ or fails academically.

When school failure is accompanied by serious and persistent antisocial behavior—conduct disorder—the risk for mental health problems in adulthood is most grave (Fergusson & Horwood, 1995; Kazdin, 1998; Walker et al., 2004). And the earlier the onset and the greater the number of antisocial behaviors, the greater the risk. Even when conduct disorder is accompanied by low intelligence and low achievement, we must be careful in drawing causal inferences; if a causal connection does exist between achievement and antisocial behavior, however, then it has implications for education, as we have long known:

> It is well known . . . that children with antisocial behavior are usually seriously retarded in academic performance. We do not know at this point whether academic failure usually preceded or followed the onset of antisocial behavior. If experiencing academic failure contributes to the occurrence of antisocial behavior disorders, then it is clear that preventive efforts should include efforts to forestall failure through programs such as those currently endeavoring to improve the IQs and academic success of disadvantaged children either by educating their parents to stimulate them as infants or through a variety of educationally oriented daycare and preschool programs. (Robins, 1974, p. 455)

To reiterate, low IQ and school failure alone are not as highly predictive of adult psychopathology as when they are combined with conduct disorder. The outlook for a youngster is particularly grim when he or she is at once relatively unintelligent, underachieving, and highly aggressive or extremely withdrawn. If conduct disorder is fostered by school failure, then programs to prevent school failure may also contribute to prevention of antisocial behavior.

INTELLIGENCE, ACHIEVEMENT, AND ANTISOCIAL BEHAVIOR

Given that antisocial behavior (for example, hostile aggression, theft, incorrigibility, running away from home, truancy, vandalism, sexual misconduct), low intelligence, and low achievement are interrelated in a complex way, it may be important to clarify their apparent interrelationship. Figure 9.2 shows a hypothetical relationship among the three characteristics. The various shaded areas in the diagram represent the approximate (hypothesized) proportions in which various combinations of the three characteristics occur. The diagram illustrates the hypothesis that relatively few youngsters who exhibit antisocial behavior are above average in IQ and achievement

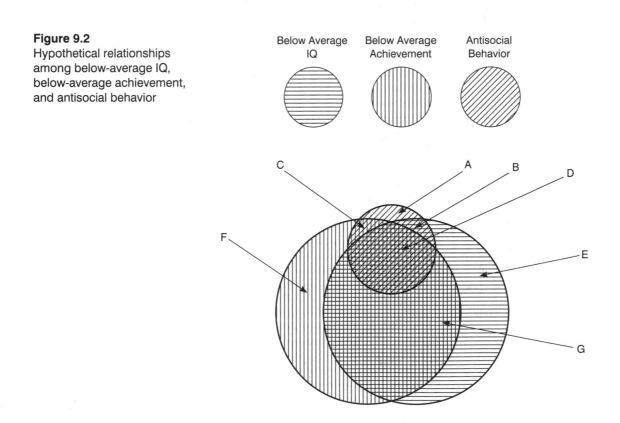

Figure 9.2
Hypothetical relationships among below-average IQ, below-average achievement, and antisocial behavior

(area A), most are below average in IQ and achievement (area D), and a few are below average in only IQ (area B) or only achievement (area C). Whereas the majority of underachieving youngsters are low in IQ (areas D and G), they are usually not antisocial (area G is much larger than area D). Some youngsters are low in IQ but not achievement (areas B and E) or vice versa (areas C and F), but relatively few of these youngsters are antisocial (area E is much larger than area B, and area F is much larger than area C).

Keep in mind that additional factors enter the picture to determine the adult outcome for children and youth with a given combination of characteristics. The severity of the antisocial behavior, the parents' behavioral characteristics, and perhaps parental socioeconomic circumstances influence the probability that behavioral difficulties will persist into adulthood. To the extent that youngsters exhibit many antisocial behaviors in a variety of settings and at high frequency, have parents who are themselves antisocial or abusive, and come from a lower social class, they have a greater chance of being hospitalized as mentally ill or incarcerated as a criminal when they become adults (Bower, 1995; Loeber, 1982; Robins, 1979; Walker et al., 2004). Also, remember that many children and youth who are low in intelligence, low in achievement, high in antisocial behavior, or some combination of these do not exhibit serious behavioral disorders as adults. Any prediction of adult behavior based on childhood behavioral characteristics is subject to substantial error in prediction for the individual case.

SCHOOL'S CONTRIBUTION TO EMOTIONAL AND BEHAVIORAL DISORDERS

The demands of school and the student's social and academic repertoire probably affect each other reciprocally. For decades, we have known that a circular reaction occurs between the student and the social context of the classroom (Glidewell, 1969; Glidewell, Kantor, Smith, & Stringer, 1966; Keogh, 2003). Students who are healthy, intelligent, upper middle class, high achieving, high in self-esteem, and adroit in interpersonal skills (likely to be perceived as "easy" and "teachable" by a teacher) enter the classroom at a distinct advantage. They are likely to make positive approaches to others, who in turn are likely to respond positively; and these advantaged students will be sensitive to others' responses toward them and be able to use their intelligence to further enhance their personal power and social status. Intelligence and achievement beget social acceptability, self-esteem, accurate social perception, and status, all of which in turn induce positive social responses from others and facilitate achievement. This perspective on the student's reciprocal interaction with the social ecology of the classroom is entirely consistent with research (cf. Colvin, Greenberg, & Sherman, 1993; Haager & Vaughn, 1997; Hess & Holloway, 1984; Keogh, 2003; Wong & Donahue, 2002). Moreover, the same coercive process found in families of antisocial boys (Patterson, 1986a, 1986b) can be found in schools (Walker et al., 2004). Educators (like parents) and classroom peers (like siblings) can become entangled in escalating contests of aversiveness, in which the individual who causes greater pain is the winner, obtaining negative reinforcement and digging in for the next round of conflict.

The same type of interaction between the student's temperament and the parents' child-rearing techniques appears to occur between the student's temperament and the school's social and academic demands. The student who is slow to approach others, has irregular work habits, is slow to adapt to new situations, and is predominantly negative in mood is most likely to have difficulty in school, although any temperamental characteristic is susceptible to modification with proper handling (Carey, 1998; Keogh, 2003; Martin, 1992; Thomas, Chess, & Birch, 1968).

The school, like the family and biological factors, does not operate unilaterally to determine students' emotional and behavioral development. However, we can identify classroom conditions and teacher reactions to pupil behavior that make behavioral difficulties more likely or could be changed to reduce the likelihood of acting out and other emotional or behavioral problems (Keogh, 2003; Kerr & Nelson, 2002; Walker, 1995). The school might contribute to disordered behavior and academic failure in one or more of the following ways:

1. Insensitivity to students' individuality
2. Inappropriate expectations for students
3. Inconsistent management of behavior
4. Instruction in nonfunctional and irrelevant skills
5. Ineffective instruction in critical skills
6. Destructive contingencies of reinforcement
7. Undesirable models of school conduct.

Besides these factors, others such as crowded and deteriorated schools and classrooms are associated with aggression and other problems. The physical conditions under which students are taught will surely affect their behavior for better or worse.

Insensitivity to Students' Individuality

Special educators of all persuasions recognize the necessity of meeting pupils' individual needs. Some speculate, in fact, that the large proportion of schoolchildren identified as having learning and behavioral disorders reflects the refusal of the education system to accommodate individual differences. Although not making reasonable accommodations to individual needs undoubtedly contributes to some students' failures or maladjustment, reasonable requirements for conformity to rules and standards clearly do not account for the failure or deviance of many others. In fact, just the opposite may be the case for some students; they may fail and behave antisocially because reasonable rules and expectations for conformity to standards of achievement and civility are not made clear (cf. Kauffman, Mostert et al., 2002; Walker, 1995; Walker et al., 2004).

However, rigidity and failure to tolerate differences do demand scrutiny. By making the same academic and behavioral requirements of each student, schools can force many students who are only slightly different from most into roles of academic failures or social deviants. Through inflexibility and stultifying insistence on sameness, schools can create conditions that inhibit or punish healthy expression of individuality. In an atmosphere of regimentation and repression, many students will respond with resentment, hostility, vandalism, or passive resistance to the system (see Keogh, 2003).

For students unfortunate enough to differ more than slightly from the norm in learning or behavior, the message in some classrooms is clear: To be yourself is to be bad, inadequate, or unacceptable. These students' self-perceptions are likely to become negative, their perceptions of social situations distorted, and their intellectual efficiency and motivation weakened. They can become caught in a self-perpetuating cycle of conflict and negative influence.

Insensitivity to individuals does not, of course, emanate from the school as an abstraction. Administrators, teachers, and other pupils are the people who are sensitive or insensitive to expressions of individuality. School administrators can create a reasonably tolerant or a repressive mood in the way they deal with students and adults. Teachers are primarily responsible for the classroom emotional climate and for how restrictive or permissive, individualized or regimented the student's school day will be. Peers may demand strict conformity regarding dress, speech, or deportment for social acceptance, especially in the higher grades. On the other hand, peers may be an easygoing, open group in which a fellow student can find acceptance even though he or she is quite different from the group.

Teachers and administrators who are sensitive to students but have clear and positive expectations for academic performance seem to foster appropriate behavior. We should not assume, however, that a positive and productive school climate is fostered merely by an emphasis on talking to students about their family and emotional problems. Teachers must not abandon their role as adult authority figures in attempts to develop better relationships with their students: "When teachers who have difficulty in maintaining basic order in the classroom treat pupils as peers, they may worsen an already bad situation" (Kasen, Johnson, & Cohen, 1990, p. 175). A critical key to generally improved student behavior is a clear, consistent plan for schoolwide discipline (Lewis & Sugai, 1999; Lewis, Sugai, & Colvin, 1998; Liaupsin, Jolivette, & Scott, 2004; Martella, Nelson, & Marchand-Martella, 2003; Rosenberg & Jackman, 2003; Walker et al., 2004).

In classic developmental studies, Thomas and Chess (1984) and Thomas et al. (1968) showed that the growth of emotional or behavioral disorders is accelerated by adults' failure to treat youngsters in accordance with their temperamental individuality (see the accompanying case book for the case of Richard, involving temperament in the context of school, and Keogh, 2003). Little experimental evidence suggests that emotional or behavioral disorders are caused by insensitivity alone. However, we can readily find anecdotal evidence that insensitivity may be a feature of many students' school experience (Epstein, 1981; see also case descriptions in Kauffman, Mostert et al., 2002). Unfortunately, insensitivity and rigidity in school environments are not relics of the past. They have always been problematic, and they remain a bane of education. Such environments appear to be a breeding ground for antisocial behavior.

The foregoing discussion is decidedly not intended as an indictment of all rules, regulations, or demands for conformity in the classroom or school. Certainly, reasonable rules must be maintained for the safety and well-being of all. No social institution can exist without some requirements of conformity, and one cannot interpret an appeal for tolerance of individual expression to mean that *anything* should be accepted. Nevertheless, insensitivity to students as individuals and needless repression of their uniqueness can contribute to emotional or behavioral problems. Students like to have a piece of the action, and allowing them to participate in self-determination of their classroom lives often results in improved behavior and academic performance (Clarke et al., 1995; Lovitt, 1977; Walker, 1995; Walker et al., 2004).

Inappropriate Expectations for Students

The expectations teachers *do* hold for their students, and the expectations they *should* hold, are continuing sources of controversy in American education (see Kauffman, 2002; Kauffman, Mostert et al., 2002; Keogh, 2003). Two facets of the problem of expectations are the effects of what teachers are led to believe about their students (especially the possible biasing effects of diagnostic or administrative labels) and teachers' classroom standards of behavior and academic performance.

Effects of Labels

Concern about labeling is decades old, and probably older than special education itself. Some claim that many of the problems of exceptional children originate with and are perpetuated by the labels we use to designate them (see Kauffman, 1999c, 2002, 2003a; Lilly, 1992). Some have assumed that a label such as "emotionally disturbed" carries with it an expectation of misbehavior and lower academic performance. The teacher's lower expectation for students labeled *exceptional* will be communicated in subtle ways to the students, and they will indeed fulfill this expectation. Moreover, there is concern about the stigma that goes with receiving a label denoting exceptionality, especially disability. Students' own expectations may also influence their performance.

Ultimately, we must face the fact that labels of some type are necessary for communication (Burbach, 1981). They simply cannot be avoided unless we refuse to discuss students' problems (Kauffman, 1999c, 2003a, 2003b). The issues, then, should be how we understand and use labels and how we work with the larger problem—our perceptions of the people whose characteristics we refer to when we use labels. There are good arguments for using labels responsibly:

> In addition to serving as an explanation for unusual behavior, the use of labels is defended on other grounds by some special educators. First, they argue that the elimination of one set of labels would only prompt development of another set. In other words, they believe that individuals with special problems will always be perceived as different. Second, these special educators contend that labels help professionals communicate with one another. In talking about a research study, for example, it helps to know with what type of population the study was conducted. Third, they assert that

labels help spotlight the special needs of people with disabilities for the general public. . . . Finally, they point out that anytime we use an intervention that is not universal—used with all students regardless of their characteristics—we automatically apply a label. That is, labels are an inescapable part of preventive practices unless those practices are universal—applied to all children without regard to their individual characteristics. (Hallahan & Kauffman, 2003, pp. 46–47)

A popular assumption is that receiving special education services destroys students' self-esteem and social status, regardless of the particular label under which they are served. Research suggests that this assumption may be unfounded for children with learning disabilities and emotional or behavioral disorders. Studies indicate that students receiving special education for learning or behavioral disorders—students receiving these labels—may have lower self-concepts or social status than do students without learning or behavioral problems. They have not, however, been found to have lower self-perceptions and status than do nonlabeled students who have academic or behavioral problems (Coleman, McHam, & Minnett, 1992; Patterson, Kupersmidt, & Griesler, 1988; Sale & Carey, 1995). Students appear to suffer damage to self-esteem and social status as a consequence of learning and behavior problems, not as a result of being labeled; the label follows the problem, not vice versa (see also Singer, 1988). In fact, a label for their difficulties appears to give many people with disabilities a sense of relief (e.g., "Finally, I know what my problem is!") and to provide others with an understandable reason for differences that, unlabeled, result in social rejection (cf. Hallahan & Kauffman, 2003). Besides, high self-esteem has not been shown to cause better academic performance, interpersonal success, or happiness (Baumeister, Campbell, Krueger, & Vohs, 2003).

Effects of Classroom Standards

The early 21st century is marked by an emphasis on higher academic and social standards in American public schools. For students with disabilities and serious academic or social problems, these increased expectations, if interpreted as universal standards demanded of all students, create the certainty of failure without extraordinary supports and a high probability of failure even with the most effective interventions known (see Hallahan & Kauffman, 2003; Hockenbury, Kauffman, & Hallahan, 1999; Kauffman, 1999e, 2002). Especially for students with emotional and behavioral disorders, alternative placements in which the expectations are adjusted to fit the students' prior learning and abilities are essential if their education is to be appropriate (see Kauffman, Bantz, & McCullough, 2002).

The research and speculation on effects of teacher bias do not lead logically to the conclusion that simply expecting normal behavior will help students with emotional or behavioral disorders improve. After all, it is quite clear that most such students are lower in tested intelligence, academic achievement, and social adjustment than are average students. Many are far below their age mates in numerous areas of development, and expecting normal performance from them is unrealistic.

For many years, we have had good reason to suspect that a discrepancy between the child's ability and adults' expectations for performance contributes directly to the development of disordered behavior (Center, Deitz, & Kaufman, 1982; Kirk, 1972). If the expectations are too high or too low, the student may become disinterested, dispirited, and disruptive. We do know that students with emotional or behavioral disorders often are motivated by negative reinforcement—by behaving in ways that allow them to escape or avoid expectations for performance (Cipani & Spooner, 1997; Gunter, Denny, Jack, Shores, & Nelson, 1993).

If expectations that are too low become self-fulfilling prophecies, and if expectations that are too high are frustrating and depressing and prompt attempts to avoid them, then what level of expectation will avoid the risk of contributing to development of disordered behavior? Expectations of improvement are always in order—assuming, of course, that the teacher knows the student's current level of academic performance or adequate social behavior and can specify a reasonable level of improvement along a measurable dimension. If pupil and teacher define *reasonable* together, then the expectations should be neither too low nor too high.

Research does not suggest that teachers' expectations and demands are well attuned to students' abilities and characteristics (Gunter et al., 1993, 1998). Investigating the standards and expectations of regular and special education teachers for students' academic performance and social–interpersonal behavior, Walker and Rankin (1983) found that teachers' expectations could be described as narrow, intense, and demanding. These findings suggest that teachers' expectations can be a significant problem for students with emotional or behavioral disorders, regardless of whether they are in a special or general education class.

Elementary and secondary school teachers' expectations and demands appear to be similar. Kerr and Zigmond (1986) studied the behavioral characteristics that high school teachers considered critical for success and those they considered intolerable; their findings were similar to those of Walker and his associates, who studied elementary teachers' standards and expectations (Hersh & Walker, 1983; Walker & Rankin, 1983; see also Walker et al., 2004). Students with externalizing problems, who act out aggressively or have conduct disorders, are extremely likely to fail to meet teachers' expectations and to violate teachers' standards of classroom decorum. Those who are compliant and productive are, predictably, well liked by teachers. The top behavioral characteristics said by teachers to be critical for success in the studies by Kerr and Zigmond (1986) and Hersh and Walker (1983) were

1. Follows established classroom rules
2. Listens to teacher instructions
3. Complies with teacher commands
4. Does in-class assignments as directed
5. Avoids breaking classroom rule(s) even when encouraged by a peer
6. Produces work of acceptable quality given his or her skill level.

The top characteristics considered by classroom teachers to be intolerable in a regular classroom were

1. Engages in inappropriate sexual behavior
2. Steals
3. Behaves inappropriately in class when corrected

4. Damages others' property
5. Refuses to obey teacher-imposed classroom rules
6. Is self-abusive
7. Makes lewd or obscene gestures
8. Ignores teacher warnings or reprimands.

Given teachers' standards and expectations, it should not be surprising that students with emotional or behavioral disorders and their teachers frequently disappoint each other, setting the stage for conflict and coercion. We should not inappropriately generalize to *all* teachers or assume that high standards and low tolerance for misbehavior are undesirable. Some teachers apparently make few demands and have great tolerance for deviance, and others are just the opposite (Kauffman, Lloyd, & McGee, 1989; Kauffman, Wong, Lloyd, Hung, & Pullen, 1991; Walker, 1986). Compared to regular classroom teachers, special education teachers may be somewhat more tolerant of misbehavior and judge students' behavior as less deviant (Fabre & Walker, 1987; Safran & Safran, 1987; Walker, 1986). Teachers' expressed tolerance for troublesome behavior may be affected by several factors, including their self-perceived competence, the availability and quality of technical assistance, and the difficulty of the particular group of students they are teaching (Safran & Safran, 1987). Teachers who have higher standards and lower tolerance for disorderly behavior may also provide more effective instruction (Gersten, Walker, & Darch, 1988). The teacher's temperament in interaction with the child's seems to be the critical factor in many school problems (Keogh, 2003).

Inconsistent Management of Behavior

A major hypothesis underlying a structured approach to educating students with emotional or behavioral disorders is that a lack of structure or order in their daily lives contributes to their difficulties. When youngsters cannot predict adults' responses to their behavior, they become anxious, confused, and unable to choose appropriate behavioral alternatives. If at one time they are allowed to engage in a certain misbehavior without penalty and at another time are punished for the same misconduct, the unpredictability of the consequences of their behavior encourages them to act inappropriately. If they cannot depend on favorable consequences following good behavior, they have little incentive to perform well.

We find strong support in the child development literature for the contention that inconsistent behavior management fosters disordered behavior (Reid & Eddy, 1997). If one can extrapolate from the findings that inconsistent parental discipline adversely affects children's behavioral development, then it seems highly likely that inconsistent behavior-management techniques in the school will also have negative effects. Capricious, inconsistent discipline in the classroom will contribute nothing toward helping students learn appropriate conduct. School-based studies of antisocial behavior such as vandalism also indicate a connection between punitive, inconsistent discipline and problem behavior (Mayer, Nafpaktitis, Butterworth, & Hollingsworth, 1987; see also Kauffman, Mostert et al., 2002; Walker et al., 2004). Even though inconsistent management may not be the root of all behavioral disorders, it obviously contributes to the perpetuation of behavioral difficulties.

Instruction in Nonfunctional and Irrelevant Skills

One way in which a school increases the probability that students will misbehave or be truant is in offering instruction for which pupils have no real or imagined use. Not only does this kind of education fail to engage pupils, but it also hinders their social adaptation by wasting their time and substituting trivial information for knowledge that would allow them to pursue rewarding activities, thus increasing the likelihood of their dropping out of school (Rylance, 1997).

The problem of making education relevant to students' lives has plagued teachers for a long time. The question we need to ask is more than whether the teacher or other adults know that instruction is important for the student's future. To resolve the question, the youngster must be convinced that the learning he or she is asked to do is or will be important. The teacher must convince the student that the instruction is in some ways worthwhile; otherwise, the classroom will be merely a place for the pupil to avoid or to disrupt. For some students with a history of school problems, convincing them will require provision of artificial reasons to learn, such as extrinsic rewards for behavior and performance.

Ineffective Instruction in Critical Skills

Social acceptance and positive self-perceptions are greatly enhanced by academic competence and skills in interacting with one's peers and authority figures. Thus, the classroom must be a place in which all class members are learning critical academic skills and the social skills critical for success in general education. Ineffective instruction in either area—academic or social learning—dooms many students to academic or social failure, or both. Nevertheless, many classrooms are not places where students are taught effectively but places where they are left to fend for themselves instructionally, to pick up whatever skills they might acquire through incidental learning or self-discovery.

We cannot overemphasize the importance of academic learning to emotional well-being and behavioral development (cf. Coleman & Vaughn, 2000; Gunter & Denny, 1998; Gunter et al., 1998; Kauffman, Mostert et al., 2002; Mooney, Epstein, Reid, & Nelson, 2003; Rhode, Jenson, & Reavis, 1992; Walker, 1995). For everyone, not just children and youth, being able to meet everyday expectations is critical to mental health. Faced with constant failure and unfavorable comparisons to peers, nearly anyone will succumb to feelings of frustration, worthlessness, irritability, and rage. Competence on the job is an elixir; incompetence compared to one's peers is an emotional and behavioral poison. The job of students is academic learning, and teachers who are not as effective as they could be in helping students achieve academic competence are contributing to students' emotional and behavioral problems.

Unfortunately, most of general public education has adopted instructional practices that are not effective, especially for students who come to school without the skills that most economically privileged students acquire outside of school (Dawson et al., 2000; Heward, 2003; Heward & Silvestri, 2004). Child-directed, "holistic," "discovery learning" approaches and heterogeneous grouping, for example, are instructional practices virtually certain to fail with students at risk of failure (see Dixon, 1994; Grossen, 1993; Heward, 2003; Heward & Silvestri, 2004). Special education classes are also too often places in which effective academic instruction is not provided (Colvin, Greenberg, & Sherman, 1993; Knitzer, Steinberg, & Fleisch, 1990). Direct instruction is effective in helping students with disabilities acquire academic skills, and using such instruction could improve the learning of students in both general and special education (Bender, 1993; Engelmann, 1997; Hallahan et al., 2005; Kauffman, 2002).

Also unfortunate is the fact that most of general public education often has failed to adopt explicit programs for teaching social skills and rewarding desirable behavior. Specific social skills need to be assessed and taught explicitly and systematically to many individuals and groups if they are to learn the basic skills needed for positive interaction with others (Mayer, 1995; Meadows, Melloy, & Yell, 1996; Walker et al., 2004). Yet few schools provide such assessment or instruction. Moreover, classrooms need to be places where desirable conduct is explicitly, frequently, and effectively rewarded (Lloyd & Kauffman, 1995). Yet most classrooms are characterized by very low rates of positive consequences for appropriate behavior (Shores, Jack, Gunter, Ellis, DeBriere, & Wehby, 1993). Popularization of the notion that rewards undermine intrinsic motivation and that positive reinforcement amounts to bribes (e.g., Kohn, 1993) has further impeded the adoption of positive behavioral strategies for managing classroom behavior (Maag, 2001). However, overwhelming empirical evidence indicates that rewards do not undermine intrinsic motivation and that rewards are essential for effective, positive classroom management, especially of difficult students (see Alberto & Troutman, 2003; Cameron & Pierce, 1994; Kazdin, 2001; Kerr & Nelson, 2002; Lewis, Lewis-Palmer, Stichter, & Newcomer, 2004; McGinnis, Friman, & Carlyon, 1999; Rhode et al., 1992; Walker, 1995; Walker et al., 2004; Walker, Forness, et al., 1998).

Destructive Contingencies of Reinforcements

From the viewpoint of behavioral psychology, the school can contribute to the development of emotional or behavioral disorders in several obvious ways:

- Providing positive reinforcement for inappropriate behavior
- Failing to provide positive reinforcement for desirable behavior
- Providing negative reinforcement for behavior that allows students to avoid their work.

The following section defines positive and negative reinforcement and gives examples of how each may work in a classroom environment.

Positive and Negative Reinforcement: A Dynamic Duo

Reinforcement—especially negative reinforcement—is often misunderstood. Many teachers do not understand how positive and negative reinforcement typically work together and how both may be involved in maintaining either desirable or trouble-some classroom behavior. In many interactions, students with emotional or behavioral disorders get a double dose of reinforcement, one positive and one negative, and often for the wrong behavior.

Reinforcement, whether positive or negative, is a reward or consequence that makes the behavior it follows more likely to recur. The "reward" may be something one gets (i.e., a positive reinforcer) or something one gets rid of or avoids (i.e., a negative reinforcer). It may be helpful to think of people looking for work and having signs stating what they want. Some signs might say, "Will work FOR ___." Other signs might say, "Will work TO GET OUT OF ___." Still others might say, "Will work FOR ___ AND TO AVOID ___." What someone will work *for* provides positive reinforcement; what someone will work *to get out of or avoid* provides negative reinforcement. Most of us will work for money, and most of us will work to get out of debt or to avoid losing our job. Most of us will work for course credit and, at the same time, work to avoid embarrassment or a bad grade. In fact, in most cases our behavior is motivated by two consequences at once: (1) something we *get,* and (2) something we *avoid* (or at least escape temporarily). We work for money and also to get out of work (the negative reinforcement—escape from work—that we call vacations).

We all experience both positive and negative reinforcement in everyday life, and both types of reinforcement play important roles in motivating our adaptive behavior. However, positive and negative reinforcement become problematic rather than helpful in the classroom or any other environment when they are misused or poorly arranged. Misuse or poor application may be the result of either of two major mistakes:

- *Misidentification.*   A teacher may believe that criticisms or reprimands are negative reinforcers that a student will work to avoid, when they are actually positive reinforcers. Being reprimanded is something the student will work to get because of the attention it brings from the teacher and classroom peers (for many of us, attention is something we crave, whether it is criticism or praise; being ignored is what we will work hardest to avoid). A teacher may also fail to see that academic assignments are negative reinforcers for a student who exhibits disruptive classroom behavior: Academic work may be something the student will misbehave to get out of. Whatever behavior allows this student to escape from the work (or postpone it) will be reinforced; the student will misbehave so that he or she does not have to do the work (see Moore & Edwards, 2003).
- *Malcontingency.*   The contingencies in a classroom are destructive if they result in either positive reinforcement or negative reinforcement for undesirable behavior. Students may learn this: I get lots of attention when I misbehave (positive reinforcement, even if the attention is in the form of intended punishment such as scolding); in addition, I get out of my academic work (negative reinforcement).

The dynamic duo of positive and negative reinforcement can be harnessed to give desirable behavior a double boost. Students get a double good deal when the classroom contingencies involving both positive and negative reinforcement are constructive: attention for desirable behavior (positive reinforcement) and little vacations from work (negative reinforcement) as a reward for work done promptly and well.

How Things Often Go Wrong

Destructive rather than constructive contingencies of reinforcement are in place in many classrooms, both in general education and in special education. Appropriate conduct typically goes unrewarded, whereas both positive and negative reinforcement for misconduct are frequent (Gunter et al., 1993, 1998; Kerr & Nelson, 2002; Shores et al., 1993; Shores & Wehby, 1999; Strain, Lambert, Kerr, Stagg, & Lenkner, 1983; Webber & Scheuermann, 1991). A great deal of evidence suggests that constructive reinforcement contingencies can be arranged to teach appropriate behavior even to students whose behavior is seriously disordered. In study after study over the past several decades, experimental studies have shown that providing teacher attention during appropriate behavior but withholding it during undesirable behavior results in improvement (see Hoff & DuPaul, 1998; Pullen, 2004; Walker, 1995; Walker et al., 2004; West et al., 1995).

Consider that in many classrooms contingencies of reinforcement are inadvertently arranged to promote the very behavior the teacher deems undesirable. Strain et al. (1983) corroborated the findings of several previous studies indicating that teachers tend to provide predominantly negative feedback to pupils and seldom reinforce appropriate behavior. The chance that any of the 130 children in their study would receive positive feedback (verbal compliment or gestural approval, such as a pat or a hug) following compliance with a teacher's command, demand, or request was only 1 in 10. In addition, Strain et al. found that the 19 regular class teachers (kindergarten through third grade) gave reinforcement (positive feedback) to poorly adjusted children following noncompliance more often than they gave reinforcement for compliance. And the teachers tended to repeat the commands, demands, and requests more often for poorly adjusted than for well-adjusted pupils. Gunter et al. (1993) and Shores et al. (1993; see also Shores & Wehby, 1999) reported similar findings. Given these conditions, which apparently are common in classrooms, it is not surprising that many children's misbehavior becomes a greater problem as they advance through the grades.

The use of constructive consequences for adaptive behavior is consistent with a conceptual model that assumes interactive effects of students' and teachers' responses. An interactional or transactional model suggests that youngsters and adults exert reciprocal influence on each other. It is reasonable to believe that teachers' and problem students' mutual praise and criticism become important factors in the maintenance of behavior and that mutual hostility could be defused beginning with either teacher or pupil. Thus, in some cases, children with developmental disabilities and problem behavior have been taught to help their teachers provide positive reinforcement for their desirable behavior (e.g., Blake et al., 2000; Craft, Alber, & Heward, 1998; Polirstok & Greer, 1977). Too often, classroom peers are allowed to provide additional reinforcement for misconduct.

Peer tutoring is another strategy designed to provide more positive reinforcement for desired behavior in the typical classroom (Tournaki & Criscitiello, 2003). Whether involving only specific pairs of students (one of whom tutors the other) or classwide peer tutoring (in which all members of the class are engaged in tutoring one another), the strategy has been shown to benefit many students whose behavior is problematic by increasing their engagement in academics and the positive interactions they have with their peers (e.g., DuPaul, Ervin, Hook, & McGoey, 1998; Gumpel & Frank, 1999). Moreover, a skillfully implemented program of peer tutoring could be a key strategy in teaching social skills to all students. Strayhorn, Strain, and Walker (1993) have suggested that peer tutoring be used as a means of teaching students nurturing responses to others, which would help make schools and the larger society kinder and gentler places in which to live. In too many cases, students are abusive of each other and their teacher, not helpful or nurturing.

Abundant empirical evidence shows that students' classroom behavior can be altered by manipulating the contingencies of reinforcement, even when the reinforcement is as natural a part of the classroom as teacher and peer attention (see Alberto & Troutman, 2003; Cullinan, 2002; Kerr & Nelson, 2002). One needs neither a great backlog of classroom observation nor great acumen to see the potential implications of this evidence in the school's contributions to the development of emotional or behavioral disorders. Students whose behavior is a problem often receive abundant attention for misbehavior but little or no attention for appropriate conduct. Even though the attention they receive for misbehavior is often in the form of criticism or punishment, it is still attention and is likely to reinforce whatever they are doing at the time it is dispensed. The effect of attention for misbehavior and nonattention for good deportment is likely to be perpetuation of the miscreant's deeds, regardless of the intentions of the teacher or another adult.

Undesirable Models of School Conduct

Children and youth are great imitators. Much of their learning is the result of watching others and mimicking their behavior. Youngsters are particularly likely to imitate the behavior modeled by people who are socially or physically powerful, attractive, and in command of important reinforcers (Bandura, 1986). Unless the modeling process is carefully controlled, students who act out and disrupt the classroom are likely to gravitate toward other peers who are disruptive. Teachers must find ways to call attention to and reward the appropriate behavior of high-status peers (Hallenbeck & Kauffman, 1995; Walker, 1995; Walker et al., 2004).

Understandably, the examples teachers set strongly influence the way in which students approach their academic work and how they behave. Rutter, Maughan, Mortimer, Ouston, and Smith (1979) pointed out that "pupils are likely to be influenced—either for good or ill—by the models of behavior provided by teachers both in the classroom and elsewhere" (p. 189). Bear (1998) listed teacher modeling of desirable behavior among the strategies known to be effective in preventing discipline problems and promoting self-discipline.

Exemplary behavior on the part of the teacher encourages like conduct in pupils. Maltreatment by the teacher of any student in the class is very likely to encourage students to treat each other with hostility or disrespect. Teachers whose attitude toward their work is cavalier or who are disorganized may foster similar carelessness and disorganization in their students. Corporal punishment—still used in some schools and classrooms—is a horrid example of aggressive misconduct by adults that may be mimicked by students in their relationships with others. A teacher's lack of self-awareness is likely to encourage a lack of self-awareness on the part of pupils (Richardson & Shupe, 2003).

Peers exert considerable social pressure on students' behavior in school, particularly at the high school level. Schools in which high-status students either refuse to perform academic tasks or exhibit serious misbehavior with impunity are likely to see the spread of academic failure and social misconduct (see Arnold & Brungardt, 1983; Farmer, 2000; Rutter et al., 1979; Walker et al., 2004).

IMPLICATIONS FOR EDUCATORS

The teacher of students with emotional or behavioral disorders must be prepared to work with pupils who are below average intellectually and academically as well as deviant in their social behavior. Some of these students are superior intellectually and academically, but not most. Teaching these students demands not only the ability to instruct pupils with an extremely wide range of intellectual and academic levels but also the ability to teach social and other nonacademic behaviors that make scholastic success possible, such as good work habits, attention strategies, and independence (Meadows & Stevens, 2004). The most crucial tasks of the teacher as a preventive agent are to foster academic success and to lessen the student's antisocial conduct. Academic failure and antisocial behavior limit future opportunities and make future maladjustment likely.

The teacher's primary task is to modulate the school environment in ways that will contribute to adaptive, prosocial behavior and academic growth. The first requirement of appropriate education for students with emotional and behavioral disorders is that they be provided with effective instruction in academic skills (Bateman, 2004; Lane, 2004; Witt, Van Der Heyden, & Gilbertson, 2004). In addition, every special education classroom should be characterized by the strategies of teachers who are also effective in preventing discipline problems and promoting self-control. Such characteristics are listed in Table 9.1.

Regrettably, many teachers of students with emotional or behavioral disorders are poorly prepared for the task. Moreover, the effectiveness of many special education programs is undercut by lack of support from administrators and parents. The challenge we face is not just preparing more and better teachers but providing the supports that will facilitate their success and keep the best in the field longer (see cases in accompanying case book for further discussion).

Table 9.1

Strategies Used by Effective Classroom Managers to Create Classroom Climates that Prevent Discipline Problems and Promote Self-Discipline

In general, effective classroom teachers

❑ Work hard to develop a classroom environment that is caring, pleasant, relaxed, and friendly, yet orderly and productive
❑ Show a sincere interest in the life of each individual student (e.g., knows their interests, family, pets, etc)
❑ Model the behaviors they desire in their students and convey that such behaviors are truly important
❑ Encourage active student participation in decision-making
❑ Strive to not only teach prosocial behavior and to reduce undesirable behavior, but to develop cognitions and emotions related to prosocial behavior
❑ Work to develop both peer acceptance, peer support, and close friendship among students
❑ Appreciate and respect diversity
❑ Appreciate and respect students' opinions and concerns
❑ Emphasize fairness by allowing for flexibility in application of consequences for rule violations
❑ Use cooperative learning activities
❑ Discourage competition and social comparisons
❑ Avoid producing feelings of shame (focusing more on pride and less on guilt)
❑ Reinforce acts of kindness in the school and community
❑ Communicate often with each child's home
❑ Provide frequent and positive feedback, encouragement, and praise, characterized by
  • Sincerity and credibility
  • Special suggestions and opportunities for good behavior
  • Highlighting the importance and value of the student's social and academic achievement
  • Attributing success to effort and ability, which implies that similar successes can be expected in the future
  • Encouraging students to believe that they behave well because they are capable and desire to do so, not because of consequences
  • A focus on both the process and the product of good behavior
  • Reference to prior behavior when commenting on improvement
  • Specification of what is being praised
  • Praise that is contingent on good behavior
❑ Establish clear rules, beginning during the first few days of school, which are characterized by
  • Clear and reasonable expectations
  • "Dos" and "Do nots" regarding classroom behavior
  • Attempts to develop student understanding of rules and their consequences
  • Highlighting the importance of a small number of important rules
  • Fairness and developmental appropriateness
  • Explanations and discussions of the rationale for each rule
  • Student input during their development
  • Clear examples of appropriate and inappropriate behavior related to each rule and direct teaching of appropriate behavior if necessary
  • Clear consequences for rule infractions
  • Distributing of a copy of rules and consequences to children and parents
  • Their consistency with school rules
  • Frequent reminders of rules and expected behaviors
  • Their nondisturbance of the learning process—the rules do not discourage healthy peer interactions such as cooperative learning or appropriate peer discussions

Source: Bear, G. G. (1998). School discipline in the United States: Prevention, correction, and long-term social development. *School Psychology Review, 27,* 20. © 1998 by the National Association of School Psychologists. Reprinted by permission of the publisher.

SUMMARY

The role of the school in causing emotional or behavioral disorders is a particularly important consideration for educators. In our society, school failure is tantamount to personal failure. The school environment is not only critically important for social development but is also the factor over which educators have direct control.

As a group, students with emotional or behavioral disorders score below average on intelligence tests and are academic underachievers. Many of them lack specific social skills. The behavior they exhibit is inimical to school success. Disordered behavior and underachievement appear to influence each other reciprocally; in an individual case, which causes the other is not as important as recognizing that they are interrelated. Academic failure and low intelligence, when combined with antisocial behavior or conduct disorder, portend social adjustment problems in adulthood. The school may contribute to the development of emotional or behavioral disorders in children in several ways:

- School administrators, teachers, and other pupils may be insensitive to the student's individuality.
- Teachers may hold inappropriate expectations of students.
- Teachers may be inconsistent in managing students' behavior.
- Instruction may be offered in nonfunctional (that is, seemingly irrelevant) skills.
- Ineffective instruction may be offered in skills that are critical for school success.
- School personnel may arrange destructive contingencies of reinforcement.
- Peers and teachers may provide models of undesirable conduct.

Teachers of students with emotional or behavioral disorders must be prepared to teach youngsters who are underachieving and difficult to instruct, and instruction must be provided in both academics and social skills.

CASE FOR DISCUSSION

You Had Better Get on Them
Bob Winters

Bob Winters had been prepared to teach preschoolers with disabilities, but he accepted a job teaching a special class of students with mild mental disabilities in a middle school. When he was hired, the principal, Mr. Dudley, had told him, "You're the expert. We'll give you a lot of leeway for making decisions about these students because you're the one who's trained to work with difficult students. Mr. Arter, the teacher last year, had lots of trouble with these kids. You'll have to come down on them hard."

Bob struggled to develop appropriate instructional programs for his students. Other teachers were coming to him for advice, but he had little or nothing to offer. He ended up assigning lots of worksheets emphasizing basic skills. He tried to keep the kids busy, but as the days and weeks rolled by his class became more and more rowdy, and he felt his classroom control slipping away. The students raced through their assignments and then wandered around the room laughing and joking in small groups and verbally abusing each other. Poor grades did not bother them. In fact, they bragged about getting bad grades and were particularly glad to show off a paper that had the lowest score in the class.

Bob's class became so unruly and noisy that Mr. Dudley occasionally came down the hall to open the classroom door and glare or shout at Bob's students. The students laughed and joked about Mr. Dudley after he left. "He thinks he's bad," one would say, and the others would shake their heads in agreement.

Bob was determined to get tougher. He simply had to get control over this class. He began trying Mr. Dudley's shouted directions. As punishment, he began requiring students to copy pages out of the dictionary, something they seemed to dread. But one Thursday he invoked this punishment when Ronnie disrupted the class as he returned from the restroom. Ronnie grinned impishly and declared, "Okay, I *love* copying the dictionary." He copied more pages than Bob had assigned. But the next day Ronnie flatly refused to copy any pages at all, and Bob eventually ordered him to the office.

Eventually, Bob decided to arrange the students' desks facing the classroom walls. Maybe this way they wouldn't distract each other so much and would get more work done, he reasoned. But then they began moving their desks together without permission. They met his reprimands with saucy comments such as "Oh, big man!" and "Yeah, he thinks he's going to do something!" When Gerald jumped out of his seat and ran over to whack Mike playfully on the back of the head, Bob lashed out. "Get your ass in the chair!" he bellowed. Gerald froze. The others stared silently at Bob as he went on, "I don't give a damn what you all want to do. You're going to do as I say." Cathy nudged Ronnie, who sat beside her, and they began to giggle. Bob descended on Cathy immediately, shouting, "Go to the office!" With flashing, angry eyes, Cathy stalked out and slammed the door. Her classmates shook their heads and exchanged scowls.

Ten minutes later, Mr. Dudley was at Bob's door. "Mr. Winters, may I see you outside?" As he walked to the door, Bob heard Amber say, "He's going to be in trouble." Bob guessed she was right.

Note: *This case was adapted from the following source: Kauffman, J. M., Mostert, M. P., Trent, S. C., Nuttycombe, D. J., & Hallahan, D. P. (1993). Managing classroom behavior: A reflective case-based approach. Boston: Allyn & Bacon.*

Questions About the Case

1. How do Bob's teaching and management strategies illustrate the concepts presented in this chapter? What was Mr. Dudley's role in contributing to the problems with this class?

2. If you were Bob's friend and colleague, what advice would you give him about improving his teaching performance?

3. Where does the responsibility lie for preventing situations like the one depicted here?

>> PERSONAL REFLECTIONS

School Factors

Rudolph E. Ford, Ph.D., is principal of the Onslow W. Minnis, Sr., Middle School, in Richmond, Virginia.

What behavioral characteristics do at-risk students exhibit in school?

At-risk students often exhibit behaviors designed to draw attention to themselves. One may attribute some of this attention-grabbing conduct to students' natural tendency to seek acceptance. This is a universal trait among all youth. However, when students are at risk, they often try to compensate for their feelings of academic inadequacy by succeeding at the popularity game. In transitions between classes, these children are often loud, obnoxious, defiant, ill mannered, and overanimated in their social interactions. They communicate in profound verbal and nonverbal ways. They may suck their teeth, roll their eyes, mouth words as if talking to themselves, or turn away from someone who approaches them. These are only a few of the gestures I often observe.

Middle and high school students seem to be more overtly interested in pursuing the opposite sex. They may dress in a more provocative way, often with the full knowledge that their dress will mean trouble with school officials. The immediate, powerful gratification that sex promises simply has more appeal to them than does avoiding trouble. Locker room talk among boys and intercepted notes of girls often reveal a level of sexual awareness or activity that surprises teachers who hold middle-class values. A male student in my school was so determined to walk his girlfriend to class and kiss her good-bye that he quickly reached the point of being a habitual offender for tardiness. In subsequent conversations with this student, he admitted to me that his girlfriend mattered more than promptness to class. He clearly and unabashedly coveted the immediate gratification of her hug, and he valued being seen with her more than any academic goal. Passing to the next grade just did not matter in his culture at home, and he had brought this culture to school. Educational pursuits did not hold much value in his world.

At-risk students often cannot see the value in education. Frequently, they do not know anyone outside of the school who has an advanced education, so they acquire an "us against them" mentality. At-risk student peer groups will sometimes socially reject those who dare to achieve. Those who strive to achieve become social pariahs who "think they are better than us," according to their peers. The social conditioning of their peer group teaches them to believe they can not achieve. Too often, those students who are at risk but want to succeed come to believe that they are not expected to achieve. Ironically, educators often contribute to these self-doubts through negative relationships with students. These self-doubts produce low effort, which then produces low achievement. The cycle of failure becomes a self-fulfilling prophecy. These students frequently do not understand the mores of middle-class, mainstream peers.

How would you characterize teachers who are likely to have special difficulty with behavior management or have negative effects on students' behavior?

Teachers who take things personally often struggle with behavior management. Predictably, these are teachers who negatively influence students' behavior. They have a low tolerance for behaviors that are dissimilar to the behaviors they learned as children. They often will not admit to being flawed themselves because they think that will reveal weakness. They rarely make apologies. Failed teachers *tell* more often than they *listen*. They rarely obtain or use feedback. They do not value what students think.

Economically deprived students and at-risk students are often the same, and they often exhibit the behaviors I have described. Teachers experiencing difficulty confuse any tolerance of such behaviors as a sign of weakness and are convinced that the strong stand they take against these behaviors is in students' long-term best interests. They do not strive to guide

231

at-risk students toward more socially acceptable behaviors through successive approximations. These teachers believe they should immediately suppress the behavior with punishment, lest they be weak. Struggling teachers establish an adversarial relationship with students. When these teachers see an unacceptable behavior, such as loud talking, they misinterpret the negative behavior as a conscious affront to their authority. In reality, students may be displaying coping mechanisms they have learned in their socioeconomically deprived subcultures at home. Teachers may be the furthest thing from their minds.

Teachers who do not understand students' modes of communication, motivation, neighborhood culture, unspoken rules, methods of giving and receiving respect, and varieties of learning styles often struggle. Teachers in at-risk schools, by design, are asked to establish relationships with students who come from subcultures different from their own. Students at risk are not regularly exposed to successful college graduates. However, all teachers must be at least minimally successful college graduates to be qualified to teach. After graduation, teachers are sorted and selected through the application process. The most civil, intelligent, poised, and charming applicants are the successful candidates for teaching positions. This process reinforces, in the mind of teachers, that how they conduct themselves is the key to success. They are appalled on the first day of school to learn that their students do not share their understanding of right and wrong. Attributes such as civility, achievement, manners, and consideration of others' feelings are not part of the rules of the street. Teachers and students must recognize the rules necessary to diffuse the dissonance that occurs when two sets of standards for behavior are in effect in the same environment. If teachers will acknowledge this duality, then they can move past it and direct students toward appropriate behaviors.

However, the importance of students learning mainstream mores cannot be overstated if they are to experience success in the workplace. Successful teachers describe for students the acceptable behavioral norm and teach students that they must learn the mainstream way of behaving to live comfortably in our society. When teachers frame this message in the context of excellent relationships with students, the odds for productive teaching and learning are increased. Teachers must gain the trust of students if they hope to direct them toward higher achievement. The teacher who is snide and sarcastic will rarely successfully establish a good rapport with students. Teachers themselves must model behaviors they expect from students. If teachers respond to students in a steady, calm, and respectful manner, then students will eventually return the favor. Teachers who bark commands, telling students what they must do rather than being a model of what they expect, often struggle with bad pupil–teacher relationships.

What do you do as a principal to try to establish a positive and supportive school climate?

The establishment of a positive and supportive school climate is paramount to the success of any school. The principal must be constantly vigilant to make sure he or she considers how decisions will affect the school climate. The stakeholders of public schools are parents, students, teachers, and administrators. Each one of these groups must feel it is a vital part of the school for the school to be successful.

As a principal, the most important thing I can do is to promote positive relationships between and among all of the stakeholder groups. I must have a highly visible presence. I must exude confidence, high energy, and a "can do" attitude with everything I do. I must model my belief in the students, faculty, and parents. I must work hard at building positive relationships with every single person with whom I come into contact—even in difficult situations such as disciplinary hearings or employee reprimands.

I ask my teachers and students and parents about their families and listen attentively until they are done telling me about them. If I am not willing to hear about Sandra hitting a home run during last Saturday's Little League game, then I should not ask. In asking, however, I show teachers, students, and parents that I care about them as individuals. I have enjoyed some very supportive and loyal colleagues as well as trusting, happy parents and students. Although I know I may not be able to establish a positive conversational rapport with everybody, I believe it is my duty to try.

As principal, I must seize each moment of each day and tweak it for all it's worth. I must embrace accountability and resist making excuses for a lack of performance, focusing instead on maximizing performance. I must convince teachers, students, and parents that we are better off with standards. I must show them that standards are a way to improve the lives of all stakeholders in our school. I must show them that standards give us a tool to measure our performances. I must ensure that the curriculum is no mystery to teachers and that they have a clear and concise understanding of what they should teach.

Teachers are a hardworking group of professionals who generally have an abundance of energy and hope.

I must ensure that the daily grind does not wear them down and demoralize them into becoming pessimists. Teachers must be included in decision making throughout the school. In positive school climates, all stakeholders feel ownership of the mission. This ownership is built through group decision making. I have witnessed better quality decisions in general when the group is involved in making that decision. The cliché "Two heads are better than one" usually holds true. As principal, I have noticed that I can feel far more confident in the decision being accepted by all stakeholders when I have included them in the decision-making process.

To build a positive school climate, I must make sure there are abundant opportunities for everyone to have fun. I must smile and ensure that everyone knows that seriousness of purpose and having a good time are not mutually exclusive.

People need to have the idea that they are free to initiate an idea or program to foster a positive school climate. They must feel that creativity is welcome. They must revel in the idea that a risk that might result in better teaching and learning is worth taking. If the principal focuses his or her dialogue on what is right about the institution, then a positive climate can be established and maintained. My goal is for everyone to be familiar with my vigor, enthusiasm, and faith in the mission, joy, and love of my profession and the people at school. I believe I am always onstage, so I must always show my very best. If I strive every day to do the things I have outlined, a positive school climate will be the eventual result or will be successfully maintained.

School climate is greatly influenced by the level of support teachers feel from the administration. Teachers have to be shown in a variety of ways how much they are valued, both individually and collectively. I accomplish this through one-on-one conversational relationship building and through a variety of enjoyable schoolwide activities designed to show appreciation. I hold a monthly teachers' coffee morning social, have monthly "goody days," give ice cream sundae treats, give single roses to teachers, hand out candy bar treats for various holidays, buy birthday corsages, go to wedding and baby showers, attend socials at various staffers' homes, and try numerous other positive, climate-boosting activities.

What do you think are the most important aspects of a student's experience at school that contribute to behavioral problems?

Lack of success is one of most important contributors to behavioral problems. When a student's life is devoid of success, he or she is certain to shut down, tune out, and rebel. The unsuccessful student will turn away from the painful failure experiences and toward social pursuits. Often, negative, attention-grabbing behaviors emerge. Therefore, opportunities for students to succeed must permeate instruction throughout the day.

When teachers lecture, do not engage students actively, do not allow students to touch anything during the lesson, focus on knowledge that is not relevant to students' real world and not connected to something students want, then students are not likely to tune in. Teachers who waste time getting started with a lesson often lose students. Students must be actively engaged as soon as they walk in the door—sometimes even before that. I recently observed a successful teacher meeting students on the sidewalk with a handout of written instructions to proceed with the lesson on entering the room. The activity had a time limit and required an oral report in just 5 minutes. The teacher handed the sheet to them without saying a word. As soon as students looked at it, they sprang into action—hurrying to their seats, swiftly unpacking, and getting to work. This was a teacher who only 1 year earlier had contemplated quitting at midyear. She says the higher level of structure she provides this year is the difference for her. She is a much happier professional now. If you are teaching fractions the day after Halloween, why not make candy the object of the fractions? Let students manipulate the candy.

Impoverished students use particular mechanisms of survival in their neighborhoods. However, teachers who refuse to recognize and control these differences often create negative tensions that contribute to behavioral problems. Schools with predominantly at-risk populations must control these tendencies through careful policies designed to teach students the right way to behave—meeting them where they are. Educators must demonstrate to at-risk students that they are advocates, not foes. At-risk students must believe their teachers are advocates. This perception is paramount for the steady academic progress that standards-based educational policy demands.

I do not advocate that we create new and special knowledge for any subgroup. The Ebonics fiasco in California was an example of the futility of that approach. To the contrary, I believe that standards are good for students. However, teachers who understand that students who exhibit unacceptable behaviors may be doing things the only way they know how experience more joy, gratification, and success.

Teachers must free themselves from feelings of resentment toward students for their actions and view misbehavior as an opportunity to teach them yet another usable skill for success in life.

Do you have any other reflections on your role in the school?

The principal must be a reflective practitioner who has a vision for the school that transcends its current efficacy. I must accept this responsibility: My leadership will steer the school to ultimate success or failure. I define success as sustained, continuous improvement. Every decision I make as principal must have this goal as its driving force. The vision I have for where we can go must be as clear in my mind as if I were looking at a sharply focused picture.

To achieve this, I must work very hard to get the best, most competent staff possible. The staff must be given an abundance of development activities to build their confidence and focus their efforts on exactly what will be tested and therefore what must be taught. For a school to be known as high performing, mediocrity must become scarce or extinct. Effective principals acquire the vision and then use the team decision-making approach to create the plans for success. Once these plans are formulated, they should be put into writing as a schoolwide improvement plan. This plan should clearly define the roles and expectations of all stakeholders, including teachers, parents, students, and administrators.

I must deliver and facilitate the delivery of service. If we develop raving fans instead of just satisfied customers, then we will have succeeded as a service organization. Traditionally, principals have not approached community relations as a marketing challenge. Too often, excellence can be observed in classrooms, but the public is not aware of the quality of the instruction students are receiving. I must seek opportunities to market our school. With the current national debate about school choice as an option, marketing our school may be more important than ever.

>> QUESTIONS FOR FURTHER REFLECTION

1. As a teacher, how can you make sure that you are aware of how you might be contributing to a student's problems?
2. If your school administrators are not supportive of what you consider to be essential or best practices, what are your best options for trying to change things?
3. How would you describe your most important goals for the students you teach, and what rationale can you provide for choosing those goals?

CHAPTER TEN

CULTURAL FACTORS

As you read this chapter, keep these guiding questions in mind:

- How do conflicts between cultures create stress for children and youth?

- What steps can educators take to avoid the problems of bias and discrimination against students whose cultures differ from their own?

- Besides family and school, what major cultural factors may contribute to behavioral deviance? Why is it difficult to evaluate the effects of these factors?

- What relationships have been established between TV viewing and children's antisocial and prosocial behavior?

- How would you characterize a neighborhood that provides support for development of children's appropriate social behavior?

APPEAL OF CULTURAL FACTORS AS CAUSAL EXPLANATIONS

Neither families nor schools include all the social influences that determine how youngsters behave. Children, families, and teachers are part of a larger culture that molds their behavior. Parents and teachers tend to hold values and set behavioral standards and expectations that are consistent with those of the cultures in which they live and work. Children's attitudes and behavior gravitate toward the cultural norms of their families, peers, and communities. We must therefore evaluate family factors in the context of cultural differences and changes. Family relationships change across time and are different in different cultures. Although we may find certain patterns or characteristics of successful child rearing that are the same across time and in all cultures, it is also clear that the same specific behaviors that are adaptive in one circumstance may not be in another (e.g., inner city versus affluent suburb; time of peace versus time of war; economic stability and growth versus economic depression; rearing by parents versus rearing by grandparents; one-parent versus two-parent families).Therefore, the findings of studies in 2000 or 2005 or 2010 may tell us less than we might imagine about American families by 2020 or later because of changing conditions and demographics (Hetherington & Martin, 1986).

Culture involves behavioral expectations, but it is more than that. Banks (1997; see also Banks & Banks, 1997) suggested that culture has many definitions but that it might be described by six elements: (1) values and behavioral styles, (2) languages and dialects, (3) nonverbal communication, (4) awareness of one's cultural distinctiveness, (5) frames of reference (normative worldviews or perspectives), and (6) identification (feeling part of the cultural group). Nations and other large social entities with a shared culture form a *macroculture*. Within the larger macroculture are many *microcultures,* smaller groups with unique values, styles, languages, dialects, ways of communicating nonverbally, awareness, frames of reference, and identification. How do we maintain American macroculture and at the same time respect the microcultures that form it? The answer is neither obvious nor easy (see Hallahan & Kauffman, 2003; Kauffman, 1999b, 1999g, 2002; Kauffman, Bantz, & McCullough, 2002, for further discussion of multiculturalism and exceptionality).

The United States has often been called a cultural melting pot—an amalgam of various nationalities and cultures. We have come to believe that its diversity of citizens makes the United States strong and good. But we realize that if we do not make a true alloy of the diverse ingredients of our culture—if we do not amalgamate our diverse elements into a single, uniquely American identity—we can be neither strong nor good as a society. *E pluribus unum* (out of many, one), a slogan stamped on our coins, seems to present an increasing paradox (see Hallahan & Kauffman, 2003; Hodgkinson, 1995; Ogbu, 1990; Osher, Cartledge, Oswald, Sutherland, Artiles, & Coutinho, 2004; Singh, 1996; Singh, Ellis, Oswald, Wechsler, & Curtis, 1997). We value cultural diversity, but common cultural values hold our society together. The tension between our separateness and our togetherness—our distinctiveness and our oneness—obviously can set the stage for disordered emotions and behavior, as well as conflicts among groups on nearly every issue. But it is togetherness, oneness, unity, and commonality that provide the glue holding any society together. An emphasis on differences to the exclusion of seeing the common sets the stage for cultural conflicts, racism, hatred, and war (see Britt, 1999; Kauffman, 2002; Raspberry, 1999; Singh, 1996).

When the child's, family's, school's, or teacher's values or expectations conflict with other cultural norms, emotional or behavioral development may be adversely affected or school behavior may become a difficult issue (see Cartledge, Kia, & Ida, 2000; Osher et al., 2004; Fisher, 2003; Nakamura, 2003). To the extent that different cultural forces tug a youngster's behavior in different directions, they create conflicting expectations and increase the probability that he or she will violate cultural norms and be labeled deviant.

Comer (1988) noted that "differences between home and school—whether of class, race, income, or culture—always create potential conflict" (p. 37). It is not surprising, therefore, that researchers have given a great deal of attention to cultural factors that contribute to disordered behavior (see Evertson & Weinstein, in press). "Race" is not a scientifically defensible biological fact. Rather, "The concept of race is a cultural invention, a culturally and historically specific way of thinking about, categorizing, and treating human beings" (Mukhopadhyay & Henze, 2003, p. 673). This is not to say that the cultural construct of race is unimportant, only that it has no basis in biology.

CONFLICTING CULTURAL VALUES AND STANDARDS

It is easy to find examples of conflicting cultural values and standards and the stress they create for children and youth. Television shows, movies, and magazines glamorize the behavior and values of high-status models that are incompatible with the standards of many children's families; youngsters' imitation of these models results in disapproval from parents. Religious groups may proscribe certain behaviors that are normative in the larger community (such as dancing, attending movies, dating, masturbating). Youngsters who conform to these religious teachings may be rejected by peers, stigmatized, or socially isolated, whereas those who violate the proscriptions may feel extreme guilt. The values children attach to certain possessions or behavior because they are highly regarded by their peers or teachers (such as wearing particular items of clothing or achieving at school) may be incomprehensible to their parents. Differences between parents' and children's values may become the focus of parental nattering.

Hitting and aggression are generally considered unacceptable in our society. However, "corporal punishment has been an integral part of how parents discipline their children throughout the history of the United States," and data suggest that almost 95% of American parents spank their young children (Gershoff, 2002, p. 539). Although some nations of the world have outlawed the corporal punishment of children, the United States has not. Attitudes among various cultural groups toward corporal punishment and knowledge of the effects of spanking remain matters of considerable controversy (Gershoff, 2002).

Children of interracial marriages may have difficulty developing a sense of identity, particularly during adolescence. They may have major problems reconciling their dual racial identifications into a single, personal identity that affirms the positive aspects of each heritage and acknowledges society's ambivalence toward biracial persons. At the same time, the demographic trends in America are toward a mixing of national, ethnic, and racial categories (Glazer, 1997; Hodgkinson, 1995).

Conflicting cultural influences on behavior are sometimes perverse; the culture provides both inducements for a given type of behavior and severe penalties for engaging in it. This kind of temptation or pressure with one hand and punishment with the other is especially evident in the areas of violent behavior and sexuality (see case of Teri Leigh in the accompanying case book). Our society fosters violence through its glorification of high-status, violent models in the mass media, yet it seeks severe punishment for youngsters' imitative social aggression. Consider teenage pregnancy—the cultural forces that foster it and society's responses to it. During the past several decades, sexual mores have changed so that adolescents now have much greater freedom and added responsibilities for preventing pregnancy. Our society tempts adolescents, offering them freedoms and responsibilities they are not equipped to handle, yet it does nothing to help them deal with these freedoms and responsibilities and in fact punishes them for abusing freedom and behaving irresponsibly. Motion pictures, MTV, and commercials highlight sex appeal and sexual encounters, providing models of behavior that are incompatible with efforts to encourage sexual abstinence and avoid pregnancy. Teenagers often pressure their peers to become sexually active; at the same time, conservative politicians have attempted to restrict sex education and make contraceptives less available to teens. Education for family life and child rearing is often inadequate.

MULTICULTURAL PERSPECTIVE

Besides the conflicts that differing cultural standards create, children's and adults' own cultural values may bias their perceptions of others. A full discussion of cultural bias in education is far beyond the scope of this chapter, but it is important to note that problems of bias and discrimination carry serious implications for evaluating youngsters' behavior. Ultimately, nearly all behavioral standards and expectations—and therefore nearly all judgments regarding behavioral deviance—are culture bound; value judgments cannot be entirely culture free. In our pluralistic society, which values multicultural elements, the central question for educators is whether they have made sufficient allowance in their judgments for behavior that is a function of a child's particular cultural heritage (see Cartledge et al., 2000; Council for Children with Behavioral Disorders, 1996; Coutinho & Oswald, 1998; Osher et al., 2004). Cultural differences that do not put the youngster at risk in the larger society should be accepted; only values and behaviors that are incompatible with achieving the larger goals of education (self-actualization, independence, and responsibility) should be modified.

Who determines the larger goals of society? We all tend to view our own cultural orientation as the standard against which others should be judged. Because the

United States has been dominated by European microcultures, the focus of multicultural concerns has been on non-European minority cultures.

It is not easy to establish rules for applying a multicultural perspective. Teachers and school administrators must make daily decisions about which standards of conduct represent their personal value systems and which represent justifiable demands for adaptation to the larger society. For example, is it really necessary for students to remove their hats in the classroom? What is "polite" English, and is it necessary that students use it to address adults in school? What values and behaviors are inconsistent with a youngster's success and happiness in society at large? When do the values of a particular culture place a student at risk for school failure? Under what conditions is risk of school failure a fault of the school itself—how it is organized and the demands it makes of students? These and similar questions have no ready answers. They will continue to be part of our struggle for fairness and justice in a multicultural society.

PROBLEMS IN EVALUATING THE EFFECTS OF CULTURAL FACTORS

Besides the family and the school, which are topics of separate chapters, the most frequently researched cultural factors include the mass media, peer group, neighborhood, ethnic origin, social class, religious institutions, urbanization, and health and welfare services. Evaluating the role of these factors in emotional or behavioral disorders is extremely difficult, primarily for three reasons.

First, the interrelationships among the many cultural influences are so strong that untangling the effects of most of the individual factors is impossible. Decades ago, Farrington (1986) noted the interaction of culture with other variables, a problem reiterated by Coutinho and Oswald (1998). Hodgkinson (1995) observed that concern with racial and ethnic differences has diverted our attention from the more pervasive effects of poverty. Although poverty may be correlated with racial or ethnic identities, the best strategy for improving the lives of children who are members of racial or ethnic minorities and those with disabilities may be to focus on poverty itself (see Park, Turnbull, & Turnbull, 2002):

> To some extent, race diverted our attention from the most urgent issue: *poverty reduces the quality of the lives of all children, regardless of race or ethnicity.* Had we spent the 40 years since the *Brown* [1954 school desegregation] decision systematically seeking to lower the poverty level for *all* American children, we would be in a different, and probably better, condition today. (emphasis in original; Hodgkinson, 1995, pp. 178–179)

Second, research related to several of the factors is limited or nearly nonexistent. Religious beliefs and institutions, for example, probably have a strong influence on family life and child behavior, yet there is little research on the effects of religion on child behavior and family life.

Third, culture and temperament are interrelated in ways that make identification of problem behavior difficult. Is the problem in the child's behavior, the teacher's expectations, or the lack of fit between the two? Keogh (2003) summarized the problem succinctly:

> The idea of culturally related differences in how temperament is viewed is especially relevant to school. Classrooms are filled with students from many different cultural and ethnic backgrounds. They come to school from homes with particular expectations about what is acceptable or unacceptable behavior, about the meaning and importance of particular temperamental characteristic. Teachers, too, come with unique temperaments that reflect their own cultural beliefs and values. In some cases, the two will mesh well; in other cases, the two will be discrepant, leading to misunderstandings and stress. (p. 35)

Despite these difficulties in understanding cultural factors, available research does suggest relationships between certain cultural characteristics and the development of behavioral deviance. For example, violence in the media and the ready availability of guns, two prominent features of contemporary American culture, are consistently linked to aggressive conduct of children and youth (Huesmann, Moise-Titus, Podolski, & Eron, 2003; Stoff, Breiling, & Maser, 1997; Walker, Ramsey, & Gresham, 2004). The challenge is to understand and sustain cultural diversity that enhances the human condition while modifying cultural patterns of behavior that destroy the human spirit (see Kauffman, Bantz, & McCullough, 2002).

Biology, Family, School, and Culture: A Tangled Web of Causal Influences

When we think of cultural factors, we think of social institutions—nations, ethnic groups, religions, schools, and families. These and other social institutions are interconnected in ways that defy simple explanations of causal influences on children's behavior. For each possible combination of social institutions, we must ask how one affects the other. To what extent does the nation make its schools, and to what extent do its schools make that nation? To what degree can schools succeed without the support of families, and to what degree can families be successful without schools that teach what their children need to learn? What are the cultural factors, other than families and schools, that shape children's behavior, and how do families and schools create, enhance, or counteract these other influences? The answers to these questions are neither simple nor obvious, but they are critical to our understanding of the roles of schools and teachers in our society.

The role of schools in American culture—the extent to which schools merely reflect our national character and the extent to which they are responsible for creating it—is frequently a matter for discussion. Perhaps the increasing use of guns in the United States is peculiarly American. If it is a part of American culture, then it is no wonder it has invaded our schools. Researchers have found that Southeast Asian refugee families adopting an orientation to certain American values—acquisition of material possessions and pursuit of fun and excitement—have children whose academic performance is lower than that of children from families maintaining traditional Southeast Asian values: persistence, achievement, and family support (Caplan, Choy, & Whitmore, 1992). From one vantage point, then, it appears that schools and teachers face a task at which they cannot succeed unless changes occur in other aspects of social context or culture. "It is clear that the U.S. educational system can work— if the requisite familial and social supports are provided for the students outside school" (Caplan et al., 1992, p. 36).

We cannot, however, ignore the fact that schools and teachers have a special responsibility to influence the families and communities for which they exist—the other parts of our culture that they also reflect. True, parents must be involved with and support the work of teachers if the schools are to succeed. "Yet we cannot expect the family to provide such support alone. Schools must reach out to families and engage them meaningfully in the education of their children" (Caplan et al., 1992, p. 42). And meaningful engagement can occur only if schools offer instruction that addresses the concerns of families and communities. Delpit (1995) noted that many poor minority children have been shortchanged by an exclusive focus on "progressive" methods of instruction that cater to the learning of middle-class White students: "I have come to believe that the 'open-classroom movement,' despite its progressive intentions, faded in large part because it was not able to come to terms with the concerns of poor and minority communities" (p. 20). The affection of the public and educators for "progressive" methods seem to other writers as well to stymie the progress of many students, especially ethnic minorities and children with disabilities or other disadvantages (see Heward, 2003; Heward & Silvestri, 2004; Hirsch, 1996; Kauffman, 2002).

Many see the role of schools in American culture changing, in large measure because of the increasingly troublesome behavior, attitudes, and social needs of students. American culture itself is shaped in significant ways by the distribution of wealth among its citizens, and increasing economic disparities are a troublesome part of American culture. Poverty is a part of American culture that we obviously have not addressed effectively (Hodgkinson, 1995; Knitzer & Aber, 1995; Park et al., 2002). The cultural context of American public schools in the 21st century includes widespread poverty among children and the deterioration of family and other social institutions that previously offered more support for schools. The role of special education for children and youth with emotional or behavioral disorders in this context will likely be a matter for increasingly hot debate because it is clear that special education has not adequately addressed the problems our society wants to see solved (see Walker, Forness, et al., 1998).

As if this were not complicated enough, genes and environments have considerable influence on behavior and the creation of culture (cf. Diamond, 1997; Pinker, 2002; Weiner, 1999; Wilson, 1998). Thus, cultures, including families, schools, and other features of societies, are partly a result of social learning and partly a result of biological fates. Wilson (1998) captured the perspective on biological and social determinants of behavior succinctly:

> All biologists speak of the interaction between heredity and environment. They do not, except in laboratory shorthand, speak of a gene "causing" a particular behavior, and they never mean it literally. That would make no more sense than its converse, the idea of behavior arising from culture without the intervention of brain activity. The accepted explanation of causation from genes to culture, as from genes to any other product of life, is not heredity alone. It is not environment alone. It is interaction between the two. (p. 149)

Genetic influences on behavior and culture seem at first consideration to suggest that cultures will always evolve so that those most "fit," in a Darwinian sense, will survive. Ultimately, perhaps, this is so, but "culture can indeed run wild for a while, and even destroy the individuals that foster it" (Wilson, 1998, p. 171). Cultures are neither immutable nor immortal.

Mass Media

Mass media include printed materials, radio, television, motion pictures, and electronic information now available on the Internet. Societal concern for the effects of mass media on the behavior of children and youth began when books and magazines became widely available (Donelson, 1987). A few generations ago, concerns about the effects of radio programs and comic books were frequently expressed. Present controversies rage over the effects of textbooks, pornographic magazines, novels, motion pictures, electronic games, and information and pornography available on the World Wide Web on the thinking and behavior of the young. That what people read, see, and hear influences their behavior is hardly questionable; yet relatively little sound research is available to explain how—with the exception of advertising material. Publishers and broadcasters do market research to show the effectiveness of sponsors' ads; they know a lot about what sells and what influences the buying habits of specific segments of their audiences, including children and adolescents. Nevertheless, the influence of the media on youngsters' social behavior is often dubious or hotly disputed. Ironically, the same individuals (television network executives) who express confidence in the behavioral effects of television commercials argue that the effects of television violence on children's social behavior is negligible (Eron & Huesmann, 1986).

Today, the effects of television on behavioral development is by far the most serious media issue. Specifically, researchers and policy makers are interested in how watching television may increase children's aggression and their prosocial behavior (for example, helping, sharing, cooperation). Research clearly links watching television to increases in aggression, but the link is a statistical probability, not a one-to-one correspondence. Some highly aggressive children do not watch much television, although some children who watch television almost incessantly are not aggressive. Yet television viewing is clearly a contributing factor in some children's antisocial conduct, and it is important to understand how television viewing can be involved in causation. One obvious way in which television violence can facilitate aggressive conduct is through observational learning; youngsters imitate what they see. This explanation is probably a gross oversimplification; however, research now suggests that much more complicated processes are involved.

The most likely explanation of the effects of television viewing fits Bandura's (1986) social cognitive model (see chapter 4). The effects involve reciprocal influence among three components: person variables (thoughts and feelings), the social environment, and behavior. In the case of television violence and aggression, Bandura's triadic reciprocality involves the child's thoughts and feelings about aggression and the television characters who perform it, the child's environment (including school, home, and community), and the child's selection of violent television programs and aggressive responses to problem situations. But general social circumstance—the social ecology in which aggression is exhibited, including friendship patterns and school performance—must also be considered (Eron & Huesmann, 1986).

Sprafkin, Gadow, and Adelman (1992) and Gadow and Sprafkin (1993) reviewed decades of research on the effects of television viewing on exceptional children. They found little evidence that watching television programs showing prosocial acts causes children with emotional or behavioral disorders to engage in more appropriate social interaction. Their review also indicated that high levels of television viewing, whether the shows contained much violence or not, have negative effects on children's behavior.

Huesmann, Moise, and Podolski (1997) reviewed research on the relationship between antisocial behavior (particularly aggression) and media violence, including dramatic violence, music videos, video games, and news violence. Their conclusions are straightforward:

> Over the past four decades, a large body of scientific literature has emerged that overwhelmingly demonstrates that exposure to media violence does indeed relate to the development of violent behavior. The emerging theories and data suggest that multiple processes are involved, but that the most important seem to involve the observational learning of attitudes, beliefs, attributional biases, and scripts that promote aggressive behavior. Desensitization of emotional processes may also play a role in long-term effects as may a cognitive justification process in which the more aggressive children use media violence to justify their acts. At the same time, powerful shorter term effects of media violence may be engendered by excitation transfer from media violence to real life and by the tendency of media violence to cue well-learned aggressive habits. These processes would seem to place children most at-risk who already live in a "culture of violence" in which there are few norms against aggressive behavior, in which there are ethnic or nationalistic forces that support violence against dehumanized targets, and in which there is little family or educational intervention to moderate the effects of media violence. (p. 190)

More recent research by Huesmann et al. (2003) has added confirmatory evidence that watching a lot of TV violence dramatically increases the risk that a child will grow up to exhibit violent interpersonal behavior in adulthood. Violent media action appears to instigate antisocial acts in some cases, to desensitize children to acts of aggression (i.e., make them more apathetic to displays of aggression and less likely to help others), and to perceive their environment as a more aggressive and dangerous place. Some violent video games appear to provide effective training in violent acts through emotional preparation and behavioral rehearsal. Although research may not indicate clearly that watching television violence consistently causes children (including those with emotional or behavioral disorders) to be violent, there are good reasons to limit children's television viewing and direct their attention toward more constructive activities. The American Psychological Association (1993) and Walker et al. (2004) concluded that decreasing the violence depicted on television and in movies would help lower the level of violent behavior among children and youth.

The role of the mass media (not just television but all print, film, video, and broadcast media) in the development of emotional or behavioral disorders is a concern to those who wish to construct a more prosocial and humane society. For example, teenage suicidal behavior appears to increase following media coverage of teen suicides (Eisenberg, 1984; Hawton, 1986). Motion pictures that glorify violent solutions to problems may add to the effects of television violence. It is difficult to conclude that print materials featuring violence and pornography play any positive role in behavioral development or conduct. Perhaps decreasing portrayal of undesirable behavior and increasing prosocial programming and reporting of prosocial acts would make our culture less self-destructive and more humane. Yet the solution to the media problem is not apparent; censorship is not compatible with the principles of a free society. Personal choice and responsibility in patronage may be the only acceptable way to approach the problem.

Peer Group

The peer group is a possible contributing factor to emotional or behavioral disorders in two ways. First, the establishment of positive, reciprocal peer relationships is critical for normal social development. Children who are unable to establish positive relationships with their classmates are at high risk because the peer group is an important link to social learning. Second, some children and youth are socially skilled and have high social status but are enmeshed in a peer group that exerts pressure toward maladaptive patterns of behavior (Farmer, 2000; Farmer, Rodkin, Pearl, & Van Acker, 1999; Walker et al., 2004).

Absence of Positive Peer Relationships

Peer relationships are extremely important for behavioral development, especially during middle childhood and early adolescence, yet until the early 1980s, research tended to focus more on family relationships than on socialization to the peer group (J. R. Harris, 1995; Hops, Finch, & McConnell, 1985). We can now identify problematic relations with peers in children as young as 5 years of age, and these problems tend to persist over time (Ialongo, Vaden-Kiernan, & Kellam, 1998; Loeber, Green, Lahey, Christ, & Frick, 1992; Walker et al., 2004). Behavioral characteristics associated with emergence and maintenance of social status in the peer group and relationships between peer status and later behavioral problems are becoming clearer (Farmer, 2000; Farmer, Farmer, & Gut, 1999).

Research indicates that, in general, high status or social acceptance is associated with helpfulness, friendliness, and conformity to rules—to prosocial interaction with peers and positive attitudes toward others. Low status or social rejection is associated with hostility, disruptiveness, and aggression in the peer group. To complicate matters, aggressive youngsters, compared to nonaggressive, seem more likely to attribute hostile intentions to their peers' behavior, and they are more likely to respond aggressively even when they interpret their peers' intentions as nonhostile. Low social status among peers is also associated with academic failure and a variety of problems in later life, including suicide and delinquency. In fact, poor peer relations, academic incompetence, and low self-esteem are among the primary factors in an empirically derived model of the development of antisocial behavior (Dishion, 1990; Patterson, 1986b; Patterson, Reid, & Dishion, 1992; Walker et al., 2004).

The evidence that antisocial children and youth are typically in conflict with their peers as well as with adult authorities is overwhelming, as is the evidence that antisocial youngsters tend to gravitate toward deviant peers (see Farmer, 2000; Farmer, Farmer, & Gut, 1999; Farmer, Rodkin, et al., 1999; Walker et al., 2004). Youngsters who do not learn about cooperation, empathy, and social reciprocity from their peers are at risk for inadequate relationships later in life. They are likely to have problems developing the intimate, enduring friendships that are necessary for adequate adjustment throughout life. Thus, the peer group is a critical factor in creating social deviance.

These generalizations do not do justice to the complexity of the research on relationships between social status among peers and children's behavioral characteristics (Farmer, Rodkin, et al., 1999). Social status can be measured using peer nominations, teacher ratings, or direct behavioral observations. Depending on the source of data, different pictures of social acceptance or rejection emerge. Normal or expected behavior in the peer group differs with age and sex, so the same type of behavior can have different implications for peer relations depending on age and sex. The social processes that lead to social rejection may be quite different from those that lead to social isolation or neglect (Coie, Dodge, & Kupersmidt, 1990; Farmer, 2000). The same classroom conditions can produce different effects on social status and friendship patterns for students of different races, and bias in peers' social perceptions can produce different outcomes in terms of social acceptability for two individuals who exhibit similar behavior.

All sources of information regarding children's social acceptance indicate that better-liked youngsters are those who are considerate, helpful, and able to appeal to group norms or rules without alienating their peers. Social rejection is related to opposite characteristics—violating rules, hyperactivity, disruption, and aggression—although the antisocial behavior that characterizes rejected youngsters changes with age. As children grow older, they tend to exhibit less overt physical aggression. The ways in which they irritate others, and so become rejected, become more complex, subtle, and verbal. Physical aggression is more often a factor leading to rejection in boys' groups than in girls'.

Social withdrawal is often associated with peer rejection, but the causal relationship is not always clear. Apparently, social withdrawal is not as prominent as aggression in young children's thinking about relations with their peers. As children grow older, however, withdrawal correlates more closely with rejection, perhaps because rejected children are acquiring a history of unsuccessful attempts to join social groups. This correlation suggests that withdrawal is the result of rejection, a way of dealing with repeated social rebuffs. Youngsters who withdraw following repeated rejection may become the targets of taunts and abuse, perpetuating a cycle of further withdrawal and further rejection.

We know less about the behavior of socially neglected children than about those who are actively rejected, partly because it is difficult to study the characteristics of children who are all but invisible to their peers. Nevertheless, it appears that their peers see them as shy and withdrawn, that they engage in solitary play more frequently than most children, and that they are less aggressive and higher achieving than even popular youngsters (Wentzel & Asher, 1995). Neglected children sometimes appear to exhibit relatively high levels of prosocial behavior and conformity to teacher expectations, but their general lack of assertiveness may result in their peers' not perceiving them as socially competent.

Given that we have identified social skills in which rejected, withdrawn, and neglected youngsters are deficient, programs to teach those skills are logical interventions. Social skills training programs are now readily available. Nevertheless, social skills training often yields equivocal results, perhaps in part because training programs are typically implemented poorly or inconsistently (Kavale, Mathur, & Mostert, 2004; Quinn, Kavale, Mathur, Rutherford, & Forness, 1999; Sridhar & Vaughn, 2001; Vaughn, Kim, Sloan, Hughes, Elbaum, & Sridhar, 2003). Moreover, we often do not know exactly what skills need to be taught. The notion that we can easily identify critical social skill deficits without careful assessment is a deceptive oversimplification (Walker et al., 2004). Research increasingly reveals that social competence is much more complex than previously thought. Social competence may relate to the ability to display specific skills in specific situations, but precise identification of skills and exact specifications of performance in given situations are extremely difficult to determine (see Pearl, 2002). Moreover, identifying social skill deficits that cause youngsters to have problems with their peers is not always possible; the causes of peer rejection or neglect are typically multiple and complex.

An important aspect of the analysis of peer relations and social skills training, and one that has not always been considered in research, is the development of expectations that bias youngsters' perceptions of their peers' behavior. If, for example, a youngster acquires a reputation among his or her peers for aggression or for popularity, others respond to this reputation. They expect behavior that is consistent with their attributions of the motives of an individual whose reputation they accept as valid, and they interpret behavioral incidents accordingly. If one child throws a ball that hits another child on the head, peers are likely to interpret the incident in terms of their beliefs about the motives of the child who threw the ball. If the child is popular and does not have a reputation for aggression, they are likely to interpret the incident as an accident; if the child has a reputation for aggression, they are likely to interpret it as aggressive. The reciprocal interaction of biased perceptions and actual behavior must be taken into account in trying to understand why some youngsters are rejected whereas others who behave similarly are not.

Effective social skills interventions must therefore include provisions for dealing with peer group response to the youngster with emotional or behavioral disorders as well as teaching skills that enhance social acceptance (Vaughn et al., 2003; Walker et al., 2004). Only when the social ecology of the peer group can be altered to support appropriate behavioral change are social skills likely to result in improved status of the target child. Knowing that a youngster lacks specific social skills necessary for social acceptance and being able to teach those skills is not enough; one must also change the youngster's reputation—the perceptions and attributions of peers.

Undesirable Peer Socialization

An important causal factor in some emotional or behavioral disorders, especially anti-social behavior and delinquency, is peer pressure and socialization to deviant peer groups. The assumption that students who exhibit antisocial tendencies will observe and imitate the desirable behavior of their regular classroom peers appears to be based on myth rather than facts about observational learning (Hallenbeck & Kauffman, 1995). Antisocial students often reject prosocial models and gravitate toward a deviant peer group (Farmer, 2000). J. R. Harris (1995) has been credited with bringing attention to the primacy of peer influences on social development, but the recognition of the importance of peers does not mean that parents have no influence on their children's socialization (Kauffman, 1999a).

Peer pressure toward rejection of academic tasks, as well as toward antisocial behavior, appears to be a serious problem in many communities. Consider the observations of R. Leon Churchill, Jr., an African American who, at the time of the following comments, was 33 years of age and the assistant city manager of Charlottesville, Virginia. He recalled that as a boy in school in Williamsburg his good study habits cost him friends. "I remember being teased constantly for getting good grades. . . . One of the major issues that Charlottesville and most schools have to deal with is the gauntlet that African-American males have to run through for achievement" (Zack, 1995, B1, B2; see also McWhorter, 2000). Peer pressure of some African American students toward academic failure and classroom disruption may involve not wanting to act or be accused of acting White; but racial and ethnic perceptions are not the only factors in such peer pressure, nor are African American students the only ones to experience peer pressure toward marginal or failing performance at school. In any ethnic or racial group and in any social stratum, we may find groups of peers who express disdain for those who are studious, high achieving, and tractable (see Farmer, Rodkin, et al., 1999; Miller-Johnson, Coie, Maumary-Gamaud, Lochman, & Terry, 1999).

Teachers must thus be aware of how their efforts to induce and maintain appropriate behavior in their students can be undermined by negative peer pressure. More important, teachers need to find ways, perhaps through peer tutoring or other means, to build a peer culture that supports kindness and achievement. Research suggests that this may be accomplished for most students when they are given regular opportunities to learn, with proper training and supervision, to nurture and teach younger children (see Farmer, Stuart, Lorch, & Fields, 1993; Strayhorn, Strain, & Walker, 1993). Moreover, special classroom settings may be required for the most effective instruction in desirable social behavior for youngsters with emotional or behavioral disorders (Farmer, 2000; Kauffman, Bantz, and Mc Cullough, 2002; Stage & Quiroz, 1998).

Neighborhood and Urbanization

Neighborhood refers not only to residents' social class and the quality of physical surroundings but to the available psychological support systems as well. Loeber, Farrington,

Stouthamer-Loeber, & Van Kammen (1998a) drew the connection between antisocial behavior and neighborhood factors explicitly:

> Externalizing problems, unlike internalizing problems, were associated with neighborhood factors. Most of the externalizing problems we studied, and particularly physical aggression and delinquency, were more prevalent in the worse neighborhoods. Therefore, interventions for externalizing problems will need to take neighborhood into account. (p. 268)

Separating the neighborhood from other causal factors in social deviance, particularly social class, has proved difficult, if not impossible (Farrington, 1986, 1995). The neighborhood and community may play important roles in the prevention of certain types of highly visible behavioral deviance, such as conduct disorder and juvenile crime (Hawkins, Arthur, & Olson, 1997; Lorion, Brodsky, Flaherty, & Holland, 1995; Short, 1997). For example, a community sense of moral order, social control, safety, and solidarity may be extremely difficult to achieve in a neighborhood in which crime rates are high. Interventions aimed at individuals will probably not succeed because of the lack of neighborhood monitoring and mutual support. Students who carry weapons to school have been found to perceive less social support from parents, teachers, classmates, and friends (Malecki & Demaray, 2003). Group-oriented, community interventions that promote a shared sense of being able to cope with deviance may be more likely to help prevent juvenile delinquency and crime in high-crime neighborhoods (Lorion et al., 1995). A neighborhood in which violence is "normative" may, actually, foster the use of violence among children and youths (see Ng-Mak, Salzinger, Feldman, & Stueve, 2002).

The belief that city life is not conducive to mental health has persisted for well over a century in spite of lack of evidence that this is the case (cf. Jarvis, 1852). Achenbach, Howell, Quay, & Conners (1991), in a national study of behavior problems, found no differences between rural and urban settings in parental ratings of children's behavior problems. However, higher behavioral problem ratings were found in areas of intermediate urbanization (i.e., urban areas of fewer than 1 million people).

Compared with rural areas, higher rates of delinquency are sometimes found to occur in urban areas; but a major difficulty in establishing urban environments as a causal factor in social deviance is that urbanization cannot be easily separated from other factors, such as crowding, quality of housing, community or neighborhood supports, social class, and so on (see Farrington, 1986, 1995). However, it is also clear that family functioning and child rearing are often quite difficult in today's urban environment.

Some people express enthusiasm for the virtues and healing powers of rural retreats and agrarian cultures, but there is not much evidence that they are superior to urban environments in producing mentally healthy and high-achieving children. The overriding factors associated with deviance appear to be low socioeconomic status and the breakdown of family and community ties. Recent reports of economic and social conditions in rural America leave no doubt that inner cities are not our only disaster areas for families and children. If rural ever meant "safe," "healthful," or "educationally superior" for children, it is clear that it does not necessarily mean those things in the present era (see the case of Andy in the accompanying case book).

Ethnicity

Ethnicity has been the focus of much contemporary concern for understanding cultural diversity and forging multicultural education. Nevertheless, ethnic identity is increasingly difficult for many Americans to define (Hodgkinson, 1995; J. M. Spencer, 1997), and we must be careful to separate ethnic influences on behavior from those of other factors such as economic deprivation, social class, the peer group, and so on (see National Research Council, 2002).

In one of the largest and most carefully controlled studies of prevalence of behavioral problems in children and adolescents, Achenbach and Edelbrock (1981) found very few racial differences. They did, however, find substantial differences in behavioral ratings from different social classes, with children of lower class exhibiting higher problem scores and lower social competence scores than did those from higher class. When the effects of social class are controlled, ethnicity apparently has little or no relationship to emotional or behavioral disorders. The risk factors that may appear to accompany ethnicity are probably a function of the poverty of many ethnic minority families (Garmezy, 1987; Hodgkinson, 1995; Park et al., 2002; Short, 1997).

Ethnicity is often suggested as a factor in juvenile delinquency because studies show higher delinquency rates among Black than among White youngsters, but we must question the meaning of differences in rate for at least two reasons. First, discrimination in processing may account for higher official delinquency rates among students of African descent. Second, ethnic origin is difficult or impossible to separate from other causal factors, including family, neighborhood, and social class. Thus, it is not clear that ethnicity is related to delinquency independently of other factors (Dinges, Atlis, & Vincent, 1997; Farrington, 1986; Yung & Hammond, 1997).

Our tendency has been to make sweeping judgments regarding ethnic groups without taking individual backgrounds and experiences into account. This leads to stereotypes based on ethnic identity alone (see Tores, Solberg, & Carlstrom, 2002). Ethnic identity plays a part in how youngsters, particularly adolescents, are treated in our society (National Research Council, 2002; Osher et al., 2004; Peterson & Ishii-Jordan, 1994; J. M. Spencer, 1997). The issues surrounding ethnicity are complex because the values, standards, and expectations of ethnic groups are shaped not only internally by members of these groups but also by external pressures from the larger macroculture of which they are part. Thus, we must be careful in analyses of the effects of ethnicity to separate the influences of ethnic background from the effects of the dominant cultural groups' treatment of other ethnic groups. Given the long history of maltreatment of ethnic groups with relatively little power by the dominant American ethnic groups, we should not be surprised to find that membership in an ethnic minority that has comparatively little political or social power presents barriers to the achievement of academic competence, economic security, and mental health. Moreover, it is important to recognize that most ethnic minority youngsters do not succumb to the risk factors they experience:

> The majority of ethnic minority youths are not members of gangs, do not abuse alcohol or other drugs, do not commit acts of violence, and do not indulge in other problem behaviors. This includes many disadvantaged youngsters who are subject to

comparable individual, family, or community-based risks that have influenced antisocial behavior in their similarly exposed peers. (Yung & Hammond, 1997, p. 491)

An important point is that the disproportionality of ethnic groups in special education or juvenile justice does not mean that a very high percentage of youngsters
from an ethnic group are in special education or juvenile justice. For example, it is an
egregious error to conclude that half of all African American students are emotionally disturbed because half of the students in special education for students with emotional disturbance are African Americans. This is the kind of logical and mathematical
error that fosters stereotypes.

Social Class and Poverty

One ordinarily measures children's social class in terms of parental occupation, with
children of laborers and domestic workers representing one of the lower classes
and children of professional or managerial workers representing one of the higher
classes. Although lower social class is often associated with psychopathology, the
meaning of this finding is controversial. The relationship between social class and
specific types of disordered behavior does not hold up as well as the relationship to
emotional and behavioral problems in general. Furthermore, family discord and disintegration, low parental intelligence, parental criminality, and deteriorated living
conditions seem to be much more influential than does parents' occupational prestige in accounting for children's behavior. Although it is true that many parents in
low-prestige occupations may be described by the characteristics just cited, it is not
clear that low social class in itself is a contributing factor in children's social deviance;
social class may be a factor only in the context of these other parental and family
characteristics.

Economic disadvantage—poverty, with all its deprivations and stress—is apparently a factor in the development of disordered behavior, but social class, at least as
measured by occupational prestige of parents, probably is not (cf. Delpit, 1995; Hart
& Risley, 1995; Hodgkinson, 1995; Park et al., 2002). Merely being poor does not
make people inadequate or destroy families or account for children's school failure
or emotional and behavioral problems. However, we do know that many of the conditions that often are part of poverty, especially in its extreme, are strong negative
influences on children's cognitive and social development: inadequate shelter, food,
and clothing; exposure to chaotic living conditions and violence; lack of opportunities to learn from nurturant, attentive adults. Nevertheless, poverty itself is the best
predictor of school failure, as Hodgkinson (1995) pointed out a conclusion that is
still valid:

If there is one universal finding from educational research, it is that poverty is at the
core of most school failures. And this is as true for white children from Appalachia as
for black and Hispanic children from inner-city slums. . . .

Consider the issue of relative deprivation. Is a child with dark skin more likely to
be disadvantaged in terms of life chances than a child born into poverty? Today, the
answer is clearly no; poverty is a more pervasive index of social disadvantage than is
minority status.

This emphatically does *not* mean that we can ignore poor minority children; it means that a successful strategy will have to lift the largest number of children out of poverty, regardless of their race. . . .

There is clear evidence from the U.S. Government Accounting Office and from other sources that a number of social programs are effective in mitigating the effects of poverty. Head Start, WIC (Women, Infants, and Children feeding program), AFDC (Aid to Families with Dependent Children), and Upward Bound are programs that reduce the effects of poverty and help reduce the number of America's youngsters who remain in poverty. In addition, the prevention agenda—ensuring that bad things do not happen to young children—is "color blind" in its effectiveness for all poor children. We have at our disposal a set of proven programs for reducing poverty for *all* children from birth to age 18. Why is this agenda not fully implemented? (pp. 176–178, emphasis on original)

Occasionally, poverty is glorified, or at least its ravages are denied and the right to be poor is defended, usually by those who have not experienced poverty or seen it up close. One middle-class man with a physical disability recalls the following in his autobiography:

I remember one night that we were at Mr. Peshkin's [the history teacher's] house . . . and we were talking about the various rights of speech and thought. And Mr. Peshkin, our very own sly Socrates, asked if we thought we had the right to be poor, and, of course, privileged middle-class youths that we were, never having seen a right we didn't like, we said yes. And we were debating this right to be poor, with great eloquence, when Mr. Lombardo, the high school Spanish teacher, dropped by the house. Mr. Lombardo, who was from South America, had been dirt poor; and he laced into this group of privileged middle-class white boys with the passion and pain of his whole life. Having silenced us, shamed us, with this dose of reality, he went on to argue for the right not to be poor. He persuaded me. (Mee, 1999, pp. 193–194)

IMPLICATIONS FOR EDUCATORS

Educators should be aware of how cultural factors may be contributing to their students' emotional or behavioral problems and of the possibility of cultural bias in evaluating behavioral problems. We can seldom untangle the effects of isolated factors from the mix of circumstances and conditions associated with disordered behavior. Parental attitudes toward behavior and its correction cannot be understood without reference to cultural and community norms, especially for such controversial issues as corporal punishment (Gershoff, 2002) and touching students (Fisher, 2003).

Sometimes, the difference between teacher and students in culture or ethnicity is jarring, and teachers are caught completely by surprise. For example, Nakamura (2003) described his surprise at the contempt students showed for him in a Japanese high school, where he found that "Just as in America, a large number of students are being left behind" (p. 31). The story of two volunteers for Teach for America (Fisher, 2003) is a tale of success and failure in a District of Columbia elementary school. The story includes this observation of one of the teachers about Josh, who was unsuccessful:

Josh's disciplinary methods were pretty much what I do," says Vest [another teacher], "but I'm an African American woman in my mid-fifties, older than many of these children's grandmothers, and I get a different kind of respect. I'm sorry, but in many of those cases, there was nothing Josh could have done differently except be born a different color. We complain a lot about it when it's the reverse, but this was the same things we face—racism. Children called the white teachers bitches and MFs, parents could threaten them, and it was okay." (Fisher, 2003, pp. 42–43)

However, this view of racism as the root problem might be challenged. Another teacher who had taught in the same school saw things differently. "Other white teachers were able to overcome the race issue . . . However, because Josh was having a tough time, race became an issue" (Fisher, 2003, p. 43). Teachers with well-honed skills in instruction and behavior management are usually successful regardless of their personal identity or that of their students.

Research on specific factors that may give rise to disorders has important implications for prevention, especially if intervention can be aimed at improving children's individual circumstances. Strong evidence now suggests a basis for corrective action in many cases. Reducing television violence and providing more prosocial television programming, for example, would probably help reduce the level of aggression in our society, as would reducing the amount of time many children spend watching television.

Much could be done to address the needs of children reared under adverse conditions in which their health and safety, not to mention intellectual stimulation and emotional development, are at stake. These kinds of social changes demand large-scale efforts that educators cannot achieve alone; indeed, the politicization of issues regarding the physical and mental health risks of children and youth calls for all Americans to speak out. Programs to serve children and youth living in poverty will have enormous consequences for the nation's future. An open question is the extent to which local, state, and national governments will ask taxpayers to fund programs for poor and disadvantaged children and youth (see in accompanying case book, "The Health and Welfare of Children: How Important Are They in American Culture?").

Of the causal factors discussed in this chapter, the peer relations of rejected and neglected students is perhaps the most important consideration for the daily work of educators. Although we now recognize the great significance of students' poor peer relations or socialization to deviant peers, we know relatively little about the most effective means of intervening to improve their status or change their social affiliations once patterns of maladaptive behavior have become well established. Developing school-based, early interventions for target children and their peers should be a priority for researchers and teachers. These interventions may play an important role in the prevention of social adjustment problems (see Evertson & Weinstein, in press; Martella, Nelson, & Marchand-Martella, 2003).

SUMMARY

Children, families, and teachers are influenced by the standards and values of the larger cultures in which they live and work. Conflicts among cultures can contribute to youngsters' stress and to their problem behavior. Not only conflicts among different cultures, but mixed messages from the same culture can be a negative influence on behavior. Cultures sometimes both encourage and punish certain types of behavior; for example, youngsters may be tempted or encouraged by the media to engage in sexual behavior, yet our society creates penalties for teenage pregnancy.

We must guard against bias and discrimination in our pluralistic, multicultural society. Cultural differences in behavior that do not put the child or youth at risk in the larger society must be accepted. Educators should seek to change only behavior that is incompatible with achievement of the larger goals of education. However, clear rules for applying a multicultural perspective have not been established. Teachers and school administrators must continue to struggle with decisions about what behavior puts a child at risk in society at large.

Besides family and school, cultural factors that influence behavior include mass media, peer group, neighborhood, urbanization, ethnicity, and social class. A major difficulty in assessing most of these and other cultural factors is that they are so intimately intertwined. It is difficult, for example, to untangle the factors of social class, ethnicity, neighborhood, urbanization, and peer groups. Social class, ethnicity, the neighborhood, and urbanization have not been shown to be, in themselves, significant causal factors in emotional and behavioral disorders. They are apparently significant only in the context of economic deprivation and family conflict.

Other cultural factors are more clearly involved in causing disordered behavior. Watching television causes rising levels of aggression among children who are already aggressive. Rejection by peers also increases the upward spiral of aggression among youngsters who are uncooperative, unhelpful, disruptive, and aggressive. Socialization to deviant peers also may be a significant factor in antisocial behavior. In both cases—television violence and peer rejection or social gravitation to bad companions—youngsters' behavior, their environments (including others' reactions to their behavior), and their perceptions are factors in the development of increasing social deviance.

The literature on peer relations and social skills training has the clearest and most direct implications for educators. Teachers must be concerned about teaching the social skills deviant students need, but they must also be concerned with the responses and perceptions of the peer group and the deviant social networks that students with behavioral disorders may establish.

A Final Note on Causal Factors

When we think about the causes of emotional or behavioral disorders, oversimplifications and overgeneralizations are great temptations (Forness, 2003; Oswald, 2003; Pinker, 2002). We are inclined to assume that highly inappropriate behavior is simply a result of inadequate parenting or teaching, physiological problems, or cultural influences. We are too often tempted to believe that _____ is destiny, whether the _____ stands for biology, culture, or anything else. Keogh (2003) noted how biological factors do not always have the negative consequences for human relationships that we might expect. She described watching preschoolers' social interactions with peers and teachers:

> One of [the] students with the most severe physical limitations was a 4-year-old boy with cerebral palsy who had no speech and only minimal locomotion. Yet he was a magnet for the other children and the staff. He was an exceptionally responsive, cheerful, and outgoing child who thrived on interactions with others and who, despite serious physical limitations, was the most popular child in the class. Other children with milder disabilities were less sought after and had fewer and less satisfactory personal relationships. The differences in these children's temperaments were striking. (pp. xiv–xv)

But it is easy to miss Keogh's message, too. Her message is not that temperament is destiny, simply that temperament must be considered for the complex role it plays in children's development—and not just the temperament of the child, but the temperament of parents and teachers as well. Oswald (2003) stated, "Causality in the world of emotional and behavioral disorders is rarely linear; it rarely proceeds unambiguously from event A to outcome B" (p. 202).

As I hope you understand from reading the four chapters in part 3, parenting, teaching, physiology, and culture can be significant causal factors, but we must be extremely cautious in drawing conclusions about the individual case. Before concluding that a student's undesirable classroom behavior is a result of the teacher's ineptitude or that the child's disorder is caused by poor parenting, we must examine carefully what transpires in the interactions between student and teacher or child and parent. However, even if we observe these interactions and find that the adult clearly is behaving toward the child in a less than admirable manner, we must be careful not to jump to the conclusion that we have found the root of the problem. A child with a serious emotional or behavioral disorder may be extremely difficult for anyone to live with; he or she may be highly effective in frustrating and bringing out the worst in just about anyone. Recognizing that causal effects are not so simple or unidirectional as they first appear should help us maintain a reasonable level of humility in evaluating our own work with children and youth and give us caution in placing blame on the other adults who work with them as well.

We know much more today about the origins of emotional or behavioral disorders than we knew 25 or even 10 years ago, but researchers now realize that causal mechanisms are far more complex than previously assumed. At the same time that research is revealing the incredible complexity and interconnectedness of causal factors, it is opening up new possibilities for intervention. Old ideas that the course of psychopathology is set by early life experiences or biology and is impervious to intervention have given way to more hopeful attitudes for most disorders. At the same time, newer ideas about the positive influences of therapeutic environments are being tempered by the realization that many patterns of behavior reflect genetics and other biophysical processes and that teachers and parents should not be blamed for them or held responsible for correcting these problems solely through interpersonal interventions.

Mark Twain said, "It is wiser to find out than to suppose" (Mark Twain Foundation, 1966, p. 943). Pinker (2002) and Tavris (2003) have reminded us also of the importance of skepticism in trying to find out why people behave as they do. The scientific frame of mind is critically important. We need also to remember Polsgrove's maxim, "Just because you *think* it doesn't make it true" (Polsgrove, 2003, p. 223), as well as the bumper sticker saying, "Don't believe everything you think."

CASE FOR DISCUSSION

What would you have done?
Contributed by Shannon Fitzsimmons

I hop on the train going toward my house and make my way past a group of kids near the door. I sit down next to a woman my age and look around me. The group of youths at the door becomes the primary focus of my attention. There are six or seven of them—one girl. I'd say they range from 10 to 13 years old. Two of the boys are engaged in a game of some sort; there is no distracting them. The language the others are using with each other is pretty coarse for public talk. As the train grows more full at each stop, the youth remain sprawled, as if the car were empty. New passengers step over their legs that are extended into the aisle.

Given the range of behaviors that one can reasonably expect from individuals in this age range, the kids that I can hear are skirting its edges. Perhaps for this reason, no one is issuing those warm smiles that adults so readily cast onto children. Perhaps for this reason also, a middle-aged woman, sitting just behind the group and across from me, stands up and moves to a seat farther back.

At this point, I notice the boy directly in front of me has an odd posture: almost a fetal position, slouched far, far down. New passengers walking by eye him curiously. After this happens several times, I lean forward to see what he is doing. He backs up, standing now, but hunched over—and resumes his activity of drawing on the seat in thick, dark ink. As I have obviously seen him, and he has obviously seen me see him, I must call him out—he's vandalizing a full train, after all.

"What are you doing?" I ask in a tone I think is curious but stern.

"I'm drawing [expletive]. What does it look like I'm doing?"

I freeze, redden. He looks up now. He is staring at me hard. I hold the stare, but I have no idea how to respond. He must be—what?—11?

"You can't do that," I say finally, and while we are not speaking loudly, everyone near us is taking note.

No one says anything.

"Listen, [expletive], if you don't want me to rob you, you'd better shut the [expletive] up."

"Excuse me?"

"I said, if you wanna keep your stuff, you'd better shut the [expletive] up."

This exchange goes on for one or two more rounds. I say nothing substantial. The 11-year-old continues to threaten me. I realize we have reached my stop. The woman beside me, who has obviously witnessed the entire event, stands up and says, "Excuse me," as she would normally to make her way out of our seat and off the train. I pick up my things. I can feel all eyes on me as I leave.

I have no idea what happened when I exited the train and began walking down the street. Maybe someone said or did something firm about the child's language or his action and got results. Maybe the kid kept on drawing in a car full of immobile adults while a handful of adolescents learned that intimidation is an effective means of achieving objectives.

After replaying the incident a number of times in my mind, I'm still not sure what I could have done or said to get the desired outcome—cessation of vandalism. I know my approach was not successful. I also

know, for me, this event illuminated greater societal problems: that some children have experienced this kind of threatening dialogue enough times in their own lives to replicate in confidently with a stranger in public and that a group of adults allowed, for whatever reason, such an event to transpire.

Questions About the Case

1. What are some ways that immediate presence of the group of peers of the vandalizing youth could have affected his behavior?

2. Of the many cultural factors discussed in chapter 10, which do you feel are most likely to have influenced the encounter described in the story?

3. What cultural bias do you think the narrator brought to her interpretation of the encounter? What cultural biases do you bring to your reading of the case?

Note: See the accompanying case book for more questions about this case.

>> PERSONAL REFLECTIONS

Cultural Factors

Lisa J. Bowman, Ph.D., is research assistant professor at the Juniper Gardens Children's Project, University of Kansas.
Barry Brown, M.Ed., is a special education administrator in the Chesapeake, Virginia, Public Schools and a Ph.D. candidate in special education at the University of Virginia.
Courtney P. Davis, Ph.D., is a research analyst at the American Institutes for Research in Washington, D.C.
Carla J. Manno, Ph.D., is assistant professor of special education at George Mason University, Fairfax, Virginia.
Rosa E. Olmeda, Ph.D., is a research analyst in the Assessment Division of the American Institutes for Research in Washington, D.C. All of these contributors have been teachers in general or special education. All were doctoral students in the Multicultural Special Education Leadership Training program at the University of Virginia.

Barry Brown, M. Ed.

Barry, at what point can you peg or identify the culture of a student?

Many educators use the words *race* and *culture* interchangeably. Race typically denotes skin color, and when we look at students, we are tempted to assume that their culture is signified simply by the color of their skin. This is an erroneous assumption. Having said that, it is increasingly important for educators to recognize that our world is culturally diverse and that our society includes many microcultures. These microcultures vary widely from group to group. All, for example, have their own rules about communication that govern language behavior as well as tremendous differences in learning styles. Therefore, unless we are aware of all the cultural differences in our society, there is no foolproof way to identify the cultures of all the students we serve.

Which aspects of culture do you think are of no significance or of only marginal significance for instruction, and which aspects are central to successful instruction?

I think that just about every aspect of culture is essential to successful instruction. My belief is that you can't teach a child you do not understand. Obviously, there is no way that one can possibly learn everything about every culture, nor is this an attainable or desir-

able goal because cultures are always in a state of flux. They're changing all the time—including whatever culture or cultures you belong to. However, some knowledge of cultures, such as the way kids typically learn things, their use of language, the expected patterns of eye contact, physical contact, and ways of responding to persons of authority, are significant to successful instruction. Otherwise, educators may misread, ignore, misinterpret, or misdiagnose significant, culturally relevant verbal and nonverbal cues from their students.

Courtney P. Davis, Ph. D.

Courtney, how do you distinguish between stereotyping and being aware of cultural differences? Can multicultural education result in stereotyping?

There is a danger in assuming that all students of a particular color or ethnicity or social class share the same qualities, such as the ability to work individually or in a group, preference for sustained eye contact, or perception of time. Generalizations based on race provide a scaffolding that acts as a framework for future interactions. Cultural ideas about race shape our initial perception, but it should not serve as the sole component for making decisions about a student. All of the decisions that a teacher makes must acknowledge the variety of contingencies and conditions that affect every child (e.g., academic ability, student personality, family and community values). Effective teachers of students of culturally diverse backgrounds are those who individualize skills to meet the needs of students. Unfortunately, inflexible generalizations and expectations have a tendency to become stereotypes. When this occurs, poorly practiced multicultural education is more likely to run the risk of encouraging stereotypes than not.

To lessen the impact of stereotypes, multicultural pedagogy proposes that successful teachers know their students as human beings in social context. By making observations, communicating with a parent, or conducting home visits, teachers further their understanding of cultural miscommunications that may occur in the classroom and can learn to avoid them. Increased knowledge about students leaves less room for educators to cling to stereotypes and helps them use observation of race, class, gender, and so on merely as an initial framework.

Lisa and Rosa, how do you think we can tell the difference between a mere cultural difference and socially deviant behavior?

A moral code for living is embedded within each culture in our society. This code reveals a correct way to live, treat others, and raise a family. The moral code we use and live by shapes our ethics or moral reasoning—that is, our thinking about what is appropriate and what is not. It also influences our values, character development, and the sum of all our virtues and vices. Although differences clearly exist among moral codes, there are similarities as well. For example, in our society, there is typically consensus about the definition of civility. Civility refers to behaviors indicative of courtesy, good manners, and respect for others. In our school systems, behaving with civility is an underlying rule. Educators must expect children to demonstrate civility because it helps maintain order and foster intellectual and social competence. The more that children's behavior deviates from civility, the more likely they are to be classified as *deviant*. Therefore, it is the responsibility of educators (and parents) to identify deviant behavior and correct it as soon as it presents itself. This may prevent the development of behavioral disorders and their detrimental consequences.

The roles of general and special educators are complicated by the fact that they must learn to tell the difference between behavior that is deviant and behavior that is merely culturally different. However, by establishing rapport with parents at the beginning of the school year, teachers can gain a better understanding of behaviors that are attributed to specific cultures. A simple example of this is a classroom scenario in which the teacher thinks a student is being disrespectful. The teacher indicates that the child is rude because, when spoken to, he or she refuses to make eye contact. However, the parent points out that in the family's culture children are taught that it is disrespectful to make eye contact with an authority figure. A more complex example involves a family whose ethics support corporal punishment for their child's misbehavior. When that child comes to school, physical aggression (e.g., fighting) may be viewed as an acceptable way to deal with conflict. Acts of physical aggression such as fighting, however, are unacceptable behaviors in school that often result in suspension. Hitting may be acceptable at home, but it is not at school. These examples illustrate the importance of teachers' communication of their expectations to parents regarding acceptable classroom behavior, namely, that some behaviors are expected and some are prohibited, regardless of children's cultural differences.

Lisa J. Bowman, Ph. D.

Rosa E. Olmeda, Ph. D.

Through collaboration with parents, educators can also develop classroom management strategies that are culturally responsive. It is important that teachers discuss behavioral interventions with parents because some strategies may be in opposition to what is acceptable at home or in the family's community. For example, the teacher may decide that time out works most effectively for a particular student's misbehavior. However, the parents may disagree, considering it an ineffective strategy because of isolation from peers.

It is imperative that teacher preparation programs expose preservice teachers to a variety of instructional practices that will meet the needs of students from culturally diverse backgrounds. In addition to a traditional lecture approach, instructional techniques such as direct instruction, cooperative learning, and mnemonic instruction can be used. Furthermore, future educators should be encouraged to examine personal biases with regard to individuals from cultural backgrounds that are different from their own. Keeping a journal of their thoughts and reflections about their interactions with students during classroom experiences may help. This is important because teachers' beliefs and biases play out, in part, during the referral process for special education. Lack of familiarity with or bias toward other cultural groups may interfere with the diagnosis of social–emotional problems because such assessment depends primarily on teacher observation and analysis of children's behavior.

Carla, when is it legitimate to ask students to overlook—or to recognize but not reject—the differences between themselves and the models or culture of those they see or read about?

Instructional leaders may request that their students overlook something (usually the instructor's own mistakes) with no assurance that their advice is followed. Concurrently, that which we notice in terms of differences between and within cultures is based on individual viewpoints developed over time and within our own ideologies. Pointing out aspects and models that we, as instructional leaders, believe our students should or should not attend to sometimes assures that those are the very points they focus on the most. A more sound approach than considering from our own vantage point what students should and should not overlook in terms of differences is to afford them the opportunity to process their own understanding of cultural complexity. I propose doing so from a perspective grounded in the theory of concept attainment.

In any learning environment, students are constantly confronted with points of dissonance before reaching a new level of understanding. In fact, this is one of the basic premises of new concept attainment. Such is the case in dealing with students from many different cultural backgrounds, whether the differences reflect socioeconomic status, ethnicity, religion,

Carla J. Manno, Ph. D.

or any of the innumerable characteristics that constitute cultural identity. Assuming that this dissonance is an accepted, necessary, and welcome aspect of new learning, we can legitimately ask our students to follow a process of recognition toward synthesis: ultimately, achieving cultural awareness and understanding through reaching individual conclusions about how to deal with a world full of fabulous differences and similarities.

We must guide our students to recognize both sameness and difference between and within cultures, and not to overlook either. In attaining any new concept, we teach by calling attention to examples (in this case, cultural sameness or similarities) and nonexamples (differences). Our goal should be to teach through modeling and discussion and to recognize the points of cultural dissonance faced by our students of different cultural backgrounds. Typically, such questions and points for growth will arise in what they see in a text, study in a curriculum, or otherwise experience in a classroom. Sometimes, however, what is omitted leads to questions surrounding cultural identity and value within the larger society. Educators, students, and families will all be served when we accept such dissonance as a natural part of the learning process leading to cultural understanding.

Difficulty in accepting cultural differences does exist for many of our students: We might as well acknowledge this by bringing it into the light of the intended rather than the unintended (i.e., unguided) curriculum.

I have learned that classrooms will always have wonderfully abundant cultural differences and similarities, whether the population is made up of students from 35 seemingly identical backgrounds, different nations, or two major ethnic groups. Our job is to allow our students the opportunities to face bravely the complex process of recognizing both the differences and the similarities of those with whom they work and learn from and to come to a level of synthesis in cultural understanding that is their own. From this, we may hope to develop communities of citizens who can comfortably face a world in which difference and similarity exist simultaneously and can be observed, understood, and supported for the benefit of all.

>> QUESTIONS FOR FURTHER REFLECTION

1. What cultural biases and preferences do *you* bring to thinking about children's behavior in school, and what can you do to minimize or eliminate your biases?
2. Under what circumstances do you see making assumptions about a student's behavior because of his or her ethnic identity becoming a stereotype?
3. In your judgment, what are the most important aspects of culture of which teachers should be aware, and how do you think teachers can best be made aware of them?

Part 4

Facets of Disordered Behavior

Introduction

In the 10 preceding chapters, we discussed emotional or behavioral disorders primarily in the general case, with only occasional and brief attention to specific types or categories of disorders. In part 4, we revisit earlier questions with which we dealt mostly in the general case, this time giving closer scrutiny to specific types of disorders. For each major type of disorder, we attempt to provide succinct answers to as many of the following questions as possible:

- How is this disorder defined? What is its prevalence?
- What do we know about its causes and its possible prevention?
- What basic strategies are used in its assessment?
- What are the primary approaches to intervention and education?

Although we are able to provide brief answers to these questions for most of the major disorders, we are not able to answer all of the questions for all of the disorders or their subtypes.

Part 4 is titled "Facets of Disordered Behavior" to indicate that the types of problems we discuss are merely different sides of what we call emotional or behavioral disorders. The classification of emotional or behavioral disorders is complex and inevitably produces ambiguous categories. Disorders of all types seem to be interconnected, so in discussing one type we necessarily consider several others as well. For example, hyperactivity, conduct disorder, and delinquency are interrelated problems. True, one might find a youngster who is hyperactive yet is not considered to have a conduct disorder and has not been designated *delinquent*. We occasionally may find a seemingly "pure" case of any given type of disorder, one in which the youngster's problem is apparently neatly limited in character. Nevertheless, these "pure" cases are atypical; in most instances, we find multiple problems, clusters of disorders, behavior that is characteristic of several different facets of what we call emotional or behavioral disorders.

How, then, shall we decide what constitutes a distinctive facet of disordered behavior? Clearly, anyone's answer to this question will be in some ways arbitrary. I have chosen to divide this part of the book into seven chapters, partly on the basis of empirical evidence of the way in which behavioral problems are clustered or factored statistically and partly according to what I believe will facilitate the clearest discussion. I have begun with the disorders that are among the most prevalent: disorders of attention and activity, often referred to as attention deficit–hyperactivity disorder (ADHD), and conduct disorders (overt aggression and covert antisocial behavior). I then turn to juvenile delinquency and substance abuse, problems closely related to conduct disorders and attention problems. In the subsequent chapter, I discuss anxiety withdrawal and a variety of other disorders that do not fit neatly under any other category (fears and phobias; obsessions and compulsions; and disorders involving speaking, eating, eliminating, moving, and sexual behavior). Depression and suicide, which I examine next, are increasingly recognized as serious problems among children and adolescents. Finally, I address the disorders known variously as psychoses, or pervasive developmental disorders, which are among the least prevalent.

I hope the chapters in part 4 bring you a better understanding of the specific ways in which children and youth can exhibit emotional or behavioral disorders. As you read these chapters, you should ask yourself how specific disorders are interrelated and how they are distinctive. Here is a sample of the kinds of questions you might ask:

- What distinguishes conduct disorder from depression?
- When we see a youngster who has a conduct disorder, for example, might we also be seeing one who is depressed (that is, might conduct disorder and depression be comorbid conditions)? Could the same set of circumstances give rise to both conduct disorder and depression?
- To what extent are interventions effective for conduct disorder appropriate or inappropriate for a student who is depressed?
- How are teenage sexual activity and teenage parenthood linked to delinquency, substance abuse, and other disorders?
- What do we know about the comorbidity of depression and excessive fears?
- Under what circumstances are we likely to see a pervasive developmental disorder and hyperactivity or attention deficits in the same person? When we do, what are the implications for teaching?

Questions such as these are not easily answered, and my brief discussion of specific disorders cannot do justice to the complexity of these problems and their interconnections.

The serious study of emotional or behavioral disorders calls to mind a statement of C. E. Ayres: "A little inaccuracy saves a world of explanation." Although I strive for all the accuracy I can bring to the time and space available, I have come to recognize the fact that eliminating every inaccuracy is an insurmountable task; it would require a world of more knowledge and explanation than any individual can muster. Contemplating the next seven chapters and the questions they leave poorly answered, or not answered at all, will, I hope, leave you with a new appreciation of the complexity of emotional or behavioral disorders and their intricate reflection of unique personal identities.

CHAPTER ELEVEN

ATTENTION AND ACTIVITY DISORDERS

As you read this chapter, keep these guiding questions in mind:

- Why do we not define *hyperactivity* simply as being highly active?

- What types of behavior are most closely associated with attention deficit–hyperactivity disorder (ADHD)?

- Why are students with attention and activity disorders typically unpopular with their peers?

- What behavioral interventions are frequently used to manage hyperactivity and related problems?

- What general conclusions have been reached regarding the use of self-monitoring to manage off-task behavior and improve academic performance?

DEFINITION AND PREVALENCE

We said in chapter 1 that youngsters with emotional or behavioral disorders often induce negative feelings and behavior in others. Among the many characteristics that are bothersome or irritating to others and induce others to respond negatively are disorders of attention and activity. During the past several decades, individuals with these disorders have been described by a variety of terms, including *hyperactive* and *hyperkinetic*. Severe and chronic problems in regulating attention and activity are now commonly known as *attention deficit–hyperactivity disorder*. The inability to control one's attention has replaced hyperactivity as the core problem of concern. The prevailing opinion is that hyperactivity usually, but not always, accompanies attention deficits. ADHD is a term about which there is still much uncertainty and controversy (see Hallahan & Kauffman, 2003; Hallahan, Lloyd, Kauffman, Weiss, & Martinez, 2005).

In this chapter, we use the term ADHD because we are concerned primarily with children and youth who have attention and activity disorders, and who have problems that are more severe than most. These youngsters with extreme attention and activity problems may also be categorized as having emotional or behavioral disorders or learning disabilities. Youngsters whose attention deficits are accompanied by hyperactivity and *impulsivity* are more likely to have conduct disorders than are those who show attention deficits and disorganization without hyperactivity. Our concern here is with youngsters who have serious social or emotional problems, whether related to hyperactivity or other manifestations of attention deficits, in addition to problems attending to their schoolwork. The varied nature of the social problems of children with disorders of attention and activity was summarized well by Whalen and Henker (1991):

> There are two truisms regarding the interpersonal difficulties of children with . . . ADHD. . . . The first is that the vast majority of these youngsters have serious social problems that pervade their everyday lives and spur frequent conflicts and confrontations. The second is that their patterns and styles of social exchange display marked heterogeneity in form as well as intensity. Many hyperactive children show a curious combination of social busyness and clumsiness, frequently initiating contact with others but in a manner perceived as immature, intrusive, or inept. A smaller number of these children show less interpersonal interest, appearing aloof and at times even oblivious as they skirt the periphery of social action. Still other hyperactive youngsters are highly aggressive, but even in this realm, heterogeneity is the rule rather than the exception. Some may engage in aggressive acts that appear planned, instrumental, and at times even hostile. For others, aggression seems to be more explosive than exploitative, linked to emotional volatility and difficulties dealing with frustration. (p. 231)

ADHD is among the most controversial disorders. Like learning disability, ADHD is seen by some people as a real and serious disability and by others as an attempt to legitimize teachers' or parents' inadequacies, or as "a fancy excuse for getting undeserved special consideration" (Bateman, 1992, p. 29). Good teaching and good discipline at home and school would, according to some skeptics, resolve the problem of

ADHD in all but a small percentage of cases. Others see ADHD as a true developmental disability for which there is no cure. Professional disagreement and public confusion have been found at almost every point of research and practice (Hallahan & Cottone, 1997; Hallahan et al., 2005).

We assume that ADHD does exist and that a consensus among professionals regarding its nature and treatment is gradually emerging. Contrary to much popular opinion, the emerging consensus, based on decades of research, is that ADHD is neither a minor problem nor a temporary characteristic of childhood that is typically outgrown. It is a distinctive set of problems, a real disorder, a real disability (Barkley, 1998, 2003; Hallahan & Kauffman, 2003; Hallahan et al., 2005; Levy & Hay, 2001; Wasserstein, Wolf, & Lefever, 2001).

Most definitions of ADHD suggest that it is a developmental disorder of attention and activity, is evident relatively early in life (before the age of 7 or 8), persists throughout the life span, involves both academic and social skills, and is frequently accompanied by other disorders.

The difficulties in focusing and sustaining attention, controlling impulsive action, and showing appropriate motivation that characterize ADHD can make a person with the disorder—regardless of his or her age—a trial for parents, siblings, teachers, classroom peers, or coworkers. Hyperactive, distractible, impulsive youngsters upset their parents and siblings because they are difficult to live with at home; at school they often drive their teachers to discomposure. They are often unpopular with their peers, and they do not typically make charming playmates or helpful workmates. Incessant movement, impulsiveness, noisiness, irritability, destructiveness, unpredictability, flightiness, and other similar characteristics of students with ADHD are not endearing to anyone—parents, siblings, teachers, and schoolmates included. The following classic description illustrates how unpleasant children with ADHD can be to those around them:

> A hyperactive child's mother might report that he has difficulty remembering not to trail his dirty hand along the clean wall as he runs from the front door to the kitchen. His peers may find that he spontaneously changes the rules while playing Monopoly or soccer. His teacher notes that he asks what he is supposed to do immediately after detailed instructions were presented to the entire class. He may make warbling noises or other strange sounds that inadvertently disturb anyone nearby. He may seem to have more than his share of accidents—knocking over the "tower" his classmates are erecting, spilling his cranberry juice on the linen tablecloth, or tripping over the television cord while retrieving the family cat, thereby disconnecting the set in the middle of the Superbowl game.
>
> A hyperactive child is all too frequently "in trouble"—with his peers, his teachers, his family, his community. His social faux pas do not seem to stem from negativism and maliciousness. In fact, he is often quite surprised when his behaviors elicit anger and rejection from others. (Whalen, 1983, pp. 151–152)

Teachers need to be aware of the developmental aspects of attention and understand what distinguishes the student with ADHD from one who exhibits normal levels of inattention and impulsivity. We frequently see a high level of seemingly undirected activity, short attention span, and impulsive behavior in normally developing young children. As children grow older, however, they gradually become better able to direct their activity into socially constructive channels, to pay attention for longer periods and more efficiently, and to consider alternatives before responding. Thus, only when attentional skills, impulse control, and motoric activity level are markedly discrepant from those expected at a particular age is the child's behavior considered to require intervention.

Children with ADHD stand out from their age peers, often from an early age (DuPaul & Stoner, 1994). Moreover, the characteristics of ADHD are not typically subtle; they tend to be "in your face" behaviors that make most of the child's peers and most adults want to exclude the child from their environment or resort to "in your face" reprisals. In fact, it is becoming more and more apparent that ADHD is frequently a component of other disorders.

Relationship to Other Disorders

Disorders of attention and activity are very frequently seen in children and youth with a wide variety of other disorders (Dulcan, 1997; Gershon, 2002; Tankersley & Landrum, 1997). Nearly all teachers, parents, and clinicians agree that many youngsters with other types of emotional or behavioral disorders—conduct disorders or autism, for example—have difficulty controlling their attention to academic and social tasks and are disruptive. Figure 11.1 shows the central role that not paying attention and disruptive behavior play in a variety of emotional and behavioral disorders, not just

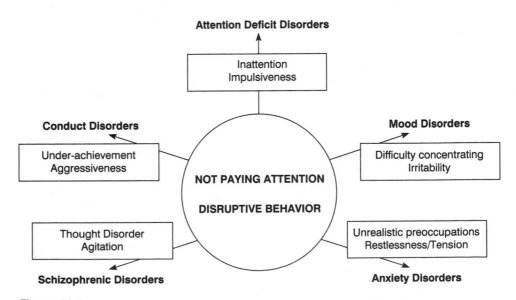

Figure 11.1
Core classroom symptoms and their possible relationships to psychiatric disorders
Source: Forness, S. R., Kavale, K. A., King, B. H., & Kasari, C. (1994). Simple versus complex conduct disorders: Identification and phenomenology. *Behavioral Disorders, 19*, 308.

ADHD. When we observe the core symptoms of inattention and disruptive behavior, therefore, we need to look further to know whether these behaviors are part of ADHD, conduct disorders, mood disorders (e.g., depression), anxiety and related disorders (e.g., obsessions, compulsions), or thought disorders such as schizophrenia. As Forness et al. (1994) have explained, not paying attention may be related to aggressiveness, impulsiveness, irritability, restlessness and emotional tension, or agitation, each of which is associated with a particular set of symptoms or diagnostic category. To complicate the picture further, a given child may have multiple disorders. Inattention may thus be part of the complex, multiple problems of an individual child.

In combination with other developmental problems such as conduct disorders or juvenile delinquency, ADHD greatly increases the risk of school failure and severity of symptoms, especially in boys (Gershon, 2002; Hallahan & Cottone, 1997). In fact, hyperactivity, inattention, and impulsiveness appear to play a key role in the development of antisocial behavior, at least for boys (Flory, Milich, Lynam, Leukefeld, & Clayton, 2003; Loeber et al., 1998).

Nearly all researchers who recognize that disorders of attention and activity exist conclude that although ADHD is a separate, distinctive disorder in its own right, there is great overlap between ADHD and other diagnostic categories (Barkley, 1998, 2003; Dulcan, 1997; Gershon, 2002). Whether ADHD should become a separate category under federal law the Individuals with Disabilities Education Act and regulations has been a matter for hot debate.

Whether there are unique features of ADHD and, if so, where the boundaries between ADHD and other disorders should be drawn are points of considerable controversy. Most experts believe that a significant percentage (perhaps about 30%) of the children with ADHD have not been served under any category of special education and that a high percentage (perhaps 50 to 70%) of those with specific learning disabilities or "emotional disturbance" (emotional or behavioral disorders) also have ADHD (cf. Bloomingdale et al., 1991; Dulcan, 1997; Fletcher et al., 1991; Hallahan et al., 2005). The confusion about the nature of ADHD and its relationship to other disorders is heightened by the fact that the children referred for mental health services often are those with extreme attention problems, with or without hyperactivity.

Children and youth with emotional or behavioral disorders typically have difficulty relating to their peers, often being actively rejected by peers because of their inappropriate social behavior. Although many children with attention deficits do not have problems with peers, some are rejected. If they have extreme attention deficits, their peer problems may be understandable: people (children or adults) do not usually prefer as companions those who are extremely "flighty." We may conclude the following:

- Many children and youth with ADHD will not be found to have emotional or behavioral disorders.
- A sizable percentage of those with extreme ADHD will be identified as having emotional or behavioral disorders.
- Many of those receiving special education because of other emotional or behavioral disorders will have ADHD.
- Learning disabilities may accompany any combination of disabilities.

Figure 11.2
Hypothetical relationships among
the populations having attention
deficit–hyperactivity disorder (ADHD),
emotional or behavioral disorders
(EBDs), and learning disabilities (LDs)

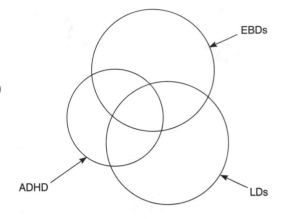

We might speculate that the relationships among the populations of individuals
having ADHD, emotional or behavioral disorders, and learning disabilities, are
approximately those shown in Figure 11.2. EBDs and LDs may occur alone or in combination with each other and with ADHD.

Prevalence

Controversy regarding definition makes the prevalence of a disorder extremely hard
to estimate, as we noted in chapter 2. Most authorities estimate the prevalence of
ADHD at 3 to 5% of the school-age population, making it one of the most common
disorders of children and youth and putting it among the most common reasons for
referral (Hallahan et al., 2005; National Institutes of Health, 1998). Moreover, ADHD
is not merely an American phenomenon (Wilens, Biederman, & Spencer, 2002).
Among those referred for ADHD and related disorders, boys far outnumber girls.
Gender bias may be a partial explanation for the predominance of boys, but the size
of the disparity suggests that there may also be biological gender differences that contribute to the disorder (Barkley, 1998, 2003; Gershon, 2002).

CAUSAL FACTORS AND PREVENTION

Historically, brain dysfunction has been the presumed cause of what is now known as
ADHD (Hallahan & Kauffman, 2003; Hallahan et al., 2005). Today, researchers are
investigating biological causes through more sophisticated anatomical and physiological tests involving blood flow to the brain, neurotransmitters, and so on (e.g., electrical potentials in brain tissue, magnetic resonance imaging). As yet, no reliable
evidence shows precisely what neurological problem is the basis of ADHD, although
many researchers suspect an underlying biological cause of most cases.

Various food substances (e.g., dyes, sugars, preservatives), environmental toxins
(e.g., lead), and allergens have been suggested as causes of hyperactivity and related

disorders. None of these has been demonstrated to be a frequent cause of ADHD, although evidence does suggest that such factors may be a cause in a very small number of cases. Claims that foods, toxins, or allergies are frequent causes are not substantiated by credible research (Barkley, 1998; DuPaul & Barkley, 1998; McLoughlin & Nall, 1994; Wolraich et al., 1995).

Genetic factors appear to increase risk for ADHD, although the genetics of the disorder are very poorly understood. We do know that ADHD is more common among the biological relatives of children who have the disorder than in the general population, suggesting that ADHD is genetically organized in some way. It is plausible that genetic factors may give some individuals a predisposition toward attention problems and impulse control and that it leads to ADHD in combination with other biological or psychological factors (see DuPaul & Barkey, 1998; Pinker, 2002).

A difficult temperament—an inborn behavioral style characterized by irritability, high activity level, short attention span, distractibility, and so on—has been suggested as a possible starting point for ADHD. Children with ADHD are often identifiable as toddlers or preschoolers (Barkley, 1998, 2003). Temperamentally, they fit the description of the "difficult child." They are children who "in the early preschool years show a mixture of problems in attention, impulse control, noncompliance, and aggression" (Campbell, Breaux, Ewing, & Szumowski, 1986, p. 232; see also Keogh, 2003). Yet temperament alone does not explain all the problems of these youngsters.

In short, evidence does not clearly and consistently link any particular biological factor to ADHD. It is plausible, however, that biological factors are involved in most cases, but precisely what they are and how they operate remain unknown (Hallahan et al., 2005).

Hypothesized psychological causes of ADHD range from psychoanalytic explanations to those involving social learning theory. For instance, numerous studies of modeling and imitation illustrate how children could acquire deviant behavior patterns through observation of frenetically active parents or siblings. The literature is replete with examples of how children's inappropriate behavior can be manipulated by social attention, suggesting that parents and teachers could inadvertently teach youngsters to behave in the manner that characterizes ADHD. Nevertheless, research has not demonstrated that ADHD is primarily a matter of undesirable social learning, and therefore it is inappropriate for us to lay responsibility for the creation of ADHD on parents or teachers (Barkley, 1998, 2003; Braswell & Bloomquist, 1991; DuPaul & Barkley, 1998; Hallahan et al., 2005).

To summarize what we know about causes, we do not know exactly why children have ADHD. There does not appear to be a single cause. In the vast majority of cases, we suspect that neurological or genetic factors launch the child toward ADHD and that these factors in combination with other influences in the child's physical and social environment produce the inattentive or hyperactive behavior.

We know more about how to control the problems related to this disorder once it has appeared than we know about its origins, so prevention is largely a matter of intervening early in the families and classrooms of youngsters who are difficult to manage (see Kauffman, 2003b). Effective primary prevention—keeping ADHD from emerging during the child's development—would require knowledge of neurology and genetics that we do not have, in addition to training in child care and management that would eliminate possible environmental causes. Secondary prevention—reduction and management of problems that have emerged—is the most feasible approach (see Kauffman, 1999c, 2003b, for further discussion of primary versus secondary prevention).

Much of the responsibility for secondary prevention falls on educators, who must manage the child's behavior in school and provide instructional programs that will foster academic success and social adjustment (Hallahan et al., 2005). ADHD appears to be a persistent set of problems that follows children into adolescence and adulthood (Barkley, 1998; Wilens, 2002). It interferes with academic achievement and peer relations. Lack of achievement, feelings of failure, social isolation or rejection, and low motivation make for high rates of socially inappropriate behavior. The student with ADHD becomes trapped in a self-perpetuating pattern of negative self-perceptions, inappropriate behavior, and negative interactions with others. Prevention of later and more serious difficulties depends on breaking this cycle.

ASSESSMENT

Assessment of ADHD usually involves a medical examination, a clinical interview by a psychologist or psychiatrist, and parent and teacher ratings of behavior (Barkley, 1998, 2003; Dulcan, 1997; Hallahan et al., 2005). The clinical assessment of ADHD by a psychologist or psychiatrist and the educational assessment of ADHD by teachers or other school personnel may differ considerably. Clinicians will likely be interested primarily in determining whether the child meets certain diagnostic criteria; teachers will be more interested in devising a plan for management of classroom behavior and instruction. Parents will want to know why their child behaves as he or she does and how they should respond. Although the characteristics of ADHD may be noticed by parents or others before the child enters school, it is often not until the child is confronted by the demands of the classroom that someone—usually a teacher—becomes aware of the seriousness of the child's problems. In the context of school, ADHD often becomes intolerable, and the child's behavior is perceived as provoking a crisis. Children with ADHD often exhibit social behavior about which teachers are understandably upset. Teachers' concerns about their students' academic performance apparently most often lead them to refer students for special education (Abidin & Robinson, 2002; Lloyd, Kauffman, et al., 1991). However, many pupils with ADHD present both behavioral and academic concerns.

The primary means of assessment of ADHD that have usefulness in school settings are teacher and peer rating scales, direct observation, and interviews. A wide variety of rating scales have been used; some are intended to be specific to ADHD, whereas others are the broader, more inclusive scales described in chapters 5 and 6. The value of any of these scales is that they allow someone to organize and quantify teachers' and peers' perceptions of the student's academic and social behavior. These perceptions are important, but they may not correspond well to direct observation of the student's behavior.

One of the problems in assessing ADHD is determining whether the youngster shows problems related to attention deficits, aggression, or both. ADHD may be distinguished by disrupting the classroom, exhibiting problems in daily academic performance, being unprepared for class, not having required materials, and so on. These problems may or may not be accompanied by aggressive behavior or other indications of additional emotional or behavioral disorders. The distinction may be important in judging the seriousness of the student's problems and designing an intervention plan.

Direct observation of the youngster's behavior in various school settings—classroom, playground, lunchroom, hallways—and careful daily records (as opposed to teacher ratings) of academic performance are critical aspects of assessment. These can pinpoint the behavioral aspects of the problem of ADHD and serve as an objective measure of the effectiveness of interventions. Both objective records of behavior and performance and subjective judgments regarding the nature and acceptability of the student's behavior and performance are important in managing ADHD.

INTERVENTION AND EDUCATION

In most cases, ADHD involves a cluster of related behavioral characteristics, including problems in regulating attention, motivation, hyperactivity, and socially inappropriate responses. Consequently, many different intervention techniques have been tried in both home and classroom settings. The two most common and successful approaches have been medication and training parents and teachers how to manage the student's behavior (psychosocial interventions). The vast majority of cases require multiple interventions involving both parents and teachers (Barkley, 1998, 2003; Hallahan et al., 2005).

Medication

No method of dealing with ADHD has been so controversial as medication (DeGrandpre, 1999; Hallahan & Kauffman, 2003; Hallahan et al., 2005). The medications usually given are psychostimulants such as Ritalin, Dexedrine, Cylert, or Adderall, or a nonstimulant drug called Strattera. Opponents of medication have described the drugs' possible negative side effects, unknown long-term effects on growth and health, possible negative effects on perceptions of personal responsibility and self-control, and possibility of encouraging drug abuse. The statements of some of the opponents of medication have been unfounded and hysterical; others have been thoughtful and cautious, based on reliable evidence that stimulant drugs are not a panacea and do, like all medications, carry risks as well as benefits. You might consider the case of John in the accompanying case book and the thoughts of his mother and her acquaintances about the management of ADHD.

Research now clearly indicates that the right dosage of the right drug results in remarkable improvement in behavior and facilitates learning (makes the student more teachable) in about 90% of youngsters with ADHD (Crenshaw, Kavale, Forness,

& Reeve, 1999; Forness, Kavale, Sweeney, & Crenshaw, 1999; Spencer, Biederman, & Wilens, 2002). It is important to recognize that higher than optimal dosage may impair learning rather than facilitate it, that a medication may not have effects on all of the youngster's problem behaviors (e.g., it may improve hyperactivity but have little or no effect on aggression), and that the effects of medication may be different in different settings (e.g., more improvement in school than at home). Children with other disorders in addition to ADHD, such as anxiety or depression, may not respond well to stimulant drugs (Tannock, Ickowicz, & Schachar, 1995).

Research clearly points to medication as the single most effective treatment of ADHD (Jensen et al., 2001). However, there is absolutely no reason to choose between medication and other interventions. As is the case with virtually all emotional and behavioral disorders, both medication and other treatments can be used to best advantage. A combination of medication and behavior management provides even better outcomes for children with ADHD than medication alone (Gully, Northup, Hupp, Spera, Levelle, & Ridgway, 2003). In fact, stimulant drugs may improve the effects of good behavior management strategies, and good behavior management may improve the effects of medication (Kolko, Bukstein, & Barron, 1999; Northrup et al., 1999).

When reasonable precautions are taken in their use and the dosage and effects are carefully monitored, stimulant drugs are a safe and sane way of augmenting parents' and teachers' other strategies for managing ADHD (Jensen et al., 2001; Spencer et al., 2002), but good psychopharmacology demands careful monitoring of the effects of medication. Teachers should offer parents and physicians their observations about the effects (or noneffects) and side effects of medications on the behavior and learning of a medicated student who is in their class.

Psychosocial Training Involving Parents and Teachers

Medication alone is not the most effective means of bringing the behavior of children with ADHD under control. Parents typically have serious difficulty managing these children at home, and teachers often have difficulty managing these children in school. Consequently, systematic training of parents and teachers in behavior management skills is an approach frequently used by psychologists who serve children with ADHD and their families (Alberto & Troutman, 2003; Barkley, 1998, 2003; Jensen et al., 2001). The objective of this training is not to cure or eliminate ADHD but help parents and teachers learn how to manage children's behavior more effectively. The training is organized around principles of behavioral psychology and involves teaching parents and teachers to interact more positively with their children during ordinary activities, avoiding the coercive interactions that are hallmarks of families with aggressive and hyperactive children and adolescents. The procedures parents and teachers are taught to use may include a token reinforcement system for encouraging appropriate behavior and response cost (withdrawing rewards) or time out (brief social isolation) for misbehavior.

Ultimately, parents may be taught techniques for managing behavior in public places and generalizing the training to new problems and settings (Barkley, 2000).

This type of training is not possible with all parents, nor is it always successful when parents are receptive to it. However, it has been used successfully with many parents. The psychologist working with parents will typically involve teachers as well in a behavior management plan because little change is likely in school unless similar behavior management procedures are used in the classroom. Parents may also need suggestions for how to manage everyday events for families, such as an adolescent's learning to drive (Snyder, 2001).

The problems of students with ADHD are usually most evident in the classroom, where compliance and focused attention to task are essential for success. Teachers should be helped to understand the likely functions of ADHD and related behavioral problems in the classroom, which they may discover through functional behavioral assessment (see chapter 6).

> The most likely function for ADHD-related behavior in school is to *escape effortful tasks,* particularly those that involve independent writing activity (e.g., seatwork) or an extended sequence of chores. This is based on the assumption that presenting independent work or a chore is an antecedent for inattention, which is then followed by a lack of work completion. A second possible function is to *gain adult and/or peer attention.* A frequent consequent event for inattention and disruption is a verbal reprimand from the adult as well as nonverbal (e.g., smiles) and verbal reactions (e.g., laughter) from the student's classmates. An additional possible function is for the ADHD-related behavior to result in *sensory stimulation* that appears more reinforcing than the stimuli that the child is expected to attend to. For example, when presented with a set of written math problems to complete, the student begins playing with a toy that was kept in his pocket. (DuPaul & Barkley, 1998, p. 152, emphasis in original)

Behavioral interventions and cognitive strategy training are the two most widely recommended approaches to managing the problems of ADHD (Barkley, 1998; Hallahan et al., 2005). Teachers must be trained in how to use these approaches if they are to have a reasonable chance of success; they are not intuitive methods or ones that every teacher learns.

Behavioral Intervention

A basic behavioral principle is that behavior is affected by its antecedents and consequences (see Alberto & Troutman, 2003; DuPaul & Barkley, 1998). Behavioral intervention is not likely to be successful unless the person who is trying to use it both understands the principles that make it work and is attuned to the student's individual characteristics and preferences. It is a powerful tool—but a good one only in the hands of a perceptive and sensitive teacher. Adept use of behavioral interventions results in warm, caring relationships between students and teachers (Cullinan, 2002; Kauffman et al., 2002, 2004; Kerr & Nelson, 2002; Walker, 1995; Walker, Ramsey, & Gresham, 2004).

Behavioral intervention means making certain that rewarding consequences follow desirable behavior and that either no consequences or punishing consequences follow undesirable behavior. As is true with parents, rearranging consequences to support desirable behavior and not support undesirable behavior may be as simple as shifting attention from inappropriate to appropriate behavior. More powerful consequences such as *token reinforcement, response cost,* and *time out* may be needed as well. In many cases, it is helpful to make the contingencies of reinforcement and punishment more explicit by writing a *contingency contract* (see chapter 12). In addition to the procedures used in the classroom, the parents may be involved in a home–school behavior modification program in which behavior at school earns the pupil rewards provided by the parents at home (see Hallahan et al., 2005). The emphasis must be on positive consequences for appropriate behavior, but prudent negative consequences for misbehavior may be necessary (DuPaul & Barkley, 1998; DuPaul & Stoner, 2002; Northrup et al., 1999; see also chapter 12).

Other behavioral intervention procedures involve altering classroom conditions or instruction to make them more attractive to students. These procedures do not in any way make consequences unimportant. They are simply an additional means of putting behavior principles to work in helping students with ADHD behave more appropriately and learn more. For example, Powell and Nelson (1997) compared the undesirable behavior of a student with ADHD under two conditions: no choice, when the teacher simply gave the student, Evan, an assignment, and a choice condition in which "the teacher presented Evan with three different language arts assignments taken from the class curriculum, and he chose one to complete" (p. 182). Figure 11.3 shows that under the choice condition, Evan's undesirable behavior was much lower. Other researchers have also found that giving students with ADHD and other emotional or behavioral disorders a say in their work (not, of course, whether to work, but perhaps which assignment to do) is helpful (e.g., Mithaug & Mithaug, 2003).

Recall the quotation (p. 273) of DuPaul and Barkley (1998) about why children may exhibit ADHD-related behavior. It is important to understand what maintains

Figure 11.3
Percentage of intervals rated as containing undesirable behaviors across conditions
Source: Powell, S., & Nelson, B. (1997). Effects of choosing academic assignments on a student with attention deficit hyperactivity disorder. *Journal of Applied Behavior Analysis, 30, 181–183.*

undesirable behavior—attention from others versus escape from effortful tasks, for example. If undesirable behavior is maintained by escape from effortful tasks, then giving a student choices of assignments may be helpful. However, if the undesirable behavior is maintained by attention from others, then giving the student choices may have no effect at all (Romaniuk, Miltenberger, Conyers, Jenner, Jurgens, & Ringenberg, 2002).

Behavioral interventions are not foolproof for controlling problems of ADHD or any other emotional or behavioral disorder, but research has demonstrated that noisy, destructive, disruptive, and inattentive behavior can usually be changed for the better by controlling the contingencies of reinforcement. Like medication or any other intervention, behavioral interventions can be abused and misused. Even when used skillfully, they can have unanticipated or undesirable outcomes, and they will not necessarily make a student with ADHD appear normal. However, behavioral interventions may be the best tool available to teachers and parents.

Cognitive Strategy Training

The interventions falling under the general rubric of cognitive training or cognitive strategy training include self-instruction, self-monitoring, self-reinforcement, and cognitive–interpersonal problem solving. All have the goal of helping individuals become more aware of their responses to academic tasks and social problems and actively engage in the control of their own responses. We describe just three strategies—mnemonics self-instruction, and self-monitoring—because they are the most widely used in classroom settings. However, other strategies that involve students cognitively and actively in their self-management, such as goal setting, are also valuable in working with ADHD (Bicard & Neef, 2002; Hallahan & Cottone, 1997; Hallahan et al., 2005; Hoff & DuPaul, 1998).

Mnemonic strategies are ways of helping students remember things. These methods include teaching students with memory problems to use first-letter strategies, key words, and peg words. For example, a teacher might use the acronym HOMES to help a student remember the names of the five Great Lakes of North America by associating the acronym with the first letters of the lakes: Huron, Ontario, Michigan, Erie, and Superior. Using key words involves choosing a picture and a phonetically similar word to retrieve a definition. For example, a teacher might help a student picture a bear acting as a lawyer to remember the meaning of the word barrister. Peg words use rhyming. For example, Washington might be remembered by thinking of (or picturing) a gun being washed, with wash and gun being the rhyming elements remembering the first president of the United States. Mnemonic strategies have been found effective in helping students with learning, emotional, and behavioral disorders remember important information (Kleinheksel & Summy, 2003; Lloyd, Forness, & Kavale, 1998).

Self-instruction involves teaching students to talk to themselves about what they are doing and what they should do. Teaching students to label stimuli and to rehearse the instructions or tasks they have been given appears to have merit as an instructional strategy in many cases. For example, a student may be told to verbalize each arithmetic problem or its operation sign while working a problem, to say each letter of a word aloud while writing it, or to rehearse a reading passage before reading it aloud to the teacher.

Typically, self-instruction training requires a series of steps in which verbal control of behavior is first modeled by an adult, then imitated by the student, and finally used independently by the student. On a given task or in a given social situation, the adult first performs the task or response while verbalizing thoughts about the task requirements or social circumstance. The adult may talk about relevant stimuli or cues, planning a response, performing as expected, coping with feelings, and evaluating performance. Then the adult and student might run through the task or response to the social situation together, with the student shadowing the adult's verbal and nonverbal behavior. Eventually, the student tries it alone while verbalizing aloud and finally with subvocal self-instruction. Teaching students to use their own language to regulate behavior has been a successful approach with some impulsive children and youth in academic or social situations. Telling impulsive students to slow down and be careful before responding may not work, yet if these same students can be taught to tell themselves in some way to stop and think before they respond, they might improve their behavior considerably.

Self-monitoring has been widely used for helping students who have difficulty staying on task in the classroom, particularly during independent seat-work time. A tape recorder is used to produce tones (prerecorded to sound at random intervals ranging from 10 to 90 seconds, with an average interval of about 45 seconds) that cue the student to ask, "Was I . . . [usually, paying attention]?" and self-record the response on a form. This simple procedure has been found effective in increasing the on-task behavior of many students, ranging from children as young as 5 years to adolescents, who have ADHD and a variety of other disorders. Variations on the procedure have been used to improve academic productivity, accuracy of work, and social behavior (Lloyd, Hallahan, Kauffman, & Keller, 1998; Mathes & Bender, 1997; Shapiro, Durnan, Post, & Levinson, 2002).

Figure 11.4 shows examples of a recording sheet that might be used with a student who is doing self-monitoring. Figure 11.5 shows examples of self-monitoring activities. Self-monitoring can be adapted to a variety of circumstances and types of behavior. For example, Hoff and DuPaul (1998) used a combination of token reinforcement, explicit feedback to students about rule following, matching self-evaluation with teacher evaluation of behavior, and self-evaluation alone to lower the disruptive behavior of several students with ADHD and related problems. The students were gradually moved from more extrinsic, teacher-determined rewards to self-management. These procedures were successful for several students in general education across different classroom settings and activities. Research on self-monitoring has led to the following general conclusions:

1. Self-monitoring procedures are simple and straightforward, but they cannot be implemented without preparing the students. Brief training is necessary, in which the teacher talks with the student about the nature of off-task and appropriate behavior, explains the procedure, role-plays the procedure, and has the student practice.

Name: _____   Date: _____

Class Preparation:
- When I hear the first beep, I will answer yes or no to questions related to my classroom preparation.

	YES	NO
Pencil on desk		
Book open to correct page		
Clean paper on desk		
All other material put away		
Sitting quietly		
Eyes on teacher		

During Class:
- When I hear the beep, I will place a check in the box if I am on-task and if I have spoken only when raising my hand.

	1	2	3	4	5
On-task					
Raised my Hand to Speak					

Classroom self-monitoring:

Name: _____   Date: _____

1. Worked without disturbing others.	1	2	3	4
2. Participated in class.	1	2	3	4
3. Listened and paid attention when the teacher was talking.	1	2	3	4
4. Asked for help when I needed it.	1	2	3	4
5. Completed class assignment.	1	2	3	4
6. Turned in completed assignment.	1	2	3	4

Figure 11.4

Example of a self-monitoring form

Source: Shapiro, E. S., Durnan, S. L., Post, E. E., & Levinson, T. S. (2002). Self-monitoring procedures for children and adolescents. In M. R. Shinn, H. M. Walker, & G. Stoner (Eds.), *Interventions for academic and behavior problems: Vol. 2. Preventive and remedial approaches* (pp. 433–454). Bethesda, MD: National Association of School Psychologists, p. 438. Copyright 2002 by the National Association of School Psychologists. Reprinted by permission of the publisher.

Name: _____   Date: _____

Assignment Checklist

	YES	NO
1. Is my name on the paper?		
2. Do all my sentences begin with a capital letter?		
3. Do my sentences end with the proper punctuation?		
4. Did I answer all the questions?		
5. Did I check my work for spelling errors?		
6. Did I turn my assigment in?		

Figure 11.5
Example of self-monitoring activities

Source: Shapiro, E. S., Durnan, S. L., Post, E. E., & Levinson, T. S. (2002). Self-monitoring procedures for children and adolescents. In M. R. Shinn, H. M. Walker, & G. Stoner (Eds.), *Interventions for academic and behavior problems: Vol. 2. Preventive and remedial approaches* (pp. 433–454). Bethesda, MD: National Association of School Psychologists, p. 439. Copyright 2002 by the National Association of School Psychologists. Reprinted by permission of the publisher.

2. Self-monitoring of on-task behavior increases time on task in most cases.
3. Self-monitoring of on-task behavior also typically increases academic productivity.
4. Improvement in on-task behavior and performance usually lasts for several months after the procedure is discontinued.
5. The beneficial effects of self-monitoring are usually achieved without the use of backup reinforcers; extrinsic rewards, such as tokens or treats for improved behavior, are seldom necessary.
6. The tape-recorded tones (cues) prompting self-monitoring are a necessary part of the initial training procedure and implementation, although they can usually be discontinued after a period of successful self-monitoring.
7. Students' self-recording—marking answers to their self-questioning—is a necessary element of initial training and implementation but can be discontinued after a period of successful self-monitoring.
8. Accuracy in self-monitoring is not critically important; some students will be in close agreement with the teacher's assessment of their on-task behavior, but others will not be.
9. The cueing tones and other aspects of the procedure are usually minimally disruptive to other students in the class.

Notwithstanding the enthusiasm with which development of cognitive strategies was greeted and the many reports of their success in dealing with a wide variety of problems, they have not produced the generalized changes in behavior and cognition in ADHD that researchers and others had hoped for. Cognitive training in all its various forms clearly is not a panacea for the problems presented by disorders of attention and activity. Moreover, cognitive training is not as simple as it might first appear. The teacher who wishes to use any of the techniques effectively must understand their theoretical basis and carefully construct procedures to fit the individual case (Hallahan et al., 2005; Shapiro et al., 2002).

A PERSPECTIVE ON INTERVENTION

Nearly every type of intervention that has been used with any kind of troublesome behavior has been tried with ADHD (cf. Barkley, 1998; Neuwirth, 1994). Perhaps that in itself is a commentary on the seriousness with which adults approach the problem. Psychotherapy, providing an optimal level of sensory stimulation, biofeedback, relaxation training, dietary control—you name it, and it has probably been experimented with or even touted as a breakthrough, a revolutionary treatment, or an outright cure.

The lure of the idea that we should be able to find a way to "fix" this common and perplexing malady of children and youth is strong, perhaps irresistible. Over the past several decades, various intervention strategies have been devised by leading scholars and researchers, investigated with initial excitement, adopted widely, and endorsed enthusiastically by many as a solution, if not the cure, for the problems we now call ADHD. Each strategy eventually has been found not to be the fix. This initial overenthusiasm for an intervention—one said to be so powerful that the developmental disorder disappears—and the eventual disappointment it leads to has been the history of our approach to every developmental disability, including mental retardation, autism, cerebral palsy, and other developmental disorders. Leading researchers now suggest that ADHD is, indeed, a developmental disability for which we have no cure, and we are not likely to find one soon (Barkley, 1998, 2003; Hallahan & Cottone, 1997; Hallahan et al., 2005).

Recognition of the fact that we have no cure for ADHD should not deter us from seeking and implementing the most effective interventions possible. We do have interventions and approaches to education that will help us reach important goals. We know that medication can be extremely helpful, especially in combination with psychological interventions. For teachers, the most important tools are a highly structured classroom where the student's attention is clearly and consistently focused, behavioral interventions are consistently and explicitly implemented, and self-management procedures are taught systematically.

Given our present level of understanding, our goal should not be to eliminate the disability known as ADHD but to manage it as effectively as possible, recognizing that it is a chronic, disabling condition.

SUMMARY

Attention deficit–hyperactivity disorder is now the most widely used term for disorders of attention and activity. There is still considerable controversy and confusion regarding terminology and definition. However, most definitions suggest that ADHD is a developmental disorder of attention and activity level that is evident before the age of 7 or 8, persists throughout the life span, involves both academic and social problems, and is frequently accompanied by other disorders. The core problems of concern are regulation of attention, cognition, motivation, and social behavior. ADHD, learning disabilities, and emotional and behavioral disorders are overlapping, interrelated categories. About 3 to 5% of the school-aged population is diagnosed with ADHD, with boys greatly outnumbering girls.

Brain injury or dysfunction has long been suspected as a cause of ADHD. Many other biological causes, including food substances, environmental toxins, genetic factors, and temperament have been researched. Various psychological causes have also been suggested, but as yet research does not clearly and reliably point to any specific biological or environmental cause. Leading researchers suggest that poorly understood neurological factors instigate the problem, which is then exacerbated by a variety of factors in the physical and social environment. Prevention of ADHD and related disorders consists primarily of managing problems once they are evident.

Assessment for teaching and assessment for clinical treatment may differ considerably. School personnel and parents are interested primarily in assessment that helps them design an intervention program. Teacher and peer rating scales and direct observation of troublesome behavior in various school settings are most useful to educators.

The most widely used and successful approaches to intervention and education with ADHD and related disorders are medication, parent training, and teacher training. Medication is very controversial, but research clearly indicates its value when it is properly managed, and alternative approaches have not been as successful as medication or medication in combination with behavioral interventions. Medication cannot teach skills or resolve all problems, but it can make the youngster more teachable. Parent and teacher training typically involves instruction in behavior management skills. Teacher training usually involves implementing behavioral interventions (e.g., token reinforcement, response cost, contingency contracts) or cognitive training strategies (e.g., self-instruction or self-monitoring). It may be important to articulate classroom behavior modification with a home-school program involving contingencies managed by parents.

Nearly every known type of intervention has been suggested and attempted with ADHD and related disorders. None has provided a cure. The goal of intervention should be to manage the youngster's problems as successfully as possible, realizing that a cure is not available and that coping strategies for parents and teachers are important for dealing with this chronic, disabling condition.

>> PERSONAL REFLECTIONS

Attention and Activity Disorders

Cleo L. Holloway, Ed. S., is an assistant principal at Huntington Middle School in Newport News, Virginia. She wrote this feature when she was a classroom teacher at the same school.

Describe the school in which you teach and your particular role in the school.

I work in an inner-city middle school (Grades 6 through 8) with a population of 873 students. There are 17 special-education classes at Huntington: three for mild mental retardation, one for severe mental retardation, two for emotional and behavioral disorders (EBDs), nine learning disabilities (LDs) self-contained classrooms, and two LD resource classes. I am one of the two LD resource teachers, but some of my students exhibit emotional and behavioral disorders, as well as learning disabilities.

Think of a particular student with an attention disorder. How does this student manifest the disorder?

Marvin was diagnosed with ADHD as a third grader and prescribed Ritalin. Now he's one of my eighth graders. He consistently complied with his medication regimen during the sixth, seventh, and now the eighth grade, but the medication has had an inconsistent effect on his behavior.

When he entered school, Marvin had difficulty maintaining self-control and following directions, behaviors that are usually disruptive to the learning environment. He is often confrontational in a loud and aggressive manner toward peers and adults. However, in a very small, highly structured instructional setting, he displays the ability and willingness to follow directions and apply himself to academic tasks.

Marvin is perceived by others as extremely oppositional and determined to have things his way. He avoids, dislikes, or is reluctant to engage in tasks that require sustained mental effort; fails to give close attention to details; has difficulty organizing tasks and activities; and will not tolerate constructive correction from anyone outside the resource setting. He apparently feels threatened by their suggestions and be-

comes argumentative. To say the least, Marvin has difficulty respecting those in authority.

Marvin's problem behaviors have escalated, and now he has been suspended as a consequence of behaviors such as using obscene language, failing to comply with requests from adults in authority and showing disrespect for them, and throwing a roll of tissue paper in the face of another student. Eventually, he was suspended in May for the remainder of the school year.

What procedures have you found most useful in working with Marvin?

My experience in working with kids who have ADHD was quite limited until I met Marvin. He is academically strong, yet his hyperactivity and impulsivity are alarming. I did for Marvin what I have always done for my students, regardless of their disability. I established rules and expectations that were clear and consistent, and I set forth consequences ahead of time and delivered them immediately, depending on behavior. A highly structured environment alleviated a lot of Marvin's inappropriate behaviors. Marvin knew what to expect and realized I would not permit him to give me excuses about why he was out of control.

My ultimate goal was to establish an environment that would nurture Marvin. I wanted to establish a routine and help him learn a habit of mind that would allow him to control his behavior and succeed academically as well as socially. I found out that Marvin was dynamic with Legos. He loved working with them. So we built every school experience around the assembling of Legos as a consequence for his doing his work. This proved to be very helpful. He would enter class, work feverishly on assignments, and then be allowed to construct whatever he wanted.

Marvin was also an avid reader, and his comprehension skills were great. I used his talents and made him the class helper. He tutored fellow classmates in literature. This improved his self-esteem and social skills. As a result, other students in the resource room changed their impressions of him. He became part of the team. However, this behavior did not transfer or generalize to regular education settings. One factor was that regular classroom peers were not as tolerant of his behavior as were the kids in the resource room.

I also found it helpful to work with Marvin's mother, a social worker, and other community agencies to plan healthy relationships at home, in the school, and in the community. This way we achieved consistency and clear expectations—a structured and predictable environment for Marvin that would help him maintain balance in his life. I emphasize that family counseling and parenting classes really facilitated this process.

What do you see as the prospects for Marvin's educational progress in the coming year?

If Marvin's behavior does not improve, I believe he will be referred to the eligibility committee, which will consider placing him in a more restrictive environment or a modified or cross-categorical program. His repeated acts of noncompliance, characterized by behaviors such as defiance of directives, use of profanity, and aggressive outbursts, have greatly impaired his ability to learn and have interfered with the learning of his classmates. He will probably receive academic support from the LD teacher as well as help in learning adolescent social skills from the EBD teacher. It is becoming increasingly difficult to request that regular education teachers make accommodations to address his needs. More support from the special educators may help Marvin have a successful school year. Thus, my recommendation is that we have discussions to address placement issues and to determine the setting best suited to Marvin's needs.

What do you see as the biggest long-term problems Marvin will face?

Marvin is a highly anxious, insecure young man whose needs for support, stability, and nurturance are considerable. Although he demonstrates notable tendencies toward aggressive, acting-out behaviors, he possesses a great longing to obtain the approval of significant others. However, as a consequence of his past behavioral patterns, coupled with a pervasive sense of inadequacy, he views himself as unable and unworthy to garner the acceptance he seeks. The latter circumstance is exacerbated by his compelling compensatory drives, aimed at gaining attention and response from others, however negative or unacceptable such attention and responses may be.

Marvin's impulsivity means that he is inclined to act without giving serious thought to the consequences of his behaviors. He became involved in the juvenile court during the summer of 1999 and was eventually placed in detention. He and his family are now receiving in-home counseling services. I hope that this intervention will help Marvin conform to rules at every level.

Cleo Holloway Interviews Marvin

Ms. H: Marvin, what has been your experience at school?

M: Okay, but it could have been better.

Ms. H: Why do you think it could have been better?

M: Because of my behavior. When somebody says something to me, I just take off. I have a quick temper.

Ms. H: What is the most difficult task for you?

M: Managing my temper.

Ms. H: What do you normally do when your temper goes off?

M: I get mad. I be ready to fight. I don't want nobody to say nothing to me. I want everybody to get along.

Ms. H: At this point, do you see yourself as successful in school?

M: Sometimes. I try, but sometimes I end up messing up.

Ms. H: How would we know when you're about to have a bad day?

M: I talk back. Get smart. Blurt out. Act up.

Ms. H: What kinds of things can we do to make you more successful in school?

M: When I get mad, you can have me be by myself or let me help y'all.

Ms. H: What do you think you need the most help in?

M: Controlling my temper. The medicine don't help.

Ms. H: When do you take your medicine?

M: In the morning when I first come to school. And it take about 30 minutes to start working.

Ms. H: If you don't take your medicine, what happens?

M: I can be bad without it, and I can be good without it.

Ms. H: Is there anything we can do about managing your behavior and getting your work done?

M: Not about my behavior.

Ms. H: Can you get your work done?

M: I try. Sometimes.

Ms. H: Name some behaviors that you do that you know keep you from having a good day.

M: Fighting, skip class. When I get here in the morning, I go to the cafeteria and take my medicine. Then I'm supposed to go to class, but I don't. When I go to class, I make jokes and people laugh.

Ms. H: How does it make you feel when people laugh at your jokes?

M: I be breaking up and liking it. I start rankin' on my friends.

Ms. H: And this is during instructional time, right?

M: Yeah. [Marvin expresses dislike for teachers and describes getting into a fight in the neighborhood before school, then resuming the fight at school and being physically restrained by a counselor.]

Ms. H: When you came in yesterday morning, none of us knew what had happened in the neighborhood. We didn't know you had a fight, and we were trying to keep you in school. And that's what we want to do because we know you're very bright. I know you have a hard time ignoring people who are saying things to you, and you feel you have to defend yourself, but how is that going to help you in school if you play into that kind of stuff every single day?

M: I didn't want to fight, but I couldn't back down because he hit me first. I know kids shouldn't fight, but sometimes you have to. But I could ignore it. But if he hits me, I'll hit him back.

Ms. H: Can you ignore him, then?

M: I can. All I gotta do is walk away.

Ms. H: What types of goals do you have for yourself?

M: Get out of this bad class. I don't care who knows I'm in the bad class.

Ms. H: How can you get out of classes that are labeled? What do you need to do?

M: Do my work. Stay out of trouble. Get to school on time every day. Stop ranking.

Ms. H: Yes, stop ranking. That's a big one. 'Cause you like to rank.

M: Yeah, I be doing stuff too, but I ain't gonna blame it all on me. It could be teachers quick to say, "Oh, he's got problems, don't pay him no mind." They're quick to say that. Or, "He's a problem child. You know, he didn't take his meds yet." You know, teachers try to put me down.

Ms. H: We need to encourage you so you can get your work done. . . . If you think about your life five years from now, in five years you'll be. . . .

M: In college. I'll be 18 and on my way to college.

Ms. H: So what do you want to be or do then?

M: I want to be a cop.

>> QUESTIONS FOR FURTHER REFLECTION

1. How would you explain to parents the difference between a child's being very active and a child's having ADHD?
2. At what point, or after what acts on your part as a teacher, should you request a student's evaluation for possible ADHD?
3. What evidence would you need before arguing with a school psychologist or other school personnel or parents that a particular student's ADHD (already identified as such) was not merely ADHD but an indication of other problems or disorders as well?

CHAPTER TWELVE

CONDUCT DISORDER
OVERT AGGRESSION

As you read this chapter, keep these guiding questions in mind:

- What distinguishes aggressive antisocial behavior from normal development?

- How and why is aggression a multicultural issue?

- What environmental conditions are associated with high risk for conduct disorder?

- When punishment is necessary, what guidelines should be followed?

- How is precorrection related to the acting-out behavior cycle?

DEFINITION, PREVALENCE, AND CLASSIFICATION

Definition

Normally developing children and adolescents occasionally exhibit antisocial behavior of various descriptions. They may throw temper tantrums, fight with their siblings or peers, cheat, lie, be physically cruel to animals or other people, refuse to obey their parents, or destroy their own or others' possessions. Normally developing youngsters do not, however, perform antisocial acts in most social contexts, nor with such frequency as to become pariahs among their peers or excessively burdensome to their parents and teachers.

A child or youth who has a conduct disorder (CD) exhibits a persistent pattern of antisocial behavior that significantly impairs everyday functioning at home or school or leads others to conclude that the youngster is unmanageable (Hinshaw & Lee, 2003; Kazdin, 1994, 1998; Walker, 1995; Walker, Ramsey, & Gresham, 2004). Many of these children are known as bullies (Tattum & Lane, 1989; Walker et al., 2004). Kazdin (1998) summarized the essential features of CD:

> Conduct disorder encompasses a broad range of antisocial behavior such as aggressive acts, theft, vandalism, firesetting, lying, truancy, and running away. Although these behaviors are diverse, their common characteristic is that they tend to violate major social rules and expectations. Many of the behaviors often reflect actions against the environment, including both persons and property. Antisocial behaviors emerge in some form over the course of normal development. Fighting, lying, stealing, destruction of property, and noncompliance are relatively common at different points in childhood and adolescence. For the most part, these behaviors diminish over time, do not interfere with everyday functioning, and do not predict untoward consequences in adulthood.
>
> The term conduct disorder is usually reserved for a pattern of antisocial behavior that is associated with significant impairment in everyday functioning at home or school, and concerns of significant others that the child or adolescent is unmanageable. (p. 199)

The children about whom we are concerned here perform noxious behaviors at a much higher rate and at a much later age than do normally developing children (see Loeber et al., 1998a, 1998b). A youngster with aggressive conduct disorder may match the noxious behaviors of the normally developing child 2 to 1 or more; and whereas the normally developing child exhibits social aggression at a decreasing rate as he or she grows older, the youngster with conduct disorder usually does not. In a now classic study, Patterson and his colleagues spent many hours observing in the homes of normally developing children and aggressive children (Patterson et al., 1975). They identified noxious behaviors, measuring the rates at which they were performed by normally developing children and contrasting them to the rates at which they were performed by aggressive children whose behavior might fit the definition of CD. They found, for example, that an aggressive child can be expected to be noncompliant about every 10 minutes, as well as to hit and to tease about every half hour. In contrast, a nonaggressive child might be expected to be noncompliant once in 20 minutes, to tease once in about 50 minutes, and to hit once in a couple of hours.

Patterson's description of Don (see the accompanying case book) illustrates the type of behavior that extremely socially aggressive young children exhibit at home and school. Don's interactions with his family are characterized by coercive exchanges. Without effective intervention to break the coercive cycle at home and school, Don seems virtually certain to experience a high rate of failure in school and continuing conflict in the community.

CD must be judged with reference to chronological age. Ordinarily, children tend to exhibit less overt aggression as they grow older. Compared to nonaggressive youngsters, children and youth with CDs typically show age-inappropriate aggression from an earlier age, develop a larger repertoire of aggressive acts, exhibit aggression across a wider range of social situations, and persist in aggressive behavior for a longer time (Patterson et al., 1992; Walker et al., 2004). A significant percentage of children and adolescents with CDs showed earlier the characteristics of oppositional defiant disorder (ODD). That is, they showed a pattern of negativistic, hostile, and defiant behavior uncharacteristic of normally developing children of the same age. Representative characteristics include having frequent temper tantrums and often arguing with adults, refusing to obey adults, deliberately annoying other people, and acting angry and resentful (Eddy, Reid, & Curry, 2002; Hinshaw & Lee, 2003; Kazdin, 1998).

CD is often comorbid with other disorders, such as attention deficit–hyperactivity disorder (ADHD). ODD, ADHD, and CD are known to be closely linked, although having one of these disorders does not necessarily mean that a youngster will have the other. In fact, several subtypes of CD are now well established; and all types of CD may be comorbid with ADHD, depression, anxiety, delinquency, substance abuse, and sexual acting out.

Prevalence

Estimates of the prevalence of CD range from 6 to 16% of boys and 2 to 9% of girls under age 18. The preponderance of boys with CD may reflect a combination of biological susceptibilities and socialization processes involving social roles, models, expectations, and reinforcement. Boys with CD tend to exhibit fighting, stealing, vandalism, and other overtly aggressive, disruptive behavior; girls are more likely to exhibit lying, truancy, running away, substance abuse, prostitution, and other less overtly aggressive behavior. The consensus among researchers is not only that the problem affects at least the officially estimated percentage of children and youth but also that the prevalence is increasing. Moreover, the severity of the disorder is perceived as increasing (see Hinshaw & Lee, 2003; Kazdin, 1998; Steiner, 1997).

Classification

One way of classifying CD is by age of onset. Researchers have frequently found that children with early onset of CD and delinquency (before age 10 or 12) typically show more severe impairment and have a poorer prognosis than do those with later onset (see Dinitz, Scarpitti, & Reckless, 1962; Eddy et al., 2002; Patterson et al., 1992; Walker, 1995; Walker et al., 2004). CD may be classified as mild (resulting in only minor harm to others), moderate, or severe (causing considerable harm to others).

CD may also be classified as undersocialized or socialized (Quay, 1986a, 1986b). *Undersocialized conduct disorder* includes characteristics such as hyperactivity, impulsiveness, irritability, stubbornness, demandingness, arguing, teasing, poor peer relations, loudness, threatening and attacking others, cruelty, fighting, showing off, bragging, swearing, blaming others, sassiness, and disobedience. *Socialized conduct disorder* is characterized by more covert antisocial acts such as negativism, lying, destructiveness, stealing, setting fires, associating with bad companions, belonging to a gang, running away, truancy, and abuse of alcohol or other drugs. However, some youngsters are described as *versatile* because they show both overt and covert forms of antisocial conduct (Loeber & Schmaling, 1985a, 1985b). In this chapter, we focus on overtly aggressive and versatile CD; covert antisocial behavior is discussed in chapter 13. As we shall see, however, antisocial behavior of all types is closely linked to delinquency and substance abuse. Much of the discussion in this chapter provides a foundation for our consideration in chapters 13 and 14 of covert antisocial behavior and delinquency.

Undersocialized aggressive CD is closely associated with violent behavior. The level of violence in our society, particularly among youth, is a widespread and long-standing concern, especially to educators and others concerned with children's development (Flannery, 1999; Flannery & Huff, 1999; Furlong & Morrison, 1994; Walker & Shinn, 2002; Walker et al., 2004). Our discussion in this chapter thus addresses both CD and the problem of violence among children and youth, including school violence.

AGGRESSION AND VIOLENCE IN SOCIAL CONTEXT

"Aggression and America have long been intimate companions" (Goldstein, Carr, Davidson, & Wehr, 1981). Aggression is not new to American children, their homes and families, or their schools. Even a cursory examination of *Children and Youth in America* (Bremner, 1970, 1971) and other similar histories quickly reveals that coercion, violence, and brutality have been practiced by and toward children and youth since the founding of this nation. Recognizing the historical presence of violence does not in any way, however, reduce the unacceptable level of aggression in the present-day lives of American children. Through the media, children are exposed to brutal acts of aggression at a rate unprecedented in the history of civilization (Huesmann, Moise-Titus, Podolski, & Eron, 2003; Sprafkin et al., 1992). Assaultive behavior, disruptiveness, and property destruction in schools have grown commonplace. Violence and weapons in schools are problems now apparent in small towns as well as big cities, in small schools as well as big ones, and in affluent as well as poor schools (Flannnery, 1999; Flannery & Huff, 1999). Incivility has become a pervasive issue in schools (Kauffman & Burbach, 1997).

Aggression as a Multicultural Issue

Aggression and violence are multicultural issues in that all subcultural groups in the United States are affected and stereotypes regarding cultural minorities are common.

African American and Latino cultures are frequently miscast as tolerant of violence (Hammond & Yung, 1994; Soriano, 1994). Violence among Native American and Asian/Pacific Island American youth is poorly understood (Chen & True, 1994; Yung & Hammond, 1994). Particularly vulnerable populations are often overlooked in discussion of violence, including children with disabilities (Levey & Lagos, 1994), girls and young women (Sorenson & Bowie, 1994; Talbott & Callahan, 1997; Talbott, Celinska, Simpson, & Coe, 2002), and lesbian, gay, and bisexual youth (D'Augelli & Dark, 1994). Without ignoring the special vulnerabilities and needs of any group, it is important to recognize the commonalities of sociocultural conditions and needs for nurturing among all children and youth regardless of color or ethnic background. Hill, Soriano, Chen, and LaFromboise (1994) noted that "the developmental mandates of all youth during adolescence are similar. But the resources for achieving developmental milestones are significantly fewer for economically disadvantaged ethnic minority youth, particularly in inner cities and particularly if they have not had the opportunity to internalize the values of their own ethnic culture that can protect against violence" (p. 86). In fact, the same risk factors for socialization appear to be operative among African American youths as among other ethnic groups (see Loeber et al., 1998a; Miller-Johnson et al., 1999; Xie et al., 1999).

Intervention programs designed for particular groups of aggressive students, such as African American males or Latino students, have been suggested (e.g., Hudley & Graham, 1995; Middleton & Cartledge, 1995; Vasquez, 1998). However, Hudley and Graham (1995) concluded that "although it has been asserted that African American children have distinct learning styles and preferred modes of instruction, in truth the data in support of these assertions are scant" (p. 193). Cultural sensitivity and multicultural competence are important, but they are no substitute for effective interventions that transcend ethnic and gender identity (Kauffman, 1999b; National Research Council, 2002). Regardless of color, ethnicity, gender, and other personal characteristics, children and youth are placed at risk by common factors such as poverty, family disruption, abuse, neglect, racism, poor schools, lack of employment opportunities, and other social blights. Likewise, the most effective remedies for these risk factors and the protective factors that increase children's resilience are essentially the same across all cultural groups.

Still, the definitions of psychopathologies are grounded in cultures. Moreover, it is important to recognize the special considerations that must be made in assessing and treating psychopathology:

> Perhaps the most important factor to consider is that the families of minority children and adolescents are not only adjusting to the general influences that affect mainstream society but also are facing the transitional stress generated by the necessary adjustment of a minority culture into American society. This process is complicated by poverty at home, lack of familiarity with English, poor schools, racism, and a community ecology that generates existential frustration, fear, and violence. (Yamamoto, Silva, Ferrari, & Nukariya, 1997, p. 51)

Cultural factors are not simply a matter of racial identity, ethnic identity, or social class but a combination of these factors:

> In American society there is an important interrelationship among ethnicity, race, and social class, with high status associated with membership in white, Anglo-Saxon,

middle-class families and low status associated with membership in nonwhite, ethnic, minority, lower-class families. . . . It follows that children and adolescents in many Asian, black, Hispanic, and American Indian families are triply stigmatized in American society because they differ from the norm in three major respects: they are nonwhite by race (except for white Hispanics), non–Anglo-Saxon by ethnicity, and predominantly non–middle-class by socioeconomic status. (Gibbs & Huang, 1998, p. 11)

Knowing the difference between pathological behavior and behavior that is simply an expression of cultural heritage is no easy matter. It is a problem of enormous consequence, because racism includes both (a) cultural bias in the attribution of pathology and (b) the dismissal of truly pathological behavior as a mere indication of cultural convention. More research is needed to help us make definitive statements about the differences between behavior that is merely cultural and behavior that represents pathology.

Aggression in the Context of School

General education teachers must be prepared to deal with aggression, for it is likely that at least one of their students will be highly disruptive, destructive, or assaultive toward other students or the teacher. Teachers of students with emotional or behavioral disorders must be ready to handle an especially large dose of aggression, for conduct disorder is one of the most common forms of exasperating deportment and psychopathology that brings students into special education. The prospective special education teacher who expects most students to be withdrawn or who believes that students with CD will quickly learn to reciprocate a kindly social demeanor will be shocked. Without effective means for controlling aggression, the teacher of students with emotional or behavioral disorders must develop a superhuman tolerance for interpersonal nastiness.

Observations in schools and studies of school records suggest that we may expect highly problematic, disruptive classroom behaviors from aggressive youngsters. These behaviors are frequently accompanied by academic failure. Not surprisingly, students who exhibit aggressive conduct disorder are often rejected by their peers and perceive their peers as hostile toward them. When children exhibit aggressive antisocial behavior and academic failure beginning in the early grades, the prognosis is particularly grim, unless effective early intervention is provided (Cullinan, 2002; Eddy et al., 2002; Flannery & Huff, 1999; Loeber et al., 1998a, 1998b; Walker & Shinn, 2002; Walker et al., 2004; Walker, Shinn, et al., 1987).

The high rates of antisocial behavior and the significant impairment of everyday functioning of youngsters with undersocialized aggressive conduct disorder do not bode well for their futures. Such youngsters tend to exhibit a relatively stable pattern of aggressive behavior over time; their problems do not tend to dissipate but continue into adulthood (Eddy et al., 2002; Kazdin, 1995, 1998; Loeber et al., 1998a, 1998b; McMahon & Wells, 1998; Olweus, 1979; Patterson et al., 1992; Robins, 1986; Walker et al., 2004). Consequently, the prognosis for later adjustment is poor, and the pattern of antisocial conduct is often transmitted over generations. Because aggressive antisocial behavior tends to keep people in contact with mental health and criminal justice systems, and because the behavior inflicts considerable suffering on victims of physical assault and property loss, the cost to society is enormous. Although for boys a history of serious antisocial conduct before age 15 increases the chances of externalizing psychopathology (aggression, criminal behavior, alcohol and drug abuse) in adulthood, for girls this kind of childhood history also increases the probability of adulthood externalizing disorders and internalizing disorders (depression, phobias; Robins, 1986). We have known this for many years: "Clearly, no other disorder of childhood and adolescence is so widespread and disruptive of the lives of those who suffer it and the lives of others" (Quay, 1986b, p. 64). Thus, finding effective interventions for conduct disorder is a priority among social scientists and educators (Eddy et al., 2002; Eron et al., 1994; Walker et al., 2004; Walker, Forness, et al., 1998). Antisocial behavior, especially when it is characterized by violent aggression, is rightfully a critical concern of all teachers but especially of special educators who teach students with emotional or behavioral disorders.

CAUSAL FACTORS AND PREVENTION

Aggression has historically been an object of study for scientists in many disciplines, and many alternative explanations have been offered for it. Psychoanalytic theories, drive theories, and simple conditioning theories have not led to effective intervention strategies, and they have been largely discounted by alternative explanations based on scientific research (Pepler & Slaby, 1994). Biological and social learning theories are supported by more reliable evidence (Dodge & Pettit, 2003). In some cases, medication for aggressive behavior may be helpful, particularly when aggression is related to ADHD (see Connor, Boone, Steingard, Lopez, & Melloni, 2003; Connor, Glatt, Lopez, Jackson, & Melloni, 2002; Konopasek & Forness, 2004; Lynn & King, 2002).

Although genetic and other biological factors apparently contribute to the most severe cases of conduct disorder, their role in milder cases of aggression is not clear; in both severe and mild forms of conduct disorder, the social environment obviously contributes to the problem (Eddy et al., 2002; Webster-Stratton & Dahl, 1995; Wells & Forehand, 1985). Furthermore, it is now apparent that there is not a single cause of conduct disorder and related problems (Burke, Loeber, & Birmaher, 2002).

Sociobiology is an intriguing and controversial topic (Pinker, 2002; Wright, 1995a, 1995b), but it has little to offer developmental psychologists who are seeking more immediate causes of aggression (Hinde, 1986; Loeber et al., 1998a, 1998b). In fact, decades of research by numerous scientists strongly suggests that an individual's social environment is a powerful regulator of neurobiological processes and behavior; social learning may be the most important determinant of aggression and prosocial behavior (Bandura, 1973; Eddy et al., 2002; Pepler & Slaby, 1994; Walker et al., 2004). The many factors that place children and youth at risk for development of a conduct disorder are shown in Table 12.1.

Among the several psychological explanations of aggression, one that stands out as most clearly supported by careful, systematic, scientific research is the *social learning theory*. Particularly relevant to our discussion here is the coercive process model constructed after decades of research by Gerald Patterson and his colleagues

Table 12.1

Factors that place youth at risk for the onset of conduct disorder

---

CHILD FACTORS

Child Temperament. A more difficult child temperament (on a dimension of "easy-to-difficult"), as characterized by more negative mood, lower levels of approach toward new stimuli, and less adaptability to change.

Neuropsychological Deficits and Difficulties. Deficits in diverse functions related to language (e.g., verbal learning, verbal fluency, verbal IQ), memory, motor coordination, integration of auditory and visual cues, and "executive" functions of the brain (e.g., abstract reasoning, concept formation, planning, control of attention).

Subclinical Levels of Conduct Disorder. Early signs (e.g., elementary school) of mild ("subclinical") levels of unmanageability and aggression, especially with early age of onset, multiple types of antisocial behaviors, and multiple situations in which they are evident (e.g., at home, school, the community).

Academic and Intellectual Performance. Academic deficiencies and lower levels of intellectual functioning.

PARENT AND FAMILY FACTORS

Prenatal and Perinatal Complications. Pregnancy and birth-related complications including maternal infection, prematurity and low birth weight, impaired respiration at birth, and minor birth injury.

Psychopathology and Criminal Behavior in the Family. Criminal behavior, antisocial personality disorder, and alcoholism of the parent.

Parent–Child Punishment. Harsh (e.g., severe corporal punishment) and inconsistent punishment increase risk.

Monitoring of the Child. Poor supervision, lack of monitoring of whereabouts, and few rules about where children can go and when they can return.

Quality of the Family Relationships. Less parental acceptance of their children, less warmth, affection, and emotional support, and less attachment.

Marital Discord. Unhappy marital relationships, interpersonal conflict and aggression of the parents.

Family Size. Larger family size, that is, more children in the family.

Sibling With Antisocial Behavior. Presence of a sibling, especially an older brother, with antisocial behavior.

Socioeconomic Disadvantage. Poverty, overcrowding, unemployment, receipt of social assistance ("welfare"), and poor housing.

SCHOOL-RELATED FACTORS

Characteristics of the Setting. Attending schools where there is little emphasis on academic work, little teacher time spent on lessons, infrequent teacher use of praise and appreciation for school work, little emphasis on individual responsibility of the students, poor working conditions for pupils (e.g., furniture in poor repair), unavailability of the teacher to deal with children's problems, and low teacher expectancies.

Source: Kazdin, A. E. (1998). Conduct disorder. In R. J. Morris & T. R. Kratochwill (Eds.), *The practice of child therapy* (3rd ed., pp. 199–230). Boston: Allyn & Bacon, p. 202.

(e.g., Eddy et al., 2002; Patterson et al., 1992). Consequently, we focus on these social learning explanations for aggression and its prevention. We first summarize the general findings of social learning research and then highlight personal, family, school, peer group, and other cultural factors and review Patterson's model of the coercive process that produces and sustains aggression.

General Conclusions from Social Learning Research

A social learning (or social cognitive) analysis of aggression includes three major controlling influences: the environmental conditions that set the occasion for behavior or that reinforce or punish it, the behavior itself, and cognitive–affective (person) variables (Bandura, 1973, 1986; Bandura & Locke, 2003; see chapter 4). Whether or not a person exhibits aggressive behavior depends on the reciprocal effects of these three factors and the individual's social history. Social learning theory suggests that aggression is learned through the direct consequences of aggressive and nonaggressive acts and through observation of aggression and its consequences. Research in social learning supports several generalizations about how aggression is learned and maintained (see Bandura, 1973; Eddy et al., 2002; Goldstein, 1983a, 1983b; McMahon & Wells, 1998; Patterson, 1986a, 1986b; Patterson et al., 1992; Pepler & Slaby, 1994; Walker et al., 2004):

- Children learn many aggressive responses by observing models or examples. The models may be family members, members of the child's subculture (friends, acquaintances, peers, and adults in the community), or individuals portrayed in the mass media (including real and fictional, human and nonhuman).
- Children are more likely to imitate aggressive models when the models are of high social status and when they see that the models receive reinforcement (positive consequences or rewards) or do not receive punishment for their aggression.
- Children learn aggressive behavior when, given opportunities to practice aggressive responses, they experience either no aversive consequences or succeed in obtaining rewards by harming or overcoming their victims.
- Aggression is more likely to occur when children experience aversive conditions (perhaps physical assault, verbal threats, taunts, or insults) or decreases in or termination of positive reinforcement. Children may learn through observation or practice that they can obtain rewarding consequences by engaging in aggressive behavior. The probability of aggression under such circumstances is especially high when alternative (appropriate) means of obtaining reinforcement are not readily available or have not been learned and when aggression is sanctioned by social authorities.
- Factors that maintain aggression include three types of reinforcement: *external reinforcement* (tangible rewards, social status rewards, removal of aversive conditions, expressions of injury or suffering by the victim), *vicarious reinforcement* (gratification obtained by observing others gain rewards through aggression), and *self-reinforcement* (self-congratulation or increased self-esteem following successful aggression).
- Aggression may be perpetuated by cognitive processes that justify hostile action: comparing one's deeds advantageously to more horrific deeds of others, appealing to

higher principles (such as protection of self or others), placing responsibility on others (the familiar "I didn't start it" and "He made me do it" ploys), and dehumanizing the victims (perhaps with demeaning labels such as *nerd, dweeb, trash, pig, drooler*).

- Punishment may also serve to heighten or maintain aggression when it causes pain, when there are no positive alternatives to the punished response, when punishment is delayed or inconsistent, or when punishment provides a model of aggressive behavior. When counterattack against the punisher seems likely to succeed, punishment maintains aggression. The adult who punishes a child by striking out not only causes pain, which increases the probability of aggression, but provides a model of aggression as well.

A social learning analysis of aggression generates testable predictions about environmental conditions that foster aggressive behavior. Research over several decades has led to the following empirically confirmed predictions about the genesis of aggression:

- Viewing televised aggression may increase aggressive behavior, especially in males and in children who have a history of aggressiveness.
- Delinquent subcultures, such as deviant peer groups or street gangs, will maintain aggressive behavior in their members by modeling and reinforcing aggression.
- Families of aggressive children are characterized by high rates of aggression on the part of all members; by coercive exchanges between the aggressive child and other family members; and by parents' inconsistent, punitive control techniques and lack of supervision.
- Aggression begets aggression. When one person presents an aversive condition for another (hitting, yelling, whining), the affronted individual is likely to reply by presenting a negative condition of his or her own, resulting in a coercive process. The coercive interaction will continue until one individual withdraws his or her aversive condition, providing negative reinforcement (escape from aversive stimulation) for the victor.

Family, school, and cultural factors involving social learning were discussed in previous chapters. These factors undoubtedly play a major role in the development of aggressive conduct disorders. By providing models of aggression and supplying reinforcement for aggressive behavior, families, schools, and the larger society teach youngsters (albeit inadvertently) to behave aggressively. This insidious teaching process is most effective for youngsters who are already predisposed to aggressive behavior by their biological endowment or their previous social learning. And the process is maintained by reciprocity of effects among the behavior, the social environment, and the child's cognitive and affective characteristics. The teaching–learning process involved in aggression includes reciprocal effects such as these:

- The social environment provides aversive conditions (noxious stimuli), including social disadvantage, academic failure, peer rejection, and rejection by parents and other adults.
- The youngster perceives the social environment as both threatening and likely to reward aggression.
- The youngster's behavior is noxious to others, who attempt to control it by threats and punitive responses.

- The youngster develops low self-concept and identifies himself or herself in primarily negative terms.
- In coercive bouts, the youngster is frequently successful in overcoming others by being more aversive or persistent, thereby obtaining reinforcement for aggression and confirming his or her perceptions of the social environment as threatening and controlled by aggressive behavior.

All of these factors contribute to the development of antisocial behavior and, over time, cement it into a pattern very resistant to change. Patterson et al. (1992) depicted the major causal factors that contribute to antisocial behavior, as shown in Figure 12.1. We next examine major contributing factors and how they are interrelated in a coercive process.

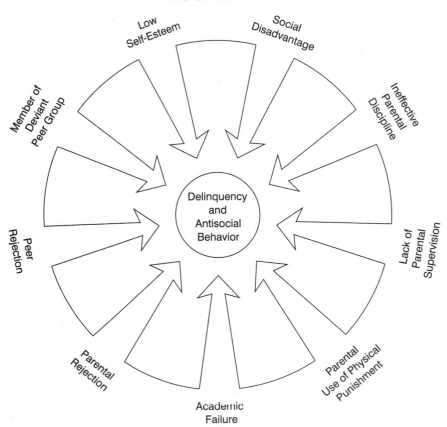

Figure 12.1
The causal wheel
Source: Patterson, G. R., Reid, J. B., & Dishion, T. J. (1992). *Antisocial Boys*. Eugene, OR: Castalia. Copyright © 1992 by Castalia Publishing Company. Reprinted by permission.

Personal Factors

As discussed in chapter 7, children are born with dispositions or temperaments that, although modifiable, tend to be fairly consistent over a period of years (see Caspi et al., 1995; Keogh, 2003; Smith & Prior, 1995). Many children with difficult, irritable temperaments are at risk for developing antisocial behavior (Center & Kemp, 2003). Their difficult temperaments as infants may evolve through social interaction with their caretakers into high rates of noncompliance and oppositional behavior in the early childhood years. These children are likely to develop low self-esteem and depressed affect as well as to have major problems in peer relations and academic achievement. In short, they may begin life with personal attributes that make social rejection likely, and these characteristics may be exacerbated by cycles of negative interaction with caretakers, peers, and teachers. Although demographic factors such as low socioeconomic status and family factors such as parental substance abuse are important, the personal characteristics of attention problems and especially fighting are predictive of the early onset of conduct disorder in boys (Keogh, 2003; Loeber et al., 1995, 1998a, 1998b).

Peer Group

From an early age, normally developing peers tend to reject their peers who are highly aggressive and disruptive of play and school activities (Guevremont & Dumas, 1994). Antisocial students may achieve high status among a subgroup of peers, but they are likely to be rejected by most of their nonantisocial peers. To achieve some sense of competence and belonging, antisocial children and youths often gravitate toward a deviant peer group (Farmer, 2000; Farmer, Farmer, & Gut, 1999). Especially given poor parental monitoring and other family risk factors and academic failure, adolescents are likely to identify with deviant peers and be drawn into delinquency, substance abuse, and antisocial behavior that limits their opportunities for further education, employment, and development of positive and stable social relationships (Loeber et al., 1998a, 1998b; Short, 1997).

Family Factors

The families of antisocial children tend to be characterized by antisocial or criminal behavior of parents and siblings. Often homes and family relationships are chaotic and unsupportive of normal social development or are characterized by physical or sexual abuse (Campbell, 1995; Green, Russo, Navratil, & Loeber, 1999; Kazdin, 1998; Lavigueur, Tremblay, & Saucier, 1995; Patterson et al., 1992). There are often many children in the family. The families are often broken by divorce or abandonment and characterized by high levels of interpersonal conflict. Parental monitoring of children's behavior tends to be lax or almost nonexistent, and discipline tends to be unpredictable but harsh—precisely the opposite of that suggested by those well versed in the topic of rearing well-socialized children (e.g., Dishion & Patterson, 1996). Often many generations live together, and grandparents or other relatives living in the home also typically lack child-rearing skills. As discussed in chapter 8, the children and parents often become enmeshed in a coercive cycle of interaction in which parent and child increase the pain they cause the other until one party "wins." We should be careful not to assume that all families of antisocial children can be so characterized. However, these are the typical family characteristics of children who are antisocial. Domestic violence, poverty, poor parental education, family members' criminality, and other adverse conditions increase the risk (i.e., chances) that a child will be aggressive or exhibit other emotional or behavioral disorders, such as depression (Yamamoto et al., 1997).

The growth, development, and perpetuation of antisocial behavior is pictured in Figure 12.2. Patterson et al. (1992) described the stages of growth of the "vile weed" of antisocial behavior. Their coercive model begins in Stage 1 with the contextual variables shown in the underground level of the diagram: difficult child temperament, stressors such as poverty and family conflict, poor discipline and monitoring by parents and grandparents, and parental antisocial behavior and substance abuse. This social context is likely to produce an antisocial child with low self-esteem. In Stage 2, school failure, parental rejection, peer rejection, and depression all contribute to one another and further strengthen the child's antisocial tendencies. In Stage 3, the youngster becomes oriented toward antisocial peers and engages in delinquency and substance abuse. Now the youth has become enmeshed in social relationships and behavioral patterns that often lead to Stage 4, in which the antisocial youth becomes an antisocial adult who is unable to hold a job and is at high risk for incarceration or other institutionalization and a disrupted marriage. Clearly, any offspring of someone in Stage 4 of this model is likely to drop into similar ground (social context) and grow through the same stages. So antisocial behavior can be passed from one generation to the next, perhaps in part through genetics but also through the conditions of the home and community. Eddy et al. (2002) depicted similar coercive interactions and conditions as causes of antisocial behavior.

School Factors

Most antisocial students experience academic failure and rejection by peers and adults in school. In many cases, they attend schools that are in deteriorated or crowded buildings. The discipline they experience in school is often little better than the parental discipline they experience at home: highly punitive, erratic, escalating, with little or no attention to their nonaggressive behavior or efforts to achieve. The academic work they are given is often not consistent with their achievement level or relevant to their eventual employment, forcing them to face failure and boredom every day they attend school (Jones & Jones, 1995; Walker et al., 2004). As for family factors, we must be careful not to accuse all teachers and school administrators of failing to teach and manage difficult students well. However, the typical school experience of antisocial students is highly negative, contributing to further maladjustment, as discussed in chapter 9.

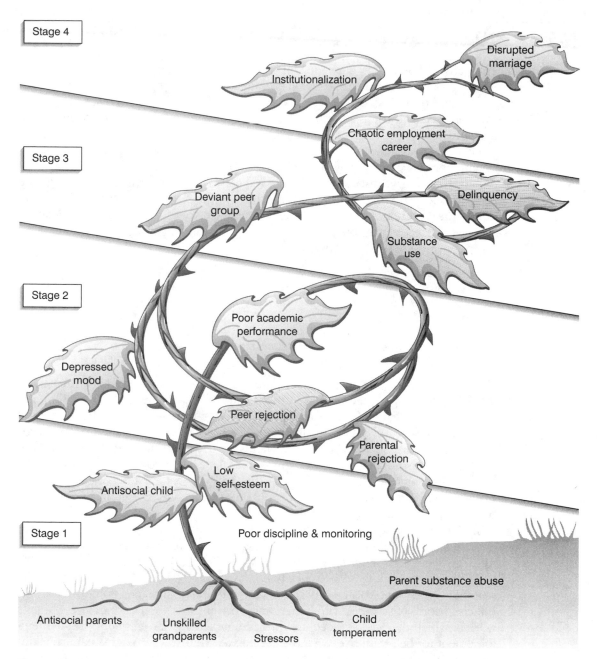

Labels within figure:

Stage 4

Stage 3

Stage 2

Stage 1

Disrupted marriage

Institutionalization

Chaotic employment career

Deviant peer group

Delinquency

Substance use

Poor academic performance

Depressed mood

Peer rejection

Parental rejection

Low self-esteem

Antisocial child

Poor discipline & monitoring

Parent substance abuse

Antisocial parents

Unskilled grandparents

Stressors

Child temperament

Figure 12.2
The vile weed: stages in the coercion model
Source: Patterson, G. R., Reid, J. B., & Dishion, T. J. (1992). *Antisocial Boys*. Eugene, OR: Castalia. Copyright © 1992 by Castalia Publishing Company. Reprinted by permission.

ASSESSMENT

The antisocial behavior characterizing conduct disorder is included on nearly all behavior problem checklists and behavior rating scales. Moreover, a variety of instruments have been designed specifically to measure the antisocial behavior of children and adolescents through self-reports or ratings of parents, teachers, or peers. These measures of antisocial behavior are often helpful, but they must always be supplemented by direct observation of the children or youth in several different settings to obtain more precise information about the problem.

In chapter 5, we discussed screening and identification instruments that might be used to select students for further study or confirm the existence of a problem requiring intervention. The instruments and practices described in chapters 5 and 6 apply to the assessment of CD. The following suggestions for assessing CD build on our prior discussion (see Kazdin, 1993, 1998, 2001):

1. Use rating scales that have multiple dimensions, because children with CD are likely to have other problems as well.
2. Make sure you assess prosocial skills (behavioral strengths or appropriate behavior) a well as CD.
3. Compare the child to norms for others of the same age and sex.
4. Assess the social contexts, including family, community, and school.
5. Make provisions for periodic reassessment to measure progress of intervention.

It is important to know what social skills a student has and what his or her standing is in peer groups (see Kavale, Mathur, & Mostert, 2004; Vaughn, Sloan, Hughes, Elbaum, & Sridhar, 2003). Another aspect of assessment is functional behavioral assessment or functional analysis: finding out what purpose the student's behavior serves, what consequences, gains, or benefits it provides (see Fox & Gable, 2004). A functional analysis can provide guidance for making alterations in the environment (e.g., tasks, commands, reinforcement) that will prevent or ameliorate problems. Unfortunately, the behavior of many disruptive students is motivated in large measure by negative reinforcement—escape from academic demands. Recall from our discussion of ADHD in chapter 11 that "the most likely function for ADHD-related behavior is to escape *effortful tasks*, particularly those that involve independent writing activity (e.g., seatwork) or an extended sequence of chores" (DuPaul & Barkley, 1998, p. 152). Gunter et al. (1998), Kyger (1999), Shores and Wehby (1999), and other researchers have found that neutral and negative teacher commands dominate the typical classrooms of students with behavioral problems. Teachers seldom give students work at which they can succeed and provide immediate and frequent positive reinforcement for behaving as expected. Teaching teachers to change this pattern is not easy (see Kyger, 1999). However, teachers must begin by asking questions related to their instruction and how their students are responding to it as well as their own (teacher's) responses to students.

As mentioned in our discussion of prevention, precorrection strategies are based on the premise that assessment of the context in which antisocial behavior is likely to occur will help teachers find ways of short-circuiting misbehavior and coercive struggles.

Ultimately, assessment is of little value unless it suggests the variables that could be changed to alter antisocial behavior (Kauffman, Mostert et al., 2002; Walker et al., 2004).

INTERVENTION AND EDUCATION

Prevention

Prediction and social control of violent behavior are among the most controversial and critical issues involving American youths. Prediction—anticipation—of antisocial behavior is essential to prevention, simply because no one can prevent what they do not anticipate (Kauffman, 2003a). Research during the past two decades has yielded a bonanza of evidence about community, family, school, peer, and personal characteristics that place children and youth at high risk of adopting antisocial behavior patterns. Nevertheless, most individuals in our society are hesitant to intervene early to prevent later problems (Kauffman, 1999c, 2003a, 2004). This is an unproductive if not maddening denial of realities that others have observed:

> Small children often exhibit the "soft" signs of antisocial behavior that are relatively trivial (e.g., noncompliance, arguing, lying) and gradually progress to much more severe "hard" signs (e.g., cruelty, aggression, bullying, harassment, violence, theft, arson) as they mature . . . Thus, it is important to address these early signs and less serious acts while we still have a chance to affect them. Far too often, we wait until it's too late to turn around vulnerable children before we define their problem behavior as in need of intervention. (Walker et al., 2004, p. 55)
>
> Preschool children, particularly boys, often engage in oppositional, overly active, and pestering behavior that may not seem serious at this developmental level. However, the manifestations of this behavior pattern in adolescence are very different and can be quite destructive . . . The myth that preschoolers will outgrow their antisocial behavior is pervasive among many teachers and early educators. Unfortunately, this belief leads many professionals to do nothing early on, when the problem can often be addressed successfully. (Walker et al., 2004, pp. 57–58)

We can now make more recommendations regarding the prevention of aggressive behavior with considerable confidence, based on research like the work we have just reviewed (see Biglan, 1995; Conduct Problems Prevention Research Group, 1999; Eddy et al., 2002; Flannery & Huff, 1999; Hester & Kaiser, 1998; Kauffman, 1994b, 1999c, 2003b; Mayer, 1995; Strain & Timm, 2001; Walker et al., 2004). However, as Biglan (1995) noted, "it is ironic that we have such high rates of serious antisocial behavior at the same time that the behavioral sciences are making so much progress in understanding and intervening in the contextual conditions that contribute to the development of antisocial behavior" (p. 479). Clearly, we need to address antisocial behavior at all levels of prevention, as Walker and Shinn (2002) suggested: *primary* (to prevent serious antisocial behavior from emerging), *secondary* (to remediate or ameliorate antisocial behavior once it is established), and *tertiary* (to accommodate or attenuate the negative effects of antisocial behavior that is unlikely to be changed).

Many members of our society, including professional practitioners in education and related disciplines as well as politicians and policymakers, have been reluctant to take the steps that we have good reason to believe would prevent or attenuate anti-social behavior (Kauffman, 1999c, 2003b). Although all may agree that the level of antisocial behavior and violence in our society is unacceptable, many are opposed to the coherent, sustained, and costly programs of government at all levels that are nec-essary to address the problem effectively. The steps research suggests we should take might be summarized as follows (see Kauffman, 1994b):

1. *Provide effective consequences to deter aggression.*   Antisocial behavior is less likely to recur if it is followed by consequences that are nonviolent but immedi-ate, certain, and proportional to the seriousness of the offense. Violence as a means of controlling aggression engenders counteraggression, setting the stage for further coercion. Aggression is reduced in the long term if the consequences are swift, assured, and restrictive of personal preferences rather than harsh or physically painful. Antisocial children and youth are typically punished capri-ciously and severely; the consequences of their behavior are often random, harsh, and unfair, cementing the pattern of counteraggression. The belief that harsher punishment is more effective is a deeply ingrained superstition. If teach-ers, parents, and others dealing with antisocial behavior learn to use effective nonviolent consequences, then the level of violence in our society will decline.

2. *Teach nonaggressive responses to problems.*   Aggressive behavior is, to a sig-nificant degree, learned. So is nonaggressive behavior. Teaching youngsters how to solve personal conflicts and other problems nonaggressively is not easy, nor will teaching nonaggression help them solve all problems. A school cur-riculum including nonaggressive conflict resolution and problem solving could lower the level of violence, but that effect would be multiplied many times were the media, community leaders, and high-profile role models to join forces with educators in teaching that nonviolence is a better way.

3. *Stop aggression early before it takes root.*   Aggression begets aggression, par-ticularly when it is successful in obtaining desired ends and when it has become well practiced. Aggression often escalates from relatively minor noncompliance and belligerence to appalling acts of violence. Nonviolent consequences are more effective when applied early in the sequence. We need intervention that is early in two ways: first, early in that we intervene with young children; sec-ond, early in that we intervene from first instances of antisocial behavior, the earliest behaviors in a chain of aggressive interactions.

4. *Restrict access to the instruments of aggression.*   Aggressors use the most ef-ficient tools available to damage their targets. True, some will show aggression with whatever tools are available. The more important truth is that having more efficient weapons (e.g., guns) enables aggressors to accomplish violent ends with less immediate risk to themselves and to escalate the level of violence eas-ily. More effective restriction of access to the most efficient tools of aggression would help to check the rise in violence: restrictions on the manufacture, dis-tribution, and possession of both the tools themselves and of the parts that make the most efficient weapons of violence operable.

5. *Restrain and reform public displays of aggression.*   The behavior one ob-serves affects one's own thinking and overt behavior. Much of the fare marketed by the entertainment industry is saturated with aggressive acts, desensitizes ob-servers to aggression and its consequences, and disinhibits expressions of ag-gression. Broadcasts of admired athletes and other public figures often depict

them bragging, intimidating their opponents, bullying, or fighting. They are often portrayed as swaggering winners or sore losers, in either case as very bad role models. Reducing the amount and type of antisocial behavior purveyed to the public as entertainment and requiring that the realistic consequences of aggression be depicted would contribute to the goal of a less violent society. Sports figures who eschew both violence and braggadocio could add immeasurably to this effect.

6. *Correct the conditions of everyday life that foster aggression.*   People tend to be more aggressive when they are deprived of basic necessities, experience aversive conditions, or perceive that there is no path to their legitimate goals other than aggression. Poverty and its attendant deprivations and aversive conditions affect an enormous proportion of American children and youth, and these conditions of everyday life provide fertile ground for aggressive conduct. Social programs that address poverty, unemployment, and related social inequities would help to remove the conditions that breed aggression. Opportunities for supervised recreation offer alternatives to antisocial behavior. A reasonably supportive society cannot abolish poverty or remove all of life's dangers, but it can keep many children from living in abject fear, misery, and hopelessness. We must have more effective social programs involving government, the private sector, local communities, religious groups, families, and individuals.

7. *Offer more effective instruction and more attractive educational options in public schools.*   Achieving academic success and engaging in study that they see as interesting and useful in their lives reduces the likelihood that youngsters will behave aggressively. By adopting instructional methods known to produce superior results—putting instruction on a solid scientific footing—schools could ensure that more students achieve success in the basic skills needed to pursue any educational option. By offering highly differentiated curricula, school systems could help more students find options that interest them and prepare them for life after high school.

Although preventive efforts may have a significant effect if implemented in only one social context (e.g., school or family), they will have maximum effect only if implemented as a coherent package of interventions involving multiple facets of the problem (see Conduct Problems Prevention Research Group, 1999; Strain & Timm, 2001). This knowledge should not deter educators or any other professionals from implementing preventive practices immediately, regardless of what happens in spheres outside their immediate responsibility or direct influence.

Most important for educators is understanding how instruction is a key tool for prevention (cf. Kauffman, Mostert et al., 2002). Being confronted daily, if not hourly, by academic and social tasks at which they are failures is known to contribute directly to students' tendency to exhibit antisocial behavior. Many antisocial students do not know how to do the academic tasks and do not have the social coping skills to be successful in the typical classroom, and each failure increases the probability of future antisocial responses to problems (Gunter et al., 1998).

The most effective approaches to school-based prevention of antisocial behavior are *proactive* and *instructive:* planning ways to avoid failure and coercive struggles regarding both academic and social behavior and actively teaching students more adaptive, competent ways of behaving. Antisocial behavior should prompt teachers to ask what prosocial skills the student needs to learn as a replacement for aggression and to devise an explicit instructional strategy for teaching those skills.

Major Features of Social Learning Interventions

Many conceptual approaches to intervention in a CD once it has emerged have been suggested. These have included psychodynamic therapies, biological treatments, and behavioral interventions. Parent management training, problem-solving training, family therapy based on systems theory and behaviorism, and treatments addressing multiple social systems (family, school, community) as well as the individual are among the most promising approaches. Interventions based on social learning principles have generally been more successful than have those based on other conceptual models (Eddy et al., 2002; Kazdin, 1994; Walker, 1995; Walker et al., 2004; Webster-Stratton & Dahl, 1995). Furthermore, a social learning approach offers the most direct, practical, and reliable implications for the work of teachers. Consequently, we confine discussion here to interventions based on social learning concepts.

A *social learning approach* to the control of aggression includes three primary components: specific behavioral objectives, strategies for changing behavior by altering the social environment, and precise measurement of behavioral change. These components allow us to judge the outcome of intervention quantitatively as well as qualitatively against an objective goal.

Social learning interventions sometimes appear quite simple, but the apparent simplicity is deceptive because it is often necessary to make subtle adjustments in technique to make them work. An exquisite sensitivity to human communication is necessary to become a virtuoso in the humane and effective application of behavior principles. The range of possible techniques for an individual case is extensive, calling for a high degree of creativity to formulate an effective and ethical plan of action.

School-based social learning interventions designed to reduce aggression may include a wide variety of strategies or procedures (Kauffman, Mostert et al., 2002). Walker (1995) discussed 12 intervention techniques for managing the acting-out student, providing guidelines for correct application, special issues, and advantages and disadvantages of each. These 12 techniques (and others) may be used individually or in combination. The following thumbnail sketches of the 12 techniques provide a beginning point for understanding how effective interventions for conduct disorder may be constructed:

- *Rules*—clear, explicit statements defining the teacher's expectations for classroom conduct. Clarity of expectations is a hallmark of corrective or therapeutic environments for students with conduct disorder. A few clear rules let students know how they should behave and what is prohibited; they are important guidelines for classroom conduct and teacher behavior as well. Positively stated rules, which should predominate, guide the teacher's praise, approval, and other forms of positive reinforcement. Negatively stated rules, which should be kept to a minimum, guide the teacher's use of punishment.
- *Teacher praise*—positive verbal, physical, gestural, or other affective indications of approval. Teacher praise for desirable, nonaggressive student conduct is one of the

key ingredients in successful behavioral management. Many teachers neglect this aspect of instruction or use praise too sparingly or unskillfully. Yet it is perhaps the most important element in a program of positive reinforcement. Moreover, rules alone are much less effective than are rules combined with frequent, skillful teacher praise for following them.

- *Positive reinforcement*—presentation of a rewarding consequence that increases the future probability or strength of the behavior it follows. Such consequences can be extremely varied in form. Rhode et al. (1992) suggested that to be most effective, praise and other forms of positive reinforcement should be given (a) immediately after appropriate behavior, (b) frequently, (c) with enthusiasm, (d) with eye contact from the teacher, (e) after or with description of the behavior that earned the reward, (f) in ways that build excitement and anticipation for obtaining them, and (g) in great variety. Sometimes, token reinforcers are given that can be exchanged later for desired objects or privileges (much like any other economic exchange or monetary system). The effective use of positive reinforcement requires differential responding to the student's behavior. That is, the desired behavior is to be reinforced; undesirable behavior is to be ignored (not reinforced). The basic idea of positive reinforcement is very simple; its skillful implementation is not, especially with difficult antisocial students.

- *Verbal feedback*—information about the appropriateness or inappropriateness of academic or social behavior. Teachers' responses to students' academic performance and conduct (the content, emotional tone, and timing of what they say and do in reaction to students' behavior) are crucial factors in how students learn to behave. Giving clear feedback, keeping it primarily positive, steering clear of arguments, and finding the most effective pace and timing are critical issues. Using verbal feedback effectively requires much experience, training, and reflection.

- *Stimulus change*—alteration of antecedent events or conditions that set the stage for behavior. Sometimes antecedents can be changed easily, resulting in a marked decrease in problem behavior. For example, making instructions or assignments shorter and clearer may result in greatly improved levels of compliance. Presenting tasks or commands in a different way may also defuse resistance to them. Increasing attention is being given to the effects of the context in which aggression occurs, and modification of the context is often found to be both feasible and effective in reducing aggression.

- *Contingency contract*—a written performance agreement between a student and teacher (or parents, or both teacher and parents), specifying roles, expectations, and consequences. Contracts must be written with the student's age and intelligence in mind. They should be simple, straightforward statements. Successful contracts are clearly written, emphasize the positive consequences for appropriate conduct, specify fair consequences to which all parties agree, and are strictly adhered to by the adults who sign the document. Contracts are not generally successful if they are used as the only or primary intervention strategy. They are useful primarily for individuals and carefully delimited problem behaviors.

- *Modeling plus reinforcing imitation*—showing or demonstrating the desired behavior and providing positive reinforcement for matching responses. Learning through watching models and imitating them—*observational learning*—is a basic social learning process. The models may be adults or peers, but it is critical that the student who is to learn more appropriate behavior be taught whom to watch, what to look for, and what to match; models without explicit instruction are not typically effective in remediating academic or social problems (see Hallenbeck & Kauffman, 1995). Effective modeling and reinforcement often must be done in private one-on-one sessions with the teacher, and procedures must be used to help students exhibit in everyday circumstances the improved behavior they learn through observational learning.

- *Shaping*—a process of building new responses by beginning with behavior the student already exhibits at some level and reinforcing successive approximations of the desired behavior. The key factor in shaping is identifying and reinforcing small increments of improvement. This typically requires careful attention to the student's current behavior in relation to a behavioral goal. It also requires ignoring behavior that does not represent progress toward the goal. As is true of positive reinforcement, the basic idea is simple, but the skillful implementation is not.

- *Systematic social skills training*—a curriculum in which the skills taught are those that help students (a) initiate and maintain positive social interactions, (b) develop friendships and social support networks, and (c) cope effectively with the social environment. Social skills involve getting along with authority figures such as teachers and parents, relating to peers in a variety of activities, and solving social problems in constructive, nonaggressive ways. They involve both skill deficits (the student does not have the skill) and performance deficits (the student has but does not use the skill). A useful social skills training program must not only be intensive and systematic but aimed at demonstration and practice of the skills in natural or everyday environments in which they are needed to avoid coercive struggles and aggressive behavior.

- *Self-monitoring and self-control training*—consistent tracking, recording, and evaluating of specific behaviors of one's own with the intention of changing those behaviors. These procedures many involve not only keeping track of one's own behavior but prompting oneself or applying consequences to oneself. These procedures require explicit training and rehearsal, as well as the motivation to use them. As discussed in chapter 11, self-monitoring is a strategy frequently used with students who have ADHD. Self-monitoring may be an inappropriate strategy for serious aggressive behavior and for students who do not have the cognitive awareness or social maturity to carry out the procedures.

- *Time out*—the removal, for a specified period of time and contingent upon a specific misbehavior, a student's opportunity to obtain positive reinforcement. Time out may involve removing a student from the group or classroom, although that is not always necessary (e.g., it may involve the teacher's turning away and refusing to respond or a time during which the student cannot earn points or other rewards). Time out should be reserved for serious behavioral problems. Like any punishment procedure, it is easily misunderstood, misused, and abused. Used knowledgeably and skillfully and in combination with other positive procedures, it is an important nonviolent tool for reducing aggressive behavior.

- *Response cost*—the removal of a previously earned reward or reinforcer (or a portion thereof) contingent on a specific misbehavior. Response cost is a fine or penalty incurred for each instance of an inappropriate behavior. Minutes of recess, free time, or access to another preferred activity or points toward earning a reinforcing item or activity may be lost for each misbehavior. Like any other punishment procedure, response cost is subject to misunderstanding and misuse. Moreover, it is ineffective without a strong program of positive reinforcement. However, of all types of punishment procedures, it is probably the least likely to engender strong emotional side effects and resistance.

The Uses and Misuses of Punishment

Many people in the United States appear to embrace corporal punishment and other highly punitive approaches to child discipline (e.g., Evans & Richardson, 1995; Gershoff, 2002; Hyman, 1995). Indeed, numerous studies have confirmed the low rates of positive reinforcement for appropriate behavior and high rates of aversive conditions for students in typical U.S. classrooms, as discussed in chapter 9 (see Bear, 1998; Gunter et al., 1998; Maag, 2001). In reaction to excessive and ineffective punishment, some have advocated a ban on all manner of punishment, arguing that positive measures alone are sufficient and punishment in any form is unethical. Research does not support a complete abandonment of punishment as a means of child management, but it does suggest great care in the use of punishment procedures.

Although teaching appropriate behavior is important in social learning interventions, some behaviors may require punishment because they are intolerable or dangerous and unresponsive to alternative positive interventions (Kazdin, 1998; Walker, 1995; Walker et al., 2004). It may be difficult or impossible to establish adequate classroom control, particularly with students who have learning and behavioral problems, without using negative consequences for misbehavior in addition to positive reinforcement of appropriate conduct. Judicious use of negative consequences for misconduct can even enhance the effectiveness of positive consequences (Lerman & Vorndran, 2002; Pfiffner & O'Leary, 1987; Pfiffner, Rosen, & O'Leary, 1985).

We must be extremely careful in the use of punishment, however, because ill-timed, vengeful, and capricious punishment, especially in the absence of incentives for appropriate behavior, provides a vicious example for youngsters and encourages their further misbehavior. Harsh punishment provokes counteraggression and coercion. Punishment is a seductive, easily abused approach to controlling behavior. Harsh punishment has an immediate effect; because it frequently results in immediate cessation of the individual's irritating or inappropriate behavior, it provides a powerful negative reinforcement for the punisher. Thus, it is often the beginning point of a coercive style of interaction in which the punished and the punisher vie for the dubious honor of winning an aversive contest. And because people mistakenly believe that punishment makes the individual suffer, physical punishment is frequently thought to be more effective than milder forms. These dangers, misconceptions, and abuses of punishment appear to underlie the coercive relationships that characterize families of aggressive antisocial children (cf. Patterson et al., 1992). Consequently, it is critical to carefully consider punishment in educational settings to avoid having the school become another battleground for aversive control.

A pervasive misconception about punishment is that it requires inflicting physical pain, psychological trauma, or social embarrassment. None of these is required; punishment can be defined as any consequence that results in a decline in the rate or strength of the punished behavior. Thus, a mild, quiet reprimand, temporary withdrawal of attention, or loss of a small privilege may often be effective punishment. For persistent and serious misbehavior, stronger punishment may be necessary, but mild forms of social punishment such as restrictions or loss of rewards are most effective if the youngster's environment also provides many opportunities for positive reinforcement of appropriate behavior.

The social learning literature clearly supports the assertion that punishment, if carefully and appropriately administered, is a humane and effective tool for controlling serious misbehavior (Lerman & Vorndran, 2002; Walker, 1995; Walker et al., 2004). Effective punishment may actually be necessary to rear a nonaggressive, socialized child (Dishion & Patterson, 1996; Patterson, 1982; Patterson et al., 1992). However, clumsy, vindictive, or malicious punishment is the teacher's or parent's downfall. And it is a mistake not to offer positive reinforcement for desired alternative behavior when punishment is employed (Maag, 2001; Thompson, Iwata, Conners, & Roscoe, 1999). We also must first give attention to what types of behavior may be legitimately punished. Punishment that is out of proportion to the seriousness of the offense has no place in humane treatment.

Before using punishment procedures, educators must be sure that a strong program of teaching and positive consequences for appropriate behavior is in place, and they must carefully consider the types of behavior that are priorities for punishment. Teachers should study the use of punishment procedures in depth before implementing them in the classroom. Following are general guidelines for humane and effective punishment:

- Punishment should be reserved for serious misbehavior that is associated with significant impairment of the youngster's social relationships and behaviors that positive strategies alone have failed to control.
- Punishment should be instituted only in the context of ongoing behavioral management and instructional programs that emphasize positive consequences for appropriate conduct and achievement.
- Punishment should be used only by people who are warm and loving toward the individual when his or her behavior is acceptable and who offer ample positive reinforcement for nonaggressive behavior.
- Punishment should be administered matter-of-factly, without anger, threats, or moralizing.
- Punishment should be fair, consistent, and immediate. If the youngster is able to understand descriptions of the contingency, punishment should be applied only to behavior that he or she has been warned is punishable. In short, punishment should be predictable and swift, not capricious or delayed.
- Punishment should be of reasonable intensity. Relatively minor misbehavior should evoke only mild punishment, and more serious offenses or problems should generally result in stronger punishment.

- Whenever possible, punishment should involve response cost (loss of privileges or rewards or withdrawal of attention) rather than aversives.
- Whenever possible, punishment should be related to the misbehavior, enabling the youngster to make restitution or practice a more adaptive alternate behavior.
- Punishment should be discontinued if it is not quickly apparent that it is effective. Unlike positive reinforcement, which may not have an immediate effect on behavior, effective punishment usually results in an almost immediate decline in misbehavior. It is better not to punish than to punish ineffectively, because ineffective punishment may merely increase the individual's tolerance for aversive consequences. Punishment will not necessarily be more effective if it becomes harsher or more intense; using a different type of punishment, making the punishment more immediate, or making the punishment more consistent may make it more effective.
- There should be written guidelines for using specific punishment procedures. All concerned parties—students, parents, teachers, and school administrators—should know what punishment procedures will be used. Before implementing specific punishment procedures, especially those involving time out or other aversive consequences, they should be approved by school authorities.

As we have discussed, children and youth with CDs have typically experienced lax monitoring and inconsistent, harsh punishment with little positive reinforcement for appropriate behavior. Their discipline has typically contributed to their CD, not because it has included punishment per se but because it has included too little positive reinforcement for the right kind of behavior and punishment that is not appropriate. Effective intervention in CDs may often require punishment, but of a different kind.

THE ACTING-OUT BEHAVIOR CYCLE AND PRECORRECTION

Social learning interventions are increasingly focused on stepping in early to prevent the escalation of aggression and the blowups in which it often terminates. One clear presentation of this approach is provided by Colvin (1992). He describes the phases children and youth typically go through in a cycle of acting-out behavior. Figure 12.3 is a graphic depiction of the seven phases.

A highly significant feature of the acting-out cycle is that it begins with a *calm* phase in which the student is behaving in ways that are expected and appropriate. The student is cooperative, compliant, and task oriented. Most students with CD exhibit appropriate behavior at least some of the time, but this behavior is typically ignored by teachers. Major emphasis should be placed on recognizing and showing approval of students in the calm phase.

An unresolved problem in school or outside of school may *trigger* the first stage in moving toward a major blowup. At this point, teachers may avert further escalation if they recognize the triggering events or conditions and move quickly to help the student resolve the problem.

If triggering problems are not resolved, the student may move into a state of *agitation*, in which overall behavior is unfocused and off task. If the teacher recognizes

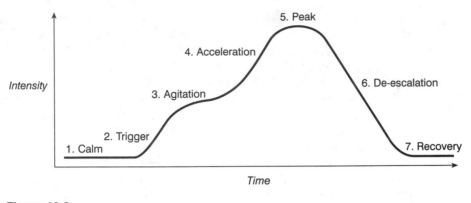

Figure 12.3
Phases of acting-out behavior
Source: Colvin, G. (1992). Managing acting-out behavior: *Behavior Associates.* Copyright © 1992 by Behavior Associates. Reprinted by permission.

indications of agitation, further escalation of aggressive behavior may be prevented by altering teacher proximity, engaging the student in alternative activities, involving the student in a plan of self-management, or using other strategies designed to help the student avoid a blowup.

Agitation may lead to *acceleration*, a phase in which the student engages the teacher in a coercive struggle. Acceleration is characterized by attempts to draw the teacher into arguments or demand teacher attention through noncompliant, highly disruptive, abusive, or destructive behavior. At this point, it is extremely important for the teacher to avoid getting drawn in, to use crisis-prevention strategies to extricate himself or herself from the struggle. By the time the student gets to this point, it is very difficult to deescalate the behavior. Clear consequences for such behavior need to be established and communicated to the student beforehand so that at this point the teacher can deliver the needed information to the student matter-of-factly and allow him or her a few seconds to make a decision (e.g., "Roger, you must stop throwing stuff around now, or I will call the principal. Take a couple of seconds to decide."). Prompt and unequivocal follow-through in applying the consequence is extremely important.

In the *peak* phase, the student's behavior is out of control. It may be necessary to call the police or the student's parents or remove the student from the classroom or school. Preparation for such out-of-control behavior is essential so that the involved adults are as calm, systematic, and effective as possible in preventing injury or damage so that the deescalation phase can be entered as quickly as possible. Frequent out-of-control behavior should be a prompt to educators to examine the environment and schoolwork for conditions that need to be changed.

During *deescalation* following a peak phase, the student typically is beginning to disengage from the struggle and is in a confused state. Behavior may range from withdrawal, to denial and blaming others for what happened, to wanting to make up, to responsiveness to directions and willingness to engage in simple tasks. It is important to take measures to help the student cool down, restore the environment as much as possible (e.g., pick up books and chairs, clean up a mess), and get back to routine activities. This is not yet the time to talk to the student about his or her behavior. Debriefing at this point in the cycle is likely to be counterproductive; the student is likely to be reluctant to talk at all or may not be able to think clearly about the incident, what led to it, and how similar problems might be avoided.

Finally, the student enters a *recovery* phase in which he or she is eager for busy work and a semblance of ordinary classwork but still reluctant to discuss what happened. It is important to provide strong reinforcement for normal routines and to avoid negotiations about the negative consequences that may have been applied to the serious misbehavior. However, it is very important at this point to *debrief* the student, to review what led up to the problem and what alternative behaviors the student might have chosen (Sugai & Colvin, 1997). Any effort of the student to problem-solve should be acknowledged, and the student should be helped to devise a step-by-step plan for avoiding repetitions of the blowup. The student needs reassurance that he or she can succeed and avoid such out-of-control incidents with help.

Educators often place a great deal of emphasis on Phases 4 and 5 of the acting-out behavior cycle, virtually ignoring the first three phases, particularly Phase 1 (calm). Walker et al. (2004) noted that this is counterproductive. The opposite emphasis is recommended by decades of research: Focus attention on the earlier phases of the cycle, on attention to and reinforcement of calm behavior, removing or ameliorating triggers, and intervening early and nonthreateningly when students begin showing signs of agitation. One systematic way of focusing attention and effort on earlier phases of the cycle is the precorrection plan described by Colvin, Sugai, and Patching (1993). Strong reinforcement for appropriate behavior is important, but precorrection begins with examination of the context in which misbehavior is likely and how conditions might be altered and instructional (as opposed to correctional) procedures used to prevent the misbehavior from occurring—how triggers and agitation can be avoided. Figure 12.4 shows a precorrection checklist and plan devised by a sixth-grade teacher for Jimmy, a student in her class.

In chapter 8, we quoted Patterson's (1986b) observation that many of the characteristics of CD emerge from "the prosaic daily round of parental mismanagement . . . something as inherently banal as family coercive exchanges. What leads to things getting out of hand may be a relatively simple affair, whereas the process itself, once initiated, may be the stuff of which novels are made" (p. 442). It is highly probable that a similar process characterizes the emergence of conduct disorder in school. Astute teachers perceive the potential for triggers and agitation and move quickly and positively to help students learn to avoid them, not just to deal appropriately with the early stages of acting out (see Kauffman, Bantz, & McCullough, 2002). Many of the most effective interventions involve expert management of ordinary events.

School Violence and Schoolwide Discipline

There is strong consensus among those who study schools and behavioral deviance that the problems of student misconduct have increased enormously in seriousness and pervasiveness during the past two decades. Such episodes will not be managed

---

A Completed Precorrection Plan

Teacher: <u>Pat Puller</u>   Student: <u>Jimmy Ott (six grade)</u>   Date: <u>Oct. 11, 2002</u>

1. Context [where and when; situation, circumstances, or conditions in which predictable behavior occurs]

   Upon entering the classroom in the morning, when at least one other student is in the room

   Predictable Behavior [the error or misbehavior that you can anticipate in the context]

   Jimmy describes his deviant behavior or deviant intentions (e.g., how he drank or did drugs or got into a fight or stole something or is going to "take someone out")

2. Expected Behavior [what you want the student to do instead of the predictable behavior]

   Jimmy will talk about appropriate topics when he enters the class

3. Context Modification [how you can change the situation, circumstances, or conditions to make the predictable behavior less likely and the expected behavior more likely to occur]

   Meet Jimmy at the door and immediately ask a question demanding appropriate talk as an answer

4. Behavior Rehearsal [practice; dry run; try out; drill]

   Practice with Jimmy coming into class and responding to my question, then talking about appropriate topics

5. Strong Reinforcement [special reward for doing the expected behavior]

   Praise for appropriate talk on coming into the classroom, plus 5 min to talk with his choice of me, principal, cook, or custodian if no inappropriate talk before first period assignment is given (principal, cook, and custodian agreed and trained is how to handle conversation)

6. Prompts [gestures or other signals indicating "remember; do it now"]

   Hand signal to Jimmy when I first see him in the morning, worked out in advance to indicate "appropriate talk"

7. Monitoring Plan [record of performance; indicator of success that you can show someone]

   Jimmy and I to record daily successful school entry talk

Figure 12.4

Precorrection checklist and plan for Jimmy

Source: Kauffman, J. M., Mostert, M. P., Trent, S. C., & Hallahan, D. P. (2002). *Managing classroom behavior: A reflective case-based approach* (3rd ed.). Boston: Allyn & Bacon, p. 63. Copyright © 2002. Reprinted by permission of the publisher.

well or lessened without a coherent schoolwide plan of behavior management in addition to strategies designed for individuals and classroom groups (Martella, Nelson, & Marchand-Martella, 2003).

In many schools today, especially middle schools, students are concerned about the violent behavior of their peers. Teaching peace and conflict-resolution skills has been suggested as an effective strategy for reducing violence (e.g., Lantieri, 1995), and perhaps such instruction can contribute to safer, less violent schools. However, it is possible that the most effective approach to school violence is focused primarily on the more ordinary, routine interactions that characterize classrooms and other school environments and that are natural extensions or refinements of basic educational practices rather than special curricula. In fact, schoolwide discipline plans may be universal interventions that help to prevent severe disorders.

An important concept in the prevention of violence is that violent acts, like the more mundane acts of aggression that characterize CD, typically follow a pattern of escalating conflict. The most effective strategies for controlling school violence, therefore, are those that modify the conditions under which lower levels of aggressive acts are most likely to occur, deal quickly and nonviolently with the earliest indications that aggressive behavior is on an escalating path, and organize the school staff to support consistent, schoolwide implementation of discipline procedures. With a good schoolwide plan, the entire school staff functions as a team to set clear behavioral expectations, establish a positive school climate in which desirable behavior is frequently recognized and reinforced, monitor student behavior continuously, apply consistent and planned consequences for unacceptable behavior, provide collegial support, and maintain clear communication about both behavioral expectations and problem incidents (see Lewis & Sugai, 1999; Liaupsin, Jolivette, & Scott, 2004; Martella et al., 2003; Walker et al., 2004).

Much of the problem of antisocial behavior in schools is in the form of bullying—coercion, intimidation, and threats that often start as mean-spirited teasing and progress to extortion and physical attack. Bullying is now recognized as a serious problem in the schools of many nations throughout the world (cf. Sheras, 2002; Walker et al., 2004). It is a serious problem that is often a precursor to school violence. Antisocial students are typically the bullies, not the victims, although they sometimes suffer the same fate as those they bully. Any student who is particularly passive, submissive, or provocative is a potential victim of bullies. Effective intervention in bullying typically requires a schoolwide, if not communitywide, effort, as well as individual intervention, because much of the bullying occurs outside the presence of any one adult. The general features of effective antibullying interventions include the following (see Olweus, 1991; Walker et al., 2004, for further discussion):

- A school climate characterized by a warm, positive, supportive school atmosphere in which adults set clear and firm limits on unacceptable behavior
- Nonhostile, nonphysical sanctions applied immediately and consistently to violations of behavioral expectations
- Continuous monitoring and surveillance of student activities in and around the school
- Adult mediation of student interactions and assumption of authority to stop bullying when it is observed
- Discussion of the issue of bullying with bullies, victims, parents, and neutral students (nonparticipants) to clarify school values, expectations, procedures, and consequences

We would like to think that all schools are responsible for all children and that no child should be excluded from a school because of his or her disability. However, some students with severe conduct disorder are disabled in ways that make their inclusion in regular classrooms and neighborhood schools inadvisable on ethical grounds, if not a mockery of social justice (see Brigham & Kauffman, 1998; Farmer,

2000; Kauffman, Bantz, & McCullough, 2002; Kauffman, Lloyd, Baker, & Riedel, 1995; Mock & Kauffman, 2003, for further discussion). Violent behavior cannot and must not be tolerated in schools if nonviolent students and their teachers are to maintain a viable social and instructional environment.

SUMMARY

Conduct disorder is characterized by persistent antisocial behavior that violates the rights of others as well as age-appropriate social norms. It includes aggression to people and animals, destruction of property, deceitfulness and theft, and serious violation of rules. We distinguish youngsters with conduct disorder from those who are developing normally by their higher rates of noxious behaviors and by the persistence of such conduct beyond the age at which most children have adopted less aggressive behavior. CD is often comorbid with other disorders. It is one of the most prevalent psychopathological disorders of childhood and youth, estimated to affect 6 to 16% of males and 2 to 9% of females under the age of 18. CD may be classified by age of onset, and those with early onset typically show more serious impairment and have a worse prognosis. Other subtypes include overt aggressive (undersocialized); covert antisocial (socialized), such as theft, lying, and arson; and versatile (socialized and undersocialized).

Aggressive behavior has long been a common phenomenon in American culture, but aggression and violence have become a much greater concern in schools during the past two decades. Aggression and violence are multicultural issues, although most contributing factors and interventions appear to apply equally across all subgroups. Both general and special education teachers must be prepared to deal with the aggressive behavior of students.

Many contributing causes of aggression have been identified, but social learning theory provides the best supported and most useful conceptualizations for educators. We know that aggression may be learned through processes of modeling, reinforcement of aggression, and ineffective punishment. The risk of aggressive behavior is increased by a wide variety of personal, family, school, peer, and other cultural factors. These factors are often combined in a coercive process leading to aggressive behavior that is passed from one generation to the next.

Steps likely to be effective in preventing CD include consequences that deter aggression, instruction in nonaggressive responses to problems, early intervention, restriction of the tools of aggression, restraint of public displays of aggression, correction of everyday living conditions, and more effective and attractive school options. A proactive, instructional approach to prevention is of greatest value to educators.

A variety of rating scales are of value in assessing CD, but direct observation of behavior in various settings must supplement the ratings. Assessment requires evaluation of a variety of domains, including both academic and social problems and behavior at home and school. Assessment must include prosocial skills as well as social deficits. Ongoing assessment to monitor progress is essential. Social skills must be assessed to guide instruction. Functional assessment of behavior to determine what consequences, gains, or benefits it provides the student will help guide intervention.

Interventions based on social learning are the most reliable and useful for teachers. These may include strategies such as rules, teacher praise, positive reinforcement, verbal feedback, stimulus change, contingency contracts, modeling and reinforcement of imitation, shaping, systematic social skills instruction, self-monitoring and self-control training, time out, and response cost. Particular care must be taken in the use of punishment because it is seductive and easily misused. The focus must be on positive strategies. The concepts of the acting-out cycle and precorrection help keep the focus of intervention on positive strategies applied early in the sequence. The acting-out cycle includes the phases *calm, trigger, agitation, acceleration, peak, deescalation,* and *recovery.* Greatest emphasis should be placed on intervention in the first three phases of the cycle. Precorrection plans help to keep the focus on earlier phases in the cycle. Schoolwide discipline plans may help decrease the level of violence in schools by focusing efforts on positive attention to appropriate behavior, clear expectations and monitoring of student behavior, staff communication and support, and consistent consequences for unacceptable behavior.

Aggressive Conduct Disorder

Evelyne Noel, M.A., is a teacher of sixth graders with emotional and behavioral disorders at Glasgow Middle School in the Fairfax County Public Schools, Alexandria, Virginia. She was formerly a classroom teacher, and then a behavior specialist, at the Phillips Programs in Annandale, Virginia, a private day school for youth with behavioral disorders. When she wrote this feature, she was a classroom teacher of nine middle school students and had one full-time assistant.

Think of a particular student who exhibits an overt conduct disorder. How does this student manifest the disorder?

Jack comes from a middle-class, intact family. Both his parents are employed, and he has two siblings. His labels when he was referred to our program were *pervasive developmental disorder*, *psychosis*, and *attention deficit–hyperactivity disorder*. At 13 years of age, Jack stands tall, and his huge smile brightens his teenage face.

Jack's honeymoon period at school, lasting about 20 days, was charming. I actually wondered for a while if he might be the miracle student who would be transformed instantly just by virtue of his placement in our school. At some point I asked him what he thought of his new placement, and he answered, "It's scary." Feeling that I had failed him as his teacher, I asked what was scary. He responded, "Everyone is so nice to me here, it's freakish." It is not the first time that one of my students has gotten nervous on immersion in a warm and loving environment. It is the novelty that scares them. As another student once said to me, "It's just that I don't know how to behave when everything is good."

I waited about 2 weeks to challenge Jack academically. This gave me time to assess him and also allowed him some respite from subject matter that had been difficult for him in the past. As I began to increase my academic expectations of Jack, his problem behaviors started to emerge.

Jack's most violent incidents involved flipping his desk over and were always related to work expectations. This caused me safety concerns for the group because of his size and strength and also because one aggressive gesture can often precede another. In ad-

dition, I never saw precursor signs. As per our classroom rules, he would then be asked to leave for a time out. He often refused and became disruptive to others. At times we had to intervene physically to escort him out of the room.

Jack had refined the art of disruption to a variety of subtle but efficient behaviors. He had figured out his peers' weak spots and mumbled offensive statements under his breath. Once he had captured their attention, he would continue to test their patience with words and discrete gestures. Jack would also quietly take his shoes off and then make sure someone noticed his "stinking feet." Throwing small items across the room was part of his repertoire, as was whining.

At times, Jack would get up and start pulling communal property and work off our classroom walls. These behaviors were impossible for our group to ignore because Jack could sustain many of them for extended periods of time.

What procedures have you found most useful in working with this student?

Rules, rules, and rules. We consistently enforced the classroom rules, always making sure that Jack knew them and understood their validity in terms of the group. There were no second chances, and behaviors that he claimed had been an accident had the same consequences, too. Of course, the best rules come with exceptions, and on a rare occasion I would break a rule if I thought it would be constructive. I never allowed excuses for behaviors that were a danger to others because I believe that a climate of safety in the room is critical for trust building.

Options and choices. Direct confrontations were avoided unless Jack was destroying property that belonged to others, was instigating something intensely, or had flipped a desk and was not calm. Often, I just waited him out, for up to 45 minutes. If he had misbehaved but was calm and not disruptive, I ignored him and carried on with my teaching. For example, we sometimes had an upside-down desk with everything tossed out of it and Jack sitting in his chair saying he would not leave. My response was "That's fine; you don't have to if you do not care to fix this situation, but I will not move on until you have taken your time out." We then withheld all social interactions from him. Sooner or later, he would get bored and simply leave. This worked with our group because we had all agreed previously that to help each other in behavioral growth we would try to refrain from giving attention to negative behaviors, and Jack's peers took their coaching role seriously. They felt good about it, too, because they knew they were supporting his progress. And they were.

Being honestly positive. If there is one thing that works magic, this is the one! It always works, sooner or later. You have to be honest about it, though, because kids are no fools. They detect lies. A day is full of little things that people do well. We would point out to Jack a day without aggressive behaviors, a moment when he had coped well, a generous gesture, a word well placed. Even after a problem, if Jack went to take his consequence promptly, I would point that out as well done: "Sure, Jack, you just messed up, but look—you're turning it around quickly. Way to go!"

Feedback and modeling. Often Jack did not even realize that he had demonstrated the behaviors that we were seeking to develop in him, so we would point them out immediately, commenting, "What you just did is exactly what we are looking for. Do it again next time!" My assistant and I would also sometimes role-play a situation he was in and act out acceptable solutions to his utter delight, which in turn anchored his attention. We would even give positive feedback when he was making progress toward eliminating a negative behavior even though it was still present. After a time out, we always debriefed with him, making sure that he understood what had happened and in what order.

Social skills training. Remember the comment "It's just that I don't know how to behave when everything is good"? Well, neither did Jack, so we taught him a repertoire of things to do and say to cope more effectively.

Contracts. Jack liked to make deals, and he liked to create his own. We let him. He would make deals with individual staff members, and the deal would get posted on an index card in his work area for the purpose of clear communication. For example, "Jack will take five time outs independently, and Grace will play 15 minutes of basketball with him." He always ensured that he would be allowed to earn his deals on work time because he hated to work.

Restitution. Jack always had to fix what he broke or destroyed, and we never forgot. (I tend to be flaky, so I write things down, particularly restitution plans, and I keep two copies in case one gets destroyed.) As with rules, we were strict and consistent with restitution. Jack once broke a doorknob in the time-out room. Because he did not have the skills to replace it, he sanded the old door down in 10-minute increments once a day for 10 days, which leads to our final strategy.

There is no negative behavior that will get you out of work. Only positive behaviors will get you breaks. This was particularly effective with Jack because most of his behaviors were precipitated by work expectations. He soon realized that teasing others instead of working or becoming violent would only make his day unpleasant and that incomplete work would come to haunt him. On the other hand, if he coped with an assignment with improved behaviors, then, lo and behold, I would come by and tell him that we would shorten the assignment on account of his good attitudes. But he never knew when I would do that.

What do you see as the prospects for this student's educational progress in the coming year?

Jack will have new teachers and new peer groups, and the question is whether he will generalize his newfound successes to new environments. That is always the true test for our students. Sometimes we succeed; sometimes we don't. If Jack can show the same levels of success in different classrooms and social groups, then he will be well on his way to a life with promises. If he cannot, then we will know that we still have a lot of work ahead of us.

What do you see as the biggest long-term problems this student will face?

In the bittersweet days of rough beginnings in a new placement, a young man slowly discovers that he is not that bad after all and not even such a failure. It is sheer relief to him but also to me, his teacher, not only because I have done my job but because violent behaviors force me to operate from a crisis modality, and that wears me down. So Jack and I are happy this year.

Behavioral improvements never happen suddenly. They happen like an onion is peeled: one thin layer at a time. When the negative shells have been stripped away, at some point an individual emerges: someone real with goodness to offer and new challenges to meet.

Jack has become well liked at the school. Staff members enjoy his sense of humor; his peers are attracted by his creativity and generosity. His strengths are emerging, and he believes in them. He is still working hard at making it every day, so we will not tell him that the challenges of coping will not end soon. For now, his behavior has become less violent, and the weaknesses in his social skills will emerge more clearly. In the future, Jack will have difficulties making friends and sustaining friendships, and he will have to work hard at developing age-appropriate leisure skills.

Evelyne Noel Interviews Jack

Ms. N: Tell me about the Phillips School.

J: They help us out because we need the help and they are very nice. They do projects with us and parties. Parties for Halloween, Valentine's Day. When the teachers in my class get good ideas, we don't like them—but they turn out to be good ones. We have a kind of café place. It's Phillips Café, where the teachers go get our lunch if we don't have any. Usually, if we have a bad day [and are not allowed to go to the café], they get us a peanut butter and jelly [sandwich]. Teachers always make deals about the café, playing basketball and bringing toys. The best part about this school is the friendly faces you see every morning.

Ms. N: What are some of the things that you personally do well?

J: I read good. In my classroom I am on my own reading level, and I am very creative. I have good ideas for the class. Today I offered [to share] my Halloween mask. They [the other students] are kind of loud, but I stop [talking] so I can get their attention.

Ms. N: Do you use your hands very well? What kinds of things do you build?

J: Cars out of other cars. I take different pieces of cars and put them together. I take toys that are broken and rebuild them with other toys, and I'm very good at Legos.

Ms. N: Yes, I agree. I've seen you. You have many, many strengths there, don't you?

J: Yep.

Ms. N: What are some of the things that are hard for you?

J: Math and writing . . . that's all.

Ms. N: How about in terms of behaviors and temper, what's hard?

J: Well, it's kinda hard when . . . the kids in the class, in the school, always question stuff. Then they always think that you're trying to get on their nerves or particularly trying to get in trouble, and there's some kids, particularly a kid in my class, I'm not going to say who, he wants to get in a high order. He wants to be the toughest and stuff. He always thinks he can work stuff out with violence and stuff and getting in trouble. But the way I learned throughout the times being in school here—and I just got here last school year after winter break, and I always had trouble with my anger and stuff. I always think I can get the way I want in the schools I've been to, but then I realized I had to do my work, I had to earn my way through all the difficulties.

Ms. N: You're really right, Jack. I've known you for a while. You have also made great progress in terms of that. Is there anything else you want to say about that question?

J: A lot of the time when kids are in trouble or are trying to get everybody to start it, I am usually quiet or kinda goofing around sometimes; most of the time, I'm quiet and ignoring everybody.

Ms. N: Yes, and I am sure that [if people were listening] to the tape [they would] notice how calm Jack's voice is now. Jack, do you think that the school rules here have helped you and help the [other] students?

J: Yeah, a lot of the school rules that I don't usually remember. . . . I get reminded now and then when I'm not really paying attention. Like, one of the rules is that you have to be safe. Staff, behavior staff, and everybody, they always try to keep other kids safe and themselves safe. If some kids are getting too aggressive, they try to calm them down. If they are too out of control, they try to restrain them. We have a locked time out with magnetic seal door, but it's for our own safety. A lot of kids don't really like it that much because it's kinda closed in, but it's always for their safety.

Ms. N: It's been a long time since you've been there. Is that right?

J: Yep.

Ms. N: Congratulations to you! Do you think it's a good idea to give students choices during the day?

J: Yeah. They like choices, but at public school we usually don't have that very many. When we do get choices at public schools, it's not the ones we like. It's kinda complicated to decide. Like, here we get enough choices so we know what to do, and a lot of the kids here always make the good decision.

Ms. N: Having choices, has that helped you improve on your behaviors—and, if so, why?

J: Yes, it does. A lot of the choices we have help us get started. When we don't make good ones, it pulls us back, but we just keep going on along the road.

Ms. N: Is school a happy, comfortable place for you? Does it feel good to be here?

J: Yeah. It's friendly people all over. A lot of time in my classroom, people want to come here because of school. Well, kids don't like school. You take a survey throughout the whole United States or the world: Half the kids or most of the kids, they say they don't really like it because it is taking up their time. You see Bill Gates and the people that make the rates by investing. We learn how to do that stuff in school. It helps us make those decisions on what to do and where to go.

Ms. N: Staff at Phillips say that they never, ever give up on students. Can you remember examples when that was true for you?

J: When I first came here, I was used to just lying around, relaxing, not doing work and stuff. The school I went to before this one, they actually gave you too many choices there. You always have a certain amount of choices, wherever you go. You can take the choice that you want. Sometimes I have a choice about doing the work or not. When I chose to do whatever I want, I kept on taking that choice actually, I got all lazy, thinking I don't have to do all this. I wasn't in the mood, but people never gave up on me because they never wanted to see me fail or anything.

Ms. N: I'm glad you feel that way. It makes us pleased to see your progress. Now we're at the last question, Jack. Is there anything else you'd like to say to the people who are going to read this book learning to become special ed. teachers?

J: When the kids give you suggestions on what to do, like projects, here we always have ideas to give the teachers and some teachers take them. Try to figure out a way to bind all the ideas and get the kids to like one. Don't always make the work boring. Have a writing assignment, do something creative. Like, I don't like writing a lot, so the teachers always make a deal with me to try out what I mean. Have contests. If you want to help a kid out, try to motivate him. Always ask what they would like to do, and then try to work out a deal with them. The best part in this school is that they always make deals with you. Never give up on ideas that would help the class. Always keep on giving ideas to the kids and let the kids give ideas to you. Never crush good ideas.

›› QUESTIONS FOR FURTHER REFLECTION

1. How would you argue with someone who insisted that overt conduct disorder is not an emotional disturbance but an indication of social maladjustment that should not be included in special education?
2. What level of aggression or violence, if any, would you argue justifies removal of a student from a regular classroom or from a typical neighborhood school?
3. What are the things you can do as a teacher to keep acting-out, aggressive behavior in your classroom to a minimum, and how are these related to cultural diversity?

CHAPTER THIRTEEN

CONDUCT DISORDER

COVERT ANTISOCIAL BEHAVIOR

As you read this chapter, keep these guiding questions in mind:

- If we conceptualize overt and covert anti-social behavior as different ends of a single dimension or continuum, what type of behavior is shared by both?

- What type of prevention programs are particularly relevant for children with covert antisocial behavior?

- What special problems does one encounter in assessing covert antisocial behavior?

- What guidelines for management of theft should school personnel follow?

- How do successful programs to decrease school vandalism differ from the usual response to increased violence and destructiveness in schools?

DEFINITION AND PREVALENCE OF COVERT ANTISOCIAL BEHAVIOR

As we saw in chapter 12, antisocial behavior may involve overt acts, such as physical and verbal aggression; covert acts, such as stealing, lying, and fire setting; or both overt and covert forms of disordered conduct. Covert antisocial behavior includes untrustworthiness and manipulation of others, running away, and concealment of one's acts. Loeber and Schmaling (1985a) suggested that overt and covert antisocial behavior may represent different ends of a single behavioral dimension, with non-compliance—sassy, negative, persistent disobedience—as the most common or key-stone characteristic of both extremes (see also Loeber et al., 1993; Loeber, Farrington, Stouthamer-Loeber, & Van Kammen, 1998a, 1998b; Patterson, Reid, & Dishion, 1992, and the case of George in the accompanying case book).

Awareness of different forms of conduct disorder has existed for decades, but re-liable empirical evidence of the different forms emerged from large-scale studies since the 1980s (Eddy, Reid, & Curry, 2002; Loeber & Schmaling, 1985a, 1985b; Quay 1986b). These studies are based on statistical probabilities. Thus, a particular child is not necessarily characterized by behavior at one end of the continuum (overt or covert antisocial behavior). As noted in chapter 12, some children are versatile in their antisocial conduct, showing both overt and covert forms. Youngsters who show versatile antisocial behavior generally have more and more severe problems, and their prognosis is usually poorer compared to those who exhibit only one type of an-tisocial behavior (Kazdin, 1998, 2001; Loeber & Schmaling, 1985a; Loeber et al., 1993, 1998a). Versatility is a matter of degree; some individuals are much more versatile or exclusive in their antisocial conduct than others are. Conduct disorder of both types is often difficult to distinguish from other disorders, especially juvenile delinquency. In fact, the socialized (covert) form typically involves delinquent activities, often with bad companions or gangs and often involving alcohol or other drug use. *Delinquency* is a legal term, however, and connotes behavior that is the topic of chapter 14. The focus of this chapter is other covert antisocial behavior problems.

Conduct disorder is one of the most common and serious behavioral problems of children and youth, with prevalence estimates ranging from 4 to 10% of the child population. The prevalence of each subtype of conduct disorder has not been esti-mated precisely. Robins (1986) indicated that conduct disorders are on the increase for both boys and girls, but boys and girls have tended to exhibit somewhat different patterns of antisocial misconduct (see Talbott & Thiede, 1999; Talbott, Celinska, Simpson, & Coe, 2002).

In Robins's research, relatively more "masculine" antisocial behaviors included van-dalism, fighting, and stealing, whereas lying, running away, and substance abuse were typed as more "feminine." Four school-related problems (truancy, expulsion, under-achievement, and discipline) clustered together for both males and females. Vandalism, lying, and stealing clustered together for girls but not for boys (Robins, 1986); that is, girls who vandalized, lied, or stole tended to do all three, whereas boys tended to per-form antisocial acts in different patterns (vandalism with fighting and substance abuse, lying with truancy and underachievement, and stealing with running away).

More recently, others have found differing patterns of antisocial behavior among samples of boys and girls (e.g., Farmer, Rodkin, Pearl, & Van Acker, 1999; Talbott & Callahan, 1997; Talbott & Thiede, 1999). Talbott and Callahan (1997) noted that measurement, prediction, and comorbidity are the critical issues in studying the antisocial behavior of girls. Moreover, "it appears that the aggressive and disruptive behavior of girls is both similar and different from that of boys, depending on the developmental period during which it is measured" (Talbott & Callahan, 1997, p. 307). Much remains to be learned about gender differences in antisocial conduct, particularly the way in which biological and social factors influence the developmental course of antisocial behavioral patterns of boys and girls.

CAUSAL FACTORS AND PREVENTION

In general, the same causal factors that we saw in chapter 12 seem to underlie covert aggression and aggressive antisocial conduct, and many of these factors influence both boys and girls in very similar ways (see Eddy et al., 2002). The contextual variables and determinants found by Patterson et al. (1992) are shown in Figure 13.1. The personal, family, and social contexts are the background for poor behavior management skills of the parents, who are unskilled in monitoring and disciplining their children and fail to use positive reinforcement and problem solving in family interactions. The outcome is social incompetence and antisocial behavior of the child. To be sure, this parental inadequacy in child rearing is not always the cause of antisocial behavior, either overt or covert. However, it is characteristic of the environments of the great majority of children and youth who exhibit antisocial behavior.

In some studies comparing overt to covert antisocial children, families of those who exhibited covert antisocial behavior are characterized by lower rates of aversive, coercive behavior on the part of parents and children and less supervision or monitoring on the part of parents. Other studies, however, have found no differences

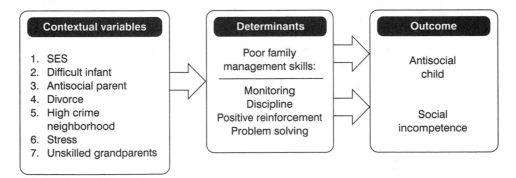

Figure 13.1
The effect of context on child adjustment
Source: From *Antisocial Boys* by Gerald R. Patterson, John B. Reid, and Thomas J. Dishion. © 1992 by Castalia Publishing Company. Reprinted by permission.

between overtly and covertly antisocial youngsters on family process variables such as parental rejection. A fairly consistent finding is that youngsters with versatile antisocial behavior come from the most disturbed families in which child-rearing practices are the most inadequate (Loeber & Schmaling, 1985a; Patterson et al., 1992).

Prevention of covert antisocial behavior in many ways parallels prevention of overt aggression. Character training or moral education seems particularly relevant to the prevention of stealing, lying, vandalism, and so on. The effects of typical moral and character education, however, have been nil or very slight. Moral behavior often does not match moral judgment. Children and youth, as well as adults, often do wrong even though they know what is right. Moral behavior tends to be controlled at least as much by situational factors as by moral or character traits; youngsters are honest or altruistic at some times and in some situations but not in others (Walker, de Vries, & Trevethan, 1987). Teachers' talk about classroom conventions, procedures, and moral issues has little effect on children's reasoning about morals. For schools to have much influence in teaching prosocial values, they must develop coherent and pervasive programs of character education that include discussion, role playing, and social-skills training to help students recognize moral dilemmas, adopt moral values, and select moral behavioral alternatives. This training may be particularly important for students with emotional or behavioral disorders (Walker, Ramsey, & Gresham, 2004).

ASSESSMENT

As with prevention, assessment of covert antisocial conduct disorder seems to parallel assessment of overt aggression. A particularly difficult problem, however, is direct observation of behavior; the behavior is, by definition, not usually observed firsthand by educators or other responsible adults. Often, the antisocial deed is not discovered until long after it is committed, and even then there may be doubts as to who was responsible. Although extremely serious, the behavior may occur at a relatively low rate compared to overt acts of aggression. This means that comparison of baseline rates to treatment may require lengthy evaluation. Assessment can therefore involve long periods of observation, and research may employ self-reports of acts such as stealing, lying, truancy, and vandalism. Laboratory assessment suggests that covert antisocial behavior, including stealing and property destruction as opposed to overt physical and verbal aggression, distinguishes specific subgroups of children with emotional and behavioral disorders (Hinshaw, Simmel, & Heller, 1995).

INTERVENTION AND EDUCATION

Because of similarities in the nature and causes of the problems, intervention and education in overt and covert forms of conduct disorder share many features, but they also have important differences (cf. Eddy et al., 2002; Loeber et al., 1998a, 1998b;

Walker et al., 2004). Consequently, the particular problems as well as the approaches to intervention may differ somewhat for specific types of covert antisocial acts. Families of children who steal, more often than families of aggressive children who do not steal, are extremely difficult treatment targets (Patterson, 1982; Patterson et al., 1992). Sometimes family therapy or parent discipline training is simply unfeasible or ineffective. Vandalism is often a particular problem in schools, and some intervention programs may therefore be primarily school based. Fire setting may be only tangentially related to school programs, but schools may be targets of arson by students with academic difficulties. Truancy is by definition an educational problem, although it is associated with delinquency, and programs to encourage school attendance may involve both the school and other community agencies.

Stealing

A common behavior problem that parents of young children report is that they do not recognize and respect the property rights of others. Many young children simply take what they want when they see it, without regard for ownership; in short, they steal. If this behavior persists beyond the age of 5 or 6, the child may become known as a stealer and get into trouble with peers and adults. The most useful analyses of the origins and management of stealing come from a behavioral or social learning perspective (Eddy et al., 2002; McMahon & Wells, 1998; Miller & Prinz, 1991; Sprick & Howard, 1995).

Reid and Patterson and their associates (see Eddy et al., 2002; Loeber et al., 1993; Moore, Chamberlain, & Mukai, 1979; Patterson, 1982; Patterson, Reid, Jones, & Conger, 1975; Reid & Hendricks, 1973; Reid & Patterson, 1976) have systematically researched the characteristics and behavior modification of aggressive children who steal. These generalizations have emerged:

- Stealers exhibit lower rates of observable out-of-control (negative–coercive and antisocial) behavior than do aggressive children who do not steal.
- Families of stealers demonstrate lower rates of both positive–friendly and negative–coercive behaviors than do families of aggressive children who do not steal.
- The differences in positive–friendly and negative–coercive behavior rates are almost completely because of the mothers' behavior.

Many stealers appear to exhibit high rates of antisocial behavior only away from home or at home when no observers are present. Many stealers are likely to confine their antisocial behavior to settings outside the home, disturbing the community rather than their parents by their theft and leaving their parents with little motivation to work on the problem. Parents of stealers tend to blame the stealing on someone else, thus refusing to recognize the problem and failing to follow through on intervention plans (see Eddy et al., 2002; Patterson, 1982; Patterson et al., 1975; Reid & Patterson, 1976).

Families of stealers appear to be loosely structured and characterized by lack of parental supervision or emotional attachment to the children (Patterson, 1982; Reid & Patterson, 1976). The stealer may, therefore, learn that taking others' possessions is acceptable behavior, that no one will care what he or she takes, and that no adverse consequences will follow theft. The child who learns to steal may be motivated to seek stimulation and reinforcement outside the family.

Despite the difficult and destructive family interaction patterns of stealers, relatively successful behavioral interventions have been devised. Patterson et al. (1975) believed that a behavioral antistealing program has several essential components. Before instituting the actual antistealing program, however, one must resolve a fundamental problem: parental definition of stealing. Parents of stealers are usually hesitant to accuse the child of theft and are loath to take disciplinary action. Because they are unlikely to observe the child in the act of taking something, the parents feel obliged to accept their child's explanation for how something came into his or her possession. Many parents blindly accept the child's claims of finding, borrowing, trading, winning, or receiving as payment whatever item was stolen. When their child is accused by teachers, peers, or police, parents of stealers argue that the child is being unjustly attacked. By blaming others—making it somebody else's problem—the parents avoid having to deal with the problem themselves. Even when the behavior occurs at home, parents often do not adequately define *stealing*. Some parents consider it theft to take food from the refrigerator without specific permission, whereas others view all family possessions as common property. The value of an item is also an issue because many parents of stealers cannot bring themselves to apply consequences for stealing something they consider to be worth very little.

The first step in dealing with theft is to recognize that the child is in difficulty because he or she steals more than other children of the same age do, may steal valuable objects, and has been labeled by others as a thief. The antitheft strategy must include steps to help the child stop being accused of theft and being viewed with suspicion. The child will not lose the stigma associated with the label until he or she learns to avoid even the appearance of wrongdoing. Following is the recommended strategy of parents (see Patterson et al., 1975, 1992):

1. Agree to define *stealing* as the child's possession of anything that does not belong to him or her or taking anything he or she does not own.
2. Only the parents decide whether a theft has occurred. They may base their judgment on either their own observation or on the report of a reliable informant.
3. When it is determined that the child has stolen, the parents state that, according to the rules, the child has taken the item and then apply the consequences. The parents must not shame or counsel the child at the time they discover the theft and apply the consequences, but they are encouraged to discuss the theft with him or her at another time.
4. Every instance of stealing must receive consequences.
5. Parents are advised to keep their eyes open and ask about "new" property rather than use detective tactics such as searching the child's room or clothing.
6. Consequences for stealing are either a specified interval of useful work or a period of grounding or restriction. Stealing more expensive items receives more severe consequences. Harsh consequences, such as humiliation or beating, are prohibited.

7. No positive reinforcement is given for periods of nonstealing because it is impossible to know that successful covert stealing has not occurred.

8. The program should stay in effect for at least 6 months following the last episode of stealing.

If the child steals both at home and at school, parents and teachers must implement consistent antitheft programs in both environments (Williams, 1985). Effective and early management of stealing is particularly important; the younger the age at which children begin stealing and the longer they persist, the more likely they are to become chronic stealers and adjudicated delinquents (Loeber et al., 1993). In general, the more severe the conduct disorder, the less likely it is that intervention will be successful (Webster-Stratton & Dahl, 1995). Management of stealing at school can present legal problems, particularly with older students, and the school must avoid illegal searches and seizures.

Lying

Parents and teachers consistently rate lying as a serious problem behavior of childhood, yet there has been little research on the subject (see Mash & Barkley, 2003; Shinn, Walker, & Stoner, 2002). In fact, McMahon and Wells (1998) stated, "To our knowledge, there have been no reports of formalized interventions to deal with lying" (p. 159). This apparently remains the case.

Developmental changes clearly occur in the understanding of lies and liars, but the relationship of these changes to the development of pathological lying is not understood. Apparently, children often lie in attempts to escape punishment. Adults consider lying a serious problem not only because it is an attempt at concealment but also because it is associated with other antisocial behaviors such as stealing and truancy. In the classroom, lying and cheating are functionally similar behaviors.

As one might expect, lying is related to the same sort of family process variables, especially lack of parental monitoring or supervision, that characterize stealing (Stouthamer-Loeber & Loeber, 1986). Although lying is a serious problem and may be a stepping-stone to the development of other conduct problems (Loeber et al., 1993), only a small body of research is available to guide intervention. However, "the cornerstone of effective management of honest behavior is the monitoring of work in progress and its subsequent verbal and written products to accurately identify occurrences of lying and cheating" (Stokes & Osnes, 1991, p. 619). In addition to careful monitoring, providing reinforcement for honest behavior and punishment of lying and cheating is necessary. It is important to determine whether the student can discriminate truth from nontruth, to find the probable reason for the student's telling untruths (e.g., to avoid consequences or work), and to avoid getting caught up in arguments about the veracity of what the student has said (see Sprick & Howard, 1995).

Fire Setting

The fires that children set frequently cause injury, loss of life, and property damage. In fact, youthful arsonists account for more than half of all set fires. Although fire setting has been a behavior of scientific interest for more than 150 years (Wooden & Berkey, 1984), we still do not understand very well the causes and management of this behavior in children (Kolko, 2002). Fanciful psychodynamic explanations that connect fire setting to sexual excitement have only recently begun to give way to conceptualizations grounded in reliable empirical evidence. Kolko and Kazdin (1986) proposed a social learning model for conceptualizing risk factors of fire play and fire setting that consists of three primary factors: learning experiences and cues, personal repertoires (cognitive, behavioral, and motivational), and parent and family influences and stressors. Kolko and Kazdin noted that children learn attitudes and behaviors from early experiences, such as watching parents or older siblings working or playing with fire. Children of fire fighters, furnace stokers, smokers, and adults who otherwise model behavior dealing with fire may be more likely to set fires.

We see interest in fire and playing with fire in a high percentage of young children. The ready availability of incendiary materials to children who are interested in fire and observe models who set or manage fires may set the stage for fire setting. Another major factor, however, is the personal repertoires that may heighten the risk of fire setting. Children may be more likely to set fires if any of the following are true:

- They do not understand the danger of fire or the importance of fire safety.
- They do not have the necessary social skills to obtain gratification in appropriate ways.
- They engage in other antisocial behaviors.
- They are motivated by anger and revenge.

Finally, stressful life events; parental psychopathology; and lack of parental supervision, monitoring, and involvement can increase the chances that a child will set fires (see Kolko, 2002; Kolko & Kazdin, 1989). Although research does not clearly distinguish different types of fire setters, all fires obviously are not set under the same conditions or for the same reasons. Some fires are set accidentally by children playing with matches or lighters, some by angry children who are seeking revenge but do not understand the awful consequences, others by delinquents who know full well the consequences of arson and are seeking to conceal another crime they have committed, some in response to deviant peer pressure, some in attempts to injure the fire setters themselves, and still others by youngsters whose behavior is related to anxiety and obsessions or compulsions.

Most school-aged youngsters who set fires have a history of school failure and multiple behavioral problems. Schools are sometimes their targets, so educators are among those who have an interest in identifying and treating fire setters. At this point, however, we can make few research-based recommendations for intervention or prevention. Both intervention and prevention will probably require efforts similar to those suggested for managing other covert antisocial behaviors such as stealing, vandalism, and truancy (McMahon & Wells, 1998). However, educators may have a unique role to play in finding out about the motivations and behavior of fire setters and finding interventions that work (Pinsonneault, Richardson, & Pinsonneault, 2002).

Vandalism

Deliberate destruction of school property costs hundreds of millions of dollars each year, and vandalism in other community settings results in much higher costs. Destructiveness and violence against people are often linked, and both are on the increase (Mayer & Sulzer-Azaroff, 2002; Walker et al., 2004). It appears to increase dramatically in antisocial boys after age 7 and to peak in the middle school years. The typical response of school administrators and justice officials to violence and vandalism is to tighten security measures and provide harsher punishment. Unfortunately, punitive measures may only aggravate the problems.

Vandalism in schools appears to be, at least in part, a response to aversive environments. More specifically, students tend to be disruptive and destructive when school rules are vague, discipline is punitive, punishment is rigidly applied regardless of students' individual differences, relationships between students and school personnel are impersonal, the school curriculum is mismatched with students' interests and abilities, and students receive little recognition for appropriate conduct or achievement. Decreasing the aversiveness of the school environment by adjusting school rules, teachers' expectations, and consequences for desirable and undesirable behavior might be more effective in preventing vandalism than will increasing security and making punishment more severe (see Mayer & Sulzer-Azaroff, 1991, 2002; Sprick & Howard, 1995; Walker et al., 2004).

Truancy

Truancy becomes a greater problem in higher grades, and it is a major factor in school failure and delinquency (see Loeber et al., 1998a). Attendance at school certainly does not guarantee academic success, but chronic unexcused absence virtually assures failure. Frequent truancy is serious not only because of probable school failure but because chronic truants are at risk for later unemployment or employment failure, criminal convictions, substance abuse, and a variety of other difficulties. Dissatisfaction with school programs and failure to attend school regularly are important signals that the student may drop out (Edgar & Siegel, 1995; Walker et al., 2004).

The problem of truancy is not new, and neither are the most effective approaches to reducing it. Interventions based on social learning principles continue to produce better results than do other approaches (see Kerr & Nelson, 2002; Walker et al., 2004). These interventions are intended to make school more attractive by recognizing and praising attendance, setting up systems in which attendance earns special rewards or privileges, giving the student work that is more interesting to him or her and at which he or she can be successful, connecting school and work or later education that is important to the student, stopping harassment by peers or other social punishment in school, and, if possible, decreasing the satisfaction or fun the student has outside of school during school hours. It is often necessary to have the cooperation of the student's parents to make school more attractive and alternatives less attractive.

SUMMARY

Covert antisocial behavior consists of acts such as stealing, lying, fire setting, vandalism, and truancy. Overt and covert antisocial behavior may represent different ends of a continuum, with noncompliance as the keystone behavior or common origin of both extremes.

Researchers note sex differences in antisocial behavior. Vandalism, fighting, and stealing are typed as "masculine," whereas lying, substance abuse, and running away are considered "feminine." Four school-related problems (truancy, expulsion, underachievement, and discipline) characterize both boys and girls with conduct disorders.

In general, the same types of causal factors seem to underlie overt and covert forms of conduct disorder. Some studies indicate, however, that families of youngsters who steal and exhibit other covert forms of antisocial behavior are characterized by lower rates of aversive, coercive behavior and lower rates of parental supervision and monitoring.

Because the acts are usually unobserved and are performed at relatively low rates, assessment of covert antisocial conduct disorder presents special problems and often involves self-reports in addition to other measures. Intervention and education for youngsters with covert antisocial problems are similar to those for overt aggression but are more complicated because covert acts are harder to detect and the consequences often cannot be applied immediately and consistently. Specific covert behaviors may thus require special treatment.

Families of stealers differ from families of aggressive youngsters who do not steal, showing less parental supervision and involvement with children. Intervention in families of stealers is often particularly difficult because the parents do not recognize or want to be bothered with the problem. Effective management of stealing includes careful supervision of the child and consistent, appropriate punishment of all instances of stealing. Theft-management procedures in schools parallel those in families.

Lying is considered a major child behavior problem because it is often part of other covert antisocial behavior. There is little research on lying and few guidelines for handling it. Fire setting is a dangerous problem among children and youth.

There is little understanding of the causes of fire-setting behavior and little research for managing it. A social learning model suggests that early learning experiences, personal repertoires (cognitive, behavioral, and motivational), and parent and family influences and stressors may put children at risk for fire setting.

Violence and destructiveness in schools are typically met by tightening security measures and applying more punitive discipline, but these measures may be counterproductive. Vandalism may represent a response to an aversive school environment. Programs to make the school environment less aversive for students by increasing positive attention to appropriate conduct, making the school curriculum more relevant, and improving school discipline practices have dramatically reduced school vandalism and truancy.

Chronic truancy virtually ensures school failure and is associated with a variety of negative outcomes in adulthood. Behavioral interventions that make school attendance more rewarding and nonattendance less attractive have been successful with many truants.

>> PERSONAL REFLECTIONS

Covert Conduct Disorder

Suzanne Newsom, M.Ed., plans professional development for special education and general education teachers in the Charlotte–Mecklenburg Schools in North Carolina. She has also been a teacher of English and drama as well as a teacher of students with severe emotional and behavioral disorders in a self-contained classroom.

Describe the school in which you teach and your particular role in the school.

Morgan School is a separate public school in the Charlotte–Mecklenburg school system, the 23rd largest system in the nation. Our students come to us in two ways. Some have been placed on a regular campus in a self-contained classroom but were still unsuccessful educationally. Others have been in secure facilities, such as training schools or psychiatric hospitals, and are reentering the public school system with the support that a small school such as Morgan can give them. Morgan's entire staff is trained to help students in crisis. Three time-out rooms are available, with a full-time crisis manager who provides guidance to students there. Each class consists of eight students with a teacher and a teaching associate. All students at Morgan manage their behavior with the help of a level system. Each class also has its own unique ways of reinforcing behavior in addition to the level system. Students remain at Morgan until they have learned appropriate behaviors that will not interfere with their learning on a regular campus.

My role as a teacher at Morgan centered around planning instruction for these students with severe behavioral and emotional disabilities. Whenever possible, I integrated lessons around central themes and imbedded social skills instruction throughout the day to support the direct instruction of social skills that occurred as a separate class. Some of my best times as a classroom teacher occurred out of the classroom. By this I mean that through experiential learning on field trips my students were engaged and motivated. Social skills were always a part of our field trip lessons. My teaching associate, Jerry Hosey, provided support in these endeavors.

Think of a particular student with a covert conduct disorder. How does this student manifest the disorder?

Billy was a student in my class for 2 years while he was in the sixth and seventh grades. In his time there and in his prior school setting, Billy developed a reputation for stealing, lying, and cheating. The items he stole were of little monetary value but of definite necessity in class: office supplies, lunch money, manipulatives for math instruction or science lab, the knob to turn the radiator on and off. He was even suspected of stealing the keys to the resource police officer's cruiser. Although the keys were never found in Billy's physical vicinity, they were discovered on the school grounds soon after he ran away from the building when confronted about the missing keys. Billy was also caught stealing small snacks in the school cafeteria when he most likely had the money to pay for them himself.

Although we knew Billy was stealing these items, it was very difficult to catch him in the act. He wore oversized clothing every day and could have played the role of the Artful Dodger in *Oliver Twist* because of his pickpocketing skills. Finally, one day in a small computer lab away from our classroom, the principal, David Kimmelman, observed Billy deftly disconnect a brand new mouse from a brand new computer system. He put it in his pocket. Soon after, the principal called Billy out of class to speak with him and the resource officer. Billy was asked to empty his pockets and could not move the stolen goods to a new hiding place quickly enough to avoid being caught. (We often suspected that Billy hid things in his underwear.) The principal chose to press charges. That way, Billy could experience real-life consequences when he went to court. The value of the computer mouse easily facilitated charging Billy with stealing school property, as did having the resource officer available as a witness.

What procedures have you found most useful in working with this student?

Providing a structured environment was very important. Keeping an inventory of class belongings and items in manipulative kits can help students with covert conduct disorders know that you intend to keep class materials organized. Anecdotal records can also provide insight into classroom behavior of students with covert antisocial behavior. After reflecting on these records, one may notice a pattern of behavior that would have gone unnoticed, even from an insider's perspective without the records.

In addition to keeping the physical aspects of the classroom organized, engaging but structured lessons are important, too. When students are involved in their learning, there is less time for covert, off-task behaviors. I always felt like I was teaching the students how to learn before I could teach them subjects required by the curriculum. Part of learning how to learn is adapting behaviors or exchanging less productive behaviors for productive ones. Shaping the behavior of a student with covert conduct disorders is easier if the class members realize that their own personal behaviors reinforce the covert behavior of their peer. For example, although it is important that students tell the teaching staff when something has been stolen from them, keeping this as low key as possible can make the act of stealing less entertaining for the thief.

Communication with home is vital. Without parental support, it is very difficult to confront covert students. Their behaviors are less obvious but can be just as disruptive to the climate of a class. Parental support can reduce the lies told by students with covert disorders. How do you get this support? My suggestion is that you make positive calls to each parent early in the school year before you are forced to make a negative one. A weekly class newsletter with updates on what is happening in the class and school, including how parents can choose to be involved, promotes communication. Find a way to reward students who deliver the newsletter to their parents or guardians. This establishes a strong, positive rapport.

What do you see as the prospects for this student's educational progress in the coming year?

I see Billy's educational progress in the image of a double helix (like the structure of DNA). His covert behaviors—lying and stealing—are intertwined with a second strand of problems—task avoidance. Billy is a very intelligent student who struggles to begin assignments. Once he begins them, completing them is not likely to be a problem. As Billy makes progress behaviorally, he makes progress academically. But in the spiral of intertwined problems, the same territory is covered again and again, albeit at a higher level.

I believe that covert patterns of behavior are especially difficult to break. As a result of Billy's court involvement stemming from the charges pressed by the principal, he is now on probation. His teacher reports that the stealing has decreased, although it has not stopped altogether. Billy reports that he absolutely no longer steals but that whenever anything "gets missing" everybody automatically blames him. Although Billy may have decreased his stealing at school, he may have increased his stealing in the community in the form of shoplifting. This I do know: Billy takes his probation seriously, a fact he alludes in the following interview. Once probation is lifted, I hope he continues on the same path. It does concern me that everyone sees Billy as a thief and treats him as such, with lack of trust being a logical long-term consequence. However, I hope that Billy does not become frustrated and revert to behaving like the thief he is believed to be. With carefully planned social skill instruction, Billy could learn ways in which to earn his classmates' trust. An issue of great concern is the increase in Billy's acting-out behaviors. He has been party to a number of fights this year.

What do you see as the biggest long-term problems this student will face?

Billy has the intelligence to do well in school. However, if he cannot find the motivation in himself to complete school, he will drop out. In his interview, he says he just doesn't really care. He can name interventions that have been put in place for him. He can name people who care about him. But Billy realizes that his future belongs to him. When I asked if he would like to go to college, Billy said he would do that to please his mother and that if he does not attend college he will be on his own. He also referred to a family pattern of dropping out of school, as if it may happen to him.

Another long-term problem Billy may face is keeping a job. Without intrinsic motivation, Billy may transfer that classroom task-avoidant behavior to a job site, where he may be fired for poor job performance.

I think that Billy will continue to have difficulty establishing relationships with peers and authority figures. Before people have a chance to connect on some level with Billy, he will demonstrate some kind of behavior that pushes them away. In his adult life, Billy may be someone who always feels that he is on the outside looking in as a result of these poor interpersonal skills.

Suzanne Newsom Interviews Billy

Ms. N: Picture this: There is a new teacher, and she's really young, like 22 years old, and she knows that hands-on activities are great, but when she does them, students start throwing materials and hiding them. What should she do?

B: Give them a consequence, make rules. Make them understand them before they put their hands on them.

Ms. N: Remember those Legos that went out the window when I was absent?

B: Oh [smiling] yeah.

Ms. N: Who threw those out the window?

B: [smiling] I don't know.

Ms. N: If you were teaching students like you, how would you show you care?

B: Just be real involved, and you could, like, do a lot of one to one.

Ms. N: What about field trips; do they help you learn?

B: Oh, yeah, they make it fun.

Ms. N: Do field trips motivate you to behave so that you can go on them?

B: Oh, yeah.

Ms. N: If you were managing behavior in a class, what is the best way to do that?

B: Tell people not to lose their temper because the kids are mean. The kids curse and call you names.

Ms. N: What could happen if the teacher loses his temper?

B: He could get in trouble and lose his job.

Ms. N: Talk about the effect on students, not on teachers.

B: Then students lose their temper, then you got a whole lot of anger in the room. Everybody gets hyped up, and they end up in time out.

Ms. N: How do you feel about suspension?

B: I don't think you should throw a kid out of school because that just adds to the problem. We should have in-school suspension here.

Ms. N: Do you think your intelligence is valued in the classroom?

B: No.

Ms. N: How can teachers get you to show your intelligence?

B: Having work and doing it.

Ms. N: What kind of work?

B: I don't know.

Ms. N: So you don't feel like you have work, or do you just choose not to do it?

B: I don't do it.

Ms. N: So it all goes back to your motivation?

B: Yeah, I guess.

Ms. N: Do you know what would motivate you?

B: No.

Ms. N: What kinds of things have been tried?

B: A level system.

Ms. N: What has your mom tried?

B: Giving and taking away privileges.

Ms. N: Did that work?

B: Yeah, for a little while.

Ms. N: Why did it stop working?

B: I just don't really care.

Ms. N: If you designed a level system, what would you put in it?

B: Rewards, like being able to have time to yourself and free time with other students. You need a break from work. Being able to play computer games, buying stuff in the school store, candy.

Ms. N: Do you know what it means to be discouraged?

B: Um-hm, like somebody gets on your nerves?

Ms. N: Or if you're doing some schoolwork and you think, "I just can't do this" or "I don't understand this," how do people help you?

B: Sometimes a student will help, and the teacher, but sometimes she won't help me.

Ms. N: Think about all of the different learning activities we did. What helped you learn the most?

B: Just, like when I would sit down and do it, that's when it would come into my head.

Ms. N: What kinds of things made you want to sit down and *do*? When you got to move stuff with your hands, a video, using a textbook, cooking, taking notes?

B: Really, it could have been anything as long as I was ready to do work, 'cause a lot of times, I just wouldn't do any work.

Ms. N: So you feel like it related more to motivation, it didn't matter what the activity was, you were motivated. Well, what motivates you to learn?

B: I don't know, just if I'm not . . . um . . . bored, I guess.

Ms. N: If you're not bored by the assignment?

B: Um-hm.

Ms. N: What makes an assignment interesting? That's what teachers really need to know.

B: If, like, I just feel like doing work, I'll do it. At the end of last year, I just didn't want to. It doesn't matter what they give me.

Ms. N: Do you like a choice in work?

B: Yeah, 'cause if you understand one assignment but not the other one, you can pick what you understand. It represents you better.

Ms. N: If you were teaching students like you, how would you do it?

B: I would just get stuff that was active instead of writing all of the time, a lot of hands-on activities.

Ms. N: What helped you stop your sneaky behavior?

B: The personal goal on the level sheet, refrain from appearing to steal and getting in trouble with the law.

Ms. N: Tell me more about the law.

B: It's no fun to be on probation. You can't do anything, or they might send you away.

Ms. N: So what kinds of things can get you suspended?

B: Fights, having stuff you're not supposed to have, like when you get searched.

Ms. N: Can you get suspended for stealing?

B: I don't know because I haven't seen it.

Ms. N: Do you feel like you still have that reputation?

B: [long silence] Yeah.

Ms. N: What about earlier today, when I couldn't find my purse? What were you thinking about then? Were you thinking about your reputation?

B: I thought it was in your car and somebody just took it.

Ms. N: You weren't worried that someone would say, "She had it before, and she was with Billy, and she thought she had it and then she couldn't find it"? Did that go through your head?

B: It crossed my mind, yeah.

Ms. N: Did it really?

B: [Nods head yes]

Ms. N: So it's hard for you to shake that reputation on yourself. Well, why did you do things like steal?

B: I don't know. Just for laughs, I guess. At first I thought it was fun, but then I got a reputation, and people always accused me of stealing when I didn't.

Ms. N: So you did it for laughs. Did it make you laugh? Was there any other value that you got out of it?

B: It made other people laugh, and sometimes they'd ask me to take stuff, and sometimes . . . um, they said they'd pay me to take stuff.

Ms. N: Did you ever get paid to take stuff?

B: No, 'cause usually, I'd just be, like, "Okay" and then never do it.

[Ms. N tries to get B to talk more about this, but he quits responding.]

Ms. N: Let's move on to something else. If you get discouraged at school about something that you are doing, about your assignments or being with other people at school, what happens? How do students handle it, and how does staff handle it?

B: Huh?

Ms. N: Sneaky behavior could get you in real trouble. How?

B: Like, in the classroom I got into trouble with the teachers. And they put it on my point sheet, and one time I got in trouble and had to go to court.

Ms. N: Because of sneaky behavior?

B: [nods yes]

Ms. N: What do you do to help other students here feel like they belong here, that this is an okay place to be?

B: Like, greet them and stuff like that. Say, "Hey," make them feel like nobody is gonna mess with them.

Ms. N: If you are a new student here, what kinds of things do you need to know about right away?

B: Like, if somebody messes with you, 'cause it's a lot of bullies at this school, you should just tell a staff when that happens.

Ms. N: So why are you here at Morgan School?

B: A lot of fights, messing with staff and students.

Ms. N: You weren't sent here because of sneaky stuff?

B: Not really, because at my old school, the only sneaky stuff I did was take locks off of lockers.

Ms. N: You never took any materials or things from other students, never told lies?

B: Well, sometimes I'd get in trouble for taking the answer book home to do my homework.

Ms. N: You wouldn't walk around and try to take everyone's pen or pencil off of their desks?

B: No!

Ms. N: I see you are smiling about that. So that was before you came here. When I was your teacher, there were sneaky things that you did in class, and there were things you did that even I was not aware of, so tell me about those things. You can't get in trouble about those things now. What were those things?

B: Like going through y'alls' desks and taking all kinds of pens and stuff like that. But sometimes it would get me in trouble, and I would have to stop because I got a reputation, and people always think I am trying to take stuff.

Ms. N: Why are students searched?

B: For safety, to make sure they didn't bring a gun.

Ms. N: Do you feel safer here than at a regular school?

B: They are probably the same because now at other schools they do locker searches and all that. They have a resource officer.

Ms. N: Tell me about times when you felt like you belonged at Morgan.

B: Getting into fights and having to be put in the TO [time-out] room.

Ms. N: Do you feel like you have friends at Morgan?

B: Yeah, sometimes, not a lot.

Ms. N: How do you know when you have a friend at Morgan?

B: If they, like, take up for you and don't, like, . . . um, get into fights with you and all that.

Ms. N: How do you know when a teacher really cares about you?

B: If they are real involved.

Ms. N: Can you give me an example?

B: Like, always trying to help you get out of trouble.

Ms. N: Can you be specific?

B: Sometimes when I want to go to TO, they sit down and talk to you and try to get a reason why you want to go to TO.

Ms. N: Describe your relationship with teachers at Morgan School.

B: Some good, and some bad.

Ms. N: What is a good relationship like?

B: Um . . . just a good relationship with the teacher.

Ms. N: How do you know that it is a good relationship?

B: If I like the teacher.

Ms. N: What makes you like the teacher?

B: If they respect the students and respect other teachers.

Ms. N: What about your relationship with the crisis manager, Mike Bragg?

B: It's okay.

Ms. N: What does the crisis manager do here?

B: He does the searches and supervises the time-out room.

Ms. N: When a student comes to time out, what's that like—the time-out room at Morgan?

B: It depends on if you cooperate and go into the time-out room, they won't shut the door and lock you in the little room. But if you don't, then you have to get restrained. That's bad.

Ms. N: When you are restrained, how does that feel?

B: It hurts.

Ms. N: Do you trust Mike Bragg?

B: With certain things.

Ms. N: Do you feel like he's looking out for your safety?

B: Sometimes.

Ms. N: Tell me about your life in 10 years. What is your life going to be like?

B: I hope I straighten up and get out, but it's hard, but a lot of people think it's easy, but it's hard. People try to get you off task. The teachers that try to help you, those are the ones I like, like you. But I didn't listen. I had a chance, but I didn't take it.

Ms. N: So at 23, you will be out of Morgan. Where will you live, where will you work? What about your transition plan? You don't want to cook, run a restaurant?

B: There's a lot of stuff. I don't see myself there.

Ms. N: What about a cop?

B: I've done too much bad stuff.

Ms. N: Do you think you'll go to college?

B: Probably, because if I don't I'll be on my own. My mom dropped out of high school and then tried to go back but it was hard. Then she ended up dropping out of college too. She told me it was hard. My grandma did that too, but not until her 40s.

Ms. N: So why do you want to go to college?

B: To please my mama.

Ms. N: What about 20 years from now?

B: I don't look at my future. I just look for what's around me now.

>> QUESTIONS FOR FURTHER REFLECTION

1. What legitimate (legal and appropriate) means can you use to assess a student's covert antisocial behavior?

2. Supposing that a student tells you of another student's covert antisocial behavior, what should you do?

3. What are the things you can do as a teacher to minimize covert antisocial behavior in your classroom?

CHAPTER FOURTEEN

PROBLEM BEHAVIORS OF ADOLESCENCE

DELINQUENCY, SUBSTANCE ABUSE, AND EARLY SEXUAL ACTIVITY

(Revised by Devery R. Mock)

As you read this chapter, keep these guiding questions in mind:

- What are the similarities and differences between conduct disorder and delinquency?

- What arguments support the view that most or all incarcerated youngsters have disabilities and need special education?

- What are the primary causes and prevention strategies related to substance abuse?

- What are the primary reasons for concern about early sexual activity?

- Which substances do children and youth most commonly abuse, and why are they not the focus of most concern about drugs?

In this chapter, we focus on delinquency, early sexual activity, and substance abuse because these particular problem behaviors often have been found to occur together. Bear in mind that the concept of adolescence continues to evolve, as do the definitions of problem behaviors associated with adolescence.

PROBLEM BEHAVIORS IN ADOLESCENCE AND EARLY ADULTHOOD

Juvenile delinquents rarely display only one isolated problem behavior. More often, they engage in a constellation of a number of interrelated problem behaviors, including delinquency, sexual precocity, and substance abuse (Jessor, 1998; Jessor, Van Den Bos, Vanderryn, Costa, & Turbin, 1995). These different problem behaviors tend to overlap with each other. That is, youngsters who are delinquent, abuse substances, and engage in early sexual behavior often participate in other antisocial activities and possess similar personality and contextual characteristics (Ensminger & Juon, 1998).

Most adolescents engage in some risky behaviors, but most stop short of serious involvement (e.g., drug addiction) and reduce the intensity of or stop such behaviors altogether by the time they are adults (Donovan & Jessor, 1985). Attention deficit–hyperactivity disorder (ADHD), lack of guilt, poor communication with parents, low achievement, and anxiety are all characteristics of adolescents who exhibit escalating levels of problem behavior that are likely to continue into adulthood (Chang, Chen, & Brownson, 2003; Chassin, Ritter, Trim, & King, 2003; Silbereisen, 1998). That is, adolescents with those characteristics are predicted to have the highest levels of problem behaviors. The presence of problem behaviors in adolescence is the strongest predictor of problem behaviors in adulthood (Brigham, Weiss, & Jones, 1998; Jessor, Donovan, & Costa, 1991).

Loeber, Farrington, Stouthamer-Loeber, and Van Kammen (1998a, 1998b) found that measures of eight forms of problem behaviors were all highly related to each other: delinquency, substance abuse, ADHD, conduct problems, physical aggression, covert behavior such as lying and manipulation, depressed mood, and shyness or being withdrawn. That is, high scores in one area of problem behavior were often accompanied by high scores in the other seven areas. Externalizing behaviors were more interrelated to each other than they were to internalizing behaviors so that physical aggression was strongly related to substance abuse but shyness and being withdrawn was not. Boys with high levels of problem behaviors were also characterized by high levels of delinquency, sexual precocity, and substance abuse. Forness, Kavale, and Walker (1999) suggested that such behaviors are often a symptom of more complex psychiatric disorders. Although many of these disorders are detected after a series of punitive interventions aimed at the most superficial aspects of the problem (Forness et al., 1999), researchers have been able to identify groups of variables that reliably predict the development of these complex disorders (Leech, Day, Richardson, & Goldschmidt, 2003). ADHD seems to put adolescents at particularly high risk for substance abuse problems (Flory, Milich, Lynam, Leukefeld, & Clayton, 2003).

Research supports the importance and plausibility of early identification. Although the remainder of this chapter is organized around different categories of problem behaviors, it is highly unlikely that any individual will display one and only one element of problem behavior. Problem behavior theory (Jessor & Jessor, 1977) and observations of comorbidity of problem behaviors with complex psychiatric disorders suggest that addressing only one or a few aspects of the problem behaviors described in this chapter will be of limited use. Rather, these problems are likely to respond only to more complex interventions that unite educational, mental health, and psychopharmocologic interventions (Forness et al., 1999).

JUVENILE DELINQUENCY

Definition and Prevalence

When someone who is not legally an adult (i.e., a juvenile) commits an act that could result in apprehension by police, he or she is said to have committed a *delinquent* act. Because many delinquent acts do not result in arrests, the extent of juvenile delinquency is difficult to determine. Some laws are vague or loosely worded so that *delinquency* is not clearly defined. Some acts are illegal if committed by a juvenile but not if they are committed by an adult (such as buying or drinking alcoholic beverages). Other delinquent acts are clearly criminal; they are considered morally wrong and punishable by law regardless of the age of the person who commits them (such as assault or murder; see cases in the accompanying case book). Many aggressive children's behavior just skirts legal delinquency. Much of the behavior of delinquents, including incarcerated youth and those at risk of incarceration, is irritating, threatening, or disruptive but not delinquent in a legal sense. Delinquent behavior may bring juveniles into contact with law enforcement.

It is important that we distinguish between delinquent behavior and official delinquency. Any act that has legal constraints on its occurrence may be considered delinquent behavior. Juveniles may commit *index crimes*—crimes that are illegal regardless of a person's age and that include the full range of criminal offenses, from misdemeanors to first-degree murder. Common index crimes committed by juveniles are vandalism, shoplifting, and various other forms of theft such as auto theft, armed robbery, and assault. Other illegal behavior may be against the law only because of the offender's age. Acts that are illegal only when committed by a minor are called *status offenses*. Status offenses include truancy, running away from home, buying or possessing alcoholic beverages, and sexual promiscuity. They also include a variety of ill-defined behaviors described by labels such as *incorrigible, unmanageable,* or *beyond parental control*. Status offenses are a grab-bag category that can be abused in determining whether or not a child is a juvenile delinquent; it is a category that encompasses serious misdeeds but that adult authorities can expand to include mere suspicion or the appearance of misconduct (Blackburn, 1993).

The differences between official delinquency and delinquent behavior are significant. Surveys in which children and adolescents report whether they engage in specific delinquent acts indicate that the vast majority (80 to 90%) have done so. Self-reports appear to be by far the best way to estimate the true extent of delinquent behavior (Siegel & Senna, 1994). Research studies have provided data indicating that self-reported delinquent behavior correlates positively with depressed mood (Beyers & Loeber, 2003) and negatively with parental awareness of child's delinquent behavior (Laird, Pettit, Bates, & Dodge, 2003). Only about 20% of all minors are at some time officially delinquent; in a given year, approximately 3% of all American children are adjudicated (Siegel & Senna, 1994). We find a disproportionate number of official delinquents among lower socioeconomic classes and ethnic minorities (Goldstein, 1991; Laub & Lauritsen, 1998; Leone, Walter, & Wolford, 1990; Loeber et al., 1998a).

Delinquent behavior, conduct disorder, and official delinquency are overlapping phenomena. Although data support a positive correlation between conduct disorder and delinquent behaviors (Vermeiren, Schwab-Stone, Ruchkin, DeClippele, & Deboutte, 2002), a youngster with conduct disorder of either the overt or covert variety may or may not engage in delinquent behavior and may or may not become an official delinquent.

Few delinquents begin their criminal behavior with extreme behaviors such as violent crime. Rather, they ease into their delinquency through a series of minor offenses. The earlier the series of behaviors begin, the more likely it is that the individual will eventually show more serious examples of problem behavior and violence. Therefore, educators must not be lulled into a sense of false security that a young misbehaving youngster will outgrow his or her behavior patterns. Quite the opposite is implied by the research conducted to date. Rather than growing out of their misbehavior, children who exhibit problem behaviors at an early age very often grow into more serious problem behaviors.

Types of Delinquents

Researchers have attempted to delineate homogeneous groups of delinquents based on behavioral characteristics, types of offenses, and membership in subcultural groups (e.g., Achenbach, 1982; Quay, 1986a). However, it may be more helpful to distinguish between those who commit one or a few delinquent acts and those who are serious repeat offenders, especially those who commit violent crimes against persons. Some have argued that because a majority of adolescents commit delinquent acts, the differences between those who are convicted and those who are not are largely a reflection of police or court biases, but "this view can be firmly rejected" (Farrington, 1995, p. 956). Farrington argued that the correspondence between official arrest records and self-reports of delinquent and criminal acts, plus the ability of self-reports to predict future convictions, indicates that both self-reports and convictions are valid measures that distinguish the worst offenders. This view is supported by the finding that prior arrest for a violent crime and a history of family violence and criminality are the best predictors (e.g., better than prior gang involvement or heavy alcohol and drug use) of a youth's likelihood of committing a violent crime (Lattimore, Visher, & Linster, 1995).

Another useful way of thinking about different types of delinquents is the age at which they commit their first offense. Prior research has indicated that the prognosis for those who begin a delinquent pattern of behavior before the age of 12 is much worse than it is for those who are late starters (Dinitz, Scarpitti, & Reckless, 1962). More recent research has suggested that this pattern typifies the trajectories of boys more so than girls (see Bryant, Rivard, Addy, Hinkle, Cowan, & Wright, 1995; Kratzer & Hodgins, 1999). The data appear to be consistent with the observation that more serious delinquent behavior is associated with a coercive family process that trains children in antisocial behavior from an early age (Patterson, Reid, & Dishion, 1992). In addition, research seems to indicate a correlation between parental dysfunction and child delinquency that is not explained by observational learning (Tapscott, Frick, Wootton, & Kruh, 1996).

Prevalence of Delinquency

Statistics regarding juvenile delinquency clearly show that most children and youth commit at least one delinquent act. But because authorities do not detect most illegal acts, hidden delinquency remains a major problem. About half the juveniles who become official delinquents are adjudicated for only one offense before they become adults. Juveniles who commit repeated offenses (*recidivists*) account for the majority of official delinquency. Recidivists commit more serious offenses, begin performing delinquent acts at an earlier age (usually before they are 12 years old), and tend to continue their antisocial behavior as adults (Farrington, 1995; Tolan, 1987; Tolan & Thomas, 1995). Males commit most juvenile offenses, particularly serious crimes against people and property. Females may be increasingly involved in major offenses, but males still far outnumber females in official delinquency statistics (Siegel & Senna, 1994). Race, drug use, poor school performance, truancy, risk-seeking, and conflicts with parents, in addition to gender, are all factors associated with delinquency recidivism (Chang et al., 2003).

The peak ages for juvenile delinquency are ages 15 to 17, after which delinquency rates decline. Orientation to drugs and delinquency related to drugs, especially alcohol abuse, are pervasive concerns of parents, educators, and other adults for this age group.

Causal Factors and Prevention

The nature of delinquency is not just law-violating behavior but also the responses of adult authority to it (Farrington, 1995). Incarceration and other forms of punishment have failed to control delinquency. Many social–cultural factors, including our society's failure to control access to firearms, contribute to delinquency. The problem is not merely young people's criminal behavior but adult responses that tend to exacerbate rather than reduce delinquency. The scope of the problem is great, and the issues in delinquency have complex legal, moral, psychological, and sociological implications. Criminologists have constructed a variety of theories of crime that include social–environmental, biological, familial, and personal causal factors (see Blackburn, 1993; Siegel & Senna, 1994). We focus here on explanations of the origins of delinquency that have the greatest implications for educators.

Longitudinal research in England and New Zealand, as well as the United States, has led to remarkably consistent findings and hypotheses about the risk factors for delinquency and suggestions for prevention (Farrington, 1995; Loeber et al., 1998a, 1998b; Loeber & Farrington, 2000; Forness et al., 1999). Research consistently reveals that the following characteristics put preadolescents at high risk for later delinquency:

- History of child abuse
- Hyperactivity, impulsivity, and problems in paying attention
- Low intelligence and low academic achievement, as well as a general pattern of disengagement from school
- Lax parental supervision and harsh authoritarian discipline
- A family history of criminality and family conflict, including aggression between siblings
- Poverty, large family size, densely populated neighborhood, poor housing
- Antisocial behavior or conduct disorder, including especially aggressive behavior and stealing.

Researchers have formed hypotheses about how these and related factors work in leading to delinquency. Three general models of influence appear in the delinquency literature: (1) delinquent behavior is the result of the stable antisocial personality traits located within the delinquent individual, (2) delinquent behavior is mostly the product of external environmental factors and circumstances, and (3) delinquent behavior is primarily the result of interactions between the personal characteristics of the individual (e.g., hyperactivity, ability) and the environment (Loeber & Stouthamer-Loeber, 1998). Most researchers endorse the third option and suggest that no single factor can account for delinquent behavior.

Steinberg and Avenevoli (1998) found that children at risk for delinquent behavior are often disengaged from school and that school disengagement appeared to precede engagement in other problem behaviors. However, their results suggested that engagement in school was more important as a protective factor than disengagement was as a risk factor. According to them, engaged students' strong bond to school (a conventional institution) serves to maintain conventional behavior and inhibit deviant behavior by increasing the costs of deviance (e.g., suspension or expulsion from school). That is, students who are engaged in school have more to lose (e.g., positive peer group, good education, entrance into college, a job) if they become involved in deviant behavior. For these reasons, "school engagement may be an important domain for delinquency prevention" (p. 420). Note that these authors do not claim that suspension and expulsion are effective deterrents to delinquency for youth who are already disengaged from school. It is only to the extent that individuals can be reengaged in schooling or prevented from becoming disengaged that such punitive processes are likely to work as deterrents to delinquency.

As we saw in Chapter 12, the parents of youngsters with conduct disorder typically do not monitor their children's behavior appropriately. Fridrich and Flannery

(1995) found that parental monitoring and susceptibility to antisocial peer influence characterized early adolescent delinquents regardless of their ethnicity. These risk factors appear to be what Patterson et al. (1992) have called "a concatenation of actions and reactions"—a series of interconnected, interdependent events and conditions leading through several stages to a criminal career. These stages and their defining characteristics, as described by Patterson et al. (1992), are shown in Figure 14.1. Not only the stages and their descriptions but the coercive process involving the exchange of mutually aversive reactions are depicted by the wavelike "his reaction, their reaction" sequence. You may recall from the discussion in chapter 12 that this "my turn, your turn" sequence is part and parcel of the acting-out cycle that we see in school. Patterson et al. (1992) see it as the essence of the coercive process leading to antisocial behavior and, left unchecked, eventually to a criminal career. It is important to note that this model does not suggest that delinquent behaviors are learned solely through parental modeling. Although such an explanation holds intuitive appeal, data do not necessarily support this conclusion (Frick & Loney, 2002).

Given these risk factors, can we predict with a high degree of accuracy which students who experience them will become delinquent? More specifically, can we make

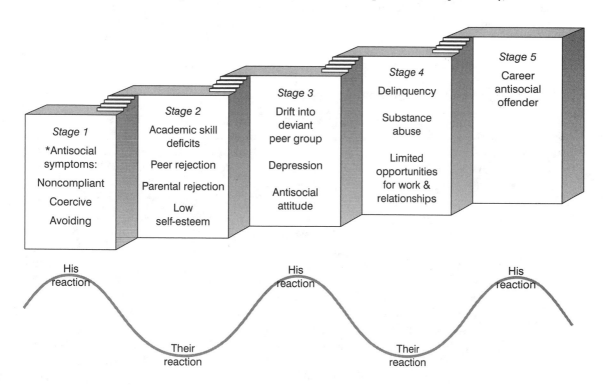

*The defining characteristics for that stage.

Figure 14.1
A concatenation of actions and reactions
Source: *Patterson, G. R., Reid, J. B., & Dishion, T. J. (1992).* Antisocial Boys *Castalia. Reprinted by permission.*

accurate enough predictions to warrant specific prevention efforts? Leech, Day, Richardson, and Goldschmidt (2003), Farrington (1995), and Sampson and Laub (1993) argued that we can; Lundman (1993) argued that we cannot and that we should abandon at least the traditional delinquency-prevention efforts and focus on more effective intervention for youth who have been apprehended for delinquent acts (as we discuss later). Loeber and Stouthamer-Loeber (1998) also argued that because many forms of delinquent behavior, particularly aggression, often appear first in the home and community before they appear at school, interventions must include strategies to deal with the behaviors in each setting where they occur.

Hamburg (1998) and others who argue for prevention programs suggest that they be aimed at relieving many of the disadvantageous conditions of life associated with delinquency: unemployment, poverty, poor housing, ineffective parental discipline, family and community disintegration, and school failure. However, currently popular approaches rely primarily on incapacitation by incarceration—earlier, more adultlike, harsher, and longer punishment. Research shows that these strategies are ineffective, at least for youth who have not committed index crimes against other people (Lundman, 1993). In addition, some crimes committed by juveniles have predictors and recidivism patterns that are quite different from those of adults committing the same crimes (Miner, 2002). Popular as they may be with social policy makers, punitive approaches are seen by many researchers as counterproductive.

Delinquency, Disabling Conditions, and the Need for Special Education

Educating juvenile delinquents presents difficult problems for public schools and correctional institutions because of unclear definitions of disabling conditions (see Nelson, Leone, & Rutherford, 2004). Are juvenile delinquents disabled and therefore included under the Individuals with Disabilities Education Act (IDEA)? We might contend that most or all incarcerated delinquents logically fall into the IDEA category of "emotionally disturbed." Unfortunately, the decision is not that clear-cut. The current federal definition specifically excludes youngsters who are "socially maladjusted but not emotionally disturbed." Thus, when delinquent behaviors are attributed to social maladjustment rather than emotional disturbance, students are denied the protections and services mandated by IDEA—unless they have mental retardation, learning disabilities, physical or sensory impairments, or mental illness as determined by a psychiatrist (see Leone, Rutherford, & Nelson, 1991; Nelson et al., 2004).

Researchers have consistently found that disabilities are common in delinquents, with learning disability the most prevalent disabling condition (Jarvelin, Daara, Rantakallio, Moilanen, & Ishohanni, 1995; Murphy, 1986; Nelson et al., 2004; Siegel & Senna, 1994; Zabel & Nigro, 1999). This finding seems reasonable given the high degree of comorbidity of emotional or behavioral disorders with learning disabilities (Glassberg, Hooper, & Mattison, 1999). Nevertheless, the ambiguous wording of the law precludes using adjudication or assignment to a correctional facility as the basis for identifying an emotional or behavioral disability. It requires curious turns of logic, however, to conclude that many incarcerated youths do not have emotional or behavioral disorders and are not entitled to special education under the law. If behavioral disorders include both overt and covert antisocial behavior, then finding incarcerated youth who do not have behavioral disorders is a logical impossibility (except, of course, children or youth who are held unjustly).

We know that mentally ill youngsters are often incarcerated and that a diagnosis of conduct disorder is often used as a rationale for incarcerating rather than providing mental health services to children and youth (see Ginsburg & Demeranville, 1999). We also know that conduct disorder is frequently accompanied by emotional or behavioral disorders of other types (Forness et al., 1999; Kazdin, 1994; Pullis, 1991; Webster-Stratton & Dahl, 1995). If higher levels of delinquent conduct indicate higher levels of psychopathology, and if youth who commit more frequent and more serious delinquent acts are more likely to be incarcerated, then the argument that all or nearly all incarcerated youth are disabled is supported. Finally, if behavioral disorders are not defined as disabling conditions under the law, then logically indefensible distinctions are drawn between emotional disturbance and social maladjustment, as we discussed in chapter 1. Wolf, Braukmann, and Ramp (1987) stated long ago that "evidence and consensus are growing that delinquent behavior, especially when persistent and serious, may often be part of a durable, significantly handicapping condition that is composed of multiple antisocial and dysfunctional behaviors, and that sometimes appears to be familially transmitted" (p. 350). The evidence and the consensus have grown that Wolf and his colleagues were correct.

Assessment of Delinquents' Educational Needs

Delinquents' disruptive behavior and bravado can make them inaccessible or uncooperative or successful in covering up their academic deficits. However, the assessment of their educational needs does not differ in any essential way from the assessment of other students' needs; evaluation should focus directly on the skills in which instruction is to be offered (see Merrell, 1994; Nelson et al., 2004; Overton, 2003). Because many delinquents have cognitive and academic deficits in addition to social and vocational skills deficits, their assessment must often be multifaceted. Assessment must often be done hurriedly and without relevant background information because delinquents are often in detention centers or special facilities where student populations are transient, educational records unavailable, and communication with other agencies difficult. Finally, because there is little agreement about the most important skills for delinquents—social, academic, or vocational—the focus of assessment is often questionable.

Intervention in Juvenile Delinquency

Juvenile delinquency—antisocial behavior that crosses the line into the illegal or criminal—presents one of the most difficult challenges for effective intervention. There are no easy or sure-fire solutions for any facet of the problem of delinquency, and the issues in treating violent juvenile delinquents are particularly complex (Hamburg, 1998; Nelson et al., 2004). The cyclic history of interventions and the failures of our legal system to deal with the problems of crime and violence, including delinquency of minors, seems characterized by a recurrent pattern of enthusiasm for proposed solutions with scant research base followed by failure to win support sufficient for success (Achenbach, 1975; Lundman, 1993; Silberman, 1978; Spergel, 1995). The 1990s were a period of pessimism regarding government social programs and enthusiasm for harsher punishment (cf. Baker, 1996). Although an exclusive reliance on harsher punishment is clearly inadvisable on scientific grounds (cf. Tate, Reppucci, & Mulvey, 1995), some have argued that we need to lower our typical expectations when working with persistent antisocial behavior. Individuals have argued that human behavior of this type is very hard to change; thus, many objectives short of a cure are worthy (Etzioni, 1994).

Effective intervention, like prevention, must include the astute, persistent, multifaceted efforts of a variety of individuals and agencies, focusing not only on risk factors but also on those factors that have demonstrated protective effects (Arthur, Hawkins, Pollard, Catalano, & Baglioni, 2002; Gavazzi, Wasserman, Partridge, & Sheridan, 2000). We make brief mention here of intervention in families and the juvenile court and corrections systems but concentrate attention on schooling.

Families

Make no mistake: Parents who are loving, nurturing, and skilled in child rearing can have delinquent children; but neglectful parents with poor discipline skills are far more likely to have delinquent children. In fact, parent–child relationships have been linked to the quality of children's social interaction into adulthood (Doyle & Markiewicz, 1996).

The typical parents of chronic delinquents do not monitor and nurture their children closely. They punish aggressive, delinquent behavior unpredictably, harshly, and ineffectively. They often show little concern when their children offend the community by stealing or fighting outside the home. As long as they do not have to deal with the misbehavior, they choose not to see their children as a serious problem. Within the home, they show little motivation to change their own behavior to decrease the coercion and violence that characterize their interactions with their children (Dishion, 1990; Patterson, 1982, 1986b; Patterson et al., 1992). Other parents may not believe that they have the ability to make a difference in the lives of their children (Bandura, 1995a, 1995b).

Intervention in the families of chronic offenders is extremely difficult. Changing longstanding patterns of coercion may be impossible in families in which parents are unmotivated and have few cognitive and social skills. Patterson and his colleagues reported success in significantly reducing aggressive behavior and stealing in many families of aggressive children; however, the long-term outcome for stealers and chronic adolescent delinquents is guarded. Although delinquent behavior may be significantly reduced during behavioral intervention, research does not show that the improvement will persist after treatment is terminated (Patterson et al., 1992). Follow-up of juvenile offenders who were placed in group homes that used a *teaching-family method* (a behaviorally oriented program designed to provide an appropriate family atmosphere) also shows that behavioral improvement during treatment is not maintained (Kirigin, Braukman, Atwater, & Wolf, 1982; Wolf et al., 1987). At this time, there appears to be no effective substitute for a family social system that has failed—at least when the criterion for effectiveness is "cure," or permanent behavioral change that requires no further treatment. Researchers have suggested that serious antisocial behavior and delinquency should be considered a social disability requiring long-term treatment (Hamburg, 1998; Walker, Ramsey, & Gresham, 2004; Wolf et al., 1987). Studies of early intervention programs with preschoolers, particularly those with parental training, consistently demonstrated that the participating children had more positive school outcomes and lower rates of violence and crime well into adolescence (Hawkins, Farrington, & Catalano, 1998). However, findings of intervention studies with older children yield less optimistic results. Unless effective child-rearing skills can be taught to the parents of a delinquent youth, effective long-term intervention in this disability may require placing the youth with a foster or surrogate family in which trained parents provide appropriate behavioral controls, models, and supports throughout adolescence and into adulthood.

Juvenile Courts and Corrections

Juvenile courts were instituted in the United States in about 1900 to offer more humane treatment of juvenile offenders than the 19th-century reform schools had provided. Judges were empowered to use their discretion in determining the consequences of a child's misconduct. Although the intent was good, the institution has become mired in an overload of cases, and the rights of children—if children are considered to have constitutional rights equal to those of all other citizens—have been blatantly abridged. Consequently, the juvenile court system and the question of children's rights have come under close scrutiny (see Bazemore & Umbreit, 1995; Siegel & Senna, 1994; Warboys & Shauffer, 1990).

Although we frequently hear proposals for drastic reform, the juvenile court system is likely to remain as it is for a considerable time. A sizable proportion of children and youth will make appearances before a juvenile court during their school years, and teachers could profit from familiarity with the court's workings. Whatever the failures in the social systems of families and schools, one can find equal disasters in the procedures and institutions devised by lawyers and judges.

Under the juvenile justice system, juvenile court judges have wide discretion in handling cases. They may release juveniles to the custody of their parents, refer youngsters to social service agencies, or assign them to a variety of correctional programs ranging from probation to restitution to community attention homes to state detention centers or even to private, less monitored wilderness-challenge experiences or boot camps. The effectiveness of the various juvenile justice and corrections options are widely and hotly debated (see Siegel & Senna, 1994), and abuses seem widespread. Most researchers conclude that harsher punishment is counterproductive in the vast majority of cases, contrary to the opinions of many holding political office.

Lundman (1993) argued persuasively for community-based intervention for all juveniles who have committed property crimes, reserving incarceration or other institutional treatment only for those who have committed index crimes against persons. (Nearly everyone agrees that juveniles who commit violent crimes against people must be placed in correctional facilities for some period of time.) Lundman (1993) suggested that *diversion* should be the standard juvenile justice response to minor property offenses and other relatively nonserious delinquency (see also Siegel & Senna, 1994). *Diversion* means that the juvenile is referred for services (e.g., family services, counseling) rather than sent to juvenile court. For moderately delinquent juveniles who are convicted of index crimes against property, Lundman recommended probation as the first and most frequent sentencing option. He also recommended abandoning efforts to scare delinquents straight through prison visits, informational seminars, and so on. Community-based interventions, including intensive monitoring and supervision, are the best approaches for most chronic property offenders, Lundman concluded.

The *restorative justice model* is a response to delinquency that is in keeping Lundman's principals. In this model, the response to crime and delinquency focuses on accountability for illegal behavior and the development of competencies that prevent reoffending (see Umbreit, Greenwood, & Coates, 2000). In this way, offenses are responded to on individual bases, focusing not on punishment, but on compensation for the victim(s). The initial data from this model offers evidence of promising results (PACER Center, 2001).

Schooling

A substantial proportion of all juvenile crime occurs in school buildings or on school grounds (Nelson et al., 2004; Siegel & Senna, 1994). Each month during the academic year, thousands of teachers and millions of children in U.S. schools are assaulted or otherwise victimized. Theft, assault, drug and alcohol abuse, extortion, sexual promiscuity, and vandalism occur all too frequently, not just in deteriorated inner-city schools but in affluent suburban and rural communities as well.

Punishment and increased focus on security are schools' usual responses to delinquent behavior. The typical punishment (detention) or exclusion (office referral, suspension, disciplinary transfer, or expulsion) is usually ineffective in reducing the problem behavior and improving the student's academic progress. In short, the typical school's response to disruptive behavior is woefully inadequate and does little more than maintain a semblance of order and prevent total abandonment of its traditional programs (Mayer, Nofpoktitis, Butterworth, & Hollingsworth, 1987; Walker et al., 2004). In chapter 12, we discussed schoolwide discipline and positive, nonpunitive procedures designed to reduce antisocial behavior. Those strategies apply also to delinquent behavior in school.

One approach to dealing with problems of students at risk for a variety of undesirable outcomes (e.g., dropping out, delinquency) is the establishment of alternative schools. In a review of research, Cox, Davidson, and Bynum (1995) found that alternative schools have had a small overall positive effect on school performance, attitude toward school, and self-esteem but not on delinquency. Alternative programs that target specific populations, such as those at risk for delinquency or low achievers, generally produced larger positive effects than did those with open admissions.

Education of children and youth with disabilities in detention is governed by the same federal laws and regulations as is education of youngsters in public schools (Nelson et al., 2004). Those in detention facilities are guaranteed all the procedural protections and requirements for nonbiased individualized assessment, individualized education programs, and so on afforded under IDEA and related laws and regulations. Ideally, therefore, assessment of students in detention is functionally related to an appropriate curriculum, and the instruction of students is data based and prepares them with critical life skills. Nevertheless, incarcerated children and youth often do not receive assessment and education. Given the following difficulties, it is not surprising that many delinquent youngsters' needs are not met:

- Criminal justice officials and the public often take the attitude that delinquent and criminal young people are not entitled to the same educational opportunities as are law-abiding citizens.
- Some psychologists, psychiatrists, and educators take the position that many incarcerated youths are not disabled.
- There is a shortage of qualified personnel to staff good special education programs in correction facilities.
- Some of the provisions of IDEA, such as regulations requiring education in the least restrictive environment and parental involvement in educational planning, are particularly difficult to implement in correctional facilities.
- The student population of correctional facilities is transient, making educational assessment and planning especially difficult.
- Interagency cooperation and understanding are often limited, which hampers obtaining student records, designating responsibility for specific services, and working out transition from detention to community.
- Administrators of correction facilities often consider security and institutional rules more important than education.
- Funds for educational programs in correction facilities are limited.

Street Gangs

An increasing problem related to delinquency is gang activities. Within the past 25 years, gangs have proliferated across the United States, and now a thousand or more cities and towns have problems with gangs and gang violence (cf. Goldstein & Glick, 1994; Klein, 1995; Spergel, 1995). Gang activity is also prevalent in many schools (Elliott, Hamburg, & Williams, 1998). However, misconceptions about gangs and gang activities abound; misunderstandings are often created or perpetuated by distorted media coverage, misinformed professionals, or both (Klein, 1995). Among the most egregious misimpressions is that most youth street gangs are organized to distribute drugs. Drug involvement by street gangs has increased, but the drug trade is not the primary activity of most street gangs.

Gangs have been an object of serious study for several decades, and we must be satisfied to summarize only a small part of the extensive and complex literature on gangs that is most relevant to educators. The definition of *gang* is difficult and controversial. Although there are many different kinds of gangs organized for different purposes, we are concerned here primarily with what are known as *street gangs,* which Klein (1995) defined as aggregations of youth who recognize themselves as a group and are oriented toward delinquent acts. It is important to recognize that some gang members are not delinquents and some delinquents are not gang members.

Gang membership is a means of obtaining affiliation, protection, excitement, and money, objects, or substances that members desire (Fagan & Wilkinson, 1998). The two characteristics that most clearly set an aggregation of youth apart as a gang are (a) commitment to a criminal orientation and (b) self-recognition as a gang, as signified by special vocabulary, clothing, signs, colors, and graffiti-marking territory (Klein, 1995). Gang members are overwhelmingly male, mostly adolescent, and predominantly homogeneous groups of ethnic minorities. Minority groups differ in the nature or focus of their gang activities (Klein, 1995; Spergel, 1995). However, increases in younger and older members, female members, and White supremacist gangs were seen in the 1990s. Early research in this area indicated that members of gangs tend to come from families that place less importance on intrafamial socialization, youth supervision, and outward expressions of affection. The typical gang member is now thought to exhibit one or more of the following characteristics, according to Klein (1995):

- A notable set of personal deficiencies—perhaps difficulty in school, low self-esteem, lower impulse control, inadequate social skills, a deficit in useful adult contacts
- A notable tendency toward defiance, aggressiveness, fighting, and pride in physical prowess
- A greater-than-normal desire for status, identity, and companionship that can be at least partly satisfied by joining a special group like a gang
- A boring, uninvolved lifestyle, in which the occasional excitement of gang exploits or rumored exploits provides a welcome respite. (p. 76)

Street gangs spend most of their time just hanging out together. Contrary to popular perception, researchers who have spent decades studying street gangs portray them as inactive most of the time:

> Street gangs through the years have done nothing more often than they have done something exciting. Their customary activities are sleeping, eating, and hanging around. Criminal acts are a minority of the activities they engage in, and violent acts are a minority of those. We must remember that despite the drama and lethality of gang violence, its prevalence does not deserve using the label *violent gang.* This only feeds a stereotype that needs no help from scholars. To repeat, most gang members' behavior is not criminal, and most gang members' crimes are not violent. And of course, most violent people are not gang members, so it's not very useful to define gangs in terms of violent crime alone. (Klein, 1995, pp. 28–29)

It is interesting that researchers have found few differences between gang-related homicides and nongang homicides (Rosenfield, Bray, & Egley, 1999). In fact, both of these types of crimes were highly concentrated in disadvantaged, racially isolated neighborhoods—suggesting more powerful predictors of violence than gang affiliation.

A variety of causal models have been constructed to explain the formation and maintenance of gangs. As Klien (1995) saw it, social and economic conditions that create an underclass are partly to blame for creating gangs. The underclass is created by industrial withdrawal from an area (typically an inner-city area), creating an absence of jobs. The failure of the educational system further contributes to joblessness in the area. Segregation of ethnic minorities also plays a role, as do other forms of racism. Opportunities for individuals in the middle class to migrate out of the depressed area result in the absence of alternative social and employment-related activities and the absence of social controls provided by important vibrant, active institutions that are necessary to maintain the social fabric. Churches, children's service agencies, business clubs, and so on suffer the loss of talented leaders, and many of those left in the community have poor skills in parental discipline and few practical skills in maintaining community organizations that control social behavior.

The onset of gang organizations is fostered by these conditions. Gang behavior then exacerbates crime, minority segregation, and other negative community conditions. Gangs are maintained by things that threaten members, legitimize the need for the gang, and increase the cohesiveness of the group (Klein, 1995). These maintaining factors include institutions that oppose the gangs (e.g., police); gang rivalries that threaten personal safety, possessions, or status; perceived barriers to alternatives to gang membership and activities; and gang intervention programs that inadvertently strengthen the gang's cohesion—for example, attempts to use the gang structure to redirect members toward noncriminal activities. Laub and Lauristsen (1998) noted that gang influence can also be spread by student transfer and busing programs. In less mobile student populations, gang influence tends to be restricted to a turf, but more mobile student populations appear to allow for spread of gang influence into a school or from a school back into a student's neighborhood.

Interventions designed to reduce gang membership and gang-related delinquent behavior are matters of considerable controversy, and to date no intervention approach has been shown to be very effective (Goldstein & Glick, 1994; Hawkins et al., 1998; Klein, 1995; Nelson et al., 2004). Gang members have extensive contact with like-minded individuals with similar behavioral, educational, and socioeconomic backgrounds (Fagan & Wilkinson, 1998). This pattern of association exacerbates the problems associated with gang memberships (e.g., exposure to violence) and insulates many gang members from interventions designed to assist them in creating more favorable life circumstances. Intervention programs typically have lacked intensity and comprehensiveness or have relied primarily on punitive measures (e.g., a crackdown by law enforcement) or other approaches that exacerbate the problem. Truly effective programs to stem the tide of gangs and gang violence would require an unlikely scenario given the current political climate. Such programs would need to include massive and sustained efforts that accomplish the following: (1) reduce poverty, (2) provide job training and well-paid jobs for youth, (3) provide decent housing in inner cities, (4) rebuild and reform deteriorated schools and their instructional programs, and (5) reduce racism and other social blights.

Many schools, Klein (1995) observed, are running scared, approaching the gang problem primarily through scare tactics, tightened security, and punitive measures, often with the help of law enforcement. Although school safety is an important, legitimate concern, schools should put their primary efforts into positive schoolwide discipline plans and restructured programs designed to meet more of the social and educational needs of students (Liaupsin, Jolivette, & Scott, 2004; Martella et al., 2003; Spergel, 1995; Walker et al., 2004). In their obsession with college-bound youth, schools fail to provide the work-oriented high school programs that keep youth in school and help them find employment (Edgar & Siegel, 1995; Spergel, 1995). Schools could play a major role in gang reduction if they focused on positive discipline, effective instruction and remediation, a differentiated curriculum with courses leading directly to work for those who are not headed for college, coordination of efforts with other community agencies, and an array of extracurricular activities designed to attract all students into meaningful alternatives.

SUBSTANCE ABUSE

We use the term *substance abuse* rather than *drug abuse* because not all abused chemicals are drugs. Abused substances other than drugs include gasoline, cleaning fluids, glue, and other chemicals that can cause psychological effects. Loeber et al. (1998a) added cigarettes to the list of substances associated with problem behavior patterns in adolescents. The substances under discussion here are those deliberately used to induce physiological or psychological effects (or both) for other than therapeutic purposes. *Abuse* usually is defined as use that contributes to health risks, disruption of psychological functioning, adverse social consequences, or some combination of these.

As Newcomb and Richardson (1995) noted, substance abuse disorders cannot exist without the availability of the substance and a willing user. Many substances are readily available, and many people are willing or anxious to use or abuse them. These facts imbue much of the discussion of substance abuse with a moralistic tone (the notion that substance abusers are simply evil or weak willed) and encourage the assumption that interdiction of supply will be effective in reducing use and abuse.

Definition and Prevalence

"Use of psychoactive substances is the norm for adolescents" (Baer, MacLean, & Marlatt, 1998, p. 183). However, prevalence studies suggest that the use of psychoactive substances is more likely to be experimental or episodic for most adolescents. What is the difference between experimentation and abuse? Does a single episode of use by a child or adolescent constitute abuse? At what level of use should an adolescent be considered to have a substance abuse disorder? It is clear that most adolescents take or use substances but that only a minority of them (perhaps 6 to 10% of users) become chronic abusers (Newcomb & Richardson, 1995). Adolescent substance abuse is in many ways similar to substance abuse in adulthood, but it is not exactly the same. Many adolescents who use or abuse substances do not become adults with substance abuse disorders. The definition of *substance abuse* is clouded by controversy regarding specific criteria, changing social attitudes, and political use of the issue (Bukstein, 1995). Baer et al. (1998) suggested that one aspect of substance use that differentiates abuse from less problematic use is the accumulation of negative consequences related to use. However, this definition is unsatisfactory because adults and adolescents face different laws, customs, and consequences related to substance use.

The topic of drug use is especially prone to distortion of fact and hysterical rhetoric because the definition of adolescent substance abuse is anchored in cultural tradition, social fad, and political positioning as well as scientific evidence. Moreover, controversy regarding definition makes many prevalence figures suspect. Nevertheless, nearly all authorities on the topic agree that substance use and abuse are alarmingly high among American children and youth and that effective measures to reduce both use and abuse of substances are needed.

A common misperception is that substance abuse has to do primarily with illegal drugs such as cocaine, marijuana, and heroin or with illicit use of prescription medications such as barbiturates; but as Werry (1986b) noted a generation ago, "alcohol and tobacco are, as ever, the real drug problem" (p. 228). Alcohol and tobacco are still the largest problems because they are readily available to adults, they are advertised for sale, most people view their use by adults as socially acceptable, and children usually receive their first exposure to and first experiment with these substances in the home (Severson & James, 2002). The earlier the child's first experience with alcohol and tobacco, the more likely he or she will become a regular user. Early use of alcohol and tobacco, as well as other substances, correlates with family problems, low socioeconomic status, school failure, and psychiatric disorders, especially conduct disorder (Upadhyaya, Brady, Wharton, & Liao, 2003). Because the negative health consequences of alcohol and tobacco are staggering, preventing children and adolescents from beginning to smoke and drink seems wise. Indeed, the most common cause of death among teenagers in the United States is auto accidents, whereas driving under the influence of alcohol and disease caused by smoking cigarettes are is the leading mortality factors among the general population of the United States. Thus, the "war on drugs" has, so far, not been focused on what likely should be its primary targets.

Another common misperception is that substance abuse is disproportionately a problem of ethnic minorities. This mistaken impression is likely an artifact of data collection procedures and intervention programs. "We may conclude that, nationwide, there are no real differences in overall patterns of use as a function of ethnicity. Nonetheless, ethnic minorities (particularly African Americans and Hispanics) are currently far *more* likely than other adolescent groups to be targeted for attention from law enforcement officials as a function of drug involvement" (Newcomb & Richardson, 1995, p. 414, emphasis in original). Contrary to many racial stereotypes, the drug ecstasy (3,4-methylenedioxymethamphetamine; MDMA) has actually been found to have higher abuse rates among White adolescents (Yacoubian, 2003). Despite racial targeting, researches have found that among individuals arrested for drug offenses, White arrestees were found more than 20 times as likely to be guilty of an ecstasy offence than non-White arrestees (Urbach, Reynolds, & Yacoubian, 2002).

Some youngsters, primarily adolescents age 15 or older, do abuse substances other than alcohol and tobacco. Following is a list of several major types of drugs of abuse, along with a few examples of each. Some of these drugs are prescribed for therapeutic purposes, so they have legitimate purposes as well as potential for abuse. We also list some of the most typical effects or symptoms of serious intoxication with the drug and of drug withdrawal:

- Depressants: alcohol, Phenobarbital, Valium, Quaalude
  Signs of intoxication: drowsiness, irritability, disinhibition, extreme relaxation or sedation
  Signs of withdrawal: tremors, fever, anxiety, hallucinations
- Stimulants: nicotine, caffeine, cocaine, amphetamines and methamphetamines
  Signs of intoxication: dilated pupils, restlessness, loss of appetite, paranoia, hallucinations
  Signs of withdrawal: fatigue, mental and physical slowness or depression
- Stimulant hallucinogens: phencyclidine (PCP), MDMA (Ecstasy), Ketamine
  Signs of intoxication: agitation, irritability, grandiosity, dilated pupils, fine tremors, sweating, rapid speech and movement, hallucinations, dry mouth and throat, uncontrolled jaw movements, repetitive movements
  Signs of withdrawal: anxiety, agitation, depression, fatigue, sleeplessness, panic attacks, increased appetite, psychosis, suicidal thoughts
- Narcotics: morphine, methadone, codeine, Darvon
  Signs of intoxication: drowsiness, slurred speech, constricted pupils, poor physical coordination, analgesia (insensitivity to pain)
  Signs of withdrawal: vomiting, cramps, fever, chills, "goose flesh"
- Inhalants: glues, aerosols, paint thinners, cleaning fluids, fuels
  Signs of intoxication: confusion, hallucinations, exhilaration or depression, poor balance
  Signs of withdrawal: inconsistent
- Marijuana: cigarettes or forms taken by mouth
  Signs of intoxication: sleepiness, poor concentration, confusion, anxiety, paranoia, distorted perceptions
  Signs of withdrawal: psychological distress
- Hallucinogens: mescaline, psilocybin, lysergic acid diethylamide (LSD)
  Signs of intoxication: dilated pupils, hallucinations, altered perceptions of body or time, problems focusing attention, emotional lability
  Signs of withdrawal: not well established

As we mentioned earlier, the substances that become popular or receive intensive media attention in any given period of time are highly variable and affected by fads and other social phenomena. For example, in the mid-1990s, Ritalin became a popular drug of abuse, and national media attention heightened concern about its prescription and control. In the late 1990s, media attention shifted to ecstasy abuse, especially among adolescents and young adults attending raves. Much of what we know about the effects of this drug is based on anecdotal evidence; clinical research has been plagued with problems including an unethical risk of neural brain injury to participants in such studies (Ricaurte, Yuan, Hatzidimitriou, Cord, & McCann, 2003). Despite varying trends in media attention, marijuana is the most widely used illicit drug in Western societies (Iversen, 1999). In addition to those we have listed, people may abuse many other preparations, including *designer drugs*—new concoctions made up in illegal laboratories and represented as well-known drugs or touted to produce euphoria. The street names of various drugs are numerous, and new names are constantly being invented.

Baer et al. (1998) reported two consistent patterns of substance abuse over time. First, experimentation with alcohol and other substances begins in adolescence and declines significantly for most individuals with transition to young adulthood. Prosocial processes associated with marriage and employment are consistently associated with declines in substance use across the early adult years. However, the second pattern suggests that there are risks for adult adjustment based on adolescent behavior. The adolescent substance abuser who becomes a substance-abusing adult typically abuses multiple substances. In addition, adolescent problem behavior and patterns of nonconformity predict adult substance abuse better than level of substance use does.

The emotional and behavioral problems associated with substance abuse include both the effects produced by using the substance and the effects of abstinence after a period of use (i.e., withdrawal). Terms commonly used in discussion of substance use include the following:

- *Intoxication* indicates symptoms of a toxic amount of substance in the bloodstream (enough to have physiological or psychological effects).
- *Tolerance* refers to physiological adaptation to a substance so that an increasing amount is required to produce the same effects; tolerance typically increases with repeated use and decreases after a period of abstinence.
- *Addiction* indicates compulsive use of a substance and that obtaining and using the substance has become a central concern and pattern of behavior.
- *Dependence* refers to the need to continue using a substance to avoid physical or emotional discomfort or both.
- *Withdrawal* designates physical or emotional discomfort associated with a period of abstinence.

An important feature of advanced substance abuse is its insidious onset, progressing through various stages. A substance abuser rarely becomes a habitual user immediately; rather, experimentation, perhaps under peer pressure, is followed by occasional social or recreational use, then use in certain circumstances or situations (perhaps to relax after a stressful event, to stay awake to perform a demanding task, or to sleep). Situational use may intensify and become part of daily routine; eventually, the substance can become the individual's central focus. Clearly, substance use and abuse do not always progress to the obsessive-dependent addiction stage (Newcomb & Richardson, 1995). However, teachers and other adults should be aware of the danger signals of the transitions from experimentation to social–recreational and to situational–circumstantial use. Teachers may first observe changes in social behavior and academic performance at the point of transition to situational use (Severson & James, 2002).

An additional concern regarding substance abuse since the 1980s is contracting the human immunodeficiency virus (HIV) through unprotected sex or the use of contaminated needles for intravenous injection of drugs. The probability of sexual activity, including sexual intercourse without a condom, is greatly increased by the use of alcohol and other substances that alter mood and cognitive control. Adolescents who are runaways, homeless, or substance abusers are a particularly high-risk group for sexual promiscuity and for contracting HIV.

It is difficult to estimate the extent of substance abuse among children and adolescents. Students with emotional or behavioral disorders are at higher risk than is the general population of students (Genaux, Morgan, & Friedman, 1995). The level of use and abuse of specific substances by adolescents reflects adult patterns and is affected by fads, social attitudes, and prohibitions (Bukstein, 1995; Newcomb & Richardson, 1995). Use of hallucinogenic drugs was lower in the 1980s than in the previous two decades, but in the 1980s cocaine became a major concern, and marijuana use, which in previous decades caused much alarm and sometimes resulted in legal penalties of absurd proportions, was considered comparatively safe (cf. Miksic, 1987). Beginning in the mid-1980s, there was a steady decrease in the use of most illicit drugs (Bukstein, 1995). The trends or fads that will appear during the next decade are impossible to predict.

Causal Factors and Prevention

A variety of theories have been said to explain adolescent substance abuse, including models that view it as a disease (metabolic or genetic abnormality), a moral issue (lack of willpower), a spiritual problem (needing the help of a higher power), or a psychological disorder (learned maladaptive behavior or intrapsychic conflicts; Bukstein, 1995; Newcomb & Richardson, 1995). Most researchers have concluded that no single cause has been or is likely to be found and that substance abuse has multiple causes. The focus is on assessing factors that heighten risk or tend to protect against risk (Severson & James, 2002).

Family factors known to increase risk are poor and inconsistent parental discipline, family conflict, and lack of emotional bonding of family members. Family members may provide models of substance abuse and introduce children to the use of substances. Undoubtedly, genetic factors contribute risk, perhaps by making some individuals more susceptible to the physiological and psychological effects of drugs (Newcomb & Richardson, 1995).

Socialization to a deviant peer group may play a major role in substance abuse, as may media exposure to substance use and abuse. All aspects of the culture in which the youngster is embedded may have a substantial influence on initiation to substance use (Kaminer, 1994).

Community conditions of joblessness and deteriorated living conditions are also risk factors. Certainly, substance abuse is no stranger to middle-class and upscale communities. Still, the lack of socioeconomic opportunity, hopelessness, crowding, and violence that characterize many poor urban communities are very significant risk factors (Bukstein, 1995).

Age of onset of substance use is a known risk factor. The earlier the age at which a youngster has his or her first experience with substance use, the greater the risk of later abuse. Risk of polydrug use, use of more than one substance within a four-week period, seems to increase with age during adolescence (Smit, Monshouwer, & Verdurmen, 2002).

Substance abuse disorders often occur with a variety of other disorders or psychiatric illnesses. Externalizing behavior problems (aggression and other characteristics of conduct disorder) are especially likely to increase risk (Lewinsohn, Gotlib, & Seeley, 1995; Steele, Forehand, Armistead, & Brody, 1995). The polysubstance abuser typically has multiple disorders, all of which are intertwined and need to be addressed. It is important to note the reciprocal influences of substance use and other disorders. Some disorders, such as schizophrenia and depression, may be precipitated by substance use. A variety of disorders may both contribute to substance abuse and be exacerbated by it (Severson & James, 2002).

Baer et al. (1998) reported that different factors were associated with drinking level compared with drinking problems. Across a number of studies, the results suggested that drinking level is more closely tied to peer group, whereas drinking problems are associated with familial and psychological problems. People who are problem drinkers experience difficulties compared to nonproblem drinkers even at the same level of consumption. "Adolescents who experience problems [in this domain] come from more aversive familial environments, associate with deviant, heavy-drinking peers, have an under-controlled behavioral style, are more heavily engaged in deviant behaviors, experience more negative affect, and are more poorly adjusted than those who drink but do not experience problems" (Baer et al., 1998, p. 190).

Protective factors include not only the opposite of family characteristics associated with high risk but personality characteristics, perhaps extending from early temperament, such as low anger and aggression, school achievement, compliance, and responsibility (Brook, Whiteman, Cohen, Shapiro, & Balka, 1995; Jessor et al., 1995; Werner, 1999). Researchers have also found that factors associated with resilience and safe sex attitudes, such as HIV/AIDS knowledge, self-esteem, and hopefulness, were in fact negatively related to drug and alcohol use among adolescents (Chang, Bendel, Koopman, McGarvey, & Canterbury, 2003). Thus, the very same strengths that may work to prevent incarceration and HIV/AIDS infection may also serve to prevent substance abuse.

Social and cultural influences such as peer support and societal disapproval can help influence children and youth to avoid substance use during adolescence or at least delay the age at which they have their first experience with substance use. Communities in which there are jobs and alternative activities to substance abuse are also protective.

Bukstein (1995) noted that a variety of targets for prevention have been suggested, including prevention of use (especially early onset of use), abuse, the consequences of use, and the risk factors associated with use and abuse. Prevention can also be aimed at increasing the protective factors that lower risk. The most effective prevention efforts we can devise will address all of these concerns. Moreover, prevention strategies should encompass and be matched with all risk factors, including peer-related factors, individual factors (e.g., poor academic and social skills, conduct disorder), family factors (e.g., parental discipline), biological factors (e.g., use of medications), and community factors (e.g., socioeconomic conditions; Baer et al., 1998). Interventions can be classified according to whether they target individuals or the larger environment. Simplistic prevention programs such as teaching children to "just say no" are doomed because alcohol and drug experimentation has become a largely normative behavior in adolescent development (Baer et al., 1998). Adolescents who break the "just say no" taboo and find no immediate negative consequences may disregard all subsequent substance abuse warnings. Clearly, a more intensive and reasoned approach to prevention is called for. General recommendations for prevention strategies are that they should be developmentally appropriate, focused on high-risk populations, comprehensive (address multiple risk factors), coordinated with changes in social policies in the community, and long-term.

Most relevant for discussion here are the skills-based interventions that form educational efforts to prevent adolescent substance abuse—interventions aimed at helping students understand the effects and consequences of substance use and abuse. Bukstein (1995) discussed curricula designed to help students learn a variety of skills that allow them to do the following things:

• Resist peer pressure
• Change attitudes, values, and behavioral norms related to substance use
• Recognize and resist adult influences toward substance use
• Use problem-solving strategies such as self-control, stress management, and appropriate assertiveness
• Set goals and improve self-esteem
• Communicate more effectively

Prevention is preferable to intervention after substance abuse has become a reality; but if it is to be effective, it must be intensive, comprehensive, and sustained, focusing on high-risk youth in high-risk neighborhoods, especially on improving the social and economic conditions in the communities of youth at highest risk (Bukstein, 1995). Unfortunately, public sentiment and social policy in the United States indicates less willingness to support effective prevention programs of the type Bukstein (1995) recommended (Kauffman, 2004).

Intervention and Education

Substance abuse prevention programs are highly desirable, but they do little to help those who are already using drugs (Baer et al., 1998). A wide range of intervention approaches and combinations of treatments are employed in treating adolescent substance abuse, including medication (see Mirza, 2002). Traditional methods include 12-step programs such as those suggested by Alcoholics Anonymous and Narcotics Anonymous. Group therapy, family therapy (either single families or groups of families), cognitive-behavior modification, and psychopharmacological treatment are alternatives frequently employed. Family involvement and programs that are consistent with cultural traditions are critical features of prevention and intervention efforts (Bukstein, 1995; Ross, 1994; Severson & James, 2002). Some programs provide a comprehensive approach to prevention and intervention involving the entire spectrum of intervention agents: schools, peer groups, families, the media, communities, law enforcement, and the business sector (e.g., Wodarski & Feit, 1995). It is important that treatment be designed for the individual case and that careful consideration be given to inpatient versus outpatient treatment (Bukstein, 1995; Newcomb & Richardson, 1995).

Our primary concern here is educational intervention. One important feature of successful substance abuse education programs is getting accurate and useful information into the hands of teachers, parents, and students in an accessible, abbreviated form. Table 14.1 is an example of the type and amount of information that can be made available.

Information alone does not necessarily change behavior, and it is therefore necessary to take more specific action. More specific action might include: (a) clear, well-defined policies for teachers and students spelling out how drug use or possession will be handled; (b) basic, simple drug education at all grade levels; (c) increased teacher awareness about local drug problems and community service agencies; (d) group discussions about topics such as adolescent development and drug use; (e) one-to-one and group counseling using community resources such as community counseling centers and drop-in centers within the school; and (f) peer-group approaches with positive role models for group or individual support.

Many students with substance abuse problems have belief systems that lead to either increased risk of substance abuse or decreased ability to respond to intervention efforts. Individuals who are at the greatest risk for initial substance abuse problems are more likely to report beliefs that they are unable to avoid using substances or to resist peer pressure. After becoming involved with drug use, problem substance users more often report beliefs that they are unable to control their drug use or minimize the harmful effects of drug use. For such individuals, treatment must involve more than information and admonitions to abstain from drug use. Supportive environments that help individuals reinterpret environmental cues and develop more positive belief systems over time, although difficult to realize, are clearly necessary. Without such supports, individuals with maladaptive efficacy beliefs on the path to management of their substance abuse are likely to experience minor setbacks and difficulties as additional evidence of their inability to affect change in their own lives and abandon their efforts to limit their substance use and its damaging effects. Treatments affecting efficacy beliefs are, for the most part, rare in schools and other public institutions. However, the high rates of relapse associated with substance abuse interventions suggest that this element is a promising addition to existing interventions.

Table 14.1
Drug information guide

Drug Used	Alcohol	Cocaine	Depressants
	Beer, wine, liquor	Coke, rock, crack, base	Barbiturates, sedatives, tranquilizers, (downers, tranks, ludes, reds, Valium, yellow jackets, alcohol)
Physical symptoms	Intoxication, slurred speech, unsteady walk, relaxation, relaxed inhibitions, impaired coordination, slowed reflexes	Brief intense euphoria, elevated blood pressure and heart rate, restlessness, excitement, feeling of well-being followed by depression	Depressed breathing and heartbeat, intoxication, drowsiness, uncoordinated movements
Look for	Smell of alcohol on clothes or breath, intoxicated behavior, hangover, glazed eyes	Glass vials, glass pipe, white crystalline powder, razor blades, syringes, needle marks	Capsules and pills, confused behavior, longer periods of sleep, slurred speech
Dangers	Addiction, accidents as result of impaired ability and judgment, overdose when mixed with other depressants, heart and liver damage	Addiction, heart attack, seizures, lung damage, severe depression, paranoia (see Stimulants)	Possible overdose, especially in combination with/ alcohol, muscle rigidity, addiction, withdrawal and overdose require medical treatment

Seven POSSIBLE Symptoms of Drug Involvement:
1. Change in school or work attendance or performance
2. Alteration of personal appearance
3. Mood swings or attitude changes

Source: Drug Information Guide. Promotional Slideguide Corp., 33 Rockwell Place, Brooklyn, NY 11217. Used with permission.

Hallucinogens	Inhalants	Marijuana	Narcotics	Stimulants
Acid, LSD, PCP, MDMA, Ecstasy, psilocybin mushrooms, peyote	Gas, aerosols, glue, nitrites, rush, white out	Pot, dope, grass, weed, herb, hash, joint	Heroin (junk, dope, black tar, China white), Demerol, Dilaudid (Ds), morphine, codeine	Speed, uppers, crank, bam, black beauties, crystal, dexies, caffeine, nicotine, cocaine, amphetamines
Altered mood and perceptions, focus on detail, anxiety, panic, nausea, synaesthesia (e.g., smell colors, see sounds)	Nausea, dizziness, headaches, lack of coordination and control	Altered perceptions, red eyes, dry mouth, reduced concentration and coordination, euphoria, laughing, hunger	Euphoria, drowsiness, insensitivity to pain, nausea, vomiting, watery eyes, runny nose (see Depressants)	Alertness, talkativeness, wakefulness, increased blood pressure, loss of appetite, mood elevation
Capsules, tablets, "microdots," blotter squares	Odor of substance on clothing and breath, intoxication, drowsiness, poor muscular control	Rolling papers, pipes, dried plant material, odor of burnt hemp rope, roach clips	Needle marks on arms, needles, syringes, spoons, pinpoint pupils, cold moist skin	Pills and capsules, loss of sleep and appetite, irritability or anxiety, weight loss, hyperactivity
Unpredictable behavior, emotional instability, violent behavior (with PCP)	Unconsciousness, suffocation, nausea and vomiting, damage to brain and central nervous system, sudden death	Panic reaction, impaired short term memory, addiction	Addiction, lethargy, weight loss, contamination from unsterile needles (hepatitis, AIDS), accidental overdose	Fatigue leading to exhaustion, addiction, paranoia, depression, confusion, possibly hallucinations

4. Withdrawal from responsibilities/family contacts
5. Association with drug-using peers
6. Unusual patterns of behavior
7. Defensive attitude concerning drugs

Teachers need to know how to manage suspected substance abuse episodes and suspected intoxication or withdrawal crises in school. Their role is to manage and refer students appropriately, not to become investigators or counselors. Although educators must be aware of indications of substance abuse, they should not automatically assume that certain physical or psychological symptoms are the result of intoxication or withdrawal. Referral to counselors or medical personnel is appropriate to determine the cause. A clear school policy regarding detection and management helps teachers and administrators respond correctly to suspected abuse and crisis situations. In the event of an emotional–behavioral crisis, the teacher should remain calm and nonconfrontational. We have known for a long time that safety is more important than demonstrating disciplinary control (Miksic, 1987).

EARLY SEXUAL ACTIVITY AND TEEN PARENTHOOD

Delinquency, substance abuse, and sexual activity are often linked. Sexual activity itself may be defined as a juvenile status offense (Udry & Bearman, 1998), but some juveniles commit index sex crimes such as rape, sodomy, or molestation (see Morenz & Becker, 1995). However, most early sexual intercourse is a concern because it is associated with a high risk of teenage pregnancy and premature parental responsibility, contracting sexually transmitted diseases (STDs), and a wide variety of psychological and health risks (Botvin, Schinke, & Orlandi, 1995). In earlier times, sexuality was less often discussed and assumed to be a feature of adult life. However, "sexuality is no longer relegated to adulthood by cultural definition and is clearly part of adolescent behavior; yet, at the same time, increases in both teen pregnancy and sexually transmitted diseases observed with the lowering of the age of first intercourse have led to continued reluctance to accept sexual behavior in adolescents" (Graber, Brooks-Gunn, & Galen, 1998, p. 279). Sexual intercourse itself is of much less concern when it is engaged in by an 18-year-old than by a 13-year-old; the level of concern is inversely proportional to the age of the child or youth (cf. Gordon & Schroeder, 1995).

Adolescents with psychological problems are at particularly high risk for contracting acquired immunodeficiency syndrome (AIDS) and other STDs through casual sexual encounters, which are often are linked with substance abuse. Sexual activity of young teenagers is also associated with social and emotional maladjustment and inadequate child-care skills (Thomas & Rickel, 1995). Many adolescents have distorted perceptions of their own high-risk behavior; they see having sex as relatively low in risk and high in benefit for them (Siegel, Cousins, Rubovits, Parsons, Lavery, & Crowley, 1994). Students with emotional or behavioral disorders tend to have distorted ideas about sexual behavior that put them at high risk of contracting AIDS (Singh, Zemitzsch, Ellis, Best, & Singh, 1994). Teenage pregnancy and parenthood present enormous problems for young people, particularly those who may already be penalized by our society's responses to ethnicity (Benson & Torpy, 1995). The problems encountered by the children of teenage mothers and fathers are often overwhelming (Scott-Jones, 1993).

The sexual behavior of teens may be motivated by a variety of factors other than physiological urges. The social and psychological conditions that encourage early sexual activity are many and complex; they include the family and cultural factors we discussed in part 3. Sexual abuse by older individuals may initiate the sexual activity of some teenagers, and they may suffer long-term psychological stress or dysfunction as a result (Gordon & Schroeder, 1995; Polunsy & Follette, 1995). Many sexually active teenagers appear to be seeking a sense of belonging, emotional closeness, or importance that they are unable to achieve in other ways. They may romanticize parenthood, believing that their child will give them the love they have not found from others. Some appear to be addicted to sex and love (Griffin-Shelley, 1994). In a study of approximately 200 adolescents aged 12 to 19 years of age, Donenberg, Bryant, Emerson, Wilson, and Pasch (2003) found that three variables enabled the researchers to predict which girls initiated sexual activity at or before 14 years of age. Those three variables were: hostile parental control, peer influence, and externalizing psychopathology. The psychological and physical risks are grave for these young teenagers. The realities and personal costs of teenage parenthood—to the teenagers and to their children—are staggering.

There are also differences in the reasons that adolescents engage in sexual intercourse that are related to the sex of the individual as well as the culture in which he or she lives. Eyre and Millstein (1999) asked 83 adolescents between the ages of 16 and 20 to list the qualities they preferred in a sexual partner as well as the reasons to have or abstain from having sexual intercourse. A core of beliefs related to reasons to have sex emerged across all of the groups included in the study. They included familiarity with the partner and the partner's sexual history, the partner's overall level of intelligence, and ease of communication as positive factors. The absence of these factors was associated with reasons not to have sex with a person. This study also found variations in attitudes and sexual behavior between males and females, as well as between African Americans and White adolescents. Males of both races described sexual arousal as a reason for engaging in intercourse, whereas females more often described concerns regarding personal respect and the individual's prospects for the future as reason to have sex. African American adolescents who were sexually active more often reported association of such activity with love, marriage, and parenthood, whereas White adolescents (particularly males) more often reported sexual activity in relation to drinking. Clearly, suggesting that all males, females, African Americans, or White adolescents express the same views on sexuality is inappropriate. However, the findings of this report suggest that several general social–motivational as well as group-specific factors may be harnessed to reduce the impact of risky sexual behavior.

The facts of teenage sexual activity and parenthood are often assumed to imply a need for education about sexuality, family life, and parenting. However, education and other interventions designed to decrease teen sexual activity have yet to demonstrate their effectiveness. Benson and Torpy (1995) studied the sexual behavior of students in Grades 6 through 8 in Chicago schools, finding that none of the following variables was related to loss of virginity: church attendance, religious affiliation, school grade-point average, type of housing, marital status of the child's natural parents, self-esteem, knowledge related to sex education, or school attendance. They concluded that current school-based efforts to reduce sexual activity and pregnancy among young teenagers are unlikely to be effective. Research on how to lower the prevalence of early sexual activity has lagged behind research on the prevention of substance abuse (Botvin et al., 1995).

Because early sexual activity and premature parenthood are often accompanied by emotional or behavioral disorders of both teenagers and their children, special educators are often involved in planning and implementing the curriculum. In addition, special educators must work with other professionals who provide supportive services to families and children in distress.

SUMMARY

Children and adolescents with emotional or behavior disorders often engage in delinquency, substance abuse, and precocious sexual behavior. These behaviors rarely occur in isolation from each other. Rather, troubled adolescents more often display a constellation of interrelated behavioral difficulties referred to as *problem behavior syndrome*. Problem behavior syndrome suggests that the severity and extent of adolescent engagement in the behaviors discussed in this chapter are related to the persistence and aggravation of such problems in adult life.

Juvenile delinquency is a legal term indicating violation of the law by an individual who is not yet an adult. Acts that are illegal only if committed by a minor are *status offenses; index crimes* are illegal regardless of the individual's age. The vast majority of youngsters commit delinquent acts; a small percentage are apprehended. Delinquent children and youth often have other emotional or behavioral disorders, especially conduct disorder. However, not all delinquents are identified as having conduct disorder, and not all youngsters with conduct disorder are delinquents. Several subtypes of delinquents (socialized-subcultural, unsocialized psychopathic, and neurotic-disturbed) have been identified, but the most important distinctions are probably between those who commit few delinquent acts and those who are chronic offenders, especially those who repeat violent offenses against persons.

About 20% of all children and youth are at some time officially delinquent, and about 3% are adjudicated each year. About half of all official delinquents commit only one offense before reaching adulthood. Recidivists account for the majority of official delinquency. Peak ages for juvenile delinquency are ages 15 to 17. Most adjudicated delinquents are male. Juvenile crime and delinquency have become more frequent and more violent in recent years.

Causal factors in delinquency are numerous and include antisocial behavior, hyperactivity and impulsivity, low intelligence and school achievement, family conflict and criminality, poverty, and poor parental discipline. Delinquency appears to grow from environmental disadvantages, weakened social bonds (to family, school, and work), and disrupted social relationships between youths and social institutions in the community. Effective prevention would have to address all of the conditions that increase risk of delinquency.

We might logically take the position that nearly all incarcerated delinquents have emotional or behavioral disorders requiring special education. Assessment of delinquents' educational needs is extremely difficult because of the behavioral characteristics of delinquents and the social agencies that serve them.

Intervention in delinquency, if it is to be successful, must involve families, juvenile justice, schools, and communities. Parents need training to monitor and discipline their children more effectively. Juvenile justice may involve a variety of strategies, ranging from diversion to incarceration. The recommendations of researchers are typically for interventions that keep all but violent offenders in the community. Schools typically respond to disruptive and delinquent behavior with heightened punishment and a focus on security, but schoolwide discipline and emphasis on attention to appropriate behavior are more successful. Education in the corrections system should include functional assessment of students' needs, a curriculum that teaches important life skills, vocational training, supportive transition back to the community, and a full range of educational and related services from collaborating agencies.

Street gangs are an increasing problem in many cities, but misperceptions of these gangs are common. Street gangs are aggregations of youth who define themselves as a group and are committed to a criminal orientation. Most do not have drug distribution as a primary focus, and most of gang members' time is spent doing noncriminal and nonviolent acts. Gang members typically have notable personal deficiencies, are antisocial, desire status and companionship, and lead mostly boring lives. The causes and approaches to prevention of gangs are similar to those for delinquency, and many of the same intervention strategies apply, especially addressing problems of poverty and joblessness. However, gangs are maintained by perceived external threats and interventions that strengthen their cohesiveness. Many schools are running scared and approach gangs in ways that are counterproductive. A particular educational need is a differentiated curriculum that includes programs for noncollege-bound youth.

Substance abuse is not easy to define. However, a substance may be considered abused when it is deliberately used to induce physiological or psychological effects (or both) for other than therapeutic purposes and when its use contributes to health risks, impaired psychological functioning, adverse social consequences, or some combination of these. The most pervasive substance abuse problems involve alcohol and tobacco. Substance abuse typically progresses through several stages: from experimentation to social–recreational use to circumstantial–situational use, which may become intensified and lead to obsessional dependency. Teachers are most likely to observe the first indications of substance use during the transition from experimentation to social–recreational or to circumstantial–situational use. The causes of substance abuse are varied and include family, peer, community, and biological factors. Substance abuse is often accompanied by other disorders. Effective prevention programs are expensive, multifaceted, and controversial. Intervention in substance abuse must be designed for the individual case. School-based interventions require clear school policies regarding drugs, systematic efforts to provide information, referral to other agencies, and involvement of families and peers. In addition, interventions related to substance abuse may need to target the individual's beliefs that they actually can affect change in their patterns of substance use.

Early sexual activity is of concern primarily because of the risk of pregnancy, sexually transmitted diseases, and psychological and health problems. The sexual activity of juveniles may be motivated by a variety of factors, but the risk of negative consequences is always high. Teachers may be involved in educational programs, but current school-based intervention programs may be ineffective.

Problem Behaviors of Adolescence

Michele M. Brigham, M.Ed., has been teaching for 28 years. She is a high school special education resource teacher and teaches practical English in Crozet, Virginia. She is also the choral director for her school and directs its musicals. As an adjunct faculty member for the University of Virginia, she teaches special education courses in Falls Church, Virginia.

How would you describe the academic needs of most of the high school students you teach?

Most of the high school students I teach face three sources of tension in dealing with their academic needs. First, my students have severe deficits in basic skills. Schools are reluctant to provide direct remediation of basic skills because to do so would mean setting up specialized treatments which would remove students from some inclusive environments and some elements of the standards-based curriculum delivered to their age mates. Second, they are not passing their classes so any time you could provide remediation is spent tutoring them on class assignments. Even with this tutorial assistance, many students still have trouble passing their classes and the state proficiency examinations. Consequently, many of them will not earn a standard high school diploma. Third, one of the results of the standards-based curriculum reform is a drastic reduction in vocational educational opportunities. In addition to it being unlikely my students can graduate with a standard high school diploma, they are unlikely to leave schools with the skills required for entry into the skilled or semiskilled labor force.

The students I work with are far behind their peers in reading and writing skills. For example, it is very common for seniors in my Practical English classes to have standard scores in the low 50s to mid-80s or third- to eighth-grade reading levels. They lack decoding skills to enable them to read fluently, and poor comprehension is the direct result of that lack of fluency. Their reading skills are so deficient that they don't consider reading a pleasurable activity or a viable way of gaining information about the world. They resist reading aloud, which is the best way to gain accuracy, and long before they get to high school most of their teachers have refrained from requiring them

to read aloud. As a result, they have been unable to make much progress in their fluency and comprehension. As reading is a primary access skill for the general curriculum, core content classes present tremendous challenges for these students.

One would expect people with poor reading skills to be deficient in writing skills also, and this is certainly the case for my students. They have difficulty in grammar, syntax and pragmatic language. Their problems with written language include basic mechanics difficulties such as spelling and punctuation. They require training in forming complete sentences and organizing ideas into complex sentences and paragraphs. Their compositions lack elaboration and provide only sketchy information about their content knowledge or the topic on which they are writing. Writing is a slow and laborious task for them, and they often have poor handwriting and keyboarding skills. Therefore, it's easy to see that skills that are automatized for most students at this level are causing distraction from the type of cognitive skills required to craft both expository and narrative prose. One of the major ways that high school students are expected to demonstrate competency in the core content classes is through writing. The writing deficiencies that characterize my students further exacerbate the problems caused by their reading difficulties as they face the demands of core content classes.

There is a complex interaction between these skill deficits and general verbal abilities. My students lack the confidence in their ability to understand other people and to express themselves. Consequently, they often mask their confusion with the appearance of belligerence or nonchalance. Many teachers base their informal judgments about what students know or students' interest level in the class on their participation in classroom discussions. Many of my students who believe they lack the ability to interact in the complex exchange of ideas may behave in ways that cause the teacher to see them as disruptive, incompetent, or aloof. Although some of them are, many of them are using these behaviors to mask their insecurity or their inability to participate competitively with their peers. These skills are rarely explicitly taught at this level in the general education curriculum. Consequently, students who have failed to acquire them before they reach high school are unlikely to extrapolate them from immediate experience or profit substantially from mere exposure to the general curriculum.

The interaction of these skill deficits leads to an even larger problem for my students, which is a deficient store of background knowledge. Their background knowledge deficits make it difficult for them to participate meaningfully in many aspects of general education classes. Put simply, they just don't understand what their teachers and peers are talking about. Consequently, many of my students dismiss the general education curriculum as "stupid" or irrelevant. Although the relevance of the curriculum is debatable, I am convinced that these problems make the curriculum far more difficult for my students than it is for most of their peers.

Most of my direct teaching is with language arts. However, in my work with students in remedial settings, I have observed similar deficits in their ability to keep up with their peers in mathematics, science, and social studies. It is easy to see how their skill deficits in reading and writing cause similar problems in these areas.

To what extent do the youngsters you teach need social skills training?

Most of the students I work with have serious problems in the social domain. However, the extent to which they would profit from direct social skills training is somewhat questionable. To many educators, social skills training means instruction in specific interactional skills such as making eye contact, shaking hands, and polite conversation. At the high school level, social skills intervention probably should be more about the students' belief that appropriate behavior is worth the effort rather than remediation of skill deficits. There is a difference between knowing the skills and using them. Most of my students know the appropriate behaviors and have the skills to employ them, but they behave in a maladaptive way because they have found that to be more effective and efficient in attaining their immediate goals. Their previous interactions have led them to believe they

will never achieve competence in the skills prized in the academic domain, so the reward structure for them has become focused on escape and avoidance.

Many of the psychologists and guidance officials who are in supportive roles construct anger management plans for my students that allow them to leave the instructional environment anytime they become upset rather than teaching them strategies to cope with demands that are difficult for them. I am not always convinced that this is the best way to support my students in reaching their long-term goals because it (a) deprives them of the instruction they need to succeed academically and (b) keeps them from learning coping skills that will allow them to achieve independence and success in employment. For example, one of the young men who was supported by such a plan was unsuccessful in work-study during his senior year and has yet to hold down a job in the 3 years since he has graduated. Whenever he is provided with negative feedback by a supervisor, he uses the same strategy he was taught in school and walks off his job. This inability to meet the demands of the working world leads me to doubt his ability to successfully meet the commitment of marriage, parenting, and other social relationships that enhance quality of life. By the time they are seniors, most of my students have experienced repeated failure in holding jobs, and I suspect that their lack of coping ability rather than deficits in specific social skills is directly related to this problem. Social skills training at the high school level would probably be better accomplished through a set of coping strategies taught through clearly established rules, expectations, and consequences that are consistently enforced, with parallels drawn to the working world.

What advice would you offer to teachers of typical high school students who are likely to have trouble with the law or need special education because of emotional or behavioral disorders?

Interestingly enough, many teachers already know the techniques that would be most successful with my students. Teacher effectiveness has been studied in depth, and teacher and lesson effectiveness variables have been identified that are crucial to students with emotional and behavioral disorders. Teachers need to consciously use the good teaching techniques that have been identified through empirical research. These include maximizing engaged time on task, with students actively participating in instructional activities; making sure the content is covered with appropriate pacing, well-defined and prioritized objectives, and structured delivery of information that includes a statement of the objectives, review and repetition of the important points, ample opportunities for practice, and frequent and explicit feedback using techniques such as curriculum-based measurement. It is important for my students to have a much higher density of feedback to allow them to see and acknowledge for themselves that they are making steps toward competency. Structure and consistency in the classroom are important for my students to feel secure enough to make attempts at learning material that has been difficult or impossible for them to learn in past attempts.

What are the most important things a teacher can do to help students who have begun to abuse substances?

Dealing with substance abuse is a bigger problem than most teachers should handle by themselves because our training prepares us for instructional-behavioral issues within the classroom. We should respect the limits as well as the competencies of our training.

Unless a teacher is trained to deal with this type of problem, the first step should always be to refer the student to the appropriate professionals. In my school, our guidance professionals, school nurse, and school psychologist are the front line for working with students with substance abuse problems. However, in thinking about things that can be done in the classroom, it's hard to imagine that the kinds of good teaching methods that help students with disabilities would be completely ineffective with students who have begun to abuse substances. Clear and explicit feedback, focus on accomplishments, high density of reinforcement for accomplishment, and helping students to understand the relationship between effective effort and successful outcome are tools teachers can use effectively with students engaging in substance abuse. It is important that the reinforcement is for legitimate accomplishment. Too often we provide reinforcement for inconsequential behaviors in our attempt to promote self-esteem. My students see through this immediately, which breaks the bond of trust required for successful instruction and creates even more concern regarding their own potential. It is vital to provide students with the skills to allow them to experience self-esteem through success.

What are the most common behavioral problems that you must deal with in your classroom?

The major problems that I have with my students are refusal to participate, truancy, and tardiness. Refusal to participate takes many forms, including gestures and language that some see as the problem instead of as serving the function of escape. I believe that whatever form the refusal to participate takes, the real problem that we should deal with is the attempt to withdraw from the instruction. I see my students in two very controlled settings outside of the core content classes—a resource–tutorial setting and a dedicated practical English class. Although many people prefer the word *segregated,* that implies involuntary separation. Most of my students are terrified that they will be forced to return to the general education settings, where they are well aware that their skill level will keep them from success and they will perceive their failure as personal humiliation. Even within these homogeneous settings, I experience high levels of resistance to instruction from many students. Task avoidance behaviors such as refusal to participate in instruction, refusal to attempt to do assignments or otherwise participate in classroom activities, tardiness, and truancy have been inadvertently rewarded in both regular and special education settings.

When students present teachers with the choice of ignoring their disengagement or dealing with the disruption that is likely to result from intervening with these behaviors, teachers who are overwhelmed by the size of their classes and the amount of material to be covered can ill afford to devote substantial amount of instructional time to that student at the expense of the rest of the class. These teachers understandably opt for the former, teaching our students that those behaviors are both effective and efficient to obtain their goals. Support staff, parents, and IEP teams too often excuse students from instructional demands rather than provide them with the requisite skills to benefit from instruction. By the time they get to high school, many of these students are so overwhelmed by their cycle of failure they are no longer willing to take the risks or make the effort required for success in learning.

What are the kids you teach actually like? Give us a thumbnail sketch of several of them.

Carrie is a sophomore, but still considered a freshman because she hasn't passed enough classes or SOLs (state exams called Standards of Learning). She is living with her grandmother. Carrie has had a lot of difficulty in her classes and has lost a job she really liked because of her inability to control her temper, work with people she doesn't like, and tell the truth. She has an emotional or behavioral disorder and a behavior plan, and she is being considered for placement in a special school but has not been placed yet because of inadequate documentation of her problems.

Kate is a junior with a learning disability (LD) and has become quite successful in her practical level classes. She takes classes half the school day and has been placed for work-study in a job she really enjoys. Though she's very proud of her job, it is currently in jeopardy because she has been unable to pass her driver's test and needs transportation (not provided by the school).

Larry is also a junior with an LD. He is probably the most successful of the three in understanding and working with his disability. He will take standard-level classes during his senior year. He is involved with his community and is active in a theater company. Larry is a very talented artist as well. Though he describes himself as a former "hoodlum," Larry has mastered the social skills he needs to be successful in school.

Michele Brigham Interviews Carrie, Kate, and Larry (individual interviews, different responses)

Ms. B.: If there was one thing you could change about school, what would it be?

Carrie: The group situation. I don't like how people are classified into different groups. You've got the Gothics, the preps, the rednecks. I don't like that. I think everybody should get along . . . You see a lot of them hang out, and you still classify them into different groups.

Ms. B.: If there was anything you could change about yourself to make school easier, what would you change?

C: I don't really think I'd actually change anything about myself. I know I have an attitude problem, and I'm working on that. But I don't think I'd change anything. Because I don't think my schooling is about me. It's my attitude, and that's just about it, and I'm working on that one.

Ms. B.: If you actually made that change, how do you think it would affect you outside of school, after you're done with school?

C: I think it would help me a whole lot if I changed my attitude, because I sometimes open my mouth about things that I really shouldn't. And I think it'd make life a little bit more easier for me.

Ms. B.: What do you think you want to be doing when you get out of school?

C: I definitely want to go to college. I either want to go and be a lawyer or a doctor. I like the whole doctor scene. I want to do something with helping people. I definitely want to do that. I'm a hands-on person helping people. I definitely want to do something like that.

Ms. B.: Is there anything in school that's helping you toward that goal?

C: Well, not at this point, but next year I'm taking a nurses class over at [the vocational–technical school] that'll give me a little feel for what I'm doing, what I'm getting into.

Ms. B.: Is there anything is school that's keeping you from that goal?

C: Not to my knowledge. No.

Ms. B.: Have you ever thought about dropping out?

C: No. I've told my father it doesn't matter how many years I'm in high school, I'm going to graduate.

Kate: No. Not ever.

Larry: Well, I'm 18 now. I became 18 last month. Pretty much no. But one of my teachers gave me the idea that maybe I could, because I'm 18, drop out and get a GED [general equivalency diploma] and completely skip my senior year and go straight to college. And I thought about that, and I asked some people, and everyone seems to agree that it's a bad idea.

Ms. B.: And you're comfortable with that?

L: Yeah. I'm a year older than I should be because I got held back in first grade. Because I was a little hoodlum back then. Caused a lot of trouble. And I really wish that hadn't happened because I won't have many friends next year. Because almost all of my friends are seniors.

Ms. B.: What's made you decide to stay in school?

C: I have a boyfriend now who didn't finish school, and he regrets it. And my father and mother dropped out of school, too. And they regret it to this day. And they tell me, "You need to finish school," but I've always promised my grandparents and everyone I'm going to make something of myself, and I am. I don't care how many years it takes me just to graduate high school, I'm going to make something of myself.

K: I don't know. It's just my goal to graduate and be with my brother. He's the only one to graduate [from high school] from my biological family.

Ms. B.: Think about the way you want to be 5 years from now. Is there anything about yourself you want to work on to get to that goal?

C: I want to work on accepting me for who I am. I really have a bad problem with doing that. Whether it's like in choir and I can't sing or, like, it's beauty pageants I go to and I don't win or something, I need to accept myself for who I am, because I really can't change myself. Which I could, but it'd be a little silly I think. But I need to work on that.

K: Have a better attitude about things. I seem to get mad if I don't understand something. They say I have attention disorder or something.

Ms. B.: When you get mad, what problems does that cause you?

K: I get frustrated and just want to stop doing whatever it is I'm doing right there at that second and start cleaning. That's the only way I can take my frustration out.

Ms. B.: Why do you have an IEP?

C: I think it's because of my . . . I call it a learning disability, I really don't know what you would call it. I think it's because of my level of reading and the way I comprehend things.

K: I have ADD.

Ms. B.: What does that mean?

K: Attention deficit disorder.

Ms. B.: Do you take medication for that?

K: No. I quit taking it because, I was taking Ritalin and it didn't help at all, and they found I was better off of it.

L: Well, the teachers, back when I was little, you know, they used to say I had ADD. My dad didn't want to believe it. And they gave me a test to check. And it turns out I didn't have ADD. I had short-term memory loss. So, you know, I have a hard time remembering things. But I think I worked things out in a way so it's not such a big problem anymore.

Ms. B.: Do you write things down?

L: No, I just . . . I don't know. It's still there, but it's not as big a problem anymore. It's something you work to overcome.

Ms. B.: How do you feel about that—having an IEP?

C: It doesn't bother me. It used to really bother me, because over at [middle school] I had two Englishes and then I was always in a study hall here, and it kind of bothered me to begin with, but then again it really didn't because I see that I needed the help. But I had to want to do it for myself. I couldn't let somebody else help me.

K: I think it's fine. I mean, it's not a regular diploma. It's not a standard or advanced, but it's a diploma.

Ms. B.: So you're going to get an IEP diploma?

K: Yeah. But it's a diploma. And it's just like a regular one. It doesn't have the word IEP on it.

Ms. B.: Do you think your IEP is helpful to you?

C: I think it is if I'd use it. Sometimes I won't use it, as you found out. I've got to want to ask for help.

K: Yes, I do.

L: Yeah. It gives me resource to get stuff done. And often times in, like, math—and math is my weak point— I'll need help, a lot of help. And that gives me help.

Ms. B.: Some people say that we should do away with special education altogether and everyone should be in a regular class. How do you feel about that?

C: I think that's a little silly, because not everybody learns the same way as somebody else would, because I definitely don't catch on to what people are saying quickly. I think we should have the special education thing because, if everybody learned at the same level school would go by so much faster, but, you know, it doesn't. And everybody comprehends things at a different pace, and we all need somebody to teach us differently.

K: I think they're wrong when they say that, because . . . Take me and [another student] who are in special education, and put them in regular classes with regular people. They're going to get made fun of if they don't know the answers. Because I'm going through that now in one of my regular classes.

L: I disagree. Because some kids are smarter, and some kids are not as smart. That's just the way things are. People like to believe that everyone's equal, but in reality they're not.

Ms. B.: Why do you think some kids abuse drugs and alcohol?

C: I think some say it has to do with their parents or peer pressure and things like that. I can honestly say, and I know you've probably heard this from a lot of kids, but I've never really done drugs. I have drank, I'll admit to that. I've been scared because my father used to do alcohol and used to do weed and stuff like that, and I've always been ascared that I'd get addicted to it, and I don't really want to ruin my life like that. I just don't understand why you would waste your life . . . But some people, they'll start off with a little weed and then it goes to worse things, and then they really realize what they did, but it's peer pressure. [This school] definitely has a lot of that, because there are parties and the parties aren't directly chaperoned. There are a lot of parties that are illegal and have so much stuff, and freshmen go to them, and, they're like, "I'm gonna be cool" and the little freshmen want to fit in with the big seniors. So they try something . . . and then it leads to something worse.

K: Because they think it's something that's going to help them, and it's not.

Ms. B.: Why do you think that?

K: Because . . . it just makes your mind light-headed. The only reason that I know that is my brother was in a bad accident a couple years ago. He had been drinking and got behind the wheel or a car, and I vowed I'd never do it.

L: It's kind of like an escape, probably. Some kids do it because it makes them feel older, it makes them feel . . . I don't know. I don't do drugs or alcohol. I've drunk before, but not often, and it's not that big a deal, and I don't do it at all anymore. I've never done drugs, and I never will. And that's because of my sister. The problem with things like drugs or weed or any of that stuff is that when you're a teenager, part of being a teenager is having these ups and downs on an emotional scale. When you're a teenager you cry a lot and laugh a lot at the same time. And what drugs do is dull that, and you go through your whole teenage life without that experience. So you don't develop like a normal person does. So you can be 34 or 40 and still be 17 mentally, because you never went through that whole stage in your life, because you dulled it. I just look at it as a complete waste of time, you know. They spend hundreds of dollars on this habit, and they just sit around with each other and smoke their weed or whatever . . . and the feelings are artificial. I believe in the good feelings that I already have. Some people get a buzz off the chemical the brain produces when you exercise a lot, they get addicted to it, and that's a good addiction . . . Sometimes I've even gotten a buzz off music, just getting good feelings, I just felt so happy, and it's uplifting. Some people get a buzz off skiing. It just depends on what part of life your drug is. I don't believe in these other things.

Ms. B.: We just finished our state testing program. Some kids will pass and some won't. Do you think these tests are good for the school and for students?

C: I think people will see them as good for the school, because they can see if teachers are doing their job. Which I don't believe. I don't think any kid really likes the SOLs. Technically, if they do, well . . . they like tests. I don't like them because I don't think they're fair to students, because students like me, I know I freak out when you have a big test coming up . . . I don't deal too well with pressure. It's not fair, because

you don't really know how the teacher's teaching, because you don't know if the teacher taught you all you should know . . . If you don't pass the SOLs, then you can't graduate, and I don't think that's too fair. It's too much pressure on us.

L: I don't really care. SOLs are a joke to me. They're so easy. If you don't pass them then you really don't deserve to pass the school, because they're so pathetically easy. They don't even mention them in advanced and honors classes. They know the kids are more than prepared to crush the tests.

Ms. B.: Do you have siblings?

L: I have an older sister. She's 4 years older than me, she's 23.

Ms. B.: Do you think school was harder for you than it was for your sister?

L: At first, she was better at school. She used to get straight As. And I used to be the one that did poorly in school. And then, ever since she hit a certain age she started mixing in with the wrong people and her grades dropped, you know, she started getting into really bad stuff, and then she had a baby and then she dropped out of school. So it was, like, for a while she was the better one, and it switched all of a sudden, and then she became the rotten apple.

Ms. B.: So, do you think you learned something from that? From seeing her get mixed up with the wrong people?

L: Oh, yes, absolutely. Because she did that, I am very firm in the belief that I'll never do any of the stuff she did, like drugs. She's completely irresponsible, and she made the worst possible choices and got with the worst people you can imagine. Like, my nephew's father is in prison right now. And I just don't ever want to become her.

Ms. B.: How about your parents and grandparents—do you know anything about how school was for them?

L: My Brazilian grandparents, I don't know them very well at all. I hardly ever see them. And I only met my grandma once, and she wasn't really my grandma. She's my step-grandmother, I suppose. My Brazilian grandpa died . . . I probably met him, but I was too young to remember . . . I don't know what the deal was with her. They probably didn't go to school much at all. My American grandparents, I know my grandmother, she only has a middle school education. So, from there, she dropped out and married my grandpa. And I'm not really sure about his education. He joined the military.

1. What are the things you can do as a teacher to help steer students away from the most serious problems of adolescence?

2. What should you do, and how should you do it, if you become aware that one of your students (of any age) is abusing substances?

3. As a teacher, how would you talk to a student who comes to you with accounts of early sexual experience? What would you ask? What would you say, and how would you say it?

CHAPTER FIFTEEN

ANXIETY AND RELATED DISORDERS

As you read this chapter, keep these guiding questions in mind:

- How is anxiety related to a variety of emotional and behavioral disorders?

- Under what conditions should educators and others be concerned when a youngster exhibits behavior characteristic of anxiety?

- What are the most effective intervention strategies in anxiety disorders, including school phobia?

- What kinds of obsessive-compulsive behavior are most often seen in children and adolescents?

- What role can the peer group play in effective intervention in social isolation?

Chapters 11 through 14 dealt mostly with problems that fall under the general dimension of *externalizing disorders*. This chapter turns to problems designated generally as *internalizing*. Although the broadband classification of *internalizing* is well established in empirical studies of behavioral dimensions, most of the specific categories and disorders that fall under it are not. In short, there is more confusion and controversy over terminology and classification for internalizing problems than for externalizing problems. Therefore, grouping internalizing problems for discussion presents unavoidable difficulties.

Regardless of how internalizing problems are grouped for discussion, it is important to recognize that they may occur along with externalizing problems. Externalizing and internalizing are not mutually exclusive, and when they occur together, the child is at particularly high risk. In fact, Loeber, Farrington, Stouthamer-Loeber, & Van Kammen (1998a) found in their longitudinal work evidence of a connection between internalizing problems and delinquency in some cases.

Anxiety, social withdrawal, and other internalizing behavior problems often occur together and sometimes are comorbid—coexisting—with externalizing behavioral problems (Albano, Chorpita, & Barlow, 2003; Brigham & Cole, 1999; Gresham & Kern, 2004; Kazdin, 2001; Tankersley & Landrum, 1997). Eating disorders and reluctant speech may both involve specific fears or anxieties, stereotyped movement disorders may involve obsessions or compulsions or both, and so on. Anxiety is a frequent component of other disorders, and anxiety disorders of all types may be comorbid with a variety of other disorders. "In general, it is important to keep in mind that comorbidity is the rule—not the exception in abnormal child psychology" (Rabian & Silverman, 1995, p. 236).

The relationships among the various problems involving anxiety and other internalizing problems are tenuous. We will not attempt to summarize definition, prevalence, causal factors, prevention, assessment, intervention, or education for the general case or for all specific disorders because these disorders are so varied and loosely related. The problems we discuss are representative of those most frequently described in the literature. We begin with anxiety disorders because they are the broadest category; anxiety appears to be a significant component of all the others.

ANXIETY DISORDERS

Anxiety—the distress, tension, or uneasiness that goes with fears and worries—is part of the normal development of young children (Albano et al., 2003; Dadds, 2002; Hintze, 2002; Morris & Kratochwill, 1998; Stevenson-Hinde & Shouldice, 1995). At birth, infants have a fear of falling and of loud noise; fear of other stimuli (strange persons, objects, situations) ordinarily develops during the first few months. These fears probably have survival value, and they are considered normal and adaptive, not deviant. As children grow into the middle childhood years they develop additional fears, especially about imaginary creatures or events. Unless the fears become excessive or debilitative and prevent the child from engaging in normal social interaction, sleep, school attendance, or exploring the environment, they are not maladaptive. Indeed, a child who has no fears at all is not only highly unusual but also likely to be hurt or killed because of inappropriate brashness.

Children's anxieties or fears may be mild and short-lived enough that they do not seriously interfere with social growth. In fact, "study of the *prevalence of anxiety* in childhood has focused on subclinical fears and school phobia" (Strauss, 1993, p. 240, emphasis in original). Most studies show that about 7 or 8% of children experience intense anxieties at some time, although not all of these anxieties require clinical intervention (see Anderson, 1994). When fear unnecessarily restricts the child's activity, however, intervention is called for. A child or youth may be in a chronic state of anxiety about a broad range of things, in which case he or she may be described as having a generalized anxiety disorder. However, a youngster may also have a more specific anxiety. It may be an extreme irrational fear that is out of proportion to reality and leads to automatic avoidance of the feared situation, which is often called a phobia. The child showing extreme anxiety and social withdrawal (often labeled *neurosis* in psychodynamic literature) has traditionally been assumed to be more disturbed and to have a worse prognosis for adult adjustment than does the hostile, acting-out child with an externalizing disorder. Research does not bear out this assumption.

Characteristics associated with anxiety and withdrawal are usually more transitory and amenable to treatment than are those associated with conduct disorder, and anxiety does not put a child at risk for later development of schizophrenia or other major psychiatric disorder in adulthood (Klein & Last, 1989; Quay & La Greca, 1986; Robins, 1966, 1986). Compared to their awareness of peers' aggressive and disruptive behavior, children's awareness of their peers' anxiety and withdrawal is not as keen or as early to develop (Safran, 1995). At least among normal children, those with high levels of anxiety appear to see themselves in more negative terms than do those whose anxiety is lower (Muris, Merckelbach, Mayer, & Snieder, 1998).

Anxiety withdrawal in its typical form is not the greatest concern to knowledgeable professionals who work with children and youth who have emotional or behavioral disorders. Nevertheless, in their extreme forms, anxiety and related disorders *do* result in serious impairment of functioning. Extreme social isolation, extreme and persistent anxiety, and persistent extreme fears, for example, can seriously endanger social and personal development and demand effective intervention. Some children and adolescents experience severe attacks of panic: "the unexpected occurrence of episodes of intense distress . . . [consisting of] a constellation of four or more cognitive and somatic symptoms (e.g., sweating, pounding heart, rapid breathing, tingling sensations, racing thoughts over losing control) and may or may not be triggered by a situational cue" (Barrios & O'Dell, 1998, p. 253). Moreover, anxiety is frequently comorbid with depression, conduct disorder, learning disabilities, and other disorders discussed later in this chapter (see Barrios & O'Dell, 1998; Newcomer, Barenbaum, & Pearson, 1995; Rabian & Silverman, 1995).

Quay and La Greca (1986) estimated that persistent anxiety may characterize 2% of the child population and that about 5% may be affected by such behavior problems at one time or another. Anxiety may be part of the problems of 20 to 30% of youngsters referred to clinics for treatment of behavioral disorders. The prevalence of anxious-withdrawn behavior appears to be approximately the same as that of conduct disorder, placing it among the most common emotional or behavioral disorders of childhood (Anderson & Werry, 1994). Boys and girls are referred for these problems in about equal percentages, but these are only rough estimates because there have been no extensive studies of prevalence in children.

Evidence suggests that much anxiety is learned but that biological factors also may contribute to anxiety disorders. Humans learn fears in a variety of ways (see Herbert, 1994; Morris & Kratochwill, 1983, 1998; Siegel & Ridley-Johnson, 1985, for detailed analyses of fear acquisition). Infants and young children especially may learn fear through classical or respondent conditioning. If an already fright-producing stimulus is paired with another object or event, the child may come to fear that object or event. Comments, remonstrations, and other verbal communications of parents (especially the mother) and other adults about objects, activities, places, persons, or situations induce fearfulness in children who have acquired language skills (see Turner, Beidel, Roberson-Nay, & Tervo, 2003). Adults' and other children's nonverbal behavior can also have a powerful influence on a child's learning fear. A child who is overly fearful of dogs may have acquired the fear in one or a combination of ways: a dog may have frightened the child by barking or growling, jumping, knocking the child down, biting, and so on; the parents or someone else may have warned the child in an emotional way about the dangers of dogs, or the child may have heard people talk about a dog's meanness and dangerousness; the child may have seen a parent, sibling, or other child (or someone in a movie or on television) attacked by or frightened by dogs.

In addition to social learning, anxiety appears in some cases to be affected by physiological factors (Harden, Pihl, Vitaro, Gendreau, & Tremblay, 1995; Morris & Kratochwill, 1998). Anxiety disorders of various types tend to run in families, and it is suspected that genetic or other physiological factors may be involved in the origins of these disorders as well as social learning. However, "at the present time, causes of anxiety and phobic disorders in childhood are not well understood and appear to be multifaceted" (Rabian & Silverman, 1995, p. 248).

Some children develop fears or phobias about separation, and leaving home or their parents—even for a short time—may be extremely traumatic for them. Some are extremely anxious about going to school. School phobia may more appropriately be called social phobia in some cases because it is a fear of the social interactions that are an expected part of school attendance (Beidel & Turner, 1998). Of course, a student may have extreme anxiety about both separation from home or parents and social interaction in school (see case of Jerry in accompanying case book).

Social learning principles can help resolve both children's and adults' excessive or irrational anxieties and fears. Three approaches, which can be used in combination, have been particularly successful: modeling, desensitization, and self-control training. With these techniques, clinicians have helped children and youth overcome a wide array of fears and phobias (see Barrios & O'Dell, 1998; Dadds, 2002; Kendall & Gosch, 1994; March, 1995; Morris & Kratochwill, 1998). Teachers may be asked to assist in implementing these procedures in school settings. Medications to reduce anxiety may also be helpful (Garland, 2002; Konopasek & Forness, 2004).

Having fearful children watch movies in which other youngsters are having fun (at a party or playing games) while approaching the feared object without hesitation (for example, the youngsters in the movie may be handling dogs or snakes while playing) reduces fear in the observers and makes them more willing to approach the thing they fear. Having individuals with phobias watch several different peer models unanxiously approach several different feared objects and showing films that display the actual feared object (rather than a replica) have increased the effectiveness of this method of fear reduction. Positive reinforcement of the fearful person's approach to the feared object adds to the fear-reducing effects of watching models. Filmed modeling procedures have been highly effective in preventing children from acquiring maladaptive fears of medical and dental procedures, as well as in dealing with children who have already become fearful (see Dadds, 2002; King, Hamilton, & Murphy, 1983).

Procedures variously referred to as systematic desensitization, reciprocal inhibition, and counterconditioning have also been effective in lowering fears of children and adults. The central feature of these procedures involves the individual's gradual and repeated exposure to the fear-provoking stimuli (either in real life or in purposeful fantasy of them), while the person remains unanxious and perhaps engaged in an activity that is incompatible with or inhibits anxiety (such as eating a favorite treat or relaxing comfortably in a chair). The gradual approach to the feared object, repeated exposure to it, and maintenance of an unanxious state during exposure are thought to weaken the conditioned or learned bond between the object and the fear response it elicits (Barrios & O'Dell, 1998; Beidel & Turner, 1998; Dadds, 2002; Morris & Kratochwill, 1998; Rabian & Silverman, 1995; Wolpe, 1975).

In self-control training, fearful individuals learn to talk through a variety of techniques for managing anxiety. They may learn relaxation, self-reinforcement, self-punishment, self-instruction, visual imagery, or problem-solving strategies. The trainer might help the individual develop mental images that represent calm or pleasant feelings that are incompatible with anxiety and that the subject can recall when he or she encounters anxiety-provoking circumstances.

Interventions based on behavioral principles have been quite successful in remediating the problem of school phobia and other social fears (Beidel & Turner, 1998; King, Ollendick, & Tonge, 1995). Specific techniques vary from case to case, but general procedures include one or more of the following:

- Desensitization of the child's fear through role playing or in vivo (real-life) approximations of attending school for an entire day
- Reinforcement for attending school even for a brief period, gradually lengthening the time the child is required to stay in school
- Matter-of-fact parental statements that the child will go back to school, avoiding lengthy or emotional discussion
- Removal of reinforcers for staying home (such as being allowed to watch television, play a favorite game, stay close to mother, or engage in other pleasurable activities).

Albano et al. (2003) and King et al. (1983) suggested that many maladaptive fears in the school setting are preventable. Prevention involves desensitizing young children to school by introducing future teachers, school routines, play activities, and so on. Transitions to middle school and senior high school similarly can be made less anxiety provoking by preparing students for their new environments and new expectations. Although many schools attempt to provide orientation experiences, they are often not carefully planned. Individual students may need to learn coping skills to deal with irrational thoughts and to learn adaptive behavior (such as asking a teacher or a peer for assistance) through modeling, rehearsal, feedback, and reinforcement.

Obsessive-Compulsive Disorders

Obsessions are repetitive, persistent, intrusive impulses, images, or thoughts about something, not worries about real-life problems. *Compulsions* are repetitive, stereotyped acts the individual feels he or she must perform to ward off a dreaded event, although these acts are not really able to prevent it. Both obsessions and compulsions may be part of ritualistic behavior by which an individual attempts to reduce anxiety. When such behavior causes marked distress, is inordinately time-consuming, or interferes with a person's routine functioning in home, school, or job, it is considered an obsessive-compulsive disorder (OCD). Children with OCD often do not understand that their behavior is excessive and unreasonable, although adults with OCD typically do.

OCD affects perhaps as many as 1 in 200 children and adolescents, making it a relatively rare disorder (see Albano et al., 2003; Johnston & March, 1992). It may involve many types of ritualistic thoughts or behaviors, such as:

• Washing, checking, or other repetitive motor behavior
• Cognitive compulsions consisting of words, phrases, prayers, sequence of numbers, or other forms of counting
• Obsessional slowness, taking excessive time to complete simple everyday tasks
• Doubts and questions that elevate anxiety.

Many children and adolescents with this disorder are not diagnosed, in part because they are often secretive about their obsessional thoughts or rituals. However, OCD can result in significant impairment in social and academic impairment. Johnston and March (1992) described a case in point:

> Betsy, an 11-year-old girl, was referred to our clinic by a local psychologist. During the initial telephone contact, Betsy's mother explained that their situation seemed desperate, as Betsy had been unable to attend school for the 2 preceding weeks. Her mother explained that Betsy repeatedly dressed and undressed and then dressed again, over and over, and was unable to stop until she was nearly exhausted. (p. 118)

Betsy's dressing rituals had begun 7 months earlier. Psychodynamic therapy was ineffective, and her symptoms worsened. Her schoolwork suffered, and her teachers reported that she was not turning in homework and completing assignments. When her parents asked her why she was having trouble, she was evasive but eventually said that it was because "she had to read each sentence three times, 'just the right way'"

(Johnston & March, 1992, p. 119). After more probing by her mother, Betsy admitted that she thought if she did not "get it right" her parents would feel hurt. Later, Betsy began repeating phrases and sentences and performing other rituals, including washing her hands up to 30 times a day to avoid contracting AIDS.

The most effective interventions are based on social learning principles, particularly strategies employed for reduction of anxiety (Albano et al., 2003; March & Mulle, 1998; Milby, Robinson, & Daniel, 1998). Medications to reduce anxiety may also be helpful (Beer, Karitani, Leonard, March, & Sweda, 2002; Garland, 2002; Johnston & March, 1992; Quintana & Birmaher, 1995). Teachers may play an important role in detecting OCD, especially when the student is secretive about thoughts or rituals and careful observation and questioning are necessary to discover why the student is having socialization or academic difficulties. Special educators may be expected to assist in intervention by implementing features of anxiety-reduction procedures in the classroom.

Posttraumatic Stress Disorder

Posttraumatic stress disorder (PTSD) refers to prolonged, recurrent emotional and behavioral reactions following exposure to an extremely traumatic event involving threatened death or serious injury to oneself or others. The person's response at the time of experiencing the event must include intense fear, helplessness, or horror (children may show disorganized or agitated behavior). PTSD is characterized by persistent cognitive, perceptual, emotional, or behavioral problems related to the event. For example, people with PTSD may reexperience the traumatic event in a variety of ways, such as through recurrent and intrusive thoughts, images, or dreams. They may avoid stimuli associated with the event or experience a general emotional numbing or unresponsiveness. Their symptoms may also include increased arousal (e.g., difficulty sleeping or concentrating; see Fletcher, 2003; Mindell & Owens, 2003; Saigh, 1998).

Until relatively recently, children's delayed emotional and behavioral reactions to extreme stress were largely ignored. PTSD was seldom studied unless the traumatic stress occurred in adulthood. Since the mid-1980s, however, mental health workers have recognized that extremely traumatic experiences can cause delayed emotional or behavioral disorders in children as well as adults (Fletcher, 2003; Terr, 1995; Yule, 1994). By the mid-1990s, it was well recognized that extreme stress or life-threatening experiences can produce not only depression, anxiety, fears, and other reactions in children but also can result in PTSD (Barrios & O'Dell, 1998; Saigh, 1998; Wolfe, 1998). Terr (1995) concluded that four characteristics are common to extreme childhood trauma:

- Visualized or otherwise repeatedly perceived memories of the trauma
- Repetitive behaviors that may be similar to obsessions or compulsions
- Fears linked specifically to the traumatic event
- Altered attitudes toward people, life, or the future, reflecting feelings of vulnerability.

There is tremendous variation in the way in which individuals respond to a given traumatic event. However, researchers are finding that accidents, wars, natural disasters such as earthquakes or hurricanes, terrorism, and the domestic and community violence commonly experienced in contemporary urban life, may often produce PTSD in children and adolescents.

Treatment of these disorders may involve a variety of approaches, such as group discussion and support activities, crisis counseling, and individual treatment to reduce anxiety and improve coping strategies. Prevention involves not only efforts to reduce accidents and violence but also planning for the traumas that are likely if not inevitable.

Events producing PTSD may occur in school or the community. Sexual and physical abuse or school shootings, for example, may give rise to PTSD. As more immigrant children from wartorn countries enter our schools, we will no doubt see an increase in the number of children showing posttraumatic stress. Regardless of the location at which the traumatic event occurs, the student with PTSD is likely to have serious problems in school. Anxiety and related responses to the trauma may make it very difficult for the student to concentrate on academic work or engage in typical social activities. Consequently, it is important that teachers be aware of the indicators of possible PTSD, refer students for evaluation, and participate in efforts to reduce anxiety to manageable levels.

Stereotyped Movement Disorders

Stereotyped movements are involuntary, repetitive, persistent, and nonfunctional acts over which the individual can exert at least some voluntary control under some circumstances but not total control in all circumstances. Stereotyped movements include self-stimulation and self-injury, as we discuss in chapter 17. However, they may also include repetitive movements related to anxiety (Albano et al., 2003; Milby et al., 1998; Werry, 1986c).

Most stereotyped movements that are not labeled self-stimulation or self-injury are referred to as tics. Tics that involve only the facial muscles and last only a short time are common; nearly one fourth of all children will at some time during their development display this kind of tic, and it is best to ignore them. Tics involving the entire head, neck, and shoulders, however, typically require intervention. Tics may be vocal as well as motor; the individual may make a variety of noises or repeat words or word sounds, with or without accompanying motor tics.

Chronic motor tics that last more than a year and involve at least three muscle groups simultaneously are more serious than those involving fewer muscles or lasting a shorter time. There are a variety of tic disorders, but the most severe variety and the one on which most research has been done is Tourette's disorder or Tourette's syndrome (TS, Spencer, Biederman, Harding, Wilens, & Faraone, 1995). The fourth edition of the *Diagnostic and Statistical Manual of Mental Disorders* (American Psychiatric Association, 2000) defines TS as a disorder with onset before age 18 in which the person has both multiple motor and one or more verbal tics occurring many times a day (usually in clusters) nearly every day or intermittently for more than a year. TS occurs in about 4 or 5 individuals per 10,000, across diverse racial and ethnic groups, and about 1.5 to 3 times more often in males than in females.

In the 1990s, TS became a focus for much research on obsessive-compulsive and anxiety disorders. Because it has been so misunderstood until recently, TS has carried extraordinary social stigma. The symptoms of TS may be very mild and not readily apparent to the casual observer. However, a person with severe symptoms may find that others respond with fear, ridicule, or hostility to their bizarre behavior (e.g., twitching, grunting, shouting obscenities or words inappropriate to the circumstances). The diagnosis of TS in two high-profile athletes (baseball player Jim Eisenreich and basketball player Mohmoud Abdul-Rauf, formerly Chris Jackson), the brilliant writing of neurologist Oliver Sacks for the popular press (see "A Surgeon's Life" in Sacks, 1995, the story of a surgeon and pilot with TS), and the work of the Tourette Syndrome Association have done much to dispel ignorance, discrimination, and cruelty shown toward children and adults with TS.

We now know that TS is a neurological disorder, although the cause and precisely what is wrong neurologically are not known. TS is a multifaceted problem with social and emotional as well as neurological features (Coffey, Miguel, Savage, & Rausch, 1994; Kerbeshian & Burd, 1994; Linet, 1995). It may have a genetic component. It can vary greatly in severity and nature of symptoms, and it is often a comorbid condition with a variety of other disorders, especially attention deficit–hyperactivity disorder (ADHD) and OCD. In fact, some researchers suggest that TS is a specific form of attentional or obsessive-compulsive disorder. Some symptoms of TS may involve ticlike ritualistic behavior (e.g., stereotyped touching or arrangement of objects, repetition of words or phrases). In some cases, the person with TS has difficulty inhibiting aggression, and TS can be mistaken for or comorbid with conduct disorder (Riddle, Hardin, Ort, Leckman, & Cohen, 1988). The symptoms of TS may become more severe under specific conditions, especially with the experience of anxiety, trauma, or social stress (Silva, Munoz, Borickman, & Friedhoff, 1995).

TS is becoming better understood as diagnosis becomes more accurate and research reveals more about its nature and treatment. The most effective treatments are cognitive-behavioral therapies and medications or a combination of the two (March, 1995; Walkup, 2002). Many individuals with TS do not like the side effects of neuroleptics and other medications that may be prescribed to attenuate their symptoms. Management of tics by other means, including allowing them to occur under many circumstances and educating others to understand and accept them, are often the preferred strategies (see the report of Kane in the accompanying case book).

Special educators are likely to encounter students with TS because it is often comorbid with other disorders and because misunderstanding of TS often leads to stigma and social rejection or isolation. Effective intervention often requires involvement of the family and school as well as the student with TS (see Albano et al., 2003; Milby et al., 1998; Riddle et al., 1988). A major aspect of the educator's role is understanding and communicating to others the nature of TS, ignoring the tics that cannot be controlled, and focusing on the student's capabilities.

Selective Mutism

Children who are extremely reluctant to speak, although they know how to converse normally, are said to exhibit *selective mutism* (SM): They choose to speak only to a certain individual or small groups of people and refuse to talk to all others. Other terms used to describe their problems include *elective mutism, speech inhibition, speech avoidance, speech phobia,* and *functional mutism.* These children present a puzzling behavior problem to teachers (Brigham & Cole, 1999; Dow, Sonies, Scheib, Moss, & Leonard, 1995; Hultquist, 1995; Rogers-Adkinson, 1999). Brigham and Cole (1999) noted that most children with SM are first identified by educators when they enter school, but "because SM is rare, it is unlikely that many individuals have much experience on which they can rely when working with children with SM. . . . Additionally, the resistance to treatment demonstrated by many children with SM can lead to feelings of ineptitude or anger on the part of the child's teacher" (p. 184).

Because the selectively mute youngster does not need to acquire normal speech but merely to learn to use speech under ordinary circumstances, remediation is often considerably easier than that of the mute or echolalic child. The selectively mute child is, at least to some degree, socially withdrawn, although he or she may be withdrawn only from adults or only from peers. Selective mutism may sometimes be a response to trauma or abuse (Jacobsen, 1995), but it appears to be a result of social anxiety in most cases, a specific fear of talking to certain individuals or groups of people (Bergman, Piacentini, & McCracken, 2002; Black & Uhde, 1995). The causes of selective mutism are apparently diverse, however, and many children who exhibit this behavior have multiple behavior problems and dysfunctional families (Brigham & Cole, 1999; Cunningham, Cataldo, Mallion, & Keyes, 1984; Hultquist, 1995). Nevertheless, parents may often assist in the assessment and treatment of selective mutism (Schill & Kratochwill, 1996). Psychopharmacological treatment may be an important adjunct of other interventions.

As with other fears, social learning principles have been the basis for the most successful approaches to selective mutism. Strategies involve alteration of the demands or conditions under which the child is expected to speak, desensitization to the fear of speaking, and reinforcement for gradual approximations of speaking freely to the person(s) in whose presence the child has been mute (see Beidel & Turner, 1998; Brigham & Cole, 1999).

Selective mutism is, as Brigham and Cole (1999) noted, poorly understood (even mysterious) and an extremely rare condition, but it can be an extraordinarily challenging problem for teachers. In some cases, the child simply starts talking more normally without treatment. Therefore, the first decision of concerned adults must be whether to implement intervention—whether the child's behavior is such a serious problem that intervention should be attempted. Evidence to date suggests that it is better to intervene than to wait for spontaneous resolution (Bergman et al., 2002; Pionek Stone, Kratochwill, Sladezcek, & Serlin, 2002). If intervention is initiated, then it is important for the teacher to work with other professionals, especially speech-language pathologists and those involved with the student's family. It is also important to implement a nonpunitive, behavioral approach to encouraging speech in the classroom and to realize that in many cases successful intervention requires long-term treatment (Beidel & Turner, 1998; Dow et al., 1995; Harris, 1996; Hultquist, 1995).

EATING DISORDERS

Eating disorders receive much attention in the press because the nation's affluence makes it acceptable to waste food and because of the near obsession many people – particularly of high social status—have with slenderness (Siegel, 1998). Among eating disorders, anorexia nervosa (or simply *anorexia*), bulimia (sometimes called *bulimarexia* or *bulimia nervosa*), binge eating, and obesity garner the most attention (Wilson, Becker, & Heffernan, 2003). These disorders are primarily, but not exclusively, problems of females, especially adolescent girls, and they appear to be more prevalent among White than among Black women (Robb & Dadson, 2002; Striegel-Moore et al., 2003). Medication is one possible treatment of such disorders (Kotler, Devlin, & Walsh, 2002; Roerig, Mitchell, Myers, & Glass, 2002).

Anorexia (literally, loss of appetite) is a misnomer, for those with the disorder do not report absence of hunger, and the problem is clearly a refusal to eat a proper diet. Individuals with anorexia are obsessively concerned with losing weight and extremely anxious about getting fat. They starve themselves down to an abnormally low weight, often exercising compulsively as well as severely restricting caloric intake. They endanger their health, sometimes dying of self-starvation. Anorexia occurs most often in females (by a ratio of about 10 to 1), usually in the early adolescent to young adult age range.

Bulimia involves binge eating followed by behavior designed to offset the food intake, such as self-induced vomiting, using laxatives or enemas, or extra exercise. People with bulimia often try to keep their eating binges and related behavior a secret. They often feel depressed and unable to control their eating habits.

Despite public fascination with anorexia and bulimia and the relatively high estimates of prevalence of these disorders among high school and college females, we have relatively little understanding of the causes or effective treatment, especially when the onset of these disorders is in childhood. Researchers now recognize that the problems are multidimensional and require multimodal treatment approaches. The cultural ideal of thinness may be a factor in precipitating some cases of eating disorders (Adams, Katz, Beauchamp, Cohen, & Zavis, 1993). Family conflicts about eating and difficulty in communicating with other family members are known to be associated with adolescents' maladaptive attitudes toward food and eating (Eme & Danielak, 1995; Mueller et al., 1995). However, genetic predisposition to eating problems is increasingly recognized by researchers (Mizes, 1995; Wilson, Becker, & Heffernan, 2003). Behavioral analyses of causes and behavioral or cognitive-behavioral interventions have been encouraging in the short run, but long-term follow-up evaluations indicate the need for more comprehensive assessment and treatment approaches (Mizes, 1995). Effective intervention requires consideration of the eating behaviors themselves and the thoughts and feelings associated with anorexia and bulimia, plus the social environment in which the patterns have developed and are maintained.

Other eating disorders include pica (eating inedible substances such as paint, hair, cloth, or dirt), rumination (self-induced vomiting, which usually begins in infancy), highly exclusive food preferences, and obesity (Foreyt & Kondo, 1985; Johnson & Hinkle, 1993; Siegel, 1998; Werry, 1986c). These problems severely limit a child's social acceptability and endanger health.

Childhood and adolescent obesity is a growing problem in most Western cultures and carries significant health risks, usually results in a poor self-image, often contributes to poor social relations, and tends to persist into adulthood (Boodman, 1995; Johnson & Hinkle, 1993; Peterson, Reach, & Grabe, 2003; Siegel, 1998; Wilson et al., 2003). Obese children often pay a heavy price in social rejection or neglect. Although causes of obesity include genetic, physiological, and environmental factors, "the basic problem is a negative imbalance between calorific intake and energy expenditure, resulting in the storage of fat in adipose cells" (Spence, 1986, p. 447). Successful management of obesity therefore requires not only changing eating habits but increasing physical activity (Johnson & Hinkle, 1993). Obesity has often been thought to be caused by learning undesirable eating patterns, and poor nutritional habits undoubtedly play a critical role. However, the discovery in 1995 of a gene that controls obesity in mice spurred public perceptions that morbid obesity in humans is often caused by genetic factors (Weiss, 1995). It is important to remember that avoidance of obesity requires a combination of proper diet and exercise—a regimen harder for some than for others but possible for nearly everyone. José Caro, chairman of the Department of Medicine at Thomas Jefferson Medical College, is quoted as saying, "Obesity is a disease . . . but it is exacerbated by a social and cultural environment that encourages consumption while minimizing physical exertion" (Weiss, 1996, p. 11).

Special educators will often deal with students who have eating disorders. These disorders are not to be addressed by special educators alone, and teachers should not independently assume responsibility for eating problems. Students with anorexia and other eating disorders may display high levels of anxious or obsessive-compulsive behavior in the classroom. The role of special education in such disorders is to provide instruction and support for proper nutrition as needed and to work with other disciplines in managing students' food intake.

ELIMINATION DISORDERS

Attitudes toward toileting vary widely among cultures and within social groups. In Western culture, toilet training is considered very important and is generally begun at a young age. Although the extreme practice of beginning toilet training in the first few weeks of life is ill advised, behavioral research shows that most children can be taught by 16 or 18 months (see O'Leary & Wilson, 1975). When children continue to wet or soil themselves after the age of 5 or 6, they are considered to have a problem that demands intervention. *Enuresis* may be either diurnal (wetting during waking hours) or nocturnal (bedwetting). About twice as many boys as girls are enuretic, and 2 or 3% of children are enuretic at age 14. At the time they begin first grade, approximately 13 to

20% of children are enuretic. *Encopresis,* or soiling, usually occurs during the day and is a rarer problem than is enuresis.

Toilet training is usually a gradual process, and stress and illness have an effect on bowel and bladder control. Thus, the younger the child and the more stressful the circumstances, the more one can expect accidents to occur. Enuresis and encopresis are not matters of infrequent accidents; the child has a chronic problem, after the age at which children are expected to be continent of urine and feces, in retaining urine or feces and releasing it only in the toilet (Peterson et al., 2003; Siegel, 1992, 1998).

Psychodynamic ideas attribute enuresis and encopresis to underlying emotional conflicts, usually conflicts involving the family. Although these psychodynamic ideas are not supported by reliable evidence, family factors obviously play an important role if the family is inconsistent or unreasonable in toilet training. At the least, wetting and soiling can sour parent–child relationships regardless of the cause of the problem. Not many parents can face these problems with complete equanimity, and rare is the child who is completely unaffected by adults' reactions to misplaced excrement. Thus, one must recognize that negative feelings about the problem often run high in families of children with elimination disorders. Treatment must be planned to avoid further parental anger and abuse of the child.

Enuresis is seldom the child's only problem; the child with enuresis often has other difficulties—perhaps stealing, overeating, or underachievement (Siegel, 1998; Vivian, Fischel, & Liebert, 1986). Nearly all children with encopresis have multiple problems, often of a severe nature. Diurnal enuresis and encopresis at school are intolerable problems for teachers and result in peer rejection (Walker & Rankin, 1983). Understandably, most youngsters with elimination disorders have low self-esteem.

In a few cases, elimination disorders have physiological causes that can be corrected by surgery or medication, but the vast majority of cases have no known anatomical defect, and medication is not particularly helpful. These disorders are in the vast majority of cases a matter of failure to learn how to control the bladder or bowels, and the effective methods of treating them involve habit training or practice. Intervention may thus involve training the child in urine retention, rapid awakening, and practice in toileting as well as reward for appropriate toileting or mild punishment for wetting. For many children, a urine alarm system in the bed or pants has successfully eliminated enuresis (Mountjoy, Ruben, & Bradford, 1984; Siegel, 1998; Taylor & Turner, 1975).

Although many approaches to enuresis have been tried and many behavioral techniques have been highly successful, no single approach has been successful for every child, and combinations of techniques are often used. Encopresis is sometimes treated by training children in biofeedback so that they learn to control their sphincters more deliberately. Those who soil themselves may be required to clean themselves rather than receive solicitous attention and cleaning from an adult. Selecting a successful technique for enuresis or encopresis depends on careful assessment of the individual case (Siegel, 1992).

Special educators who work with students having more severe disorders are particularly likely to encounter those who have elimination disorders. These disorders can be extremely troublesome in school, making students unwelcome to adults and peers alike and becoming the central issue in behavior management. Special educators need to work with professionals from other disciplines, particularly psychology and social work, to address the problems created by elimination disorders in the classroom.

SEXUAL PROBLEMS

Promiscuous sexual conduct is often thought to connote moral misjudgment, and promiscuity is often involved in delinquency. Early sexual intercourse and teenage pregnancy are serious problems for teenagers and their children, as discussed in chapter 14. Dating and related heterosexual relationships are of great concern to teens and their adult caretakers. Sexual relationships and sexual behavior can be sources of enormous anxiety and obsessive-compulsive behavior for children and teens. Scarcely anyone condones exhibitionism, sadomasochism, incest, prostitution, fetishism, and sexual relations involving children; and these behaviors usually carry serious social penalties. American social mores do not condone all sex practices—some sexual behavior is clearly taboo, and incest is taboo in nearly every society (see Becker & Bonner, 1998; Wilson, 1998). However, most people now recognize the wide variety of normal sexual expression that is a matter of preference or biological determination. Graziano and Dorta (1995) noted types of behavior that brings children and youth to therapy:

> Intense, excessive, and inappropriate masturbation (e.g., public), cross-sex dressing and other behavior, sexual promiscuity in young adolescents, homosexuality, and paraphilia (bizarre/perverted sexual behavior) are examples of sex-related child/youth problems treated in behavior therapy. Unlike most of the others listed, homosexuality in children is defined as a problem based largely on parents' personal values and whether the child or adolescent feels the homosexual urges are threatening. (pp. 174–175)

Autoerotic activity is not inherently maladaptive, although it is viewed as undesirable or prohibited by some religious groups. When carried to excess or done publicly, sexual self-stimulation is considered disordered behavior by nearly everyone. Although many or most teachers have observed children masturbating publicly, little research has been done on the problem of children's public masturbation, perhaps because masturbation has for so long been looked upon as evil (Hare, 1962; Stribling, 1842) and is still condemned by some religions as is homosexuality.

Classifying gender-related behavior of any kind as a disorder raises serious questions of cultural bias and discrimination. The consensus is that some forms of sexual expression are deviant and should be prevented—incest, sexual sadism or masochism, pedophilia, and public masturbation, for example. Today, however, many people feel there is nothing deviant about other sex-related behaviors, such as preference for clothing styles, stereotypical masculine or feminine mannerisms, and homosexuality. Clothing styles and accepted sex roles have changed dramatically since about 1970. *Androgyny* (having the characteristics of both sexes) is apparent in many fashions and in role models. Problems related to sexual preference may be seen as primarily a matter of cultural or personal intolerance, so we must be sensitive to the possibility of cultural and personal bias in judging sex-related behavior, just as we must be aware of personal biases toward racial and ethnic identity. In children, *gender identity disorder* may be manifested by an insistent desire to be the opposite sex, strong preference for or insistence on dressing like the other sex or adopting the opposite sex role, strong preference for playmates of the other sex, and persistent wishes to have the physical features of the opposite sex. If such characteristics cause significant distress or impairment of social functioning, then they may be considered a disorder (see American Psychiatric Association, 2000; Gordon & Schroeder, 1995; Zucker & Bradley, 1995).

Sexual behavior that involves intimidation, harassment, and other forms of aggression are, as noted in prior chapters, more accurately associated with conduct disorder and delinquency. However, many individuals who exhibit sexual aggression may experience high levels of anxiety as a comorbid condition (Araji, 1997).

Special educators, especially those who deal with adolescents, are certain to be confronted by students' sexual behavior and knowledge (or lack of it) that are of great concern. Maintaining an open mind about sexual preferences and alternative modes of sexual expression is important; so is an understanding of pathological behavior and the necessity of addressing it. Teachers must be ready to work with psychologists, psychiatrists, social workers, and other professionals in identifying and managing deviant sexual behavior (see Soutter, 1996).

SOCIAL ISOLATION AND INEPTITUDE

Social isolation may result from excessive behavior, such as hyperactivity or aggression, that drives others away, or it may result from deficiencies in behavior, such as lack of social initiative (see Farmer, 2000; McFadyen-Ketchum & Dodge, 1998; Rubin, Burgess, Kennedy, & Stewart, 2003). Some socially isolated youngsters lack social approach skills, such as looking at, initiating conversation with, asking to play with, and appropriately touching their peers or adults. Usually, they also lack responsiveness to others' initiations of social contact. Others may be neglected by their peers for reasons that are not well understood. However, rejected, socially isolated children do not engage in the *social reciprocity* (exchange of mutual and equitable reinforcement between pairs of individuals) that is characteristic of normal social development. The isolated or neglected student usually lacks specific social skills for making and keeping friends and may be rejected by peers.

Social isolation is not an all-or-nothing problem. All children and youth sometimes exhibit withdrawn behavior and are socially inept. This behavior may occur with any degree of severity, ranging along a continuum from a normal social reticence in new situations to the profound isolation of psychosis. In nearly any classroom, from preschool through adulthood, however, some individuals are distinguished by their lack of social interaction. Their social isolation is often accompanied by immature or inadequate behavior that makes them targets of ridicule or taunts. They are friendless loners who are apparently unable to avail themselves of the joy and satisfaction of social reciprocity. Unless their behavior and that of their peers can be changed, they are likely to remain isolated from close and frequent human contact and the attendant developmental advantages afforded by social interaction. Their prognosis, then, is not good without intensive intervention (McEvoy & Odom, 1987).

Causal Factors and Prevention

Social learning theory predicts that some children, particularly those who have not been taught appropriate social interaction skills and those who have been punished for attempts at social interaction, will be withdrawn. A mildly or moderately withdrawn youngster is likely to be anxious and have a low self-concept, but the conclusion that anxiety and low self-concept cause withdrawal and social isolation is not justifiable. It is more plausible that anxiety and low self-concept result from the child's lack of social competence.

Parental overrestrictiveness or social incompetence, lack of opportunity for social learning, and early rebuffs in social interaction with peers may contribute to a child's learning to play in isolation from others and to avoid social contact. Parents who are socially obtuse are likely to have children whose social skills are not well developed, probably because socially awkward parents provide models of undesirable behavior and are unable to teach their children the skills that will help them become socially attractive (Dadds, 2002; Putallaz & Heflin, 1990). Aversive social experiences, including abuse by parents or siblings, may indeed produce anxious children who have little self-confidence and evaluate themselves negatively. Anxiety and self-derogation may thereafter contribute to reticence in social situations and help to perpetuate social incompetence. Nevertheless, the child's temperamental characteristics, in combination with early socialization experiences and the nature of the current social environment, probably account for the development of social isolation (Keogh, 2003; Kochanska, 1995). The social learning view of isolate behavior, which focuses on the factors of reinforcement, punishment, and imitation, carries direct implications for intervention and suggests ways in which to remediate isolation by teaching social skills. Effective prevention of social isolation, however, involves more than teaching youngsters how to approach and respond to others; it requires arranging a social environment that is conducive to positive interactions.

ASSESSMENT

The definition of *social isolation* includes active rejection by peers or neglect of peers (Wentzel & Asher, 1995). Measurement of rejection and acceptance frequently includes use of a questionnaire or sociometric game that asks youngsters to choose or nominate classmates for various roles. Students may be asked to indicate which of their peers they would most like to play, sit, work, or party with and with whom they would least like to interact. The results of this procedure are then analyzed to see which individuals have high social status in the group (to whom many peers are attracted), those who are isolates (not chosen as playmates or workmates by anyone), and those who are rejected (with whom peers want to avoid social contact). More precise measurement of social interaction may be obtained by direct daily observation and recording of behavior. We can thus define *social isolates* as children who have a markedly lower number of social interactions than do their peers.

Sociometric status and direct measurement of social interactions, although both valuable in assessment, do not necessarily reveal what causes a youngster to experience social isolation. A student could, for example, have a relatively high rate of positive social interaction and still be a relative social isolate; his or her interactions might involve relatively few peers and be characterized by a superficial or artificial quality (Hundert, 1995; Walker, Ramsey, & Gresham, 2004). Consequently, assessment should also include teacher ratings and self-reports. Thus, adequate measurement of social skills or social isolation requires attention to the rate of interactive behaviors, qualitative aspects of social interaction, and children's perceptions of social status (see Cartledge & Milburn, 1995).

As social skills research becomes more sophisticated, the nuances of appropriate social interaction become more difficult to capture. Much of our knowledge about the nature of children's social skills is superficial. Children's social intentions (*why* as well as *what* they do) may be an important area to research; we may need to assess their pragmatic reasons for interacting with peers in specified ways to fully understand social isolation and social acceptance.

Intervention and Education

One approach to the problem of withdrawal is to try to improve the youngster's self-concept, on the assumption that this will result in a tendency to engage more often in social interactions. We can encourage children to express their feelings about their behavior and social relationships in play therapy or in therapeutic conversations with a warm, accepting adult. As they come to feel accepted and able to express their feelings openly, their self-concepts will presumably become more positive. The incidence of positive social interactions should then increase as well. Attempts to remediate social isolation without teaching specific social skills or manipulating the social environment are usually ineffectual, however. Few data show that self-concept can be improved without first improving behavior. If youngsters' appraisals of their own behavior are unrealistic, then bringing self-perceptions into line with reality is, to be sure, a worthy goal. If youngsters are indeed socially isolated, then attempting to convince them of their social adequacy without first helping them learn the skills for social reciprocity may be misleading. After their behavior has been improved, however, there is a foundation for improving self-image.

Arranging appropriate environmental conditions helps teach socially isolated youngsters to reciprocate positive behavior with their peers. Situations that are conducive to social interaction, contain toys or equipment that promote social play and bring the isolated youngster into proximity with others who have social interaction skills or who require social interaction from the target child. Specific intervention strategies based on social learning principles include these:

- Reinforcing social interaction (perhaps with praise, points, or tokens)
- Providing peer models of social interaction

- Providing training (models, instruction, rehearsal, and feedback) in specific social skills
- Enlisting peer confederates to initiate social interactions and reinforce appropriate social responses.

Of course, all four strategies may be used together, and experimental research shows the effectiveness of these procedures in modifying certain behaviors (Walker, Schwarz, et al., 1994). Social learning strategies for defining, measuring, and changing disabled youngsters' deficient social behavior show great promise. Nevertheless, current social skills training methods do not adequately address the problems of producing behavioral changes that actually make disabled children and youth more socially acceptable, that generalize across a variety of social situations, and that are maintained after intervention is terminated. As Strain, Odom, and McConnell (1984) noted, social skills involve *reciprocity*—an exchange of behavior between two people. Interventions that focus exclusively on changing the isolated individual's behavior miss that vital aspect of social adaptation: social interaction. The goal of intervention must be to help the socially isolated individual become enmeshed or entrapped in positive, reciprocal, self-perpetuating social exchanges, which can be done only by carefully choosing the target skills. One must select target skills with these questions in mind:

- Are the particular social behaviors likely to be maintained after intervention is terminated?
- Are the skills likely to generalize across different settings (as in different areas of the school and during different types of activities)?
- Do the target skills relate to peers' social behavior so that peer behavior prompts and reinforces performance of the skill (that is, are the skills part of naturally occurring, positive social interactions)?

If these questions generate affirmative answers, then social skills training is more likely to last (McConnell, 1987).

Some children and youth are not social isolates but still do not fit in well with their peers and are hampered by inadequate social sensitivity or ineptness in delicate social situations. Children whose previous social experience is at odds with the majority of their peers, adolescents making their first approaches to members of the opposite sex, and adolescents interviewing for their first jobs are often quite tactless or unskilled in the social graces demanded for acceptance. Some individuals have irritating personal habits that detract from social adequacy. The results of social ineptitude may be negative self-image, anxiety, and withdrawal.

One can often eliminate or avoid bungling social behaviors by teaching important social cues and appropriate responses. Offering group and individual counseling, showing the youngster videotaped replays of his or her own behavior, modeling appropriate behavior, and providing guided practice (or some combination of these strategies) have been used to teach social skills (see Blake, Wang, Cartledge, & Gardner, 2000; Gresham, 2000; Kavale, Mathur, & Mostert, 2004). A social learning view of the origin and remediation of interpersonal ineptness is clearly a functional view for the special educator, for it implies that direct instruction is most effective.

The design of intervention strategies depends partly on the age of the student and the nature of the student's relationship to peers. Older students with a long history of socialization difficulties and victimization by peers may need a safe haven, such as a special school or class, in which to learn new skills (as illustrated by the case of Pauline in the accompanying case book).

SUMMARY

Grouping anxiety and related disorders for discussion is problematic because the disorders are loosely interrelated. Subcategories of anxiety disorders are not well defined, and anxiety disorders are frequently comorbid with a variety of other disorders.

Anxiety—uneasiness, fears, and worries—is part of normal development. However, extreme anxiety and fears (phobias) can be seriously debilitating. Anxiety disorders are generally more transient and are associated with lower risk for adulthood psychiatric disorder than are behaviors related to externalizing disorders. Excessive anxiety may characterize 2 to 5% of the child population and 20 to 30% of youngsters referred to clinics for behavior problems. Boys and girls are affected about equally. Anxiety disorders appear to have both social and biological causes and to be most amenable to social learning approaches to intervention, sometimes combined with medication.

Anxiety appears to play a significant role in a variety of related disorders. Obsessive-compulsive disorder involves ritualistic thinking or behavior intended to ward off feared events. It may take many forms and is potentially a serious detriment to school attendance and performance. Posttraumatic stress disorder is now recognized as a disorder of children and adolescents as well as adults. The anxiety and other problems associated with PTSD can seriously impede students' progress in school. Stereotyped movement disorders include Tourette's syndrome, a disorder involving multiple motor and vocal tics and now recognized as a neurological problem. TS is often comorbid with other disorders and appears to be particularly closely associated with anxiety, attention disorders,

and obsessive-compulsive disorders. *Selective mutism* is extreme, persistent anxiety about speaking in the presence of certain individuals. Intervention is typically designed to reduce anxiety in situations demanding speech.

Eating disorders include anorexia, bulimia, and compulsive overeating, which often involve anxiety about food, eating, and body weight. Elimination disorders include enuresis and encopresis. These disorders are extremely problematic in school settings and must be resolved if children are to develop normal peer relations. Sexual problems are difficult to define because of societal attitudes toward sexual behavior. However, some types of sexual behavior, such as public masturbation, incest, and masochism, are clearly taboo.

Socially isolated children and youth do not have the social approach and response skills necessary to develop reciprocally reinforcing relationships. They may lack these skills because of inappropriate models of social behavior at home, inadequate instruction or opportunity to practice social skills, or other circumstances that inhibit social development. Intervention and prevention call for teaching social skills that are assumed important for social development, but there is a great deal of controversy concerning which are the most appropriate skills and the most effective instructional methods. In general, social skills training involves modeling, rehearsal, guided practice, and feedback, either for individual students or for groups. Peer-mediated interventions that alter both the socially isolated youngster's behaviors and those of peers in naturally occurring interactions may be the most effective strategies.

>> PERSONAL REFLECTIONS

Anxiety and Related Disorders

Jill Jakulski, Ph.D., is principal of the Herndon Center, a special cofacility for middle school students with emotional and behavioral disorders in Herndon, Virginia. When these reflections were written, she was an assistant principal in charge of special education at James Madison High School in Vienna, Virginia.

Describe the school in which you work and your professional role in the school.

James Madison High School is located in Vienna, Virginia, and is part of Fairfax County Public Schools. It enrolls 1,600 students, approximately 185 of whom receive special education services. Of those receiving special education, 60 students receive services from either the emotional disabilities resource program or the self-contained emotional disabilities program. I work as one of four assistant principals in the building and am the supervising administrator of all special education programs.

Madison's special education programs provide students with opportunities to be included in general education classes and extracurricular activities to the maximum extent appropriate. As determined by the IEP (individualized education program) team, students can access a self-contained classroom setting within the emotional disabilities program for up to six of their seven classes each day. These self-contained classrooms offer a student–teacher ratio of no more than 10 to 1, with an instructional assistant, and provide specialized support and instruction paced to meet their individual needs. Most of the teachers in the self-contained classrooms are certified in both emotional disabilities and learning disabilities.

Incorporating instructional strategies that focus on students' strengths and interests, teachers within the emotional disabilities center program follow the prescribed program of studies as dictated by the Fairfax schools. Accommodations and modifications are implemented on a case-by-case basis depending on the needs of each student. Creative classroom and behavior management techniques (such as incentive programs, after-school activities, snacks during break time, etc.) are implemented in a way that has resulted in improved performance on the part of students.

The clinical workers—a psychologist and a social worker—establish weekly counseling groups for students to examine topics such as positive social skills, coping strategies, and so on. They provide individual counseling on an as-needed basis for students and are available for on-the-spot life-space crisis intervention. They meet with the self-contained teachers twice weekly to conduct a mini-staffing, providing teachers with an update of students' emotional states and family dynamics and allowing time for teachers to ask questions or discuss issues specific to a particular student. In addition, they frequently make contact with students' mainstream teachers so that they can keep the lines of communication open and clear.

Think of a particular student in your school who exhibits severe anxiety. How does the student's behavior demonstrate anxiety?

Salina was born in Mexico in 1984 and moved with her parents to the United States when she was three years old. Although she spoke only Spanish until she entered preschool, Salina was described by her teachers as a good student who learned quickly. She also excelled socially and academically. She had many friends and became a very social young girl.

Salina was initially identified as a student with a learning disability and a speech-language disorder but was found ineligible for continued special education services when she was in the eighth grade. Shortly after that time, Salina was hospitalized for self-destructive behaviors and suicidal ideation. After her release from the hospital, Salina's emotional status deteriorated again, resulting in another hospitalization.

By the beginning of her ninth-grade year, Salina was too afraid and anxious to go to school, even

388

though she indicated that she wanted to. At that time, Salina reported having significant fears and anxieties associated with social problems; however, school staff had not been aware of problems of that nature in the past. With careful planning on the part her guidance counselor, a plan was devised to help Salina get to school. This plan was only partially successful in that she was only able to attend two classes. Furthermore, because of her overwhelming feelings of anxiety, she needed to be released from her classes 10 minutes early so that she could move from one class to another without seeing other students.

Salina's anxiety about her problems with peers continued to increase. During the first few weeks of her attending school, she experienced several anxiety attacks, which resulted in regression to the point that she was cutting herself and contemplating suicide. A thorough evaluation was recommended, and Salina was subsequently found eligible for special education services as a student with emotional disabilities. Following the eligibility determination, the IEP team also determined that Salina needed a more restrictive setting than could be provided in her base school. A change of placement was then made to James Madison High School, where she would be able to access more specialized services.

When Salina began attending Madison, she was able to go to school on the bus every day and initially was mainstreamed into general education classes for math, world history, and health–physical education. Salina's teachers reported positive observations of her performance in those classes and were optimistic about her chances for success. However, Salina soon began to exhibit the symptoms of anxiety and quickly began to regress emotionally. At times, even though she indicated a strong desire to go to her mainstream classes, Salina would tremble before leaving to go to one. In addition, she was irritable with her peers and teachers, she became compulsive about her worries and fears related to her classes, and she often cried.

The program's social worker, lead teacher, and I worked with Salina daily. We also held strategy meetings with her parents. Salina reported that although she felt our efforts were helpful, her anxiety and overwhelming feelings of fear were too much for her. Some days, Salina needed intensive support several times during the course of the 7-period day. Within 3 weeks, her IEP had been amended to reflect direct special education services in self-contained classes for six of her seven classes. (Health/physical education was not offered as a self-contained class.)

What strategies have you found most helpful in working with Salina?

The most important variable provided for Salina at Madison was an unconditional guarantee of (a) a safe place to which she could retreat when feeling too overwhelmed to cope and (b) an adult who would always be there to assist her as she processed her feelings. (The adults available to her included the social worker, the lead teacher, and myself.)

Through our ongoing efforts to assist Salina in coping with her emotional turmoil, deeper issues began to surface. Specifically, she had experimented with marijuana, heroin, alcohol, and cigarettes in the past and was extremely uncomfortable with the fact that she had chosen to participate in such activities. Furthermore, Salina reported having been sexually assaulted on two occasions, both of which she had reported only to her psychiatrist.

When working with Salina, we found that it was critical to provide her with the time needed to express how she was feeling. When she was afforded the opportunity to do so, she was receptive to guidance and would work to formulate a plan of action. Salina demonstrated a commitment to conquer what she called her "demons" and remained faithful to our procedure, which dictated that she seek out one of us as needed.

What are your biggest concerns about Salina's future?

My biggest concern for Salina—and others like her—centers around her need for a very strong support network. In the special education program she is currently in at Madison, all of the staff are knowledgeable about anxiety disorders and have been trained to work with students who exhibit all kinds of emotional disabilities. In addition to the supportive, therapeutic environment provided for students, there are two clinical resources—the psychologist and the social worker—who are available at all times. Salina has made so much progress that, although she is no longer dependent on those supports, she finds comfort in knowing that they are there, which has been very helpful to her.

As long as specialized services are restricted to specialized programs, success for students like Salina may be limited in typical mainstream settings. It is my hope that in the near future, public school officials will provide the support needed to offer a more comprehensive system of services in all educational settings. These services would be for all students, regardless of their eligibility for special education services. In the meantime, I take comfort in knowing that Fairfax County Public Schools do have a numbers of special education schools (centers) designed to meet the very diverse needs presented by students with emotional and behavioral disabilities.

Jill Jakulski Interviews Salina

Ms. J: Salina, tell me about yourself.

S: Well, I'm a very outspoken person now. I used to be very quiet and had trouble sharing my feelings. I used to keep everything inside of me, and nothing seemed to make me feel happiness. But now I do feel happiness, even though it's not all of the time, and even though it's not to the extent that I want it to be. I have an anxiety disorder, so I have to just be patient.

Ms. J: What does anxiety feel like to you?

S: Anxiety feels bad to me—like I am out of control and have nothing good to think about. Usually, it has to do with worrying about something I did or didn't do, or something a person has said about me. In the past, when I had to go to the hospital, I felt helpless and thought a lot about suicide. I even attempted suicide once; other times I just cut on myself—that's why I have all of these scars on my arms and legs.

Ms. J: Do you feel that way now when you are having trouble dealing with your anxiety?

S: Now, when I am having trouble controlling the anxiety, I get really quiet and I shake a lot. I don't really think about suicide anymore, but I usually can't stop myself from thinking about the situation that is causing the anxiety. That only makes it worse to deal with, but I can't seem to help it. During those times, it's like an obsession. So it's, like, even though I know that there are things I can do to help myself when I'm really having a problem with the anxiety, I can't always do those things because I'm so focused on the problem. Also, I feel like crying when I have problems with anxiety. Nothing feels good or right, and I can't let go.

Ms. J: What kinds of situations trigger anxiety problems for you?

S: Little things can make me crazy. Like a few weeks ago when I was doing the laundry and I accidentally put my brother's colored shirt in a load of white clothes. The color faded onto the white clothes, and I was so upset with myself for doing something so stupid. My mother kept telling me that it was okay and that she had made the same mistake earlier that week, but I couldn't help being upset. I became nervous and was shaking, and I couldn't stop crying. All weekend long I was sad and kept thinking about my mistake. After that day I didn't feel like I could trust myself with the laundry. And now, when I know I have to wash clothes, I become very nervous and upset when I think about it. It takes a very long time for those feelings to leave me. I'll probably worry about how I should do the laundry for another 6 months, unfortunately.

My dad also causes me to feel a lot of anxiety. He is a very traditional Hispanic man, and he has problems with communication—especially when it involves emotions. It's hard for him to open up to me or my mom in the way we wish. He was not from a family or a culture where men talked about emotions or showed sensitivity. So whenever I need to talk to my parents, or when he brings up an issue with me, it's very difficult for me. When I know it's coming, I have the same symptoms as I already told you about— nervousness, shaking, crying, feeling sad, and constantly thinking about it. Sometimes my mind tells me it will be okay, but I can't trust that. That's why I worry so much. I worry a lot at home.

Ms. J: How does school affect your anxiety level?

S: That's the good part; school is much better for me this year. Up until the end of last year, I looked at school as a social situation. I didn't think of school as a place I came to learn; I was more interested in stuff teenagers like. I was always worrying about what others were thinking or saying about me, and I even thought the girls wanted to fight me. Because of that, I worried all of the time. This year, I'm focused on just being a good student. That has been really helpful for me because I don't have to spend my time thinking about the problems I might have with others.

Now, when I think about how I came back into the center for my classes, I have anxiety because I now know I should have been able to handle things. They weren't that bad now that I think about them, but even now I don't think I'm ready to handle being out in the mainstream for any of my classes—except for PE, of course.

Ms. J: Why does school seem so much better for you this year?

S: Well, coming to the center was the best thing that ever happened to me. I think that the teachers—and everyone—are the most caring people that I have ever met. I know that if I'm upset, I don't have to talk about it, but on the other hand, I know I can if I want to. . . . Everyone is so knowledgeable and understanding, and they are supportive of everyone. That has helped me with other kids, too.

Ms. J: What do you mean?

S: Well, before, up until the end of ninth grade, I had problems with other kids. But now, because I'm better, and because the people here have helped almost everyone else to be better too, I feel like everyone is pretty supportive of each other. When I'm really having a hard time, everyone just leaves me alone; that really helps. And when I feel like I need to, I can come talk to you or someone else.

Another thing is that since I've come here and felt so comforted, I think my parents feel the same way, too. They loved it when they came here for the tour that first time and then for my IEP. They said that they felt supported by everyone here. But they wondered why it had taken so long for them to find the right help for me. They think it's wrong that there are so few programs like this. If you think about it, I could have been getting better starting in the eighth grade, but no one in my school knew how hard it was for me. They just didn't know any better. It's hard to believe that teachers cannot notice stuff like that, but. . . .

Ms. J: But what?

S: Well, I don't know. . . . I guess it's just hard for me to think that teachers can be teachers without knowing how to work with all kinds of kids. I'm not embarrassed to be in special education, but lots of kids are. I feel like some kids might not need to be in centers if the teachers knew better.

Ms. J: Has being here had any effect on your interactions with your parents at home?

S: Oh, yeah. I'm doing so much better, so obviously they are doing much better. I was crazy to live with before. . . . I feel sorry for my mom—I put her through a lot, but she never complained. My mother has always been there for me, no matter what.

Now I don't think I get so anxious at home or upset, and I know I can always talk to my mother about

things—or my psychiatrist. My mother will always listen to me and, even though he's not very good with emotional things, my dad is more patient with me, and he does try to talk with me when I'm upset.

Ms. J: What advice can you give students who have anxiety problems in school?

S: The first thing I would say is to try to relax. I know that is easy for me to say, but once a person learns how to do it, it really does help. The second thing is to understand that it takes time to get over things like that. Finally, I would say that it's important that they feel like they have safe people to go to when upset and to let them help you. Kids have to be willing to trust the adults who are trying to help them. There has to be people like all of you for this to happen though, and I don't think many kids are this lucky.

Ms. J: What advice can you give to people who work in schools and might be working with a student who has an anxiety disorder?

S: Adults have to understand that they cannot push us when we are struggling like that. It's not like we do it on purpose, and it's not like we can just snap out of it—at least it isn't that way for me, and I really don't think most kids fake it. Teachers sometimes try to make it like we are upset over nothing. I know it may seem that way to them, but not to us. We don't want to be this way; but unless the adults understand that it will take a lot of time, patience, and understanding, we're all going to suffer—I know we make it difficult for teachers when we are having problems.

The only other thing I would say is that every school should have a program like this. I like it here, and I don't want to leave. But I don't think we should have to leave our base school just because we have problems. We aren't bad kids. I think that if teachers would just try to understand what life feels like to us, things would be better. The schools should put programs like this in every school so that every student has access to people when they need them. It makes me sad when I think about my lost time.

>> QUESTIONS FOR FURTHER REFLECTION

1. What indications would lead you to believe that a student of yours is anxious to the point of having an emotional or behavioral disorder?
2. Given your information to this point, what possible changes in behavior might you anticipate if a student who is taking medication

for an anxiety-related disorder discontinues taking it?
3. If a student of yours were socially inept, how would you approach this student (what would you try to accomplish, and what would you say to him or her)?

CHAPTER SIXTEEN

DEPRESSION AND SUICIDAL BEHAVIOR

As you read this chapter, keep these guiding questions in mind:

- How does the federal definition of "emotionally disturbed" include internalizing disorders and depression?

- How do comorbidity and the episodic nature of mood disorders complicate the assessment of depression?

- What are the major theories or models of depression that guide intervention?

- What is the relationship between age, gender, ethnicity, and suicide rates?

- How can teachers help reduce suicide risk, and how should they manage students following a suicide threat or attempt?

One of the five distinguishing characteristics of children defined in federal regulations as having serious emotional disturbance is "a general, pervasive mood of unhappiness or depression" (see chapter 1). Just which youngsters federal officials meant to identify by this characteristic is not clear (Cullinan, 2004; Duncan, Forness, & Hartsough, 1995; Forness, 1988b; Forness & Kavale, 1997). A general, pervasive mood of unhappiness or depression is more narrow and restrictive than the broadband behavioral dimension of *internalizing,* yet it does not correspond exactly with narrower dimensions, such as social withdrawal (see chapters 5 and 15). Neither is it consistent with the clinical criteria for a major depressive episode but approximates a less severe condition referred to by clinicians as *dysthymia.* However, depressed mood might be considered the prototypical internalizing disorder (Reynolds, 1992). A reasonable conclusion is that the federal definition of "emotionally disturbed" should be interpreted to include a wide range of internalizing disorders such as anxiety withdrawal and clinical depression.

Depression has been relatively neglected in special education research, yet its close relationship to a variety of other disorders and to academic and social difficulties is now clear. It is recognized as an important disorder of childhood and adolescence that increases in prevalence with age, often coexists with other disorders, and is associated with long-term risks of mental illness and suicide (Carr, 2002; Geller & DelBello, 2003; Kaslow, Morris, & Rehm, 1998; Kazdin & Marciano, 1998; Shaffer & Waslick, 2002; Spirito & Overholser, 2003). The relationship between depression and suicidal behavior—a concern of all educators but especially those who work with psychologically disturbed students—makes these important related topics.

DEPRESSION

Definition and Prevalence

Childhood depression has been a controversial topic for several decades. Traditional psychoanalytic theory suggests that depression cannot occur in childhood because psychological self-representation is not sufficiently developed. Some scholars suggest that children's depression is masked by other symptoms—expressed indirectly through symptoms such as enuresis, temper tantrums, hyperactivity, learning disabilities, truancy, and so on. However, most researchers now agree that depression in childhood parallels adult depression in many ways, but the specific types of behavior the depressed person exhibits will be developmentally age appropriate (Kaslow, Morris, & Rehm, 1998; Kazdin & Marciano, 1998; Stark, Ostrander, Kurowski, Swearer, & Bowen, 1995). Both children and adults can thus be characterized by depressed mood and loss of interest in productive activity, but adults may develop problems around work and marriage, whereas children may have academic problems and exhibit a variety of inappropriate conduct such as aggression, stealing, social withdrawal, and so forth.

The assumption that depression in childhood is similar to depression in adulthood is evident in the fourth edition of the *Diagnostic and Statistical Manual of Mental Disorders* (*DSM–IV;* American Psychiatric Association, 2000). Depression is not listed among the disorders that are usually first diagnosed in infancy, childhood, or adolescence, but special notes on depression in children are included under the section on adults' mood disorders. To some extent, however, the assumption that depression is the same phenomenon in children and adults may be misleading. We must remember that children are not merely scaled-down versions of adults, that childhood depression may be accompanied by other disorders (attention deficit–hyperactivity disorder, conduct disorder, anxiety disorders, learning disabilities, school failure, and so on), and that children's limited experience and cognitive capacity may give them perceptions of depression that differ from adults'.

Childhood depression was at one time looked on as just a normal part of human development, an idea we now realize is erroneous. After the abnormality of childhood depression had been recognized, it was seen by some as the underlying problem behind all other childhood disorders, another view that clearly is not tenable. If aggression, hyperactivity, noncompliance, learning disabilities, school failure, and other problems of nearly any sort are all attributed to underlying depression in the absence of core features of depressed behavior (depressed mood, loss of interest in most or all normal activities), then depression becomes meaningless as a concept and diagnostic category. A more defensible perspective is that childhood depression is a serious disorder in its own right that may or may not be accompanied by other maladaptive behavior or be comorbid with other disorders (Hammen & Rudolph, 2003; Seeley, Rohde, Lewinsohn, & Clarke, 2002; Waslick, Kandel, & Kakouros, 2002).

Depression is part of a larger category of *mood disorders* delineated in the *DSM–IV*. One's mood may be elevated or depressed, and mood disorders may involve different levels of severity of symptoms in both directions (or toward both poles). Depressed mood is characterized by *dysphoria,* feelings of unhappiness or unwellness not consistent with one's circumstances. In children and adolescents, dysphoria may be shown as irritability as well as by unhappiness. Elevated mood is characterized by the opposite—*euphoria,* a feeling of extraordinary and often unrealistic happiness or wellness. Dysphoric mood or irritability that lasts for a protracted period of time (a year or more for children and adolescents) but does not reach an intense level is called *dysthymia*. Euphoria and frenetic activity are known as *mania*. Some mood disorders are *unipolar,* such as depressive disorder in which mood varies between normal and extreme dysphoria (depression) or normal and extreme euphoria (mania). Others are *bipolar,* in which mood swings from one extreme to the other (Geller & DelBello, 2003). (*Bipolar* has largely replaced the earlier terminology, *manic-depressive*.)

Although the *DSM–IV* sets out detailed diagnostic criteria for the clinical diagnosis of various mood disorders in adults and makes notes regarding diagnosis in children and adolescents, considerable uncertainty remains about just how these criteria should apply to children and adolescents. The same general characteristics apply to adults and children, but the exact characterization of these disorders in children awaits much more research. Generally speaking, the symptoms one looks for in depression and related mood disorders in children and adolescents include the following:

- Anhedonia (inability to experience pleasure in all or nearly all activities)
- Depressed mood or general irritability
- Disturbance of appetite and significant weight gain or loss

- Disturbance of sleep (insomnia or hypersomnia)
- Psychomotor agitation or retardation
- Loss of energy, feelings of fatigue
- Feelings of worthlessness, self-reproach, excessive or inappropriate guilt, or hopelessness
- Diminished ability to think or concentrate; indecisiveness
- Ideas of suicide, suicide threats or attempts, recurrent thoughts of death.

These symptoms indicate depression only if several are exhibited over a protracted period of time and if they are not temporary, reasonable responses to life circumstances (e.g., as a consequence of a death in the family, we would expect several symptoms associated with depression during a period of grieving; see the case of Bryan in the accompanying case book for an example of childhood depression.)

Depression and other mood disorders tend to be episodic and of long duration. People tend to have repeated bouts with depression and related disorders, and those who have a major episode are at high risk for more. Children and adolescents with long-standing depression (2 years or longer) have been found to have more significant impairments, greater anxiety, and lower self-esteem and to show more acting-out behavior (Dubois, Felner, Bartels, & Silverman, 1995). Depressive behavior may result in peer rejection, particularly if it is exhibited under conditions of low stress and there is no apparent reason for depressive behavior (Little & Garber, 1995).

Depression affects a substantial percentage of children and adolescents, and many young people who are depressed remain untreated for the disorder (Kazdin & Marciano, 1998; Seeley et al., 2002). In prepubescent children, the prevalence of these disorders is about the same in boys and girls, with prepubescent boys being perhaps even slightly more likely than girls the same age to be depressed. By age 15, however, girls are twice as likely as boys to be depressed, and this high female–male ratio of about 2 to 1 remains constant for the next 35 to 40 years (Seeley et al., 2002; Stark et al., 1995). Although there is still considerable uncertainty about the definition and diagnosis of many mood disorders, bipolar disorder is increasingly diagnosed in adolescents with major mental health problems and recognized as a topic needing research. Also, the comorbidity of depressive disorders with other disorders, particularly conduct disorder and attention deficit–hyperactivity disorder, is increasingly recognized (Kazdin & Marciano, 1998; Papolos, 2003; Seeley et al., 2002). Depression has also been found to affect some children diagnosed with autism or other forms of pervasive developmental disorder (DeJong & Frazier, 2003; Ghaziuddin & Greden, 1998).

Assessment

The diagnosis of depression and other mood disorders in children and adolescents is generally left to psychologists or psychiatrists. However, educators can play a key role in aiding the assessment of these disorders (Cullinan, 2004). Competent assessment requires a multimodal approach in which several sources of information are tapped:

self-reports, parental reports, peer nominations, observation, and clinical interviews. A substantial number of devices are available for assessing depression, including rating scales and structured interviews (Kaslow et al., 1998; Merrell, 1994). However, the most important contribution of teachers to assessment may be careful observation of students' behavior that may reflect depression.

The types of behavior indicating possible depression include four categories of problems: affective, cognitive, motivational, and physiological. We may expect the depressed student to show depressed affect—to act unusually sad, lonely, and apathetic. Cognitive characteristics may include negative comments about oneself that indicate low self-esteem, excessive guilt, and pessimism. Depressed students often avoid demanding tasks and social experiences, show little interest in normal activities, and seem not to be motivated by ordinary or special consequences. Finally, depressed students often have physical complaints of fatigue or illness or problems with sleeping or eating. If a student exhibits such characteristics frequently for a period of weeks, the teacher should consider the possibility that the student is suffering from a mood disorder and refer him or her for evaluation. However, it is important not to overlook the possibility that other behaviors, such as general irritability or acting out, are also sometimes signs of depression, especially in children and adolescents. Difficulty in expressing anger appropriately is one characteristic associated with depression (Kashani, Dahlmeier, Borduin, Soltys, & Reid, 1995), so a student's behavior might be thought mistakenly to reflect an externalizing disorder.

Comorbidity of depression with other disorders sometimes makes assessment particularly difficult, as does the episodic nature of mood disorders and the fact that an individual can have more than one mood disorder. If the student exhibits conduct disorder or attention deficit–hyperactivity disorder, for example, it may be easy to overlook indications of depression. When an individual is recovering a more normal mood after a depressive episode, it is easy to assume that the depression was not serious or that the risk of another episode is nil. If the student has a dysthymic disorder but is going through a major depressive episode, the low-grade depression may be misinterpreted as normal.

Causal Factors, Relationship to Other Disorders, and Prevention

In most cases, we do not know exactly what causes depression. Some cases are evidently *endogenous* (a response to unknown genetic, biochemical, or other biological factors); other cases are apparently *reactive* (a response to environmental events, such as death of a loved one or academic failure). Predictably, child abuse, parental psychopathology, and family conflict and disorganization are frequently linked to children's depression. Research provides some suggestion that childhood depression and adult religiosity may be related (Miller, Weissman, Gur, & Greenwald, 2002).

Evidence is accumulating that there is a significant correlation between parents' depression and a variety of problems in their children, including depression (see Beardslee, Versage, Van de Velde, Swatling, & Hoke, 2002; Joiner & Coyne, 1999; Kaslow et al., 1998; Kazdin & Marciano, 1998; Seeley et al., 2002). This relationship undoubtedly reflects genetic influences on behavior. However, the fact that depression runs in families may reflect family interactions as well. Depressed parents may provide models of depressed behavior (which their children imitate), reinforce depressive behaviors in their children, or create a home environment that is conducive to depression (by setting unreasonable expectations, providing few rewards for achievement or initiative, emphasizing punishment, or providing noncontingent rewards and punishments). Depressed mothers are known to lack parenting skills, which could account for at least some of their children's behavioral and affective problems. Cummings and Davies (1999) noted: "On the one hand, in comparison to nondepressed parents, depressed parents are more inconsistent, lax, and generally ineffective in child management and discipline. On the other hand, when they are not yielding to the child's demands, they are more likely to engage in direct, forceful control strategies and are less likely to end disagreements in compromise" (p. 307).

Educators are in a particularly good position to identify depression and should give special attention to the ways in which a student's depression may affect and be affected by school performance (Seeley et al., 2002). Young children who are depressed engage in less play and exhibit more undirected activity than do typical children (Lous, de Wit, De Bruyn, & Riksen-Walraven, 2002). Depression appears to be associated with lowered performance on some cognitive tasks, lowered self-esteem, lowered social competence, deficits in self-control, and a depressive attributional style in which children tend to believe that bad outcomes are a result of their own unmodifiable and global inadequacies. There is an inverse relationship between depressive symptoms and problem-solving abilities: Better problem solvers tend to show fewer depressive symptoms (Goodman, Gravitt, & Kaslow, 1995), and depression appears to be related to poor academic self-image (Masi, Sbrana, Poli, Tomaiuolo, Favilla, & Marcheschi, 2000).

These findings suggest that school failure and depression may be reciprocal causal factors: depression makes the student less competent and less confident, both academically and socially; failing academically and socially makes the student feel and act more depressed and reinforces the attribution of failure to unalterable personal characteristics (Patterson & Capaldi, 1990). Depression and failure may thus become a vicious cycle that is hard to break. This cycle may often be a part of conduct disorder and, to a lesser extent, learning disabilities. Yet teachers and other school personnel have been slow to recognize the signs of depression and even slower to provide intervention. Kazdin and Marciano (1998) noted in discussion of the underidentification of depression:

> In school settings, for example, it is likely that teachers may not view withdrawal and moodiness as possible signs of serious dysfunction. Also, because depression is so often comorbid with externalizing disorders (e.g., Conduct Disorder, Substance Abuse), it is likely to be overshadowed in the clinical picture. Even when systematically assessed and identified, the depression may not receive much explicit attention. (p. 240)

Preventing depression is important because childhood depression, at least in its severe and chronic form, is linked to adult maladjustment and sometimes to suicidal behavior. However, research provides little guidance for preventive efforts (Kazdin & Marciano, 1998). We might guess that an accumulation of major stressful life events is an important factor in some youngsters' depression and suicide. However, more typical daily hassles can also put adolescents at risk for depression, particularly in the late childhood and early adolescent years (Lewinsohn et al., 1995). Primary prevention may therefore involve efforts to reduce all manner of stressful life events for all children, but such broad-based, unfocused efforts are unlikely to receive much political or fiscal support. There is a better chance for support and success if efforts focus on relieving stress for abused and neglected youngsters and others whose lives are obviously extremely stressful. Another approach to primary prevention, somewhat more focused and feasible, is parenting training for depressed parents (Beardslee et al., 2002). Secondary and third-level prevention are still more focused and feasible, giving depressed youngsters behavioral or cognitive-behavioral training in overcoming their specific difficulties. This training is preventive in that it keeps the child's current situation from worsening and may forestall the development of long-term negative outcomes and recurrent episodes of depression.

Intervention and Education

Antidepressant drugs are often prescribed for childhood depression, although there has been inadequate research on their effectiveness and the side effects can be problematic (Hamnen & Rudoph, 2003; Kaslow et al., 1998; Konopasek & Forness, 2004; Kusumakar, Lazier, MacMaster, & Santor, 2002; Ryan, 2002). When medications are prescribed, teachers need to carefully monitor the effects on behavior and learning. As is the case in nearly every type of disorder, successful intervention requires collaborative, multimodal treatment involving a variety of professionals.

Teachers are most likely to be directly involved in interventions that are behavioral or cognitive-behavioral. These interventions are based on theories of depression that highlight the roles of social skills, productive and pleasurable activity, causal attributions, cognitive assertions, and self-control (see Kaslow et al., 1998; Kazdin & Marciano, 1998; Seeley et al., 2002).

Kaslow et al. (1998) outlined a general decision-making model for approaching the treatment of depression. First, if a student appears to be depressed, it is important to ask whether there are associated disorders. If so, then interventions should be implemented to address them first because depression might be relieved if the other disorders are ameliorated; if not, then intervention for depression is necessary. In designing interventions for depression, Kaslow et al. suggested assessing the student's problems in the following order and providing intervention if significant problems of that type are found:

1. Low activity level
2. Social skills deficits
3. Self-control deficits
4. Depressive attributional style
5. Low self-esteem and feelings of hopelessness
6. Limited self-awareness and interpersonal awareness.

In their schema, the priority for assessment and intervention is activity level and the second target for intervention is social skills. Teachers can be extremely helpful, if not the key players, in implementing both of these strategies.

SUICIDAL BEHAVIOR

Definition and Prevalence

The definition of *completed suicide* is straightforward: to kill oneself intentionally. However, determining that a death was a suicide is often difficult because the circumstances, particularly the intentions of the deceased, are in question. Suicide is socially stigmatizing, so the label *suicide* is likely to be avoided if death can be attributed to accident (Madge & Harvey, 1999). Accidents are the leading cause of death among adolescents in the 15 to 24 age bracket, and many researchers suspect that, in this age group, many deaths attributed to accident are disguised or misreported suicides (e.g., Madge & Harvey, 1999).

The term parasuicide sometimes refers to unsuccessful or uncompleted suicidal behavior. *Attempted suicide* is difficult to define because studies often differ in distinctions between suicidal gestures (suicidal behavior that is interpreted as not serious in intent), thoughts of suicide, threats of suicide, and self-inflicted injury requiring medical treatment (see Spirito & Overholser, 2003).

Regardless how we define them, suicide and suicide attempts of adolescents (and, to a lesser extent, younger children) have increased dramatically during the past several decades (Spirito, 2003). Only accidents and homicides are more often the cause of death among youth between the ages of 15 and 24. Suicidal behavior among children and adolescents is a major public health problem, not only in this country but in many countries of the world (Spirito & Overholser, 2003). Adolescent males have a higher suicide rate than do females, and this sex difference becomes more marked with age. Among older adolescents and young adults, parasuicides are more common for females than for males. Among children, the gender difference is reversed, with suicide attempts more common for boys than for girls. In the United States, until recently, Black males have had significantly lower suicide rates than did White males; rates for Native American youth are higher than are rates for Whites (Wyche & Rotheram-Borus, 1990). However, suicide rates for Black males have increased markedly since 1986, and it may no longer be accurate to say that Black males are at lower risk of suicide than are White males (Shaffer, Gould, & Hicks, 1994). The accurate assessment of suicide risk may require particular sensitivity to particular minority populations (Goldston, 2003). Suicide rates are higher for married than for unmarried teenagers. Suicide methods appear to relate to the availability of means; firearms are more commonly used in the United States than they are in most other countries.

Although suicide is rarely reported in children under 10 years old and is relatively infrequent even in prepubertal children (Shaffer & Hicks, 1994; Smith, 1992), we do occasionally encounter reports of suicide attempts and successful suicides of very young children (e.g., Rosenthal & Rosenthal, 1984). However, rising suicidal behavior among young people and the high rate at which children and youth kill or attempt to kill themselves are alarming. "It appears . . . that by late adolescence, teenagers' tendency toward self-destructiveness has mushroomed from a rare event to a phenomenon that is at least passingly considered by most teens and is acted on by 1 out of 12 of them" (Smith, 1992, p. 257). Greater understanding of the causes and more effective prevention programs must be priorities. We also need better means of dealing with suicidal individuals after an attempted suicide and with survivors after a completed suicide.

Causal Factors and Prevention

Most authorities agree that biological and nonbiological factors interact in complex ways in the causation of suicide and depression. There appear to be genetic and other physiological contributions to depressive behavior, as we have already noted, and these factors may increase risk for suicidal behavior as well. However, educators focus primarily on the environmental factors involved. The many complex factors that contribute to children's and adolescents' suicidal behavior include major psychiatric problems, feelings of hopelessness, impulsivity, naive concepts of death, substance abuse, social isolation, abuse and neglect by parents, family conflict and disorganization, a family history of suicide and parasuicide, and cultural factors, including stress caused by the educational system and attention to suicide in the mass media. Youth with emotional or behavioral disorders, especially those who use alcohol or illicit drugs, are at particularly high risk of suicidal behavior (Carr, 2002; Spirito & Overholser, 2003).

The common thread among all causal factors is that suicidal individuals believe they have little impact on the world around them. They often do not know that help is available for dealing with their problems, believing that no one cares and that they must deal with their problems alone. Gulp, Clyman, and Culp (1995) studied 220 students in Grades 6 through 12. Nearly half of those who reported feelings of depression did not ask for help, most often because they did not know about services available to them in the school or, if they did, believed they had to take care of their problems by themselves. Feelings of loneliness and especially hopelessness appear to be among the best predictors of suicidal thoughts and intentions (Spirito & Overholser, 2003).

Hopelessness has long been recognized as a primary characteristic of the thinking of those prone to suicide. Hopelessness and intent to commit suicide correlate more highly than do depression and suicide intent. Apparently, all individuals who feel hopeless are depressed, but not all who are depressed feel hopeless. Those who feel hopeless are convinced that things will not get better, cannot get better, so they might as well give up hope. Hopelessness may represent the final stage of depression that tends to precede suicidal intent, the stage at which an individual concludes that suicide is justified.

Many children and adolescents who commit suicide or parasuicide have a history of emotional or behavioral disorders and school failure. In fact, school performance of adolescents who show suicidal behavior is almost uniformly poor, and most teenagers' suicides and parasuicides occur in the spring months, when school problems (grades, graduation, college admission) are highlighted.

Other factors increasing the likelihood of suicide attempts, besides mood disorders, include high levels of stress related to parents (e.g., having been physically hurt by a parent, running away, living apart from both parents), sexuality (e.g., concerns regarding pregnancy, sexually transmitted diseases, and pressure to become sexually active), police contacts, and lack of adult support outside the home (Flisher, 1999; Wolfe, 1998). Some have suspected that social stress related to homosexuality is a factor in suicide, but research has found no reliable connection between sexual orientation and suicide (Shaffer et al., 1994). Unsurprisingly, suicidal behavior appears to be learned, at least in part, through observation of the behavior of others in family and social contexts. Families that do not form emotional bonds and parents whose discipline style is chaotic are also factors increasing risk for suicidal behavior (Bush & Pargament, 1995). Outbreaks of suicide attempts are particularly likely to occur in institutional settings and psychiatric hospitals, probably partly as a result of imitation or competitive bids for attention and status.

Ordinarily, we think of depression as the primary disorder associated with suicidal behavior. However, the role of aggressive behavior is increasingly recognized (Spirito & Overholser, 2003). Primary suicide prevention presents enormous problems of identifying individuals who are at risk because, in any attempt to make predictions, the number of false positives is extremely high and the consequences of false negatives are extremely severe. Because only a relatively small percentage of the population commits or attempts suicide, and because suicidal and nonsuicidal individuals have many common characteristics, any general screening procedure turns up many false positives—individuals who are not actually at high risk. But the consequence of identifying as "not at risk" those who are in fact likely to attempt or commit suicide (the false negatives) are obviously grim. Consequently, most primary prevention programs are aimed at entire school populations.

Assessment

Suicidal behavior is not always preceded by recognizable signals, although some characteristics and circumstances are danger signals that educators and other adults should be on the lookout for. Adults' and peers' awareness of indications that a child or youth might be at risk for suicidal behavior is an important aspect of assessing the general school population (Carr, 2002; Popenhagen & Qualley, 1998; Spirito & Overholser, 2003). These are some indications of risk in the general school population:

- Sudden changes in usual behavior or affect
- Serious academic, social, or disciplinary problems at school
- Family or home problems, including parental separation or divorce, child abuse, or running away from home
- Disturbed or disrupted peer relations, including peer rejection and breakup of romantic relationships or social isolation
- Health problems, such as insomnia, loss of appetite, sudden weight change, and so on
- Substance abuse
- Giving away possessions or talk of not being present in the future
- Talk of suicide or presence of a suicide plan
- Situational crisis such as death of a family member or close friend, pregnancy or abortion, legal arrest, loss of employment of self or family member.

Part of any assessment of risk involves systematic evaluation of the characteristics of individuals who are thought to be at higher than usual risk. A personal characteristic associated with most suicides, parasuicides, and thoughts of suicide is depression, so it is important to assess depression. However, depression may be accompanied by aggressive behavior, conduct disorder, or a variety of other problems.

Intervention and Education

Adults should do the following:

* Take all suicide threats and attempts seriously
* Seek to reestablish communication
* Provide emotional support or sustenance that relieves alienation.

Although dealing adequately with the problem of suicidal behavior requires a complex, multifaceted effort, the general notion is that the suicidal individual must be helped to establish and maintain as many points of contact as possible with significant others, including adults and peers. The child or adolescent must be shown ways that are not self-destructive to solve problems and get attention from others. Teachers can aid in suicide prevention by realizing that they can identify students who are at risk; school systems can play a part in prevention by providing curricula that acquaint students with others' experience of normal physical and social development (Seeley et al., 2002; Spirito & Overholser, 2003).

The educator's role in intervention is primarily to provide information about suicide and refer students who appear at risk to other professionals. A comprehensive program of suicide awareness and prevention has several parts: administrative guidelines specifying school policy, faculty inservice to obtain support of teachers and provide them with basic information and skills in dealing with students, and curricular programs for students. In addition, hot lines, peer counseling, and programs designed to reduce and manage stress may be implemented.

Managing children and adolescents after their suicide attempts or threats is the joint responsibility of counselors or other mental health personnel and teachers. Although teachers should not attempt to offer counseling or therapy themselves, they can provide critical support by encouraging students and families to obtain help from qualified counselors or therapists. Teachers can also help by reducing unnecessary stress on students and being willing and empathic listeners.

SUMMARY

The federal definition of "emotionally disturbed" suggests that youngsters with internalizing problems, including depression, should be eligible for special education, although the definition describes depression and related disorders ambiguously. Childhood depression has only recently become a topic of serious research. Consensus is emerging that depression is a major disorder of childhood that parallels adult depression in many respects, but particular behaviors exhibited in response to depressed affect will be developmentally age appropriate. Both adults and children who are depressed experience depressed moods and lose interest in productive activity. Depressed children may exhibit a variety of inappropriate behavior, and depression is often comorbid with other conditions.

Depression is part of the larger category of mood disorders, which includes unipolar and bipolar disorders involving elevated or depressed mood. Indications of depression include anhedonia, depressed mood or irritability, disturbances of sleep or appetite, psychomotor agitation or retardation, loss of energy or fatigue, feelings of self-derogation or hopelessness, difficulty thinking or concentrating, and suicidal ideation or attempts. Several of these symptoms are exhibited for a protracted period and are not a reasonable response to life events. Prevalence of depression is higher among older adolescents than young children, and girls are more affected at older ages. Depression may be found in 2 to 8% of the child population, and researchers suspect that many cases are not identified.

Assessment of depression must be multifaceted and should include self-reports, parental reports, peer nominations, observations, and clinical interviews. The judgments of teachers should not be overlooked. Teachers should be on the lookout for four categories of problems: affective, cognitive, motivational, and physiological.

Some cases of depression clearly result from unknown biological factors, but the causal factors in most cases are indeterminable. In some cases, depression represents a reaction to stressful or traumatic environmental events. We find significant correlations between parents' depression and problems of their children, including depression. Educators should give special attention to how depression and school failure can be reciprocal causal factors. Prevention of depression is important because severe chronic depression is associated with adult maladjustment and suicidal behavior. Prevention may involve reducing stress, training in parenting, or teaching specific cognitive or behavioral skills.

Antidepressant drugs may be useful in some cases of depression, but their effects and side effects should be monitored carefully. Interventions are based on theories that attribute depression to inadequate social skills, maladaptive thought patterns, and lack of self-control. Selecting intervention strategies depends on analyzing the depressed individual's specific cognitive and social characteristics. Teachers can play a major role in teaching social skills and engaging students in higher levels of productive activities as well as assisting in other approaches.

Suicide and suicidal behavior (parasuicide) of children and youth, especially of adolescents and young adults, have increased dramatically in the past several decades. Factors increasing the risk of suicidal behavior include biological and environmental factors, especially a history of difficulty or failure in school, stress related to family dysfunction or abuse, substance abuse, family members or acquaintances who have completed suicide, depression and feelings of hopelessness, and aggressive behavior.

Prevention of suicide is extremely difficult because of the problems associated with false positives and false negatives. Prevention programs are typically aimed at entire school populations and consist of guidelines for teaching, in-service for teachers, and instructional programs for students and parents. Assessment of suicide risk involves recognizing danger signals and evaluating the individual's sense of hopelessness (Esposito, Johnson, Wolfsdorf, & Spirito, 2003). Evaluation of statistically based risk factors and the student's ability to perform specific coping tasks are required to determine whether a suicide attempt is imminent.

Teachers and other adults should take all suicide threats and attempts seriously, seek to reestablish communication with students who feel alienated and help them establish as many points of contact as possible with significant others, and provide emotional sustenance and support. Schools should have a plan for follow-up intervention when a suicide occurs but must be careful in implementing prevention and intervention programs so that suicide risk is not inadvertently increased.

Depression and Suicidal Behavior

Tezella G. Cline, B.S., Winston-Salem State University, works with the professional development team as a full-time, senior mentor with the Charlotte–Mecklenburg New Teacher Program and is enrolled in the school administration master's program at Gardner-Webb University. She taught at the Spaugh Middle School of Math, Science, and Technology in Charlotte, North Carolina, when she wrote this feature.

Describe the school in which you teach and your particular role in the school.

I teach in an inner-city magnet school that focuses on math, science, and technology. The technology-rich curriculum is designed to stimulate student interest and enhance student learning. The school's population is balanced racially. We have about 700 students enrolled in Grades 6 through 8. Our school population is 63% male, 44% Black, and 56% other ethnicities (Asian, Hispanic, Native American, multiracial, or White). About 45% of the students receive free or reduced-cost lunch, 18% are identified as gifted and talented, and 11% receive resource services or are in special classes. Students identified as "exceptional" number about 70, with 20 of these being classified as behaviorally and emotionally handicapped. The exceptional classes at my school include two resource classes and two self-contained classes. The resource classes serve mostly the learning disabled students, and the self-contained classes serve behaviorally and emotionally disabled students.

I am presently teaching sixth- and seventh-grade students in a self-contained setting. My eight students (five boys and three girls) have behavioral and emotional disorders. I also serve as team leader for our department as well as mentor for new special education teachers. I am a part of the Charlotte–Mecklenburg School Division's Teacher Leader Program, which works with the staff development department to offer training sessions for professional growth for all teachers. This year, I was awarded an Impact II grant.

Think of a particular student who exhibits depression or suicidal behavior. How does this student manifest the disorder?

I want to preface my answer with some general observations about teaching. A classroom teacher has a very important responsibility: to teach all students. Another important part of this responsibility is to observe each student for possible behavioral, emotional, academic, or social difficulties. This task means that teachers must be willing to establish one-to-one as well as group relationships with students. The better the teacher knows individuals and their families, the better he or she can serve the student. Careful daily observation and analysis of behaviors is essential. Another vital part of a successful educational program is communication. The teacher must communicate what has been observed with the parent or caretaker and with other professionals. This will allow us to better meet the needs of the student with behavioral or emotional difficulties.

George, one of my students who exhibits depression and suicidal behaviors, has the following five characteristics. First, he lacks appropriate social skills. This child has difficulty presenting himself in a socially acceptable way. When placed in a positive situation, he acts out—behaves in a negative, inappropriate way. When those around him react to his behavior, he usually responds with negative verbal statements about himself or others. He then blames others for being "stupid" enough to think that he could perform in that particular situation. Additional negative verbal responses from him include "I don't care," "So?" and "Nobody cares." Whenever he is faced with a challenge (good or bad), he seems to become frightened and try to avoid the challenge by being so negative that he will have to be removed from the situation. He seems to try to push friends, loved ones, and those who care away. He tries to isolate himself. Once this is done, however, he experiences depressed feelings.

Second, George becomes aggressive. He tries to create conflict situations, at times simply to have an excuse to become aggressive and avoid the challenge of the moment. For example, he will lie about someone hitting him or complain that other students are looking at him or making threats toward him. He often puts himself in conflict situations and then complains that no one ever helps him.

Third, George withdraws from or avoids social activity with his peers. Even when he's with a group, he will isolate himself by doing something to irritate others in the group. I have seen this occur even during fun, seemingly nonthreatening activities. At the beginning of the activity or event he will be overly excited and anxious to participate. Then, as he gets more involved, he becomes progressively negative and finally withdraws by giving up. Once this has occurred, his anger sets in.

Fourth, George exhibits mood swings. Within moments, this student can go from being happy, excited, and cheerful to being sad, angry, and aggressive. For example, recently we were having our classroom project presentations for parents and other adult visitors. George had presented successfully for the principal, teachers, and his parent. It was the last day of school before the winter holiday. He had been given gifts and food during class, and everyone seemed to be having fun and smiling. George even shared a gift with teachers and explained that the gift was something that he had made himself, especially for the teachers. His mom was proud of his success, and she told him so as they kissed each other good-bye. Less than 30 minutes later his mood changed drastically. He became very active and disruptive to students around him. He was angry and cursing and on the verge of fighting with another student. The fact that other adults and a school administrator were in the room did not matter. Although I reminded him of what a great day he was having and how proud we all were of him, he proceeded to tell me that he did not care about any of this stuff. He also informed me that he wanted his gifts back. He continued making threats of aggression and arguing with staff. When we sent him to the time-out area in the room, he rolled on the floor and made loud noises. Later, when calm, he appeared sad and lonely. He made negative statements about himself and asked to go home, stating that he was tired.

Fifth, George picks friends and activities that are dangerous. He makes poor decisions about most things. He knows what's right, but he does the opposite. He often lies to himself and others about his choices. There are times when George will do anything to get peers to like him. He will also try to "buy" friendships.

What procedures have you found most useful in working with this student?

I have found that George responds best when he gets additional one-on-one attention. This attention can come from me or from our security officer. I believe that this male influence sometimes reaches him in a way that I cannot.

I believe it is important for students with emotional or behavioral disorders to build positive relationships with a variety of adults in their school or community environment. These relationships may prove helpful in crisis situations. When I notice a mood swing or an aggressive episode coming on, I try to ask another significant adult in the child's life to take the student for a walk to talk to him. This strategy has been most effective because it removes the student from the environment that he or she is having difficulty with. In addition, it removes the audience (the other students). Both (environment and audience) are factors that can prolong or intensify a problem. When a student is removed, he or she is no longer the center of peer attention yet has the attention that he or she is seeking.

Another way that I have been successful with George is by keeping up my daily communication with his mother. I believe that this gives him a feeling of family and consistency. He feels secure when he knows that what happens at home will be communicated to me and that all events from school will be shared with his mother. This also lets him know how important he is.

In addition, I also plan special, exciting, fun activities at least every 2 weeks. Also, my daily instruction includes activities that allow students to interact with each other as they use hands-on materials and engage themselves in discovery learning. I build in choices for students, and this gives them all a feeling of control and something to look forward to. We have special events or snacks at the end of the school day. Doing this helps to address feelings of hopelessness and encourages students to be motivated to stay focused on their tasks and to try to get the reward at the end of the day. Another benefit of planning special events is that they may relieve some of the stress that middle school students feel, especially those dealing with depression.

Another strategy I use with George is to listen when he asks to talk. Often, he comes to me and says, "I need to talk to you outside." I always set aside a time during the day to just listen to his concerns or ideas. The information that he shares is usually very helpful and enlightening. My role here is to support him by listening.

What are the prospects for this student's educational progress in the coming year?

Academically, George is average. He enjoys math and has just been mainstreamed into a regular math class on a trial basis. If he can be successful in this class, I will work toward placing him into another mainstream class. This depends, of course, on how well he adjusts and how consistent he can be. The challenge for me is to monitor him closely. Because I know his pattern of behavior, I expect that after the second week he will probably feel the pressure and will begin doing things to get himself put out of the class. He will then develop an "I don't care" attitude and begin to make negative statements about going to the class. I will be proactive by establishing a reward system and by communicating with the home to get his mother to do the same. This will, I hope, assist in keeping his interest and motivation level high.

George's prospects for the future are good if he continues to get support from parents, teachers, and other professionals. He does not deal well with changes in his environment, especially if he feels neglected. Academically, he is able to succeed, but he will need continued emotional support to progress. He presently gets professional counseling weekly with an outside agency (not in school). This will need to continue if progress is to occur.

What are the biggest long-term problems this student faces?

It is difficult for George to be consistent because of his mood swings. This will probably cause continued difficulty for him. Also, a major area of concern is his lack of appropriate social skills needed to obtain reinforcement from his social environment. He functions within the controlled environment of the special classroom, but my concern is how he will make it when out on his own.

George must be able to deal with changes in his environment and in relationships to the point that he can manage and control his negative responses to those changes. He must deal with changes in his world without giving up.

Tezella Cline Interviews George

Ms. C: How are you feeling today?

G: Good.

Ms. C: How would you describe yourself?

G: Trapped up in feelings.

Ms. C: Can you tell me about any of those?

G: Like, different ones. Like, wanting to go home, but my mom hadn't came yet.

Ms. C: Name and describe things that make you feel the best about yourself.

G: I like working alone. And . . . when I'm doing a good job and the teacher says that I'm doing a good job.

Ms. C: Describe your personality.

G: I think I'm a nice guy. When you get to know me a good bit. And generous.

Ms. C: Tell me about your life.

G: There have been ups and downs all through it. I had to go to Alexander.

Ms. C: What's Alexander?

G: Children's' Center . . . and then I had to go back home to live with my mom. I was in regular classes, then I went to BEH [behaviorally and emotionally handicapped classes], and that's all. There have been ups and downs in my life.

Ms. C: How do you feel about those ups and downs?

G: Well, when I went to Alexander, I didn't like it. It was a childrens' center where they kept me overnight for 60 days.

Ms. C: When did you go there?

G: I think when I was like 4 or 5. I was out of control.

Ms. C: Out of control? What do you mean by that?

G: I was, like, being too bad to stay at home.

Ms. C: And at school? What was it like there?

G: I was in a regular class, and I didn't do very good in school. I got suspended a lot.

Ms. C: How often do you think you got suspended?

G: I got in trouble with the teacher, like, more than once every day.

Ms. C: Can you describe for me some of the types of things that you did?

G: I would not follow directions and not respect the teachers. I would mostly talk to my peers. Not listen to the teacher.

Ms. C: But all kids do that sometimes, right?

G: Yeah.

Ms. C: But what made you different?

G: I was doing it constantly.

Ms. C: Tell me the best thing about your life right now.

G: That I have a loving family that cares about me.

Ms. C: Do you have friends?

G: Yeah! I do!

Ms. C: Tell me about your friends.

G: They're fun, and I talk to them.

Ms. C: You don't have to name them, but describe your friends.

G: Some of them are bad, and some of them are good.

Ms. C: Which ones do you like to be with the most? Be honest.

G: Sometimes the bad.

Ms. C: What makes you say that they are bad?

G: Their actions are bad.

Ms. C: For example. . . .

G: Like they do bad things when they know it's wrong. Then they try to cover up for it.

Ms. C: What kinds of things?

G: Like, they throw spit balls or something like that.

Ms. C: What do you like best about being in school?

G: The math.

Ms. C: Why?

G: Because that's my favorite subject.

Ms. C: How do you feel when you're doing your favorite subject?

G: It makes me feel good 'cause I know what I'm doing most of the time.

Ms. C: What kinds of expressions do you have when you're doing math?

G: Like algebra and stuff like that?

Ms. C: No, I mean what kinds of emotions?

G: I'm feeling good because I know that I know how to do this and it's fun.

Ms. C: What do you like best about being at home?

G: All the privileges that I get, and I know I can't do that in a group home or something like that.

Ms. C: So you do think about that sometimes?

G: Yes, when my mom reminds me about it a lot.

Ms. C: How do you feel when you have to do subjects that you do not want to do?

G: I feel mad sometimes at the teacher, but I try to do it the best I can.

Ms. C: When you do those subjects that you don't like, tell me what you might be thinking.

G: I'm thinking that I don't want to do it, but I've got to 'cause I want to learn.

Ms. C: How do you handle those feelings when you feel them coming?

G: I try to ignore them because I need to do my work.

Ms. C: Do you talk to yourself?

G: Yes.

Ms. C: What do you say?

G: I can do it. I give myself strategies saying that I can do it and stuff like that.

Ms. C: What kind of strategies have you learned through the years?

G: That if you talk to yourself enough that you will convince yourself that you can do it.

Ms. C: Tell me the things that you say, specifically.

G: I can do it, and you're the one that can do it.

Ms. C: Now, think about when you are angry and you're not saying those things to yourself. What kinds of things are you saying?

G: When I'm angry, I'm mostly angry at somebody and it gets me really mad. And I'm not thinking about nothing, and I just say things that I don't really mean.

Ms. C: Right. What kinds of things come out?

G: Sometimes I curse.

Ms. C: After you've said things that you don't really mean, then what are you feeling? Do you feel good, or do you feel bad?

G: I feel bad because I've blown up at my mom a lot, and then at the end I'm really sad that I did that, and I can't live with myself sometimes doing that. So I need to stop doing it.

Ms. C: You have a lot of emotions going on there. Think now specifically about how you feel when you're getting angry or upset. What's usually the first feeling on up to where it's the top feeling?

G: That I'm really getting mad at somebody . . . like I'm saying I can cool down a little bit. Whenever I get to the top of it, I get really, really mad, and then I get like saying, "*rurrrr*," and I get, like, shaking all over and my face starts to turn red and stuff like that.

Ms. C: When you reach that point, what are you thinking?

G: That I should, like, sometimes I think that I need to hit the person, but I know in myself that I shouldn't because I'll get suspended from school.

Ms. C: So what do you do?

G: I tell myself that you shouldn't hit 'cause it's not the right thing to do.

Ms. C: Have you ever told yourself the right thing but then done the other?

G: Yeah. I do that a lot. Then I think I know the right thing, then whenever I be bad I think it's a little more funner, sometimes.

Ms. C: So it makes you feel. . . .

G: Happy sometimes when I be bad, but whenever I get the consequences, it don't make sense to me.

Ms. C: Okay. Think about when you're angry. You told me what you're telling yourself. What ways do you show others that you're angry?

G: I really have a high temper. I mean, I yell a lot. Sometimes I throw things.

Ms. C: So explain this to me. Are you saying that it's not always when you have to do work, or you have to do things that other people tell you to do that get you angry?

G: No, it's not like that. It's like almost every day I try to deal with it to a certain extent.

Ms. C: So sometimes, even when you're doing something that you like to do, you get mad?

G: Yeah, I get angry then, too.

Ms. C: Do you ever get mad at yourself?

G: Yeah. I get mad at myself 'cause I can't do it myself, sometimes. That makes me mad at myself.

Ms. C: When you get mad at yourself, how does that make you feel toward yourself? Do you ever do things to yourself or say negative things to yourself?

G: Yeah, like right after I get done yelling at my mom when we have a big fight, I say, I tell it to myself, I say, "Why did you do that? You shouldn't have done that 'cause she's your mom. And you shouldn't say those kind of things to your mom." And I get real mad at myself sometimes.

Ms. C: Do you ever feel like hurting yourself or something like that?

G: At one point in my life I did. I thought I couldn't live with myself doing this. And I thought that I should kill myself, but I didn't.

Ms. C: Do you remember how old you were when you thought that?

G: I think I was around 6 or 5.

Ms. C: That young?

G: Yeah.

Ms. C: Since then, have you ever tried to hurt yourself in any way?

G: Well, there was this one time I was sitting in a car and I had a knife. I cut my finger. Right across here.

Ms. C: Have you ever felt just really, really low or really sad?

G: Yes.

Ms. C: Have you ever felt, would you say, depressed?

G: Yes. I felt that way a lot when I was really young.

Ms. C: Can you use any words to describe how that feels?

G: It feels like you can't go any lower than you go. You're, like, real low and you're saying to yourself, "Why can't I go on? What have I done?" And I just got so low, and it's hard to like, do stuff 'cause you're so depressed and you don't know what to do next.

Ms. C: What do teachers do that makes you feel this way sometimes?

G: When they tell you to do something over and over. They keep doing that over and over, and that gets me mad.

Ms. C: What do teachers do sometimes that makes you feel depressed or sad or low?

G: Whenever a teacher makes fun of me, it makes me feel sad or low.

Ms. C: What could teachers do to help make you feel better or feel lifted or happy once you're feeling depressed or sad or low?

G: Like, do my favorite subject, like math or something like that.

Ms. C: Name some things that you do at school that seem to get you into trouble.

G: I tend to hang with some bad people, bad friends. I shouldn't do that. I should know better.

Ms. C: Anything else that you do at school that gets you into trouble? What about in the classroom?

G: Yeah. I talk back, and I don't follow the teacher's directions.

Ms. C: What happens when you talk back or don't follow the teacher's directions? What comes after that?

G: I usually lose points or I get, like, a time out.

Ms. C: How do you feel when that happens?

G: I feel angry at myself along with them [bad friends] because I didn't follow directions. And with them because they made me have to do it.

Ms. C: So even though you understand the rules and you know what is expected, then when you don't do what is expected and you get the consequence you still feel angry when you get the consequence?

G: Yes.

Ms. C: Now, is that anger directed to the teacher, do you think, or is it to yourself?

G: Mostly toward myself and also a little bit toward the teacher.

Ms. C: How do you react when you get caught doing something wrong?

G: Most of the time I say, "I didn't do it" or "It wasn't me."

Ms. C: Do you accept responsibility for your own behavior?

G: Sometimes. But I do not accept it more than I do accept it.

Ms. C: Do you tell the truth?

G: Sometimes.

Ms. C: Do you tell the truth about serious things?

G: Yes.

Ms. C: What kinds of things do you think you do not tell the truth about?

G: My behavior or something I did wrong.

Ms. C: Do you do your homework?

G: Sometimes, when I feel like it.

Ms. C: What makes you feel like doing it?

G: I want to get it over with so I can have time to play.

Ms. C: How do you feel about your school?

G: I feel like the school has lived up to its potential because it's been here so long and I think it's done good in all subjects. It teaches kids how to do good.

Ms. C: How do you feel about your class right now? The situation in your [self-contained] class right now?

G: I think we're not doing too good toward making the school's name that it's already got. Because we have a lot of problems in class. Behavior problems.

Ms. C: Describe the problems. What kinds of problems?

G: Behavior problems and temper moods. Tempers fly up, and we get mad at each other and mad at the teachers and stuff like that.

Ms. C: What do you think the teacher should do when the moods and tempers fly up?

G: The teacher should give them consequences and redirect them.

Ms. C: What are the things about your class that help you the most?

G: That some people in my class help me do my work. Group work.

Ms. C: What are some things in your class that upset you or make you angry?

G: When their tempers fly up at me and they think I did something and I didn't.

Ms. C: Do you have a routine in your class?

G: Yes. It's on our point system where we have to do math or social studies.

Ms. C: Do you think that's good for you?

G: Yeah. I like to know what is after each other so I can prepare for it. I think that's a good routine.

Ms. C: When you're feeling sad or depressed, how long does that feeling usually last?

G: Feeling angry and depressed, well, I'm never like that for a long period of time. For some reason my feelings never stay the same. They never keep going on and on and on like some people. They last 5 minutes or less.

Ms. C: Do you always know what makes you sad or depressed? Or does it just sometimes come upon you?

G: It sometimes just comes on me at different times of the day.

Ms. C: When do you think you're the most up or happy?

G: In the morning.

Ms. C: Then when does that feeling of lowness or depression come on you?

G: In the afternoon. Especially after lunch 'cause that's when I have to take my medicine.

Ms. C: How does that make you feel?

G: It makes me feel not good 'cause I know I can't control my behavior without it. Makes me feel kind of depressed because I can't do it without it. It makes me feel not good at all.

Ms. C: How can teachers or other adults help you when you feel like hurting yourself or becoming aggressive?

G: Probably restrain the person.

Ms. C: How does that make you feel?

G: Angry.

Ms. C: How do you think it makes the teacher feel when they have to restrain you?

G: They are probably thinking the same thing.

Ms. C: What would you say to a person who was feeling hopeless and trying to hurt themselves?

G: You shouldn't do that because you have a life to live and God put you on this earth so you could live this life.

Ms. C: Think about a time when you were having a great day and then suddenly everything changed within you and you began feeling angry or sad. Can you explain why or how that happened?

G: Yeah. Like, when I was all happy and then I thought about my rabbit died 'cause my dog killed it. I started to feel sad, and then I got all angry at everybody and I took my anger out on them.

Ms. C: So, sounds like what causes you to have sad or depressed feelings is sometimes on the outside, but sometimes they are on the inside too. And they have the same effect on you just like it's happening now. So it sounds like it's important to talk about your feelings before . . . to let people know what's going on.

G: Yeah, I think it is because you can let people know before you explode. So they'll know what to expect.

Ms. C: Is talking to your teacher important?

G: Yes, I think it is because you can let your feelings out and you can express to them how you feel.

Ms. C: Name three things that you love about school.

G: Math, science, and technology.

Ms. C: Name three things that you really dislike about school.

G: Social studies and reading.

Ms. C: How do rules make you feel?

G: Feels like we are trapped. You can do this, but you can't do that. It makes you feel like you're restricted to certain things.

Ms. C: And then, as a result of that feeling, what other feelings come? What do you feel like doing if you feel trapped?

G: It feels like you can't get out of here, you can't move, and stuff like that.

>> QUESTIONS FOR FURTHER REFLECTION

1. How would you tell the difference between depression and other problems that one of your students is experiencing?

2. In your opinion, what are the kinds of events that would cause your students to legitimately experience a depressed mood?

3. What are the most helpful things you could do as a teacher to prevent depression and suicide attempts among your students?

CHAPTER SEVENTEEN

SCHIZOPHRENIA AND PERVASIVE DEVELOPMENTAL DISORDERS

As you read this chapter, keep these guiding questions in mind:

- What does *psychotic* mean, and how might schizophrenia and autism fit or not fit a definition?

- What are the signs or symptoms of schizophrenia, and how might they be mistaken for other disorders in children?

- How would you characterize autism, and what is the prognosis for a child with this disorder?

- Why is a full range of educational interventions required for students with schizophrenia and autism?

- What are the primary causes of and interventions for stereotypies?

We have already sketched major features of schizophrenia and autism, primarily in chapters 5 and 7. This chapter briefly recaps information regarding the nature and causes of these severe disorders but focuses primarily on the educational implications of several characteristics common to many individuals who have psychotic disorders or pervasive developmental disorders.

Schizophrenia is explicitly included in the federal category "emotionally disturbed," as discussed in chapter 1. Schizophrenia is typically referred to as a psychotic disorder, and autism and other pervasive developmental disabilities have often been called psychoses as well. However, the term *psychotic* has had many definitions, none of which is universally accepted. The narrowest definition includes childhood schizophrenia but not autism; the broadest definition includes both.

Besides autism, pervasive developmental disorders include *Asperger's disorder* (much like autism but without significant delays in cognition and language), *Rett's disorder* (normal development for 5 months to 4 years followed by regression and retardation), and *childhood disintegrative disorder* (normal development for at least 2 and up to 10 years followed by significant loss of skills; see Schopler, Mesibov, & Kunce, 1998; Zwaigenbaum & Szatmati, 1999). Because these additional disorders are rare and their characteristics overlap considerably with autism, we discuss only autism and Asperger's disorder under separate headings.

Much controversy has surrounded the inclusion of autism in special education categories (see Sweeney & Hoffman, 2004). As noted in chapter 1, autism has been excluded from the category "emotionally disturbed" and has been made a separate category of its own under federal special education regulations. Nevertheless, we discuss autism in this book because children and youth with autism typically exhibit behaviors that are severely problematic and may be considered emotional or behavioral disorders in their own right (e.g., mutism, extreme self-stimulation, or self-injury). An important point about the emotional and behavioral problems associated with both autism and schizophrenia is that they are now recognized as having their origins primarily in biological factors, as noted in chapter 7.

We first discuss schizophrenia, autism, and Asperger's disorder under separate headings. Then we turn our attention to behavior often seen in youngsters with severe disabilities, regardless of their diagnostic labels: socialization problems, communication disorders, and stereotypy, especially self-stimulation and self-injury. Behavior of these types is severely debilitating and often presents persistent challenges to teachers and others who work with children and youth who have schizophrenia, autism, severe mental retardation, or other severe developmental disabilities.

SCHIZOPHRENIA

Definition and Prevalence

Schizophrenia is a disorder in which people usually have two or more of the following symptoms:

- Delusions
- Hallucinations
- Disorganized speech (e.g., they may frequently get derailed or be incoherent)
- Grossly disorganized or catatonic behavior
- Negative symptoms such as lack of affect, inability to think logically, or inability to make decisions (American Psychiatric Association, 2000; see also Asarnow & Asarnow, 2003).

The definition is not simple. "Schizophrenia is a complex, multifaceted disorder (or group of disorders), which has escaped precise definition after almost a century of study" (Russell, 1994, p. 631). Defining schizophrenia in children is even more problematic than defining it in adults (the usual age of onset is between ages 18 and 40 years) because children usually have more difficulty explaining themselves (see Erlenmeyer-Kimling, Roberts, Rock, Adamo, Shapiro, & Pape, 1998). Nevertheless, "there is no longer any question that schizophrenia can be reliably diagnosed in children using the same criteria used with adults" (Asarnow & Asarnow, 1994, p. 595; see also Asarnow & Asarnow, 2003). Moreover, children can have schizophrenia and another disability, including mental retardation (Lee, Moss, Friedlander, Donnelly, & Honer, 2003).

Schizophrenia affects about 1 in 100 adults, but it is increasingly rare in ages lower than 18. Delusional thinking is rare in children, but sometimes young children are convinced of the reality of their fantasies or the delusions of other people. They may engage in fantasies during play, and these fantasies may interfere with their socialization or academic learning. The case of Wanda (see the accompanying case book) illustrates the extent to which children with schizophrenia can become caught up in their fantasies.

Table 17.1 shows examples of the hallucinations, delusions, and thought disorders seen in children. The hallucinations and delusions take a wide variety of forms. The delusions of children and adolescents frequently have sexual or religious content. Children having delusions and hallucinations are not always diagnosed as having schizophrenia. They may be diagnosed as having bipolar disorder (Isaac, 1995), or they may have comorbid disorders, such as schizophrenia along with conduct disorder, attention deficit–hyperactivity disorder (ADHD), depression or bipolar disorder, or another diagnosable psychiatric disorder (Asarnow & Asarnow, 2003). In many cases, the diagnosis is difficult because the onset is insidious—slow, perhaps beginning with conduct problems, anxiety disorders, or ADHD. Symptom patterns may go unrecognized or be confused (Asarnow, Thompson, & Goldstein, 1994; Russell, 1994). Some children who are diagnosed with autism or other pervasive developmental disorders are later diagnosed as having schizophrenia, but this is not typically the case. Most children with schizophrenia never lose their symptoms completely, although some do (Asarnow & Asarnow, 1994, 2003).

Causes and Prevention

As discussed in chapter 7, the causes of schizophrenia are known to be in large measure biological, but the exact biological mechanisms responsible for the illness are not known (Asarnow, Asamen, et al., 1994; Asarnow & Asarnow, 2003; Gottesman,

Table 17.1
Examples of psychotic symptoms

Hallucinations

Unrelated to affective state

A 7-year-old boy stated, "Everything is talking, the walls, the furniture, I just know they're talking."

Command

An 11-year-old boy heard both "good" and "bad" voices. The bad voices tell him to hit others and that they will kill the good voices if he does not obey. The "good" voices say things like "Help your mom with dinner."

Conversing

An 8-year-old boy stated, "I can hear the devil talk—God interrupts him and the devil says 'shut up to God.' God and the devil are always fighting."

Religious

An 11-year-old boy heard God's voice saying, "Sorry D., but I can't help you now, I am helping someone else." He also reported hearing Jesus and the devil.

Persecutory

A 9-year-old boy reported voices calling him bad names, and threatening that if he doesn't do what he is told something bad will happen to him.

Commenting

An 8-year-old girl reported an angel saying things like "You didn't cry today" and "You've been a very nice girl today."

Visual

A 9-year-old girl reported, "If I stare at the wall I see monsters coming toward me. If I stop staring, they'll come faster."

Tactile

An 5-year-old boy felt snakes and spiders on his back (and was so convincing he was taken to the emergency room by his parents).

Somatic

An 8-year-old girl reported feeling an angel, babies, and devil inside her arm, and that she could feel them fighting.

Source: Russell, A. T. (1994). The clinical presentation of childhood-onset schizophrenia. *Schizophrenia Bulletin, 20,* 634–635.

1991; Lenzenweger & Dworkin, 1998). Genetic factors are known to play a critical role, but which genes are involved and how they work is not understood. It is quite likely that schizophrenia is not a single disease entity but a cluster of highly similar disorders in the same way that cancer is not a single disease. The same causal factors seem to operate whether schizophrenia is first diagnosed in childhood or adulthood (Asarnow & Asarnow, 1995, 2003). However, onset of schizophrenia in childhood or

Table 17.1
(continued)

Delusions

Bizarre

A 7-year-old boy believed that there were "memory boxes" in his head and body and reported that he could broadcast his thoughts from his memory boxes with a special computer using radar tracking.

Persecutory

A girl believed that the "evil one" was trying to poison her orange juice.

Somatic

One 7-year-old boy believed that there were boy and girl spirits living inside his head: "They're squishing on the whole inside, they're touching the walls, the skin."

Reference

An 8-year-old girl believed that people outside of her house were staring and pointing at her trying to send her a message to come outside. She also believed that people on the TV were talking to her because they used the word *you*.

Grandiose

An 11-year-old boy had the firm belief that he was "different" and able to kill people. He felt that when "God zooms through me [him]" he became very strong and developed big muscles.

Thought Disorder

"I used to have a Mexican dream. I was watching TV in the family room. I disappeared outside of this world and then I was in a closet. Sounds like a vacuum dream. It's a Mexican dream. When I was close to that dream earth, I was turning upside down. I don't like to turn upside down. Sometimes I have Mexican dreams and vacuum dreams. It's real hard to scream in dreams."

---

adolescence seems to carry a worse prognosis than adult-onset schizophrenia, particularly when the symptoms of the disease are severe (Eggers, Bunk, & Drause, 2000; Lay, Blanz, Hartmann, & Schmidt, 2000).

We know that in the vast majority of cases, if not all, biological and environmental factors work together to cause schizophrenia. Families in which the parents exhibit deviant behavior may contribute to the development of schizophrenia (Asarnow, Thompson, & Goldstein, 1994). Primary prevention consists of assessing genetic risks and avoiding behavior that may trigger schizophrenia in vulnerable persons, especially substance abuse and extreme stress (Gottesman, 1987). Secondary prevention consists mainly of psychopharmacological treatment and structured environments in which symptoms can be managed most effectively.

Education and Related Interventions

Educational intervention for children and youth with schizophrenia is nearly impossible to describe because the symptoms and educational needs of these students vary so greatly. We are safe in saying that education will be only one of several interventions because pharmacological treatment and social work with the family will be critical as well (see Forness, Kavale, Sweeney, & Crenshaw, 1999; Konopasek & Forness, 2004; Sweeney, Forness, Kavale, & Levitt, 1997). When special education is necessary, it appears that a highly structured, individualized program provides a feeling of safety and allows the student to keep symptoms in check as much as possible.

The outcomes for children and youth with schizophrenia are extremely variable. A substantial proportion of these students do not make a good overall adjustment as they progress into adulthood. Some cases, however, turn out quite well (as illustrated by the case of Bill in the accompanying case book).

Schizophrenia is nearly always treated with antipsychotic drugs (neuroleptics) such as Haldol (haloperidol) or Mellaril (thioridazine), which are designed to reduce hallucinations and other symptoms (see Figure 7.1). "Children with schizophrenia show a positive treatment response to some of the same pharmacologic treatments that have demonstrated efficacy with adults with schizophrenia" (Asarnow & Asarnow, 1995, p. 595). However, these drugs do not work well for all children and youth (or adults), and they may have serious side effects (Asarnow & Asarnow, 2003).

In summary, schizophrenia is a rare and disabling disorder of childhood. The onset is often insidious and confused with other disorders. Intervention nearly always involves psychopharmacology, along with social and educational interventions (Forness, Walker, & Kavale, 2003). A structured, individualized educational program is often necessary. With appropriate intervention, some children and youth with schizophrenia lose many or most of their symptoms.

AUTISM

Definition and Prevalence

Autism is distinguished by its early onset. It is ordinarily diagnosed by the time the child is 30 months old. The primary definition of autism is detailed in the extensive criteria listed in the *Diagnostic and Statistical Manual of Mental Disorders* (*DSM–IV*, American Psychiatric Association, 2000; see also Klinger, Dawson, & Renner, 2003; National Research Council, 2001). However, S. L. Harris (1995a) summarized the essential features: "Although the subtle details of the diagnosis continue to be debated, the basic symptoms of autism remain consistent. These symptoms fall under three broad headings: social, communication, and behavior" (p. 305). The symptoms may range from mild to severe.

Children with autism differ greatly in their specific abilities and disabilities; autism is something one may have in degrees, just as people may have varying degrees of conduct disorder, cerebral palsy, mental retardation, or any other special ability or disabling condition (see Charlop-Christy, Schreibman, Pierce, & Kurtz, 1998; Klinger et al., 2003; Newsom, 1998; Simpson & Myles, 1998). Hence, the terminology of the field is changing to *autistic spectrum disorder* (see National Research Council, 2001; Sweeney & Hoffman, 2004).

Impairment of social relatedness to others is a prime characteristic of autistic spectrum disorder, including full-blown autism. Parents of children with autism often notice that their babies or toddlers do not respond normally to being picked up or cuddled. They may show little or no interest in other people but be preoccupied with objects. They may not learn to play normally. These characteristics persist and prevent the child from developing attachments to their parents (Buitelaar, 1995) or friendships with their peers. Some children with autism, but not all, improve somewhat as they progress through later childhood and adolescence in their ability to relate to other people. However, even those who do improve may seem unable to catch the nuances of social relationships or comprehend many ordinary social meanings. They may remain distant and unable to develop intimate relationships.

Autism also involves impairments in verbal and nonverbal communication. A substantial proportion of children with autism, perhaps half, have no functional language. Autism may often involve failure to establish normal eye-to-face gaze or the inability to read the emotions and intentions expressed by people's eyes and other facial features (Arbelle, Sigman, & Kasari, 1994; Baroncohen, Campbell, Karmiloff-Smith, Grant, & Walker, 1995), and children with autism may lack facial expressions that communicate their feelings effectively or accurately. Those who do develop speech typically show abnormalities in intonation, rate, volume, and content of their oral language. Their speech may sound like that of a robot, or they may exhibit *echolalia,* a parroting of what they hear. They may reverse pronouns (e.g., confuse *you* and *I,* or refer to themselves as "he" or "she" rather than "I" or "me"). The pragmatics of language—using language as a tool for social interaction—is particularly difficult for most people with autism. Those who do acquire the mechanics of language, especially those who are older and higher functioning, may have considerable difficulty using language appropriately because they are unaware of the reactions of their listeners. For example, they may not realize that the people they are talking to are not interested in all the details of stock quotes that they have committed to memory.

Stereotyped, ritualistic behavior is a common feature of autism. So is aggression directed at others and self-injury. In fact, the behavioral problems associated with autism are legion. More extreme behavioral problems are generally linked to more severe disabilities in children with autism and mental retardation (Emerson & Bromley, 1995). Self-stimulation and self-injury may be caused by a variety of physiological and social factors and be used to communicate a variety of wants or needs (e.g., "Pay attention to me," "Let me out of here," "There's nothing to do," "There's too much to do"; see Dunlap, Robbins, & Kern, 1994; Repp & Deitz, 1990). The interrelationships among the social, communication, and behavioral characteristics are critically important for conceptualizing autism and designing effective, humane interventions (Klinger et al., 2003).

The prevalence of autism has increased dramatically in the past decade, and autistic spectrum disorder may now be diagnosed in about 1 in 100 children (Gross, 2003; Sheehan, 2003). It occurs more often in boys than in girls. It is not a phenomenon of American culture; children with autism are found among children around the world. It may occur across the entire range of intelligence, although the majority of children with autism test below the criterion for mental retardation (70) and relatively few score above average. Besides mental retardation, autism may be comorbid with a variety of other disabilities, such as learning disabilities, epilepsy, or conduct disorder.

Some people with autism have provided descriptions of their experiences, and these can help us understand more about the nature of this disorder as well (e.g., Grandin, 1995; see also Sacks, 1995). It is important to recognize that individuals with autism and other pervasive developmental disabilities experience anxiety, stress, and the other internal states that all of us share as human beings (Groden, Cautela, Prince, & Berryman, 1994).

Causes and Prevention

The causes of autism remain mostly unknown (National Research Council, 2001). We do know that the blame heaped on parents by psychoanalytic interpretations of the disorder was unwarranted, a horrid consequence of the arrogant disregard of scientific methodology (Mesibov, Adams, & Klinger, 1997; Sheehan, 2003). As noted in chapter 7, there is a consensus among scientific researchers that autism is a brain disorder, probably having multiple causes, none of which is very well understood (Charlop-Christy & Kelso, 1999; Charlop-Christy et al., 1998; S. L. Harris, 1995a; Klinger et al., 2003). Various neurochemicals and brain structures have been researched for many years, yet no definitive findings have emerged for a single cause—only hypotheses that seem partially supported in some cases. We do know that genetics plays a role in the disorder. One bit of evidence that genes are important is that identical twins are far more likely than fraternal twins to be concordant for autism (i.e., both to have the disorder). A reasonable guess, given the range of symptoms and associated conditions, is that autism has no single cause.

The only primary, physiological prevention strategies are genetic counseling and prenatal care, but these are not very specific because so little is understood about the biology of autism. Secondary prevention consists of early identification and intervention. Early intervention involves treatment of family problems as well as treatment of the child with autism. As we have noted, the effect of a child with disabilities on the family varies enormously from one family to another. Having a child with autism can be a very stressful experience for parents and siblings. The child with autism may precipitate family problems, but family discord or disorganization may affect the outcomes for the child. "These two factors may intertwine, with family dysfunction heightening the child's needs, and the child's behavior problems intensifying family difficulties" (S. L. Harris, 1994, p. 161). Educational programs may play an important role in secondary prevention, as we discuss later.

Education and Related Interventions

Educational work with children who have autism must be both early and intense, and it must be focused on helping children overcome their greatest disability: inability to communicate effectively (Harris & Weiss, 1998; Sheuermann & Webber, 2002). True, these children have social and behavioral problems that need attention as well. However, it is increasingly clear that communication skills are at the heart of the disability of autism. Communication skills are essential for establishing and maintaining social relatedness. Moreover, many of the behavioral problems associated with autism may represent socially unacceptable attempts to communicate with others. Communication disorders are not peculiar to autism but are a common problem among children with a wide range of developmental disabilities, hence our later discussion of communication disorders under a separate heading.

In addition to the focus on communication, many children and youth with autism need intensive instruction in daily living skills (Bondy & Frost, 1995; S. L. Harris, 1995a, 1995b; Harris & Weiss, 1998; Scheuermann & Webber, 2002; Schopler, Mesibor, & Kunce, 1995; Simpson & Myles, 1998; Sweeney & Hoffman, 2004). Effective instruction in both language and other functional daily living skills requires a highly structured, directive approach that uses basic principles of behavioral psychology as the basis for analyzing tasks and teaching procedures. The principles and techniques most often employed successfully include positive and negative reinforcement, modeling and imitation training, shaping, prompting, extinction, and a variety of punishment procedures, as we discuss later under the heading of socialization problems (see Charlop-Christy et al., 1998; Klinger et al., 2003; Newsom, 1998; Schreibman, 1994).

However, emphasis is increasingly on using these behavioral principles and techniques in natural settings and interactions. Researchers are constantly seeking to make better instructional use of the natural interactions by which children normally learn language and other social skills. For example, at the preschool level, the emphasis is on natural interactions with normal peers in regular classrooms (e.g., Bondy & Frost, 1995; Charlop-Christy et al., 1998; Strain, Danko, & Kohler, 1995). At the elementary level, children with autism have sometimes been included in cooperative learning groups with their normal peers in regular classrooms (e.g., Dugan, Kamps, Leonard, Watkins, Rheinberger, & Stackhaus, 1995). Educators are looking for ways in which to help students with autism learn at any age, including the teen years, the skills of self-management (e.g., Klinger et al., 2003; Koegel, Frea, & Surratt, 1994; Newman, Buffington, O'Grady, McDonald, Poulson, & Hemmes, 1995; Scheuermann & Webber, 2002).

In part because of the emphasis on finding more natural ways of teaching children with autism, an increasing percentage of such students are being taught in neighborhood schools and general education classrooms, especially at younger ages (Bondy & Frost, 1995; Dunlap, Robbins, & Kern, 1994; Strain, Danko, & Kohler, 1995). Still, the majority of students with autism are not taught in regular classrooms.

Understanding the parental role in autism has resulted in recruiting parents as therapeutic agents in many treatment programs (e.g., Bondy & Frost, 1995; Butera & Haywood, 1995; Charlop-Christy et al., 1998; S. L. Harris, 1994; Harris & Weiss, 1998; Lovaas, 1987; Scheuermann & Webber, 2002; Simpson & Zionts, 1992). If early intervention is to have the intensive, pervasive character that makes it effective, then family involvement is essential. Without parental participation in training, children with autism are unlikely to acquire and maintain the functional communication and daily living skills they need for social development and eventual independence. Siblings may also play an important role in developing and sustaining the social learning of children with autism. For example, Strain and Danko (1995) used a social skills training program, originally developed for the preschool classroom, to teach parents and other caretakers how to increase the positive social interactions of children age 3 to 5 with their preschool-aged siblings who had autism.

Psychopharmacological interventions in autism consist of a wide variety of experimental drugs, including *neuroleptics* (antipsychotic drugs) such as Haldol (haloperidol) and stimulants such as Ritalin (methylphenidate; Fisman, 2002; Konopasek & Forness, 2004; Marriage, 2002). Although these medications may give symptomatic relief in some cases (e.g., reducing self-injurious behavior or hyperactivity), responses to the drugs are idiosyncratic; the effects tend to be unpredictable and depend on individual sensitivities. Even when drugs are helpful, behavior management and instruction by parents and teachers are still critical; medications may sometimes make the individual more tractable or teachable, but they are not sufficient themselves to address the disorder.

In summary, education and related interventions for students with autism must be early, intensive, highly structured, and involve families if they are to be most effective. Early, intensive intervention may produce remarkable gains in many young children with autism, although no intervention yet can claim universal success in enabling children with autism to overcome their disabilities (S. L. Harris, 1995a, 1995b; Lovaas, 1987). The early intervention program of Lovaas and his colleagues at UCLA has been widely seen as the most effective program available (see Harris & Weiss, 1998; Smith & Lovaas, 1997), although its research methodology is clearly open to criticism (see Gresham & MacMillan, 1997a, 1997b). Education is increasingly focused on using natural interactions to teach students in natural environments, including regular classrooms. All interventions must address problems in socialization, communication disorders, and stereotypy.

ASPERGER SYNDROME

Definition and Education

We include specific discussion of Asperger syndrome because it is an increasingly common diagnosis for children who show some, but not all, of the characteristics typical of autism. The characteristics or diagnostic criteria include qualitative impairment in social interaction and restricted, repetitive, and stereotyped patterns of behavior, interests, and activities. These are similar to those that define autism. However, children with Asperger syndrome do not show clinically significant general delay in language, nor do they show significant delay in cognitive development or the development of age-appropriate self-help skills or adaptive behavior. Thus, although they have significant problems in socialization and manifest some of the peculiarly obsessive or repetitive behaviors of children with autism, their language and cognitive development are much more normal than is typical for autism (see Klinger et al., 2003; National Research Council, 2001).

High-functioning children with autism may exhibit socially strange behavior but have normal or even superior language and cognitive abilities. Thus, distinguishing between high-functioning autism and Asperger syndrome is typically difficult if not sometimes impossible on entirely objective grounds (see Schopler et al., 1998). Predictably, there is as yet no basis for distinguishing between high-functioning autism and Asperger syndrome in education (Kunce & Mesibov, 1998; see also Scheuermann & Webber, 2002; Simpson & Myles, 1998). However, the outcomes for children with Asperger seem to be better than for children with other pervasive developmental disorders (Starr, Szatmari, Bryson, & Zwaigenbaum, 2003).

SOCIALIZATION PROBLEMS

As we have noted, socialization depends to a great extent on competence in communication. However, children and youth with schizophrenia or pervasive developmental disorders may fail to develop other social skills besides language. Their odd, unresponsive, and rejecting patterns of behavior may disable them in learning to play with, befriend, and be befriended by others.

One social skill in which many children with autism have difficulty is eye gaze. Failure to establish eye contact with others makes children with autism seem to look through or beyond other people or to appear "out of it." Rather than focus on others' faces, they often rely on peripheral vision and quick, furtive glances to interpret social cues. This gaze aversion makes adults feel ill at ease and shut out. Failing to look at people's faces could also be one reason these children have difficulty interpreting others' emotions and learning communication skills (Baroncohen, Campbell, Karmiloff-Smith, Grant, & Walker, 1995). Infants and toddlers with autism may have great difficulty learning to imitate adults in part because they do not look at their faces and eyes like normally developing infants and young children do. Because gaze aversion is obviously a disturbing and debilitating social behavior, one of the first steps in teaching children who avert their gaze must be to establish appropriate eye contact. Methods for overcoming averted gaze include games that require looking at another person, prompts, imitating the child's behavior, and reinforcement for eye contact (see Bondy & Frost, 1995; Butera & Haywood, 1995; Charlop-Christy et al., 1998; Scheuermann & Webber, 2002).

Many children with pervasive developmental disorders have extreme problems with social skills of nearly every type. "Children with autism often have to be taught in considerable detail all of the complexities of social interactions such as how to play a game with another child, how to express affection, to wait one's turn, to console another child who is crying, or to initiate a play interaction" (S. L. Harris, 1995b, p. 312). Many critical social skills cannot be taught one-on-one by an adult teacher or with a group of other equally unskilled children, so it is not surprising that most intervention requires interaction with normally developing peers. Peers may be trained to serve as models, to initiate interactions, and to respond appropriately to the student with autism in home, classroom, or community settings (see Charlop-Christy & Kelso, 1999; Pierce & Schreibman, 1995; Strain & Danko, 1995; Strain et al., 1995).

As discussed previously, students with schizophrenia and pervasive developmental disorders exhibit a wide range of emotional and behavioral problems and often have comorbid disorders. Consequently, the full range of interventions used with disorders discussed in other chapters, including attention deficit disorder, hyperactivity, conduct disorder, depression, and so on, may be needed.

COMMUNICATION DISORDERS

Teaching children with autism and other pervasive developmental disorders to use communication effectively is one of the greatest challenges in their education. Enormous progress has been made since the 1960s, when the first systematic attempts were made in teaching language to children with autism.

Educational programs of the 1960s and 1970s used an operant conditioning approach to teach, step-by-step, approximations of functional language. The child's responses at each step in the sequence were rewarded, typically with praise, hugs, and food given by the teacher immediately following the child's performance of the desired behavior. For example, at the earliest step in the sequence, a child might be reinforced for establishing eye contact with the teacher. The next step might be making any vocalization while looking at the teacher, next making a vocalization approximating a sound made by the teacher, then imitating words spoken by the teacher, and finally replying to the teacher's questions. Of course, this description is a great simplification of the procedures that were employed, but through such methods nonverbal children were taught basic oral language skills.

A disappointing outcome of early language training was that few of the children acquired truly useful or functional language, even after intensive and prolonged training. Their speech tended to have a mechanical quality, and they often did not learn to use their language for many social purposes. A current trend in language intervention is emphasis on pragmatics (making language more functional in social interaction) and motivating children to communicate (Koegel & Koegel, 1995). Instead of training children to imitate words in isolation or to use syntactically and grammatically correct forms, we might train them to use language to obtain a desired result. For example, the child might be taught to say, "I want juice" (or a simplified form: "juice" or "want juice") to get a drink of juice. Increasingly, language intervention in autism involves structuring opportunities to use language in natural settings (Sigafoos, Kerr, Roberts, & Couzens, 1994). For example, the teacher may set up opportunities for children to make requests by using a missing item strategy (e.g., give the child a coloring book but not crayons, prompting a request for the crayons), interrupting a chain of behavior (e.g., stopping the child on her way out to play, prompting a request to go out), or delaying assistance with tasks (e.g., waiting to help a child put on his coat until he asks for assistance). This approach is compatible with today's emphasis on inclusion of children with autism in regular preschool and elementary school programs (S. L. Harris, 1995b).

People with autism have special difficulty understanding the communication of social and emotional meanings (see Charlop-Christy & Kelso, 1999; Happe, 1994; Happe & Frith, 1995; Newsom, 1998; Rogers-Adkinson & Griffith, 1999; Sigman, 1994). They may not be able to form a coherent picture of social contexts; use social imagination; accurately attribute mental states or feelings to others; or understand jokes, pretense, lies, or figures of speech. In fact, the core disability in autism may be an absence of a "theory of mind"—the inability to understand the existence of subjective mental states (e.g., beliefs, desires, intentions) and how these help people explain and make sense of behavior (Happe, 1994; Happe & Frith, 1995). Language intervention, then, might focus on helping children with autism understand more about how language is used to communicate about subjective mental states as well as more object-centered social interactions.

Some children with autism do not acquire truly functional oral language under an operant training regimen, and training is extremely time-consuming in the face of slow progress. For these children, alternatives to speech such as sign language or augmentative communication systems may be necessary (S. L. Harris, 1995b). Augmentative and alternative communication includes systems in which people use pictures, picture boards, signing, or computerized systems to "talk." Researchers are attempting to make it more likely that children who use alternative communication will talk about the same kinds of things other youngsters talk about (see Marvin, Beukelman, Brockhaus, & Kast, 1994). It is important to train users of alternative communication systems to understand the pragmatics of language. Whether communication is through speech or other language systems, the primary purpose of training is social interaction.

Autism and other severe developmental disabilities are developmental puzzles that many people would like to solve, for obvious reasons. Progress comes slowly through careful, programmatic research. Claims of breakthrough interventions are almost always misleading and disappointing. In the early 1990s, there were claims of the discovery of normal or extraordinary intelligence and communicative ability in children and adults with autism using a procedure called facilitated communication (e.g., Biklen, 1990; Biklen & Schubert, 1991). However, by the mid-1990s, researchers had accumulated overwhelming evidence that facilitated communication is not a reliable and efficient means of communication. In the vast majority of cases, research has shown that facilitated communication is a complete hoax in which the facilitator, not the person with a developmental disability, does the communicating. If not an outright fraud, facilitated communication has been found to be very limited and inefficient (Gardner, 2001; Mostert, 2001; Shane, 1994).

The language training procedures based on operant conditioning applied to natural language contexts has not led to dramatic breakthroughs or a cure. However, reliable research over a period of decades now supports their use as highly effective in helping children with autism learn to communicate more effectively (e.g., Charlop-Christy et al., 1998; Klinger et al., 2003; Koegel & Koegel, 1995; Scheuermann & Webber, 2002; Lovaas, 1987).

STEREOTYPY

Children and adults with severe emotional, behavioral, or cognitive disabilities may engage in persistent, repetitive, seemingly meaningless behavior. Their stereotypical patterns of behavior, or *stereotypy,* may or may not result in serious self-injury. Often it seems to serve the primary or sole purpose of providing sensory feedback, and it is therefore called self-stimulation. We briefly discuss both noninjurious self-stimulation and self-injury.

Self-stimulation

Self-stimulation can take an almost infinite variety of forms, such as staring blankly into space, body rocking, hand flapping, eye rubbing, lip licking, or repeating the same vocalization over and over. Depending on the *topography* (particular movements) of self-stimulation and the rate or intensity, it can result in physical injury—for example, eye rubbing at a high rate and pressure.

Self-stimulation is apparently a way to obtain self-reinforcing or self-perpetuating sensory feedback (Rapp, Miltenberger, Galensky, Ellingson, & Long, 1999). It is not likely to stop for long unless demands for other incompatible responses are made or it is actively suppressed. This appears to be true of some self-stimulatory behavior (such as nail biting) of ordinary people. As Sroufe, Steucher, and Stutzer (1973) suggested long ago, we could probably find some form of self-stimulation in everyone's behavior, varying only in subtlety, social appropriateness, and rate. It is a pervasive characteristic of normally developing infants, and nearly everyone engages in higher rates of self-stimulatory behavior when bored or tired. Thus, like most behaviors, self-stimulation is considered normal or pathological depending on its social context, intensity, and rate.

High rates of self-stimulation sometimes require highly intrusive, directive intervention procedures because students are unlikely to learn academic or social tasks when engaged in such behavior. Many procedures have been researched, among them using self-stimulation or alternative sensory stimulation as a reinforcer for appropriate behavior and a variety of punishing consequences (see Charlop, Kurtz, & Casey, 1990). As we learn more about the nature of self-stimulation and related behavior, we are coming to understand that the context in which it occurs (e.g., highly structured tasks or relatively unstructured recreation) has much to do with the success of the procedures used to control it (Haring & Kennedy, 1990; Newsom, 1998; Scheuermann & Webber, 2002).

The best method of controlling self-stimulation varies according to the individual. Intervention is not always justified; for some, reducing self-stimulation may serve no therapeutic purpose. When self-stimulation does not result in physical injury or deformity, interfere significantly with learning, or prevent participation in normal activities, then intervention may not be justified. Whether to intervene depends on the topography, rate, duration, and typical social consequences of the behavior.

Self-injury

Some youngsters injure themselves repeatedly and deliberately in the most brutal fashion. We find this kind of *self-injurious behavior* (SIB) in some individuals with severe mental retardation, but it is a characteristic often associated with multiple disabilities—for example, mental retardation and autism or schizophrenia and another disorder. Very rarely does an individual with SIB have well-developed oral language. Most people who show SIB of the type we are discussing here are either mute or have very limited language abilities. In fact, one frequent approach to SIB is to try to figure out what function such behavior has, what it communicates, and what noninjurious consequences it produces (e.g., attention or escape from adults' demands, sensory stimulation; see Repp et al., 1999; Scheuermann & Webber, 2002).

Nevertheless, some children and youth with normal intelligence and language skills deliberately injure themselves without the intent of killing themselves. The prevalence of such behavior may be as high as 2 to 3% of adolescents (Garrison, Addy, McKeown, Cuffe, Jackson, & Waller, 1993). Such behavior may include "skin cutting, skin burning, self-hitting, interfering with wound healing, severe skin scratching, hair pulling and bone breaking" (Garrison et al., 1993, p. 343). As noted in chapter 14, such behavior is closely associated with depression and thoughts of suicide.

Whatever their causes or functions, the atavistic (primitive) behaviors known as SIBs take a variety of forms, but left unchecked, they share the consequence of bodily injury. Without physical restraint or effective intervention, there is risk that the youngster will permanently disfigure, incapacitate, or kill himself or herself.

The deviant aspects of SIBs are its rate, intensity, and persistence. Perhaps 10% of young, nondisabled children under the age of 5 occasionally engage in some form of self-injurious behavior (Zirpoli & Lloyd, 1987). It is considered normal, for example, for young children in fits of temper to bang their heads or hit themselves. Deviant self-injury, however, occurs so frequently and is of such intensity and duration that the youngster cannot develop normal social relationships or learn self-care skills and is in danger of becoming even more severely disabled.

Evidence indicates that SIBs could in some cases be a result of deficiencies in biochemicals required for normal brain functioning, inadequate development of the central nervous system, early experiences of pain and isolation, sensory problems, insensitivity to pain, or the body's ability to produce opiatelike substances in response to pain or injury. But no single biological explanation is now supported by research (Iwata, Zarcone, Vollmer, & Smith, 1994; Oliver, 1995). However, biological factors need not, and probably usually do not, operate independently of social factors in causing SIBs. Perhaps, in many cases, biological factors cause initial self-injury, but social learning factors exacerbate and maintain the problem. Self-injury, like other types of behavior, may be reinforced by social attention. This notion has important implications for intervention because it suggests ways of teaching alternatives to self-injury.

Some children appear to use SIBs as a means of getting adults to withdraw demands for performance, which the children experience as aversive. When presented with a task that demands their attention and performance, these children begin to injure themselves; the demands are then withdrawn. The social interaction and attention involved in teaching and learning is reinforcing for some children, and withdrawal of attention contingent upon SIBs is, for some, an effective extinction or punishment procedure. The same type of interaction and attention is apparently aversive for other children, and withdrawal of attention contingent on SIBs is negatively reinforcing for them; it makes the problem worse instead of better (see Oliver, 1995).

The assessment of self-injury is at once straightforward and complex. It is straightforward in that assessment involves direct observation and measurement: self-injurious behaviors should be defined, observed, and recorded daily in the different environments in which they occur. It is complex in that the causes are not well understood, and care must be taken to assess possible biological and subtle environmental causes (see Iwata et al., 1994; Lerman, Iwata, Zarcone, & Ringdahl, 1994). Possible biological causes include genetic anomalies and factors such as ear infections and sensory deficits. SIBs may occur more often in some environments than in others, and a change in environmental conditions (such as demands for performance) may dramatically alter the problem. It is thus important to assess the quality of the youngster's surroundings and social environment as well as the behavior itself, and it is particularly important to assess the social consequences of SIBs (Belcher, 1995; Scheuermann & Webber, 2002).

Many different approaches to reducing SIBs have been tried. No approach has been entirely successful, although some show much better results than others do. Among the least successful have been various forms of psychotherapy, "sensory-integration therapy," and "gentle teaching," approaches that are nonaversive (i.e., do not involve punishment) but are supported by very little scientific evidence that they reduce SIBs (see Scheuermann & Webber, 2002, for a succinct listing of controversial treatments of autism and evidence of their effectiveness). The most effective nonaversive strategies yet devised involve functional analysis (to find the purpose the behavior serves) and arranging an environment in which alternative behaviors are taught or SIB is less likely to occur (see Klinger et al., 2003; Scheuermann & Webber, 2002). The emphases of research and practice in the early 21st century are on functional analysis, nonaversive procedures, and pharmacological treatments.

Some have suggested that all behavioral problems are resolvable without the use of punishment or aversive consequences (e.g., LaVigna & Donnellan, 1986). However, nonaversive approaches are not always successful, and in some cases punishing consequences (e.g., electric shock or time out) have been quickly and highly effective in reducing self-injury (see Iwata et al., 1994; Schreibman, 1994). Controversy continues regarding the use of aversives, partly because *aversive* and *successful treatment* are difficult to define. Although everyone agrees that the use of nonaversive interventions is preferable, not everyone agrees that aversive interventions should be strictly and totally prohibited (Lerman & Vorndran, 2002).

SUMMARY

In the federal category "serious emotional disturbance," schizophrenia is explicitly included and autism is excluded (it is a separate category under the Individuals with Disabilities Education Act [IDEA]). However, both are rare, severe disorders of children and youth in which emotional and behavioral disorders are manifested. Schizophrenia is a major psychiatric disorder falling under the category of "psychotic disorders." Autism is one of several pervasive developmental disorders. Both autism and schizophrenia may occur with other disorders. Asperger's disorder is difficult to distinguish from high-functioning autism. A variety of disorders related to autism are now referred to as autistic spectrum disorder.

Symptoms of schizophrenia include hallucinations, delusions, and grossly aberrant behavior or thinking. It affects about 1 in 100 adults. It is unusual in individuals under 18 years of age, especially in preteens. The onset is often insidious and may be confused with other disorders. However, schizophrenia seems to be essentially the same disorder in children and adults. The causes appear to be primarily biological, although they are not well understood. Effective education is usually highly structured and individualized. Psychopharmacological treatment is essential. Some children with schizophrenia recover, although many make little improvement and continue to have major symptoms in adulthood.

Autism is defined by the early onset of severe problems in socialization, communication, and behavior. It occurs across the entire range of intelligence, although most children with autism show mental retardation. Children with autism are severely impaired in building social relationships and in verbal and nonverbal communication, and they often exhibit stereotyped patterns of behavior. Autism affects about 0.5 of 1% of children under the age of three and more boys than girls. Its causes are known to be brain dysfunction, but the nature of the dysfunction is not known. Educational intervention focuses on building communication skills, daily living skills, and management of inappropriate behavior; programs increasingly emphasize education involving interaction with normal peers. Early, intensive intervention produces good outcomes for some children with autism, but many continue to have serious disabilities throughout adolescence and adulthood.

Asperger's disorder is difficult or impossible to distinguish from high-functioning autism and is part of autistic spectrum disorder. Education and other intervention procedures are similar to those recommended for individuals with autism who function at a relatively high level.

The socialization problems of children and youth with schizophrenia and pervasive developmental disorders are extremely varied. Bizarre behavior, problems with eye-to-face gaze, and lack of understanding of social interactions are characteristics associated with autism. Schizophrenia may be comorbid with a wide variety of other disorders, such as conduct disorder, ADHD, or depression. A full range of intervention strategies is needed to address the socialization problems of these children and youth.

Communication disorders are a central feature of autism. About half of children with autism have no functional oral language. Interventions now focus on naturalistic applications of operant conditioning principles in communication training. Some children with autism need to rely on alternative means of communication, such as signing.

Stereotypy consists of repetitive, stereotyped acts that seem to provide reinforcing sensory feedback. Stereotypies may be merely self-stimulatory or self-injurious. Self-stimulation may interfere with learning. The best method of control depends on its topography and function. Self-injurious behavior appears to have multiple causes, both biological and social. It may serve the function of getting attention from others or allowing the individual to escape from demands. Current trends in research and intervention emphasize functional analysis, nonaversive procedures, and psychopharmacological treatment.

>> PERSONAL REFLECTIONS

Schizophrenia and Pervasive Developmental Disorders

Linda Brandenburg, M.S.Ed., is a program director at the Kennedy Krieger School in Baltimore and a doctoral student in special education at Johns Hopkins University.

Describe the school in which you teach and your particular role in the school.

I work at the Kennedy Krieger School in Baltimore, Maryland. Kennedy Krieger is a nonpublic special education facility that serves students between the ages of 6 and 21 who may have any of the following disabilities: learning disabilities (with secondary language, behavioral, medical, or emotional components), emotional disturbances, neurological impairments, physical disabilities, autism and other pervasive developmental disorders, and traumatic brain injury. The students who come to our school are referred to us by the local education agencies (i.e., school districts) when they feel they are unable to meet the needs of the students in the public school setting. Because IDEA says that students are entitled to a free, appropriate public education, when students are referred and subsequently accepted into our program, the referring agency is then responsible for paying the tuition. Thus, although we are not a public school, we operate using public education funds. For several years, I have been the principal and director of the LEAP (Life Skills and Education for Students with Autism and Pervasive Behavior Disorders) program, which serves approximately 55 students with severe autism. Prior to that, I was a special education teacher in the middle school program, which serves approximately 70 students. So I have been working primarily with students who have autism and other pervasive development disorders.

Think of a particular student with a pervasive developmental disorder. How does this student manifest the disorder?

Joe is a young man (currently 15 years old) with whom I have been working for several years. He is diagnosed as having a pervasive developmental disorder with some evidence of emotional disturbance as a secondary disability. External manifestations of this disorder include communication deficits, processing difficulties, behavioral challenges, and overall difficulties with attention and self-monitoring. Joe is a friendly young man who, because of his communication deficits, has difficulty establishing socially appropriate relationships with his peers. Not knowing how to make appropriate contact with them, he usually attempts to engage them in ways that make them uncomfortable. In the past year, he has discovered girls. In particular, he has a crush on one of his classmates, Sue. In his efforts to make contact with Sue, he frequently asks her if he can touch her shoes or her earrings. Sue, understandably, is put off by these attempts at socialization. Joe, unfortunately, is unable to control his obsessions with Sue and her shoes and earrings, so he continues to ask her several times a day if he can touch these items. Sue continues to refuse, so Joe becomes agitated and subsequently engages in maladaptive forms of expressing his frustrations (e.g., verbal perseveration—saying the same thing over and over—or stomping, slamming things, and occasionally throwing things). These behaviors are usually the result of his cognitive perseveration—going over and over the same thought—on some (seemingly) small incident or occurrence, such as Sue's shoes and earrings.

One such incident occurred when Joe was about 12 years old. While he was preparing for afternoon homeroom, he suddenly became very angry and explosive. He started stomping around the room and repeating "wrong color" over and over to himself. When asked what the problem was, he was unable to communicate but continued to escalate until we removed him to the quiet room, where he was eventually able to calm down. After calming down, he was able to tell us that he was angry because he could not locate the exact shade of blue crayon he needed to complete a Power Rangers drawing. Apparently, the blue that was

428

available was the wrong color. Again, this explosive incident occurred as a result of a seemingly small issue (the wrong crayon) and was exacerbated by his inability to communicate the problem he was having.

Most frequently, Joe engages in these maladaptive behaviors because he is unable to communicate his problems verbally. Thus, his behaviors serve as his communication. His communication deficits, which are a function of the pervasive development disorder, are what most frequently get him into trouble. In addition to trouble at school, Joe is also reported as having difficulty getting along with his sister at home. He has been known to steal or destroy her things as well as tease her relentlessly. On rare occasions, Joe has exhibited aggression toward others.

As Joe has matured, his ability to communicate more appropriately has improved. Although he still obsesses on odd things, such as shoes and earrings, he is better able to control his behaviors and communicate his frustrations. His peers, however, still see him as different and are therefore reluctant to socialize with him.

What procedures have you found most useful in working with this student?

In my years of working with students who have pervasive developmental disorders, the biggest thing I've learned is to be consistent. Joe, as well as many of his peers, requires a highly structured environment in which classroom procedures as well as behavioral protocols must be implemented predictably and consistently. He responds well to routines that include clear, concise directions so that he may have some control over his own learning environment and processes. A key to providing Joe with instruction and behavioral support is providing him with clear expectations as well as predictable rewards and consequences. Our program has implemented a schoolwide level system for behavior management. During the course of the day, students earn points for completing work and managing their behaviors. As they earn points, the points correspond to levels. As students climb the level ladder, they earn more privileges and rewards. The system is designed to provide them with incentives to do well while teaching them that the choices are theirs to make. If they choose well, they will earn. If they choose poorly, there are consequences in place. Ultimately, the objective of the system is to help them shift their locus of control from external (e.g., you made me lose points) to internal (e.g., I will work harder to earn my points). As they become better able to manage behaviors, they become more accessible to learning.

A few key factors have contributed to the effectiveness of the behavior management system over the years. One factor is that the entire staff has been trained in the principles and techniques of behavior and crisis management. When the staff members are able to act as a unified team and respond consistently to all students, the students learn that they will get the same messages and responses from every adult they come in contact with. Everyone must be consistent about enforcing rules. Another factor that has contributed to the success of the program is communication with parents and families. It's one thing to be consistent in school, but if the student goes home and is greeted with lack of structure and inconsistency, he or she will likely experience setbacks. Of course, not all parents are able or willing to enforce certain rules at home. But for those who are, we have provided them with training as well as constant feedback regarding their child's education and behavior protocols. This system has worked well for Joe, and over the years he has demonstrated remarkable improvements in his ability to manage and take responsibility for his own behaviors.

What do you see as the prospects for this student's educational progress in the coming year?

Joe is beginning his first year at the Kennedy Krieger High School program. In some ways, the high school program is very similar to the Kennedy Krieger Middle School program, which Joe is transitioning from. The high school, like the middle school, also operates on a schoolwide level system for behavior management. The system has been modified so that the students must work harder and for longer periods of time to earn rewards and privileges. The mission of the high school is to provide students with the skills and opportunities necessary for successful employment and transition to adult life. With that in mind, one of the privileges that the students work for is the privilege of being placed on a job site outside of the actual high school campus. Through the level system, students have the opportunity to demonstrate that they can not only do the assigned work but manage their own behavior that so they can perform in a socially acceptable manner at a workplace. For many of these students, social and behavioral deficits are the primary reasons behind failure to achieve and maintain successful employment. The system provides them with the structure they need to develop more appropriate professional behaviors as well as monitor their progress as they do so.

429

In addition to promoting professional behaviors, the high school program is designed to provide students with a variety of experiences within a career cluster. Career clusters include hospitality and tourism, retail and consumer sales, information technology, manufacturing and construction, and graphic arts and communication. Each cluster represents a variety of jobs. For example, in the hospitality and tourism cluster there are hotel jobs (bellhop, desk clerk, housekeeping, etc.), restaurant jobs (waiter, hostess, dishwasher, etc.), and other service jobs. The students are trained to do several jobs within a cluster rather than one job (as they would be in a traditional vocational program). The classroom curriculums are designed so that students learn basic academics within the context of the career cluster. Being exposed to a variety of workplace experiences and complementary school-based curriculum, the students become more well rounded and better prepared to enter the workforce.

Having had the opportunity to watch Joe's educational and behavioral progress during his middle school years, I feel confident that he will continue to benefit from the structured programming in the high school. In many ways, Joe's educational progress depends on his behavioral progress. It will be Joe's responsibility to continue to demonstrate his ability to maintain and take responsibility for his own behaviors. As he continues to do so, we will have more opportunities to provide him with the skills he will need to become gainfully employed. As he progresses, we look forward to placing him on actual job sites where he will have opportunities to perform independently. When Joe came to our middle school program, the prognosis for progress appeared bleak at times. Today the prospects for his progress in the high school years are good.

What do you see as the biggest long-term problems this student will face?

In the long term, Joe's biggest problems will be the result of his inability to approach new people in socially appropriate ways. He is unable to assess the dynamics of a social situation and determine how to appropriately integrate himself into it. I believe that Joe will be able to manage his own frustrations and anxieties well enough so that he can function effectively in a school or work environment. I believe his biggest difficulty will continue to be his social interactions with others. As a result, he may even become somewhat of a loner, despite his intense desire to have friends.

Linda Brandenburg Interviews Joe

Ms. B: Joe, how old are you?

J: Fifteen.

Ms. B: What grade are you in?

J: Ninth.

Ms. B: Do you know what kind of school Kennedy Krieger is?

J: It's for handicapped students.

Ms. B: Right, for kids with disabilities. Do you know why you're here?

J: Because it makes me . . . it helps me.

Ms. B: Okay. Can you describe the class you are in?

J: A high school class.

Ms. B: Well, why do you think you are in this school and in this class?

J: I need to get myself together.

Ms. B: What do you mean, "get yourself together"?

J: Like, stop acting crazy. No giggling. No teasing.

Ms. B: You mean behavior problems? What problems have you had in school?

J: I go to resource. Talk back to teachers.

Ms. B: Sounds like behavior problems. What can you do to help resolve or fix these problems?

J: Calm down. Get myself under control.

Ms. B: Okay. What does "under control" mean? How do you feel if you're under control?

J: Calm.

Ms. B: Calm. So how do you feel if you're out of control?

J: Not calm.

Ms. B: Uh huh. Do you feel angry?

J: Yes. I always hate being when I'm not calm.

Ms. B: So what kind of things make you feel out of control?

J: Like, "No, you're not getting breakfast today!" Not going to computer. No fun.

Ms. B: When you can't do something you want to do? How about with other kids your age? How do you get along with them?

J: Good sportsmanship.

Ms. B: Good sportsmanship is a good thing. But do you have problems with other students? Tell me about them. What do you do?

J: Like, Donald. I touch his Legos.

Ms. B: So who's causing the problem there, you or Donald?

J: Donald.

Ms. B: When you touch his stuff?

J. Me.

Ms. B: What other problems do you have with your friends?

J: Touching Susan's face.

Ms. B: Okay, so what have your teachers done to help you do better?

J: Go to resource.

Ms. B: Resource. What things do you think you are good at or do a good job with?

J: Reading. Computers. Science.

Ms. B: Why do you think you are good at those things?

J: I study them. Like, I search the Web sites.

Ms. B: Where will you go to school next year?

J: The Krieger High School.

Ms. B: The whole name of the school is the Career and Technology Center. What do you think you'll learn in that high school program?

J: Technologies. Computers and electronics.

Ms. B: What do you want to do when you finish high school? What kind of job do you want?

J: Be a computer repairer.

Ms. B: What kinds of skills do you think you'll need to do that job?

J: Get some tools and fix computers. Fix them up if they have a problem.

Ms. B: Joe, what kinds of problems do you think you may have with that job? What will be the hard part?

J: The computer's broke?

Ms. B: How to figure out if it's broken?

J: Yes.

Ms. B: What do you think you can do to work on those problems?

J: Thinking.

Ms. B: So you want to get a job as a computer repairer. What else would you like to do with your life?

J: Have lunch with friends.

Ms. B: Where do you think you might live?

J: In a house.

>> QUESTIONS FOR FURTHER REFLECTION

1. What behavioral characteristics would indicate to you as a teacher that a student might be developing schizophrenia?
2. If you are going to teach students with schizophrenia or autistic spectrum disorder, what kinds of behavior should you be prepared to deal with, and how would you characterize your best preparation for the task?
3. Under what circumstances, if any, do you believe punishment is justified with students who have schizophrenia or pervasive developmental disorders?

Part 5

Implications: A Beginning Point

Introduction

To this point, we have concentrated on the characteristics of emotional or behavioral disorders. We turn now to the role of teachers in the amelioration or resolution of these problems. What can teachers do to help students with emotional or behavioral disorders? What might they expect as outcomes of their work? With what basic assumptions should one approach the tasks of teaching and managing these students in school? What teaching and management strategies are most likely to be successful? These and related questions are logical extensions of what we have discussed in prior chapters, but their answers demand more space than a single chapter—or a single book—can offer. My comments in the final chapter are therefore only a preface or brief orientation to educational methodology, based primarily on my understanding of the research findings I have summarized in the other sections of the book.

My purpose in this final chapter is to sketch what I consider to be a conceptual or philosophical foundation for educating children and youth with emotional or behavioral disorders. To the extent that my sketching is successful, you will be able to describe the essence of my views of good teaching after you have read chapter 18. I suggest that as teachers we must begin by examining our expectations, not only of the students we teach but of ourselves and others who live and work with these students. Within the context of our expectations, we must try to make sense of causal factors and our role in them. As professional educators, we also have an obligation to accomplish these tasks:

- Define and measure each student's behavior precisely enough to monitor progress and communicate that progress clearly to others.
- Design appropriate and corrective experiences for students.
- Communicate effectively with students about their behavior.
- Teach students self-control through modeling and direct instruction.

I offer a synopsis of my views on teaching because I feel it is important that every professional educator work out a basic philosophy regarding what teachers can and should do to help students with emotional or behavioral disorders. I do not mean to suggest that when you have done so you will stop questioning yourself and others. Although I have written a statement revealing something of my own philosophical orientation to teaching, I do not consider it final or immutable. It is by necessity a tentative statement, open to revision as I learn more about teaching and about students with special problems. As I suggested in my introduction to part 1, I hope that reading this book will launch you on an adventure of self-questioning. I also hope that you will question the discernment of my comments in part 5 in the light of what you have experienced firsthand and what you have read, not only in this book but in many other sources as well. Ultimately, my hope is that you will work toward articulating your own views on teaching particularly challenging students and that your self-questioning adventure will never stop.

CHAPTER EIGHTEEN

A PERSONAL STATEMENT

As you read this chapter, keep these guiding questions in mind:

- What should I expect of myself as a teacher and of my students?

- What causal factors should I be most concerned about, and what is my role as a teacher?

- How should I define and measure the behavior of my students?

- What roles do communication, directness, honesty, self-control, and modeling play in effective education for students with emotional or behavioral disorders?

- Why must instruction be the primary concern of teachers of students with emotional or behavioral disorders?

SETTING EXPECTATIONS

What we expect of our students and ourselves is a critical factor in our choice of educational strategies, and our expectations determine in part what we and our students achieve. Furthermore, our expectations greatly influence how we evaluate what we and our students accomplish. Setting appropriate expectations is not only important but surprisingly difficult—if we take the task seriously. Unfortunately, the early 21st century may be remembered as an era of hollow slogans and trite pronouncements regarding educators' expectations. "All children can learn," for example, may be recalled as a particularly popular but banal phrase that was seldom followed by important questions regarding what all children can learn or at what rate, to what degree of proficiency, with what allocation of resources, or for what purpose (Kauffman, 1999f, 2002; Kauffman & Hallahan, 1993). Likewise, holding "the same high expectations for all students" may be remembered as a gross oversimplification that ignores the need to recognize students' individual differences (Kauffman, 1999e; Kauffman, Mostert, Trent, & Hallahan, 2002). Setting appropriate expectations for others and ourselves requires considerable reflection on what we know about human development and learning, the nature of each student's problems, and our own limitations and biases. Let us hope that the next decade brings a more serious and reflective attitude toward what we should anticipate from ourselves and others.

Educators are sometimes impulsive in setting their expectations for students, neglecting the questions that might help them establish a constructive and realistic foundation for teaching and its evaluation. The special educator working with students who have emotional or behavioral disorders must begin with the same questions that every teacher must ask before designing a behavior management plan:

- Could this problem be a result of inappropriate curriculum or teaching strategies?
- What do I demand and prohibit—and what should I?
- Why do certain behaviors bother me, and what should I do about them?
- Is the behavior I am concerned about developmentally significant?
- Should I focus on a behavioral excess or a deficiency?
- Will resolution of this problem solve any others?

A reflective approach demands much additional self-questioning to arrive at academic and behavioral expectations that do not sell the student short, set the student up for failure, or impose improper personal or cultural biases (Kauffman, Mostert, et al., 2002).

Teachers are sometimes acculturated during their training or by others in the school system to expect too little or too much of themselves and other adults who live and work with children. The primary objectives of some teachers seem to be survival and self-serving behavior, with little apparent concern for their role in improving the achievement and social behavior of their students. They accept little responsibility for their students' failure, expecting of themselves only that they "put in their time." They typically get what they expect and leave the world no better than they found it. Other teachers see themselves as martyrs or saviors, sacrificing nearly all other personal desires for the sake of their students. Their students' failure becomes their personal failure, and they expect to achieve a cure that will make their students "normal." They seldom get what they expect, and they tend to leave education—often prematurely—embittered by human failure.

Predictably, those who expect too little of themselves tend to excuse the abuse, neglect, and incompetence of other adults; those who expect too much of themselves are often disparaging of others who are unable or unwilling to measure up to their extraordinary personal standards of goodness. Self-understanding is a prequisite for teaching children with emotional or behavioral disorders (Richardson & Shupe, 2003). Finding a level of expectation for oneself and others that facilitates personal growth, fosters hope and persistence in the face of failure, and allows one to develop supportive relationships with parents and other teachers is no small accomplishment. These are particularly daunting tasks for the many teachers who begin teaching students with emotional or behavioral disorders without adequate training (see Clark-Chiarelli & Singer, 1995; Heward & Silvestri, 2003; Lloyd & Kauffman, 1995).

Teachers' expectations of themselves as well as of the children they teach are often shaped by their culture, particularly the way teachers and teaching are viewed by others. Although he was describing the attitudes of Egyptian parents (in Egypt, about 1930), the Nobel Prize–winning novelist Naguib Mahfouz wrote dialogue that is representative of many Americans' attitudes today. In Mahfouz's story, the family patriarch tells his son Kamal, who wants to become a teacher, that teaching is "a miserable profession, which wins respect from no one." Kamal's father goes on to describe a teaching career as "utterly devoid of grandeur or esteem," and he suggests that none of the teachers Kamal knows deserves even to be called a human being (see Mahfouz, 2001, pp. 586–596). True, some teachers are inhumane. However, the wife of the patriarch, Kamal's mother, offers a different perspective on being a teacher. She does not understand why anyone would disparage teaching and recalls the saying, "I become the slave of anyone who teaches me even a single syllable" (Mahfouz, 2001, p. 597).

Some people understand the power of teaching, but it is important to enter teaching with the knowledge that some disparage it as a profession. It is also important to focus attention on the insights of people like Kamal's mother. Many teachers are shocked by the contempt some parents show for them. One parent of a student is reported to have said of a District of Columbia school, "You had parents roaming the halls and threatening teachers. In front of the children, even during school, parents would berate the teachers loudly" (Fisher, 2003, p. 37). Such contempt can shake one's confidence in expectations for students and for oneself as a teacher.

UNDERSTANDING CAUSAL FACTORS AND THE ROLE OF THE TEACHER

The first or ultimate causes of emotional or behavioral disorders almost always remain unknown. A realistic and productive approach is to consider contributing factors that may interact to cause disorder. Contributing factors may be predisposing or precipitating; both increase the probability that a disorder will occur under given circumstances. Precipitating factors may trigger a maladaptive response, given a set of predisposing variables. An important task of the teacher is to identify the contributing factors that account for the student's current emotional or behavioral status. We know that a variety of biological factors are important, but experience—including the experience a teacher can provide in school—is not only at least as important as biology but a factor the teacher can do something about. Hart and Risley (1995) noted:

> The fundamental consensus among scientists has not changed: Experience and heredity contribute about equally to human functioning. Of course in the human species, genetics contributes both to the general competence of parents and children and to specific social behaviors of parenting and childing that influence the experience children receive. But beyond the contribution of genetics, all societies assume that experience can be enhanced and supplemented to improve the competencies of children and that those competencies will become part of the inheritance they pass on to their children. (p. xvi)

The primary focus of the special educator must be on the contributing factors that the teacher can alter (see Pullen, 2004). Factors over which the teacher has no control may determine how children or youth are approached initially, but the teacher is called on to begin working with specific pupils after disorders have appeared. The special educator has two primary responsibilities: first, to make sure that he or she does no further disservice to the student; and second, to manipulate the student's present environment to foster development of more appropriate behavior in spite of unalterable past and present circumstances. Emphasis must be on the present and future, not the past. Although other environments may be important, the teacher's focus must be on the classroom environment. Certainly teachers may profitably extend their influence beyond the classroom, perhaps working with parents to improve the home environment or using community resources for the child's benefit. But talk of influence beyond the classroom, including such high-sounding phrases as *ecological management* and *wraparound services,* is patent nonsense until the teacher has demonstrated that he or she can make the classroom environment conducive to improved behavior (see Heward, 2003).

This is not to say that collaboration of school personnel with families and communities is unimportant. Yet we must recognize that many teachers work under conditions in which administrators and consultants do not facilitate home–school or community–school ties. Teachers are often on their own, and the individual contribution they can make outside the classroom is limited.

The stance of the special educator, therefore, must be that behavior is predictable and controllable; in the case of disordered behavior, enough controlling factors can be found and changed in the classroom to produce a therapeutic result in that context. We cannot change the past, and the teacher alone cannot alter many of the contributing factors operating in the present. Educators must have faith that the proper classroom environment alone *can* make a difference in the student's life, even if nothing else can be altered. We must also hope that more than classroom environment can be changed, and we must work toward that end. But we cannot escape our responsibility for implementing best practices in the classroom or atone for our "implementational sins" by pointing the finger at other factors such as the structure of education or the lack of comprehensive, integrated, collaborative services (cf. Kauffman, 1994a,

2003b; Whelan, 1998). We must light the candle we can, even though we know that it does not dispel all the darkness in our students' lives (Kauffman, 1999c).

DEFINING AND MEASURING BEHAVIOR

Teachers must have the primary role in determining students' eligibility for special education and deciding how children and youth will be served. Teachers' tolerance for and knowledge of individual students' behavior in the context of their classrooms must become the ultimate criteria for deciding which students need special help and where a student can be educated appropriately (Gerber, 1988; see also Kauffman et al., 1995a).

Defining and classifying emotional or behavioral disorders are persistent problems—enigmas that appear always to defy a truly satisfactory resolution. The intractability of defining and classifying youngsters' disorders does not, fortunately, preclude useful definition and measurement of behavior. The teacher can define and measure precisely the behaviors that bring children and youths into conflict with others and are self-defeating. Indeed, the teacher who cannot or will not pinpoint and measure the relevant behaviors of the students he or she is teaching is probably not going to be very effective. As we have seen in previous chapters, students are considered to need help primarily because they exhibit behavioral excesses or deficiencies. Not to define precisely and to measure these behavioral excesses and deficiencies, then, is a fundamental error; it is akin to the malpractice of a nurse who decides not to measure vital signs (heart rate, respiration rate, temperature, and blood pressure), perhaps arguing that he or she is too busy, that subjective estimates of vital signs are quite adequate, that vital signs are only superficial estimates of the patient's health, or that vital signs do not signify the nature of the underlying pathology. The teaching profession is dedicated to the task of changing behavior demonstrably for the better. What can one say, then, of educational practice that does not include precise definition and reliable measurement of the behavior change induced by the teacher's methodology? It is indefensible. Measurement need not be sophisticated to be extremely valuable, but it is indispensable in assessing needs and progress (see also Heward, 2003; Heward & Silvestri, 2003).

The technology of behavioral definition and measurement is readily available to teachers—and has been for decades (e.g. Alberto & Troutman, 2003; Howell & Hyatt, 2004; Kazdin, 2001; Kauffman, Landrum, & Sayeski, in press; Kerr & Nelson, 2002; Lewis, Lewis-Palmer, Stichter, J., & Newcomer, 2004). With relatively little investment of effort, the teacher can learn behavior-measurement techniques and teach them to students. When students know how to define and measure their own behavior and the responses of those with whom they live, two additional benefits accrue:

1. The teacher is relieved of some of the mechanical aspects of teaching.
2. The students have an opportunity to gain an extra degree of control over their own environments.

My suggestion is not that every behavior of every student should be measured or that the teacher should become preoccupied with measurement to the exclusion of other crucial concerns (Kauffman, Mostert, et al., 2002). Teaching is much more than measurement. A mechanical approach to teaching that excludes affective concerns is no more justifiable than an approach that neglects cognitive and behavioral goals. If the student's most important behavioral characteristics are not monitored, however, then it will be almost impossible for the teacher to communicate anything of substance about the student's progress to the youngster or to anyone else.

The importance of behavioral measurement is demonstrated so clearly and frequently that one is prompted to ask why many teachers still do not measure their pupils' behavior. Measurement has probably been neglected for at least these reasons (see also Heward, 2003):

- There has been a strong bias among some special educators in support of theoretical models that do not include direct measurement of behavior and, in fact, include the presumption that measurable responses are unimportant or a superficial aspect of psychopathology.
- Parents have placidly accepted less than adequate evidence of teachers' effectiveness as the best that the education profession can offer.
- Many teachers are still uninformed about the value of direct measurement of behavior or are untutored in the appropriate methodology.
- Some teachers are incompetent and negligent.
- Although measurement of behavior is invaluable for precise assessment of therapeutic effects, measurement is often not a prerequisite for behavioral change.
- Informal and subjective estimates of students' behavioral status, which include anecdotal records and statements such as "She is much improved this week" without any objective data to back up the claim, give the impression that more precise measurement is unnecessary.

Admittedly, some qualitative or affective aspects of pupil's behavior and teachers' methodology cannot be measured directly, and these affective variables may be extremely important. I do not mean to imply that one should ignore everything that cannot be measured. But for a teacher of students with emotional or behavioral disorders not to ask, "Exactly what is it this student does or does not do that is causing a problem?" and then not set about measuring the behavior in question as objectively and precisely as possible is unconscionable. Without direct measurement of behavior, the teacher risks being misled by subjective impressions of the student's responses and the effects of instructional and behavioral management techniques. It is reasonable to expect that the teacher show objective and precise evidence of pupils' behavioral change, as well as describe the quality of his or her relationship to students in more subjective and affective terms.

HELPING STUDENTS EXPERIENCE WORK, PLAY, LOVE, AND FUN

It does not take great wisdom to see that children and youth with emotional or behavioral disorders often do not do productive work or know how to play, give and receive love, and have fun. Yet these four experiences—work, play, love, and fun—are nearly the essence of a satisfying and meaningful existence. Education of these students requires a curriculum that brings these essential experiences into sharp focus. This is not to imply that a curriculum must try to teach these experiences directly; in fact, someone who wishes to teach a youngster how to work, play, love, or have fun must have a curriculum with a content of useful specific skills, but the skills in themselves do not constitute essential life experiences. The vapid antics of "fun seekers" and the desperate "play" of professional athletes illustrate the difficulty in apprehending fun and play through concentrated effort alone. Relations among events—the structure of experience as well as events themselves—teach a person to work, play, love, and enjoy.

The teacher's primary task is to structure or order the environment for the pupil in such a way that work is accomplished, play is learned, love is felt, and fun is enjoyed—by the student and the teacher. The teacher does not provide structure and order by allowing the student complete freedom to choose what to do. Youngsters with emotional or behavioral disorders are in difficulty because they make unguided and unfortunate choices about how to conduct themselves. One must make value judgments about what a student should learn. Hobbs (1974, p. 156) wrote: "A child simply must know how to read, write, spell, and do arithmetic, and it is good for him to know how to hit a ball, to play a guitar, to scull a canoe, . . . and to travel by bus across town." The teacher must have confidence in his or her own judgment about what is good for the youngster to learn and how the student should behave, or effective structuring of the student's environment is impossible. This does not mean the teacher should determine every skill the pupil learns or every way of behaving. The point is not to make students mindlessly conform to ridiculous behavioral standards but to require a reasonable standard of conduct and learning that will allow them greater personal choice and fulfillment in a free society.

In addition to the value judgments and difficult decisions one must make about what to teach, questions remain about how to best arrange the teaching environment. Two fundamental principles guide the organization of an effective teaching environment: choosing tasks that are appropriate for the pupil (tasks that are at the right level and at which the student can usually succeed) and arranging appropriate consequences for performance. One does not learn work, play, love, and fun through failure but through success and mastery. We do not learn pride, dignity, self-worth, and other attributes of good mental health by having our wishes immediately gratified but by struggling to overcome difficulties, meeting requirements, and finding that our own efforts will achieve desired goals.

We cannot depend on our students to learn by some magical, mysterious, internally guided process; their learning will be assured only by a skillful and sensitive adult who makes the expectations for their behavior appropriately difficult. Hobbs (1974) described the appropriate level of expectation as the "Principle of Just Manageable Difficulties." The "J.M.D. Principle" is that people are most well adjusted or in the best mental health when they choose for themselves problems or tasks that are just about, but not quite, insurmountable. The J.M.D. Principle remains worthy of our efforts to live by it:

> Part of the art of choosing difficulties is to select those that are indeed just manageable. If the difficulties chosen are too easy, life is boring; if they are too hard, life is defeating. The trick is to choose trouble for oneself in the direction of what he would like to become at a level of difficulty close to the edge of his competence. When one achieves this fine tuning of his life, he will know zest and joy and deep fulfillment. (Hobbs, 1974, p. 165)

The teacher's task is to choose at first just manageable tasks for students and then gradually allow them to set their own goals as they become attuned to their true capabilities and desires.

Ample evidence indicates that the order in which events are structured has a profound influence on students' learning—specifically, that making highly preferred events (play) contingent or dependent on less preferred events (such as work) improves the individual's work performance (cf. Bandura, 1986; Kerr & Nelson, 2002; Walker, 1995; Walker, Ramsey, & Gresham, 2004). The expectation "work before play (or pay)" is a fundamental principle of behavior modification. An environment in which rewards and privileges (beyond those that are everyone's right) are gratis is stultifying. "Earning your way," on the other hand, builds self-esteem. Long ago, Rothman (1970), who worked with disturbed and delinquent girls in New York City, commented on the value of work and pay:

> If I had my way, all children would work and be paid for the work they do. If the work of children is to learn, then children should be paid for learning. Money is a powerful motivator. I daresay that truancy might decrease and that more children would learn, even those children who have been relegated to the substratum of the nonachiever, if they were paid for services rendered. Someday, I would like a fund to pay girls for increasing their reading and arithmetic skills. Supposing I could say to a girl, "You increased your reading from fourth grade to fifth. You have earned five dollars." How great! If only we could do it. (p. 211)

It *can* be done, if not with money then with special privileges, goods, or services that are meaningful to the child. Meaningful reward for accomplishment is a time-honored means of teaching and encouraging students to do their best, notwithstanding the ignorance of those who consider rewards inherently demeaning (e.g., Kohn, 1993). Properly used rewards for performance have not been found to decrease intrinsic motivation (see McGinnis et al., 1999). The fundamental principle underlying a token economy is payment of a fair wage for work. Rothman (1970) also noted one of the usual outcomes of work: "Pride—an essential personal ingredient. All the girls who work find it" (p. 232).

I will not be so presumptuous as to try to define play, love, or fun; a definition of *work*—purposeful and necessary expenditure of effort to achieve a desired goal—is daring enough. For the emotionally healthy individual, work, play, love, and fun are inextricably intertwined, and for someone with emotional or behavioral disabilities, they are unrelated or unattainable. When a youngster's emotions and behavior have become disordered, the most effective strategy for restoring a "vital balance" or "zest, joy, and deep fulfillment" is to provide appropriate work and consistent consequences for performance. Play, love, and fun are likely to follow the experience of accomplishing a valued task and earning a reward by one's own labor. To work is to build a sound basis for self-esteem.

COMMUNICATING DIRECTLY AND HONESTLY

Some advocates of a structured approach and some behavior-modification enthusiasts imply that consistent consequences for behavior alone will be enough to bring about therapeutic change. Teaching is more than just providing a structured relationship among events, however. How the environment is arranged may be as important as the structure itself in determining the outcome for the student.

How one listens and talks to students will have an effect on their perceptions and their responses to other environmental events (Kauffman, Mostert, et al., 2002). In describing the consequences of behavior, for example, the teacher can emphasize either the positive or the negative aspects of an arrangement. A teacher may say, "You may not go to recess until your math is finished." Another teacher might phrase it, "You may go to recess as soon as you finish your math." Both teachers have described the response–consequence relationship, and both statements are equally correct; but the second draws attention to the positive consequences of appropriate performance and the first to the negative results of nonperformance. Each statement may affect the student differently. Nonverbal communication, too, is important and should be consistent with what is said. To be therapeutic, teachers must listen, talk, and act in ways that communicate respect, caring, and confidence, both in themselves and in their students.

It does not follow that the teacher must always communicate approval or positive regard for the student's behavior. In fact, the teacher must communicate disapproval with great clarity. We cannot expect a youngster to learn to behave appropriately if we respond to all behavior with approval or equanimity. Candor, including honest appraisal of inappropriate behavior, will serve the teacher well. Consistent follow-through with positive and negative consequences for desirable and undesirable behavior, combined with extremely clear communication of expectations, will be successful in managing most behavioral problems.

Communication is a two-way affair, and teachers will not be successful unless they learn to listen skillfully, to watch students' behavior with understanding, and to interpret accurately the relationship between children's verbal and nonverbal behavior. Youngsters who do not believe they are being listened to will go to extreme lengths to make themselves understood, often getting into additional trouble by their efforts to establish communication.

Directness in talking to children and youth facilitates communication. Many teachers and parents tend to be tentative, noncommittal, and obfuscatory in their conversations with youngsters, perhaps out of fear of rejecting or being rejected or perhaps from the misguided notion that to help youngsters who have emotional or behavioral disorders one must never direct them (cf. O'Leary, 1995). These youngsters do not profit from having to guess about adults' wishes or intentions. A few, in fact, will improve their behavior almost immediately if the teacher merely states clearly, forthrightly, and unequivocally how they are to behave.

Students with emotional or behavioral disorders are sure to test the teacher's honesty. Honesty is more than candor in expressing opinions and reporting facts accurately. Students want to know whether teachers are as good as their word. A teacher who makes idle threats or fails to deliver positive and negative consequences as promised will surely run afoul of his or her students.

MODELING AND TEACHING SELF-CONTROL

There is overwhelming evidence that children learn much through observing others' behavior (Bandura, 1986; Cullinan, 2002; Hallenbeck & Kauffman, 1995; Kerr & Nelson, 2002). Teachers whose own behavior is not exemplary may corrupt rather than help students, regardless of their finesse with other teaching strategies. To be blunt, teaching students with emotional or behavioral disorders is not an appropriate job for social misfits or the psychologically unstable. Imitating the teacher should lead to behavioral improvement, not to maladaptive conduct. These statements should not be taken to mean that the teacher must be a model of perfection. The expectation of perfection in oneself or others is itself maladaptive, a problem that the teacher will need to help many students with emotional or behavioral disorders overcome. Being able to accept imperfections in oneself and others and to cope constructively with one's own and others' failures are among the emotional and behavioral characteristics that the teacher must demonstrate. Hobbs (1966) summed up the kind of model a teacher (in this example a teacher counselor in Project Re-ED) should provide, and it remains a guiding ideal:

> But most of all a teacher–counselor is a decent adult; educated, well trained; able to give and receive affection, to live relaxed, and to be firm; a person with private resources for the nourishment and refreshment of his own life; not an itinerant worker but a professional through and through; a person with a sense of the significance of time, of the usefulness of today and the promise of tomorrow; a person of hope, quiet confidence, and joy; one who has committed himself to children and to the proposition that children who are emotionally disturbed can be helped by the process of re-education. (pp. 106–107)

A teacher of students with emotional or behavioral disorders should be a model of self-control. Not only should one model self-control; one should also teach through direct instruction. Every pupil, those with emotional or behavioral disorders included, should be allowed free choice and self-determination, for appropriate self-guidance is both inherent in the concept of individual rights and inimical to the loss of control that characterizes disordered behavior. This statement does not mean that students should always be allowed to behave as they will without interference or that the teacher is always wrong to require a pupil to behave willy-nilly. Students should be allowed to choose for themselves how they will behave except when they choose to behave in ways that are self-defeating, ways that clearly are not in their best interests, or in ways that violate the rights of others. The teacher's role should be to structure the classroom environment so that the student is aware of options, can exercise choice in as many areas of behavior as possible, and is tutored in and rewarded for appropriate decisions. Students should be taught cognitive behavior-modification techniques, such as self-instruction, rehearsal, and guided practice, to make them as self-sufficient as possible in controlling their own behavior. External control may be required at first to humanize the pupil, but the task of truly humanistic education is not completed until control is internalized to the greatest extent possible.

INSTRUCTION: REFOCUSING ON THE BUSINESS OF EDUCATION

One of the most important lessons we have learned during the past three decades as educators of students with emotional or behavioral disorders is that academic instruction must not be ignored or even made secondary (see Heward, 2003; Kauffman & Landrum, 2005; Lane, 2004). The observation that the education of these students too often relegates academic instruction to a secondary concern and focuses on control or containment of misbehavior is a serious indictment that must not be allowed to characterize our work.

We must refocus our efforts on instruction for two reasons. First, academic achievement is so fundamental to emotional and social adjustment that it is foolish not to make it a capstone of educational intervention. Enhancing their academic achievement is the single most reliable way of improving students' self-appraisal and social competence. Second, managing or modifying students' behavior is best approached, at least by teachers, as an instructional problem (Kauffman, Mostert et al., 2002; Pullen, 2004; Walker et al., 2004). This means placing more emphasis on the antecedents of problems—the settings or contexts in which behavioral problems predictably occur. It means thinking of social or emotional problems much as one would think of problems in teaching reading or math or any another academic subject. It means paying very careful attention to specifying precisely the behavior that is expected, modifying the contexts in which misbehavior happens, and rehearsing and prompting expected behavior. Strong reinforcement for desirable behavior is important, but it will be maximally effective only if the other instructional components are well implemented.

THINKING ABOUT REAL PEOPLE

It is one thing to think of emotional and behavioral disorders in the abstract, but quite another thing to observe them in reality. It is one thing to observe these disorders happening in other peoples' lives, but quite another thing when they become a part of your own life. Too often, we forget to consider the lives of the parents and families as well as the lives of the teachers and students involved. We forget to consider what it is like to have a disorder and what it is like to have and be responsible for parenting or teaching a child or youth with a disorder.

I offer the culminating case in the accompanying case book, the case of John as written by his mother. You may recall that the case of John was introduced in chapter 11 and that ADHD is both a common problem and a difficulty accompanying a variety of other disabilities. This case is much longer and more complex than those in the rest of the case book. In this sense it is more realistic, because emotional and behavioral disorders are not simple and do not have simple solutions. It is a case that asks us to think about all of the preceding chapters and what they mean for John, his mother, his family, and his teachers.

REMEMBERING THE PAST WHEN THINKING ABOUT THE FUTURE

Textbooks often end with speculation about the future. I have chosen instead to comment on the past because I believe the best prediction of future developments derives from analysis of past events. In the past, we have seen an ebb and flow of concern for the plight of students with emotional or behavioral disorders and periods of progress and regression in effective intervention. Professionals have expressed enthusiasm for new methods and disillusionment when the solution turns out to be less than final. A solely legal-bureaucratic approach to fulfilling society's obligation to disabled students has failed in the past and shows no particular promise for the future. The Individuals With Disabilities Education Act and its successors may set forth legal standards and promises, and these may be extremely important, but they can be circumvented or changed. Effective and humane education of students with disabilities has always depended on the individual actions of competent, caring teachers and other individuals, and this will be the case in the future regardless of legal mandates or prohibitions.

What *has* happened is always a harbinger of what *will* happen, and it is wise to know how today's problems are related to the past. We are living today with the backdraft of reductions in human services and supports for those in need—reductions defended with rhetoric intended to cover the painful consequences for children and their families. Children and youth at risk do not benefit from the sloganeering, denial, self-contradiction, posturing, and irrational, antiscientific, or unintelligible statements that have become popular in talk of reforming education (Kauffman, 2002, 2003a, 2004; Kauffman, Brigham, & Mock, 2004).

It is also wise to remember that special education and related disciplines solve more problems than they create, are greater sources of hope than of despair, and stand more for healing wounds than for making them (Kauffman & Hallahan, 2005b; Walker, Forness, et al., 1998). One leader in the field of emotional and behavioral disorders put it this way in accepting a significant award for his many years of service:

> Our society is now reaping a bitter harvest of our own making of damaged children and youth that is sown with the seeds of domestic violence, neglect and abuse and made much worse by the toxic conditions of our society. Collectively, we seem to have a greatly reduced capacity to safely raise and socialize our children.
>
> I believe our field stands as a lighthouse beacon of hope, caring and unconditional support for these at-risk children and youth to whom life has dealt such a cruel hand. I have been a researcher in the area of school-related behavior disorders for over three decades. During that time, I have been proud to call myself a member of the BD field which brings together dedicated professionals from diverse backgrounds who work together so well on behalf of at-risk children. Our field models and demonstrates positive values and best practice(s) that can make a real difference in the lives of children and youth with emotional and behavioral disorders and those of their families. (Walker, 2003, p. 2)

The issues today parallel those of the last century, although the potential for helping students with emotional or behavioral disorders is greater today than it was then because of our broader base of scientific knowledge and experience. We have reason, then, for guarded optimism. Quick and easy cures are not possible for most problems. People must care but go beyond caring to search diligently for reliable answers to the questions of how youngsters come to have emotional or behavioral disorders. Even more important is finding out how children can be helped to learn appropriate behavior. To the extent that people dedicate themselves to finding such answers and putting those answers to work in practice, we can have confidence that progress will ultimately outweigh regression.

>> GLOSSARY

Adjustment disorders   Maladaptive reactions to an identifiable and stressful life event or circumstance. Includes impairment of social and/or occupational functioning. Maladaptive behavior is expected to change when stress is removed.

Affective disorders   *See* Mood disorders.

Amnesia   Chronic or severe inability to remember; loss of memory that is general or more than temporary.

Anorexia nervosa   Severe self-starvation and marked weight loss that may be life threatening. Occurs most often in adolescent girls.

Anoxia; hypoxia   Deprivation of oxygen for a long enough time to result in brain trauma.

Anxiety disorders   Disorders in which anxiety is the primary feature. Anxiety may focus on specific situations, such as separation or social contact with strangers, or it may be generalized and pervasive.

Anxiety withdrawal   Behavior characterized by anxiety, feelings of inadequacy, embarrassment, shyness, and withdrawal from social contact.

Asperger syndrome   Impairment of social behavior (e.g., eye-to-eye gaze, facial expression, peer relationships, sharing of experience, social reciprocity) and restricted, repetitive, stereotyped patterns of behavior or interests but without significant delay in language or cognitive development.

Athetoid movement   Involuntary, jerky, writhing movements (especially of the fingers and wrists) associated with athetoid cerebral palsy.

Attentional strategies   Use of verbal labeling, rehearsal, self-instruction, or other techniques to improve a child's ability to attend efficiently to appropriate stimuli.

Attention deficit and disruptive behavior disorders   Includes attention deficit–hyperactivity disorder, conduct disorder, oppositional defiant disorder, and disruptive behavior disorder.

Attention deficit–hyperactivity disorder (ADHD)   A disorder that includes inattention, impulsivity, and hyperactivity, beginning before age 7 and of sufficient severity and persistence to result in impairment in two or more settings (e.g., home and school) in social, academic, or occupational functioning. May be primarily hyperactive–impulsive type or primarily inattentive type.

Autism; autistic   *See* Autistic spectrum disorder.

Autistic spectrum disorder   Autism is a pervasive developmental disorder with onset before age three in which there is qualitative impairment of social interaction and communication and restricted, repetitive, stereotyped patterns of behavior, interests, and activities. Autistic spectrum disorder includes the full range of autism symptoms, from classic autism as just defined, to Asperger's syndrome and autisticlike behavior.

Aversive conditioning   A form of punishment; presenting an aversive (painful or unpleasant) consequence following a behavior to reduce the frequency or probability of its recurrence.

Behavior intervention plan (BIP)   A plan for changing a problem behavior.

Behavior modification   Systematic control of environmental events, especially of consequences, to produce specific changes in observable responses. May include reinforcement, punishment, modeling, self-instruction, desensitization, guided practice, or any other technique for strengthening or eliminating a particular response.

Behavioral model   Assumptions that emotional or behavioral disorders result primarily from inappropriate learning and that the most effective preventive actions and therapeutic interventions involve controlling the child's environment to teach appropriate responses.

Biological model   Assumptions that emotional or behavioral disorders result primarily from dysfunction of the central nervous system (because of brain lesions, neurochemical irregularities, or genetic defects) and that the most effective preventive actions and therapeutic interventions involve prevention or correction of such biological defects.

Bipolar disorder   Major mood disorder characterized by both manic and depressive episodes. *See also* Depression, Manic.

Brain syndrome   *See* Organic brain syndrome.

Bulimia   Recurrent episodes of binge eating followed by purging (by vomiting or enemas) or other compensatory behavior (e.g., fasting or excessive exercise) intended to prevent weight gain, accompanied by preoccupation with body shape or weight.

Case   An example. A story describing a problem and information relevant to understanding it.

Catatonic Behavior   Characterized by muscular rigidity and mental stupor, sometimes alternating with periods of extreme excitement; inability to move or interact normally; "frozen" posture or affect.

Catharsis   In psychoanalytic theory, the notion that it is therapeutic to express one's feelings freely under certain

449

conditions (e.g., that aggressive drive can be reduced by free expression of aggression in a safe way, such as hitting a punching bag or a doll).

Cerebral palsy   A developmental disability resulting from brain damage before, during, or soon after birth and having as a primary feature weakness or paralysis of the extremities. Often accompanied by mental retardation, sensory deficiencies, and/or behavioral disorders.

Cerebral trauma   *See* Traumatic brain injury.

Character disorder   Acting-out, aggressive behavior with little or no indication of associated anxiety or guilt.

Childhood disintegrative disorder   Normal development followed by significant loss, after age 2 but before age 10, of previously acquired social, language, self-care, or play skills with qualitative impairment in social interaction or communication and stereotyped behavior.

Childhood psychosis   Used to denote a wide range of severe and profound disorders of children, including autism, schizophrenia, and symbiotic psychosis.

Choreoathetoid movement   Involuntary, purposeless, uncontrolled movement characteristic of some types of neurological disorders.

Comorbid condition   A condition or disorder occurring simultaneously with another.

Comorbidity   Two or more disorders occurring together, as in comorbidity of depression and conduct disorder.

Conceptual model   A theory. In emotional or behavioral disorders, a set of assumptions regarding the origins and nature of the problem and the nature of therapeutic mechanisms; a set of assumptions guiding research and practice.

Conduct disorder; conduct problem   Repetitive, persistent pattern of behavior violating basic rights of others or age-appropriate social norms or rules, including aggression toward people and animals, destruction of property, deceitfulness or theft, and serious violation of family or school rules. Onset may be in childhood or adolescence, and severity may range from mild to severe.

Contingency contract   In behavior modification, a written agreement between a child and an adult (or adults) specifying the consequences for specific behavior.

Counterconditioning   Behavior therapy that teaches, by means of classical and operant conditioning, adaptive responses that are incompatible with maladaptive responses.

Countertheorists   *See* Humanistic education.

Craniocerebral trauma   *See* Traumatic brain injury.

Criterion referenced   Assessment or testing based on a standard or criterion that the student should be able to reach rather than an average or norm.

Curriculum-based evaluation; curriculum-based assessment; curriculum-based measurement   Evaluation or assessment based on the student's performance in the actual curriculum with the materials (texts, problems) that the teacher is using for instruction. Requires frequent, brief measurement of the student's performance using regular instructional materials.

Cyclothymia; cyclothymic disorder   Fluctuation of mood alternating between depression and mania but with symptoms not severe enough to be considered bipolar disorder. *See also* Bipolar disorder; Depression; Manic.

Delinquency   The illegal behavior of a minor.

Delusion   Abnormal mental state in which something is falsely believed.

Delusional disorder   Disorder characterized by nonbizarre (i.e., potentially true) delusions without schizophrenia.

Depression; depressive episode   Depressed mood and loss of interest or pleasure in nearly all normal activities; episode lasting for at least 2 weeks.

Desensitization; systematic desensitization   Elimination of fears or phobias by gradually subjecting the fearful individual to successively more anxiety-provoking stimuli (real or imagined) while the individual remains relaxed and free of fear.

Developmental disorders   Disorders apparently caused by the child's failure to develop at a normal rate or according to the usual sequence.

***Diagnostic and Statistical Manual of the American Psychiatric Association* (*DSM*)**   Editions designated by roman numerals, as *DSM–IV* for the fourth edition. Revised third edition is referred to as *DSM–III–R*.

Distractibility   Inability to direct and sustain attention to the appropriate or relevant stimuli in a given situation. *See also* Selective attention.

Down syndrome   A genetic defect in which the child is born with an extra chromosome (number 21 in the 22 pairs; hence, trisomy 21) in each cell; a syndrome associated with mental retardation.

Dynamic psychiatry   The study of emotional processes, mental mechanisms, and their origins; study of evolution, progression, or regression in human behavior and its motivation. Distinguished from *descriptive psychiatry,* in which focus is on static clinical patterns, symptoms, and classification.

Dysphoria   General feeling of unhappiness or unwellness, especially when disproportionate to its cause or inappropriate to one's life circumstances. Opposite of *euphoria*.

Dysthymia   Feeling of depressed mood on most days for at least 2 years but not of the severity required for diagnosis of a major depressive episode or clinical depression.

Echolalia; echolalic   The parroting repetition of words or phrases either immediately after they are heard or later. Typical in very young children who are learning to talk. Among older children and adults, usually observed only in individuals with schizophrenia or autism.

Ecobehavioral analysis   A procedure in which naturally occurring, functional events are identified and employed to improve instruction and behavior management.

Ecological model   Assumptions that emotional or behavioral disorders result primarily from flaws in a complex social system in which various elements of the system (e.g., child, school, family, church, community) are highly interdependent and that the most effective preventive actions and therapeutic interventions involve changes in the entire social system.

Educateur   An individual broadly trained to enhance social development of children and youth in various community contexts. Someone trained in education and related disciplines to intervene in the social ecology of troubled children and youth.

Ego   The conscious mind. In Freudian psychology, the volitional aspect of behavior.

Ego psychology   Psychological theories or models emphasizing the ego.

Elective mutism   *See* Selective mutism.

Electroencephalogram (EEG)   A graphic record of changes in the electrical potential of the brain. Used in neurological and psychiatric research.

Emotional intelligence   Adeptness in assessing and managing emotions, including skills in awareness of one's own emotions, recognition of others' emotional states, regulation of one's own emotions and motivation, and management of interpersonal relationships.

Emotional lability   Unstable or rapidly shifting emotional states.

Encephalitis   Inflammation of the brain, usually as a result of infection and often accompanied by behavioral manifestations such as lethargy.

Encopresis   Incontinence of feces, which may consist of passing feces into the clothing or bed at regular intervals or leaking mucus and feces into the clothing or bed almost continuously.

Endogenous depression   Depression apparently precipitated by biological factors rather than adverse environmental circumstances.

Enuresis; enuretic   Incontinence of urine, which may be diurnal (wetting oneself during the day) or nocturnal (bed-wetting).

Epilepsy   Recurrent abnormal electrical discharges in the brain that cause seizures. A person is not considered to have epilepsy unless repeated seizures occur.

Ethology   Scientific comparative study of animal and human behavior, especially study of the development of human character.

Eugenics   Belief that human qualities can be improved through selective mating. A science dealing with improving inherited characteristics of a race or breed.

Euphoria   Feeling of elation. Extreme and unrealistic happiness.

Externalizing behavior   Acting-out behavior, such as fighting. Sometimes called conduct disorder.

Facilitated communication   A procedure said to allow persons who are unable to communicate through speech to communicate by using a keyboard. A facilitator assists communication by giving emotional and physical support as the disabled person types.

Feeding disorder of infancy or early childhood   Feeding disturbance, occurring before age 6, characterized by persistent failure to eat adequately and gain weight but not due to gastrointestinal or other general medical conditions.

Follow-back studies   Studies in which adults with a given disorder are "followed back" in time in an attempt to find the antecedents of their condition in their medical, educational, or social histories.

Fragile X syndrome   A genetic disorder, associated primarily with mental retardation but also a variety of other mental or behavioral problems, in which part of the X chromosome shows variations, such as breaks or gaps.

Frustration–aggression hypothesis   Hypothesis that frustration always produces aggression and that aggression is always the result of frustration.

Functional analysis   Assessment of behavior to determine the purposes, goals, or function of behavior.

Functional behavioral assessment   Procedures designed to find out why a student exhibits problem behavior, including assessment of the antecedents and consequences of behavior and the apparent purpose of the problem behavior.

General intelligence   The totality of skills and knowledge that enable a person to solve problems and meet social expectations. The theory that intelligence consists of general problem-solving abilities rather than abilities to perform specific tasks.

Heightened risk   A higher chance or risk than is true for the general population that an individual will experience an event or condition (e.g., use drugs, acquire a traumatic head injury, become delinquent, fail in school, be diagnosed with schizophrenia, etc.).

Holistic education   An approach emphasizing individuals' construction of their own realities based on personal experience and rejecting traditional analytic and quantitative views of reality.

Humanistic education   Education suggested by countertheorists, who call for radical school reform and/or greater self-determination by the child. Education in which freedom, openness, innovation, self-direction, and self-evaluation by students and mutual sharing between students and teachers are practiced.

Hyperactivity; hyperactive   High level of motor activity accompanied by socially inappropriate behavior, often including conduct disorder, distractibility, and impulsivity.

Hyperkinesis   Excessive motor activity.

Hyperthyroidism   Enlargement of and excessive secretion of hormones from the thyroid gland that may result in nervousness, weakness, and restless overactivity.

Hypoglycemia   Abnormally low level of blood sugar that may produce behavioral symptoms such as irritability, fretfulness, confusion, negativism, or aggression. May be associated with diabetes.

Hypomanic   *See* Manic.

Hypoxia   Severely reduced supply of oxygen. *See* Anoxia.

Immaturity–inadequacy   Disorder characterized by social incompetence, passivity, daydreaming, and behavior typical of younger children.

Impulsivity   Tendency to react quickly and inappropriately to a situation rather than take time to consider alternatives and choose carefully.

Incidence   The rate of occurrence (as new cases) of a specific disorder in a given population during a given period of time (e.g., 25 per 1,000 per year).

Incontinence; incontinent   The release of urine or feces at inappropriate times or places. Lack of control of bladder or bowel function.

Index crime   An act that is illegal regardless of the person's age. Crimes for which the FBI keeps records, including the range from misdemeanors to murder.

Individuals With Disabilities Education Act (IDEA)   The federal special education law, enacted in 1990, that amended the Education for All Handicapped Children Act of 1975 (which was also known as Public Law 94–142), most recently reauthorized in 2004.

Induction approach   Use of reasoning, explanation, modeling, and expressions of love and concern in discipline, especially in teaching or enforcing moral standards.

Infantile autism   *See* Autistic spectrum disorder.

Interactional–transactional model   Assumptions that emotional or behavioral disorders result primarily from the mutual influence of the child and other people on each other and that the most effective preventive actions and therapeutic interventions involve changing the nature of interactions and transactions between the child and others.

Internalizing behavior   Behavior typically associated with social withdrawal, such as shyness, anxiety, or depression.

Intervention   Method or strategy used in treatment of an emotional or behavioral disorder.

Intrapsychic; intrapsychic causal factors   Having to do with the mind; in the mind itself. Conflict or disequilibrium between parts of the mind (in psychoanalytic theory, the id, the ego, and the superego), especially conflict in the unconscious.

Kanner's syndrome; early infantile autism   Originally described by Leo Kanner in 1943. *See also* Autistic spectrum disorder.

Lability   *See* Emotional lability.

Life-impact curriculum   A special curriculum intended to change students' thinking about their experiences and choices. A curriculum based on humanistic or holistic philosophy.

Life space crisis intervention   Ways of talking with children based on psychoeducational theory to help them understand and change their behavior through reflection and planning. *See also* Life space interview.

Life space interview (LSI)   Therapeutic way of talking with disturbed children about their behavior. A set of techniques for managing behavior by means of therapeutic communication.

Locus of control   Belief that one's behavior is under internal or external control. Individuals have an internal locus to the extent that they believe they are responsible for their actions, an external locus to the extent that they believe chance or others' actions determine their behavior.

Macroculture   A nation or other large social entity with a shared culture.

Mania   Excessive excitement or enthusiasm, usually centered on a particular activity or object.

Manic; manic episode   Persistently elevated, expansive, or irritable mood. Episode of such mood lasting at least 1 week.

Megavitamin therapy   Administration of extremely large doses of vitamins in the hope of improving or curing behavior disorders.

Metacognition; metacognitive   Thinking about thinking. Awareness and analysis of one's thought processes. Controlling one's cognitive processes.

Microculture   A smaller group existing within a larger cultural group and having unique values, style, language, dialect, ways of communicating nonverbally, awareness, frame of reference, and identification.

Minimal brain dysfunction; minimal brain damage   Term applied to children who exhibit behavioral characteristics (e.g., hyperactivity, distractibility) thought to be associated with brain damage, in the absence of other evidence that their brains have been damaged.

Minimal cerebral dysfunction   *See* Minimal brain dysfunction.

Modeling   Providing an example to imitate. Behavior modification technique in which a clear model of the desired behavior is provided. (Typically, reinforcement is given for imitation of the model.)

Mood disorders   Disorders of emotion that color outlook on life. Usually characterized by either elation or depression. May be episodic or chronic, manic or depressive.

Moral therapy; moral treatment   Treatment provided in the late 18th and early 19th centuries characterized by humane and kindly care, therapeutic activity, and consistent consequences for behavior.

Multiaxial assessment   A system used in the *DSM–IV* in which the client is rated on five axes: clinical disorders, personality disorders or mental retardation, general medical conditions, psychosocial and environmental problems, and global assessment of functioning.

Multiple intelligences   Highly specific types of problem-solving abilities (e.g., analytical, synthetic, and practical abilities) or intelligence in specific areas (e.g., linguistic, musical, spatial, interpersonal, intrapersonal, bodily–kinesthetic, or logical–mathematical). The theory that persons do not have a general intelligence but specific intelligences in various areas of performance.

Negative reinforcement   Withdrawal or postponement of a negative reinforcer (aversive event or stimulus) contingent upon a behavior, which increases the probability that the behavior will be repeated.

Neologism   A coined word that is meaningless to others. A meaningless word in the speech of a person with a psychotic disorder or a pervasive developmental disorder.

Neuroleptics   Antipsychotic drugs. Drugs that suppress or prevent symptoms of psychosis. Major tranquilizers.

Neurosis; neurotic behavior   Emotional or behavioral disorder characterized by emotional conflict but not loss of contact with reality.

Normative   Based on a norm, a sample assumed to provide a normal distribution of scores. Based on comparison to a statistical average for a representative sample of individuals.

Operant conditioning   Changing behavior by altering its consequences. Altering the future probability of a response by providing reinforcement or punishment as a consequence.

Oppositional defiant disorder (ODD)   A pattern of negativistic, hostile, and defiant behavior that is unusual for the individual's age and developmental level, lasting at least 6 months and often characterized by fits of temper, arguing with adults, refusing to comply with adults' requests or rules, and deliberately annoying others and resulting in significant impairment of social, academic, or occupational functioning.

Organic brain syndrome; organic psychosis   Disorder caused by brain damage.

Organic mental disorders   Disorders caused by transient or permanent brain dysfunction, often resulting from *anoxia,* ingestion of drugs or other toxic substances, or injury to brain tissue.

Organicity   Behavioral indications of brain damage or organic defects.

Orthomolecular therapy   Administration of chemical substances, vitamins, or drugs on the assumption that they will correct a basic chemical or molecular error that causes emotional or behavioral disorders.

Overcorrection   Set of procedures designed to overcorrect behavioral errors. May be *positive practice* overcorrection (requiring the individual to practice a more adaptive or appropriate form of behavior) or *restitution*

overcorrection (requiring the individual to restore the environment to a condition better than its status before the misbehavior occurred).

Overselective attention   *See* Selective attention.

Parasuicide   Attempted suicide.

Permissive approach to education   Allowing children to behave as they wish within broad or loosely defined limits, on the assumption that it is therapeutic to allow them to act out their feelings (unless they endanger someone) and that the teacher must be permissive to build a sound relationship with children. Derived mostly from psychoanalytic theory.

Personal agency   The assumption, based on social learning theory, that a person is self-conscious and can make predictions and choices.

Person variables   Thoughts, feelings, and perceptions. Private events or states.

Personality disorders   Deeply ingrained, inflexible, maladaptive patterns of relating to, perceiving, and thinking about the environment and oneself that impair adaptive functioning or cause subject distress.

Personality problem   Disorder characterized by neurotic behavior, depression, and withdrawal.

Pervasive developmental disorder   Distortion of or lag in all or most areas of development, as in autism. *See also* Rett's disorder; Asperger's disorder; Childhood disintegrative disorder.

Phenomenological model   Assumptions that emotional or behavioral disorders result primarily from inadequate or distorted conscious experience with life events and that the most effective preventive actions and therapeutic interventions involve helping individuals examine their conscious experience of the world.

Phobia   Irrational and debilitating fear.

Pica   Persistent eating of nonnutritional substances (e.g., paint, plaster, cloth).

Play therapy   Therapeutic treatment in which the child's play is used as the theme for communication between therapist and child.

Positive practice   *See* Overcorrection.

Positive reinforcement   Presentation of a positive reinforcer (reward) contingent upon a behavior, which increases the probability that the behavior will be repeated.

Postencephalitic behavior syndrome   Abnormal behavior following encephalitis (inflammation of the brain).

Posttraumatic stress disorder (PSD)   Disorder in which after experiencing a highly traumatic event the individual persistently reexperiences the event, avoids stimuli associated with the event, becomes generally unresponsive, or has persistent symptoms of arousal (e.g., hypervigilant, irritable, difficulty concentrating, difficulty sleeping), resulting in significant impairment of everyday functioning.

Pragmatics   The practical use of language in social situations. The functional use rather the mechanics of language.

Precorrection   The strategy of anticipating and avoiding misbehavior by identifying and modifying the context in which it is likely to occur. Using proactive procedures to teach desired behavior rather than focusing on correction of misbehavior.

Premorbid; premorbid personality   Condition or personality characteristics predictive of later onset of illness or disorder.

Prevalence   The total number of individuals with a specific disorder in a given population (e.g., 2%).

Primary prevention   Procedures designed to keep a disorder (or disease) from occurring.

Primary process thinking   Psychoanalytic concept that disorganized or primitive thought or activity represents direct expression of unconscious mental processes. Distinguished from *secondary process* (rational, logical) thinking.

Prosocial behavior   Behavior that facilitates or maintains positive social contacts. Desirable or appropriate social behavior.

Pseudoretardation   Level of functioning associated with mental retardation that increases to normal level of functioning when environmental factors are changed. Falsely diagnosed mental retardation.

Psychoactive substance use disorders   Disorders involving abuse of mood-altering substances (e.g., alcohol or other drugs).

Psychoanalytic model   Assumptions that emotional or behavioral disorders result primarily from unconscious conflicts and that the most effective preventive actions and therapeutic interventions involve uncovering and understanding unconscious motivations.

Psychodynamic model   *See* Psychoanalytic model.

Psychoeducational model   Approach to education that takes into account psychodynamic concepts such as unconscious motivation but focuses intervention on the ego processes by which the child gains insight into his or her behavior.

Psychoneurosis; psychoneurotic   *See* Neurosis.

Psychopath; psychopathic   An individual who exhibits mostly amoral or antisocial behavior and is usually impulsive, irresponsible, and self-gratifying without consideration for others. Also called *sociopath* or *sociopathic*.

Psychopathology   Mental illness. In psychiatry, the study of significant causes and development of mental illness. More generally, emotional or behavioral disorder.

Psychophysiological   Physical disorder thought to be caused by psychological (emotional) conflict.

Psychosexual disorder   Disorders involving sexual functioning or sex-typed behavior.

Psychosis   A major mental illness in which thought processes are disordered (e.g., schizophrenia).

Psychosomatic; psychosomaticization   *See* Psychophysiological.

Psychotherapy   Any type of treatment relying primarily on verbal and nonverbal communication between patient and therapist rather than on medical procedures. Not typically defined to include behavior modification. Typically administered by a psychiatrist or a clinical psychologist.

Psychotic disorder; psychotic behavior   Emotional or behavioral disorder characterized by major departure from normal patterns of acting, thinking, and feeling (e.g., schizophrenia). *See also* Schizophrenic disorder, Substance-induced psychotic disorder.

Punishment   Consequences that reduce future probability of a behavior. May be *response cost* (removal of a valued object or commodity) or *aversive conditioning* (presentation of an aversive stimulus such as a slap or an electric shock).

Rave   Dance party frequented by adolescents and young adults, generally involving "techno-dance music" and abuse of the drug Ecstasy and other controlled substances.

Reactive attachment disorder of infancy or early childhood   Markedly disturbed and developmentally inappropriate social behavior beginning before age 5 and assumed to be caused by neglect of the child's basic emotional and physical needs or by repeated changes in primary caregiver (e.g., frequent changes in foster placement).

Reactive depression   Depression apparently precipitated by a specific event. Depression that is a reaction to adverse circumstances.

Reactive disorders   Emotional or behavioral disorders apparently caused by reaction to stressful circumstances.

Reciprocal inhibition   *See* Desensitization.

Reinforcement   Presenting or removing stimuli following a behavior to increase its future probability. *Positive reinforcement* refers to presenting positive stimuli (rewards). *Negative reinforcement* refers to removing negative stimuli (punishers) contingent on a response. Both positive and negative reinforcement increase the rate or strength of the response.

Respondent behavior   An elicited response. Reflexive behavior elicited automatically by presenting a stimulus (e.g., pupillary contraction elicited by shining a light in the eye).

Respondent conditioning   Process by which a previously neutral stimulus comes to elicit a respondent behavior after the neutral stimulus has been paired with presentation of another stimulus (an unconditioned stimulus that already elicits a response) on one or more trials.

Response cost   Punishment technique consisting of taking away a valued object or commodity contingent on a behavior. A fine. Making an inappropriate response "cost" something to the misbehaving child.

Response topography   The particular movements that comprise a response. How the response looks to an observer as opposed to the effect of the response on the environment.

Restitution   *See* Overcorrection.

Rett's disorder   Apparently normal development through at least age 5 months, followed by deceleration of head growth between ages 5 months and 48 months, loss of psychomotor skills, and severe impairment of expressive and receptive language. Usually associated with severe mental retardation.

Risk   The chance or probability that a specified outcome or set of outcomes will occur. A risk factor is an event or condition increasing the probability of a specified outcome.

Rumination; mercyism   Regurgitation with loss of weight or failure to thrive.

Schizoaffective disorder   An episode of mood disorder concurrent with schizophrenia.

Schizoid; schizophrenic spectrum behavior   *See* Schizophreniform disorder.

Schizophrenia   *See* Schizophrenic disorder.

Schizophrenic disorder   Psychotic disorder characterized by distortion of thinking, abnormal perception, and bizarre behavior and emotions lasting at least 6 months.

Schizophreniform disorder   Behavior like that seen in schizophrenia but not as long in duration or accompanied by decline in functioning. *See also* Schizophrenic disorder.

Schizophrenogenic   Someone (in psychoanalytic theory, typically the mother) or something that causes schizophrenia.

School phobia   Fear of going to school, usually accompanied by indications of anxiety about attendance, such as abdominal pain, nausea, or other physical complaints just before leaving for school in the morning.

Secondary prevention   Procedures implemented soon after a disorder (or disease) has been detected. Designed to reverse or correct a disorder or prevent it from becoming worse.

Selective attention   Ability to direct and sustain one's attention to the appropriate and relevant stimuli in a given situation. Disorders of selective attention include *underselective attention* (inability to focus attention only on relevant stimuli or to disregard irrelevant stimuli) and *overselective attention* (inability to attend to all the relevant stimuli or tendency to focus on an irrelevant stimulus).

Selective mutism   Consistent failure to speak in specific social circumstances in which speaking is expected, such as school (and in spite of speaking in other situations, e.g., home) but not due to lack of knowledge of or ability to use language.

Self-instruction   Telling oneself what to do or how to perform. Technique for teaching children self-control or how to improve their performance by talking to themselves about what they are doing.

Self-stimulation   Any repetitive, stereotyped activity that seems only to provide sensory feedback.

Sensitization approach   Use of harsh punishment, threats, and overpowering force in discipline, especially in teaching or enforcing moral standards.

Separation anxiety disorder   Developmentally inappropriate and excessive anxiety about separation from home or those to whom the individual is attached lasting at least 4 weeks, beginning before age 18, and causing significant distress or impairment of social or academic functioning.

Sequela   Something that follows. A consequence. The lingering effect of an injury or disease (pl. *sequelae*).

Social-cognitive theory   *See* Social learning theory.

Social learning theory   Assumptions that antecedent or setting events (e.g., models, instructions), consequences (rewards and punishments), and cognitive processes (perceiving, thinking, feeling) influence behavior. Includes features of behavioral model or behavior modification with additional consideration of cognitive factors.

Social validity   The acceptability and significance of a treatment procedure as judged by parents or other consumers.

Socialized delinquency; Subcultural delinquency   Delinquent behavior in the context of an antisocial peer group.

Sociological model   Approximate equivalent of *ecological model*.

Sociopath; sociopathic   *See* Psychopath.

Soft neurological signs   Behavioral indications, such as uncoordination, distractibility, impulsivity, perceptual problems, and certain patterns of nerve reflexes, that may occur in individuals who are not brain damaged as well as in those who are. Signs that an individual may be brain damaged but that cannot be said to indicate the certainty of brain damage.

Somatic   Physical. Of or relating to the body.

Somatoform disorders   Physical symptoms suggesting a physical disorder, in the absence of demonstrable organic findings to explain the symptoms.

Status offense   An act that is illegal only if committed by a minor (e.g., buying or drinking alcohol).

Stereotype   A simplified, standardized concept or image with particular meaning in describing a group. A routine or persistently repeated behavior.

Stereotypic behavior   Persistent repetition of speech or motor activity.

Stereotypic movement disorder   Repetitive, seemingly driven, nonfunctional motor behavior that markedly interferes with normal activities or results in self-inflicted injury requiring medical treatment.

Stereotypy   A persistent, repetitive behavior or vocalization associated with self-stimulation, self-injury, or tic.

Strauss syndrome   Group of emotional and behavioral characteristics, including hyperactivity, distractibility, impulsivity, perceptual disturbances, no family history of mental retardation, and medical history suggestive of brain damage. Named after Alfred A. Strauss.

Structured approach to education   Making the classroom environment highly predictable by providing clear directions for behavior, firm expectations that students will behave as directed, and consistent consequences for behavior. Assumes that children lack order and predictability in everyday life and will learn self-control in a highly structured (predictable) environment. Derives primarily from learning theory.

Substance-induced psychotic disorder   Delusions or hallucinations caused by intoxication with or withdrawal from drugs or other substances.

Systematic desensitization   *See* Desensitization.

Target assessment   Definition and direct measurement (counting) of behaviors that are considered to be a problem (as opposed to administering psychological tests designed to measure behavioral traits or mental characteristics).

Temperament   Inborn emotional or behavioral style, including general level of activity, regularity or predictability, approach or withdrawal, adaptability, intensity of reaction, responsiveness, mood, distractibility, and persistence.

Tertiary prevention   Procedures designed to keep a severe or chronic disorder (or disease) from causing complications or overwhelming the individual or others.

Therapeutic milieu   Total treatment setting that is therapeutic. Environment that includes attention to therapeutic value of both physical and social surroundings.

Tic   Sudden, rapid, recurrent, nonrhythmic, stereotyped movement or vocalization.

Tic disorder   Stereotyped movement disorder in which there is disregulation of gross motor movement. Recurrent, involuntary, repetitive, rapid, purposeless movement. May be transient or chronic.

Time out   Technically, time out from positive reinforcement. Interval during which reinforcement (rewards) cannot be earned. In classroom practice, usually a brief period of social isolation during which the child cannot receive attention or earn rewards.

Token economy; token reinforcement; token system   System of behavior modification in which tangible or token reinforcers, such as points, plastic chips, metal washers, poker chips, or play money, are given as rewards and later exchanged for backup reinforcers that have value in themselves (e.g., food, trinkets, play time, books). A miniature economic system used to foster desirable behavior.

Topography   *See* Response topography.

Tourette's disorder   Multiple motor and vocal tics occurring many times daily (not necessarily together), with onset before age 18 and causing marked distress or significant impairment of social or occupational functioning.

Tourette's syndrome (TS)   *See* Tourette's disorder.

Transactions   Exchanges.

Transference   Unconscious redirection of feelings toward a different person (e.g., responding to teacher as if to parent). In psychoanalytic theory, responding to the therapist as if to another person, usually a parent.

Traumatic brain injury   Injury to the brain caused by an external force, not caused by a degenerative or congenital condition, and resulting in a diminished or altered state of consciousness and neurological or neurobehavioral dysfunction.

Traumatic head injury   *See* Traumatic brain injury.

Triadic reciprocality   The mutual influences of environment, person variables (thoughts, feelings), and behavior in social development.

Underselective attention   *See* Selective attention.

Unipolar   In psychology, feelings characterized by mood swings in one direction (e.g., swings from normal feelings to feelings of depression without swings to manic behavior or feelings of euphoria).

Unsocialized aggression   Unbridled aggressive behavior characterized by hostility, impulsivity, and alienation.

Vicarious extinction   Extinction of a fear response by watching someone else engage in an anxiety-provoking activity without apparent fear. Loss of fear (or other response) by observing others' behavior.

Vicarious reinforcement   Reinforcement obtained by watching someone else obtain reinforcers (rewards) for a particular response.

▶▶ REFERENCES

Abidin, R. R., & Robinson, L. L. (2002). Stress, biases, or professionalism: What drives teachers' referral judgments of students with challenging behaviors? *Journal of Emotional and Behavioral Disorders, 10,* 204–212.

Abrams, L. A. (1995). Strengthening the fabric of child and family policies: Interweaving the threads of research. In D. Baumrind (Ed.), *Child maltreatment and optimal caregiving in social contexts* (pp. 101–116). New York: Garland.

Achenbach, T. M. (1975). The historical context of treatment for delinquent and maladjusted children: Past, present, and future. *Behavioral Disorders, 1*(1), 3–14.

Achenbach, T. M. (1982). Assessment and taxonomy of children's behavior disorders. In B. B. Lahey & A. E. Kazdin (Eds.), *Advances in clinical child psychology* (Vol. 5, pp. 2–38). New York: Plenum.

Achenbach, T. M. (1985). *Assessment and taxonomy of child and adolescent psychopathology.* Beverly Hills, CA: Sage.

Achenbach, T. M. (1991). *Manual for the Child Behavior Checklist/4–18 and 1991 profile.* Burlington: University of Vermont, Department of Psychiatry.

Achenbach, T. M., & Edelbrock, C. S. (1981). Behavior problems and competencies reported by parents of normal and disturbed children aged four through sixteen. *Monographs of the Society for Research in Child Development, 46*(1, Serial No. 188).

Achenbach, T. M., & Edelbrock, C. S. (1989). Diagnostic, taxonomic, and assessment issues. In T. H. Ollendick & M. Hersen (Eds.), *Handbook of child psychopathology* (2nd ed., pp. 53–69). New York: Plenum.

Achenbach, T. M., & Edelbrock, C. S. (1991). *Child behavior checklist—Teacher's report.* Burlington, VT: University Associates in Psychiatry.

Achenbach, T. M., Howell, C. T., Quay, H. C., & Conners, C. K. (1991). National survey of problems and competencies among four- to sixteen-year-olds. *Monographs of the Society for Research in Child Development, 56*(3, Serial No. 225).

Ackerson, L. (1942). *Children's behavior problems.* Chicago: University of Chicago Press.

Adamczyk-Robinette, S. L., Fletcher, A. C., & Wright, K. (2002). Understanding the authoritative parenting–early adolescent tobacco use link: The mediating role of peer tobacco use. *Journal of Youth and Adolescence, 31,* 311–318.

Adams, P. J., Katz, R. C., Beauchamp, K., Cohen, E., & Zavis, D. (1993). Body dissatisfaction, eating disorders, and depression: A developmental perspective. *Journal of Child and Family Studies, 2,* 37–46.

Alaghband-Rad, J., McKenna, K., Gordon, C. T., Albus, K., Hamburger, S. D., Rumsey, et al. (1995). Childhood-onset schizophrenia: The severity of premorbid course. *Journal of the American Academy of Child and Adolescent Psychiatry, 34,* 1273–1283.

Albano, A. M., Chorpita, B. F., & Barlow, D. H. (2003). Childhood anxiety disorders. In E. J. Mash & R. A. Barkley (Eds.), *Child psychopathology* (2nd ed., pp. 279–329). New York: Guilford.

Alberto, P., & Troutman, A. (2003). *Applied behavior analysis for teachers* (6th ed.). Upper Saddle River, NJ: Merrill/Prentice Hall.

Allison, M. (1992). The effects of neurologic injury on the maturing brain. *Headlines, 3*(5), 2–10.

American Educational Research Association, American Psychological Association, & National Council on Measurement in Education. (1985). *Standards for educational and psychological testing.* Washington, DC: Authors.

American Psychiatric Association. (1994). *Diagnostic and statistical manual of mental disorders* (4th ed.). Washington, DC: Author.

American Psychiatric Association. (2000). *Diagnostic and statistical manual of mental disorders.* (4th text rev. ed.). Washington, DC: American Psychiatric Publishing.

American Psychological Association. (1993). *Violence and youth: Psychology's response: Vol. 1. Summary report of the American Psychological Association Commission on Violence and Youth.* Washington, DC: Author.

Anderson, J., & Werry, J. S. (1994). Emotional and behavioral problems. In I. B. Pless (Ed.), *The epidemiology of childhood disorders* (pp. 304–338). New York: Oxford University Press.

Anderson, J. C. (1994). Epidemiological issues. In T. H. Ollendick, N. J. King, & W. Yule (Eds.), *International handbook of phobic and anxiety disorders in children and adolescents* (pp. 43–65). New York: Plenum.

Anderson, M. G., & Webb-Johnson, G. (1995). Cultural contexts, the seriously emotionally disturbed classification, and African American learners. In B. A. Ford, F. E. Obiakor, & J. M. Patton (Eds.), *Effective education of African American exceptional learners: New perspectives* (pp. 151–187). Austin, TX: Pro-Ed.

Anonymous. (1994). First person account: Schizophrenia with childhood onset. *Schizophrenia Bulletin, 20,* 587–590.

Araji, S. K. (1997). *Sexually aggressive children: Coming to understand them.* Thousand Oaks, CA: Sage.

Arbelle, S., Sigman, M. D., & Kasari, G. (1994). Compliance with parental prohibition in autistic children. *Journal of Autism and Developmental Disorders, 24,* 693–702.

Armstrong, M. I., & Evans, M. E. (1992). Three intensive community-based programs for children and youth with serious emotional disturbance and their families. *Journal of Child and Family Studies, 1,* 61–74.

Armstrong, S. W., & Kauffman, J. M. (1999). Functional behavioral assessment: Introduction to the series. *Behavioral Disorders, 24,* 167–168.

Arnold, W. R., & Brungardt, T. M. (1983). *Juvenile misconduct and delinquency.* Boston: Houghton Mifflin.

Arthur, M. W., Hawkins, D. J., Pollard, J. A., Catalano, R. F., & Baglioni, A. J. (2002). Measuring risk and protective factors for substance use, delinquency, and other adolescent problem behaviors: The Communities That Care Youth Survey. *Evaluation Review, 26,* 575–601.

Asarnow, J. R., & Asarnow, R. F. (2003). Childhood-onset schizophrenia. In E. J. Mash & R. A. Barkley (Eds.), *Child psychopathology* (2nd ed., pp. 455–485). New York: Guilford.

Asarnow, J. R., Thompson, M. C., & Goldstein, M. J. (1994). Childhood-onset schizophrenia: A follow-up study. *Schizophrenia Bulletin, 20,* 599–617.

Asarnow, R. F., Asamen, J., Granholm, E., Sherman, T., Watkins, J. M., & Williams, M. E. (1994). Cognitive/neuropsychological studies of children with schizophrenic disorders. *Schizophrenia Bulletin, 20,* 647–669.

Asarnow, R. F., & Asarnow, J. R. (1994). Childhood-onset schizophrenia: Editors' introduction. *Schizophrenia Bulletin, 20,* 591–597.

Azar, S. T., & Wolfe, D. A. (1998). Child physical abuse and neglect. In E. J. Mash & R. A. Barkley (Eds.), *Treatment of childhood disorders* (2nd ed., pp. 501–544). New York: Guilford.

Baer, J. S., MacLean, M. G., & Marlatt, G. A. (1998). Linking etiology and treatment for adolescent substance abuse: Toward a better match. In R. Jessor (Ed.), *New perspectives on adolescent risk behavior* (pp. 182–220). New York: Cambridge University Press.

Baker, E. M., & Stullken, E. H. (1938). American research studies concerning the "behavior" type of exceptional child. *Journal of Exceptional Children, 4,* 36–45.

Baker, H. J. (1934). Common problems in the education of the normal and the handicapped. *Exceptional Children, 1,* 39–40.

Baker, P. (1996, January 16). Virginia joins movement to get tough on violent youths. *The Washington Post,* pp. B1, B4.

Bandura, A. (1977). *Social learning theory.* Upper Saddle River, NJ: Prentice Hall.

Bandura, A. (1978). The self-system in reciprocal determinism. *American Psychologist, 33,* 344–358.

Bandura, A. (1986). *Social foundations of thought and action: A social cognitive theory.* Upper Saddle River, NJ: Prentice Hall.

Bandura, A. (1995a). Comments on the crusade against the causal efficacy of human thought. *Journal of Behavior Therapy and Experimental Psychiatry, 26,* 179–190.

Bandura, A. (1995b). Exercise of personal and collective efficacy in changing societies. In A. Bandura (Ed.), *Self-efficacy in changing societies* (pp. 1–45). New York: Cambridge University Press.

Bandura A., & Locke, E. A. (2003). Negative self-efficacy and goal effects revisited. *Journal of Applied Psychology, 88,* 87–99.

Banks, J. A. (1995). The historical reconstruction of knowledge about race: Implications for transformative teaching. *Educational Researcher, 24*(2), 15–25.

Banks, J. A. (1997). *Teaching strategies for ethnic studies* (6th ed.). Boston: Allyn & Bacon.

Banks, J. A., & Banks, C. A. (Eds.). (1997). *Multicultural education: Issues and perspectives* (3rd ed.). Boston: Allyn & Bacon.

Barkley, R. A. (Ed.). (1998). *Attention-deficit hyperactivity disorder: A handbook for diagnosis and treatment* (2nd ed.). New York: Guilford.

Barkley, R. A. (2000). *Taking charge of ADHD: The complete, authoritative guide for parents* (Rev. ed.). New York: Guilford.

Barkley, R. A. (2003). Attention-deficit/hyperactivity disorder. In E. J. Mash & R. A. Barkley (Eds.), *Child psychopathology* (2nd ed., pp. 75–143). New York: Guilford.

Barlow, Z. (2003, July 19). When gangs come to town: Small towns like Staunton are "virgin territory." *The Roanoke Times,* pp. A1, A6, A7.

Baroncohen, S., Campbell, R., Karmiloff-Smith, A., Grant, J., & Walker, J. (1995). Are children with autism blind to the mentalistic significance of the eyes? *British Journal of Developmental Psychology, 13,* 379–398.

Barrett, R. P. (Ed.). (1986). *Severe behavior disorders in the mentally retarded.* New York: Plenum.

Barrios, B. A. (1993). Direct observation. In T. H. Ollendick & M. Hersen (Eds.), *Handbook of child and adolescent assessment* (pp. 140–164). New York: Pergamon.

Barrios, B. A., & O'Dell, S. L. (1998). Fears and anxieties. In E. J. Mash & R. A. Barkley (Eds.), *Treatment of childhood disorders* (2nd ed., pp. 249–337). New York: Guilford.

Bateman, B. D. (1992). Learning disabilities: The changing landscape. *Journal of Learning Disabilities, 25,* 29–36.

Bateman, B. D. (1994). Who, how, and where: Special education's issues in perpetuity. *Journal of Special Education, 27,* 509–520.

Bateman, B. D. (2004). *Elements of successful teaching: General and special education students*. Verona, WI: IEP Resources.

Bateman, B. D., & Chard, D. J. (1995). Legal demands and constraints on placement decisions. In J. M. Kauffman, J. W. Lloyd, D. P. Hallahan, & T. A. Astuto (Eds.), *Issues in educational placement: Students with emotional and behavioral disorders* (pp. 285–316). Hillsdale, NJ: Erlbaum.

Bateman, B. D., & Linden, M. A. (1998). *Better IEPs: How to develop legally correct and educationally useful programs* (3rd ed.). Longmont, CO: Sopris West.

Bates, J. E., & Wachs, T. D. (Eds.). (1994). *Temperament: Individual differences at the interface of biology and behavior*. Washington, DC: American Psychological Association.

Baumeister, R. F., Campbell, J. D., Krueger, J. I., & Vohs, K. D. (2003). Does high self-esteem cause better performance, interpersonal success, happiness, or healthier lifestyles? *Psychological Science in the Public Interest, 4*(1), 1–44.

Baumgartner, T. A., & Jackson, A. S. (1991). *Measurement for evaluation in physical education and exercise science*. Dubuque, IA: Brown.

Baumrind, D. (1995). *Child maltreatment and optimal caregiving in social contexts*. New York: Garland.

Baumrind, D. (1996). The discipline controversy revisited. *Journal of Applied Family and Child Studies, 45*, 405–414.

Baumrind, D. (1997). Necessary distinctions. *Psychological Inquiry, 8*, 176–182.

Bazemore, S. G., & Umbreit, M. (1995). Rethinking the sanctioning function of juvenile court: Retributive or restorative responses to youth crime. *Crime and Delinquency, 41*, 296–316.

Bear, G. G. (1998). School discipline in the United States: Prevention, correction, and long-term social development. *School Psychology Review, 27*, 14–32.

Beardslee, W. R., Versage, E. M., Van de Velde, P., Swatling, S., & Hoke, L. (2002). Preventing depression in children through resiliency promotion: The preventive intervention project. In R. J. McMahon & R. D. Peters (Eds.), *The effects of parental dysfunction on children* (pp. 71–86). New York: Kluwer.

Beck, S. J. (1995). Behavioral assessment. In M. Hersen & R. T. Ammerman (Eds.), *Advanced abnormal child psychology* (pp. 157–170). Hillsdale, NJ: Erlbaum.

Becker, J. V., & Bonner, B. (1998). Sexual and other abuse of children. In R. J. Morris & T. R. Kratochwill (Eds.), *The practice of child therapy* (3rd ed., pp. 367–389). Boston: Allyn & Bacon.

Becker, W. C. (1964). Consequences of different kinds of parental discipline. In M. L. Hoffman & L. W. Hoffman (Eds.), *Review of child development research* (Vol. 1, pp. 169–208). New York: Russell Sage Foundation.

Beer, D. A., Karitani, M., Leonard, H. L., March, J. S., & Sweda, S. E. (2002). Obsessive-compulsive disorder. In S. Kutcher (Ed.), *Practical child and adolescent psychopharmacology* (pp. 159–186). New York: Cambridge University Press.

Begali, V. (1992). *Head injury in children and adolescents* (2nd ed.). Brandon, VT: Clinical Psychology.

Beidel, D. C., & Turner, S. M. (1998). *Shy children, phobic adults: Nature and treatment of social phobia*. Washington, DC: American Psychological Association.

Belcher, T. L. (1995). Behavioral treatment vs. behavioral control: A case study. *Journal of Developmental and Physical Disabilities, 7*, 235–241.

Bell, R. Q. (1968). A reinterpretation of the direction of effects in studies of socialization. *Psychological Review, 75*, 81–95.

Bell, R. Q., & Harper, L. V. (1977). *Child effects on adults*. Hillsdale, NJ: Erlbaum.

Bender, R. (1993). What makes a pull-out program work? *Effective School Practices, 12*(1), 16–19.

Benson, M. D., & Torpy, E. J. (1995). Sexual behavior in junior-high-school students. *Obstetrics and Gynecology, 85*, 279–284.

Bergland, M., & Hoffbauer, D. (1996). New opportunities for students with traumatic brain injuries. *Teaching Exceptional Children, 28*(2), 54–56.

Bergman, R. L., Piacentini, J., & McCracken, J. T. (2002). Prevalence and description of selective mutism in a school-based sample. *Journal of the American Academy of Child and Adolescent Psychiatry, 41*, 938–946.

Berry, C. S. (1936). The exceptional child in regular classes. *Exceptional Children, 3*, 15–16.

Bettelheim, B. (1967). *The empty fortress*. New York: Free Press.

Beyers, J. M., & Loeber, R. (2003). Untangling developmental relations between depressed mood in male adolescents. *Journal of Abnormal Child Psychology, 31*, 247–266.

Beyth-Marom, R., Lichtenstein, S., & Marom, B. (1985). *An elementary approach to thinking under uncertainty*. Hillsdale, NJ: Lawrence Erlbaum Associates.

Bicard, D. F., & Neef, N. A. (2002). Effects of strategic versus tactical instructions on adaptation to changing contingencies in children with ADHD. *Journal of Applied Behavior Analysis, 35*, 375–389.

Bickman, L., Heflinger, C. A., Lambert, E. W., & Summerfelt, W. T. (1996). The Fort Bragg managed care experiment: Short term impact on psychopathology. *Journal of Child and Family Studies, 5*, 137–160.

Bielinski, J. (2001). Overview of test accommodations. *Assessment for Effective Intervention, 26*(2), 17–20.

Bierman, K. L., Coie, J. D., Dodge, K. A., Greenberg, M. T., Lochman, J. E., McMahon, R. J., et al. (2002). Using the Fast Track randomized prevention trial to test the early-starter model of the development of serious conduct problems. *Development and Psychopathology, 14,* 925–943.

Biglan, A. (1995). Translating what we know about the context of antisocial behavior into lower prevalence of such behavior. *Journal of Applied Behavior Analysis, 28,* 479–492.

Biklen, D. (1990). Communication unbound: Autism and praxis. *Harvard Educational Review, 60,* 291–314.

Biklen, D., & Schubert, A. (1991). New words: The communication of students with autism. *Remedial and Special Education, 12*(6), 46–57.

Black, B., & Uhde, T. W. (1995). Psychiatric characteristics of children with selective mutism. *Journal of the Academy of Child and Adolescent Psychiatry, 34,* 847–856.

Blackburn, R. (1993). *The psychology of criminal conduct: Theory, research, and practice.* New York: Wiley.

Blair, R. J. (1992). Application of the life-impact curriculum. *Journal of Emotional and Behavioral Problems, 1*(2), 16–21.

Blake, C., Wang, W., Cartledge, G., & Gardner, R. (2000). Middle school students with serious emotional disturbances serve as social skills trainers and reinforcers for peers with SED. *Behavioral Disorders, 25,* 280–298.

Blanton, S. (1925). The function of the mental hygiene clinic in schools and colleges. *New Republic, 122,* 93–101.

Bloomingdale, L., Swanson, J. M., Barkley, R. A., & Satterfield, J. (1991, March). *Response to the ADD notice of inquiry by the Professional Group for ADD and Related Disorders (PGARD).* Scarsdale, NY: PGARD.

Bockoven, J. S. (1956). Moral treatment in American psychiatry. *Journal of Nervous and Mental Disease, 124,* 167–194, 292–321.

Bockoven, J. S. (1972). *Moral treatment in community mental health.* New York: Springer.

Bolgar, R., Zweig-Frank, H., & Paris, J. (1995). Childhood antecedents of interpersonal problems in young adult children of divorce. *Journal of the American Academy of Child and Adolescent Psychiatry, 34,* 143–150.

Bolger, K. E., Patterson, C. J., & Kupersmidt, J. B. (1998). Peer relationships and self-esteem among children who have been maltreated. *Child Development, 69,* 1171–1197.

Bondy, A. S., & Frost, L. A. (1995). Educational approaches in preschool: Behavior techniques in a public school setting. In E. Schopler & G. B. Mesibov (Eds.), *Learning and cognition in autism* (pp. 311–333). New York: Plenum.

Boodman, S. G. (1995, June 13). Researchers study obesity in children. *Washington Post Health,* pp. 10, 13, 15.

Boodman, S. G. (2003, June 3). Whose voice? Schizophrenia Digest lets drug makers speak. *The Washington Post,* pp. F1, F4.

Bortner, M., & Birch, H. G. (1969). Patterns of intellectual ability in emotionally disturbed and brain-damaged children. *Journal of Special Education, 3,* 351–369.

Botvin, G. J., Schinke, S., & Orlandi, M. A. (1995). School-based health promotion: Substance abuse and sexual behavior. *Applied and Preventive Psychology, 4,* 167–184.

Bower, B. (1995). Criminal intellects: Researchers look at why lawbreakers often brandish low IQs. *Science News, 147,* 232–233, 239.

Bower, E. M. (1960). *Early identification of emotionally handicapped children in school.* Springfield, IL: Thomas.

Bower, E. M. (1981). *Early identification of emotionally handicapped children in school* (3rd ed.). Springfield, IL: Thomas.

Bower, E. M. (1982). Defining emotional disturbance: Public policy and research. *Psychology in the Schools, 19,* 55–60.

Bower, E. M., Shellhammer, T. A., & Daily, J. M. (1960). School characteristics of male adolescents who later became schizophrenic. *American Journal of Orthopsychiatry, 30,* 712–729.

Braden, J. P., & Kratochwill, T. R. (1997). Treatment utility of assessment: Myths and realities. *School Psychology Review, 26,* 475–485.

Brandenburg, N. A., Friedman, R. M., & Silver, S. E. (1990). The epidemiology of childhood psychiatric disorders: Prevalence findings from recent studies. *Journal of the American Academy of Child and Adolescent Psychiatry, 29,* 76–83.

Brannan, P. A., Hall, J., Bor, W., Najman, J. M., & Williams, G. (2003). Integrating biological and social processes in relation to early-onset persistent aggression in boys and girls. *Developmental Psychology, 39,* 309–323.

Braswell, L., & Bloomquist, M. L. (1991). *Cognitive-behavioral therapy with ADHD children: Child, family, and school interventions.* New York: Guilford.

Bremner, R. H. (Ed.). (1970). *Children and youth in America: A documentary history: Vol. 1. 1600–1865.* Cambridge, MA: Harvard University Press.

Bremner, R. H. (Ed.). (1971). *Children and youth in America: A documentary history: Vol. 2. 1866–1932.* Cambridge, MA: Harvard University Press.

Brigham, F. J., & Cole, J. E. (1999). Selective mutism: Developments in definition, etiology, assessment and treatment. In T. Scruggs & M. Mastropieri (Eds.), *Advances in learning and behavioral disabilities* (Vol. 13, pp. 183–216). Greenwich, CT: JAI.

Brigham, F. J., & Kauffman, J. M. (1998). Creating supportive environments for students with emotional or behavioral disorders. *Effective School Practices, 17*(2), 5–35.

Brigham, F. J., Tochterman, S., & Brigham, M. S. P. (2000). Students with emotional and behavioral disorders and their teachers in test-linked systems of accountability. *Assessment for Effective Intervention, 26*(1), 19–27.

Brigham, F. J., Weiss, M., & Jones, C. D. (1998, April). *Synthesis of follow-along and outcome studies of students with mild disabilities.* Paper presented at the annual meeting of the Council for Exceptional Children, Minneapolis, MN.

Brigham, M. M., Brigham, F. J., & Lloyd, J. W. (2002, November). *Accommodations and assessment: Supporting, distracting or enabling?* Paper presented at the annual conference of Teacher Educators of Children with Behavior Disorders, Scottsdale, AZ.

Britt, D. (1999, October 1). Finding gold in differences of others. *The Washington Post*, pp. B1, B7.

Brook, J. S., Whiteman, M., Cohen, P., Shapiro, J., & Balka, E. (1995). Longitudinally predicting late adolescent and young adult drug use: Childhood and adolescent precursors. *Journal of the American Academy of Child and Adolescent Psychiatry, 34,* 1230–1238.

Brown, F. (1943). A practical program for early detection of atypical children. *Exceptional Children, 10,* 3–7.

Brown, J. L., & Pollitt, E. (1996). Malnutrition, poverty, and intellectual development. *Scientific American, 274*(2), 38–43.

Brown, L. L., & Hammill, D. D. (1990). *Behavior rating profile: An ecological approach to behavioral assessment* (rev. ed.). Austin, TX: Pro-Ed.

Brown, W. H., Musick, K., Conroy, M., & Schaffer, E. H. (2001). A proactive approach for promoting young children's compliance. *Beyond Behavior, 11*(20), 3–8.

Brown, W. H., Odom, S. L., & Buysse, V. (2002). Assessment of preschool children's peer-related social competence. *Assessment for Effective Intervention, 27*(4), 61–71.

Bryant, E. S., Rivard, J. C., Addy, C. L., Hinkle, K. T., Cowan, T. M., & Wright, G. (1995). Correlates of major and minor offending among youth with severe emotional disturbance. *Journal of Emotional and Behavioral Disorders, 3,* 76–84.

Buitelaar, J. K. (1995). Attachment and social withdrawal in autism—Hypotheses and findings. *Behaviour, 132,* 319–350.

Bukstein, O. G. (1995). *Adolescent substance abuse: Assessment, prevention, and treatment.* New York: Wiley.

Bullis, M., & Cheney, D. (1999). Vocational and transition interventions for adolescents and young adults with emotional or behavioral disorders. *Focus on Exceptional Children, 31*(7), 1–24.

Burbach, H. J. (1981). The labeling process: A sociological analysis. In J. M. Kauffman & D. P. Hallahan (Eds.), *Handbook of special education* (pp. 361–377). Upper Saddle River, NJ: Prentice Hall.

Burke, D. (1972). Countertheoretical interventions in emotional disturbance. In W. C. Rhodes & M. L. Tracy (Eds.), *A study of child variance: Vol. 2. Interventions* (pp. 573–657). Ann Arbor: University of Michigan.

Burke, J. D., Loeber, R., & Birmaher, B. (2002). Oppositional defiant disorder and conduct disorder: A review of the past 10 years, part II. *Journal of the Academy of Child and Adolescent Psychiatry, 41,* 1275–1293.

Burns, J. M., & Swerdlow, R. H. (2003). Right orbitofrontal tumor with pedophilia symptom and constructional apraxia sign. *Archives of Neurology, 60,* 437–440.

Burns, M. K., & Symington, T. (2002). A meta-analysis of prereferral intervention teams: Student and systemic outcomes. *Journal of School Psychology, 40*(5), 437–447.

Busch, T. W., & Espin, C. A. (2003). Using curriculum-based measurement to prevent learning and assess learning in content areas. *Assessment for Effective Intervention, 28*(3/4), 49–58.

Bush, E. G., & Pargament, K. I. (1995). A quantitative and qualitative analysis of suicidal preadolescent children and their families. *Child Psychiatry and Human Development, 25,* 241–252.

Butera, G., & Haywood, H. C. (1995). Cognitive education of young children with autism: An application of Bright Start. In E. Schopler & G. B. Mesibov (Eds.), *Learning and cognition in autism* (pp. 269–292). New York: Plenum.

Cameron, J., & Pierce, W. D. (1994). Reinforcement, reward, and intrinsic motivation: A meta-analysis. *Review of Educational Research, 64,* 363–423.

Campbell, S. B. (1983). Developmental perspectives in child psychopathology. In T. H. Ollendick & M. Hersen (Eds.), *Handbook of child psychopathology* (pp. 13–40). New York: Plenum.

Campbell, S. B. (1995). Behavior problems in preschool children: A review of recent research. *Journal of Child Psychology and Psychiatry, 36,* 113–149.

Campbell, S. B., Breaux, A. M., Ewing, L. J., & Szumowski, E. K. (1986). Correlates and predictors of hyperactivity and aggression: A longitudinal study of parent-referred problem preschoolers. *Journal of Abnormal Child Psychology, 14,* 217–234.

Caprara, G., Barbarnelli, C., Pastorelli, C., Bandura, A., & Zimbardo, P. (2000). Prosocial foundations of children's academic achievement. *Psychological Science, 11,* 302–326.

Caplan, N., Choy, M. H., & Whitmore, J. K. (1992, February). Indochinese refugee families and academic achievement. *Scientific American, 266*(2), 36–42.

Caplan, R. B. (1969). *Psychiatry and the community in nineteenth century America.* New York: Basic Books.

Carey, G., & Goldman, D. (1997). The genetics of antisocial behavior. In D. M. Stoff, J. Breiling, & J. D. Maser (Eds.), *Handbook of antisocial behavior* (pp. 243–254). New York: Wiley.

Carey, W. B. (1998). Temperament and behavior problems in the classroom. *School Psychology Review, 27,* 522–533.

Carey, W. B., & McDevitt, S. C. (1995). *Coping with children's temperament: A guide for professionals.* New York: Basic Books.

Carlberg, C., & Kavale, K. (1980). The efficacy of special versus regular class placement for exceptional children: A meta-analysis. *Journal of Special Education, 29,* 155–162.

Carlson, P. (2003, January 26). The psychotic bank robber: A schizophrenic teen takes desperate measures. His parents want help. The law wants prison. *The Washington Post,* pp. F1, F4–F5.

Carr, A. (2002). *Depression and attempted suicide in adolescence.* Malden, MA: BPS Blackwell.

Cartledge, G., Kea, C. D., & Ida, D. J. (2000). Anticipating differences—celebrating strengths: Providing culturally competent services for students with serious emotional disturbance. *Teaching Exceptional Children, 32*(3), 30–37.

Cartledge, G., & Milburn, J. F. (Eds.). (1995). *Teaching social skills to children: Innovative approaches* (3rd ed.). Boston: Allyn & Bacon.

Caspi, A., Henry, B., McGee, R. O., Moffitt, T. E., & Silva, P. A. (1995). Temperamental origins of child and adolescent behavior problems: From age three to age fifteen. *Child Development, 66,* 55–68.

Center, D. B., Deitz, S. M., & Kaufman, M. E. (1982). Student ability, task difficulty, and inappropriate classroom behavior: A study of children with behavior disorders. *Behavior Modification, 6,* 355–374.

Center, D. B., & Kemp, D. (2003). Temperament and personality as potential factors in the development and treatment of conduct disorders. *Education and Treatment of Children, 26,* 75–88.

Chang, J. J., Chen, J. J., & Brownson, R. C. (2003). The role of repeat victimization in adolescent delinquent behaviors and recidivism. *Journal of Adolescent Health, 32,* 272–280.

Chang, V. Y., Bendel, T. L., Koopman, C. McGarvey, E. L., & Canterbury, R. J. (2003). Delinquents' safe sex attitudes. *Criminal Justice and Behavior, 30,* 210–229.

Charlop, M. H., Kurtz, P. F., & Casey, F. G. (1990). Using aberrant behaviors as reinforcers for autistic children. *Journal of Applied Behavior Analysis, 23,* 163–181.

Charlop-Christy, M. H., & Kelso, S. E. (1999). Autism. In V. L. Schwean & D. H. Saklofske (Eds.), *Handbook of psychosocial characteristics of exceptional children* (pp. 247–273). New York: Plenum.

Charlop-Christy, M. H., Schreibman, L., Pierce, K., & Kurtz, P. F. (1997). Childhood autism. In R. J. Morris & T. R. Kratochwill (Eds.), *The practice of child therapy* (3rd ed., pp. 271–302). Boston: Allyn & Bacon.

Chassin, L., Ritter, J., Trim, R. S., & King, K. M. (2003). Adolescent substance use disorders. In E. J. Mash & R. A. Barkley (Eds.), *Child psychopathology* (2nd ed., pp. 199–230). New York: Guilford.

Chen, S. A., & True, R. H. (1994). Asian/Pacific Island Americans. In L. D. Eron, J. H. Gentry, & P. Schlegel (Eds.), *Reason to hope: A psychosocial perspective on violence and youth* (pp. 145–162). Washington, DC: American Psychological Association.

Cheney, D., & Bullis, M. (2004). Research findings and issues in the school-to-community transition of adolescents with emotional or behavioral disorders. In R. B. Rutherford, M. M. Quinn, & S. R. Mathur (Eds.), *Handbook of research in emotional and behavioral disorders.* New York: Guilford.

Chesapeake Institute. (1994, September). *National agenda for achieving better results for children and youth with serious emotional disturbance.* Washington, DC: Author.

Chess, S., & Thomas, A. T. (2003). Foreword. In B. K. Keogh, *Temperament in the classroom: Understanding individual differences* (pp. ix–xii). Baltimore: Brookes.

Chubb, J. E., Evers, W. M., Finn, C. E., Jr., Hanushek, E. A., Hill, P. T., Hirsch, E. D., Jr., et al. (2003). Our schools and our future: Are we still at risk? *Education Next, 3*(2), 9–15.

Cicchetti, D., & Toth, S. L. (1995). A developmental psychopathology perspective on child abuse and neglect. *Journal of the American Academy of Child and Adolescent Psychiatry, 34,* 541–565.

Cipani, E. (1999). *A functional analysis of behavior (FAB) model for school settings.* Visalia, CA: Cipani.

Cipani, E., & Spooner, F. (1997). Treating problem behaviors maintained by negative reinforcement. *Research in Developmental Disabilities, 18,* 329–342.

Clark, H. B., & Clarke, R. T. (1996). Research on the wraparound process and individualized services for children with multiple-system needs. *Journal of Child and Family Studies, 5,* 1–5.

Clark, H. B., Prange, M. E., Lee, B., Boyd, A., McDonald, B. A., & Stewart, E. S. (1994). Improving adjustment outcomes for foster children with emotional and behavioral disorders: Early findings from a controlled study of individualized services. *Journal of Emotional and Behavioral Disorders, 2,* 207–218.

Clark-Chiarelli, N., & Singer, J. D. (1995). Teachers of students with emotional or behavioral disorders: Who they are and how they view their jobs. In J. M. Kauffman, J. W. Lloyd, D. P. Hallahan, & T. A. Astuto (Eds.), *Issues in educational placement: Students with emotional and behavioral disorders* (pp. 145–168). Hillsdale, NJ: Erlbaum.

Clarke, R. T., Schaefer, M., Burchard, J. D., & Welkowitz, J. W. (1992). Wrapping community-based mental health services around children with a severe behavioral disorder: An evaluation of Project Wraparound. *Journal of Child and Family Studies, 1,* 241–261.

Clarke, S., Dunlap, G., Foster-Johnson, L., Childs, K. E., Wilson, D., White, R., et al. (1995). Improving the conduct of students with behavioral disorders by incorporating student interests into curricular activities. *Behavioral Disorders, 20,* 221–237.

Cline, D. H. (1990). A legal analysis of policy initiatives to exclude handicapped/disruptive students from special education. *Behavioral Disorders, 15,* 159–173.

Cluett, S. E., Forness, S. R., Ramey, S., Ramey, C., Hsu, C., Kavale, K. A., et al. (1998). Consequences of differential diagnostic criteria on identification rates of children with emotional or behavior disorders. *Journal of Emotional and Behavioral Disorders, 6,* 130–140.

Coffey, B. J., Miguel, E. C., Savage, C. R., & Rauch, S. L. (1994). Tourette's disorder and related problems: A review and update. *Harvard Review of Psychiatry, 2,* 121–132.

Coie, J. D. (1990). Toward a theory of peer rejection. In S. R. Asher & J. D. Coie (Eds.), *Peer rejection in childhood* (pp. 365–401). New York: Cambridge University Press.

Coie, J. D., Dodge, K. A., & Kupersmidt, J. (1990). Peer group behavior and social status. In S. R. Asher & J. D. Coie (Eds.), *Peer rejection in childhood* (pp. 17–59). New York: Cambridge University Press.

Coleman, J. M., McHam, L. A., & Minnett, A. M. (1992). Similarities in the social competencies of learning disabled and low-achieving elementary school children. *Journal of Learning Disabilities, 25,* 671–677.

Coleman, M., & Vaughn, S. (2000). Reading interventions for students with emotional/behavioral disorders. *Behavioral Disorders, 25,* 93–104.

Collins, F. (2003, April 22). A common thread. *The Washington Post,* p. A19.

Collins, F., Green, E. D., Guttmacher, A. E., & Guyer, E. S. (2003). A vision for the future of genomics research. *Nature, 422,* 835–847.

Colvin, G. (1992). *Managing acting-out behavior.* Video and workbooks. Eugene, OR: Behavior Associates.

Colvin, G., Greenberg, S., & Sherman, R. (1993). The forgotten variable: Improving academic skills for students with serious emotional disturbance. *Effective School Practices, 12*(1), 20–25.

Colvin, G., Sugai, G., & Patching, B. (1993). Precorrection: An instructional approach for managing predictable problem behaviors. *Intervention in School and Clinic, 28,* 143–150.

Comer, J. P. (1988). Is "parenting" essential to good teaching? *NEA Today, 6*(6), 34–40.

Conduct Problems Prevention Research Group. (1999). Initial impact of the Fast Track prevention trial for conduct problems: II Classroom effects. *Journal of Consulting and Clinical Psychology, 67,* 648–657.

Connor, D. F., Boone, R. T., Steingard, R. J., Lopez, I. D., & Melloni, R. (2003). Psychopharmacology and aggression: II. A meta-analysis of nonstimulant medication effects on overt aggression-related behaviors in youth with SED. *Journal of Emotional and Behavioral Disorders, 11,* 157–168.

Connor, D. F., Glatt, S., J. Lopez, I. D., Jackson, D., & Melloni, R. H. (2002). Psychopharmacology and aggression. I: A meta-analysis of stimulant effects on overt/covert aggression-related behaviors in ADHD. *Journal of the American Academy of Child and Adolescent Psychiatry, 41,* 253–261.

Conroy, M. A., Clark, D., Fox, J. J., & Gable, R. A. (2000). Building competence in FBA: Are we headed in the right direction? *Preventing School Failure, 44*(4), 169–173.

Conroy, M. A., & Davis, C. A. (2000). Early elementary-aged children with challenging behaviors: Legal and educational issues related to IDEA and assessment. *Preventing School Failure, 44*(4), 163–168.

Conroy, M. A., Davis, C. A., Fox, J. J., & Brown, W. H. (2002). Functional assessment of behavior and effective supports for young children with challenging behaviors. *Assessment for Effective Intervention, 27*(4), 35–47.

Conroy, M. A., Hendrickson, J. M., & Hester, P. P. (2004). Early identification and prevention of emotional and behavioral disorders. In R. B. Rutherford, M. M. Quinn, & S. R. Mathur (Eds.). *Handbook of research in emotional and behavioral disorders.* New York: Guilford.

Cook, B. G., Landrum, T. J., Tankersley, M., & Kauffman, J. M. (2003). Bringing research to bear on practice: Effecting evidence-based instruction for students with emotional or behavioral disorders. *Education and Treatment of Children, 26,* 345–361.

Costello, E. J., Messer, S. C., Bird, H. R., Cohen, P., & Reinherz, H. Z. (1998). The prevalence of serious emotional disturbance: A re-analysis of community studies. *Journal of Child and Family Studies, 7,* 411–432.

Costenbader, V., & Buntaine, R. (1999). Diagnostic discrimination between social maladjustment and emotional disturbance: An empirical study. *Journal of Emotional and Behavioral Disorders, 7,* 2–10.

Coulton, C. J., Korbin, J. E., Su, M., & Chow, J. (1995). Community level factors and child maltreatment rates. *Child Development, 66,* 1262–1276.

Council for Children with Behavioral Disorders. (1996). Guidelines for providing appropriate services to culturally diverse youngsters with emotional and/or behavioral disorders: Report of the Task Force of the CCBD Ad Hoc Committee on Ethnic and Multicultural Concerns. *Behavioral Disorders, 21,* 137–144.

Council for Children with Behavioral Disorders Executive Committee. (1987). Position paper on definition and identification of students with behavioral disorders. *Behavioral Disorders, 13,* 9–19.

Council for Exceptional Children. (1997–1999). *CEC standards for professional practice in special education.* Reston, VA: Council for Exceptional Children.

Coutinho, M. J., & Oswald, D. P. (1998). Ethnicity and special education research: Identifying questions and methods. *Behavioral Disorders, 24,* 66–73.

Cox, S. M., Davidson, W. S., & Bynum, T. S. (1995). A meta-analytic assessment of delinquency-related outcomes of alternative education programs. *Crime and Delinquency, 41,* 219–234.

Craft, M. A., Alber, S. R., & Heward, W. L. (1998). Teaching elementary students with developmental disabilities to recruit teacher attention in a general education classroom: Effects on teacher praise and academic productivity. *Journal of Applied Behavior Analysis, 31,* 399–415.

Crawford, L., & Tindal, G. (2002). Curriculum-based collaboration in secondary schools. In M. R. Shinn, H. M. Walker, & G. Stoner (Eds.), *Interventions for academic and behavior problems II: Preventive and remedial approaches* (pp. 825–853). Bethesda, MD: National Association of School Psychologists.

Crenshaw, T. M., Kavale, K. A., Forness, S. R., & Reeve, R. E. (1999). Attention deficit hyperactivity disorder and the efficacy of stimulant medication: A meta-analysis. In T. Scruggs & M. Mastropieri (Eds.), *Advances in learning and behavioral disabilities* (Vol. 13, pp. 135–165). Greenwich, CT: JAI.

Crijnen, A. A. M., Achenbach, T. M., & Verhulst, F. C. (1997). Comparisons of problems reported by parents of children in 12 cultures: Total problems, externalizing, and internalizing. *Journal of the Academy of Child and Adolescent Psychiatry, 36,* 1269–1277.

Crimmins, C. (2000). *Where is the mango princess?* New York: Knopf.

Crockett, J. B. (Ed.). (2001). The meaning of science and empirical rigor in the social sciences [Special issue]. *Behavioral Disorders, 27*(1).

Crockett, J. B., & Kauffman, J. M. (1999). *The least restrictive environment: Its origins and interpretations in special education.* Mahwah, NJ: Erlbaum.

Cuban, L. (2000). Why is it so hard to get "good" schools? In L. Cuban & D. Shipps (Eds.), *Reconstructing the common good in education: Coping with intractable dilemmas.* Stanford, CA: Stanford University Press.

Cullinan, D. (2002). *Students with emotional and behavior disorders: An introduction for teachers and other helping professionals.* Upper Saddle River, NJ: Merrill/Prentice Hall.

Cullinan, D. (2004). Research issues on classification and definition of emotional and behavioral disorders. In R. B. Rutherford, M. M. Quinn, & S. R. Mathur (Eds.). *Handbook of research in emotional and behavioral disorders.* New York: Guilford.

Cullinan, D., & Epstein, M. H. (1979). Administrative definitions of behavior disorders: Status and directions. In F. H. Wood & K. C. Lakin (Eds.), *Disturbing, disordered, or disturbed? Perspectives on the definition of problem behavior in educational settings* (pp. 17–28). Minneapolis: University of Minnesota, Department of Psychoeducational Studies, Advanced Training Institute.

Cullinan, D., & Epstein, M. H. (1985). Adjustment problems of mildly handicapped and nonhandicapped students. *Remedial and Special Education, 6*(2), 5–11.

Cullinan, D., Epstein, M. H., & Kauffman, J. M. (1982). The behavioral model and children's behavior disorders: Foundations and evaluation. In R. L. McDowell, G. W. Adamson, & F. H. Wood (Eds.), *Teaching emotionally disturbed children* (pp. 15–46). Boston: Little, Brown.

Cullinan, D., Epstein, M. H., & Kauffman, J. M. (1984). Teachers' ratings of students behaviors: What constitutes behavior disorder in schools? *Behavioral Disorders, 10,* 9–19.

Cullinan, D., Epstein, M. H., & Lloyd, J. W. (1991). Evaluation of conceptual models of behavior disorders. *Behavioral Disorders, 16,* 148–157.

Cummings, E. M., & Davies, P. (1999). Depressed parents and family functioning: Interpersonal effects and children's functioning and development. In T. Joiner & J. C. Coyne (Eds.), *The interactional nature of depression* (pp. 299–327). Washington, DC: American Psychological Association.

Cunningham, C. E., Cataldo, M. F., Mallion, C., & Keyes, J. B. (1984). A review and controlled single case evaluation of behavioral approaches to the management of elective mutism. *Child and Family Behavior Therapy, 5*(4), 25–49.

Dadds, M. R. (2002). Learning and intimacy in the families of anxious children. In R. J. McMahon & R. D. Peters (Eds.), *The effects of parental dysfunction on children* (pp. 87–104). New York: Kluwer.

Daly, P. M. (1985). The educateur: An atypical childcare worker. *Behavioral Disorders, 11,* 35–41.

Danforth, S. (1997). On what basis hope? Modern progress and postmodern possibilities. *Mental Retardation, 35,* 93–106.

Danforth, S. (2001). A pragmatic evaluation of three models of disability in special education. *Journal of Developmental and Physical Disabilities, 13,* 343–359.

Danforth, S., & Rhodes, W. C. (1997). Deconstructing disability: A philosophy for education. *Remedial and Special Education, 18,* 357–366.

D'Augelli, A. R., & Dark, L. J. (1994). Lesbian, gay, and bisexual youths. In L. D. Eron, J. H. Gentry, & P. Schlegel (Eds.), *Reason to hope: A psychosocial perspective on violence and youth* (pp. 177–196). Washington, DC: American Psychological Association.

Davids, L. (1975). Therapeutic approaches to children in residential treatment: Changes from the mid-1950s to the mid-1970s. *American Psychologist, 30,* 809–814.

Deaton, A. V., & Waaland, P. (1994). Psychosocial effects of acquired brain injury. In R. C. Savage & G. F. Wolcott

(Eds.), *Educational dimensions of acquired brain injury* (pp. 239–255). Austin, TX: Pro-Ed.

DeCatanzaro, D. A. (1978). Self-injurious behavior: A biological analysis. *Motivation and Emotion, 2,* 45–65.

DeGrandpre, R. (1999) *Ritalin nation: Rapid-fire culture and the transformation of human consciousness.* New York: Norton.

DeJong, S., & Frazier, J. A. (2003). Bipolar disorder in children with pervasive developmental disorder. In B. Geller & M. P. DelBello (Eds.), *Bipolar disorder in childhood and early adolescence* (pp. 51–75). New York: Guilford.

Dell Orto, A. E., & Power, P. W. (2000). *Brain injury and the family: A live and living perspective* (2nd ed.). Washington, DC: CRC.

Delpit, L. (1995). *Other people's children: Cultural conflict in the classroom.* New York: New Press.

Dembinski, R. J., Schultz, E. W., & Walton, W. T. (1982). Curriculum intervention with the emotionally disturbed student: A psychoeducational perspective. In R. L. McDowell, G. W. Adamson, & F. H. Wood (Eds.), *Teaching emotionally disturbed children* (pp. 206–234). Boston: Little, Brown.

DeMyer, M. K. (1975). The nature of neuropsychological disability in autistic children. *Journal of Autism and Childhood Schizophrenia, 5,* 109–128.

DeMyer, M. K., Barton, S., Alpern, G. D., Kimberlin, C., Allen, J., & Steele, R. (1974). The measured intelligence of autistic children. *Journal of Autism and Childhood Schizophrenia, 4,* 42–60.

Denham, S., Blair, K., Schmidt, M., & DeMulder, E. (2002). Compromised emotional competence: Seeds of violence sown early? *American Journal of Orthopsychiatry, 72,* 70–82.

Dennison, G. (1969). *The lives of children.* New York: Random House.

Deno, S. L. (1985). Curriculum-based measurement: The emerging alternative. *Exceptional Children, 52,* 219–232.

Deno, S. L. (2003). Curriculum-based measures: Development and perspectives. *Assessment for Effective Intervention, 28*(3/4), 3–12.

DeRosier, M. E., Kupersmidt, J. B., & Patterson, C. J. (1995). Children's academic and behavioral adjustment as a function of the chronicity and proximity of peer rejection. *Child Development, 65,* 1799–1813.

Deutsch, A. (1948). *The shame of the states.* New York: Harcourt, Brace, & World.

Diamond, J. (1997). *Guns, germs, and steel: The fates of human societies.* New York: Norton.

Diamond, S. C. (1993). Special education and the great god, inclusion. *Beyond Behavior, 4*(2), 3–6.

Dinges, N. G., Atlis, M. M., & Vincent, G. M. (1997). Cross-cultural perspectives on antisocial behavior. In D. M. Stoff, J. Breiling, & J. D. Maser (Eds.), *Handbook of antisocial behavior* (pp. 463–473). New York: Wiley.

Dinitz, S., Scarpitti, F. R., & Reckless, W. C. (1962). Delinquency vulnerability: A cross group and longitudinal analysis. *American Sociological Review, 27,* 515–517.

Dishion, T. J. (1990). The peer context of troublesome child and adolescent behavior. In P. E. Leone (Ed.), *Understanding troubled and troubling youth* (pp. 128–153). Newbury Park, CA: Sage.

Dishion, T. J., & Patterson, S. G. (1996). *Preventive parenting with love, encouragement and limits.* Eugene, OR: Castalia.

Dixon, B. (1994). What's worse: An evil conspiracy or a very bad accident? *Effective School Practices, 12*(4), 10–23.

Dodge, K. A., & Pettit, G. S. (2003). A biopsychosocial model of the development of chronic conduct problems in adolescence. *Developmental Psychology, 39,* 349–371.

Donelson, K. (1987). Six statements/questions from the censors. *Phi Delta Kappan, 69,* 208–214.

Donenberg, G. R., Bryant, F. B., Emerson, E., Wilson, H. W., & Pasch, K. E. (2003). Tracing the roots of early sexual debut among adolescents in psychiatric care. *Journal of the American Academy of Child and Adolescents in Psychiatric Care, 42,* 594–608.

Donovan, J., & Jessor, R. (1985). Structure of problem behavior in adolescence and young adulthood. *Journal of Consulting and Clinical Psychology, 53,* 890–904.

Dornbusch, S. M., Ritter, P. L., Leiderman, P. H., Roberts, D. F., & Fraleigh, M. J. (1987). The relation of parent style to adolescent school performance. *Child Development, 58,* 1244–1257.

Dow, S. P., Sonies, B. C., Scheib, D., Moss, S. E., & Leonard, H. L. (1995). Practical guidelines for the assessment and treatment of selective mutism. *Journal of the American Academy of Child and Adolescent Psychiatry, 34,* 836–846.

Doyle, A. B., & Markiewicz, D. (1996). Parents' interpersonal relationships and children's friendships. In W. M. Bukowski, A. F. Newcomb, & W. W. Hartup (Eds.), *The company they keep: Friendship in childhood and adolescence* (pp. 115–136). Cambridge, England: Cambridge University Press.

Doyle, C. (2003). Child emotional abuse: The role of educational professionals. *Educational and Child Psychology, 20,* 8–21.

Dubois, D. L., Felner, R. D., Bartels, C. L., & Silverman, M. M. (1995). Stability of self-reported depressive symptoms in a community sample of children and adolescents. *Journal of Clinical Child Psychology, 24,* 386–396.

Dugan, E., Kamps, D., Leonard, B., Watkins, N., Rheinberger, A., & Stackhaus, J. (1995). Effects of cooperative learning groups during social studies for students with autism and fourth-grade peers. *Journal of Applied Behavior Analysis, 28,* 175–188.

Dulcan, M. (1997). Practice parameters for the assessment and treatment of children, adolescents, and adults with attention-deficit/hyperactivity disorder. *Journal of the American Academy of Child and Adolescent Psychiatry, [Suppl. 36]*(10), 85S–121S.

Duncan, B. B., Forness, S. R., & Hartsough, C. (1995). Students identified as seriously emotionally disturbed in day treatment: Cognitive, psychiatric, and special education characteristics. *Behavioral Disorders, 20,* 238–252.

Dunlap, G., & Kern, L. (1993). Assessment and intervention for children within the instructional curriculum. In J. Reichle & D. P. Wacker (Eds.), *Communication alternatives to challenging behavior: Integrating functional assessment and intervention strategies* (pp. 177–203). Baltimore: Brookes.

Dunlap, G., Kern, L., dePerczel, M., Clarke, S., Wilson, D., Childs, K. E., et al. (1993). Functional analysis of classroom variables for students with emotional and behavioral disorders. *Behavioral Disorders, 18,* 275–291.

Dunlap, G., Robbins, F. R., & Kern, L. (1994). Some characteristics of nonaversive intervention for severe behavior problems. In E. Schopler & G. B. Mesibov (Eds.), *Behavioral issues in autism* (pp. 227–245). New York: Plenum.

DuPaul, G. J., & Barkley, R. A. (1998). Attention-deficit hyperactivity disorder. In R. J. Morris & T. R. Kratochwill (Eds.), *The practice of child therapy* (3rd ed., pp. 132–166). Boston: Allyn & Bacon.

DuPaul, G. J., Ervin, R. A., Hook, C. L., & McGoey, K. E. (1998). Peer tutoring for children with attention deficit hyperactivity disorder: Effects on classroom behavior and academic performance. *Journal of Applied Behavior Analysis, 31,* 579–592.

DuPaul, G. J., & Stoner, G. (2002). Interventions for attention problems. In M. R. Shinn, H. M. Walker, & G. Stoner (Eds.), *Interventions for academic and behavior problems II: Preventive and remedial approaches* (pp. 913–938). Bethesda, MD: National Association of School Psychologists.

Dupre, A. P. (1996). Should students have constitutional rights? Keeping order in the public schools. *George Washington Law Review, 65*(1), 49–105.

Dupre, A. P. (1997). Disability and the public schools: The case against "inclusion." *Washington Law Review, 72,* 775–858.

Dupre, A. P. (2000). A study in double standards, discipline, and the disabled student. *Washington Law Review, 75,* 1–96.

DuRant, R. H., Getts, A., Cadenhead, C., Emans, S. J., & Woods, E. R. (1995). Exposure to violence and victimization and depression, hopelessness, and purpose in life among adolescents living in and around public housing. *Developmental and Behavioral Pediatrics, 16,* 233–237.

Dwyer, K. P., & Bernstein, R. (1998). Mental health in the schools: "Linking islands of hope in a sea of despair." *School Psychology Review, 27,* 277–286.

Eber, L., & Keenan, S. (2004). Collaboration with other agencies: Wrap around and systems of care and alternative educational placements for children and youth with EBD. In R. B. Rutherford, M. M. Quinn, & S. R. Mathur (Eds.), *Handbook of research in emotional and behavioral disorders.* New York: Guilford.

Eddy, J. M., Reid, J. B., & Curry, V. (2002). The etiology of youth antisocial behavior, delinquency, and violence and a public health approach to prevention. In M. R. Shinn, H. M. Walker, & G. Stoner (Eds.), *Interventions for academic and behavior problems II: Preventive and remedial approaches* (pp. 27–52). Bethesda, MD: National Association of School Psychologists.

Edgar, E. B. (1987). Secondary programs in special education: Are many of them justifiable? *Exceptional Children, 53,* 555–561.

Edgar, E., & Siegel, S. (1995). Postsecondary scenarios for troubled and troubling youth. In J. M. Kauffman, J. W. Lloyd, D. P. Hallahan, & T. A. Astuto (Eds.), *Issues in educational placement: Students with emotional and behavioral disorders* (pp. 251–283). Hillsdale, NJ: Erlbaum.

Edgerton, R. B. (1984). Mental retardation: An anthropologist's changing view. In B. Blatt & R. J. Morris (Eds.), *Perspectives in special education: Personal orientations* (pp. 125–156). Glenview, IL: Scott, Foresman.

Eggers, C., Bunk, D., & Drause, D. (2000). Schizophrenia with onset before the age of eleven: Clinical characteristics of onset and course. *Journal of Autism and Developmental Disorders, 30,* 29–38.

Ehrensaft, M. K., Wasserman, G. A., Verdelli, L., Greenwald, S., Miller, L. S., & Davies, M. (2003). Maternal antisocial behavior, parent practices, and behavior problems in boys at risk for antisocial behavior. *Journal of Child and Family Studies, 12,* 27–40.

Eiduson, B. T., Eiduson, S., & Geller, E. (1962). Biochemistry, genetics, and the nature–nurture problem. *American Psychologist, 119,* 342–350.

Eisenberg, L. (1984). The epidemiology of suicide in adolescents. *Pediatric Annals, 13,* 47–54.

Elkind, D. (1998). Behavioral disorders: A postmodern perspective. *Behavioral Disorders, 23,* 153–159.

Elliott, D. S., Hamburg, B., & Williams, K. R. (1998). Violence in American schools: An overview. In D. S. Elliott, B. A. Hamburg, & K. R. Williams (Eds.), *Violence in American schools* (pp. 31–54). New York: Cambridge University Press.

Ellwood, M. S., & Stolberg, A. L. (1993). The effects of family composition, family health, parenting behavior and environmental stress on children's divorce adjustment. *Journal of Child and Family Studies, 2,* 23–36.

Eme, R. F., & Danielak, M. H. (1995). Comparison of fathers of daughters with and without maladaptive eating attitudes. *Journal of Emotional and Behavioral Disorders, 3,* 40–45.

Emerson, E., & Bromley, J. (1995). The form and function of challenging behavior. *Journal of Intellectual Disability Research, 39,* 388–398.

Emery, R. E., Binkoff, J. A., Houts, A. C., & Carr, E. G. (1983). Children as independent variables: Some clinical implications of child effects. *Behavior Therapy, 14,* 398–412.

Engelmann, S. (1997). Theory of mastery and acceleration. In J. W. Lloyd, E. J. Kameenui, & D. Chard (Eds.), *Issues in educating students with disabilities* (pp. 177–195). Mahwah, NJ: Erlbaum.

Ensminger, M. E., & Juon, H. S. (1998). Transition to adulthood among high-risk youth. In R. Jessor (Ed.), *New perspectives on adolescent risk behavior* (pp. 365–391). New York: Cambridge University Press.

Epstein, J. L. (1981). *The quality of school life.* Lexington, MA: Heath.

Epstein, M. H. (2000). The Behavioral and Emotional Rating Scale: A strength-based approach to assessment. *Diagnostique, 25*(3), 249–256.

Epstein, M. H., & Cullinan, D. (1998). *Scale for Assessing Emotional Disturbance.* Austin, TX: Pro-Ed.

Epstein, M. H., Cullinan, D., & Polloway, E. A. (1986). Patterns of maladjustment among the mentally retarded. *American Journal of Mental Deficiency, 91,* 127–134.

Epstein, M. H., Hertzog, M. A., & Reid, R. (2001). The Behavioral and Emotional Rating Scale: Long-Term Test–Retest Reliability. *Behavioral Disorders, 26*(4), 314–320.

Epstein, M. H., Kutash, K., & Duchnowski, A. (Eds.). (1998). *Outcomes for children and youth with emotional and behavioral disorders and their families: Programs and evaluation of best practices.* Austin, TX: Pro-Ed.

Epstein, M. H., & Sharma, J. (1998). *The Behavioral and Emotional Rating Scale: A strength-based approach to assessment.* Austin, TX: Pro-Ed.

Erlenmeyer-Kimling, L., Roberts, S. A., Rock, D., Adamo, U. H., Shapiro, B. M., & Pape, S. (1998). Prediction from longitudinal assessments of high-risk children. In M. F. Lenzenweger & R. H. Dworkin (Eds.), *Origins and development of schizophrenia: Advances in experimental psychopathology* (pp. 427–445). Washington, DC: American Psychological Association.

Eron, L. D., Gentry, J. H., & Schlegel, P. (Eds.). (1994). *Reason to hope: A psychosocial perspective on violence and youth.* Washington, DC: American Psychological Association.

Eron, L. D., & Huesmann, L. R. (1986). The role of television in the development of prosocial and antisocial behavior. In D. Olweus, J. Block, & M. Radke-Yarrow (Eds.), *Development of antisocial and prosocial behavior: Research, theories, and issues* (pp. 285–314). New York: Academic Press.

Esposito, C., Johnson, B., Wolfsdorf, B. A., & Spirito, A. (2003). Cognitive factors: Hopelessness, coping, and problem solving. In A. Spirito, A. & J. C. Overholser (Eds.), *Evaluating and treating adolescent suicide attempters: From research to practice* (pp. 89–112). New York: Academic Press.

Etzioni, A. (1994, July). Incorrigible: Bringing social hope and political rhetoric into instructive contact with what it means to be human. *Atlantic Monthly, 274,* 14–16.

Evans, E. D., & Richardson, R. C. (1995). Corporal punishment: What teachers should know. *Teaching Exceptional Children, 27*(2), 33–36.

Evans, M. E., Armstrong, M. I., Dollard, N., Kuppinger, A. D., Huz, S., & Wood, V. M. (1994). Development and evaluation of treatment foster care and family-centered intensive case management in New York. *Journal of Emotional and Behavioral Disorders, 2,* 228–239.

Evertson, C., & Weinstein, C. (Eds.). (in press). *Handbook of classroom management: Research, practice, and contemporary issues.* Mahwah, NJ: Erlbaum.

Eyre, S. L., & Millstein, S. G. (1999). What leads to sex? Adolescents preferred partners and reasons for sex. *Journal of Research on Adolescence, 9,* 277–307.

Fabre, T. R., & Walker, H. M. (1987). Teacher perceptions of the behavioral adjustment of primary grade level handicapped pupils within regular and special education settings. *Remedial and Special Education, 8*(5), 34–39.

Fagan, J., & Wilkinson, D. L. (1998). Social contexts and functions of adolecent violence. In D. S. Elliott, B. A. Hamburg, & K. R. Williams (Eds.), *Violence in American schools* (pp. 31–54). New York: Cambridge University Press.

Fagen, S. A. (1979). Psychoeducational management and self-control. In D. Cullinan & M. H. Epstein (Eds.), *Special education for adolescents: Issues and perspectives* (pp. 235–271). Upper Saddle River, NJ: Merrill/Prentice Hall.

Farmer, T. W. (2000). Misconceptions of peer rejection and problem behavior: A social interactional perspective of the adjustment of aggressive youth with mild disabilities. *Remedial and Special Education, 21,* 194–208.

Farmer, T. W., Farmer, E. M. Z., & Gut, D. (1999). Implications of social development research for school-based interventions for aggressive youth with emotional and behavioral disorders. *Journal of Emotional and Behavioral Disorders, 7,* 130–136.

Farmer, T. W., & Hollowell, J. H. (1994). Social networks in mainstream classrooms: Social affiliations and behavioral characteristics of students with EBD. *Journal of Emotional and Behavioral Disorders, 2,* 143–155.

Farmer, T. W., Leung, M.-C., Pearl, R., Rodkin, P. C., Cadwallader, T. W., & Van Acker, R. (2002). Deviant or diverse peer groups? The peer affiliations of aggressive students. *Journal of Educational Psychology, 94,* 611–620.

Farmer, T. W., Rodkin, P. C., Pearl, R., & Van Acker, R. (1999). Teacher-assessed behavioral configurations, peer assessments, and self-concepts of elementary students with mild disabilities. *Journal of Special Education, 33,* 66–80.

Farmer, T. W., Stuart, C. B., Lorch, N. H., & Fields, E. (1993). The social behavior and peer relations of emotionally and behaviorally disturbed students in residential treatment: A pilot study. *Journal of Emotional and Behavioral Disorders, 1,* 223–234.

Farrington, D. P. (1986). The sociocultural context of childhood disorders. In H. C. Quay & J. S. Werry (Eds.), *Psychopathological disorders of childhood* (3rd ed., pp. 391–422). New York: Wiley.

Farrington, D. P. (1995). The development of offending and antisocial behaviour from childhood: Key findings from the Cambridge Study in Delinquent Development. *Journal of Child Psychology and Psychiatry, 36,* 929–964.

Farson, M. R. (1940). Education of the handicapped child for social competency. *Exceptional Children, 6,* 138–144, 150.

Feil, E. (1999). Using the preschool age as a developmental leverage to prevent behavior problems with early screening and intervention. *Effective School Practices, 17*(3), 50–55.

Feldman, R. S., Salzinger, S., Rosario, M., Alvardo, L., Caraballo, L., & Hammer, M. (1995). Parent, teacher, and peer ratings of physically abused and nonmaltreated children's behavior. *Journal of Abnormal Child Psychology, 23,* 317–334.

Felner, R. D., Brand, S., DuBois, D., Adan, A. M., Mulhall, P. F., & Evans, E. G. (1995). Socioeconomic disadvantage, proximal environmental experiences, and socioemotional and academic adjustment in early adolescence: Investigation of a mediated effects model. *Child Development, 66,* 774–792.

Fenichel, C. (1974). Carl Fenichel. In J. M. Kauffman & C. D. Lewis (Eds.), *Teaching children with behavior disorders: Personal perspectives* (pp. 50–75). Upper Saddle River, NJ: Merrill/Prentice Hall.

Fergusson, D. M., & Horwood, L. J. (1995). Early disruptive behavior, IQ, and later achievement and delinquent behavior. *Journal of Abnormal Child Psychology, 23,* 183–199.

Fisher, M. (2003, April 6). Pass/fail. *The Washington Post Magazine,* 14–18, 37–48.

Fisman, S. N. (2002). Pervasive development disorder. In S. Kutcher (Ed.), *Practical child and adolescent psychopharmacology* (pp. 265–304). New York: Cambridge University Press.

Fitzgerald, H. E., Davies, W. H., & Zucker, R. A. (2002) Growing up in an alcoholic family: Structuring pathways for risk aggregation and theory-driven intervention. In

R. J. McMahon & R. D. Peters (Eds.). *The effects of parental dysfunction on children* (pp. 127–146). New York: Kluwer.

Fizzell, R. L. (1987). Inside a school of choice. *Phi Delta Kappan, 68,* 758–760.

Flannery, D. J., & Huff, C. R. (Eds.). (1999). *Youth violence: Prevention, intervention, and social policy.* Washington, DC: American Psychiatric Press.

Flannery, R. B. (1999). *Preventing youth violence: A guide for parents, teachers, and counselors.* New York: Continuum.

Fletcher, J. M., Morris, R. D., & Francis, D. J. (1991). Methodological issues in the classification of attention-related disorders. *Journal of Learning Disabilities, 24,* 72–77.

Fletcher, K. E. (2003). Childhood posttraumatic stress disorder. In E. J. Mash & R. A. Barkley (Eds.), *Child psychopathology* (2nd ed., pp. 330–371). New York: Guilford.

Flisher, A. J. (1999). Mood disorder in suicidal children and adolescents: Recent developments. *Journal of Child Psychology and Psychiatry and Allied Disciplines, 40,* 315–324.

Flory, K., Milich, R., Lynam, D. R., Leukefeld, C., & Clayton, R. (2003). The relationship between disruptive behavior disorders and substance use and dependence symptoms in young adulthood: Individuals with symptoms of attention-deficit/hyperactivity disorder are uniquely at risk. *Psychology of Addictive Behaviors, 17,* 151–158.

Flowers, A. L., Hastings, T. L., & Kelley, M. L. (2000). Development of a screening instrument for exposure to violence in children: The KID-SAVE. *Journal of Psychopathology & Behavioral Assessment, 22*(1), 91–104.

Flowers, A. L., Lanclos, N. F., & Kelley, M. L. (2002). Validation of a screening instrument for exposure to violence in African American children. *Journal of Pediatric Psychology, 27,* 351–361.

Ford, A. D., Olmi, D. J., Edwards, R. P., & Tingstrom, D. H. (2001). The sequential introduction of compliance training components with elementary-aged children in general education classroom settings. *School Psychology Quarterly, 16*(2), 142–157.

Forehand, R., & McKinney, B. (1993). Historical overview of child discipline in the United States: Implications for mental health clinicians and researchers. *Journal of Child and Family Studies, 2,* 221–228.

Foreyt, J. P., & Kondo, A. T. (1985). Eating disorders. In P. H. Bornstein & A. E. Kazdin (Eds.), *Handbook of clinical behavior therapy with children* (pp. 309–344). Homewood, IL: Dorsey.

Forness, S. R. (1988a). Planning for the needs of children with serious emotional disturbance: The national special education and mental health coalition. *Behavioral Disorders, 13,* 127–133.

Forness, S. R. (1988b). School characteristics of children and adolescents with depression. In R. B. Rutherford, C. M. Nelson, & S. R. Forness (Eds.), *Bases of severe behavioral disorders of children and youth* (pp. 177–203). Boston: Little, Brown.

Forness, S. R. (2002). Barriers to evidence-based treatment: Developmental psychopathology and the interdisciplinary disconnect in school mental health practice. *Journal of School Psychology, 351,* 1–8.

Forness, S. R. (2003). Parting reflections on education of children with emotional or behavioral disorders. *Behavioral Disorders, 28,* 198–201.

Forness, S. R., & Kavale, K. A. (1997). Defining emotional or behavioral disorders in school and related services. In J. W. Lloyd, E. J. Kameenui, & D. Chard (Eds.), *Issues in educating students with disabilities* (pp. 45–61). Mahwah, NJ: Erlbaum.

Forness, S. R., & Kavale, K. A. (2001a). Ignoring the odds: Hazards of not adding the new medical model to special education decisions. *Behavioral Disorders, 26,* 269–281.

Forness, S. R., & Kavale, K. A. (2001b). Reflections on the future of prevention. *Preventing School Failure, 45*(2), 75–81.

Forness, S. R., Kavale, K. A., King, B. H., & Kasari, C. (1994). Simple versus complex conduct disorders: Identification and phenomenology. *Behavioral Disorders, 19,* 306–312.

Forness, S. R., Kavale, K. A., & Lopez, M. (1993). Conduct disorders in school: Special education eligibility and comorbidity. *Journal of Emotional and Behavioral Disorders, 1,* 101–108.

Forness, S. R., Kavale, K. A., Sweeney, D. P., & Crenshaw, T. M. (1999). The future of research and practice in behavioral disorders: Psychopharmacology and its school implications. *Behavioral Disorders, 24,* 305–318.

Forness, S. R., Kavale, K. A., & Walker, H. M. (1999). Identifying children at risk for antisocial behavior: The case for comorbidity. In R. Gallimore, L. P. Bernheimer, D. L. MacMillan, D. L. Speece, & S. Vaughn (Eds.), *Developmental perspectives on children with high-incidence disabilities* (pp. 135–155). Mahwah, NJ: Erlbaum.

Forness, S. R., & Knitzer, J. (1992). A new proposed definition and terminology to replace "serious emotional disturbance" in Individuals With Disabilities Education Act. *School Psychology Review, 21,* 12–20.

Forness, S. R., Walker, H. M., & Kavale, K. A. (2003). Psychiatric disorders and treatment. *Teaching Exceptional Children, 36*(2), 42–49.

Fox, J., & Gable, R. A. (2004). Functional behavioral assessment. In R. B. Rutherford, M. M. Quinn, & S. R. Mathur (Eds.), *Handbook of research in emotional and behavioral disorders.* New York: Guilford.

Freedman, J. (1993). *From cradle to grave: The human face of poverty in America.* New York: Atheneum.

Frick, P. J., & Loney, B. R. (2002). Understanding the association between parent and child antisocial behavior. In R. J. McMahon & R. D. Peters (Eds.), *The effects of parental dysfunction on children* (pp. 105–126). New York: Kluwer Academic.

Fridrich, A. H., & Flannery, D. J. (1995). The effects of ethnicity and acculturation on early adolescent delinquency. *Journal of Child & Family Studies, 4,* 69–87.

Friesen, B. J., & Stephens, B. (1998). Expanding family roles in the system of care: Research and practice. In M. H. Epstein, K. Kutash, & A. Duchnowski, (Eds.), *Outcomes for children and youth with emotional and behavioral disorders and their families: Programs and evaluation of best practices* (pp. 231–259). Austin, TX: Pro-Ed.

Fuchs, D., & Fuchs, L. S. (1994). Inclusive schools movement and the radicalization of special education reform. *Exceptional Children, 60,* 294–309.

Fuchs, D., & Fuchs, L. S. (1995). Special education can work. In J. M. Kauffman, J. W. Lloyd, D. P. Hallahan, & T. A. Astuto (Eds.), *Issues in educational placement: Students with emotional and behavioral disorders* (pp. 363–377). Hillsdale, NJ: Erlbaum.

Fuchs, L. S., & Fuchs, D. (2001). Helping teachers formulate sound test accommodation decisions for students with learning disabilities. *Learning Disabilities Research & Practice, 16*(3), 174–181.

Fuchs, L. S., Fuchs, D., Eaton, S. B., Hamlett, C., Binkley, E., & Crouch, R. (2000). Using objective data sources to enhance teacher judgments about test accommodations. *Exceptional Children, 67,* 67–81.

Fujiura, G. T., & Yamaki, K. (2000). Trends in demography of childhood poverty and disability. *Exceptional Children, 66,* 187–199.

Furlong, M. J., & Morrison, G. M. (1994). Introduction to the mini-series: School violence and safety in perspective. *School Psychology Review, 23,* 139–150.

Furlong, M. J., Morrison, G. M., & Jimerson, S. (2004). Externalizing behaviors of aggression and violence. In R. B. Rutherford, M. M. Quinn, & S. R. Mathur (Eds.). *Handbook of research in emotional and behavioral disorders.* New York: Guilford.

Gable, R. A. (1999). Functional assessment in school settings. *Behavioral Disorders, 24,* 246–248.

Gable, R. A., Quinn, M. M., Rutherford, R. B., & Howell, K. (1998). Addressing problem behaviors in schools: Use of functional assessments and behavior intervention plans. *Preventing School Failure, 42,* 106–119.

Gadow, K. D., & Sprafkin, J. (1993). Television "violence" and children with emotional and behavioral disorders. *Journal of Emotional and Behavioral Disorders, 1,* 54–63.

Gallagher, D. J. (Ed.). (2004). *Challenging orthodoxy in special education: Dissenting voices.* Denver, CO: Love.

Gardner, H., & Hatch, T. (1989). Multiple intelligences go to school: Educational implications of the theory of multiple intelligences. *Educational Researcher, 18*(8), 4–9.

Gardner, M. (2001, January/February). Facilitated communication: A cruel farce. *Skeptical Inquirer,* 17–19.

Garland, E. J. (2002). Anxiety disorders. In S. Kutcher (Ed.), *Practical child and adolescent psychopharmacology* (pp. 187–229). New York: Cambridge University Press.

Garmezy, N. (1987). Stress, competence, and development. Continuities in the study of schizophrenic adults, children vulnerable to psychopathology, and the search for stress-resistant children. *American Journal of Orthopsychiatry, 57,* 159–174.

Garrison, C. Z., Addy, C. L., McKeown, R. E., Cuffe, S. P., Jackson, K. L., & Waller, J. L. (1993). Nonsuicidal physically self-damaging acts in adolescents. *Journal of Child and Family Studies, 2,* 339–352.

Garrison, W. T., & Earls, F. J. (1987). *Temperament and child psychopathology*. Newbury Park, CA: Sage.

Gavazzi, S. M., Wasserman, D., Partridge, C., & Sheridan, S. (2000). The Growing Up FAST Diversion Program: An example of juvenile justice program development for outcome evaluation. *Aggression and Violent Behavior, 5,* 159–175.

Gay, G. (1998, Winter). Coming of age ethnically: Teaching young adolescents of color. *Prevention Researcher,* pp. 7–9.

Gay, L. R., & Airasian, P. (2003). *Educational research: Competencies for analysis and applications* (4th ed.). Upper Saddle River, NJ: Merrill/Prentice Hall.

Geller, B., & DelBello, M. P. (Eds.). (2003). *Bipolar disorder in childhood and early adolescence*. New York: Guilford.

Genaux, M., Morgan, D. P., & Friedman, S. G. (1995). Substance use and its prevention: A summary of classroom practices. *Behavioral Disorders, 20,* 279–289.

Gerber, M. M. (1988). Tolerance and technology of instruction: Implications for special education reform. *Exceptional Children, 54,* 309–314.

Gerber, M. M., & Semmel, M. I. (1984). Teacher as imperfect test: Reconceptualizing the referral process. *Educational Psychologist, 19,* 137–148.

Gergen, K. (2001). Psychological science in a postmodern context. *American Psychologist, 56,* 803–813.

Germann, G., & Tindal, G. (1985). An application of curriculum-based assessment: The use of direct and repeated measurement. *Exceptional Children, 52,* 244–265.

Gershoff, E. T. (2002). Corporal punishment by parents and associated child behaviors and experiences: A meta-analytic and theoretical review. *Psychological Bulletin, 128,* 539–579.

Gershon, J. (2002). A meta-analytic review of gender differences in ADHD. *Journal of Attention Disorders, 5,* 143–154.

Gesten, E. L., Scher, K., & Cowen, E. L. (1978). Judged school problems and competencies of referred children from varying family background characteristics. *Journal of Abnormal Child Psychology, 6,* 247–255.

Gersten, R., Walker, H. M., & Darch, C. (1988). Relationships between teachers' effectiveness and their tolerance for handicapped students. An exploratory study. *Exceptional Children, 54,* 433–438.

Ghaziuddin, M., & Greden, J. (1998). Depression in children with autism/pervasive developmental disorders: A case-control family history study. *Journal of Autism and Developmental Disorders, 28,* 111–115.

Gibbs, J. T., & Huang, L. N. (Eds.). (1997). *Children of color: Psychological interventions with culturally diverse youth*. San Francisco: Jossey-Bass.

Ginsburg, C., & Demeranville, H. (1999). Sticks and stones: The jailing of mentally ill kids. *Nation, 269*(21), 17–20.

Glassberg, L. A., Hooper, S. R., & Mattison, R. E. (1999). Prevalence of learning disabilities at enrollment in special education students with behavioral disorders. *Behavioral Disorders, 25*(1), 9–21.

Glazer, N. (1997). *We are all multiculturalists now*. Cambridge, MA: Harvard University Press.

Glidewell, J. C. (1969). The child at school. In J. G. Howells (Ed.), *Modern perspectives in international child psychiatry*. New York: Brunner/Mazel.

Glidewell, J. C., Kantor, M. B., Smith, L. M. & Stringer, L. A. (1966). Socialization and social structure in the classroom. In L. W. Hoffman & M. L. Hoffman (Eds.), *Review of child development research* (Vol. 2, pp. 221–256). New York: Russell Sage Foundation.

Goldstein, A. P. (1983a). Behavior modification approaches to aggression prevention and control. In A. P. Goldstein (Ed.), *Prevention and control of aggression* (pp. 156–209). New York: Pergamon.

Goldstein, A. P. (1983b). United States: Causes, controls, and alternatives to aggression. In A. P. Goldstein & M. H. Segall (Eds.), *Aggression in global perspective* (pp. 435–474). New York: Pergamon.

Goldstein, A. P. (1991). *Delinquent gangs: A psychological perspective*. Champaign, IL: Research Press.

Goldstein, A. P., Carr, E. G., Davidson, W. S., & Wehr, P. (Eds.). (1981). *In response to aggression*. New York: Pergamon.

Goldston, D. B. (2003). *Measuring suicidal behavior and risk in children and adolescents*. Washington, DC: American Psychological Association.

Goleman, D. (1995). *Emotional intelligence*. New York: Bantam.

Good, R. H., & Jefferson, G. (1998). Contemporary perspectives on curriculum-based measurement validity. In M. R. Shinn (Ed.), *Advanced applications of curriculum-based measurement* (pp. 61–88). New York: Guilford.

Goodman, S. H., Gravitt, G. W., & Kaslow, N. J. (1995). Social problem solving: A moderator of the relation between negative life stress and depression symptoms in children. *Journal of Abnormal Child Psychology, 23,* 473–485.

Gordon, B. N., & Schroeder, C. S. (1995). *Sexuality: A developmental approach to problems.* New York: Plenum.

Gottesman, I. (1987). Schizophrenia: Irving Gottesman reveals the genetic factors. *University of Virginia Alumni News, 75*(5), 12–14.

Gottesman, I. I. (1991). *Schizophrenia genesis: The origins of madness.* New York: Freeman.

Gould, S. J. (1996). *The mismeasure of man* (Rev. ed.). New York: Norton.

Graber, J. A., Brooks-Gunn, J., & Galen, B. R. (1998). Betwixt and between: Sexuality in the context of adolescent transitions. In R. Jessor (Ed.), *New perspectives on adolescent risk behavior* (pp. 270–316). New York: Cambridge University Press.

Graham, P. J. (1979). Epidemiological studies. In H. C. Quay & J. S. Werry (Eds.), *Psychopathological disorders of childhood* (2nd ed., pp. 185–209). New York: Wiley.

Grandin, T. (1995). How people with autism think. In E. Schopler & G. B. Mesibov (Eds.), *Learning and cognition in autism* (pp. 137–156). New York: Plenum.

Graubard, P. S. (1964). The extent of academic retardation in a residential treatment center. *Journal of Educational Research, 58,* 78–80.

Graziano, A. M., & Dorta, N. J. (1995). Behavioral treatment. In M. Hersen & R. T. Ammerman (Eds.), *Advanced abnormal child psychology* (pp. 171–187). Hillsdale, NJ: Erlbaum.

Green, L., Fein, D., Joy, S., & Waterhouse, L. (1995). Cognitive functioning in autism. In E. Schopler & G. B. Mesibov (Eds.), *Learning and cognition in autism* (pp. 13–31). New York: Plenum.

Green, S. M., Russo, M. F., Navratil, J. L., & Loeber, R. (1999). Sexual and physical abuse among adolescent girls with disruptive behavior problems. *Journal of Child and Family Studies, 8,* 151–168.

Greenwood, C. R., Carta, J. J., & Dawson, H. (2000). Ecobehavioral assessment system software (EBASS): A system for observation in education settings. In T. Thompson, D. Felce., & F. J. Symons (Eds.), *Behavioral observation: Technology and applications in developmental disabilities* (pp. 229–251). Baltimore: Brookes.

Gresham, F. M. (2000). Assessment of social skills in students with emotional and behavioral disorders. *Assessment for Effective Intervention, 26*(1), 51–58.

Gresham, F. M., & Elliott, S. N. (1990). *Social Skills Rating System.* Circle Pines, MN: American Guidance Service.

Gresham, F. M., Elliott, S. N., & Evans-Fernandez, S. E. (1993). *Student Self-Concept Scale.* Circle Pines, MN: American Guidance Service.

Gresham, F. M., & Kern, L. (2004). Internalizing behavior problems in children and adolescents. In R. B. Rutherford, M. M. Quinn, & S. R. Mathur (Eds.), *Handbook of research in emotional and behavioral disorders.* New York: Guilford.

Gresham, F. M., & Little, S. G. (1993). Peer-referenced assessment strategies. In T. H. Ollendick & M. Hersen (Eds.), *Handbook of child and adolescent assessment* (pp. 165–179). New York: Pergamon.

Gresham, F. M., & MacMillan, D. L. (1997a). Autistic recovery? An analysis and critique of the empirical evidence on the Early Intervention Project. *Behavioral Disorders, 22,* 185–201.

Gresham, F. M., & MacMillan, D. L. (1997b). Denial and defensiveness in the place of fact and reason: Rejoinder to Smith and Lovaas. *Behavioral Disorders, 22,* 219–230.

Gresham, F. M., MacMillan, D. L., & Bocain, K. M. (1996). Behavioral earthquakes: Low frequency, salient behavioral events that differentiate students at-risk for behavioral disorders. *Behavioral Disorders, 21,* 277–292.

Gresham, F. M., MacMillan, D. L., Bocain, K. M., & Ward, S. L. (1998). Comorbidity of hyperactivity–impulsivity–inattention and conduct problems: Risk factors in social, affective, and academic domains. *Journal of Abnormal Child Psychology, 26,* 393–406.

Gresham, F. M., Quinn, M. M., & Restori, A. (1999). Methodological issues in functional analysis: Generalizability to other disability groups. *Behavioral Disorders, 24,* 180–182.

Griffin-Shelley, E. (1994). *Adolescent sex and love addicts.* Westport, CT: Praeger.

Grinder, R. E. (1985). The gifted in our midst: By their divine deeds, neuroses, and mental test scores we have known them. In F. D. Horowitz & M. O'Brien (Eds.), *The gifted and talented: Developmental perspectives* (pp. 5–35). Washington, DC: American Psychological Association.

Grob, G. N. (1973). *Mental institutions in America: Social policy to 1875.* New York: Free Press.

Groden, J., Cautela, J., Prince, S., & Berryman, J. (1994). The impact of stress and anxiety on individuals with autism and developmental disabilities. In E. Schopler & G. B. Mesibov (Eds.), *Behavioral issues in autism* (pp. 177–194). New York: Plenum.

Gronna, S. S., Jenkins, A. A., & Chin-Chance, S. A. (1998). Who are we assessing? Determining state-wide participation rates for students with disabilities. *Exceptional Children, 64,* 407–418.

Grosenick, J. K., & Huntze, S. L. (1979). *National needs analysis in behavior disorders: A model for a comprehensive needs analysis in behavior disorders.* Columbia: University of Missouri, Department of Special Education.

Grosenick, J. K., & Huntze, S. L. (1983). *More questions than answers: Review and analysis of programs for behaviorally disordered children and youth*. Columbia: University of Missouri, Department of Special Education.

Gross, J. (2003, November 19). Government develops strategy to fight autism. *New York Times,* A1, A16.

Grossen, B. (1993). Child-directed teaching methods: A discriminatory practice of Western education. *Effective School Practices, 12*(2), 9–20.

Guevremont, D. C., & Dumas, M. C. (1994). Peer relationship problems and disruptive behavior disorders. *Journal of Emotional and Behavioral Disorders, 2,* 164–172.

Gully, V., Northup, J., Hupp, S., Spera, S., LeVelle, J., & Ridgway, A. (2003). Sequential evaluation of behavioral treatments and methylphenidate dosage for children with attention deficit hyperactivity disorder. *Journal of Applied Behavior Analysis, 36,* 375–378.

Gulp, A. M., Clyman, M. M., & Culp, R. E. (1995). Adolescent depressed mood, reports of suicide attempts, and asking for help. *Adolescence, 30,* 827–837.

Gumpel, T. P., & Frank, R. (1999). An expansion of the peer-tutoring paradigm: Cross-age peer tutoring of social skills among socially rejected boys. *Journal of Applied Behavior Analysis, 32,* 115–118.

Gunter, P. L., & Denny, R. K. (2004). Data collection in research and application involving students with emotional and behavioral disorders. In R. B. Rutherford, M. M. Quinn, & S. R. Mathur (Eds.), *Handbook of research in emotional and behavioral disorders*. New York: Guilford.

Gunter, P. L., Denny, R. K., Jack, S. L., Shores, R. E., & Nelson, C. M. (1993). Aversive stimuli in academic interactions between students with serious emotional disturbance and their teachers. *Behavioral Disorders, 18,* 265–274.

Gunter, P. L., Hummel, J. H., & Conroy, M. A. (1998). Increasing correct academic responding: An effective intervention strategy to decrease behavior problems. *Effective School Practices, 17*(2), 36–54.

Haager, D., & Vaughn, S. (1997). Assessment of social competence in students with learning disabilities. In J. W. Lloyd, E. J. Kameenui, & D. Chard (Eds.), *Issues in educating students with disabilities* (pp. 129–152). Mahwah, NJ: Erlbaum.

Hallahan, D. P., & Cottone, E. A. (1997). Attention deficit hyperactivity disorder. In T. E. Scruggs & M. A. Mastropieri (Eds.), *Advances in learning and behavioral disabilities* (Vol. 11, pp. 27–67). Greenwich, CT: JAI.

Hallahan, D. P., & Kauffman, J. M. (1977). Categories, labels, behavioral characteristics: ED, LD, and EMR reconsidered. *Journal of Special Education, 11,* 139–149.

Hallahan, D. P., & Kauffman, J. M. (2003). *Exceptional learners: Introduction to special education* (9th ed.). Boston: Allyn & Bacon.

Hallahan, D. P., Keller, C. E., & Ball, D. W. (1986). A comparison of prevalence rate variability from state to state for each of the categories of special education. *Remedial and Special Education, 7*(2), 8–14.

Hallahan, D. P., Lloyd, J. W., Kauffman, J. M., Weiss, M., & Martinez, E. (2005). *Introduction to learning disabilities* (3rd ed.). Boston: Allyn & Bacon.

Hallenbeck, B. A., & Kauffman, J. M. (1995). How does observational learning affect the behavior of students with emotional or behavioral disorders? A review of research. *Journal of Special Education, 29,* 45–71.

Hallfors, D., Fallon, T., & Watson, K. (1998). An examination of psychotropic drug treatment for children with serious emotional disturbance. *Journal of Emotional and Behavioral Disorders, 6,* 56–64.

Hamburg, M. (1998). Youth violence is a public health concern. In D. S. Elliott, B. A. Hamburg, & K. R. Williams (Eds.), *Violence in American schools* (pp. 31–54). New York: Cambridge University Press.

Hammen, C., & Rudolph, K. D. (2003). Childhood mood disorders. In E. J. Mash & R. A. Barkley (Eds.), *Child psychopathology* (2nd ed., pp. 233–278). New York: Guilford.

Hammond, W. R., & Yung, B. R. (1994). African Americans. In L. D. Eron, J. H. Gentry, & P. Schlegel (Eds.), *Reason to hope: A psychosocial perspective on violence and youth* (pp. 105–118). Washington, DC: American Psychological Association.

Hanson, M. J., & Carta, J. J. (1996). Addressing the challenges of families with multiple risks. *Exceptional Children, 62,* 201–212.

Hanson, M. J., & Lynch, E. W. (1992). Family diversity: Implications for policy and practice. *Topics in Early Childhood Special Education, 12,* 283–306.

Happe, F. G. E. (1994). An advanced test of theory of mind: Understanding of story characters' thoughts and feelings by able autistic, mentally handicapped, and normal children and adults. *Journal of Autism and Developmental Disorders, 24,* 129–154.

Happe, F. G. E., & Frith, U. (1995). Theory of mind in autism. In E. Schopler & G. B. Mesibov (Eds.), *Learning and cognition in autism* (pp. 177–197). New York: Plenum.

Harden, P. W., Pihl, R. O., Vitaro, F., Gendreau, P. L., & Tremblay, R. E. (1995). Stress response in anxious and nonanxious disruptive boys. *Journal of Emotional and Behavioral Disorders, 3,* 183–190.

Hare, E. H. (1962). Masturbatory insanity: The history of an idea. *Journal of Mental Science, 108,* 1–25.

Haring, N. G., & Phillips, E. L. (1962). *Educating emotionally disturbed children*. New York: McGraw-Hill.

Haring, T. G., & Kennedy, C. H. (1990). Contextual control of problem behavior in students with severe disabilities. *Journal of Applied Behavior Analysis, 23,* 235–243.

Harrington, R. (2001). Cognitive behaviour therapy. In H. Remschmidt (Ed.), *Psychotherapy with children and adolescents* (pp.113–123). New York: Cambridge University Press.

Harris, H. F. (1996). Elective mutism: A tutorial. *Language, Speech, and Hearing Services in Schools, 27,* 10–15.

Harris, J. R. (1995). Where is the child's environment? A group socialization theory of development. *Psychological Review, 102,* 458–489.

Harris, S. L. (1994). Treatment of family problems in autism. In E. Schopler & G. B. Mesibov (Eds.), *Behavioral issues in autism* (pp. 161–175). New York: Plenum.

Harris, S. L. (1995a). Autism. In M. Hersen & R. T. Ammerman (Eds.), *Advanced abnormal child psychology* (pp. 305–317). Hillsdale, NJ: Erlbaum.

Harris, S. L. (1995b). Educational strategies in autism. In E. Schopler & G. B. Mesibov (Eds.), *Learning and cognition in autism* (pp. 293–309). New York: Plenum.

Harris, S. L., & Weiss, M. J. (1998). *Right from the start: Behavioral intervention for young children with autism. A guide for parents and professionals.* Bethesda, MD: Woodbine House.

Hart, B., & Risley, T. R. (1995). *Meaningful differences in the everyday experience of young American children.* Baltimore: Brookes.

Hartman, C., Hox, J., Mellenbergh, G. J., Boyle, M. H., Offord, D. R., Racine, Y., et al. (2001). DSM–IV internal construct validity: When a taxonomy meets data. *Journal of Child Psychology & Psychiatry & Allied Disciplines, 42,* 817–836.

Hastings, T. L., & Kelley, M. L. (1997). Development and validation of the Screen for Adolescent Violence Exposure (SAVE). *Journal of Abnormal Child Psychology, 25*(7), 511–520.

Haugaard, J. J. (1992). Epidemiology and family violence involving children. In R. T. Ammerman & M. Hersen (Eds.), *Assessment of family violence: A clinical and legal sourcebook* (pp. 89–107). New York: Wiley.

Hawkins, J. D., Arthur, M. W., & Olson, J. J. (1997). Community interventions to reduce risks and enhance protection against antisocial behavior. In D. M. Stoff, J. Breiling, & J. D. Maser (Eds.), *Handbook of antisocial behavior* (pp. 365–374). New York: Wiley.

Hawkins, J. D., Farrington, D. P., & Catalano, R. F. (1998). Reducing violence through the schools. In D. S. Elliott, B. A. Hamburg, & K. R. Williams (Eds.), *Violence in American schools* (pp. 188–216). New York: Cambridge University Press.

Hawton, K. (1986). *Suicide and attempted suicide among children and adolescents.* Beverly Hills, CA: Sage.

Hay, D. A., & Levy, F. (2001). Implications of genetic studies of attentional problems for education and intervention. In F. Levy & D. A. Hay (Eds.), *Attention, genes and ADHD* (pp. 214–224). Philadelphia: Taylor & Francis.

Hayes, S. C., Nelson, R. O., & Jarrett, R. B. (1987). The treatment utility of assessment: A functional approach to evaluating assessment quality. *American Psychologist, 42,* 963–974.

Hayes, S. C., Nelson, R. O., & Jarrett, R. B. (1989). The applicability of treatment utility. *American Psychologist, 44,* 1242–1243.

Hendershott, A. B. (2002). *The politics of deviance.* San Francisco: Encounter.

Henderson, H. A., & Fox, N. A. (1998). Inhibited and uninhibited children: Challenges in school settings. *School Psychology Review, 27,* 492–505.

Henggeler, S. W., Schoenwald, S. K., & Munger, R. L. (1996). Families and therapists achieve clinical outcomes, systems of care mediate the process. *Journal of Child and Family Studies, 5,* 177–183.

Henry, N. B. (Ed.). (1950). The education of exceptional children. *Forty-ninth yearbook of the National Society for the Study of Education, Part II.* Chicago: University of Chicago Press.

Herbert, M. (1994). Etiological considerations. In T. H. Ollendick, N. J. King, & W. Yule (Eds.), *International handbook of phobic and anxiety disorders in children and adolescents* (pp. 3–20). New York: Plenum.

Hersen, M., & Ammerman, R. T. (Eds.). (1995). *Advanced abnormal child psychology.* Hillsdale, NJ: Erlbaum.

Hersh, R. H., & Walker, H. M. (1983). Great expectations: Making schools effective for all students. *Policy Studies Review, 2*(1), 147–188.

Hess, F. M., & Brigham, F. (2000). None of the above: The promise and peril of high-stakes testing. *American School Board Journal, 187*(1), 26–29.

Hess, R. D., & Holloway, S. D. (1984). Family and school as educational institutions. In R. D. Parke (Ed.), *Review of child development research* (Vol. 7, pp. 179–222). Chicago: University of Chicago Press.

Hester, P. P., & Kaiser, A. P. (1998). Early intervention for the prevention of conduct disorder: Research issues in early identification, implementation, and interpretation of treatment outcomes. *Behavioral Disorders, 24,* 57–65.

Hetherington, E. M., & Camara, K. A. (1984). Families in transition: The process of dissolution and reconstruction. In R. D. Parke (Ed.), *Review of child development research* (Vol. 7, pp. 398–439). Chicago: University of Chicago Press.

Hetherington, E. M., & Martin, B. (1986). Family factors and psychopathology in children. In H. C. Quay & J. S. Werry (Eds.), *Psychopathological disorders of childhood* (3rd ed., pp. 332–390). New York: Wiley.

Heuchert, C. M., & Long, N. J. (1980). A brief history of life-space interviewing. *Pointer, 25*(2), 5–8.

Heward, W. L. (2003). Ten faulty notions about teaching and learning that hinder the effectiveness of special education. *The Journal of Special Education, 36,* 186–205.

Heward, W. L., & Silvestri, S. M. (2004). The neutralization of special education. In J. W. Jacobson, J. A. Mulick, & R. M. Foxx (Eds.), *Fads: Dubious and improbable treatments for developmental disabilities*. Mahwah, NJ: Erlbaum.

Hewett, F. M. (1968). *The emotionally disturbed child in the classroom*. Boston: Allyn & Bacon.

Hewett, F. M. (1974). Frank M. Hewett. In J. M. Kauffman & C. D. Lewis (Eds.), *Teaching children with behavior disorders: Personal perspectives* (pp. 114–140). Upper Saddle River, NJ: Merrill/Prentice Hall.

Hewitt, L. E., & Jenkins, R. L. (1946). *Fundamental patterns of maladjustment: The dynamics of their origin*. Springfield: State of Illinois.

Hill, H. M., Soriano, F. I., Chen, S. A., & LaFromboise, T. D. (1994). Sociocultural factors in the etiology and prevention of violence among ethnic minority youth. In L. D. Eron, J. H. Gentry, & P. Schlegel (Eds.), *Reason to hope: A psychosocial perspective on violence and youth* (pp. 59–97). Washington, DC: American Psychological Association.

Hinshaw, S. P., & Lee, S. S. (2003). Conduct and oppositional defiant disorders. In E. J. Mash & R. A. Barkley (Eds.), *Child psychopathology* (2nd ed., pp. 144–198). New York: Guilford.

Hinshaw, S. P., Simmel, C., & Heller, T. L. (1995). Multimethod assessment of covert antisocial behavior in children: Laboratory observations, adult ratings, and child self-reports. *Psychological Assessment, 7,* 209–219.

Hintze, J. M. (2002). Interventions for fears and anxiety problems. In M. R. Shinn, H. M. Walker, & G. Stoner (Eds.), *Interventions for academic and behavior problems II: Preventive and remedial approaches* (pp. 939–960). Bethesda, MD: National Association of School Psychologists.

Hirsch, E. D., Jr. (1996). *The schools we need and why we don't have them*. New York: Anchor.

Hobbs, N. (1966). Helping the disturbed child: Psychological and ecological strategies. *American Psychologist, 21,* 1105–1115.

Hobbs, N. (1974). Nicholas Hobbs. In J. M. Kauffman & C. D. Lewis (Eds.), *Teaching children with behavior disorders: Personal perspectives* (pp. 142–167). Upper Saddle River, NJ: Merrill/Prentice Hall.

Hobbs, N. (1975a). *The futures of children*. San Francisco: Jossey-Bass.

Hobbs, N. (1975b). *Issues in the classification of children* (Vols. 1 & 2). San Francisco: Jossey-Bass.

Hockenbury, J. C., Kauffman, J. M., & Hallahan, D. P. (1999). What's right about special education. *Exceptionality, 8*(1), 3–11.

Hodges, K., & Zeman, J. (1993). Interviewing. In T. H. Ollendick & M. Hersen (Eds.), *Handbook of child and adolescent assessment* (pp. 65–81). New York: Pergamon.

Hodgkinson, H. L. (1995). What should we call people? Race, class, and the census for 2000. *Phi Delta Kappan, 77,* 173–179.

Hoff, K. E., & DuPaul, G. J. (1998). Reducing disruptive behavior in general education classrooms: The use of self-management strategies. *School Psychology Review, 27,* 290–303.

Hoffman, E. (1974). The treatment of deviance by the educational system: History. In W. C. Rhodes & S. Head (Eds.), *A study of child variance: Vol. 3. Service delivery systems* (pp. 81–144). Ann Arbor: University of Michigan.

Hoffman, E. (1975). The American public school and the deviant child: The origins of their involvement. *Journal of Special Education, 9,* 415–423.

Hollinger, J. D. (1987). Social skills for behaviorally disordered children as preparation for mainstreaming: Theory, practice, and new directions. *Remedial and Special Education, 8*(4), 17–27.

Hooper, S. R., Roberts, J. E., Zeisel, S. A., & Poe, M. (2003). Core language predictors of behavioral functioning in early elementary school children: Concurrent and longitudinal findings. *Behavioral Disorders, 29,* 10–24.

Hops, H., Finch, M., & McConnell, S. (1985). Social skills deficits. In P. H. Bornstein & A. E. Kazdin (Eds.), *Handbook of clinical behavior therapy with children* (pp. 543–598). Homewood, IL: Dorsey.

Howe, K. R., & Miramontes, O. B. (1992). *The ethics of special education*. New York: Teachers College Press.

Howell, K. W. (1985). Functional assessment in correctional settings. In C. M. Nelson, R. B. Rutherford, & B. I. Wolford (Eds.), *Special education in the criminal justice system* (pp. 165–186). Upper Saddle River, NJ: Merrill/Prentice Hall.

Howell, K. W., Fox, S. L., & Morehead, M. K. (1993). *Curriculum-based evaluation for teaching and decision making* (2nd ed.). Pacific Grove, CA: Brooks/Cole.

Howell, K. W., & Hyatt, K. (2004). Curriculum-based measurement of students with EBD: Assessment for data based decision making. In R. B. Rutherford, M. M. Quinn, & S. R. Mathur (Eds.). *Handbook of research in emotional and behavioral disorders*. New York: Guilford.

Howells, J. G., & Guirguis, W. R. (1984). Childhood schizophrenia 20 years later. *Archives of General Psychiatry, 41,* 123–128.

Hudley, C., & Graham, S. (1995). School-based interventions for aggressive African-American boys. *Applied and Preventive Psychology, 4,* 185–195.

Huefner, D. S. (1994). The mainstreaming cases: Tensions and trends for school administrators. *Educational Administration Quarterly, 30,* 27–55.

Huefner, D. S. (2000). *Getting comfortable with special education law: A framework for working with children with disabilities*. Norwood, MA: Christopher-Gordon.

Huesmann, L. R., Moise, J. F., & Podolski, C. (1997). The effects of media violence on the development of antisocial behavior. In D. M. Stoff, J. Breiling, & J. D. Maser (Eds.), *Handbook of antisocial behavior* (pp. 181–193). New York: Wiley.

Huesmann, L. R., Moise-Titus, J., Podolski, C., & Eron, L. (2003). Longitudinal relations between children's exposure to TV violence and their aggressive and violent behavior in young adulthood: 1977–1992. *Developmental Psychology, 39,* 201–221.

Hultquist, A. M. (1995). Selective mutism: Causes and interventions. *Journal of Emotional and Behavioral Disorders, 3,* 100–107.

Hundert, J. (1995). *Enhancing social competence in young students: School-based approaches.* Austin, TX: Pro-Ed.

Hyman, I. A. (1995). Corporal punishment, psychological maltreatment, violence, and punitiveness in America: Research, advocacy, and public policy. *Applied and Preventive Psychology, 4,* 113–130.

Hynd, G. W. (2001). Foreword. In J. Wasserstein, L. E. Wolf, & F. F. Lefever (Eds.), *Adult attention deficit disorder: Brain mechanisms and life outcomes* (pp. ix–x). New York: New York Academy of Sciences.

Ialongo, N. S., Vaden-Kiernan, N., & Kellam, S. (1998). Early peer rejection and aggression: Longitudinal relations with adolescent behavior. *Journal of Developmental and Physical Disabilities, 10,* 199–213.

Institute of Medicine. (1989). *Research on children and adolescents with mental, behavioral and developmental disorders: Mobilizing a national initiative.* Washington, DC: National Academy Press.

Isaac, G. (1995). Is bipolar disorder the most common diagnostic entity in hospitalized adolescents and children? *Adolescence, 30,* 273–276.

Iversen, L. (1999). High time for cannabis research. *Proceedings of the National Academy of Science, 96,* 5338–5339.

Iwata, B. A., Zarcone, J. B., Vollmer, T. R., & Smith, R. G. (1994). Assessment and treatment of self-injurious behavior. In E. Schopler & G. B. Mesibov (Eds.), *Behavioral issues in autism* (pp. 131–159). New York: Plenum.

Jackson, C., Henriksen, L., & Foshee, V. A. (1998). The authoritative parenting index: Predicting health risk behaviors among children and adolescents. *Health Education and Behavior, 25,* 319–337.

Jackson, J. F. (1995). Hit by friendly fire: Iatrogenic effects of misguided social policy interventions on African American families. In D. Baumrind (Ed.), *Child maltreatment and optimal caregiving in social contexts* (pp. 89–99). New York: Garland.

Jacobsen, T. (1995). Case study: Is selective mutism a manifestation of identity disorder? *Journal of the Academy of Child and Adolescent Psychiatry, 34,* 863–866.

Jakubecy, J. J., Mock, D. R., & Kauffman, J. M. (2003). Special education, current trends. In J. W. Guthrie (Ed.), *Encyclopedia of education* (2nd ed., pp. 2284–2290). New York: Macmillan Reference.

James, M., & Long, N. (1992). Looking beyond behavior and seeing my needs: A red flag interview. *Journal of Emotional and Behavioral Problems, 1*(2), 35–38.

Janko, S. (1994). *Vulnerable children, vulnerable families: The social construction of child abuse.* New York: Teachers College Press.

Jarvelin, M. R., Daara, E., Rantakallio, P., Moilanen, I., & Ishohanni, M. (1995). Juvenile delinquency, education, and mental disability. *Exceptional Children, 61,* 230–239.

Jenkins, J. M., Rasbash, J., & O'Connor, T. G. (2003). The role of the shared family context in differential parenting. *Developmental Psychology, 39,* 99–113.

Jensen, P. S., Hinshaw, S. P., Swanson, J. M., Greenhill, L. L., Conners, C., Arnold, L., et al. (2001). Findings from the NIMH Multimodal Treatment Study of ADHD (MTA): Implications and applications for primary care providers. *Journal of Developmental & Behavioral Pediatrics, 22,* 60–73.

Jessor, R. (1998). New perspectives on adolescent risk behavior. In R. Jessor (Ed.), *New Perspectives on adolescent risk behavior* (pp. 1–10). New York: Cambridge University Press.

Jessor, R., Donovan, J. E., & Costa, F. M. (1991). *Beyond adolescence: Problem behavior and young adult development.* New York: Cambridge University Press.

Jessor, R., & Jessor, S. L. (1977). *Problem behavior and psycho-social development: A longitudinal study of youth.* New York: Academic Press.

Jessor, R., Van Den Bos, J., Vanderryn, J., Costa, F. M., & Turbin, M. S. (1995). Protective factors in adolescent problem behavior: Moderator effects and developmental change. *Developmental Psychology, 31,* 923–933.

Johnson, J. H. (1986). *Life events as stressors in childhood and adolescence.* Beverly Hills, CA: Sage.

Johnson, W. G., & Hinkle, L. K. (1993). Obesity. In T. H. Ollendick & M. Hersen (Eds.), *Handbook of child and adolescent assessment* (pp. 364–383). New York: Pergamon.

Johnson-Powell, G., Yamamoto, J., Wyatt, G. E., & Arroyo, W. (Eds.). (1997). *Transcultural child development: Psychological assessment and treatment.* New York: Wiley.

Johnston, H. F., & March, J. S. (1992). Obsessive–compulsive disorders in children and adolescents. In W. R. Reynolds (Ed.), *Internalizing disorders in children and adolescents* (pp. 107–148). New York: Wiley.

Joiner, T., & Coyne, J. C. (Eds.). (1999). *The interactional nature of depression.* Washington, DC: American Psychological Association.

Jones, E. D., Southern, W. T., & Brigham, F. J. (1998). Curriculum-based assessment: Testing what is taught and teaching what is tested. *Intervention in School & Clinic, 33*(4), 239–249.

Jones, V. R., & Jones, L. S. (1995). *Comprehensive classroom management: Creating positive learning environments for all students.* Boston: Allyn & Bacon.

Jordan, D. (1995). *Honorable intentions: A parent's guide to educational planning for children with emotional or behavioral disorders.* Minneapolis: PACER Center.

Jordan, D., Goldberg, P., & Goldberg, M. (1991). *A guidebook for parents of children with emotional or behavioral disorders.* Minneapolis: PACER Center.

Judson, O. (2002). *Dr. Tatiana's sex advice to all creation.* New York: Holt.

Juul, K. D. (1986). Epidemiological studies of behavior disorders in children: An international survey. *International Journal of Special Education, 1,* 1–20.

Kagan, J., Gibbons, J. L., Johnson, M. O., Reznick, J. S., & Snidman, N. (1990). A temperamental disposition to the state of uncertainty. In J. Rolf, A. S. Masten, D. Cicchetti, K. H. Nuechterlein, & S. Weintraub (Eds.), *Risk and protective factors in the development of psychopathology* (pp. 164–178). New York: Cambridge University Press.

Kaminer, Y. (1994). *Adolescent substance abuse: A comprehensive guide to theory and practice.* New York: Plenum.

Kamps, D. M., Leonard, B. R., Dugan, E. P., Boland, B., & Greenwood, C. R. (1991). The use of ecobehavioral assessment to identify naturally occurring effective procedures in classrooms serving students with autism and other developmental disabilities. *Journal of Behavioral Education, 1,* 367–397.

Kamps, D. M., & Tankersley, M. (1996). Prevention of behavioral and conduct disorders: Trends and research issues. *Behavioral Disorders, 22,* 41–48.

Kane, M. J. (1994). Premonitory urges as "attentional tics" in Tourette's syndrome. *Journal of the American Academy of Child and Adolescent Psychiatry, 33,* 805–808.

Kanner, L. (1943). Autistic disturbances of affective contact. *Nervous Child, 2,* 217–250.

Kanner, L. (1960). Child psychiatry: Retrospect and prospect. *American Journal of Psychiatry, 117,* 15–22.

Kanner, L. (1964). *History of the care and treatment of the mentally retarded.* Springfield, IL: Thomas.

Kanner, L. (1973). Historical perspective on developmental deviations. *Journal of Autism and Childhood Schizophrenia, 3,* 187–198.

Kasen, S., Johnson, J., & Cohen, P. (1990). The impact of school emotional climate on student psychopathology. *Journal of Abnormal Child Psychology, 18,* 165–177.

Kashani, J. H., Dahlmeier, J. M., Borduin, C. M., Soltys, S., & Reid, J. C. (1995). Characteristics of anger expression in depressed children. *Journal of the American Academy of Child and Adolescent Psychiatry, 34,* 322–326.

Kaslow, N. J., Morris, M. K., & Rehm, L. P. (1998). Childhood depression. In R. J. Morris & T. R. Kratochwill (Eds.), *The practice of child therapy* (3rd ed., pp. 48–90). Boston: Allyn & Bacon.

Katsiyannis, A. (1994). Pre-referral practices: Under Office of Civil Rights scrutiny. *Journal of Developmental and Physical Disabilities, 6,* 73–76.

Katz, M. (1997). *On playing a poor hand well: Insights from the lives of those who have overcome childhood risks and adversities.* New York: Norton.

Kamphaus, R. W., & Frick, P. J. (1996). *Clinical assessment of child and adolescent personality and behavior.* Boston: Allyn & Bacon.

Kauffman, J. M. (1974). Severely emotionally disturbed. In N. G. Haring (Ed.), *Behavior of exceptional children* (pp. 377–410). Upper Saddle River, NJ: Merrill/Prentice Hall.

Kauffman, J. M. (1976). Nineteenth-century views of children's behavior disorders: Historical contributions and continuing issues. *Journal of Special Education, 10,* 335–349.

Kauffman, J. M. (1979). An historical perspective on disordered behavior and an alternative conceptualization of exceptionality. In F. H. Wood & K. C. Lakin (Eds.), *Disturbing, disordered, or disturbed? Perspectives on the definition of problem behavior in educational settings* (pp. 49–70). Minneapolis: University of Minnesota, Department of Psychoeducational Studies, Advanced Training Institute.

Kauffman, J. M. (1981). Historical trends and contemporary issues in special education in the United States. In J. M. Kauffman & D. P. Hallahan (Eds.), *Handbook of special education* (pp. 3–23). Upper Saddle River, NJ: Prentice Hall.

Kauffman, J. M. (1984). Saving children in the age of Big Brother: Moral and ethical issues in the identification of deviance. *Behavioral Disorders, 10,* 60–70.

Kauffman, J. M. (1986a). Educating children with behavior disorders. In R. J. Morris & B. Blatt (Eds.), *Special education: Research and trends* (pp. 249–271). New York: Pergamon.

Kauffman, J. M. (1986b). Growing out of adolescence: Reflections on change in special education for the behaviorally disordered. *Behavioral Disorders, 11,* 290–296.

Kauffman, J. M. (1987). Research in special education: A commentary. *Remedial and Special Education, 8*(6), 57–62.

Kauffman, J. M. (1988). Lessons in the nonrecognition of deviance. In R. B. Rutherford, C. M. Nelson, & S. R. Forness (Eds.), *Bases of severe behavioral disorders of children and youth* (pp. 3–19). Boston: Little, Brown.

Kauffman, J. M. (1989). The regular education initiative as Reagan–Bush education policy: A trickle-down theory of education of the hard-to-teach. *Journal of Special Education, 23,* 256–278.

Kauffman, J. M. (1992). Foreword. In K. R. Howe & O. B. Miramontes, *The ethics of special education* (pp. xi–xvii). New York: Teachers College Press.

Kauffman, J. M. (1993). How we might achieve the radical reform of special education. *Exceptional Children, 60,* 6–16.

Kauffman, J. M. (1994a). Places of change: Special education's power and identity in an era of educational reform. *Journal of Learning Disabilities, 27,* 610–618.

Kauffman, J. M. (1994b, March 16). Taming aggression in the young: A call to action. *Education Week, 13*(25), 43.

Kauffman, J. M. (1995). Why we must celebrate a diversity of restrictive environments. *Learning Disabilities Research and Practice, 10,* 225–232.

Kauffman, J. M. (1997). Conclusion: A little of everything, a lot of nothing is an agenda for failure. *Journal of Emotional and Behavioral Disorders, 5,* 76–81.

Kauffman, J. M. (1999a). Comments on social development research in emotional and behavioral disorders. *Journal of Emotional and Behavioral Disorders, 7,* 189–191.

Kauffman, J. M. (1999b). Educating students with emotional or behavioral disorders: What's over the horizon? In L. M. Bullock & R. A. Gable (Eds.), *Educating students with emotional and behavioral disorders: Historical perspective and future directions* (pp. 38–59). Reston, VA: Council for Children with Behavioral Disorders.

Kauffman, J. M. (1999c). How we prevent the prevention of emotional and behavioral disorders. *Exceptional Children, 65,* 448–468.

Kauffman, J. M. (1999d). The role of science in behavioral disorders. *Behavioral Disorders, 24,* 265–272.

Kauffman, J. M. (1999e). The special education story: Obituary, accident report, conversion experience, reincarnation, or none of the above? *Exceptionality, 8*(1), 3–11.

Kauffman, J. M. (1999f). Today's special education and its messages for tomorrow. *Journal of Special Education, 32,* 244–254.

Kauffman, J. M. (1999g). What we make of difference and the difference we make. Foreword in V. L. Schwean & D. H. Saklofske (Eds.), *Handbook of psychosocial characteristics of exceptional children* (pp. ix–xii). New York: Plenum.

Kauffman, J. M. (2002). *Education deform: Bright people sometimes say stupid things about education.* Lanham, MD: Scarecrow Education.

Kauffman, J. M. (2003a). Appearances, stigma, and prevention. *Remedial and Special Education, 24,* 195–198.

Kauffman, J. M. (2003b). Reflections on the field. *Behavioral Disorders, 28,* 205–208.

Kauffman, J. M. (2003c, November 22). *The president's commission and the devaluation of special education.* Paper presented at the 27th annual conference of Teacher Educators of Children With Behavior Disorders, Tempe, AZ.

Kauffman, J. M. (2004). How we prevent the prevention of emotional and behavioral difficulties in education. In P. Garner, F. Yuen, P. Clough, & T. Pardeck (Eds.), *Handbook of emotional and behavioral difficulties in education.* London: Sage.

Kauffman, J. M., Bantz, J., & McCullough, J. (2002). Separate and better: A special public school class for students with emotional and behavioral disorders. *Exceptionality, 10,* 149–170.

Kauffman, J. M., Boland, J., Hopkins, N., & Birnbrauer, J. S. (1980). *Managing and teaching the severely disturbed and retarded: A guide for teachers.* Columbus, OH: Special Press.

Kauffman, J. M., Brigham, F. J., & Mock, D. R. (2004). Historical and contemporary perspectives in the field of behavioral disorders. In R. B. Rutherford, M. M. Quinn, & S. R. Mathur (Eds.), *Handbook of research in emotional and behavioral disorders.* New York: Guilford.

Kauffman, J. M., & Burbach, H. J. (1997). On creating a climate of classroom civility. *Phi Delta Kappan, 79,* 320–325.

Kauffman, J. M., Cullinan, D., & Epstein, M. H. (1987). Characteristics of students placed in special programs for the seriously emotionally disturbed. *Behavioral Disorders, 12,* 175–184.

Kauffman, J. M., Gerber, M. M., & Semmel, M. I. (1988). Questionable assumptions underlying the regular education initiative. *Journal of Learning Disabilities, 21*(1), 6–11.

Kauffman, J. M., & Hallahan, D. P. (1993). Toward a comprehensive service delivery system. In J. I. Goodlad & T. C. Lovitt (Eds.), *Integrating general and special education* (pp. 73–102). Upper Saddle River, NJ: Merrill/Prentice Hall.

Kauffman, J. M., & Hallahan, D. P. (1997). A diversity of restrictive environments: Placement as a problem of social ecology. In J. W. Lloyd, E. J. Kameenui, & D. Chard (Eds.), *Issues in educating students with disabilities* (pp. 325–342). Hillsdale, NJ: Erlbaum.

Kauffman, J. M., & Hallahan, D. P. (Eds.). (2005a). *The illusion of full inclusion: A comprehensive critique of a current special educational bandwagon* (2nd ed.). Austin, TX: Pro-Ed.

Kauffman, J. M., & Hallahan, D. P. (2005b). *What special education is and why we need it.* Boston: Allyn & Bacon.

Kauffman, J. M., & Kneedler, R. D. (1981). Behavior disorders. In J. M. Kauffman & D. P. Hallahan (Eds.), *Handbook of special education* (pp. 165–194). Upper Saddle River, NJ: Prentice Hall.

Kauffman, J. M., & Landrum, T. J. (2005). Educational service interventions and reforms. In J. W. Jacobson & J. A. Mulick (Eds.), *Handbook of intellectual and developmental disabilities.* New York: Kluwer.

Kauffman, J. M., Landrum, T. J., & Sayeski, K. L. (in press). Behavioral approaches to classroom management. In C. Evertson & C. Weinstein (Eds.), *Handbook of classroom management: Research, practice, and contemporary issues*. Mahwah, NJ: Erlbaum.

Kauffman, J. M., & Lewis, C. D. (Eds.). (1974). *Teaching children with behavior disorders: Personal perspectives*. Upper Saddle River, NJ: Merrill/Prentice Hall.

Kauffman, J. M., & Lloyd, J. W. (1995). A sense of place: The importance of placement issues in contemporary special education. In J. M. Kauffman, J. W. Lloyd, D. P. Hallahan, & T. A. Astuto (Eds.), *Issues in educational placement: Students with emotional and behavioral disorders* (pp. 3–19). Hillsdale, NJ: Erlbaum.

Kauffman, J. M., Lloyd, J. W., Baker, J., & Riedel, T. M. (1995). Inclusion of all students with emotional or behavioral disorders? Let's think again. *Phi Delta Kappan, 76*, 542–546.

Kauffman, J. M., Lloyd, J. W., Hallahan, D. P., & Astuto, T. A. (Eds.). (1995a). *Issues in educational placement: Students with emotional and behavioral disorders*. Hillsdale, NJ: Erlbaum.

Kauffman, J. M., Lloyd, J. W., Hallahan, D. P., & Astuto, T. A. (Eds.). (1995b). Toward a sense of place for special education in the 21st century. In J. M. Kauffman, J. W. Lloyd, D. P. Hallahan, & T. A. Astuto (Eds.), *Issues in educational placement: Students with emotional and behavioral disorders* (pp. 379–385). Hillsdale, NJ: Erlbaum.

Kauffman, J. M., Lloyd, J. W., & McGee, K. A. (1989). Adaptive and maladaptive behavior: Teachers' attitudes and their technical assistance needs. *Journal of Special Education, 23*, 185–200.

Kauffman, J. M., McGee, K., & Brigham, M. (in press). Enabling or disabling? Observations on changes in the purposes and outcomes of special education. *Phi Delta Kappan*.

Kauffman, J. M., Mostert, M. P., Trent, S. C., & Hallahan, D. P. (2002). *Managing classroom behavior: A reflective case-based approach* (3rd ed.). Boston: Allyn & Bacon.

Kauffman, J. M., & Pullen, P. L. (1996). Eight myths about special education. *Focus on Exceptional Children, 28*(5), 1–12.

Kauffman, J. M., & Smucker, K. (1995). The legacies of placement: A brief history of placement options and issues with commentary on their evolution. In J. M. Kauffman, J. W. Lloyd, D. P. Hallahan, & T. A. Astuto (Eds.), *Issues in educational placement: Students with emotional and behavioral disorders* (pp. 21–44). Hillsdale, NJ: Erlbaum.

Kauffman, J. M., Wong, K. L. H., Lloyd, J. W., Hung, L., & Pullen, P. L. (1991). What puts pupils at risk? An analysis of teachers' judgments of pupils' behavior. *Remedial and Special Education, 12*(5), 7–16.

Kaufman, A. S., & Ishikuma, T. (1993). Intellectual and achievement testing. In T. H. Ollendick & M. Hersen (Eds.), *Handbook of child and adolescent assessment* (pp. 192–207). New York: Pergamon.

Kavale, K. A., & Forness, S. R. (1995). Social skill deficits and training: A meta-analysis of the research in learning disabilities. In T. E. Scruggs & M. A. Mastropieri (Eds.), *Advances in learning and behavioral disabilities* (pp. 119–160). Greenwich, CT: JAI.

Kavale, K. A., & Forness, S. R. (2000). History, rhetoric and reality: An analysis of the inclusion debate. *Remedial and Special Education, 21,* 279–296.

Kavale, K. A., Mathur, S. R., & Mostert, M. P. (2004). Social skills training and teaching social behavior. In R. B. Rutherford, M. M. Quinn, & S. R. Mathur (Eds.). *Handbook of research in emotional and behavioral disorders*. New York: Guilford.

Kavale, K. A., & Mostert, M. P. (2003). River of ideology, islands of evidence. *Exceptionality, 11,* 191–208.

Kazdin, A. E. (1977). Assessing the clinical or applied importance of behavior change through social validation. *Behavior Modification, 1,* 427–452.

Kazdin, A. E. (1993). Conduct disorder. In T. H. Ollendick & M. Hersen (Eds.), *Handbook of child and adolescent assessment* (pp. 292–310). New York: Pergamon.

Kazdin, A. E. (1994). Interventions for aggressive and anti-social children. In L. D. Eron, J. H. Gentry, & P. Schlegel (Eds.), *Reason to hope: A psychosocial perspective on violence and youth* (pp. 341–382). Washington, DC: American Psychological Association.

Kazdin, A. E. (1995). *Conduct disorders in childhood and adolescence* (2nd ed.). Thousand Oaks, CA: Sage.

Kazdin, A. E. (1998). Conduct disorder. In R. J. Morris & T. R. Kratochwill (Eds.), *The practice of child therapy* (3rd ed., pp. 199–230). Boston: Allyn & Bacon.

Kazdin, A. E. (2001). *Behavior modification in applied settings* (6th ed.). Belmont, CA: Wadsworth.

Kazdin, A. E., & Marciano, P. L. (1998). Childhood and adolescent depression. In E. J. Mash & R. A. Barkley (Eds.), *Treatment of childhood disorders* (2nd ed., pp. 211–248). New York: Guilford.

Kendall, P. C., & Gosch, E. A. (1994). Cognitive-behavioral interventions. In T. H. Ollendick, N. J. King, & W. Yule (Eds.), *International handbook of phobic and anxiety disorders in children and adolescents* (pp. 415–438). New York: Plenum.

Keogh, B. K. (2003). *Temperament in the classroom: Understanding individual differences*. Baltimore: Brookes.

Kerbeshian, J., & Burd, L. (1994). Tourette's syndrome: A developmental psychobiologic view. *Journal of Developmental and Physical Disabilities, 6,* 203–218.

Kerr, M. M., & Nelson, C. M. (2002). *Strategies for addressing behavior problems in the classroom* (4th ed.). Upper Saddle River, NJ: Merrill/Prentice Hall.

Kerr, M. M., Nelson, C. M., & Lambert, D. L. (1987). *Helping adolescents with learning and behavior problems*. Upper Saddle River, NJ: Merrill/Prentice Hall.

Kerr, M. M., & Zigmond, N. (1986). What do high school teachers want? A study of expectations and standards. *Education and Treatment of Children, 9*, 239–249.

King, C. I. (1999, July 10). Where are the fathers? *The Washington Post*, p. A19.

King, N. J., Hamilton, D. I., & Murphy, G. C. (1983). The prevention of children's maladaptive fears. *Child and Family Behavior Therapy, 5*(2), 43–57.

King, N. J., Ollendick, T. H., & Tonge, B. J. (1995). *School refusal: Assessment and treatment*. Boston: Allyn & Bacon.

Kingery, P. M., & Walker, H. M. (2002). What we know about school safety. In M. R. Shinn, H. M. Walker, & G. Stoner (Eds.), *Interventions for academic and behavior problems II: Preventive and remedial approaches* (pp. 71–88). Bethesda, MD: National Association of School Psychologists.

Kirigin, K. A., Braukman, C. J., Atwater, J. D., & Wolf, M. M. (1982). An evaluation of Teaching–Family (Achievement Place) group homes for juvenile offenders. *Journal of Applied Behavior Analysis, 15*, 1–16.

Kirk, S. A. (1972). *Educating exceptional children* (2nd ed.). Boston: Houghton Mifflin.

Klein, M. W. (1995). *The American street gang: Its nature, prevalence, and control*. New York: Oxford University Press.

Klein, R. G., & Last, C. G. (1989). *Anxiety disorders in children*. Newbury Park, CA: Sage.

Kleinheksel, K. A., & Summy, S. E. (2003). Enhancing student learning and social behavior through mnemonic strategies. *Teaching Exceptional Children, 36*(2), 30–35.

Klinger, L. G., Dawson, G., & Renner, P. (2003). Autistic disorder. In E. J. Mash & R. A. Barkley (Eds.), *Child psychopathology* (2nd ed., pp. 409–454). New York: Guilford.

Klorman, R. (1995). Psychophysiological determinants. In M. Hersen & R. T. Ammerman (Eds.), *Advanced abnormal child psychology* (pp. 59–85). Hillsdale, NJ: Erlbaum.

Knapp, M. S. (1995). How shall we study comprehensive, collaborative services for children and families? *Educational Researcher, 24*(4), 5–16.

Knitzer, J. (1982). *Unclaimed children: The failure of public responsibility to children and adolescents in need of mental health services*. Washington, DC: Children's Defense Fund.

Knitzer, J., & Aber, J. L. (1995). Young children in poverty: Facing the facts. *American Journal of Orthopsychiatry, 65*, 174–176.

Knitzer, J., Steinberg, Z., & Fleisch, F. (1990). *At the schoolhouse door: An examination of programs and policies for children with behavioral and emotional problems*. New York: Bank Street College of Education.

Knoblock, P. (1970). A new humanism for special education: The concept of the open classroom for emotionally disturbed children. In P. A. Gallagher & L. L. Edwards (Eds.), *Educating the emotionally disturbed: Theory to practice* (pp. 68–85). Lawrence: University of Kansas.

Knoblock, P. (1973). Open education for emotionally disturbed children. *Exceptional Children, 39*, 358–365.

Knoblock, P. (1979). Educational alternatives for adolescents labeled emotionally disturbed. In D. Cullinan & M. H. Epstein (Eds.), *Special education for adolescents: Issues and perspectives* (pp. 273–304). Upper Saddle River, NJ: Merrill/Prentice Hall.

Knoblock, P. (1983). *Teaching emotionally disturbed children*. Boston: Houghton Mifflin.

Kochanska, G. (1995). Children's temperament, mothers' discipline, and security of attachment: Multiple pathways to emerging internalization. *Child Development, 66*, 597–615.

Koegel, L. K., & Koegel, R. L. (1995). Motivating communication in children with autism. In E. Schopler & G. B. Mesibov (Eds.), *Learning and cognition in autism* (pp. 73–87). New York: Plenum.

Koegel, R. L., Frea, W. D., & Surratt, A. V. (1994). Self-management of problematic social behavior. In E. Schopler & G. B. Mesibov (Eds.), *Behavioral issues in autism* (pp. 81–97). New York: Plenum.

Kohn, A. (1993). *Punished by rewards*. New York: Houghton Mifflin.

Kolko, D. (2002). (Ed.). *Handbook on firesetting in children and youth*. New York: Academic Press.

Kolko, D. J., Bukstein, O. G., & Barron, J. (1999). Methylphenidate and behavior modification in children with ADHD and comorbid ODD or CD: Main and incremental effects across settings. *Journal of the American Academy of Child and Adolescent Psychiatry, 38*, 578–586.

Kolko, D. J., & Kazdin, A. E. (1986). A conceptualization of fire setting in children and adolescents. *Journal of Abnormal Child Psychology, 14*, 49–61.

Kolko, D. J., & Kazdin, A. E. (1989). The Children's Firesetting Interview with psychiatrically referred and nonreferred children. *Journal of Abnormal Child Psychology, 17*, 609–624.

Konopasek, D. E. (1996). *Medication fact sheets: A medication reference guide for the non-medical professional*. Anchorage, AK: Artic Tern.

Konopasek, D., & Forness, S. R. (2004). Research regarding the use of psychopharmacology in the treatment of emotional and behavioral disorders. In R. B. Rutherford, M. M. Quinn, & S. R. Mathur (Eds.), *Handbook of research in emotional and behavioral disorders*. New York: Guilford.

Kornberg, L. (1955). *A class for disturbed children: A case study and its meaning for education*. New York: Teachers College Press.

Kotler, L. A., Devlin, M. J., & Walsh, B. T. (2002). Eating disorders and related disturbances. In S. Kutcher (Ed.),

Practical child and adolescent psychopharmacology (pp. 410–430). New York: Cambridge University Press.

Kovaleski, J. F., Gickling, E. E., Morrow, H., & Swank, P. R. (1999). High versus low implementation of instructional support teams: A case for maintaining program fidelity. *Remedial & Special Education, 20,* 170–183.

Kratochwill, T. R., & McGivern, J. E. (1996). Clinical diagnosis, behavioral assessment, and functional analysis: Examining the connection between assessment and intervention. *School Psychology Review, 25,* 342–355.

Kratzer, L., & Hodgins, S. (1999). A typology of offenders: A test of Moffitt's theory among males and females from childhood to age 30. *Criminal Behavior and Mental Health, 9,* 57–73.

Krueger, J. I. (2002). Postmodern parlor games. *American Psychologist, 57,* 461–462.

Kruger, D. J. (2002). The deconstruction of constructivism. *American Psychologist, 57,* 456–457.

Kunce, L. J., & Mesibov, G. B. (1998). Educational approaches to high-functioning autism and Asperger's syndrome. In E. Schopler, G. B. Mesibov, & L. J. Kunce, (Eds.), *Asperger syndrome or high functioning autism?* (pp. 227–261). New York: Plenum.

Kupersmidt, J. B., Griesler, P. C., DeRosier, M. E., Patterson, C. J., & Davis, P. W. (1995). Childhood aggression and peer relations in the context of family and neighborhood factors. *Child Development, 66,* 360–375.

Kupersmidt, J. B., & Patterson, C. J. (1987). *Interim report to the Charlottesville Public Schools on children at risk.* Unpublished manuscript, University of Virginia, Charlottesville.

Kusumakar, V., Lazier, L., MacMaster, F. P., & Santor, D. (2002). Bipolar mood disorders: diagnosis, etiology, and treatment. In S. Kutcher (Ed.), *Practical child and adolescent psychopharmacology* (pp. 106–133). New York: Cambridge University Press.

Kutcher, S. (Ed.). (2002). *Practical child and adolescent psychopharmacology.* New York: Cambridge University Press.

Kyger, M. M. (1999). *Fix it before it breaks: Training teachers to use precorrection procedures.* Unpublished doctoral dissertation, University of Virginia, Charlottesville.

Laird, R. D., Pettit, G. S., Bates, J. E., & Dodge, K. A. (2003). Parents' monitoring-relevant knowledge and adolescents' delinquent behavior: Evidence of correlated developmental changes and reciprocal influences. *Child Development, 74,* 752–768.

Lambros, K. M., Ward, S. L., Bocain, K. M., MacMillan, D. L., & Gresham, F. M. (1998). Behavioral profiles of children at-risk for emotional and behavioral disorders: Implications for assessment and classification. *Focus on Exceptional Children, 30*(5), 1–16.

Landrum, T. J. (2000). Assessment for eligibility: Issues in identifying students with emotional or behavioral disorders. *Assessment for Effective Intervention, 26*(1), 41–49.

Landrum, T. J., & Kauffman, J. M. (1992). Characteristics of general education teachers perceived as effective by their peers: Implications for inclusion of children with learning and behavioral disorders. *Exceptionality, 3,* 147–163.

Landrum, T. J., & Kauffman, J. M. (2003). Emotionally disturbed, education of. In J. W. Guthrie (Ed.), *Encyclopedia of education* (2nd ed., pp. 726–728). New York: Macmillan Reference.

Landrum, T. J., & Tankersley, M. (1999). Emotional and behavioral disorders in the new millennium: The future is now. *Behavioral Disorders, 24,* 319–330.

Landrum, T. J., Tankersley, M., & Kauffman, J. M. (2003). What's special about special education for students with emotional and behavioral disorders? *The Journal of Special Education, 37,* 148–156.

Lane, K. L. (2004). Academic instruction and tutoring interventions for students with emotional/behavioral disorders 1990 to present. In R. B. Rutherford, M. M. Quinn, & S. R. Mathur (Eds.), *Handbook of research in emotional and behavioral disorders.* New York: Guilford.

Lantieri, L. (1995). Waging peace in our schools: Beginning with the children. *Phi Delta Kappan, 76,* 386–388.

Lattimore, P. K., Visher, C. A., & Linster, R. L. (1995). Predicting rearrest for violence among serious youthful offenders. *Journal of Research in Crime and Delinquency, 32,* 54–83.

Laub, J. H., & Lauritsen, J. L. (1998). The interdependence of school violence with neighborhood and family conditions. In D. S. Elliott, B. A. Hamburg, & K. R. Williams (Eds.), *Violence in American schools* (pp. 127–155). New York: Cambridge University Press.

LaVigna, G. W., & Donnellan, A. M. (1986). *Alternatives to punishment: Solving behavior problems with nonaversive strategies.* New York: Irvington.

Lavigueur, S., Tremblay, R. E., & Saucier, J. (1995). Interactional processes in families with disruptive boys: Patterns of direct and indirect influence. *Journal of Abnormal Child Psychology, 23,* 359–378.

Lay, B., Blanz, B., Hartmann, M., & Schmidt, M. H. (2000). The psychosocial outcome of adolescent-onset schizophrenia: A 12-year followup. *Schizophrenia Bulletin, 26,* 801–816.

Lee, P., Moss, S., Friedlander, R., Donnelly, T., & Honer, W. (2003). Early-onset schizophrenia in children with mental retardation: Diagnostic reliability and stability of clinical features. *Journal of the American Academy of Child and Adolescent Psychiatry, 42,* 162–169.

Leech, S. L., Day, N. L., Richardson, G. A., & Goldschmidt, L. (2003). Predictors of self-reported delinquent behavior in a sample of young adolescents. *Journal of Early Adolescence, 23,* 78–106.

Lenzenweger, M. F., & Dworkin, R. H. (Eds.). (1998). *Origins and development of schizophrenia: Advances in experimental psychopathology.* Washington, DC: American Psychological Association.

Leone, P. E., Rutherford, R. B., & Nelson, C. M. (1991). *Special education in juvenile corrections.* Reston, VA: Council for Exceptional Children.

Leone, P. E., Walter, M. B., & Wolford, B. I. (1990). Toward integrated responses to troubling behavior. In P. E. Leone (Ed.), *Understanding troubled and troubling youth* (pp. 290–298). Newbury Park, CA: Sage.

Lerman, D. C., Iwata, B. A., Zarcone, J. R., & Ringdahl, J. (1994). Assessment of stereotypic and self-injurious behavior as adjunctive responses. *Journal of Applied Behavior Analysis, 27,* 715–728.

Lerman, D. C., & Vorndran, C. M. (2002). On the status of knowledge for using punishment: Implications for treating behavior disorders. *Journal of Applied Behavior Analysis, 35,* 431–464.

Leve, L. D., Winebarger, A. A., Fagot, B. I., Reid, J. B., & Goldsmith, H. H. (1998). Environmental and genetic variance in children's observed and reported maladaptive behavior. *Child Development, 69,* 1286–1298.

Levendosky, A. A., Okun, A., & Parker, J. G. (1995). Depression and maltreatment as predictors of social competence and social problem-solving skills in school-aged children. *Child Abuse and Neglect, 19,* 1183–1195.

Levey, J. C., & Lagos, V. K. (1994). Children with disabilities. In L. D. Eron, J. H. Gentry, & P. Schlegel (Eds.), *Reason to hope: A psychosocial perspective on violence and youth* (pp. 197–213). Washington, DC: American Psychological Association.

Levin, H. M., Guthrie, J. W., Kleindorfer, G. B., & Stout, R. T. (1971). School achievement and post-school success: A review. *Review of Educational Research, 41,* 1–16.

Levy, F., & Hay, D. A. (Eds.). (2001). *Attention, genes and ADHD.* Philadelphia: Taylor & Francis.

Lewinsohn, P. M., Gotlib, I. H., & Seeley, J. R. (1995). Adolescent psychopathology. IV: Specificity of psychosocial risk factors for depression and substance abuse in older adolescents. *Journal of the American Academy of Child and Adolescent Psychiatry, 34,* 1221–1229.

Lewis, C. D. (1974). Introduction: Landmarks. In J. M. Kauffman & C. D. Lewis (Eds.), *Teaching children with behavior disorders: Personal perspectives* (pp. 2–23). Upper Saddle River, NJ: Merrill/Prentice Hall.

Lewis, T. J., Lewis-Palmer, T., Stichter, J., & Newcomer, L. L. (2004). Applied behavior analysis and the education and treatment of students with emotional and behavioral disorders. In R. Rutherford, M. M. Quinn, & S. Mathur (Eds.), *Handbook of research in emotional and behavioral disorders.* New York: Guilford.

Lewis, T. J., & Sugai, G. (1999). Effective behavior support: A systems approach to proactive schoolwide management. *Focus on Exceptional Children, 31*(6), 1–24.

Lewis, T. J., Sugai, G., & Colvin, G. (1998). Reducing problem behavior through a school-wide system of effective behavioral support: Investigation of a school-wide social skills training program and contextual interventions. *School Psychology Review, 27,* 446–459.

Lewis, W. W. (1982). Ecological factors in successful residential treatment. *Behavioral Disorders, 7,* 149–156.

Liaupsin, C. J., Jolivette, K., & Scott, T. M. (2004). School-wide systems of behavior support: Maximizing student success in schools. In R. B. Rutherford, M. M. Quinn, & S. R. Mathur (Eds.), *Handbook of research in emotional and behavioral disorders.* New York: Guilford.

Light, R., McCleary, C., Asarnow, R., Zaucha, K., & Lewis, R. (1998). Mild closed-head injury in children and adolescents: Behavior problems and academic outcomes. *Journal of Consulting and Clinical Psychology, 66,* 1023–1027.

Lilly, M. S. (1992). Labeling: A tired, overworked, yet unresolved issue in special education. In W. Stainback & S. Stainback (Eds.), *Controversial issues confronting special education: Divergent perspectives* (pp. 85–95). Boston: Allyn & Bacon.

Lincoln, A. J., Kaufman, J., & Kaufman, A. S. (1995). Intellectual and cognitive assessment. In M. Hersen & R. T. Ammerman (Eds.), *Advanced abnormal child psychology* (pp. 137–155). Hillsdale, NJ: Erlbaum.

Linet, L. S. (Ed.). (1995). *Medical letter: 1995 summary of the recent literature.* Bayside, NY: Tourette Syndrome Association.

Linnoila, M. (1997). On the psychobiology of antisocial behavior. In D. M. Stoff, J. Breiling, & J. D. Maser (Eds.), *Handbook of antisocial behavior* (pp. 336–340). New York: Wiley.

Lipsky, D. K., & Gartner, A. (1991). Restructuring for quality. In J. W. Lloyd, N. N. Singh, & A. C. Repp (Eds.), *The regular education initiative: Alternative perspectives on concepts, issues, and models* (pp. 43–56). Sycamore, IL: Sycamore.

Little, S. A., & Garber, J. (1995). Hyperaggression, depression, and stressful life events predicting peer rejection in children. *Development and Psychopathology, 7,* 845–856.

Lloyd, J. W., Forness, S. R., & Kavale, K. A. (1998). Some methods are more effective than others. *Intervention in School and Clinic, 33*(4), 195–200.

Lloyd, J. W., Hallahan, D. P., Kauffman, J. M., & Keller, C. E. (1998). Academic problems. In T. R. Kratochwill & R. J. Morris (Eds.), *Practice of child therapy* (3rd ed., pp.167–198). Boston: Allyn & Bacon.

Lloyd, J. W., & Kauffman, J. M. (1995). What less restrictive placements require of teachers. In J. M. Kauffman, J. W. Lloyd, D. P. Hallahan, & T. A. Astuto (Eds.), *Issues in educational placement: Students with emotional and behavioral disorders* (pp. 317–334). Hillsdale, NJ: Erlbaum.

Lloyd, J. W., Kauffman, J. M., Landrum, T. J., & Roe, D. L. (1991). Why do teachers refer pupils for special education? An analysis of referral records. *Exceptionality, 2,* 115–126.

Locke, E. A. (2002). The dead end of postmodernism. *American Psychologist, 57,* 458.

Loeber, R. (1982). The stability of antisocial and delinquent child behavior: A review. *Child Development, 53,* 1431–1446.

Loeber, R., & Farrington, D. P. (2000). Young children who commit crime: Epidemiology, developmental origins, risk factors, early interventions, and policy implications. *Development and Psychopathology, 12,* 737–762.

Loeber, R., Farrington, D. P., Stouthamer-Loeber, M., & Van Kammen, W. B. (1998a). *Antisocial behavior and mental health problems: Explanatory factors in childhood and adolescence.* Mahwah, NJ: Erlbaum.

Loeber, R., Farrington, D. P., Stouthamer-Loeber, M., & Van Kammen, W. B. (1998b). Multiple risk factors for multi-problem boys: Co-occurrence of delinquency, substance use, attention deficit, conduct problems, physical aggression, covert behavior, depressed mood, and shy/withdrawn behavior. In R. Jessor (Ed.), *New perspectives on adolescent risk behavior* (pp. 90–149). New York: Cambridge University Press.

Loeber, R., Green, S. M., Keenan, K., & Lahey, B. B. (1995). Which boys will fare worse? Early predictors of the onset of conduct disorder in a six-year longitudinal study. *Journal of the American Academy of Child and Adolescent Psychiatry, 34,* 499–509.

Loeber, R., Green, S. M., Lahey, B. B., Christ, M. A. G., & Frick, P. J. (1992). Developmental sequences in the age of onset of disruptive child behaviors. *Journal of Child and Family Studies, 1,* 21–41.

Loeber, R., & Schmaling, K. B. (1985a). Empirical evidence for overt and covert patterns of antisocial conduct problems: A meta analysis. *Journal of Abnormal Child Psychology, 13,* 337–352.

Loeber, R., & Schmaling, K. B. (1985b). The utility of differentiating between mixed and pure forms of antisocial child behavior. *Journal of Abnormal Child Psychology, 13,* 315–336.

Loeber, R., & Stouthamer-Loeber, M. (1998). *Juvenile aggression at home and at school.* In D. S. Elliott, B. A. Hamburg, & K. R. Williams (Eds.), *Violence in American schools: A new perspective* (pp. 94–126). New York: Cambridge University Press.

Loeber, R., Wung, P., Keenan, K., Giroux, B., Stouthamer-Loeber, M., Van Kammen, W., & Maughan, B. (1993).

Developmental pathways in disruptive child behavior. *Development and Psychopathology, 5,* 103–134.

Long, N. J. (1974). Nicholas J. Long. In J. M. Kauffman & C. D. Lewis (Eds.), *Teaching children with behavior disorders: Personal perspectives* (pp. 168–196). Upper Saddle River, NJ: Merrill/Prentice Hall.

Long, N. J., & Newman, R. G. (1965). Managing surface behavior of children in school. In N. J. Long, W. C. Morse, & R. G. Newman (Eds.), *Conflict in the classroom* (pp. 352–362). Belmont, CA: Wadsworth.

Long, N. J., Wood, M. M., & Fecser, F. A. (2001). *Life space crisis intervention: Talking with students with in conflict.* Austin, TX: Pro-Ed.

Lorion, R. P., Brodsky, A., Flaherty, M. J., & Holland, C. C. (1995). Community and prevention. In M. Hersen & R. T. Ammerman (Eds.), *Advanced abnormal child psychology* (pp. 213–230). Hillsdale, NJ: Erlbaum.

Lous, A. M., de Wit, C. A. M., De Bruyn, E. E. J., & Riksen-Walraven, J. M. (2002). Depression markers in young children's play: A comparison between depressed and nondepressed 3- to 6-year-olds in various play situations. *Journal of Child Psychology and Psychiatry and Allied Disciplines, 43,* 1029–1038.

Lovaas, O. I. (1987). Behavioral treatment and normal educational and intellectual functioning in young autistic children. *Journal of Consulting and Clinical Psychology, 55,* 3–9.

Lovaas, O. I., Koegel, R. L., Simmons, J. Q., & Long, J. S. (1973). Some generalization and follow-up measures on autistic children in behavior therapy. *Journal of Applied Behavior Analysis, 6,* 131–166.

Lovitt, T. C. (1977). *In spite of my resistance—I've learned from children.* Upper Saddle River, NJ: Merrill/Prentice Hall.

Lundman, R. J. (1993). *Prevention and control of juvenile delinquency* (2nd ed.). New York: Oxford University Press.

Lynam, D. R. (1996). Early identification of chronic offenders: Who is the fledgling psychopath? *Psychological Bulletin, 120,* 209–234.

Lynn, D., & King, B. H. (2002). Aggressive behavior. In S. Kutcher (Ed.), *Practical child and adolescent psychopharmacology* (pp. 305–327). New York: Cambridge University Press.

Lyons, D. F., & Powers, V. (1963). Follow-up study of elementary school children exempted from Los Angeles City Schools during 1960–1961. *Exceptional Children, 30,* 155–162.

Maag, J. W. (2001). Rewarded by punishment: Reflections on the disuse of positive reinforcement in schools. *Exceptional Children, 67,* 173–186.

Madge, N., & Harvey, J. G. (1999). Suicide among the young—The size of the problem. *Journal of Adolescence, 22,* 145–155.

Mahfouz, N. (2001). *The Cairo trilogy* (W. M. Hutchins, O. E., Kenny, L. M. Kenny, & A. B. Samaan, Trans.). London: Everyman.

Mahoney, M. J. (1995). Cognition and causation in human experience. *Journal of Behavior Therapy and Experimental Psychiatry, 26,* 275–278.

Malecki, C. K., & Demaray, M. K. (2003). Carrying a weapon to school and perceptions of social support in an urban middle school. *Journal of Emotional and Behavioral Disorders, 11,* 169–178.

Malone, J. C. (2003). Advances in behaviorism: It's not what it used to be. *Journal of Behavioral Education, 12,* 85–89.

Manno, C. J., Bantz, J., & Kauffman, J. M. (2000). Cultural causes of rage and violence in children and youth. *Reaching Today's Youth, 4*(2), 54–59.

March, J. S. (1995). Cognitive-behavioral psychotherapy for children and adolescents with OCD: A review and recommendations for treatment. *Journal of the American Academy of Child and Adolescent Psychiatry, 34,* 7–18.

March, J. S., & Mulle, K. (1998). OCD in children and adolescents: A cognitive-behavioral treatment manual. New York: Guilford.

Mark Twain Foundation. (1966). Mark Twain: Collected tales, sketches, speeches, & essays, 1891–1910. New York: Library of America.

Marriage, K. (2002). Schizophrenia and related psychoses. In S. Kutcher (Ed.), *Practical child and adolescent psychopharmacology* (pp. 134–158). New York: Cambridge University Press.

Martella, R. C., Nelson, J. R., & Marchand-Martella, N. E. (2003). *Managing disruptive behaviors in the schools: A schoolwide, classroom, and individualized learning approach*. Boston: Allyn & Bacon.

Martens, E. H., & Russ, H. (1932). *Adjustment of behavior problems of school children: A description and evaluation of the clinical program in Berkeley, Calif.* Washington, DC: U.S. Government Printing Office.

Martin, J. A. (1981). A longitudinal study of the consequences of early mother–infant interaction: A microanalytic approach. *Monographs of the Society for Research in Child Development, 43*(3, Serial No. 190).

Martin, R. P. (1992). Child temperament effects on special education process and outcomes. *Exceptionality, 3,* 99–115.

Marvin, C. A., Beukelman, D. R., Brockhaus, J., & Kast, L. (1994). "What are you talking about?": Semantic analysis of preschool children's conversational topics in home and preschool settings. *Augmentative and Alternative Communication, 10,* 75–86.

Mash, E. J., & Barkley, R. A. (Eds.). (2003). *Child psychopathology* (2nd ed.). New York: Guilford.

Masi, G., Sbrana, B., Poli, P., Tomaiuolo, F., Favilla, L., & Marcheschi, M. (2000). Depression and school functioning in non-referred adolescents: A pilot study. *Child Psychiatry and Human Development, 30,* 161–171.

Mathes, M. Y., & Bender, W. N. (1997). The effects of self-monitoring on children with attention-deficit/hyperactivity disorder. *Remedial and Special Education, 18,* 121–128.

Mattison, R. E. (2004). Psychiatric and psychological assessment of EBD during school mental health consultation. In R. B. Rutherford, M. M. Quinn, & S. R. Mathur (Eds.), *Handbook of research in emotional and behavioral disorders*. New York: Guilford.

Mayer, G. R. (1995). Preventing antisocial behavior in the schools. *Journal of Applied Behavior Analysis, 28,* 467–478.

Mayer, G. R., Nafpaktitis, M., Butterworth, T., & Hollingsworth, P. (1987). A search for the elusive setting events of school vandalism: A correlational study. *Education and Treatment of Children, 10,* 259–270.

Mayer, G. R., & Sulzer-Azaroff, B. (1991). Interventions for vandalism. In G. Stoner, M. R. Shinn, & H. M. Walker (Eds.), *Interventions for achievement and behavior problems* (pp. 559–580). Silver Spring, MD: National Association of School Psychologists.

Mayer, G. R., & Sulzer-Azaroff, B. (2002). Interventions for vandalism and aggression. In M. R. Shinn, H. M. Walker, & G. Stoner (Eds.), *Interventions for academic and behavior problems II: Preventive and remedial approaches* (pp. 853–884). Bethesda, MD: National Association of School Psychologists.

McCloskey, L. A., Figueredo, A. J., & Koss, M. P. (1995). The effects of systemic family violence on children's mental health. *Child Development, 66,* 1239–1261.

McConaughy, S. H. (1993). Evaluating behavioral and emotional disorders with the CBCL, TRF, and YSR cross-informant scales. *Journal of Emotional and Behavioral Disorders, 1,* 40–52.

McConaughy, S. H., Kay, P. J., & Fitzgerald, M. (1998). Preventing SED through parent–teacher action research and social skills instruction: First-year outcomes. *Journal of Emotional and Behavioral Disorders, 6,* 81–93.

McConnell, M. E., Cox, C. J., Thomas, D. D., & Hilvitz, P. B. (2001). *Functional behavioral assessment*. Denver, CO: Love.

McConnell, S. R. (1987). Entrapment effects and the generalization and maintenance of social skills training for elementary school students with behavioral disorders. *Behavioral Disorders, 12,* 252–263.

McDowell, R. L., Adamson, G. W., & Wood, F. H. (Eds.). (1982). *Teaching emotionally disturbed children*. Boston: Little, Brown.

McEvoy, M. A., & Odom, S. L. (1987). Social interaction training for preschool children with behavioral disorders. *Behavior Disorders, 12,* 242–251.

McFadyen-Ketchum, S. A., & Dodge, K. A. (1998). Problems in social relationships. In E. J. Mash & R. A. Barkley (Eds.), *Treatment of childhood disorders* (2nd ed., pp. 338–365). New York: Guilford.

McGinnis, J. C., Friman, P. C., & Carlyon, W. D. (1999). The effect of token rewards on "intrinsic" motivation for doing math. *Journal of Applied Behavior Analysis, 32,* 375–379.

McGuffin, P., & Thapar, A. (1997). Genetic basis for bad behavior in adolescents. *Lancet, 350,* 411–412.

McIntyre, T. (1992). The "invisible culture" in our schools: Gay and lesbian youth. *Beyond Behavior, 3*(3), 6–12.

McIntyre, T., & Silva, P. (1992). Culturally diverse childrearing practices: Abusive or just different? *Beyond Behavior, 4*(1), 8–12.

McLoughlin, J. A., & Nall, M. (1994). Allergies and learning/behavioral disorders. *Intervention in School and Clinic, 29,* 198–207.

McMahon, R. J., & Wells, K. C. (1998). Conduct problems. In E. J. Mash & R. A. Barkley (Eds.), *Treatment of childhood disorders* (2nd ed., pp. 111–207). New York: Guilford.

McMaster, K., Fuchs, D., Fuchs, L. S., & Copton, D. L. (2002). Monitoring the academic progress of children who are unresponsive to generally effective early reading intervention. *Assessment for Effective Intervention, 27*(4), 23–34.

McWhorter, J. H. (2000). Explaining the black education gap. *The Wilson Quarterly, 24*(3), 73–92.

Meadows, N. B., Melloy, K. J., & Yell, M. L. (1996). Behavior management as a curriculum for students with emotional and behavior disorders. *Preventing School Failure, 40,* 124–130.

Meadows, N. B., & Stevens, K. B. (2004). Teaching alternative behaviors to students with emotional/behavioral disorders. In R. B. Rutherford, M. M. Quinn, & S. R. Mathur (Eds.), *Handbook of research in emotional and behavioral disorders.* New York: Guilford.

Mee, C. L. (1999). *A nearly normal life.* Boston: Little, Brown.

Menninger, K. (1963). *The vital balance.* New York: Viking.

Menolascino, F. J. (1990). The nature and types of mental illness in the mentally retarded. In M. Lewis & S. M. Miller (Eds.), *Handbook of developmental psychopathology* (pp. 397–408). New York: Plenum.

Merrell, K. W. (1994). *Assessment of behavioral, social, and emotional problems: Direct and objective methods for use with children and adolescents.* New York: Longman.

Mesibov, G. B., Adams, L. W., & Klinger, L. G. (1997). *Autism: Understanding the disorder.* New York: Plenum.

Meyers, A. W., & Cohen, R. (1990). Cognitive-behavioral approaches to child psychopathology. In M. Lewis & S. M. Miller (Eds.), *Handbook of developmental psychopathology* (pp. 475–485). New York: Plenum.

Middleton, M. B., & Cartledge, G. (1995). The effects of social skills instruction and parental involvement on the aggressive behavior of African American males. *Behavior Modification, 19,* 192–210.

Miksic, S. (1987). Drug abuse management in adolescent special education. In M. M. Kerr, C. M. Nelson, & D. L. Lambert, *Helping adolescents with learning and behavior problems* (pp. 226–253). Upper Saddle River, NJ: Merrill/Prentice Hall.

Milby, J. B., Robinson, S. L., & Daniel, S. (1998). Obsessive compulsive disorders. In R. J. Morris & T. R. Kratochwill (Eds.), *The practice of child therapy* (3rd ed., pp. 5–47). Boston: Allyn & Bacon.

Miller, G. E., & Prinz, R. J. (1991). Designing interventions for stealing. In G. Stoner, M. R. Shinn, & H. M. Walker (Eds.), *Interventions for achievement and behavior problems* (pp. 593–616). Silver Spring, MD: National Association of School Psychologists.

Miller, L., Weissman, M., Gur, M., & Greenwald, S. (2002). Adult religiousness and history of childhood depression: Eleven-year follow-up study. *Journal of Nervous and Mental Disease, 190,* 86–93.

Miller-Johnson, S., Coie, J. D., Maumary-Gremaud, A., Lochman, J., & Terry, R. (1999). Peer rejection and aggression in childhood and severity and type of delinquency during adolescence among African-American youth. *Journal of Emotional and Behavioral Disorders, 7,* 137–146.

Mindell, J. A., & Owens, J. A. (2003). *A clinical guide to pediatric sleep: Diagnosis and management of sleep problems.* New York: Lippincott Williams & Wilkins.

Miner, M. H. (2002). Factors associated with recidivism in juveniles: An analysis of serious juvenile sex offenders. *Journal of Research and Crime and Delinquency, 39,* 421–436.

Minty, B. (1999). Outcomes in long-term foster family care. *Journal of Child Psychology and Psychiatry and Allied Disciplines, 40,* 991–999.

Mirza, K. A. H. (2002). Adolescent substance use disorder. In S. Kutcher (Ed.), *Practical child and adolescent psychopharmacology* (pp. 328–381). New York: Cambridge University Press.

Mithaug, D. K., & Mithaug, D. E. (2003). Effects of teacher-directed versus student-directed instruction on self-management of young children with disabilities. *Journal of Applied Behavior Analysis, 36,* 133–136.

Mizes, J. S. (1995). Eating disorders. In M. Hersen & R. T. Ammerman (Eds.), *Advanced abnormal child psychology* (pp. 375–391). Hillsdale, NJ: Erlbaum.

Mock, D., & Kauffman, J. M. (2002). Preparing teachers for full inclusion: Is it possible? *The Teacher Educator, 37,* 202–215.

Mock, D. R., & Kauffman, J. M. (2004). The delusion of full inclusion. In J. W. Jacobson, J. A. Mulick, & R. M. Foxx

(Eds.), *Fads: Dubious and improbable treatments for developmental disabilities*. Mahwah, NJ: Erlbaum.

Mooney, P., Epstein, M. H., Reid, R., & Nelson, J. R. (2003). Status and trends of academic research for students with emotional disturbance. *Remedial and Special Education, 24,* 273–287.

Moore, D. R., Chamberlain, P., & Mukai, L. H. (1979). Children at risk for delinquency: A follow-up comparison of aggressive children and children who steal. *Journal of Abnormal Child Psychology, 7,* 345–355.

Moore, K. J., & Chamberlain, P. (1994). Treatment foster care: Toward development of community-based models for adolescents with severe emotional and behavioral disorders. *Journal of Emotional and Behavioral Disorders, 2,* 22–30.

Moore, J. W., & Edwards, R. P. (2003). An analysis of aversive stimuli in classroom demand contexts. *Journal of Applied Behavior Analysis, 36,* 339–348.

Morenz, B., & Becker, J. (1995). The treatment of youthful sexual offenders. *Applied and Preventive Psychology, 4,* 247–256.

Morris, R. J., & Kratochwill, T. R. (1983). *Treating children's fears and phobias*. New York: Pergamon.

Morris, R. J., & Kratochwill, T. R. (1998). Childhood fears and phobias. In R. J. Morris & T. R. Kratochwill (Eds.), *The practice of child therapy* (3rd ed., pp. 91–131). Boston: Allyn & Bacon.

Morse, W. C. (1974). William C. Morse. In J. M. Kauffman & C. D. Lewis (Eds.), *Teaching children with behavior disorders: Personal perspectives* (pp. 198–216). Upper Saddle River, NJ: Merrill/Prentice Hall.

Morse, W. C. (1985). *The education and treatment of socioemotionally impaired children and youth*. Syracuse, NY: Syracuse University Press.

Morse, W. C. (1994). Comments from a biased point of view. *Journal of Special Education, 27,* 531–542.

Morse, W. C., Cutler, R. L., & Fink, A. H. (1964). *Public school classes for the emotionally handicapped: A research analysis*. Washington, DC: Council for Exceptional Children.

Mostert, M. P. (2001). Facilitated communication since 1995: A review of published studies. *Journal of Autism and Developmental Disorders, 31,* 287–313.

Mostert, M. P., Kauffman, J. M., & Kavale, K. R. (2003). Truth and consequences. *Behavioral Disorders, 28,* 333–347.

Motto, J. J., & Wilkins, G. S. (1968). Educational achievement of institutionalized emotionally disturbed children. *Journal of Educational Research, 61,* 218–221.

Mountjoy, P. T., Ruben, D. H., & Bradford, T. S. (1984). Recent technological advancements in the treatment of enuresis. *Behavior Modification, 8,* 291–315.

Mueller, C., Field, T., Yando, R., Harding, J., Gonzalez, K. P., Lasko, D., et al. (1995). Under-eating and over-eating concerns among adolescents. *Journal of Child Psychology and Psychiatry, 36,* 1019–1025.

Mukhopadhyay, C., & Henze, R. C. (2003). How real is race? Using anthropology to make sense of human diversity. *Phi Delta Kappan, 84,* 669–678.

Muris, P., Merckelbach, H., Mayer, B., & Snieder, N. (1998). The relationship between anxiety disorder symptoms and negative self-statements in normal children. *Social Behavior and Personality, 26,* 307–316.

Murphy, D. M. (1986). The prevalence of handicapping conditions among juvenile delinquents. *Remedial and Special Education, 7*(3), 7–17.

Muskal, F. (1991). Sociological/ecological theories of emotional disturbance. *Journal of Developmental and Physical Disabilities, 3,* 267–288.

Najman, J. M., Behrens, B. C., Andersen, M., Bor, W., O'Callaghan, M., & Williams, G. M. (1997). Impact of family type and family quality on child behavior problems: A longitudinal study. *Journal of the American Academy of Child and Adolescent Psychiatry, 36,* 1357–1365.

Nakamura, D. (2003, April 6). Fast times at Asakita High. *The Washington Post Magazine,* 28–31, 48–51.

National Mental Health Association. (1986). *Severely emotionally disturbed children: Improving services under Education of the Handicapped Act (P.L. 94–142)*. Washington, DC: Author.

National Research Council. (2001). *Educating children with autism*. Washington, DC: National Academy Press.

National Research Council. (2002). *Minority students in special and gifted education*. (M. S. Donovan & C. T. Cross, Eds.,) Committee on Minority Representation in Special Education. Washington, DC: National Academy Press, Division of Behavioral and Social Sciences Education.

Neill, A. S. (1960). *Summerhill*. New York: Hart.

Nelson, C. M., Leone, P. E., & Rutherford, R. B. (2004). Youth delinquency: Prevention and intervention. In R. B. Rutherford, M. M. Quinn, & S. R. Mathur (Eds.). *Handbook of research in emotional and behavioral disorders*. New York: Guilford.

Nelson, C. M., & Pearson, C. A. (1991). *Integrating services for children and youth with emotional and behavioral disorders*. Reston, VA: Council for Exceptional Children.

Nelson, C. M., Rutherford, R. B., & Wolford, B. I. (Eds.). (1987). *Special education in the criminal justice system*. Upper Saddle River, NJ: Merrill/Prentice Hall.

Nelson, J. R., Benner, G. J., & Rogers-Adkinson, D. L. (2003). An investigation of the characteristics of K–12 students with co-morbid emotional disturbance and significant language deficits served in public school settings. *Behavioral Disorders, 29,* 25–33.

Nelson, J. R., Roberts, M. L., Mathur, S R., & Rutherford, R. B. (1999). Has public policy exceeded our knowledge base? A review of the functional behavioral assessment literature. *Behavioral Disorders, 24,* 169–179.

Neuwirth, S. (1994). *Attention-deficit hyperactivity disorder: Decade of the brain* (National Institutes of Health Pub. No. 94-3572). Washington, DC: National Institutes of Health.

Newcomb, M. D., & Richardson, M. A. (1995). Substance use disorders. In M. Hersen & R. T. Ammerman (Eds.), *Advanced abnormal child psychology* (pp. 411–431). Hillsdale, NJ: Erlbaum.

Newcomer, P. L., Barenbaum, E., & Pearson, N. (1995). Depression and anxiety in children and adolescents with learning disabilities, conduct disorders, and no disabilities. *Journal of Emotional and Behavioral Disorders, 3,* 27–39.

Newman, B., Buffington, D. M., O'Grady, M., McDonald, M. E., Poulson, C. L., & Hemmes, N. S. (1995). Self-management of schedule following in three teenagers with autism. *Behavioral Disorders, 20,* 190–196.

Newsom, C. (1998). Autistic disorder. In E. J. Mash & R. A. Barkley (Eds.), *Treatment of childhood disorders* (2nd ed., pp. 416–467). New York: Guilford.

Ng-Mak, D. S., Salzinger, S., Feldman, R., & Stueve, A. (2002). Normalization of violence among inner-city youth: A formulation for research. *American Journal of Orthopsychiatry, 72,* 92–101.

Nicol, S. E., & Erlenmeyer-Kimling, L. (1986). Genetic factors and psychopathology: Implications for prevention. In B. A. Edelstein & L. Michelson (Eds.), *Handbook of prevention* (pp. 21–41). New York: Plenum.

Northrup, J., Fusilier, I., Swanson, V., Huete, J., Bruce, T., Freeland, J., Gulley, V., & Edwards, S. (1999). Further analysis of the separate and interactive effects of methylphenidate and common classroom contingencies. *Journal of Applied Behavior Analysis, 32,* 35–50.

Odden, A., Monk, D., Nakib, Y., & Picus, L. (1995). The story of the education dollar: No academy awards and no fiscal smoking guns. *Phi Delta Kappan, 77,* 161–168.

Ogbu, J. U. (1990). Understanding diversity: Summary comments. *Education and Urban Society, 22,* 425–429.

O'Hanlon, A. (1998, June 21). Time out for Alan. *Washington Post Magazine,* pp. 8–15, 23–25.

O'Leary, K. D., & Wilson, G. T. (1975). *Behavior therapy: Applications and outcomes.* Upper Saddle River, NJ: Prentice Hall.

O'Leary, S. G. (1995). Parental discipline mistakes. *Current Directions in Psychological Science, 4,* 11–13.

Oliver, C. (1995). Annotation: Self-injurious behaviour in children with learning disabilities: Recent advances in assessment and intervention. *Journal of Child Psychology and Psychiatry, 30,* 909–927.

Ollendick, T. H., & Hersen, M. (1983). A historical overview of child psychopathology. In T. H. Ollendick & M. Hersen (Eds.), *Handbook of child psychopathology* (pp. 3–11). New York: Plenum.

Olsson, C. A., Bond, L., Burns, J. M., Vella-Brodrick, D. A., & Sawyer, S. M. (2003). Adolescent resilience: A concept analysis. *Journal of Adolescence, 26,* 1–11.

Olweus, D. (1979). Stability of aggressive reaction patterns in males: A review. *Psychological Bulletin, 86,* 852–875.

Olweus, D. (1991). Bully/victim problems among school children: Basic facts and effects of a school-based intervention program. In D. J. Pepler & K. H. Rubin (Eds.), *The development of childhood aggression* (pp. 411–446). Hillsdale, NJ: Erlbaum.

O'Neil, J. (1995). Can inclusion work? A conversation with Jim Kauffman and Mara Sapon-Shevin. *Educational Leadership, 52*(4), 7–11.

O'Neill, R. E., Horner, R. H., Albin, R. W., Sprague, J. R., Storey, K., & Newton, J. S. (1997). *Functional assessment and program development for problem behavior.* Pacific Grove, CA: Brooks/Cole.

Osher, D., Cartledge, G., Oswald, D., Sutherland, K. S., Artiles, A. J., & Coutinho, M. (2004). Issues of cultural and linguistic competency in disproportionate representation. In R. B. Rutherford, M. M. Quinn, & S. R. Mathur (Eds.), *Handbook of research in emotional and behavioral disorders.* New York: Guilford.

Oswald, D. (2003). Response to Forness: Parting reflections on education of children with emotional or behavioral disorders. *Behavioral Disorders, 28,* 202–204.

Oswald, D. P., Best, A. M., Coutinho, M. J., & Nagle, H. A. L. (2003). Trends in the special education identification rates of boys and girls: A call for research and change. *Exceptionality, 11,* 223–237.

Oswald, D. P., Coutinho, M. J., Best, A. M., & Singh, N. N. (1999). Ethnic representation in special education: The influence of school-related economic and demographic variables. *Journal of Special Education, 32,* 194–206.

Overton, T. (2000). *Assessing students with special needs: An applied approach* (4th ed.). Upper Saddle River, NJ: Merrill/Prentice Hall.

PACER Center. (2001). *Unique challenges, hopeful responses: A handbook for professionals working with youth with disabilities in the juvenile justice system.* Minneapolis, MN: Author.

Palmer, D. S., Fuller, K., Arora, T., & Nelson, M. (2001). Taking sides: Parent views on inclusion for their children with severe disabilities. *Exceptional Children, 67,* 467–484.

Papolos, D. F. (2003). Bipolar disorder and comorbid disorders: The case for a dimensional nosology. In B. Geller & M. P. DelBello (Eds.), *Bipolar disorder in childhood and early adolescence* (pp. 76–106). New York: Guilford.

Park, J., Turnbull, A. P., & Turnbull, H. R. (2002). Impacts of poverty on quality of life in families of children with disabilities. *Exceptional Children, 68,* 151–170.

Parker, H., & Parker, S. (1986). Father–daughter sexual abuse: An emerging perspective. *American Journal of Orthopsychiatry, 56,* 531–549.

Pataki, C. S., & Carlson, G. A. (1995). Childhood and adolescent depression: A review. *Harvard Review of Psychiatry, 3,* 140–151.

Patterson, C. J., Kupersmidt, J. B., & Griesler, P. C. (1988). *Self-concepts of children in regular education and in special education classes.* Unpublished manuscript, University of Virginia, Charlottesville.

Patterson, G. R. (1973). Reprogramming the families of aggressive boys. In C. Thoresen (Ed.), *Behavior modification in education.* Chicago: University of Chicago Press.

Patterson, G. R. (1975). The aggressive child: Victim or architect of a coercive system? In L. A. Hammerlynck, L. C. Handy, & E. J. Mash (Eds.), *Behavior modification and families* (pp. 267–316). New York: Brunner/Mazel.

Patterson, G. R. (1980). Mothers: The unacknowledged victims. *Monographs of the Society for Research in Child Development, 45*(5, Serial No. 186).

Patterson, G. R. (1982). *Coercive family process.* Eugene, OR: Castalia.

Patterson, G. R. (1986a). The contribution of siblings to training for fighting: A microsocial analysis. In D. Olweus, J. Block, & M. Radke-Yarrow (Eds.), *Development of antisocial and prosocial behavior: Research, theories, and issues* (pp. 235–262). New York: Academic Press.

Patterson, G. R. (1986b). Performance models for antisocial boys. *American Psychologist, 41,* 432–444.

Patterson, G. R., & Capaldi, D. M. (1990). A mediational model for boys' depressed mood. In J. Rolf, A. S. Masten, D. Cicchetti, K. H. Nuechterlein, & S. Weintraub (Eds.), *Risk and protective factors in the development of psychopathology* (pp. 141–163). New York: Cambridge University Press.

Patterson, G. R., & Forgatch, M. (1987). *Parents and adolescents living together.* Eugene, OR: Castalia.

Patterson, G. R., Reid, J. B., & Dishion, T. J. (1992). *Antisocial boys.* Eugene, OR: Castalia.

Patterson, G. R., Reid, J. B., Jones, R. R., & Conger, R. E. (1975). *A social learning approach to family intervention: Vol. 1. Families with aggressive children.* Eugene, OR: Castalia.

Peacock Hill Working Group. (1991). Problems and promises in special education and related services for children and youth with emotional or behavioral disorders. *Behavioral Disorders, 16,* 299–313.

Pearl, R. (2002). Students with learning disabilities and their classroom companions. In B. Y. L. Wong & M. Donahue (Eds.), *The social dimensions of learning disabilities: Essays in honor of Tanis Bryan* (pp. 77–91). Mahwah, NJ: Erlbaum.

Pepler, D. J., & Slaby, R. G. (1994). Theoretical and developmental perspectives on youth and violence. In L. D. Eron, J. H. Gentry, & P. Schlegel (Eds.), *Reason to hope: A psychosocial perspective on violence and youth* (pp. 27–58). Washington, DC: American Psychological Association.

Pescara-Kovach, L. A., & Alexander, K. (1994). The link between food ingested and problem behavior: Fact or fallacy? *Behavioral Disorders, 19,* 142–148.

Peterson, L., Reach, K., & Grabe, S. (2003). Health-related disorders. In E. J. Mash & R. A. Barkley (Eds.). *Child psychopathology* (2nd ed., pp. 716–749). New York: Guilford.

Peterson, R., & Ishii-Jordan, S. (Eds.). (1994). *Multicultural issues in the education of students with behavioral disorders.* Cambridge, MA: Brookline.

Pfiffner, L. J., & O'Leary, S. G. (1987). The efficacy of all-positive management as a function of the prior use of negative consequences. *Journal of Applied Behavior Analysis, 20,* 265–271.

Pfiffner, L. J., Rosen, L. A., & O'Leary, S. G. (1985). The efficacy of an all-positive approach to classroom management. *Journal of Applied Behavior Analysis, 18,* 257–261.

Piacentini, J. (1993). Checklists and rating scales. In T. H. Ollendick & M. Hersen (Eds.), *Handbook of child and adolescent assessment* (pp. 82–97). New York: Pergamon.

Pierce, K., & Schreibman, L. (1995). Increasing the complex social behaviors in children with autism: Effects of peer-implemented pivotal response training. *Journal of Applied Behavior Analysis, 28,* 285–295.

Pilowsky, D. (1995). Psychopathology among children placed in family foster care. *Psychiatric Services, 46,* 906–910.

Pionek Stone, B., Kratochwill, T. R., Sladezcek, I., & Serlin, R. C. (2002). Treatment of selective mutism: A best-evidence synthesis. *School Psychology Quarterly, 17,* 168–190.

Pinker, S. (2002). *The blank slate: The modern denial of human nature.* New York: Viking.

Pinsonneault, I. L., Richardson, J. P., & Pinsonneault, J. (2002). Three models of educational interventions for child and adolescent firesetters. In D. Kolko (Ed.), *Handbook on firesetting in children and youth* (pp. 261–278*).* New York: Academic Press.

Place, M., Reynolds, J., Cousins, A., & O'Neill, S. (2002). Developing a resilience package for vulnerable children. *Child and Adolescent Mental Health, 7,* 162–167.

Plasencia-Peinado, J., & Alvarado, J. L. (2000). Assessing students with emotional and behavioral disorders using curriculum-based measurement. *Assessment for Effective Intervention, 26*(1), 59–66.

Plomin, R. (1989). Environment and genes: Determinants of behavior. *American Psychologist, 44,* 105–111.

Plomin, R. (1995). Genetics and children's experiences in the family. *Journal of Child Psychology and Psychiatry, 36,* 33–68.

Polirstok, S. R., & Greer, R. D. (1977). Remediation of mutually aversive interactions between a problem student and four teachers by training the student in reinforcement techniques. *Journal of Applied Behavior Analysis, 10,* 707–716.

Polsgrove, L. (2003). Reflections on past and future. *Behavioral Disorders, 28,* 221–226.

Polsgrove, L., & Ochoa, T. (2004). Trends and issues in behavioral interventions. In A. D. McCray, H. J. Rieth, & P. T. Sindelar (Eds.), *Critical issues in special education: Access, diversity, and accountability* (pp. 156–182). Boston: Allyn & Bacon.

Polsgrove, L., & Smith, S. W. (2004). Informed practice in teaching behavioral self-control to children with E/BD. In R. B. Rutherford, M. M. Quinn, & S. R. Mathur (Eds.), *Handbook of research in emotional and behavioral disorders.* New York: Guilford.

Pomeroy, J. C., & Gadow, K. D. (1998). An overview of psychopharmacotherapy for children and adolescents. In R. J. Morris & T. R. Kratochwill (Eds.), *The practice of child therapy* (3rd ed., pp. 419–470). New York: Pergamon.

Popenhagen, M. P., & Qualley, R. M. (1998). Adolescent suicide: Detection, intervention, and prevention. *Professional School Counseling, 1*(4), 30–36.

Postel, H. H. (1937). The special school versus the special class. *Exceptional Children, 4,* 12–13, 18–19.

Poulin, F., & Boivin, M. (1999). Proactive and reactive aggression and boys' friendship quality in mainstream classrooms. *Journal of Emotional and Behavioral Disorders, 7,* 168–177.

Powell, S., & Nelson, B. (1997). Effects of choosing academic assignments on a student with attention deficit hyperactivity disorder. *Journal of Applied Behavior Analysis, 30,* 181–183.

Prior, M., & Werry, J. S. (1986). Autism, schizophrenia, and allied disorders. In H. C. Quay & J. S. Werry (Eds.), *Psychopathological disorders of childhood* (3rd ed., pp. 156–210). New York: Wiley.

Pullen, P. (2004). *Brighter beginnings for teachers.* Lanham, MD: Scarecrow Education.

Pullis, M. (1991). Practical considerations of excluding conduct disordered students: An empirical analysis. *Behavioral Disorders, 17,* 9–22.

Pungello, E. P., Kupersmidt, J. B., Burchinal, M. R., & Patterson, C. J. (1996). Environmental risk factors and children's achievement from middle childhood to early adolescence. *Developmental Psychology, 32,* 755–767.

Putallaz, M., & Heflin, A. H. (1990). Parent–child interaction. In S. R. Asher & J. D. Coie (Eds.), *Peer rejection in childhood* (pp. 189–216). New York: Cambridge University Press.

Quay, H. C. (1986a). Classification. In H. C. Quay & J. S. Werry (Eds.), *Psychopathological disorders of childhood* (3rd ed., pp. 1–34). New York: Wiley.

Quay, H. C. (1986b). Conduct disorders. In H. C. Quay & J. S. Werry (Eds.), *Psychopathological disorders of childhood* (3rd ed., pp. 35–72). New York: Wiley.

Quay, H. C., & La Greca, A. M. (1986). Disorders of anxiety, withdrawal, and dysphoria. In H. C. Quay & J. S. Werry (Eds.), *Psychopathological disorders of childhood* (3rd ed., pp.73–110). New York: Wiley.

Quinn, K. P., Epstein, M. H., & Cumblad, C. L. (1995). Developing comprehensive, individualized, community-based services for children and youth with emotional and behavior disorders: Direct service providers' perspectives. *Journal of Child and Family Studies, 4,* 19–42.

Quinn, K. P., & McDougal, J. L. (1998). A mile wide and a mile deep: Comprehensive interventions for children and youth with emotional and behavioral disorders and their families. *School Psychology Review, 27,* 191–203.

Quinn, M. M., Kavale, K. A., Mathur, S. R., Rutherford, R. B., & Forness, S. R. (1999). A meta-analysis of social skill interventions for students with emotional or behavioral disorders. *Journal of Emotional and Behavioral Disorders, 7,* 54–64.

Quintana, H., & Birmaher, B. (1995). Pharmacological treatment. In M. Hersen & R. T. Ammerman (Eds.), *Advanced abnormal child psychology* (pp. 189–212). Hillsdale, NJ: Erlbaum.

Rabian, B., & Silverman, W. K. (1995). Anxiety disorders. In M. Hersen & R. T. Ammerman (Eds.), *Advanced abnormal child psychology* (pp. 235–252). Hillsdale, NJ: Erlbaum.

Radke-Yarrow, M. (1990). Family environments of depressed and well parents and their children: Issues of research methods. In G. R. Patterson (Ed.), *Depression and aggression in family interaction* (pp. 169–184). Hillsdale, NJ: Erlbaum.

Rao, S., Hoyer, L., Meehan, K., Young, L., & Guerrera, A. (2003). Using narrative logs: Understanding students' challenging behaviors. *Teaching Exceptional Children, 35*(5), 22–29.

Rapp, J. T., Miltenberger, R. G., Galensky, T. L., Ellingson, S. A., & Long, E. S. (1999). A functional analysis of hair pulling. *Journal of Applied Behavior Analysis, 32,* 329–337.

Raspberry, W. (1999, April 12). An end to our American argot? *Charlottesville Daily Progress,* p. A23.

Ravitch, D. (2003). *The language police: How pressure groups restrict what students learn.* New York: Knopf.

Reddy, L. A., & Pfieffer, S. I. (1997). Effectiveness of treatment foster care with children and adolescents: A review of outcome studies. *Journal of the American Academy of Child and Adolescent Psychiatry, 36,* 581–588.

Redl, F. (1966). Designing a therapeutic classroom environment for disturbed children: The milieu approach. In P. Knoblock (Ed.), *Intervention approaches in educating emotionally disturbed children* (pp. 79–98). Syracuse, NY: Syracuse University Press.

Reid, J. (1993). Prevention of conduct disorder before and after school entry: Relating intervention to developmental findings. *Development and Psychopathology, 5,* 243–262.

Reid, J. B., & Eddy, J. M. (1997). The prevention of antisocial behavior: Some considerations in the search for effective interventions. In D. M. Stoff, J. Breiling, & J. D. Maser (Eds.), *Handbook of antisocial behavior* (pp. 343–356). New York: Wiley.

Reid, J. B., & Hendricks, A. (1973). Preliminary analysis of the effectiveness of direct home intervention for the treatment of predelinquent boys who steal. In L. A. Hammerlynck, L. C. Handy, & E. J. Mash (Eds.), *Behavior change: Methodology, concepts and practice* (pp. 209–219). Champaign, IL: Research Press.

Reid, J. B., & Patterson, G. R. (1976). The modification of aggression and stealing behavior of boys in the home setting. In A. Bandura & E. Ribes (Eds.), *Behavior modification: Experimental analyses of aggression and delinquency* (pp. 123–145). Hillsdale, NJ: Erlbaum.

Reid, R., Epstein, M. H., Pastor, D. A., & Ryser, G. R. (2000). Strengths-based assessment differences across students with LD and EBD. *Remedial & Special Education, 21,* 346–355.

Reitman, D., & Gross, A. M. (1995). Familial determinants. In M. Hersen & R. T. Ammerman (Eds.), *Advanced abnormal child psychology* (pp. 87–104). Hillsdale, NJ: Erlbaum.

Reitman, D., Hummek, R., Franz, D. Z., & Gross, A. M. (1998). A review of methods and instruments for assessing externalizing disorders: Theoretical and practical considerations in rendering a diagnosis. *Clinical Psychology Review, 18,* 555–584.

Remschmidt, H., & Quaschner, K. (2001). Psychodynamic therapy. In H. Remschmidt (Ed.), *Psychotherapy with children and adolescents* (pp. 81–97). New York: Cambridge University Press.

Remschmidt, H. E., Schulz, E., Martin, M., Warnke, A., & Trott, G. (1994). Childhood-onset schizophrenia: History of the concept and recent studies. *Schizophrenia Bulletin, 20,* 727–745.

Repp, A. C., & Deitz, D. E. D. (1990). Using an ecobehavioral analysis to determine a taxonomy for stereotyped responding. In S. R. Schroeder (Ed.), *Ecobehavioral analysis and developmental disabilities: The twenty-first century* (pp. 122–140). New York: Springer.

Reppucci, N. D., Britner, P. A., & Woodard, J. L. (1997). *Preventing child abuse and neglect through parent education.* Baltimore: Brookes.

Reschley, D. J. (1988). Special education reform: School psychology evolution. *School Psychology Review, 17,* 459–475.

Reschly, D. J. (1997). Utility of individual ability measures and public policy choices for the 21st century. *School Psychology Review, 26,* 234–241.

Reynolds, C. R., & Kamphaus, R. W. (1992). *Behavioral Assessment System for Children.* Circle Pines, MN: American Guidance Service.

Reynolds, W. M. (1992). Depression in children and adolescents. In W. R. Reynolds (Ed.), *Internalizing disorders in children and adolescents* (pp. 149–253). New York: Wilcy.

Reynolds, W. M. (1993). Self-report methodology. In T. H. Ollendick & M. Hersen (Eds.), *Handbook of child and adolescent assessment* (pp. 98–123). New York: Pergamon.

Rezmierski, V. E., Knoblock, P., & Bloom, R. B. (1982). The psychoeducational model: Theory and historical perspective. In R. L. McDowell, G. W. Adamson, & F. H. Wood (Eds.), *Teaching emotionally disturbed children* (pp. 47–69). Boston: Little, Brown.

Rhode, G., Jenson, W. R., & Reavis, H. K. (1992). *The tough kid book: Practical classroom management strategies.* Longmont, CA: Sopris West.

Rhodes, W. C. (1965). Institutionalized displacement and the disturbing child. In P. Knoblock (Ed.), *Educational programming for emotionally disturbed children: The decade ahead* (pp. 42–57). Syracuse, NY: Syracuse University Press.

Rhodes, W. C. (1967). The disturbing child: A problem of ecological management. *Exceptional Children, 33,* 449–455.

Rhodes, W. C. (1970). A community participation analysis of emotional disturbance. *Exceptional Children, 37,* 309–314.

Rhodes, W. C., & Doone, E. M. (1992). One boy's transformation. *Journal of Emotional and Behavioral Problems, 1*(2), 10–15.

Rhodes, W. C., & Head, S. (Eds.). (1974). *A study of child variance: Vol. 3. Service delivery systems.* Ann Arbor: University of Michigan.

Rhodes, W. C., & Tracy, M. L. (Eds.). (1972a). *A study of child variance: Vol. 1. Theories.* Ann Arbor: University of Michigan.

Rhodes, W. C., & Tracy, M. L. (Eds.). (1972b). *A study of child variance: Vol. 2. Interventions.* Ann Arbor: University of Michigan.

Ricaurte, G. A., Yuan, J., Hatzidimitriou, G., Cord, B. J. & McCann, U. D. (2003). "MDMA ("Ecstasy") and neurotoxicity": Response. *Science, 300,* 1504–1505.

Rich, H. L., Beck, M. A., & Coleman, T. W. (1982). Behavior management: The psychoeducational model. In R. L. McDowell, G. W. Adamson, & F. H. Wood (Eds.),

Teaching emotionally disturbed children (pp. 131–166). Boston: Little, Brown.

Richardson, G. A., McGauhey, P., & Day, N. L. (1995). Epidemiologic considerations. In M. Hersen & R. T. Ammerman (Eds.), *Advanced abnormal child psychology* (pp. 37–48). Hillsdale, NJ: Erlbaum.

Richardson, B. G., & Shupe, M. J. (2003). The importance of teacher self-awareness in working with students with emotional and behavioral disorders. *Teaching Exceptional Children, 36*(2), 8–13.

Riddle, M. A., Hardin, M. T., Ort, S. I., Leckman, J. F., & Cohen, D. J. (1988). Behavioral symptoms in Tourette's syndrome. In D. J. Cohen, R. D. Brunn, & J. F. Leckman (Eds.), *Tourette's syndrome and disorders* (pp. 151–162). New York: Wiley.

Robb, A. S., & Dadson, M. J. (2002). Eating disorders in males. *Child and Adolescent Psychiatric Clinics of North America, 11,* 399–418.

Robins, L. N. (1966). *Deviant children grown up.* Baltimore: Williams & Wilkins.

Robins, L. N. (1974). Antisocial behavior disturbances of childhood: Prevalence, prognosis, and prospects. In E. J. Anthony & C. Koupernik (Eds.), *The child in his family: Children at psychiatric risk* (pp. 447–460). New York: Wiley.

Robins, L. N. (1979). Follow-up studies. In H. C. Quay & J. S. Werry (Eds.), *Psychopathological disorders of childhood* (2nd ed., pp. 483–513). New York: Wiley.

Robins, L. N. (1986). The consequences of conduct disorder in girls. In D. Olweus, J. Block, & M. Radke-Yarrow (Eds.), *Development of antisocial and prosocial behavior: Research, theories, and issues* (pp. 385–414). New York: Academic Press.

Roerig, J. L., Mitchell, J. E., Myers, T. C., & Glass, J. B. (2002). Pharmacotherapy and medical complications of eating disorders in children and adolescents. *Child and Adolescent Psychiatric Clinics of North America, 11,* 365–385.

Rogers, C. (1983). *Freedom to learn for the 80s.* Upper Saddle River, NJ: Merrill/Prentice Hall.

Rogers-Adkinson, D. (1999). Psychiatric disorders in children. In D. Rogers-Adkinson & P. Griffith (Eds.), *Communication disorders and children with psychiatric and behavioral disorders* (pp. 39–68). San Diego: Singular.

Rogers-Adkinson, D., & Griffith, P. (Eds.). (1999). *Communication disorders and children with psychiatric and behavioral disorders.* San Diego: Singular.

Romaniuk, C., Miltenberger, R., Conyers, C., Jenner, N., Jurgens, M., & Ringenberg, C. (2002). The influence of activity choice on problem behaviors maintained by escape versus attention. *Journal of Applied Behavior Analysis, 35,* 349–362.

Rosenberg, M. S., & Jackman, L. A. (2003). Development, implementation, and sustainability of comprehensive school-wide behavior management systems. *Intervention in School and Clinic, 39,* 10–21.

Rosenblatt, A., & Attkisson, C. C. (1992). Integrating systems of care in California for youth with severe emotional disturbance. I: A descriptive overview of the California AB377 Evaluation Project. *Journal of Child and Family Studies, 1,* 93–113.

Rosenfield, R., Bray, T. M., & Egley, A. (1999). Facilitating violence: A comparison of gang-motivated, gang-affiliated and nongang youth homicides. *Journal of Quantitative Criminology, 15,* 495–516.

Rosenthal, P. A., & Rosenthal, S. (1984). Suicidal behavior by preschool children. *American Journal of Psychiatry, 141,* 520–525.

Ross, G. R. (1994). *Treating adolescent substance abuse: Understanding the fundamental elements.* Boston: Allyn & Bacon.

Rotenberg, K. J. (1991). *Children's interpersonal trust: Sensitivity to lying, deception, and promise violations.* New York: Springer-Verlag.

Rothman, D. (1971). *The discovery of the asylum: Social order and disorder in the new republic.* Boston: Little, Brown.

Rothman, E. P. (1970). *The angel inside went sour.* New York: McKay.

Rothman, E. P., & Berkowitz, P. H. (1967). The clinical school—a paradigm. In P. H. Berkowitz & E. P. Rothman (Eds.), *Public education for disturbed children in New York City* (pp. 355–369). Springfield, IL: Thomas.

Rubin, K. H., Burgess, K. B., Kennedy, A. E., & Stewart, S. L. (2003). Social withdrawal in childhood. In E. J. Mash & R. A. Barkley (Eds.), *Child psychopathology* (2nd ed., pp. 372–406). New York: Guilford.

Rubin, R. A., & Balow, B. (1978). Prevalence of teacher identified behavior problems: A longitudinal study. *Exceptional Children, 45,* 102–111.

Russell, A. T. (1994). The clinical presentation of childhood-onset schizophrenia. *Schizophrenia Bulletin, 20,* 631–646.

Rutherford, R. B., Quinn, M. M., & Mathur, S. R. (Eds.). (2004). *Handbook of research in emotional and behavioral disorders.* New York: Guilford.

Rutter, M. (1979). Maternal deprivation, 1972–1978: New findings, new concepts, new approaches. *Child Development, 50,* 283–305.

Rutter, M. (1995). Clinical implications of attachment concepts: Retrospect and prospect. *Journal of Child Psychology and Psychiatry, 36,* 549–571.

Rutter, M., & Bartak, L. (1973). Special educational treatment of autistic children: A comparative study—II: Follow-up findings and implications for services. *Journal of Child Psychology and Psychiatry, 14,* 241–270.

Rutter, M., Maughan, B., Mortimer, P., Ouston, J., & Smith, A. (1979). *Fifteen thousand hours: Secondary schools and their effects on children*. Cambridge, MA: Harvard University Press.

Rutter, M., & Schopler, E. (1987). Autism and pervasive developmental disorders: Concepts and diagnostic issues. *Journal of Autism and Developmental Disorders, 17,* 159–186.

Ryan, N. D. (2002). Depression. In S. Kutcher (Ed.), *Practical child and adolescent psychopharmacology* (pp. 91–105). New York: Cambridge University Press.

Rylance, B. J. (1997). Predictors of high school graduation or dropping out for youths with severe emotional disturbances. *Behavioral Disorders, 23,* 5–17.

Sabornie, E. J. (1985). Social mainstreaming of handicapped students: Facing an unpleasant reality. *Remedial and Special Education, 6*(2), 12–16.

Sabornie, E. J. (2004). Qualitative research and its contributions to knowledge of behavior disorders. In R. B. Rutherford, M. M. Quinn, & S. R. Mathur (Eds.), *Handbook of research in emotional and behavioral disorders*. New York: Guilford.

Sabornie, E. J., & Kauffman, J. M. (1985). Regular classroom sociometric status of emotionally disturbed adolescents. *Behavioral Disorders, 10,* 268–274.

Sacks, O. (1995). *An anthropologist on Mars*. New York: Knopf.

Sacks, P. (1999). *Standardized minds: the high price of America's testing culture and what we can do to change it*. Cambridge, MA: Perseus.

Safran, J. S., & Safran, S. P. (1987). Teacher's judgments of problem behaviors. *Exceptional Children, 54,* 240–244.

Safran, S. P. (1995). Peers' perceptions of emotional and behavioral disorders: What are students thinking? *Journal of Emotional and Behavioral Disorders, 3,* 66–75.

Saigh, P. A. (1998). Posttraumatic stress disorder. In R. J. Morris & T. R. Kratochwill (Eds.), *The practice of child therapy* (3rd ed., pp. 390–418). Boston: Allyn & Bacon.

Sale, P., & Carey, D. M. (1995). The sociometric status of students with disabilities in a full-inclusion school. *Exceptional Children 62,* 6–19.

Salvia, J., & Ysseldyke, J. E. (1991). *Assessment in special and remedial education* (5th ed.). Boston: Houghton Mifflin.

Sameroff, A. J., & Chandler, M. J. (1975). Reproductive risk and the continuum of caretaking casualty. In F. D. Horowitz (Ed.), *Review of child development research* (Vol. 4, pp. 187–244). Chicago: University of Chicago Press.

Sampson, R. J., & Laub, J. H. (1993). *Crime in the making: Pathways and turning points through life*. Cambridge, MA: Harvard University Press.

Sasso, G. M. (2001). The retreat from inquiry and knowledge in special education. *The Journal of Special Education, 34,* 178–193.

Sasso, G. M., Conroy, M. A., Stichter, J. P., & Fox, J. J. (2001). Slowing down the bandwagon: The misapplication of functional assessment for students with emotional and behavioral disorders. *Behavioral Disorders, 26,* 282–296.

Scheuermann, B., & Webber, J. (2002). *Autism: Teaching does make a difference*. Belmont, CA: Wadsworth.

Schill, M. T., & Kratochwill, T. R. (1996). An assessment protocol for selective mutism: Analog assessment using parents as facilitators. *Journal of School Psychology, 34,* 1–21.

Schopler, E., & Mesibov, G. B. (Eds.). (1987). *Neurobiological issues in autism*. New York: Plenum.

Schopler, E., & Mcsibov, G. B. (Eds.). (1994). *Behavioral issues in autism*. New York: Plenum.

Schopler, E., & Mesibov, G. B. (Eds.). (1995). *Learning and cognition in autism*. New York: Plenum.

Schopler, E., Mesibov, G. B., & Hearsey, K. (1995). Structured teaching in the TEACCH system. In E. Schopler & G. B. Mesibov (Eds.), *Learning and cognition in autism* (pp. 243–268). New York: Plenum.

Schopler, E., Mesibov, G. B., & Kunce, L. J. (Eds.). (1998). *Asperger syndrome or high functioning autism?* New York: Plenum.

Schreibman, L. (1994). General principles of behavior management. In E. Schopler & G. B. Mesibov (Eds.), *Behavioral issues in autism* (pp. 11–38). New York: Plenum.

Schroeder, S. R. (Ed.). (1990). *Ecobehavioral analysis and developmental disabilities: The twenty-first century*. New York: Springer-Verlag.

Schwartz, I. S., & Baer, D. M. (1991). Social validity assessments: Is current practice state of the art? *Journal of Applied Behavior Analysis, 24,* 189–204.

Schweitzer, R. D., Hier, S. J., & Terry, D. (1994). Parental bonding, family systems, and environmental predictors of adolescent homelessness. *Journal of Emotional and Behavioral Disorders, 2,* 39–45.

Scott, T. M., Liaupsin, C. J., Nelson, C. M., & Jolivette, K. (2003). Ensuring student success through team-based functional behavioral assessment. *Teaching Exceptional Children, 35*(5), 16–21.

Scott, T. M., & Nelson, C. M. (1999). Functional behavioral assessment: Implications for training and staff development. *Behavioral Disorders, 24,* 249–252.

Scott-Jones, D. (1993). Adolescent childbearing: Whose problem? What can we do? *Phi Delta Kappan, 75,* K1–K12.

Seeley, J. R., Rohde, P., Lewinsohn, P. M., & Clarke, G. N. (2002). Depression in youth: Epidemiology, identification, and intervention. In M. R. Shinn, H. M. Walker, & G. Stoner (Eds.), *Interventions for academic and behavior problems II: Preventive and remedial approaches* (pp. 885–911). Bethesda, MD: National Association of School Psychologists.

Serbin, L. A., Stack, D. M., Schwartzman, J. C., Bentley, V., Saltaris, C., & Ledingham, J. E. (2002). A longitudinal study of aggressive and withdrawn children in adulthood: Patterns of parenting and risk to offspring. In R. J. McMahon & R. D. Peters (Eds.), *The effects of parental dysfunction on children* (pp. 43–69). New York: Kluwer.

Serna, L. A., Lambros, K., Nielsen, E., & Forness, S. R. (2002). Head Start children at risk for emotional or behavioral disorders: Behavior profiles and clinical implications of a primary prevention program. *Behavioral Disorders, 27,* 137–141.

Serna, L., Nielsen, E., Lambros, K., & Forness, S. (2000). Primary prevention with children at risk for emotional or behavioral disorders: Data on a universal intervention for Head Start classrooms. *Behavioral Disorders, 26,* 70–84.

Severson, H. H., & James, L. (2002). Prevention and early interventions for addictive behaviors: Health promotion in the schools. In M. R. Shinn, H. M. Walker, & G. Stoner (Eds.), *Interventions for academic and behavior problems II: Preventive and remedial approaches* (pp. 681–702). Bethesda, MD: National Association of School Psychologists.

Shaffer, D., Gould, M., & Hicks, R. C. (1994). Worsening suicide rates in Black teenagers. *American Journal of Psychiatry, 151,* 1810–1812.

Shaffer, D., & Hicks, R. (1994). Suicide. In I. B. Pless (Ed.), *The epidemiology of childhood disorders* (pp. 339–365). New York: Oxford University Press.

Shaffer, D., & Waslick, B. D. (Eds.). (2002). *The many faces of depression in children and adolescents.* Washington, DC: American Psychiatric Publishing.

Shane, H. C. (Ed.). (1994). *Facilitated communication: The clinical and social phenomenon.* San Diego: Singular.

Shapiro, E. S., Durnan, S. L., Post, E. E., & Levinson, T. S. (2002). Self-monitoring procedures for children and adolescents. In M. R. Shinn, H. M. Walker, & G. Stoner (Eds.), *Interventions for academic and behavior problems II: Preventive and remedial approaches* (pp. 433–454). Bethesda, MD: National Association of School Psychologists.

Shaw, D. S., & Winslow, E. B. (1997). Precursors and correlates of antisocial behavior from early infancy to preschool. In D. M. Stoff, J. Breiling, & J. D. Maser (Eds.), *Handbook of antisocial behavior* (pp. 148–158). New York: Wiley.

Sheehan, S. (1993a, January 11). A lost childhood. *New Yorker,* pp. 54–85.

Sheehan, S. (1993b, January 18). A lost motherhood. *New Yorker,* pp. 52–79.

Sheehan, S. (2003, December 1). The autism fight. *The New Yorker,* 76–87.

Sheras, P. (2002). *Your child: Bully or victim? Understanding and ending school yard tyranny.* New York: Skylight.

Shinn, M. R., Shinn, M. M., Hamilton, C., & Clarke, B. (2002). Using curriculum-based measurement in general education classrooms to promote reading success. In M. R. Shinn, H. M. Walker, & G. Stoner (Eds.), *Interventions for academic and behavior problems II: Preventive and remedial approaches* (pp. 113–142). Bethesda, MD: National Association of School Psychologists.

Shinn, M. R., Walker, H. M., & Stoner, G. (Eds.). (2002), *Interventions for academic and behavior problems II: Preventive and remedial approaches.* Bethesda, MD: National Association of School Psychologists.

Shores, D., & Wehby, J. H. (1999). Analyzing the social behavior of students with emotional and behavioral disorders in classrooms. *Journal of Emotional and Behavioral Disorders, 7,* 194–199.

Shores, R. E. (1987). Overview of research on social interaction: A historical and personal perspective. *Behavioral Disorders, 12,* 233–241.

Shores, R. E., Jack, S. L., Gunter, P. L., Ellis, D. N., DeBriere, T. J., & Wehby, J. H. (1993). Classroom interactions of children with behavior disorders. *Journal of Emotional and Behavioral Disorders, 1,* 27–39.

Short, J. F. (1997). *Poverty, ethnicity, and violent crime.* New York: Westview.

Siegel, A. W., Cousins, J. H., Rubovits, D. S., Parsons, J. T., Lavery, B., & Crowley, C. L. (1994). Adolescents' perceptions of the benefits of their own risk taking. *Journal of Emotional and Behavioral Disorders, 2,* 89–98.

Siegel, B. (1995). Assessing allegations of sexual molestation made through facilitated communication. *Journal of Autism and Developmental Disorders, 25,* 319–326.

Siegel, L. J. (1992). Somatic disorders of childhood and adolescence. In W. R. Reynolds (Ed.), *Internalizing disorders in children and adolescents* (pp. 283–310). New York: Wiley.

Siegel, L. J. (1998). Somatic disorders. In R. J. Morris & T. R. Kratochwill (Eds.), *The practice of child therapy* (3rd ed., pp. 231–302). Boston: Allyn & Bacon.

Siegel, L. J., & Ridley-Johnson, R. (1985). Anxiety disorders of childhood and adolescence. In P. H. Bornstein & A. E. Kazdin (Eds.), *Handbook of clinical behavior therapy with children* (pp. 266–308). Homewood, IL: Dorsey.

Siegel, L. J., & Senna, J. J. (1994). *Juvenile delinquency: Theory, practice, and law* (5th ed.). St. Paul, MN: West.

Sigafoos, J., Kerr, M., Roberts, D., & Couzens, D. (1994). Increasing opportunities for requesting in classrooms serving children with developmental disabilities. *Journal of Autism and Developmental Disorders, 24,* 631–645.

Sigman, M. (1994). What are the core deficits in autism? In S. H. Broman & J. Grafman (Eds.), *Atypical cognitive deficits in developmental disorders: Implication for brain function* (pp. 139–157). Hillsdale, NJ: Erlbaum.

Silberberg, N.E., & Silberberg, M. C. (1971). School achievement and delinquency. *Review of Educational Research, 41,* 17–32.

Silbereisen, R. K. (1998). Lessons we learned—problems still to be solved. In R. Jessor (Ed.), *New perspectives on adolescent risk behavior* (pp. 518–543). New York: Cambridge University Press.

Silberman, C. E. (1978). *Criminal violence, criminal justice.* New York: Random House.

Silva, R. R., Munoz, D. M., Barickman, J., & Friedhoff, A. J. (1995). Environmental factors and related fluctuation of symptoms in children and adolescents with Tourette's disorder. *Journal of Child Psychology and Psychiatry, 36,* 305–312.

Simpson, R. L. (1999). Children and youth with emotional and behavioral disorders: A concerned look at the present and a hopeful eye for the future. *Behavioral Disorders, 24,* 284–292.

Simpson, R. L., & Myles, B. S. (Eds.). (1998). *Educating children and youth with autism: Strategies for effective practice.* Austin, TX: Pro-Ed.

Simpson, R. L., & Zionts, P. (1992). *Autism: Information and resources for parents, families, and professionals.* Austin, TX: Pro-Ed.

Sinclair, E., Forness, S. R., & Alexson, J. (1985). Psychiatric diagnosis: A study of its relationship to school needs. *Journal of Special Education, 19,* 333–344.

Singh, A. N., Zemitzsch, A. A., Ellis, C. R., Best A. M., & Singh, N. N. (1994). Seriously emotionally disturbed students' knowledge and attitudes about AIDS. *Journal of Emotional and Behavioral Disorders, 2,* 156–163.

Singh, N. N. (1996). Cultural diversity in the 21st century: Beyond E Pluribus Unum. *Journal of Child and Family Studies, 5,* 121–136.

Singh, N. N., Ellis, C. R., Oswald, D. P., Wechsler, H. A., & Curtis, W. J. (1997). Value and address diversity. *Journal of Emotional and Behavioral Disorders, 5,* 24–35.

Smit, F., Monshouwer, K., & Verdurmen, J. (2002). Polydrug use among secondary school students: Combinations, prevalences and risk profiles. *Drug Education Prevention & Policy, 9,* 355–365.

Smith, C. R., Wood, F. H., & Grimes, J. (1988). Issues in the identification and placement of behaviorally disordered students. In M. C. Wang, M. C. Reynolds, & H. J. Walberg (Eds.), *Handbook of special education: Research and practice* (Vol. 2, pp. 95–124). New York: Pergamon.

Smith, J., & Prior, M. (1995). Temperament and stress resilience in school-age children: A within-families study. *Journal of the American Academy of Child and Adolescent Psychiatry, 34,* 168–179.

Smith, K. (1992). Suicidal behavior in children and adolescents. In W. R. Reynolds (Ed.), *Internalizing disorders in children and adolescents* (pp. 255–282). New York: Wiley.

Smith, T., & Lovaas, O. I. (1997). The UCLA Young Autism Project: A reply to Gresham and MacMillan. *Behavioral Disorders, 22,* 202–218.

Smith, R. G., & Churchill, R. M. (2002). Identification of environmental determinants of behavior disorders through functional analysis of precursor behaviors. *Journal of Applied Behavior Analysis, 35,* 125–136.

Smucker, K. S., Kauffman, J. M., & Ball, D. W. (1996). School-related problems of special education foster care students with emotional or behavioral disorders: Comparison to other groups. *Journal of Emotional and Behavioral Disorders, 4,* 30–39.

Snow, J. H., & Hooper, S. R. (1994). *Pediatric traumatic brain injury.* Thousand Oaks, CA: Sage.

Snyder, J. M. (2001). *AD/HD & driving. A guide for parents of teens with AD/HD.* Whitefish, MT: CHAAD. Also retrieved from www.whitefishconsultants.com

Sorenson, S. B., & Bowie, P. (1994). Girls and young women. In L. D. Eron, J. H. Gentry, & P. Schlegel (Eds.), *Reason to hope: A psychosocial perspective on violence and youth* (pp. 167–176). Washington, DC: American Psychological Association.

Soriano, F. I. (1994). U.S. Latinos. In L. D. Eron, J. H. Gentry, & P. Schlegel (Eds.), *Reason to hope: A psychosocial perspective on violence and youth* (pp. 119–132). Washington, DC: American Psychological Association.

Soutter, A. (1996). A longitudinal study of 3 cases of gender identity disorder of childhood successfully resolved in the school setting. *School Psychology International, 17,* 49–57.

Spence, S. H. (1986). Behavioural treatments of childhood obesity. *Journal of Child Psychology and Psychiatry, 27,* 447–453.

Spencer, E. K., & Campbell, M. (1994). Children with schizophrenia: Diagnosis, phenomenology, and pharmacotherapy. *Schizophrenia Bulletin, 20,* 713–725.

Spencer, J. M. (1997). *The new colored people: The mixed-race movement in America.* New York: New York University Press.

Spencer, T., Biederman, J., Harding, M., Wilens, T., & Faraone, S. (1995). The relationship between tic disorders and Tourette's syndrome revisited. *Journal of the American Academy of Child and Adolescent Psychiatry, 34,* 1133–1139.

Spencer, T., Biederman, J., & Wilens, T. (2002). Attention-deficit/hyperactivity disorder. In S. Kutcher (Ed.), *Practical child and adolescent psychopharmacology* (pp. 230–264). New York: Cambridge University Press.

Spergel, I. A. (1995). *The youth gang problem: A community approach.* New York: Oxford University Press.

Spirito, A. (2003). Understanding attempted suicide in adolescence, In A. Spirito, A. & J. C. Overholser (Eds.), *Evaluating and treating adolescent suicide attempters: From research to practice* (pp. 1–18). New York: Academic Press.

Spirito, A., & Overholser, J. C. (Eds.). (2003). *Evaluating and treating adolescent suicide attempters: From research to practice*. New York: Academic Press.

Sprafkin, J., Gadow, K. D., & Adelman, R. (1992). *Television and the exceptional child: A forgotten audience*. Hillsdale, NJ: Erlbaum.

Sprick, R. S., & Howard, L. M. (1995). *The teacher's encyclopedia of behavior management*. Longmont, CO: Sopris West.

Sridhar, D., & Vaughn, S. (2001). Social functioning of students with learning disabilities. In D. P. Hallahan & B. K. Keogh (Eds), *Research and global perspectives in learning disabilities: Essays in honor of William M. Cruickshank* (pp. 65–91). Mahwah, NJ: Erlbaum.

Sroufe, L. A., Steucher, H. U., & Stutzer, W. (1973). The functional significance of autistic behaviors for the psychotic child. *Journal of Abnormal Child Psychology, 1*, 225–240.

Stage, S. A., & Quiroz, D. R. (1997). A meta-analysis of interventions to decrease disruptive classroom behavior in public education settings. *School Psychology Review, 26*, 333–368.

Stainback, W., & Stainback, S. (1991). A rationale for integration and restructuring: A synopsis. In J. W. Lloyd, N. N. Singh, & A. C. Repp (Eds.), *The Regular Education Initiative: Alternative perspectives on concepts, issues, and models* (pp. 226–239). Sycamore, IL: Sycamore.

Stark, K. D., Ostrander, R., Kurowski, C. A., Swearer, S., & Bowen, B. (1995). Affective and mood disorders. In M. Hersen & R. T. Ammerman (Eds.), *Advanced abnormal child psychology* (pp. 253–282). Hillsdale, NJ: Erlbaum.

Starr, E., Szatmari, P., Bryson, S., & Zwaigenbaum, L. (2003). Stability and change among high-functioning children with pervasive developmental disorders: A 2-year outcome study. *Journal of Autism and Developmental Disorders, 33*, 15–22.

Steele, R. G., Forehand, R., Armistead, L, & Brody, G. (1995). Predicting alcohol and drug use in early adulthood: The role of internalizing and externalizing behavior problems in early adolescence. *American Journal of Orthopsychiatry, 65*, 380–388.

Stein, E., Raegrant, N., Ackland, S., & Avison, W. (1994). Psychiatric disorders of children in care: Methodology and demographic correlates. *Canadian Journal of Psychiatry, 39*, 341–347.

Steinberg, L., & Avenevoli, S. (1998). Disengagement from school and problem behavior in adolescence: A developmental–contextual analysis of the influences of family and part-time work. In R. Jessor (Ed.), *New perspectives on adolescent risk behavior* (pp. 392–424). New York: Cambridge University Press.

Steiner, H. (1997). Practice parameters for the assessment and treatment of children and adolescents with conduct disorder. *Journal of the American Academy of Child and Adolescent Psychiatry, Supplement, 36*(10), 122S–139S.

Sternberg, R. J. (1991). Giftedness according to the triarchic theory of human intelligence. In N. Colangelo & G. A. Davis (Eds.), *Handbook of gifted education* (pp. 45–54). Boston: Allyn & Bacon.

Sternberg, R. J., & Grigorenko, E. L. (2002). Difference scores in the identification of children with learning disabilities: It's time to use a different method. *Journal of School Psychology, 40*, 65–83.

Stetter, G. M. T. (1995). *The effects of pre-correction on cafeteria behavior*. Unpublished manuscript, University of Virginia, Charlottesville.

Stevenson, D. L., & Baker, D. P. (1987). The family–school relation and child's school performance. *Child Development, 58*, 1348–1357.

Stevenson-Hinde, J., Hinde, R. A., & Simpson, A. E. (1986). Behavior at home and friendly or hostile behavior in preschool. In D. Olweus, J. Block, & M. Radke-Yarrow (Eds.), *Development of antisocial and prosocial behavior: Research, theories, and issues* (pp. 127–148). New York: Academic Press.

Stevenson-Hinde, J., & Shouldice, A. (1995). 4.5 to 7 years: Fearful behaviour, fears and worries. *Journal of Child Psychology and Psychiatry, 36*, 1027–1038.

Stoff, D. M., Breiling, J., & Maser, J. D. (Eds.). (1997). *Handbook of antisocial behavior*. New York: Wiley.

Stokes, T. F., & Osnes, P. G. (1991). Honesty, lying, and cheating: Their elaboration and management. In G. Stoner, M. R. Shinn, & H. M. Walker (Eds.), *Interventions for achievement and behavior problems* (pp. 617–631). Silver Spring, MD: National Association of School Psychologists.

Stone, F., & Rowley, V. N. (1964). Educational disability in emotionally disturbed children. *Exceptional Children, 30*, 423–426.

Stouthamer-Loeber, M., & Loeber, R. (1986). Boys who lie. *Journal of Abnormal Child Psychology, 14*, 551–564.

Strain, P. S., & Danko, C. D. (1995). Caregivers' encouragement of positive interaction between preschoolers with autism and their siblings. *Journal of Emotional and Behavioral Disorders, 3*, 2–12.

Strain, P. S., Danko, C. D., & Kohler, F. (1995). Activity engagement and social interaction development in young children with autism: An examination of "free" intervention effects. *Journal of Emotional and Behavioral Disorders, 3*, 108–123.

Strain, P. S., Lambert, D. L., Kerr, M. M., Stagg, V., & Lenkner, D. A. (1983). Naturalistic assessment of children's compliance to teachers' requests and consequences for compliance. *Journal of Applied Behavior Analysis, 16*, 243–249.

Strain, P. S., Odom, S. L., & McConnell, S. (1984). Promoting social reciprocity of exceptional children:

Identification, target behavior selection, and intervention. *Remedial and Special Education, 5*(1), 21–28.

Strain, P. S., & Timm, M. A. (2001). Remediation and prevention of aggression: An evaluation of the Regional Intervention Program over a quarter century. *Behavioral Disorders, 26,* 297–313.

Strand, P. S., Barnes-Holmes, Y., & Barnes-Holmes, D. (2003). Educating the whole child: Implications of behaviorism as a science of meaning. *Behavioral Education, 12,* 103–117.

Strauss, C. C. (1993). Anxiety disorders. In T. H. Ollendick & M. Hersen (Eds.), *Handbook of child and adolescent assessment* (pp. 239–250). New York: Pergamon.

Strayhorn, J., Strain, P. S., & Walker, H. M. (1993). The case for interaction skills training in the context of tutoring as a preventative mental health intervention in the schools. *Behavioral Disorders, 19,* 11–26.

Stribling, F. T. (1842). Physician and superintendent's report. In *Annual Reports to the Court of Directors of the Western Lunatic Asylum to the Legislature of Virginia* (pp. 1–70). Richmond, VA: Shepherd & Conlin.

Striegel-Moore, R. H., Dohm, F. A., Kraemer, H. C., Taylor, C. B., Daniels, S., Crawford, P. B., et al. (2003). Eating disorders in white and black women. *American Journal of Psychiatry, 160,* 1326–1331.

Sugai, G., & Colvin, G. (1997). Debriefing: A transition step for promoting acceptable behavior. *Education and Treatment of Children, 20,* 209–221.

Sugai, G., Horner, R. H., & Gresham, F. M. (2002). Behaviorally effective school environments. In M. Shinn, H. Walker, & G. Stoner (Eds.), *Interventions for achievement and behavior problems II: Preventative and remedial approaches* (pp. 315–350). Bethesda, MD: National Association of School Psychologists.

Sugai, G., Horner, R. H., & Sprague, J. R. (1999). Functional assessment-based behavior support planning: Research to practice. *Behavioral Disorders, 24,* 253–257.

Sugai, G. & Lewis, T. J. (2004). Social skills instruction in the classroom. In C. B. Darch & E. J. Kame'enui (Eds.), *Instructional classroom management: A positive approach to behavior management* (2nd ed., pp. 152–173). White Plains, NY: Longman.

Suzman, K. B., Morris, R. D., Morris, M. K., & Milan, M. A. (1997). Cognitive-behavioral remediation of problem solving deficits in children with acquired brain injury. *Journal of Behavior Therapy and Experimental Psychiatry, 28,* 203–212.

Swap, S. (1974). Disturbing classroom behaviors: A developmental and ecological view. *Exceptional Children, 41,* 163–172.

Swap, S. (1978). The ecological model of emotional disturbance in children: A status report and proposed synthesis. *Behavioral Disorders, 3,* 186–196.

Swap, S., Prieto, A. G., & Harth, R. (1982). Ecological perspectives on the emotionally disturbed child. In R. L. McDowell, G. W. Adamson, & F. H. Wood (Eds.), *Teaching emotionally disturbed children* (pp. 70–98). Boston: Little, Brown.

Sweeney, D. P., Forness, S. R., Kavale, K. A., & Levitt, J. G. (1997). An update on psychopharmacologic medication: What teachers, clinicians, and parents need to know. *Intervention in School and Clinic, 33*(1), 4–21, 25.

Sweeney, D. P., & Hoffman, C. D. (2004). Research issues in autism spectrum disorders in children and adolescents. In R. B. Rutherford, M. M. Quinn, & S. R. Mathur (Eds.), *Handbook of research in emotional and behavioral disorders*. New York: Guilford.

Talbott, E., & Callahan, K. (1997). Antisocial girls and the development of disruptive behavior disorders. In J. W. Lloyd, E. J. Kameenui, & D. Chard (Eds.), *Issues in educating students with disabilities* (pp. 305–322). Mahwah, NJ: Erlbaum.

Talbott, E., Celinska, D., Simpson, J., & Coe, M. G. (2002). "Somebody else making somebody else fight": Aggression and the social context among urban adolescent girls. *Exceptionality, 10,* 203–220.

Talbott, E., & Thiede, K. (1999). Pathways to antisocial behavior among adolescent girls. *Journal of Emotional and Behavioral Disorders, 7,* 31–39.

Tamkin, A. S. (1960). A survey of educational disability in emotionally disturbed children. *Journal of Educational Research, 53,* 313–315.

Tankersley, M., & Landrum, T. J. (1997). Comorbidity of emotional and behavioral disorders. In J. W. Lloyd, E. J. Kameenui, & D. Chard (Eds.), *Issues in educating students with disabilities* (pp. 153–173). Mahwah, NJ: Erlbaum.

Tankersley, M., Landrum, T. J., & Cook, B. G. (2004). How research informs practice in the field of emotional and behavioral disorders. In R. B. Rutherford, M. M. Quinn, & S. R. Mathur (Eds.), *Handbook of research in emotional and behavioral disorders*. New York: Guilford.

Tanner, E. M., & Finn-Stevenson, M. (2002). Nutrition and brain development: Social policy implications. *American Journal of Orthopsychiatry, 72,* 182–193.

Tannock, R., Ickowicz, A., & Schachar, R. (1995). Differential effects of methylphenidate on working memory in ADHD children with and without comorbid anxiety. *Journal of the American Academy of Child and Adolescent Psychiatry, 34,* 886–896.

Tapscott, M., Frick, P. J., Wootton, J. M., & Kruh, I. (1996). The intergenerational link to antisocial behavior: Effects of paternal contact. *Journal of Child and Family Studies, 5,* 229–240.

Tasker, F., & Golombok, S. (1995). Adults raised as children in lesbian families. *American Journal of Orthopsychiatry, 65,* 203–215.

Tate, D. C., Reppucci, N. D., & Mulvey, E. P. (1995). Violent juvenile delinquents: Treatment effectiveness and implications for future action. *American Psychologist, 50,* 777–781.

Tattum, D. P., & Lane, D. A. (Eds.). (1989). *Bullying in schools.* Stoke-on-Trent, England: Trentham.

Tavris, C. (2003, February 28). Mind games: Psychological warfare between therapists and scientists. *Chronicle of Higher Education, 49*(25), 137.

Taylor, P. D., & Turner, R. K. (1975). A clinical trial of continuous, intermittent, and overlearning "bell and pad" treatments for nocturnal enuresis. *Behaviour Research and Therapy, 13,* 281–293.

Taylor, R. L. (1997). *Assessment of exceptional students: Educational and psychological procedures* (4th ed.). Boston: Allyn & Bacon.

Teare, J. F., Smith, G. L., Osgood, D. W., Peterson, R. W., Authier, K., & Daly, D. L. (1995). Ecological influences in youth crisis shelters: Effects of social density and length of stay on youth problem behaviors. *Journal of Child and Family Studies, 4,* 89–101.

Teglasi, H. (1998). Temperament constructs and measures. *School Psychology Review, 27,* 564–585.

Terr, L. C. (1995). Childhood traumas: An outline and overview. In G. S. Everly & J. M. Lating (Eds.), *Psychotraumatology: Key papers and core concepts in post-traumatic stress* (pp. 301–320). New York: Plenum.

Thomas, A., & Chess, S. (1984). Genesis and evolution of behavioral disorders: From infancy to early adult life. *American Journal of Psychiatry, 141,* 1–9.

Thomas, A., Chess, S., & Birch, H. G. (1968). *Temperament and behavior disorders in children.* New York: New York University Press.

Thomas, A., Chess, S., & Korn, S. J. (1982). The reality of difficult temperament. *Merrill-Palmer Quarterly, 28,* 1–20.

Thomas, E. A., & Rickel, A. U. (1995). Teen pregnancy and maladjustment: A study of base rates. *Journal of Community Psychology, 23,* 200–215.

Thompson, R. A., & Wilcox, B. L. (1995). Child maltreatment research: Federal support and policy issues. *American Psychologist, 50,* 789–793.

Thompson, R. H., Iwata, B. A., Conners, J., & Roscoe, E. M. (1999). Effects of reinforcement for alternative behavior during punishment of self-injury. *Journal of Applied Behavior Analysis, 32,* 317–328.

Thompson, S. J., & Thurlow, M. L. (2001). Participation of students with disabilities in statewide assessment systems. *Assessment for Effective Intervention, 26*(2), 5–8.

Thompson, S. J., Thurlow, M. L., Esler, A., & Whetsone, P. J. (2001). Addressing standards and assessments on the IEP. *Assessment for Effective Intervention, 26*(2), 77–84.

Tindal, G., Heath, B., Hollenbeck, K., Almond, P., & Harniss, M. (1998). Accommodating students with disabilities on large-scale tests: An experimental study. *Exceptional Children, 64,* 439–450.

Tobin, T. J., & Sugai, G. M. (1999). Using sixth-grade school records to predict school violence, chronic discipline problems, and high school outcomes. *Journal of Emotional and Behavioral Disorders, 7,* 40–53.

Tolan, P. H. (1987). Implications of age of onset for delinquency risk. *Journal of Abnormal Child Psychology, 15,* 47–65.

Tolan, P. H., & Thomas, P. (1995). The implications of age of onset for delinquency risk. II: Longitudinal data. *Journal of Abnormal Child Psychology, 23,* 157–181.

Tores, J. B., Solberg, S. H., & Carlstrom, A. H. (2002). The myth of sameness among Latino men and their machismo. *American Journal of Orthopsychiatry, 72,* 163–181.

Tournaki, N., & Criscitiello, E. (2003). Using peer tutoring as a successful part of behavior management. *Teaching Exceptional Children, 36*(2), 22–29.

Trent, S. C., & Artiles, A. J. (1995). Serving culturally diverse students with emotional or behavioral disorders: Broadening current perspectives. In J. M. Kauffman, J. W. Lloyd, D. P. Hallahan, & T. A. Astuto (Eds.), *Issues in educational placement: Students with emotional and behavioral disorders* (pp. 215–249). Hillsdale, NJ: Erlbaum.

Trout, A., Epstein, M. H., Mickelson, W. T., Nelson, J. R., & Lewis, L. M. (2003). Effects of a reading intervention for kindergarten students at-risk of emotional disturbance and reading deficits. *Behavioral Disorders, 28,* 313–321.

Trout, A. L., Nordness, P. D., Pierce, C. D., & Epstein, M. H. (2003). Research on the academic status of children and youth with emotional and behavioral disorders: A review of the literature from 1961–2000. *Journal of Emotional and Behavioral Disorders, 11,* 198–210.

Turnbull, A. P., & Turnbull, H. R. (1990). *Families, professionals, and exceptionality: A special partnership* (2nd ed.). Upper Saddle River, NJ: Merrill/Prentice Hall.

Turner, S. M., Beidel, D. C., Roberson-Nay, R., & Tervo, K. (2003). Parenting behaviors in parents with anxiety disorders. *Behaviour Research and Therapy, 41,* 541–554.

Tyler, J. S., & Colson, S. (1994). Common pediatric disabilities: Medical aspects and educational implications. *Focus on Exceptional Children, 27*(4), 1–16.

Tyler, J. S., & Mira, M. P. (1993). Educational modifications for students with head injuries. *Teaching Exceptional Children, 25*(3), 24–27.

Tyler, J. S., & Mira, M. P. (1999). *Traumatic brain injury in children and adolescents: A sourcebook for teachers and other school personnel* (2nd ed.). Austin, TX: Pro-Ed.

Udry, F. R., & Bearman, P. S. (1998). New methods for new research on adolescent sexual behavior. In R. Jessor (Ed.), *New perspectives on adolescent risk behavior* (pp. 242–269). New York: Cambridge University Press.

Ullmann, L., & Krasner, L. (1969). *A psychological approach to abnormal behavior*. Upper Saddle River, NJ: Prentice Hall.

Umbreit, M. S., Greenwood, J., & Coates, R. (2000). *Restorative justice and mediation series*. Washington, DC: U.S. Department of Justice, Office for Victims of Crime.

Upadhyaya, H., P., Brady, K. T., Wharton, M., & Liao, J. (2003). Psychiatric disorders and cigarette smoking among child and adolescent psychiatry inpatients. *American Journal of Addictions, 12,* 144–152.

Urbach, B. J., Reynolds, K. M. Yacoubian, G. S. Jr. (2002). Exploring the relationship between race and ecstasy involvement among a sample of arrestees. *Journal of Ethnicity in Substance Abuse, 1,* 49–61.

U.S. Department of Education. (1991). *Thirteenth annual report to Congress on the implementation of the Individuals with Disabilities Education Act*. Washington, DC: Author.

U.S. Department of Education. (1994). *Sixteenth annual report to Congress on implementation of the Individuals with Disabilities Education Act*. Washington, DC: Author.

U.S. Department of Education. (1995). *Seventeenth annual report to Congress on implementation of the Individuals with Disabilities Education Act*. Washington, DC: Author.

U.S. Department of Education. (2002). *Twenty-fourth annual report to Congress on implementation of the Individuals with Disabilities Education Act*. Washington, DC: Author.

U.S. Department of Health and Human Services. (2001). *Report of the Surgeon General's conference on children's mental health: A national action agenda*. Washington, DC: Author.

Vaden-Kiernan, N., Ialongo, S., Pearson, J., & Kellam, S. (1995). Household family structure and children's aggressive behavior: A longitudinal study of urban elementary school children. *Journal of Abnormal Child Psychology, 23,* 553–568.

Van Den Berg, J. E., & Grealish, E. (1996). Individualized services and supports through the wraparound process: Philosophy and procedures. *Journal of Child & Family Studies, 5,* 7–21.

Vanderwood, M., McGrew, K. S., & Ysseldyke, J. E. (1998). Why we can't say much about students with disabilities during education reform. *Exceptional Children, 64,* 359–370.

Van Dyke, R., Stallings, M. A., & Colley, K. (1995). How to build an inclusive school community: A success story. *Phi Delta Kappan, 76,* 475–479.

Van Hasselt, V. B., & Hersen, M. (Eds.). (1991a). *Journal of Developmental and Physical Disabilities, 3*(3, Special issue).

Van Hasselt, V. B., & Hersen, M. (Eds.). (1991b). *Journal of Developmental and Physical Disabilities, 3*(4, Special issue).

Vasquez, J. A. (1998, Winter). Dinstinctive traits of Hispanic students. *Prevention Researcher,* pp. 1–4.

Vaughn, S., & Dammann, J. E. (2001). Science and sanity in special education. *Behavioral Disorders, 27,* 21–29.

Vaughn, S., Kim, A., Sloan, C. V. M., Hughes, M. T., Elbaum, B., & Sridhar, D. (2003). Social skills interventions for young children with disabilities. *Remedial and Special Education, 24,* 2–15.

Vermeiren, R., Schwab-Stone, M., Ruchkin, V., De Clippele, A., & Deboutte, D. (2002). Predicting recidivism in delinquent adolescents from psychological and psychiatric assessment. *Comprehensive Psychiatry, 43,* 142–149.

Vigil, J. D., & Yun, S. C. (1984). Familiar correlates of gang membership: An exploratory study of Mexican American youth. *Hispanic Journal of Behavioral Sciences, 6,* 65–76.

Vivian, D., Fischel, J. E., & Liebert, R. M. (1986). Effect of "wet nights" on daytime behavior during concurrent treatment of enuresis and conduct problems. *Journal of Behavior Therapy and Experimental Psychiatry, 17,* 301–303.

Votel, S. M. (1985). Special education in France for the emotionally/behaviorally disordered as it relates to that of the United States. In S. Braaten, R. B. Rutherford, & W. Evans (Eds.), *Programming for adolescents with behavioral disorders* (Vol. 2, pp. 127–135). Reston, VA: Council for Children With Behavioral Disorders.

Waldman, I. D., & Lillenfeld, S. O. (1995). Diagnosis and classification. In M. Hersen & R. T. Ammerman (Eds.), *Advanced abnormal child psychology* (pp. 21–36). Hillsdale, NJ: Erlbaum.

Walker, H. M. (1986). The Assessment for Integration into Mainstream Settings (AIMS) assessment system: Rationale, instruments, procedures, and outcomes. *Journal of Clinical Child Psychology, 15,* 55–63.

Walker, H. M. (1995). *The acting-out child: Coping with classroom disruption* (2nd ed.). Longmont, CO: Sopris West.

Walker, H. M. (2003, February 20). *Comments on accepting the Outstanding Leadership Award from the Midwest Symposium for Leadership in Behavior Disorders*. Kansas City, KS: Author.

Walker, H. M., Block-Pedego, A., Todis, B., & Severson, H. (1991). *School Archival Records Search (SARS)*. Longmont, CO: Sopris West.

Walker, H. M., & Buckley, N. K. (1973, May). Teacher attention to appropriate and inappropriate classroom behavior. *Focus on Exceptional Children,* pp. 5–12.

Walker, H. M., & Bullis, M. (1991). Behavior disorders and the social context of regular class integration: A conceptual dilemma? In J. W. Lloyd, N. N. Singh, & A. C. Repp

(Eds.), *The Regular Education Initiative: Alternative perspectives on concepts, issues, and models* (pp. 75–93). Sycamore, IL: Sycamore.

Walker, H. M., Forness, S. R., Kauffman, J. M., Epstein, M. H., Gresham, F. M., Nelson, C. M., et al. (1998). Macro-social validation: Referencing outcomes in behavioral disorders to societal issues and problems. *Behavioral Disorders, 24,* 7–18.

Walker, H. M., Hops, H., & Fiegenbaum, E. (1976). Deviant classroom behavior as a function of combinations of social and token reinforcement and cost contingency. *Behavior Therapy, 7,* 76–88.

Walker, H. M., Hops, H., & Greenwood, C. R. (1981). RECESS: Research and development of a behavior management package for remediating social aggression in the school. In P. S. Strain (Ed.), *The utilization of classroom peers as behavior change agents* (pp. 261–303). New York: Plenum.

Walker, H. M., Kavanagh, K., Stiller, B., Golly, A., Severson, H., & Feil, E. G. (1998). First Step to Success: An early intervention approach for preventing school antisocial behavior. *Journal of Emotional and Behavioral Disorders, 6,* 66–80.

Walker, H. M., & McConnell, S. (1988). *The Walker–McConnell Scale of Social Competence and School Adjustment: A social skills rating scale for teachers.* Austin, TX: Pro-Ed.

Walker, H. M., McConnell, S., Holmes, D., Todis, B., Walker, J., & Golden, N. (1983). *The Walker social skills curriculum: The ACCEPTS program.* Austin, TX: Pro-Ed.

Walker, H. M., Nishioka, V. M., Zeller, R., Severson, H. H., & Feil. (2000). Causal factors and potential solutions for the persistent under-identification of students having emotional or behavioral disorders in the context of schooling. *Assessment for Effective Intervention, 26*(1), 29–39.

Walker, H. M., Ramsey, E., & Gresham, F. M. (2004). *Antisocial behavior in school: Strategies and best practices* (2nd ed.). Pacific Grove, CA: Brooks/Cole.

Walker, H. M., & Rankin, R. (1983). Assessing the behavioral expectations and demands of less restrictive settings. *School Psychology Review, 12,* 274–284.

Walker, H. M., Reavis, H. K., Rhode, G., & Jenson, W. R. (1985). A conceptual model for delivery of behavioral services to behavior disordered children in educational settings. In P. H. Bornstein & A. E. Kazdin (Eds.), *Handbook of clinical behavior therapy with children* (pp. 700–741). Homewood, IL: Dorsey.

Walker, H. M., Schwarz, I. E., Nippold, M. A., Irvin, L. K., & Noell, J. W. (1994). Social skills in school-age children and youth: Issues and best practices in assessment and intervention. *Topics in Language Disorders, 14*(3), 70–82.

Walker, H. M., & Severson, H. H. (1990). *Systematic Screening for Behavior Disorders (SSBD): A multiple gating procedure.* Longmont, CO: Sopris West.

Walker, H. M., Severson, H. H., & Feil, E. G. (1994). *The Early Screening Project: A proven child-find process.* Longmont, CO: Sopris West.

Walker, H. M., Severson, H. H., Nicholson, F., Kehle, T., Jenson, W. R., & Clark, E. (1994). Replication of the Systematic Screening for Behavior Disorders (SSBD) procedure for the identification of at-risk children. *Journal of Emotional and Behavioral Disorders, 2,* 66–77.

Walker, H. M., Severson, H., Stiller, B., Williams, G., Haring, N., Shinn, M., et al. (1988). Systematic screening of pupils in the elementary age range at risk for behavior disorders: Development and trial testing of a multiple gating model. *Remedial and Special Education, 9*(3), 8–14.

Walker, H. M., & Shinn, M. R. (2002). Structuring school-based interventions to achieve integrated primary, secondary and tertiary prevention goals for safe and effective schools. In M. R. Shinn, H. M. Walker, & G. Stoner (Eds.), *Interventions for academic and behavior problems II: Preventive and remedial approaches* (pp. 1–26). Bethesda, MD: National Association of School Psychologists.

Walker, H. M., Shinn, M. R., O'Neill, R. E., & Ramsey, E. (1987). A longitudinal assessment of the development of antisocial behavior in boys: Rationale, methodology, and first year results. *Remedial and Special Education, 8*(4), 7–16.

Walker, H. M., & Sprague, J. R. (1999a). Longitudinal research and functional behavioral assessment issues. *Behavioral Disorders, 24,* 335–337.

Walker, H. M., & Sprague, J. R. (1999b). The path to school failure, delinquency, and violence: Causal factors and some potential solutions. *Interventions in School and Clinic, 35,* 67–73.

Walker, H. M., Zeller, R. W., Close, D. W., Webber, J., & Gresham, F. (1999). The present unwrapped: Change and challenge in the field of behavior disorders. *Behavioral Disorders, 24,* 293–304.

Walker, L. J., de Vries, B., & Trevethan, S. D. (1987). Moral stages and moral orientations in real-life and hypothetical dilemmas. *Child Development, 58,* 842–858.

Walkup, J. T. (2002). Tic disorders and Tourette's syndrome. In S. Kutcher (Ed.), *Practical child and adolescent psychopharmacology* (pp. 382–409). New York: Cambridge University Press.

Wallerstein, J. S. (1987). Children of divorce: Report of a ten-year follow-up of early latency-age children. *American Journal of Orthopsychiatry, 57,* 199–211.

Warboys, L. M., & Shauffer, C. B. (1990). Protecting the rights of troubled and troubling youth: Understanding attorneys' perspectives. In P. E. Leone (Ed.), *Understanding troubled and troubling youth* (pp. 25–37). Newbury Park, CA: Sage.

Waslick, B. D., Kandel, R., & Kakouros, A. (2002). Depression in children and adolescents. In D. Shaffer, & B. D. Waslick, B. D. (Eds.), *The many faces of depression in children and adolescents* (pp. 1–36). Washington, DC: American Psychiatric Publishing.

Wasserstein, J., Wolf, L. E., & Lefever, F. F. (Eds.). (2001). *Adult attention deficit disorder: Brain mechanisms and life outcomes.* New York: New York Academy of Sciences.

Waters, E., Hay, D. F., & Richters, J. E. (1986). Infant–parent attachment and the origins of prosocial and antisocial behavior. In D. Olweus, J. Block, & M. Radke-Yarrow (Eds.), *Development of antisocial and prosocial behavior: Research, theories, and issues* (pp. 97–126). New York: Academic Press.

Watt, N. F., Moorehead-Slaughter, O., Japzon, D. M., & Keller, G. G. (1990). Children's adjustment to parental divorce: Self-image, social relations, and school performance. In J. Rolf, A. S. Masten, D. Cicchetti, K. H. Nuechterlein, & S. Weintraub (Eds.), *Risk and protective factors in the development of psychopathology* (pp. 281–303). New York: Cambridge University Press.

Watt, N. F., Stolorow, R. D., Lubensky, A. W., & McClelland, D. C. (1970). School adjustment and behavior of children hospitalized for schizophrenia as adults. *American Journal of Orthopsychiatry, 40,* 637–657.

Webb, M. W., II. (1983). A scale for evaluating standardized reading tests, with results for *Nelson-Denny, Iowa,* and *Stanford. Journal of Reading, 26*(5), 424–429.

Webber, J., & Scheuermann, B. (1991). Accentuate the positive . . . Eliminate the negative. *Teaching Exceptional Children, 24,* 13–19.

Webster-Stratton, C. (1985). Comparison of abusive and nonabusive families with conduct-disordered children. *American Journal of Orthopsychiatry, 55,* 59–69.

Webster-Stratton, C., & Dahl, R. W. (1995). Conduct disorder. In M. Hersen & R. T. Ammerman (Eds.), *Advanced abnormal child psychology* (pp. 333–352). Hillsdale, NJ: Erlbaum.

Wehby, J. H., & Lane, K. L. (Eds.). (2003). Special series: Academic status of children with emotional disturbance. *Journal of Emotional and Behavioral Disorders, 11* (4, Whole issue).

Wehby, J. H., Symons, F. J., & Canale, J. A. (1998). Teaching practices in classrooms for students with emotional and behavioral disorders: Discrepancies between recommendations and observations. *Behavioral Disorders, 24,* 51–56.

Wehmeyer, M. L. (2001). Assessment in self-determination: Guiding instruction and transition planning. *Assessment for Effective Intervention, 26*(4), 41–49.

Weiner, J. (1999). *Time, love, memory: A great biologist and his quest for the origins of behavior.* New York: Knopf.

Weiss, R. (1995, June 13). Gene studies fuel the nature-nurture debate. *The Washington Post (Health section),* pp. 11, 13.

Weiss, R. (1996, January 9). The perfect fat pill is still a long weigh off: As discoveries mount, so does evidence of the body's complexity. *The Washington Post (Health section),* p. 11.

Wells, K. C., & Forehand, R. (1985). Conduct and oppositional disorders. In P. H. Bornstein & A. E. Kazdin (Eds.), *Handbook of clinical behavior therapy with children* (pp. 218–265). Homewood, IL: Dorsey.

Wentzel, K. R., & Asher, S. R. (1995). The academic lives of neglected, rejected, and controversial children. *Child Development, 66,* 754–763.

Werner, E. E. (1999). Risk and protective factors in the lives of children with high-incidence disabilities. In R. Gallimore, L. P. Bernheimer, D. L. MacMillan, D. L. Speece, & S. Vaughn (Eds.), *Developmental perspectives on children with high-incidence disabilities* (pp. 15–31). Mahwah, NJ: Erlbaum.

Werry, J. S. (1986a). Biological factors. In H. C. Quay & J. S. Werry (Eds.), *Psychopathological disorders of childhood* (3rd ed., pp. 294–331). New York: Wiley.

Werry, J. S. (1986b). Organic and substance use disorders. In H. C. Quay & J. S. Werry (Eds.), *Psychopathological disorders of childhood* (3rd ed., pp. 211–230). New York: Wiley.

Werry, J. S. (1986c). Physical illness, symptoms and allied disorders. In H. C. Quay & J. S. Werry (Eds.), *Psychopathological disorders of childhood* (3rd ed., pp. 232–293). New York: Wiley.

Werry, J. S. (1994). Diagnostic and classification issues. In T. H. Ollendick, N. J. King, & W. Yule (Eds.), *International handbook of phobic and anxiety disorders in children and adolescents* (pp. 21–42). New York: Plenum.

Werry, J. S., McClellan, J. M., Andrews, L. K., & Ham, M. (1994). Clinical features and outcome of child and adolescent schizophrenia. *Schizophrenia Bulletin, 20,* 619–630.

West, R. P., Young, K. R., Callahan, K., Fister, S., Kemp, K., Freston, J., et al. (1995). The musical clocklight: Encouraging positive classroom behavior. *Teaching Exceptional Children, 27*(2), 46–51.

Whalen, C. K. (1983). Hyperactivity, learning problems, and the attention deficit disorders. In T. H. Ollendick & M. Hersen (Eds.), *Handbook of child psychopathology* (pp. 151–199). New York: Plenum.

Whalen, C. K., & Henker, B. (1991). Social impact of stimulant treatment for hyperactive children. *Journal of Learning Disabilities, 24,* 231–241.

Whelan, R. J. (Ed.). (1998). *Emotional and behavioral disorders: A 25-year focus.* Denver, CO: Love.

Whelan, R. J. (1999). Historical perspective. In L. M. Bullock & R. A. Gable (Eds.), *Educating students with emotional and behavioral disorders: Historical perspective and future directions* (pp. 3–36). Reston, VA: Council for Children With Behavioral Disorders.

White, D. A., & Breen, M. (1998). Edutainment: Gifted education and the perils of misusing multiple intelligences. *Gifted Child Today, 21*(2), 12–17.

Wickman, E. K. (1929). *Children's behavior and teachers' attitudes.* New York: Commonwealth Fund, Division of Publications.

Widom, C. S. (1997). Child abuse, neglect, and witnessing violence. In D. M. Stoff, J. Breiling, & J. D. Maser (Eds.), *Handbook of antisocial behavior* (pp. 159–170). New York: Wiley.

Wilens, T.E., Biederman, J., & Spencer, T.J. (2002). Attention deficit/hyperactivity disorder across the lifespan. *Annual Review of Medicine, 53,* 113–131.

Williams, R. (2003, June 16). "I wish they were still here to make me crazy:" For parents of teens charged with murder, love prevails. *Charlottesville Daily Progress,* pp. A1, A8.

Williams, R. L. M. (1985). Children's stealing: A review of theft-control procedures for parents and teachers. *Remedial and Special Education, 6*(2), 17–23.

Willis, D. J., Swanson, B. M., & Walker, C. E. (1983). Etiological factors. In T. H. Ollendick & M. Hersen (Eds.), *Handbook of child psychopathology* (pp. 41–63). New York: Plenum.

Wilson, E. O. (1998). *Consilience: The unity of knowledge.* New York: Vintage.

Wilson, G. T., Becker, C. B., & Heffernan, K. (2003). Eating disorders. In E. J. Mash & R. A. Barkley (Eds.). *Child psychopathology* (2nd ed., pp. 687–715). New York: Guilford.

Witt, J. C., Van Den Heyden, A. M., & Gilbertson, D. (2004). Instruction and classroom management. In R. B. Rutherford, M. M. Quinn, & S. R. Mathur (Eds.). *Handbook of research in emotional and behavioral disorders.* New York: Guilford.

Wodarski, J. S., & Feit, M. D. (1995). *Adolescent substance abuse: An empirical-based group preventive health paradigm.* New York: Haworth.

Wodrich, D. L, Stobo, N., & Trca, M. (1998). Three ways to consider educational performance when determining serious emotional disturbance. *School Psychology Quarterly, 13,* 228–240.

Wolf, M. M., Braukmann, C. J., & Ramp, K. A. (1987). Serious delinquent behavior as part of a significantly handicapping condition: Cures and supportive environments. *Journal of Applied Behavior Analysis, 20,* 347–359.

Wolfe, V. V. (1998). Child sexual abuse. In E. J. Mash & R. A. Barkley (Eds.), *Treatment of childhood disorders* (2nd ed., pp. 545–597). New York: Guilford.

Wolpe, J. (1975). Laboratory-derived clinical methods of deconditioning anxiety. In T. Thompson & W. S. Dockens (Eds.), *Applications of behavior modification* (pp. 33–41). New York: Academic Press.

Wolraich, M. L., Wilson, D. B., & White, J. W. (1995). The effect of sugar on behavior or cognition in children. *Journal of the American Medical Association, 274,* 1617–1621.

Wong, B. Y. L., & Donahue, M. (Eds.). (2002). *The social dimensions of learning disabilities: Essays in honor of Tanis Bryan.* Mahwah, NJ: Erlbaum.

Wood, F. H. (Ed.) (1990). When we talk with children: The life space interview. *Behavioral Disorders, 15,* 110–126.

Wood, F. H. (1999). CCBD: A record of accomplishment. *Behavioral Disorders, 24,* 273–283.

Wood, F. H., Smith, C. R., & Grimes, J. (Eds.). (1985). *The Iowa assessment model in behavioral disorders: A training manual.* Des Moines: Iowa Department of Public Instruction.

Wood, M. M., & Long, N. J. (1991). *Life space intervention: Talking with children and youth in crisis.* Austin, TX: Pro-Ed.

Wooden, W. S., & Berkey, M. L. (1984). *Children and arson: America's middle class nightmare.* New York: Plenum.

Woodson, S. A. (2003, July 3). Letter to the editor: This is aberrant, not normal behavior. *Charlottesville Daily Progress,* A8.

Wright, R. (1995a, March 13). The biology of violence. *New Yorker, 71*(3), 68–77.

Wright, R. (1995b, August 28). The evolution of despair. *Time 146*(9), 50–57.

Wyche, K. F., & Rotheram-Borus, M. J. (1990). Suicidal behavior among minority youth in the United States. In A. R. Stiffman & L. E. Davis (Eds.), *Ethnic issues in adolescent mental health* (pp. 323–338). Newbury Park, CA: Sage.

Xie, H., Cairns, R. B., & Cairns, B. D. (1999). Social networks and social configurations in inner-city schools: Aggression, popularity, and implications for students with EBD. *Journal of Emotional and Behavioral Disorders, 7,* 147–155.

Yacoubian, G. S. (2003). Correlates of ecstasy use among students surveyed through the 1997 College Alcohol Study. *Journal of Drug Education, 33,* 61–69.

Yamamoto, J., Silva, J. A., Ferrari, M., & Nukariya, K. (1997). Culture and psychopathology. In G. Johnson-Powell, J. Yamamoto, G. E. Wyatt, & W. Arroyo (Eds.), *Transcultural child development: Psychological assessment and treatment* (pp. 34–57). New York: Wiley.

Yell, M. L. (1998). *The law and special education.* Upper Saddle River, NJ: Merrill/Prentice Hall.

Yell, M. L., Bradley, R., & Shriner, J. G. (1999). The IDEA amendments of 1997: A school-wide model for conducting functional behavioral assessments and developing behavior intervention plans. *Education and Treatment of Children, 22,* 244–266.

Yell, M. L., & Drasgow, E. (2000). Legal requirements for assessing students with emotional and behavioral disorders. *Assessment for Effective Intervention, 26*(1), 5–17.

Yell, M. L., Katsiyannis, A. A., Bradley, R., & Rozalski, M. (2000). Ensuring compliance with disciplinary provisions of IDEA 97: Challenges and opportunities. *Journal of Special Education Leadership, 13,* 3–18.

Yell, M. L., Rogers, D., & Rogers, E. L. (1998). The legal history of special education: What a long, strange trip it's been! *Remedial and Special Education, 19,* 219–228.

Yell, M. L., & Shriner, J. G. (1997). The IDEA amendments of 1997: Implications for special and general education teachers, administrators, and teacher trainers. *Focus on Exceptional Children, 30*(1), 1–19.

Yell, M. L., & Stecker, P. M. (2003). Developing legally correct and educationally meaningful IEPs using curriculum-based measurement. *Assessment for Effective Intervention, 28*(3/4), 73–88.

Yule, W. (1994). Posttraumatic stress disorder. In T. H. Ollendick, N. J. King, & W. Yule (Eds.), *International handbook of phobic and anxiety disorders in children and adolescents* (pp. 223–240). New York: Plenum.

Yung, B. R., & Hammond, W. R. (1994). Native Americans. In L. D. Eron, J. H. Gentry, & P. Schlegel (Eds.), *Reason to hope: A psychosocial perspective on violence and youth* (pp. 133–144). Washington, DC: American Psychological Association.

Yung, B. R., & Hammond, W. R. (1997). Antisocial behavior in minority groups: Epidemiological and cultural perspectives. In D. M. Stoff, J. Breiling, & J. D. Maser (Eds.), *Handbook of antisocial behavior* (pp. 474–495). New York: Wiley.

Zabel, R. H., & Nigro, F. A. (1999). Juvenile offenders with behavioral disorders, learning disabilities, and no disabilities: Self-reports of personal, family, and school characteristics. *Behavioral Disorders, 25,* 22–40.

Zack, I. (1995, October 11). UVA forums to focus on roles of black males. *Charlottesville Daily Progress,* pp. B1, B2.

Zanglis, I., Furlong, M. J., & Casas, J. M. (2000). Case study of a community mental health collaborative: Impact on identification of youths with emotional or behavioral disorders. *Behavioral Disorders, 25,* 359–371.

Zayas, L. H. (1995). Family functioning and child rearing in an urban environment. *Developmental and Behavioral Pediatrics, 16*(3, Supplement), S21–S24.

Zigler, E. F., & Finn-Stevenson, M. (1997). Policy efforts to enhance child and family life: Goals for 2010. In R. P. Weissberg, T. P. Gullotta, R. L. Hampton, B. A. Ryan, & G. R. Adams (Eds.), *Establishing preventive services* (pp. 27–60). Thousand Oaks, CA: Sage.

Zigmond, N. (1996). Organization and management of general education classrooms. In D. L. Speece & B. K. Keogh (Eds.), *Research on classroom ecologies: Implications for the inclusion of children with learning disabilities* (pp. 163–190). Mahwah, NJ: Erlbaum.

Zirpoli, T. J. (1986). Child abuse and children with handicaps. *Remedial and Special Education, 7*(2), 39–48.

Zirpoli, T. J., & Lloyd, J. W. (1987). Understanding and managing self-injurious behavior. *Remedial and Special Education, 8*(5), 46–57.

Zwaigenbaum, L., & Szatmari, P. (1999). Psychosocial characteristics of children with pervasive developmental disorders. In V. L. Schwean & D. H. Saklofske (Eds.), *Handbook of psychosocial characteristics of exceptional children* (pp. 275–298). New York: Plenum.

Zucker, K. J., & Bradley, S. J. (1995). *Gender identity disorder and psychosexual problems in children and adolescents.* New York: Guilford.

>> AUTHOR INDEX

>> SUBJECT INDEX